DISPUTE MANAGEMENT

Dispute management processes are becoming the norm as a precursor, or an alternative, to traditional court-based litigation. *Dispute Management* is a clear and concise introduction to an expansive range of dispute processes. Beginning with communication theory and practice, and the historical, philosophical and cultural considerations of dispute management, the book then addresses the traditional topics of negotiation, mediation and litigation, as well as interviewing, Collaborative Practice, facilitation, conciliation and arbitration. Each topic is well researched, offering the necessary depth, socio-legal considerations and balanced coverage of theory and practice.

The textbook addresses relevant ethical and cultural issues and is supported by an array of interesting examples that promote discussion. Case studies at the end of each chapter link theory to practice and present disputes between, inter alia, neighbours, conflict in the workplace, and cases that make it to trial.

Offering a combination of theoretical insights and practical information *Dispute Management* is a vital resource for students, lawyers and dispute practitioners.

Pauline Collins is Professor in the School of Law and Justice at the University of Southern Queensland.

Dalma Demeter is a law academic and practitioner and has taught at the University of Canberra Law School and Bond University.

Susan Douglas is a retired academic and now works as a dispute management practitioner and (volunteer) legal practitioner.

Cambridge University Press acknowledges the Australian Aboriginal and Torres Strait Islander peoples of this nation. We acknowledge the traditional custodians of the lands on which our company is located and where we conduct our business. We pay our respects to ancestors and Elders, past and present. Cambridge University Press is committed to honouring Australian Aboriginal and Torres Strait Islander peoples' unique cultural and spiritual relationships to the land, waters and seas and their rich contribution to society.

DISPUTE MANAGEMENT

Pauline Collins

Dalma Demeter

Susan Douglas

CAMBRIDGE UNIVERSITY PRESS

CAMBRIDGE
UNIVERSITY PRESS

University Printing House, Cambridge CB2 8BS, United Kingdom

One Liberty Plaza, 20th Floor, New York, NY 10006, USA

477 Williamstown Road, Port Melbourne, VIC 3207, Australia

314–321, 3rd Floor, Plot 3, Splendor Forum, Jasola District Centre, New Delhi – 110025, India

103 Penang Road, #05–06/07, Visioncrest Commercial, Singapore 238467

Cambridge University Press is part of the University of Cambridge.

It furthers the University's mission by disseminating knowledge in the pursuit of education, learning and research at the highest international levels of excellence.

www.cambridge.org
Information on this title: www.cambridge.org/9781108794718

First published 2021

Cover designed by Anne-Marie Reeves
Typeset by Straive

A catalogue record for this publication is available from the British Library

A catalogue record for this book is available from the National Library of Australia

ISBN 978-1-108-79471-8 Paperback

Additional resources for this publication at https://www.cambridge.org/highereducation/isbn/9781108794718/resources.

Please be aware that this publication may contain several variations of Aboriginal and Torres Strait Islander terms and spellings; no disrespect is intended. Please note that the terms 'Indigenous Australians' and 'Aboriginal and Torres Strait Islander peoples' may be used interchangeably in this publication.

To Cleo, Anna, Daniel and Olivia.
Pauline Collins

To my parents, Ferenc and Erzsebet Demeter.
Dalma Demeter

To members of the Australian Dispute Resolution Research Network and the wider dispute management community of practice.
Susan Douglas

FOREWORD

This book is fresh and thorough. Everyone has experienced the problems of dispute, but now we know there are processes that help us manage these problems. These processes have exploded in use, variety, and flexibility in the last few decades. They have become a comprehensive field of action and study. This book is a significant step in that development.

Dispute is a normal consequence of the mass of activities in which busy humans can engage, but we know how corrosive unresolved dispute can be. The authors expressly recognise that not all disputes can be resolved, but can be managed to minimise damage.

Dispute occurs everywhere – between parent and child, within or among businesses, clubs and organisations, between citizen and government, and among nations. Where there is human activity, there is a risk of dispute. It helps to know what makes a dispute, how it forms, and what shape it may take for management purposes, a topic with which this book opens. Virtually all dispute involves a need for careful communication. The authors examine the role of communication as it applies to dispute, with a new and helpful focus on how we can all communicate in a more effective and empathetic way.

Most disputes, whether in the family, between international trading partners or among anyone else, can be managed between the disputants on a negotiated basis. Only a small number of disputes must be litigated. Between those two groups, there is a vast array that will benefit from mediation, conciliation, facilitation, expert determination, arbitration or any of the other processes. Most of them require a trained dispute practitioner. This textbook, however, has a wider scope than simply to teach the practitioner the skills – it extends to the theory, philosophy, and legal understanding required to understand when and what processes to use, and why.

Any reader of this textbook, whether a student, an experienced dispute practitioner, a specialist regularly exposed to dispute such as lawyers, psychologists, mentors, counsellors, human resources officers or even an existing disputant, will find the textbook helpful and filled with useful theoretical insights and practical information. The same applies to those managing dispute in the workplace, on boards or in community organisations. Any dispute is amenable to management by those skilled and informed about how to do it.

The authors of this textbook are eminently qualified to produce a work on dispute management. The background of each has made the book theoretically strong, highly practical and very readable. Dr Pauline Collins is a Professor teaching dispute management in law degree courses, including for higher degrees, at the University of Southern Queensland and has actively written in the field in published books and articles. In addition, and just as importantly, she has practised as a lawyer – the law being one of those areas where managing dispute is a central task. She is also a National Mediator Accreditation Scheme (NMAS) Mediator, conducting mediations for the Queensland Civil and Administrative Tribunal.

Dr Dalma Demeter is an academic and law practitioner with expertise in arbitration and international business law. She has taught at the Canberra University Law School and is teaching for Bond University Faculty of Law. She is a founding director of the UNCITRAL National Coordination Committee for Australia (UNCCA), of which she was the Deputy Chair for three years. She has extensive experience as a commercial arbitrator and adjudictator and was a founding partner of the Australasian Dispute Resolution Centre.

Dr Susan Douglas is likewise a highly qualified academic who has published widely on dispute management. She has taught in the School of Law at the University of the Sunshine Coast, is a founding member of, and has served as President of the Australian Dispute Resolution Network. Susan is a NMAS-accredited mediator with experience in private practice and family mediation. Her research and practice in dispute management is informed by her professional qualifications and experience in law and social work.

The result of the collaboration of the three authors is a textbook which describes individual dispute processes distinctly and makes clear the theoretical reasons for the operation of each. At the same time, the textbook abounds in real examples and case studies of the management of disputes. The authors have used practical themes when examining various dispute management processes. For example, in the analysis of Negotiation, the theme used is workplace dispute. Plainly, negotiation can be used in any form of dispute but it helps to explore negotiation in an applied detailed context. When examining Mediation, the theme of Elders and inheritance is used. In the emerging field of Collaborative Practice, widely used in family law but which could expand further, family dispute is used to explain the process. Arbitration is examined in the book in the context of commercial and building disputes. That is a useful approach in Australia, where arbitration is heavily used in those fields. The option of litigating, which involves the final determinative forum, is examined in the context of civil compensation dispute in tort. The thematic approach in each of these cases, allows the study of dispute management processes in an applied context.

The textbook does not suggest that these are the only processes available. It also deals with conciliation, into which ADRAC (Australian Dispute Resolution Advisory Council) – the body of which I am a member – is currently completing a major study to be released in early 2021. The book recognises that numerous other processes are available and refers to the fluidity and to the flexibility of dispute management generally. These are matters that occupied the time of the National Alternative Dispute Resolution Council (NADRAC), of which I was a Chair, and its successor ADRAC, now chaired by the Hon. Ruth McColl AO SC.

Australia is a leader in the theory of dispute management because both its academic authors and entities like NADRAC and ADRAC have elucidated dispute management theory and processes and have helped make the field accessible. This textbook, likewise, provides great insights and in addition has provided new ways of presenting ideas and examples of dispute management that will be of assistance to anyone interested in the field; that would be a large group of people as we are all capable of experiencing dispute and having to find ways to manage it.

I congratulate the authors and commend the textbook to anyone interested in human conflict.

Jeremy Gormly SC
Former Chair of NADRAC
Immediate Past President of ADRAC
Denman Chambers
Sydney

CONTENTS

ABOUT THE AUTHORS

Pauline Collins is Professor in the School of Law and Justice at the University of Southern Queensland. She teaches dispute management and international humanitarian law. Pauline has been widely published on matters such as legal education, dispute management, military discipline, international law and private military companies. Pauline has also been a legal practitioner in South Australia working in general practice, Parliamentary Counsel, the Crown Solicitors Office, and the office of the Director of Public Prosecution. She has degrees in law, visual arts, public relations and is a Nationally Qualified Mediator. Pauline was National Mediation Conference Board member helping organise the National Mediation Conference, Gold Coast, 2016. Pauline conducts mediations for the Dispute Resolution Branch in the Queensland Civil and Administrative Tribunal.

Dalma Demeter is a law academic, researcher, and practitioner with expertise in international commercial law and dispute resolution. Her teaching combines professional skills and practical application with theory and her pedagogy is recognised by several teaching awards. As a researcher and author, Dalma's publications focus primarily on dispute management and legal development. She is frequently invited to present at international conferences and to provide capacity building training in the Asia-Pacific Region. As a legal practitioner, Dalma serves as independent arbitrator, adjudicator, and consultant. Her expertise in commercial arbitration, international commercial law, and contracts cover both civil law and common law systems. As an adjudicator, she is accredited to decide construction payment claims. Dalma is a tireless supporter of dispute management and of legal development and harmonisation in international trade law. She serves on several Boards and Committees for organisations working in these areas and she has been the Deputy Chair of the UNCITRAL National Coordination Committee for Australia (UNCCA) between 2017-2020.

Susan Douglas is a retired law academic who worked at the University of the Sunshine Coast for over 20 years. She has degrees in Arts, Social Work (with Honours) and Law; a PhD based upon an empirical investigation of mediation; a qualification in University Learning and Teaching; and she is a NMAS-accredited mediator. Sue identifies as a socio-legal scholar and her research includes publication of empirical and critical studies in dispute management, with a focus on mediation. Her teaching has included Business Law, Employment Law and Alternative Dispute Resolution (ADR). Sue continues to publish and to contribute to the ADR Research Network, of which she is a founding member and has served as President. She is currently a consultant editor for the *Australasian Dispute Resolution Journal* (ADJR). She contributed as a Design Committee Member of the Australian National Mediation Conference in 2019 and is committed to a similar role for the Conference in 2021. Sue continues to volunteer as a solicitor with the Suncoast Community Legal Service and as a Management Committee member with the Maroochy Neighbourhood Centre where she offers a mediation service.

TABLE OF CASES

500 Burwood Highway Pty Ltd v Australian Unity Ltd [2012] VSC 596, **78**
789TEN v Westpac Banking Corporation [2004] NSWSC 594, **180**
Atkins v iiNet Pty Ltd [2019] SASC 83, **184**
BC v Minister for Immigration and Multicultural Affairs [2002] FCAFC 221, **351**
Burns v The Queen (1975) CLR 258, **131**
Calderbank v Calderbank [1975] 3 WLR 586, **346**
Carter v Walker (2010) 32 VR 1, **351**
Casaceli v Natuzzi SpA (2012) 292 ALR 143, **298**
CDJ v VAJ (1998) 197 CLR 172, **348**
Clone Pty Ltd v Players Pty Ltd (in liq) (2018) 264 CLR 165, **347**
Coco v AN Clark (Engineers) Ltd [1969] RPC 41, **270**
Collins v Queensland (2020) 61 Fam LR 160, **93**
Conomy v Maden [2019] HCATrans 41, **346**
Donoghue v Stevenson [1932] AC 562, **85**
Ebatarinja v Deland (1998) 194 CLR 444, **129, 131**
Egan v Motor Services (Bath) Ltd [2008] 1 WLR 1589, **22–3**
Ellis v Trustees of the Roman Catholic Church for the Archdiocese of Sydney [2007] HCATrans 697, **336**
Enka Insaat ve Sanayi AS v OOO Insurance Company Chubb [2020] EWCA Civ 574, **304**
Field v Commissioner for Railways for New South Wales (1957) 99 CLR 285, **180**
Galaxy Development Pty Ltd v Civil Contractors (Australia) Pty Ltd [2020] QSC 51, **364**
Glencore International AG v Commissioner of Taxation (2019) 265 CLR 646, **344**
Henderson v Henderson (1843) 67 ER 313, **351**
Hera Resources Pty Ltd v Gekko Systems Pty Ltd [2019] NSWSC 37, **344**
Hickie v Hunt & Hunt [1998] HREOCA 8, **161**
House v The King (1936) 55 CLR 499, **347**
Hulley Enterprises Limited (Cyprus) v Russia, UNCITRAL, PCA Case No. AA 226, **382**
Interpharma Pty Ltd v Eli Lilly and Company [2008] FCA 1422, **345**
Jones v National Coal Board [1957] 2 QB 55, **338**
Kruger v Commonwealth (1996) 3 Leg Rep 14, **349**
Ku-ring-gai Council v Ichor Constructions Pty Ltd [2018] NSWSC 610, **324**
Legal Services Commissioner v Mullins [2006] QLPT 12, **214–15**
Ling v Commonwealth (1996) 139 ALR 159, **351**
Liprini v McIntyre [2019] NSWSC 355, **178**
Mabo v Queensland (No 2) (1992) 175 CLR 1, **366**
McDermott v The Queen (1948) 76 CLR 501, **131**
Murphy v Murphy [2007] FamCA 795, **128**
National Australia Bank Ltd v Freeman [2000] QSC 295, **96**
Oceanic Sun Line Special Shipping Co Inc v Fay (1988) 165 CLR 197, **341**

Orr v Holmes (1948) 76 CLR 632, **348**
Ostwald Brothers Pty Ltd v Jaylon Pacific Pty Ltd [2016] QSC 240, **363**
Pearce v The Queen (1998) 194 CLR 610, **351**
Pell v The Queen (2020) 376 ALR 478, **347**
R v Ireland (1970) 126 CLR 321, **131**
R v Lee (1950) 82 CLR 133, **131**
Secure Funding Pty Ltd v Bee [2016] NSWSC 521, **365**
Spadaccini v Grice (2012) 32 NTLR 1, **35**
Strickland v Commonwealth Director of Public Prosecutions (2018) 266 CLR 325, **131–2**
Subway Systems Australia Pty Ltd v Ireland([2014) 46 VR 49, **301**
Sulamérica Cia Nacional De Seguros SA v Enesa Engenheria SA [2013] 1 WLR 102, **304**
TCL Air Conditioner (Zhongshan) Co Ltd v Judges of the Federal Court of Australia (2013) 251 CLR 533, **349**
Veteran Petroleum Limited (Cyprus) v Russia, UNCITRAL, PCA Case No. AA 228, **382**
Yukos Universal Limited (Isle of Man) v Russia, UNCITRAL, PCA Case No. AA 227, **382**

TABLE OF STATUTES

Australia

Australian Capital Territory

New South Wales

Northern Territory

Queensland

South Australia

Tasmania

ACKNOWLEDGEMENTS

Pauline would like to acknowledge dispute management colleagues and her many students who have inspired her and expanded her knowledge. Thanks also to Lucy Russell and Rose Albiston from Cambridge University Press for their guidance and support throughout the development of this textbook, and to Ellie Gleeson (freelance editor) for her editorial assistance.

Dalma would like to acknowledge the moral support and ongoing encouragement that her partner, Dr David Cashman, provided throughout the writing process over what has been a challenging year. His book on *Performing Popular Music* (Taylor & Francis, 2019) also served as an inspiration for the last section of this textbook giving an insight into the good and bad realities of working in a profession. She also expresses her gratitude to Professor Tibor Varady, whose teaching and practice are the source of her love for arbitration, and to Tim Sullivan who introduced her to the world of adjudication.

Susan would like to acknowledge the support and encouragement of friends and colleagues in mediation research and practice, particularly, Mary Riley, Christine Jones and Alysoun Boyle, who have inspired her with their critical perspectives and innovative practice in dispute management.

The authors and Cambridge University Press would like to thank the following for permission to reproduce material in this book.

Figure 1.2: Reproduced with permission of Taylor & Francis through the Copyright Clearance Centre.

Figure 2.1: Reproduced from Celeste Lawson et al, *Communication Skills for Business Professionals* (Cambridge University Press, 2nd ed, 2019)

Figure 11.2: Reproduced with permission of the Parliamentary Education Office.

Table 5.4: Reproduced under Creative Commons Attribution 4.0 International (CC BY 4.0) licence (https://creativecommons.org/licenses/by/4.0/).

Extract from *Egan v Motor Services [Bath] Ltd* [2007] EWCA Civ 1002: Licensed for use under the Open Government Licence, UK.

Extract from Australian Dispute Resolution Advisory Council, 'Conciliation: A Discussion Paper' (2019) 12: © Australian Dispute Resolution Advisory Council 2019.

Every effort has been made to trace and acknowledge copyright. The publisher apologises for any accidental infringement and welcomes information that would redress this situation.

INTRODUCTION

Welcome to *Dispute Management*. This textbook is designed to introduce you to the range of processes lawfully available to manage disputes. It provides an overview of the many possible processes – both for those entering the profession and those already engaged as dispute practitioners. The approach adopted in this textbook is outlined here.

The manner of addressing disputes has been rapidly changing in the last couple of decades in Australia and many places in the world. New dispute processes provide options that vary from the traditional process of court litigation and these are swiftly becoming the norm for society. Practitioners of law in particular need to understand more about the nature and dynamics of conflict and disputes as they develop, rather than just dealing with the end result of a dispute. This understanding will assist when dispute practitioners are selecting the most appropriate process or model for managing a dispute. Before an adversarial or litigious process can occur in most Australian courts and tribunals, parties will have gone through some other process in attempting to manage their dispute. This textbook will aid readers in deciding on an appropriate or required process to manage a dispute, and address the skills and knowledge required when choosing to follow a particular approach.

First, a note on commonly used terms and phrases. This textbook refers to 'management' of disputes by means that are lawful. We deliberately do not use the term 'resolution', as we acknowledge not all disputes can or will be resolved. Some disputes can only be managed. 'Managed' is also a term that describes the dispute practitioners' role in ensuring the selection of the process most appropriate for the nature of the dispute presenting, in order for the parties to have the best chance at having their dispute addressed. This is noting always that dispute management may require a mixture of processes at different times in the dispute cycle. We use the term 'dispute practitioner' acknowledging that those working in this field can have diverse backgrounds and qualifications. Many are lawyers, but many have training as psychologists, social workers, and social scientists. The textbook addresses accepted lawful processes as opposed to unlawful. For instance, holding a duel at dawn to settle a dispute is no longer lawful.

The textbook provides a grounding in the fundamentals of dispute management in the Australian legal system. It presents the array of possible processes for managing disputes, including using litigation. It is designed to assist dispute practitioners identify the most appropriate process, or in some cases processes, to assist the parties in managing a dispute to achieve a desirable outcome. Readers are provided with knowledge on important skills in dispute theory and communication skills, such as listening, interviewing and negotiating. Specific legal, ethical, and cultural concerns are addressed in an integrated manner as they arise within the chapters.

This is a holistic textbook, adopting an integrative approach to dispute management. The opening three chapters delve into overarching considerations relevant in the disputing domain. Chapter 1 provides an introduction to understanding what causes disputes and how they develop from an initial conflict phase. It adopts an approach to disputes that flows through the whole textbook and utilises the attitude of a body that has been influential in Australian dispute management – the National Alternative Dispute Resolution Advisory Council (NADRAC) – by dividing disputes along monadic (single party), dyadic (two party) and triadic (three or more parties with a neutral third person) basis. The textbook covers the breadth of dispute management processes and techniques from the monadic self-help approaches through to litigation – the most formalised process for dispute management. While NADRAC no longer exists, it has had a major influence on the development of dispute management in Australia. NADRAC as an independent advisory body to the Federal Government was abolished in 2013 under the then Abbott Government. The wealth of material it was responsible for creating can be found at the Federal Attorney-General's website.[1] Since then, a group of senior specialists have reformed under the name of Australian Dispute Resolution Advisory Council (ADRAC)[2] and this body fills an autonomous role in supporting the world of dispute management.

Chapter 2 addresses communication, which is at the heart of all human interaction and something that requires specialised understanding for those engaged in dispute management. Chapter 3 addresses the history and philosophy underpinning the dispute management culture, which has aided understanding for managing human interaction when in dispute. Cultural considerations must factor into understanding and addressing dispute management, as must an understanding of the context and place in which the dispute exists.[3] The textbook discusses different values and cultures, including Indigenous cultures and their methods of managing disputes and experience of the justice system, making the text more readily accessible in different jurisdictions and providing a greater depth of understanding in a globalised environment. Bringing this concentration of awareness to the management of disputes provides a richness of knowledge that is more likely to augur well for the practitioner in the management of disputes and in the ability to choose the most apt process to achieve proper management.

Chapters 4–11 each focus on a particular dispute management process, or area, and bring cultural, ethical, and relevant special considerations into the discussion. This reflects life and practice in which all these matters intermingle, rather than creating separate chapters or textbooks on ethics or particular types of disputes, such as family or workplace disputes. Each chapter also focuses on a particular type of dispute area as its example in the knowledge exercises. This ensures a range of types of disputes are discussed and humanised. While the dispute management process addressed in a chapter can be used in a range of dispute types, the example dispute type is used to demonstrate its application. For instance, the collaborative process uses the example of family disputes, as this is the area in which Collaborative Practice is predominantly used. The negotiation chapter (Chapter 5) uses the example of workplace disputes as such disputes entail significant negotiation and can be addressed across all three bases – monadic, dyadic and triadic.

Each chapter follows a consistent approach, adopting similar headings throughout. This is in order to provide an easy-to-follow layout guiding the reader by addressing their expectations as the chapters unfold. The textbook provides a wealth of referenced materials in order to direct the reader to further resources and learning material. An opportunity to apply the knowledge gained is provided through exercises at the end of each chapter to reinforce the reader's knowledge and understanding of the different processes. Teachers are also provided with online resources and PowerPoints to assist with their development of the reader's knowledge and skills. These are available on a separate password-protected site.

1 See Australian Government Attorney-General's Department, *Alternative Dispute Resolution* (Web Page) <https://www.ag.gov.au/legal-system/alternative-dispute-resolution>.

2 Australian Dispute Resolution Advisory Council (ADRAC) <https://www.adrac.org.au/>.

3 See, eg, Pauline Collins, Victor Igreja and Patrick Danaher (eds), *Nexus between Place, Conflict and Communication in a Globalising World* (Palgrave Macmillan, 2019).

A praxis approach in which learning is capable of being translated into action is utilised in the textbook. Praxis combines the learning of theory with the understanding and practice of skills and techniques necessary to activate the theory. Relevant cases and vignettes are given as examples, demonstrating the material presented. This helps the reader see the principles in operation, and the facts of the story aid the memory.

The referencing adopts the Australian Guide to Legal Citation (AGLC). As those trained in or training in law may predominantly be readers of the textbook, this will model the correct mode of citation to those readers. This reference style supports a rich set of information and websites to be identified to enable the reader to pursue at their leisure in order to gain a web of growing knowledge. As a relatively new discipline area, the management of disputes sees a great deal of change as legislation develops, cases arise, and new processes are established.

The final chapter discusses certain statutory schemes implementing dispute management processes through legislation. It also provides the dispute practitioner with relevant information when stepping into the disputing world in order that they may have some confidence that they have the knowledge and resources required. Turn the page and commence your journey!

1 UNDERSTANDING DISPUTES

Learning aims

- Classify conflicts and disputes
- Demonstrate knowledge of the components and causes of disputes
- Identify appropriate theory and models to analyse disputes
- Describe the disputing cycle
- Recognise special factors that can influence a dispute
- Demonstrate an ability to diagnose a suitable process for addressing individual disputes
- Explain the impact of disputes on society
- Recognise special considerations applicable to disputes

Understanding disputes

This section will provide a short introduction to disputes by describing a dispute as opposed to a conflict, identifying components of a dispute and the dispute cycle, and identifying parties to a dispute.

A dispute as opposed to conflict

Conflict: a different view of a situation or circumstance that is creating a cost, be it emotional disharmony, breakdown in relationships, financial or personal reputational loss, or identity harm. It operates in a latent unacknowledged stage.

How one defines a dispute gives insight into how to approach and deal with a dispute. Disputes may develop out of an initial **conflict**. A conflict brews as an underlying issue that can reach a point where claims are made, or action taken. At this point, a conflict becomes a dispute. How one deals with the dispute once it becomes manifest constitutes the dispute management process. Until the underlying conflict becomes manifest through overt action, it is described as being 'latent'. There may be signs and symptoms that disagreement exists. This early stage is addressed as a conflict; it will not have reached a stage where action has occurred that announces there is a dispute.

Conflicts involve a different view of a situation or circumstance that is creating a cost, be it emotional disharmony, breakdown in relationships, financial or personal reputational loss, or identity harm. When a conflict is at this stage, it is likely to demand management. How that can occur raises many possibilities and this text addresses those options. However, before we dig into these, you need to be able to diagnose the underlying causes of a dispute to ensure you adopt the most appropriate process that can assist the parties to move past their impasse.

You are encouraged at this stage to arrive at your own definition of both conflict and disputes. You may like to revisit your definition at the end of the chapter to see if you would change it in any way.

Dispute: requires a minimum of two parties with incompatible goals that create an obstacle that becomes manifest and acknowledged.

Components of a dispute and the dispute cycle

A **dispute** is not necessarily identified through parties emotionally venting or having an argument, even a physical one, although this can perhaps be symptomatic of an underlying conflict. Such events, while seen as undesirable, are not necessarily a dispute. A dispute, at its simplest, requires a minimum of two parties. The key components include incompatible goals as perceived by one or both parties; these create an obstacle to the party's future progress and an assertion of a dispute is made.[1] An identified dispute can ultimately lead to positive change in people's lives.

Disputes also can rotate through a cycle. They are not necessarily one-directional in their development. A conflict may take time to develop into a dispute and, even when it gets to a disputing stage, inviting the need for management and perhaps engagement of third parties, it can de-escalate and return to a low-level conflict. This can reignite and grow into a dispute again. If a dispute is not managed well, or through the most suitable process, it can even redevelop after application of a dispute management process. For instance, litigation is seen as a process that resolves a dispute. However, the resolution refers to the courts having reached an end point in addressing the dispute. For the parties, particularly the 'losing' party, in litigation they may not feel that the dispute is resolved personally. From this, more disputes can arise. Conflicts can lie dormant for many years before they are brought to the surface as a dispute and then perhaps become hidden again.

New disputes can develop out of past disputes. If all facets of a dispute and its underlying causes and the interests of parties are not addressed, then off-shoots from the initial dispute can grow – a bit like digging out a weed: if not all of it is removed, then new sprouts can shoot. When managing a dispute, practitioners should ensure any final agreement clearly identifies the components of the dispute on which agreement has been reached. This enables any off-shoot disputes to be addressed as a separate matter. However, making sure the causal factors are addressed in the initial process is the ideal.

Identifying parties to a dispute

There is no limit on the number of **parties** that can be involved in a dispute. These can escalate to whole societies, particularly in international disputes, or large groups seeking change through disputes in their communities, such as around environmental issues. When identifying the key parties in larger disputes, several factors need to be considered. If the wrong parties are brought into the management process, then the possibility of settlement will not arise. This requires some assessment by the practitioner of who are the most influential or powerful persons that can speak on behalf of others in a group. In some cultures, this is not immediately apparent. For instance, in Pacific Islander cultures, the headman or woman should be identified. To engage in a process that does not address this person will be offensive. Therefore, cultural sensitivity is important to consider when identifying the relevant parties. If there are multiple parties, it is useful to talk to a number of members of the group and listen carefully for any person who is referred to often, as this is likely a central person. They may not be a CEO or easily identified leader, but they are a person the group respects as influential and someone they will follow. Moore describes this as a reputational approach.[2]

Parties: these can be identified by the party seeking dispute management; by their position within an organisation; or, in multi-party disputes, they can be identified based on their reputation among the group, or their role in prior disputes involving the party.

1 Deborah Borisoff and David A Victor, *Conflict Management: A Communication Skills Approach* (Allyn and Bacon, 2nd ed, 1997); William W Wilmot and Joyce L Hocker, *Interpersonal Conflict* (McGraw-Hill, 5th ed, 1998).

2 See Christopher W Moore, *The Mediation Process: Practical Strategies for Resolving Conflict* (John Wiley & Sons, 4th ed, 2014) 245–6, where he talks of a positional approach (a key position); reputational approach (who do others identify as people 'central'; and decision-making approach (who has been involved on behalf of the group or organisation in managing similar disputes.

Other obvious parties are the person who raises the matter by identifying a dispute and seeking dispute management. It is also clear that a party to a dispute, such as corporations, organisations, or a state, can be a legal entity. In such cases, the person involved in the dispute management process is a representative of the legal entity. The CEO of an organisation is a necessary party where they hold a key position that demonstrates they are a person with clear authority to agree to any management of a dispute. There may be more than one person with such authority, depending on the organisational structure of the entity involved. In such large organisations, a person, or persons, may hold a designated position that provides them with the necessary authority to speak on behalf of the organisation and they are the person with authority to reach agreement on behalf of others. Moore describes this as the decision-maker approach.[3] Once parties to a dispute are identified, it is then necessary to move to consideration of an appropriate dispute management process to use.

In this text, we use a well-accepted classification of disputes based on monadic, dyadic and triadic dispute management approaches.[4] You will see this classification referred to throughout this textbook. Using such a device assists when identifying an appropriate management process.

Dispute management: three approaches include monadic (single party management); dyadic (generally two-party management); triadic (bringing in a third party to assist in management). The third-party neutral can act in a facilitative, advisory or determinative manner or a hybrid combination of these.

Classification of dispute management approaches

This textbook follows a **dispute management** classification based on three approaches. These are monadic (involving one party response), dyadic (involving the parties, usually two parties, working to manage their dispute with each other), and triadic (which brings in a third party to assist the disputing parties to manage their dispute).

Monadic dispute management

Rational thinking: requires activating the cognitive brain, rather than operating from the emotional primitive brain.

Monadic dispute management is often identified as a 'self-help' approach. This can take various forms. We are all aware of things annoying us on a daily basis; for example, the way the neighbour fails to control their weeds, the way colleagues at work talk about certain topics, the way our partners may fail to communicate clearly. All these conflicts have the potential to escalate and ultimately manifest as a dispute. If that were the case, there would be so many disputes it would be hard for society to function meaningfully, if at all. Therefore, common methods for addressing such potential disputes include thinking about a matter in a rational way which yields greater perspective so that the issue does not become an incompatible goal or obstacle to future progress. **Rational thinking** requires activating the cognitive brain, rather than operating from the emotional

3 Ibid.

4 See National Alternative Dispute Resolution Advisory Council, *Alternative Dispute Resolution Definitions* (1997) cited in Laurence Boulle, *Mediation: Principles Process Practice* (LexisNexis Butterworths, 2nd ed, 2005) 109.

primitive brain.[5] For instance, a good relationship with my neighbour is more beneficial than a dispute over some weeds. If they appear in my garden, I can take care of the weeds and know my garden is neat. The monadic approach can, however, lead to a form of denial;[6] for instance, not reflecting on one's own personality or concerns that trigger anger or other reactions and addressing these factors. If the issue is a signifier of other concerns, then it is likely to return. Seemingly, small matters can be indications, like the tip of an iceberg, that there is something far more substantial underlying an otherwise small issue.

Another monadic manner for addressing a dispute, but one that can ultimately lead to an escalation in the dispute, is through either coercion or submission. A coercive party, through psychological manipulation or threatened violence, will dominate the other party into compliance. A submission arises when one party decides to go along with the other party's desires, often through the coercive practices of the other party, 'for the sake of peace'. Submission will not necessarily end the conflict but may internalise it with ongoing consequences for the submitting party.

Ultimately, the submissive party may decide that another way to deal with the dispute in a monadic manner is to walk away from it. For instance, one could sell their property and move away from the weed-filled garden next door, and the worker who does not like the way colleagues talk on certain topics can withdraw from the conversation, or even go as far as leaving that workplace.

In this text, we talk about negotiation and having difficult conversations. We also talk about what neuroscience is teaching us about our brains and how we respond differently to conflict and disputes. Some individuals like to take on a 'fight' when an issue arises that requires management; others engage in 'flight' and remove themselves from the conflict; some just 'freeze'. The reaction is driven by a part of our brain known as the 'amygdala'. The freeze state has only more recently been uncovered and tends to operate like a pause function prepatory to deciding whether to fight or take flight.[7]

The **amygdala** is a small almond-shaped sub-cortical part of the primitive emotional centre of the brain with 12 sub-nuclei providing a highway of connectivity to other parts of the brain. This multi-functional structure is vital to consider when addressing how humans behave in disputes, as it is an essential interface between the emotive human response mechanisms and the cognitive rational brain. The workings of the amygdala are still being uncovered, although magnetic resonance imaging used by neuroscientists has helped dispute practitioners to better understand human response to conflicts and disputes.

Amygdala: a small almond-shaped sub-cortical part of the primitive emotional centre of the brain providing a highway of connectivity to other parts of the brain, including between the emotive human response mechanisms and the cognitive rational brain. It can produce a fight, flight or freeze response.

Walking away is an example of flight. In such a situation, the other party or parties may have no idea that there was any issue. They will not necessarily be aware as to why one party has left. Such actions do not address the conflict, which remains latent. There is no change in behaviour and therefore no growth in

5 For those interested in investigating rational thinking further, see Ralph Wedgwood, *The Value of Rationality* (Oxford University Press, 2017).

6 See, eg, Eviatar Zerubavel, *The Elephant in the Room: Silence and Denial in Everyday Life* (Oxford University Press, 2006).

7 See, eg, Karin Roelofs, 'Freeze for Action: Neurobiological Mechanisms in Animal and Human Freezing' (2017) 372(1718) *Philosophical Transactions of the Royal Society. Series B Biological Sciences* 1.

understanding by those engaging in the undesired conduct. The party walking away, or staying but acting in a non-responsive or submissive manner, carries the cost of the burden of an unaddressed obstacle that can lead to the need to seek counselling to manage the issues that may arise internally for that party. Ultimately, it may lead the party to deciding to address the initial conflict by taking a next step and raising it to a dispute. This then leads to an increased scale of management. Alternatively, a fight response can lead to further trouble, particularly if it is a physical response, but it can also result in a drawn-out emotive legal battle. Being aware when one is in an amygdala state and allowing time for it to pass and then responding from a cognitive rational position enables opportunity for appropriate responses to the initial trigger.

Dyadic (two-party) management

A dyadic approach occurs when the parties to the dispute work together to manage the dispute without a third-party intervention. This is the most common form of dispute management. The main tool for management is the parties being able to communicate appropriately. To do this successfully, so both parties can live with the outcome, requires a sound understanding of how effective communication is used. The next chapter will provide the building blocks required for good communication.

When the disputing parties directly engage in managing their dispute, the process provides the parties with the greatest control over the outcome. It is also less costly, relatively quick and, if done well, can help maintain relationships. As noted, the process used by the two parties is heavily reliant on communication ability, and good will. To be truly effective, the parties must have a genuine willingness to compromise. It can be described as a process of 'unassisted negotiation'. This is a technique described in Chapter 5 and is the process by which dyadic dispute management occurs. The process is generally informal, but it can also be formal depending on how and where the negotiation takes place and whether there is assistance from advisors on either or both sides. When others are involved, then we move to the third approach to dispute management.

Triadic dispute management

This approach is the level where most processes covered in this text occur and is the one at which dispute management professionals are engaged. The triadic approach simply means that there is a non-disputing third party included by the disputing parties to assist them in managing their dispute. This can occur in several different ways. The following breaks these down into processes used under the triadic approach. Each is based on the nature of the role of the third party. This can occur at three broad levels. These are:

1. Facilitative – where the third party assists the parties but does not provide advice or a determination
2. Advisory – where the third party investigates and may advise on matters regarding the facts, the law, the evidence or likely outcomes
3. Determinative – where the third party may investigate or hear evidence and make an enforceable determination.

Each approach operates in different dispute management processes that fall under these broad headings. The facilitative third-party intervention engages processes such as mediation (Chapter 6), facilitation (Chapter 7), and conciliation (Chapter 8). Mediation and conciliation can also be in the advisory category depending on the nature of the model followed. The advisory third party is used in processes that require collecting evidence or hearing arguments in relation to the dispute or an aspect of the dispute. They include processes such as expert case appraisal, mini trial, counselling, and **early neutral evaluation**. These processes are not given dedicated chapters in this textbook but are mentioned where they relate closely to a process that is described.

Early neutral evaluation: a process (like a mini trial) that involves parties presenting their case to a dispute practitioner. This is a triadic neutral process, and it can be either advisory or determinative. The dispute practitioner can also be an expert or a judge, magistrate, or registrar of a court.

The third determinative process includes a third party conducting an investigation or hearing, assessing the parties' submissions, and weighing evidence presented that enables a final determination to be made outside of the disputing parties' control. The decision may, or may not, be binding; that is, not all determinative processes are adjudicative, but any adjudicative process is determinative. Such processes include arbitration (Chapter10) and litigation (Chapter 11).

The collaborative law process (Chapter 9) is unique in that it uses aspects of facilitative processes but also the advisory process. Negotiation (Chapter 5) and interviewing (Chapter 4) fit in each of the three levels depending on the nature of the arrangement with the third party.

Figure 1.1 Range of conflict

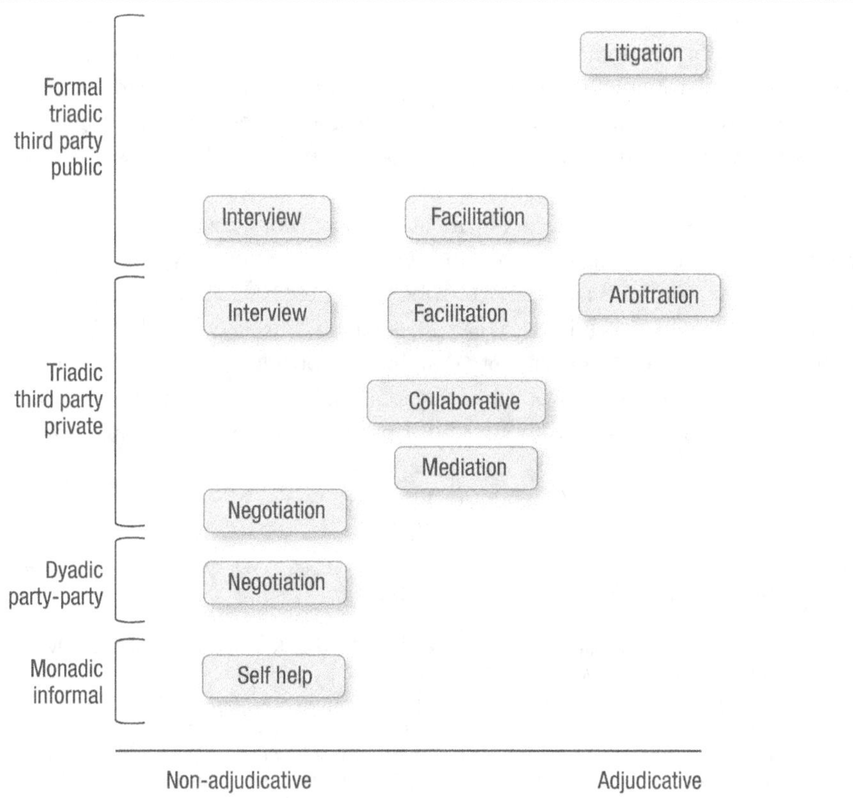

Using theory and models to dissect disputes

Furlong[8] describes two essential aspects to managing disputes:

1. Providing an effective diagnosis of the dispute, and
2. Based on the correct diagnosis, taking the appropriate action to manage the dispute.

A correct diagnosis relies on both the theory and the application of relevant dispute or conflict models and tools. The theory is founded on research that produces principles or hypotheses derived from research. This research depends on correct methods applied to produce sound evidence. Models, on the other hand, are not so reliant on proving the reliability of the results of their application, but on how helpful they can be in assisting the practitioner to diagnose a dispute and its underlying causes.[9] A model will enable the practitioner to understand the underlying causes of a dispute and so direct their focus. A model also provides the tool by which the practitioner can assess the best process to use and the procedures and techniques required that will aid in the dispute management.[10]

There are many theories and models on the causes of disputes. This text will focus on just a few of the more utilised that cover a range of approaches to identifying the possible causes of a dispute. Research theory acknowledges that many factors impinge on the causes of disputes. These factors may include power, resources, gender, ethnicity, religion, culture, place, and communication. Disputes are often not one dimensional. To isolate causes, the third party gains information from the parties with the aim of developing a hypothesis that is tested through using the appropriate tools and interventions. Practitioners should maintain their awareness of the research to inform their depth of knowledge. This work provides references to research and examples to support the reader in exploring further learning in this regard. For instance, research from neuroscience is providing a greater understanding of how the brain reacts to factors, such as difference in appearance or facial expressions of emotion, and communication responses.[11]

Power and resources underpin many international conflicts but can also relate to structural conflict and personal conflict. Bartos and Wehr[12] describe three types of resources. These are power, wealth, and prestige. They describe power as the ability to coerce others into doing their bidding by adjusting the weaker party's payoff. This can be either through a reward for behaviour or a threat of punishment. At an international level, this is often witnessed where a dominant state has power over other states through economic and trade dependencies that favour the dominant state, or through sheer physical military or economic power.

8 Gary T Furlong, *The Conflict Resolution Toolbox: Models & Maps for Analyzing, Diagnosing, and Resolving conflict* (John Wiley & Sons, 2005) 2.

9 Ibid 9.

10 Pauline Collins, 'Mediators' Authentic Presence: Ways of Knowing our Primitive Selves' (2010) 21(2) *Australasian Dispute Resolution Journal* 85.

11 See, eg, JS Winston et al, 'Automatic and Intentional Brain Responses During Evaluation of Trustworthiness of Faces' (2002) 5(3) *Nature Neuroscience* 277; Roberto E Mercadillo, and Nallely A Arias, 'Violence and Compassion: A Bioethical Insight into their Cognitive Bases and Social Manifestations' (2011) 61(200–201) *International Social Science Journal* 221.

12 Otomar J Bartos and Paul Wehr, *Using Conflict Theory* (Cambridge University Press, 2002) 30.

Moore's Conflict Model

When looking to models, Moore's Circle of Conflict[13] (Figure 1.2) is often used in Australian dispute management. This model is particularly useful as it divides the causes of dispute into five key types, adding the main attributes in each type and suggesting the focus that any intervention should take. The third party develops a **hypothesis** based on knowledge of the parties and the dispute information, together with the theory about factors like values, communication, or psychological aspects. Disputes are often not one-dimensional, such as only a communication dispute, but have multiple causes. To isolate these causes, the third party gains information from the parties to establish the likely causes and creates a hypothesis that enables the use of the best process and interventions. These are then adjusted as the results of the interventions are observed and assessed. Moore advises that, to be effective, a dispute must have the appropriate process applied – one that is a suitable intervention for the dispute as diagnosed. Cultural considerations also need to be factored into any hypothesis-building.

Hypothesis: a surmised explanation that can be tested with further investigation to either prove or disprove its accuracy.

Other models are referred to here to introduce the practitioner to a range of possible models. There are more,[14] and it is suggested that practitioners access these and learn to use a selection that work effectively for them. The different models apply to different dispute types and cater to different practitioner needs.

Power/Rights/Interest Model

A significant model is the Power/Rights/Interest Model (Figure 1.3). Fisher and Ury proposed this model first in 1981 in their text *Getting to Yes: Negotiating Agreement Without Giving In.*[15] It focuses on the approach a party may take to a dispute, rather than on deeper causes. The model shows all disputes are approached from one of three aspects and each aspect has identifiable characteristics that assist in choosing an appropriate process to adopt in managing the dispute.

A power aspect is an approach that relies on power resources that can take many forms, such as financial, technological, physical and mental capacity, hierarchical structural positions, and social influence. A party with any of these power attributes is often not incentivised to collaborate or compromise. They tend to seek to be a winner, leaving the less powerful party to be the loser. However, more power for one party does not always reduce the power for the other; both can achieve increased power and the amount of power resources a party holds can fluctuate. Power is recognition that each party has some ability to influence the other. For example, parties are often at least sensitive to concerns such as reputation. When there is such an incentive, or a reason to look beyond the power aspect, parties may turn to their rights.

13 Christopher W Moore, *The Mediation Process: Practical Strategies for Resolving Conflict* (Jossey-Bass, 3rd ed, 2003) 64–65. See Moore (n 2) 110: his latest version of the Conflict Circle 110 (the 2003 version is reproduced in this text as the authors prefer the intervention guidance provided).

14 See Nadja M Spegel, Bernadette Rogers and Ross P Buckley, *Negotiation: Theory and Techniques* (Butterworths, 1998) 104; Peter Condliffe, *Conflict Management: A Practical Guide* (LexisNexis Butterworths, 5th ed, 2016) 5–7.

15 Roger Fisher, William Ury and Bruce Patton, *Getting To Yes: Negotiating Agreement Without Giving In* (Penguin Books, rev ed, 2011); see Anne Lytle, Jeanne Brett and Debra Shapiro, 'The Strategic Use of Interests, Rights, and Power to Resolve Disputes' (1999) 15(1) *Negotiation Journal* 31.

Figure 1.2 Moore's Circle of Conflict[16]

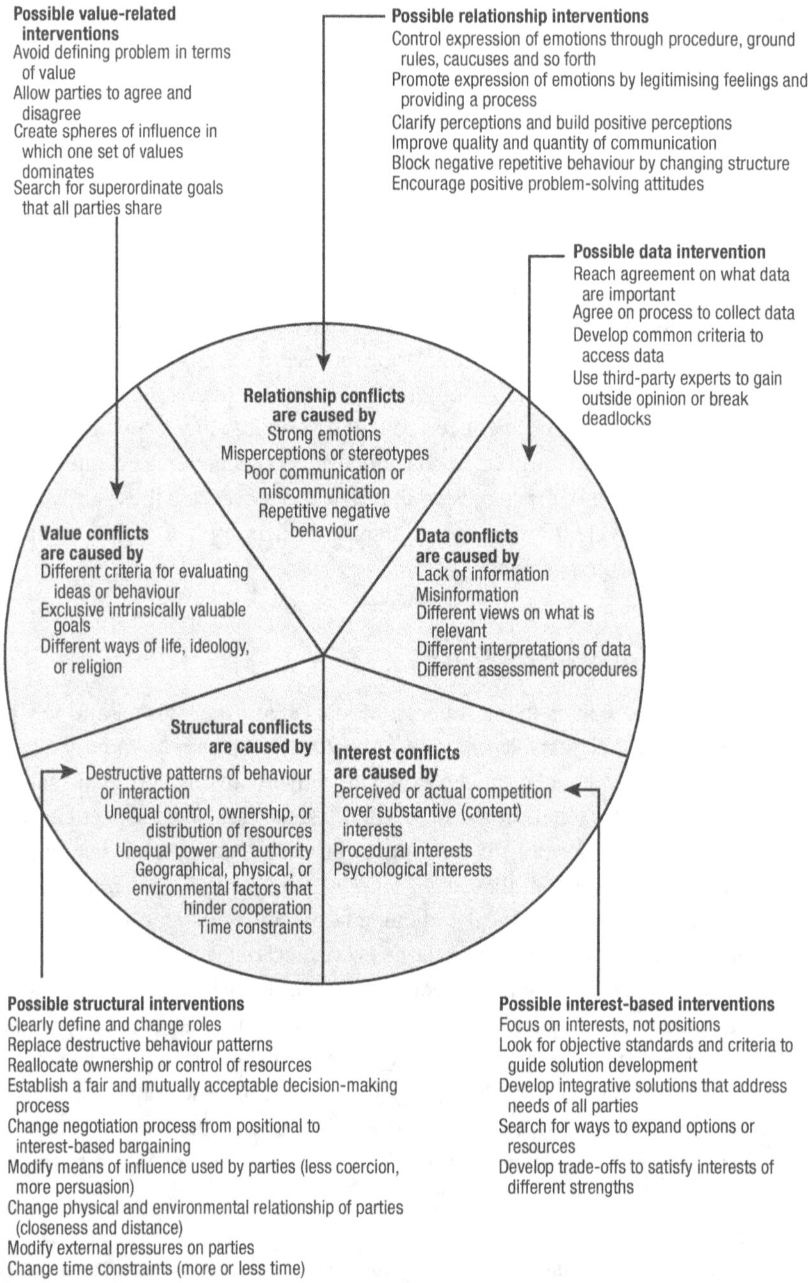

16 Moore (n 13).

Figure 1.3 Power/Rights/Interest Model

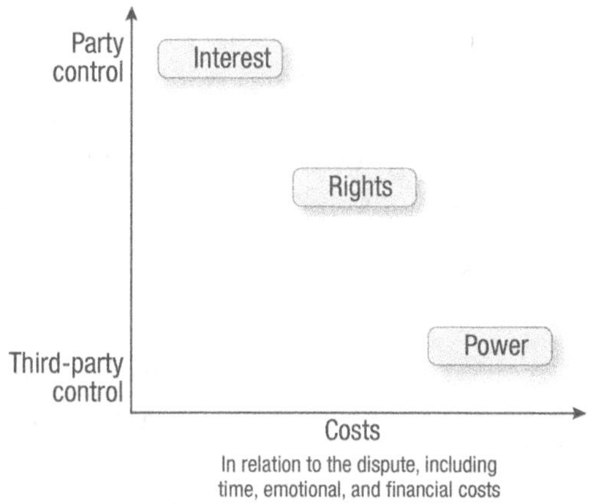

A rights aspect is based on an approach that draws on the concept of an objective set of laws, rules or customs (often based on moral claims) to which all are subject. When these are applied to the facts in a dispute, a decision as to the outcome should be possible. This relies on a perception of equality in treatment, regardless of one's power or status. Minority groups find a rights-based approach useful to equalise power and to ensure their entitlements according to the law are observed. A third party making a decision in applying the law, rules, or customs to the facts usually determines these rights. This can be bodies such as a court, tribunal, arbitrator or complaints body. A rights approach is an ideal, which can fail if the laws, rules, or customs have an embedded inequality or the third-party decision-maker has an unconscious bias. When enforcing a right under the law, it again means there is a winner and loser as a rights-based approach enables parties to speak from a position of entitlement that often results in an assertion over the other party's interests. This has led to the rise in approaches that seek to find another way, such as a win/win solution where both parties can have their interests satisfied, without necessarily addressing their legal rights.

The interest aspect is based on an approach that signifies a move to different methods of managing disputes. It helps parties find more common ground to achieve an outcome that may satisfy each party more than a winner and loser approach. It generally will involve compromise but not always, as sometimes both parties' interests can be satisfied 100 per cent. Interests are discoverable by asking parties why they want what they claim. It explores the underlying needs and desires through a process of open questions or conversation to understand what may be driving a dispute, irrespective of their expressed claims and rights-based positions. Once the parties express their driving motivations in detail, they can 'expand the pie' by considering a greater range of possible options than their rights and claims may allow. This can lead to solutions that may result in both parties' interests being met. This is where brainstorming can produce a creative dispute management solution. In most cases, it will require a concession or trade-off based on working with the parties' different prioritising of their respective interests.

Far from the objective basis of rights application, or the blunt power approach, an interest-based approach focuses on the specificities of every person's unique situation. This allows a substantive tailored way to managing a dispute. To be successful, this approach requires parties being ready to find a solution in a way that works best for all parties. A good practitioner will be able to assist the parties by using their communication techniques and understanding of dispute management processes to uncover the party's true interests and genuine needs and by enabling the parties to express these and move to creative solutions.

Dimensions Model

The Dimensions Model (Figure 1.4) is based on Bernard Mayer's[17] research. This model divides disputes along three dimensions, responding to how an individual feels, thinks, and behaves when in a dispute. This assists a practitioner to adopt appropriate intervention processes suited to the parties. The three dimensions are based on the parties' feelings, perceptions, and actions:

1. Emotional – the feeling aspects parties have regarding a dispute
2. Cognitive – the perceptive and thinking aspects parties have about a dispute
3. Behavioural – what the parties do, or how they act in relation to the conflict.

Generally, a person first experiences emotional response, such as frustration, fear, sadness and so on. Dealing with emotion is a special consideration when analysing a dispute and emotion must be acknowledged. The cognitive or thinking brain then perceives that another's wants, interests, needs or values are incompatible, resulting in communicative action or behaviour.

The way a party thinks about the objective facts and the other party in dispute is based on subjective assumptions, both conscious and unconscious, memory, and designation of motives. These can be verified, checked, and challenged. Overt behaviour can lead to an escalation in responses in a tit-for-tat manner. Identifying behaviour and the effect it has on the other party can assist in reducing the impact. By addressing the behaviour and acknowledging emotions, parties can make a perceptive cognitive change.

Figure 1.4 Dimensions Model

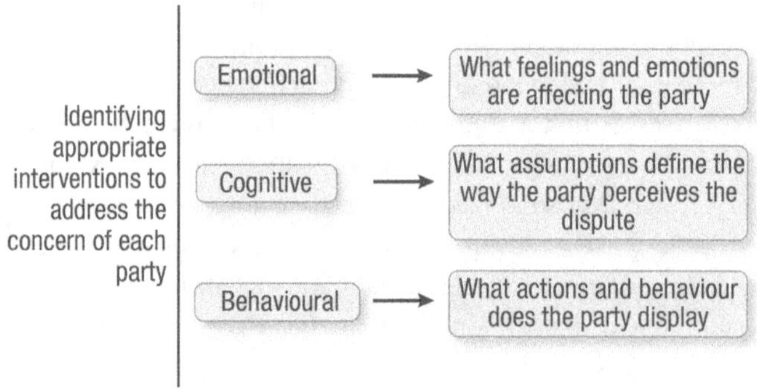

17 Bernard S Mayer, *The Dynamics of Conflict: A Guide to Engagement and Intervention* (Jossey-Bass, 2nd ed, 2012); see Gary Furlong, 'The Dimensions Model' in Furlong (n 8) 24.

Social Style Model

A very different model, the Social Style Model[18] addresses personality types. This focus considers how different personalities can approach or see the world in a different manner. Our personality filters our communication style and so many personality assessment tools will focus on this aspect of the expression of **personality**.

Personality: an individual's distinctive qualities.

Many tools exist to aid in assessing personality. Myers-Briggs[19] is a ubiquitous personality-typing tool derived from the work of Carl Jung and created by Isabel Briggs Myers and Katharine Cook Briggs. It categorises personal traits based on opposites: extraversion (E) and introversion (I); sensing (S) and intuition (N); thinking (T) and feeling (F); judging (J) and perceiving (P). An individual will be able to find a stronger emphasis in each pair to deduce a four-letter personality that leads to 16 different personality typings.

Many personality models exist. Digman's work, the Five-Factor Model, draws together research identifying a general consistency in assessing personality that involves five traits. He describes these as:

1. Extraversion/introversion (or Surgency)
2. Friendliness/hostility (or Agreeableness)
3. Conscientiousness (or Will)
4. Neuroticism/emotional stability (or Emotional Stability), and
5. Intellect (or Openness).[20]

A lesser-known tool is the Enneagram (Table 1.1).[21] This is an ancient tool with its source buried in the mists of time. It is a tool that identifies personality types through a process of storytelling to enable recognition of behaviour patterns that identify a person's worldview based on nine dominate typologies. The nine typologies are linked evenly in groups of three between the head, the heart, or the gut. Each has an animal totem to signify their most significant traits. Once these are known, it can assist in broaching an understanding of each parties' worldview, leading to greater communicative understanding. The tool has been very useful when applied in workplaces.

A practitioner that understands their personality and what drives their self and their approach to disputing situations will have a better ability to be able to assist disputing parties. As a practitioner, it is essential to ensure you do not contribute to the dispute through your own projections, style, and values, but rather keep your focus on the process and ensuring a cognitive constructive approach is modelled for the parties. Self-understanding not only aides the practitioner's ability to be effective as a dispute manager, but also gives a depth of awareness and understanding to the parties' motivations and approaches to a dispute.

18 Furlong (n 8) 24.

19 See Myers-Briggs Organisation, *The 16 MBTI Types* (Web Page) <https://www.myersbriggs.org/my-mbti-personality-type/mbti-basics/the-16-mbti-types.htm?bhcp=1>.

20 John M Digman, 'Personality Structure: Emergence of the Five-Factor Model' (1990) 41(1) *Annual Review of Psychology* 417.

21 Don Richard Riso, *Personality Types: Using the Enneagram for Self-discovery* (Houghton Mifflin, 1987); Don Richard Riso, *Understanding the Enneagram: the Practical Guide to Personality Types* (Houghton Mifflin, 1990); Hannah Nathans and Han Van der Meer, 'The Enneagram and Styles of Problem-Solving' (2009) 2(1) *Enneagram Journal* 62.

Table 1.1 The Enneagram

Head	Heart	Gut
Experience life through sight	*Experience life through touch and taste*	*Experience life through hearing and smell*
No 5. Owl (The Observer)	No 2. Dog (The Giver)	No 8. Tiger (The Boss)
No 6. Wolf (The Devil's advocate)	No 3. Beaver (The Performer)	No 9. Bear (The Mediator)
No 7. Otter (The Epicure)	No 4. Cat (The tragic Romantic)	No 1. Eagle (The Perfectionist)

All conflict models exist as tools to assist practitioners as a third-party dispute manager to adopt the best process suited to the dispute before them. This includes legal practitioners when advising their client. Practitioners are encouraged to explore the models that best suit their area of work.

Using dispute knowledge to assist in dispute management

This section will develop understanding of (1) causes; (2) latent/manifest disputes; (3) entrapment; (4) analysing a dispute; and how to use this knowledge to take an appropriate dispute management approach. The section will engage with a clear understanding of positions, rights, interests, needs, wants and emotion.

Understanding causes of disputes

Meta-level: understanding something from a bigger perspective, beyond the thing (dispute) itself.

Approaching disputes with a philosophical understanding of the causes can provide a **meta-level** awareness of a dispute and its analysis. The following thoughts are drawn from Kenneth Cloke.[22] As noted in the Dimensions Model, when we know the way we see conflict, it can help identify the causes of disputes that arise from this and can give perspective on the way parties may perceive a dispute. It can also help challenge the parties to approach their dispute from a different perspective.

For instance, many who have travelled extensively, or had an epiphany, or cathartic moment – perhaps a near-death experience – will gain a perspective that places many issues at a lower order in the spectrum of importance. Sometimes, if a party could consider their dispute from the perspective that the world may end tomorrow, they will realise the level of importance (or non-importance) their issues seemingly have.

Proxemics: the study of personal human space.

Disputes can arise because a party feels they are not respected or valued, or their personal space has been breached. This speaks of **proxemics** – the personal space distance a person prefers. Different cultures have different proxemics. In Australia, we are said to require considerable space, we do not like 'people in our face' – looking at us or touching us in an uninvited manner. Whole societies can engage in

22 Kenneth Cloke, *Mediating Dangerously: The Frontiers of Conflict Resolution* (Jossey-Bass, 2001).

fighting when boundaries are violated. By taking time to understand the needs of others in this regard and their differences, respect can arise, and the dispute can diminish.

Some parties like to play the 'victim or martyr' and enlist their friends and others as a resource support to go into 'battle' with the other party. Demonising the other is a standard tactic used in conflicts and disputes. Again, this occurs in both interpersonal and international disputes. Such activity needs scrutiny to avoid groupthink and to uncover the truth. In the **post-truth** society, much misinformation is used to promote certain party's agendas, and this can lead to false conflicts. Post-truth is a developing phenomenon driven by the burgeoning media channels of communication in which stories can be created by anyone for their own and varied purposes. No longer are news and information reliant on reporting through journalists subject to a code of reporting independently verifiable and objective facts.[23] While the possibility of spreading false information to further individual purposes has existed since humans could communicate, it has not, in previous centuries, been supported by the medium of technology that circulates stories globally and instantly. The controllers of the technology driven communication channels have become powerful bureaucracies influencing society in a manner that diminishes room for individual participative discussion and understanding:

Post-truth: the preference for personal opinions over scientific or objectively verifiable facts.

> This transfer of rationality and power from individuals to organizations is strongly fuelled by digital systems and platforms, and it is not by chance that people now think of these systems and platforms, operated by the 'custodians of the internet' . . . as the most powerful entities operating in present-day societies. The big enterprises and administrative bodies, namely the big bureaucracies, have made use of a powerful tool of formal rationality – algorithms – whose inhuman, hidden rationality can decide the fate of enterprises, people, and financial arrangements without having to explain or be accountable to anyone.[24]

The post-truth information is also reliant on groupthink and this, in turn, has become relevant in the context of unconscious bias research.[25] **Groupthink** arises when implied or even explicit pressure exists to conform to thinking by group influencers, where dissent is frowned upon, and reputation is guarded at the cost of truth. It creates a pressure for conformity in a close-minded approach that prohibits good decision-making by consideration of diverse voices. In the corporate world, it is found that groupthink leads to very poor decision-making at executive levels, which can lead to breach of legal and ethical duties.[26] Unconscious or even conscious bias can also contribute to conflict where in reality there is none.

Groupthink: arises when implied or explicit pressure by group influencers creates conformity in thinking, where dissent is frowned upon, and reputation is guarded at the cost of truth.

23 See, eg, Stephan Lewandowsky, 'Beyond Misinformation: Understanding and Coping with the "Post-Truth" Era' (2017) 6(4) *Journal of Applied Research in Memory and Cognition* 353.

24 Maddalena Giovanni and Guido Gili, *The History and Theory of Post-Truth Communication* (Palgrave Macmillan, 2020) 7 (references omitted).

25 See, eg (in the context of different dispute processes), Sai On Cheung and Keyao Li, 'Biases in Construction Project Dispute Resolution' (2019) 26(2) *Engineering, Construction and Architectural Management* 321; SI Strong, 'Truth in a Post-Truth Society: How Sticky Defaults, Status Quo Bias, and the Sovereign Prerogative Influence the Perceived Legitimacy of International Arbitration' (2018) 2 *University of Illinois Law Review* 533; see Chapter 7, 226.

26 Australian Prudential Regulation Authority, *Prudential Inquiry into the Commonwealth Bank of Australia: Final Report* (2018) <https://www.apra.gov.au/sites/default/files/CBA-Prudential-Inquiry_Final-Report_30042018.pdf>.

False disputes generally involve just one party. These occur when a party has a misperception, perhaps due to their unconscious bias, personality or psychological disposition. False conflicts can also include those who take a 'victim' approach in gathering others to their team, much like a groupthink influencer, or there is just a misunderstanding based on data or other false information.

Expectations of parties, particularly when unmet, can also foster dispute. Research has shown that the most common time for disputes amongst couples is post a special holiday period, such as Christmas or New Year, or a special occasion, such as a birthday. The problem is the couple's expectations for a time they are most likely to spend together have not been met.[27] Negotiating realistic expectations – or, better still, avoiding having too many expectations, by instead being open to possibility – is likely to reduce disputes.

Much conflict, and therefore dispute development, comes down to communication. The aspects of communication that lead to this include an inability to listen at a deep level to hear the subtle cues in communication, including from the non-verbal, or paralanguage. Other aspects include failure to communicate, concealing, lying or sending conflicting messages.[28]

Cloke refers to structural level disputes. Often these occur in organisations, or at an international level, but also at the interpersonal family level. He describes these disputes as 'the sound made by cracks in a system, the manifestation of contradictory forces existing in a single space' or 'the voice of a new paradigm, a demand for change in a system that has outlived its usefulness'.[29] These type of disputes, if managed appropriately, can lead to positive change; however, if mismanaged, much pain and damage can occur before change eventually arrives. An example of the former is provided by the changes eventually achieved by the 'Same Sex Marriage' movement in Australia, with a change in paradigm bringing a relatively peaceful transition to update a system that had not previously been responsive to changes in society.[30] An example of the consequences of mismanagement at an international level is the Arab Spring in 2011,[31] and the unfolding of the hugely destructive Syrian war, among other conflicts within surrounding countries. Institutions and certain social practices can provide safe harbours for the relief of societal tensions in non-destructive forms, just as a healthy democracy allows free expression of different perspectives to enable society to form a consensus opinion.[32]

Parties can hold onto their grievances as if they are property – their dispute becomes their life, and they can neglect to learn from past errors, project their own unknown failings on to others, or bring ghosts into a current relationship. The latter two are false disputes, as they

27 Marianna Papadakis, 'Unhappy Married Women Driving Divorce, Survey Finds' *The Financial Review* (online, 16 January 2015) <https://www.afr.com/business/health/unhappy-married-women-driving-divorce-survey-finds-20150116-12rddh>; see Courtney Thompson, 'This is the Time When Your Partner is Most Likely to Cheat' *New York Post* (online, 28 August 2017) <https://nypost.com/2017/08/28/this-is-the-time-when-your-partner-is-most-likely-to-cheat/?utm_campaign=SocialFlow&utm_source=NYPTwitter&utm_medium=SocialFlow&sr_share=twitter>.

28 Robert Bolton, *People Skills* (Simon & Schuster, 1986); see Chapter 2, 46: Bolton's common barriers to communication.

29 Cloke (n 22) 8.

30 See, eg, TB Gravelle and A Carson, 'Explaining the Australian marriage equality vote: An aggregate-level analysis' (2019) 39(2) *Politics* 186.

31 Tansa George Massoud, John A Doces and Christopher Magee, 'Protests and the Arab Spring: An Empirical Investigation' (2019) 51(3) *Polity* 429.

32 Lewis A Coser, *The Function of Social Conflict* (Free Press, 1956) 40.

involve one party bringing their psychological aspects to bear on the other. Projections can be understood in terms of Carl Jung's[33] theory on the unknown aspects of self – our own shadow side that we project onto others. When this occurs, we will tend to have an inexplicable dislike for the person on whom we project our unaccepted self. For instance, you may not like a person because you think they are loud and too talkative. In such a case, if you ask yourself honestly 'Is that something I do?', you may find it is. This is a shadow projection. Generally, this is identifiable where other people do not have an issue with the person in the way you do. Ghosts occur where a person from one party's past – perhaps a parent – works as a voice in their head, demanding certain responses that are not appropriate to the context of the matter at hand. A perceptive practitioner will be alert to these possibilities when they are diagnosing a dispute. Identifying these underlying causes assists in directing the practitioner to the best process and tools for management.

The stages of dispute development: latent and manifest

A matter often remains latent while still at the conflict stage. This is when everyone keeps smiling, but there is definite unease, a 'grit your teeth and bear it' situation. At this point, it is a hidden conflict. Others are likely to feel a tension surrounding those who may be in a latent conflict. The parties, or any one of them, may lack awareness of the conflict and the possibility it could erupt into a dispute. They may be aware that something is bothering them (or the other party), but there is no appetite to do anything to change their perceptions or the situation.

Eventually, however, a latent conflict has the propensity to surface and become a manifest dispute (Figure 1.5). This is usually as a result of an overt activating event. When a dispute manifests, it is most likely to require some form of management. A manifest dispute can escalate in many ways.[34]

If the parties do not manage the dispute through monadic or dyadic processes, they will generally seek a third-party intervener to address their dispute and aid with communication. This third party may be anyone from a friend operating in an informal manner, or person known and respected by both parties, through to an expert or independent, unknown, and impartial third person, such as a dispute practitioner.

Moore,[35] when introducing the concepts of latent and manifest, refers to an additional 'emergent stage'. This is where the parties are known and most of the issues are known, but it is unclear how the dispute can be managed. Parties may adopt a perceived hostile process in this emergent phase in an attempt to manage the dispute towards their advantage. This risks the dispute escalating and is a crucial time for practitioners to identify the importance of suggesting an appropriate approach to manage the dispute.

Entrapment

A classic dilemma for parties in dispute is described by **entrapment** theory. Entrapment arises when a person invests a great deal in some thing or

Entrapment: becoming so invested in a situation that it makes it hard to acknowledge and address or withdraw.

33 See CG Jung, *The Spirit in Man, Art and Literature*, tr REC Hull (Ark Paperbacks, 1967).

34 See also Laurence Boulle and Nadja Alexander, *Mediation Skills and Techniques* (LexisNexis, Butterworths, 3rd ed, 2019) specifically chapter 4; Mayer (n 17).

35 Moore (n 2) 23–4.

Figure 1.5 Circle of latent conflict and manifest dispute

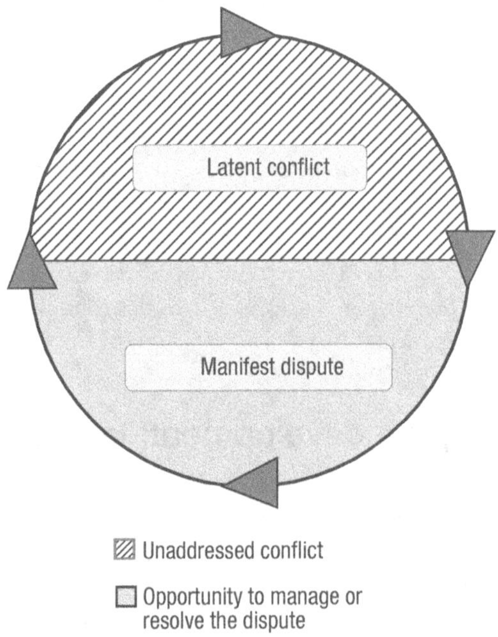

relationship. This investment can be personal, emotional, resource intensive, and interest-based. For instance, a personal relationship has an investment of all these aspects: for this reason it can be hard for parties to acknowledge there is a dispute that requires addressing. The question arises at what point it should be acknowledged that by investing more emotion, resources, and interest in the situation any improvement will result.

Some people will purposefully tell others of their intentions to set up a social entrapment. This type of entrapment may rely on telling people they are giving up an addiction, such as smoking, eating unhealthy food, or drinking alcohol. The more people that they inform, the harder it becomes to renege without 'losing face' socially for being unreliable.

A classic example of entrapment is found in the following case in which the parties have pursued expensive litigation to prove their position.

EGAN V MOTOR SERVICES (BATH) LTD [2008] 1 WLR 1589

Facts: Darren Egan purchased a brand-new Audi motor car in March 2004. The vehicle did not perform to his satisfaction.

Issue: Egan sought to vacate the contract. In the month following, he wished to return the vehicle and get his money back, claiming it was unsatisfactory as it had a tendency to veer to the left when driving. Bath Motor Services denied there was any problem with the car's steering and refused to accept Egan's claims. Egan sued for the return of the purchase price and damages in 2006. The claim failed in the first instance and the appeal was dismissed.

The judge held that there was nothing wrong with the Audi and Egan was not entitled to reject it. After Egan had sold the vehicle, the amount in issue was around £6,000.

Decision: On appeal, Lord Justice Ward said:

> What I have found profoundly unsatisfactory, and made my views clear in the course of argument, is the fact that the parties have between them spent in the region of £100,000 arguing over a claim which is worth about £6,000. In the florid language of the argument, I regarded them, one or other, if not both, of them, as 'completely cuckoo' to have engaged in such expensive litigation with so little at stake. At the time of writing this judgment I rightly do not know whether any, or if so what, attempts have been made to settle this case and the remarks that follow are of general application. I raise that matter again in this judgment to make the point, as firmly as I can, that this is a paradigm case which, if it could not have been settled by the parties themselves, customer and dealer, then it behoved both solicitors to take the firmest grip on the case from the first moment of instruction. That, I appreciate, may not always be easy, but perhaps a copy of this judgment can, at the first meeting, be handed to the client, bristling with righteous indignation, in this case the customer who has paid a small fortune for a motor car which does not meet his satisfaction, and the dealer anxious to preserve the reputation of his prestige product. "This case cries out for mediation", should be the advice given to both the claimant and the defendant. Why? Because it is perfectly obvious what can happen. Feelings are running high, early positions are taken, positions become entrenched, the litigation bandwagon will roll on, experts are inevitably involved, and, before one knows it, there will be two/three day trial and even, heaven help them, an appeal. It is on the cards a wholly disproportionate sum, £100,000, will be to fight over a tiny claim, £6,000. And what benefit can mediation bring? It brings an air of reality to negotiations that, I accept, may well have taken place in this case, though, for obvious reasons, we have not sought to enquire further into that at this stage. Mediation can do more for the parties than negotiation. In this case the sheer commercial folly could have been amply demonstrated to both parties sitting at the same table but hearing it come from somebody who is independent. At the time this dispute crystallised, the car was practically brand new. It would not have been vastly different from any demonstration car. The commercial possibilities are endless for finding an acceptable solution which would enable the parties to emerge, one with some satisfaction, perhaps a replacement vehicle and the other with its and Audi's good name intact and probably enhanced, but perhaps with each of them just a little less wealthy. The cost of such a mediation would be paltry by comparison with the costs that would mount from the moment of the issue of the claim. In so many cases, and this is just another example of one, the best time to mediate is before the litigation begins. It is not a sign of weakness to suggest it. It is the hallmark of common sense. Mediation is a perfectly proper adjunct to litigation. The skills are now well developed. The results are astonishingly good. Try it more often [53].

When dissecting a dispute, it is helpful to break it down and consider from different angles. When doing this, it is useful to consider the aspects of a dispute to determine the practitioner's role as a third-party intervener. The following section considers further positions: wants, rights, interests-needs, and emotions. The Power/Rights/Interest Model outlined previously is useful to consider in this context.

Analysing a dispute

The following are factors that should be considered in analysing a dispute.

Positions

Positions are what parties identify as a want. They desire a certain outcome, to win, to receive a certain level of compensation for a perceived wrong. This can often become entrenched and parties can be reluctant to move from their position. Levels of power and resources available will often determine the degree of entrenchment a party will take in holding onto their position. As you have read, a power-based approach enables the adoption of a dominate position based on the parties' perceived want. Sometimes, positions are backed by a party arguing it is their right – be it legal or moral.

Rights

Rights develop out of a claim based on legislation or sometimes morals. Objective information assists a third party to decide whose rights prevail, thus providing for a winner. The adjudicator as a third-party decision-maker in a triadic manner can be a tribunal member, arbitrator or judge. Generally, the process requires deciding an outcome – either by the third-party inquiring through an inquisitorial style of questioning, or hearing evidence produced through an adversarial process. These processes can take longer and cost more than a process that focuses on facilitating an agreement based on an understanding of each party's interests.

Interests

Uncovering parties' interests requires moving the parties from their position – what they say they want, to explore fully the underlying interests by asking why they want something and addressing the need that sustains their interests. Interests can be many, and this enables an expanding of the pie from an entrenched combat over often singularly expressed wants to broaden the possibility of finding some common interests or at least areas of aligned concern. Once some common ground can be uncovered, it enables the parties to move to a problem-solving mode and jointly attack their common problem. To get to this stage, one must always be aware of first acknowledging the emotions that parties feel and express.

Emotion

Humans cannot function without emotional activation that operates from their primitive brain. A decision is impossible without this emotional involvement. Therefore, trying to deny emotions is ineffectual. It is better to appropriately acknowledge other's emotions by identifying as accurately as possible what they express – not by saying 'I understand'. Saying you 'understand' is a form of denial of the other person and can escalate their emotional state. Knowing that the amygdala has been activated, giving rise to tensed muscles, increased breathing and heart rate, flushed skin, hair follicles rising, and raised pitch of voice signifies that trying to reason will not be possible until the amygdala has calmed down. This rate varies across individuals and genders. It can be observable both by others and by the individual concerned once they have returned to a restful normal state.

By matching some of the person's paralanguage, such as their breathing and vocal tone, or hand and other gestures – a process known as **isopraxism** – they can be brought back to a calmer state. Such actions must be done with a deal of caution so as not to mimic the other in a way that can be interpreted as demeaning. It is a subtle process. If the upset party is yelling, one does not yell back but can raise the pitch of the voice in a controlled manner. Isopraxism is the mirroring or following of the other's paralanguage. It has also been referred to as the 'Chameleon affect'.[36] Once in a calmer state, the cognitive reasoning brain can be accessed and the possibility of entering a dialogue is open.

Isopraxism: consciously mirroring another's bodily movements and other physiological actions, such as breathing.

Anger is an emotion most often associated with disputes and is underpinned by fear. If anger escalates, it can bring about a spiralling effect in which both parties retaliate in a tit-for-tat escalation. This spiral needs to be halted to avoid the escalation and instead enter a more collaborative process by attacking the problem rather than the people involved. A party's ability to identify their emotions through self-awareness can help detect and control anger before it becomes uncontrolled. Practitioners and conflict coaches can assist parties with appropriate techniques to intervene in the spiral.[37]

Positives and negatives of disputes

As Kenneth Cloke states, disputes 'are both a creative and destructive force'.[38] So why should society be so concerned with dispute management? The answer may seem obvious to many: the right degree of harmony should be sought. Having indicated the essential aspect of allowing for disputes, for positive change to arise, it is also important to keep this in balance.

Positives

Many fail to see the positives in disputes. They experience a dispute that they are involved in as painful. It costs emotionally, financially, and often depletes or destroys relationships. However, the very nature of human interaction entails communicating with each other. This can inevitably lead to misunderstandings and pressure points. If identified early, these can often be addressed in a simple manner that prevents escalation.

Conflict and the disputes arising out of conflict are an inherent part of human nature and are essential in human and business relationships. Without disputes, we as individuals would not grow and change. Our self-awareness would stagnate. Society would become bland. Creative ideas and development would decline perpetuating an unhealthy complacency.

Conflicts and disputes should not be repressed. Without allowance for expressions of grievance, this can ferment in hidden places and explode in catastrophic ruptures. Enabling

36 See TL Chartrand and JA Bargh, 'The Chameleon Effect: The Perception-Behaviour Link and Social Interaction' (1999) 76(6) *Journal of Personality and Social Psychology* 893.

37 Ana Shetach, 'The Four-Dimensions Model' (2009) 39(3) *International Studies of Management & Organization* 82, 88; see also Noelene Salmon, 'Cutting Edge . . . Cutting the Cost: The Business Case for Conflict Coaching in a Government Workplace' (2017) 28(1) *Australasian Dispute Resolution Journal* 64.

38 Kenneth Cloke, 'Journeys into the Heart of Conflict' (2004) 4(2) *Pepperdine Dispute Resolution Journal* 219.

free expression of disputes ensures a transparency and openness in society so the issues can be managed and addressed before they become explosive demands. The Arab Spring, as noted previously, is an example of suppression of society's demands in ridged and controlled political systems. This suppression results in rupture as the society tears itself apart, often in deadly and explosive ways, to seek a change that addresses the people's interests, wants, needs, and rights.

The cycle of communication can lead to points where, much as storm clouds burst, the need for emotional release occurs. Without this tension, the awareness of concerns and how one affects those one is in contact with, would remain unknown. Without disputes, humans would not look for solutions and change behaviour, often to achieve improved outcomes. Lack of awareness would lead to many remaining oppressed and unheard. By bringing the concerns to the surface and addressing them, society has an inbuilt cycle for growth and positive change.

Wild law movement: a movement to give personal legal recognition to nature and animals.

Environmental disputes are particularly useful to demonstrate this. Animals and places have not had 'voice' in the disputing world until recently. The **wild law movement**[39] is an example of a dispute that recognises more than just the human dimensions of our planet. It contests anthropocentric beliefs that humans are the centre of the world and nature exists to exploit for human benefit alone. Nature and the natural kingdom in the anthropocentric view is seen as property, much like females were and still may be seen as property in some places, and Earth was once seen as being the centre of the Universe. These notions are now heavily contested.[40] Rivers and animals are being acknowledged as having inherent rights, including the right to be treated as equal to humans in our world.

Negatives

Disputes bring disharmony and this disrupts the ability for individuals to function to their full capacity. This in turn diminishes the ability of society to flourish. This view is based on economic notions, as societies are dependent on contract as the means of legalising relations in the process of producing capital. Without enforceable meaningful contracts and smoothly functioning businesses, along with workers operating at their best capacity, the economy will decline. Trade between private commercial entities and states is disrupted. However, managing disputes brings us much more than this. Disputes, if left unmanaged, can lead to crimes. Domestic violence is a major concern in Australia.[41] This affects children and therefore carries over to the next generation. Individuals each have a right to enjoy life and to be the best they can. A peaceful and harmonious society supports this entitlement.

It is interesting that the Happiness World Survey finds some of the poorer countries high up on the happiness scale.[42] Satisfaction is a relative perception based on who a party compares

39 See, eg, Cormac Cullinan, *Wild Law: A Manifesto for Earth Justice* (Green Books, 2nd ed, 2011).

40 See, eg, Peter Burden, 'Wild Law' (2009) 100 *Arena Magazine* 49-50; Abigail Hutchison, 'The Whanganui River as a Legal Person' (2014) 39(3) *Alternative Law Journal* 179.

41 See Australian Institute of Health, 'Domestic Violence' (Web Page) <https://www.aihw.gov.au/reports-data/behaviours-risk-factors/domestic-violence/overview>.

42 United Nations, 'Sustainable Development Solutions Network's 2019 World Happiness Report', (Web Page) <https://worldhappiness.report/>.

themselves with and the factors by which happiness is evaluated. Bhutan's King Jigme Singye Wangchuck has been an advocate for a different measurement than the economic emphasis on gross domestic product (GDP) for a country's success. His alternative was to judge the success and wellbeing of a community through a gross national happiness (GNH) measure. This has led to the annual world survey of countries' GNH, rather than the economic scale of GDP. Other countries' leaders are also advocating this approach.[43]

Arriving at this point does not mean all disputes have to be managed immediately and that disputes are a bad thing.

Special considerations

This section includes coverage of some areas deserving of special consideration when considering disputes. These are culture, neuroscience, and ethics. How these factors affect the nature of a dispute and its diagnosis along with applying a suitable management process are raised.

Culture

Culture, whether ethnic, generational, religious, gender, or organisational, impacts on how parties perceive a dispute, relate to each other, or understand whether and what dispute management system may be useful in a given scenario. Cultural differences affecting both procedure and substance have been repeatedly identified in dispute management, mainly from the practical perspective of skills development for negotiation, mediation, or arbitration advocacy. Dispute management is affected by differences between the disputing parties' cultural background and education, but also the background of the third-party neutral.

Culture has been defined as 'the total accumulation of an identifiable group's beliefs, norms, activities, institutions, and communication patterns'.[44] These aspects can identify a group of people as belonging to a specific culture. Hoftsede, Hoftsede and Minkov have suggested that there is a 'collective programming of the mind that distinguishes the members of one group or category of people from others'.[45] While an individual has their own personality, in identifying as belonging to a group, they carry the influence of that group. In this sense, culture is described as '... a series of lenses that shape what we see and don't see, how we perceive and interpret, and where we draw boundaries ... Cultural messages whisper to us from the many groups of which we are a part'.[46] These groups can be associations,

43 James Ellsmoor, 'New Zealand Ditches GDP for Happiness and Wellbeing' (11 July 2019) *Forbes* <https://www.forbes.com/sites/jamesellsmoor/2019/07/11/new-zealand-ditches-gdp-for-happiness-and-wellbeing/#641a92b31942>.

44 Carley H Dodd, *Dynamics of Intercultural Communication* (William C Brown, 3rd ed, 1991) 41.

45 Geert H Hofstede, Gert Jan Hofstede and Michael Minkov, *Cultures and Organizations: Software of the Mind: Intercultural Cooperation and its Importance for Survival* (McGraw-Hill, 3rd ed, 2010) 6.

46 Michelle LeBaron and Vinashri Pillay (eds), *Conflict Across Cultures: A Unique Experience of Bridging Differences* (Intercultural Press, 2006) 14.

organisations, ethnic, or religious in nature. The notion of 'culture' is a construct used to identify groups in order to anticipate some of the group's behaviour.

Bringing personality types and cultural scores together is not a simple matter. Hoftsede, Hoftsede and Minkov[47] have researched differences in societies based on a scale comprised of six dimensions, namely:

- power distance
- individualism
- masculinity/femininity
- uncertainty avoidance
- long-term orientation
- indulgence/restraint.

Expression of emotions will vary across cultural groups. This includes what are acceptable emotions and what level of emotional expression can occur. While basic values are shared across cultures, these may sit in a different hierarchy and the expression of these occur through different norms. Different cultural groupings adopt different processes for managing disputes. For instance, Indigenous cultures tend to a restorative justice approach in which the offender is marked by punishment, but then integrated back into the community. This was because offenders, often being young males, were needed in the community for survival. An example of a cultural grouping within an organisational structure is found in the military in Western countries, which retain the ability to conduct criminal hearings in a court-martial system outside the normal civilian criminal system.

Low-context culture: a culture that values the individual and direct communication.

High-context culture: a culture that seeks to maintain group cohesion and relationships.

Often cultures are identified as falling into one of two identifiable forms of communication. This is based on differences identified as either **low-context** or **high-context cultures** (Table 1.2). Low-context cultures value the individual and direct communication that seeks to resolve disputes through a solution orientated outcome. High-context cultures avoid confrontation and seek to maintain group cohesion and relationships.[48] How these translate into and affect the management of a particular dispute will depend on the nature of that dispute and the nature of the cultural differences. For example, a low-context communicator will formulate more direct, straightforward claims; while a high-context communicator will appear to be vague in comparison. A confrontational party will more likely prefer a rights-based determinative dispute management method; while a confrontation-avoiding party will prefer a collaborative approach. A party from a high-context trust-based society will be more open to dispute management and solutions aiming to maintain a long-term relationship; while a party from a low-context task-based culture will put greater emphasis on the contracted rights and obligations of the parties. Cultural differences can be both a source of dispute and a solution once

47 Hofstede, Hofstede and Minkov (n 45) 35; see also Geert Hofstede and Robert R McCrae, 'Personality and Culture Revisited: Linking Traits and Dimensions of Culture' (2004) 38(1) *Cross-Cultural Research* 52.

48 Elizabeth G Chua and William B Gudykunst, 'Conflict Resolution Styles in Low and High Context Cultures' (1987) 4(1) *Communication Research Reports* 32.

recognised and are likely to be a significant factor in determining both the process and the outcome of dispute management.[49]

Table 1.2 Differences between low-context and high-context cultures[50]

Low-context	High-context
Direct communicator	Implicitly embeds meanings in context
Values individualism	Values group cohesion and sense
Tends to develop transitory personal relationships	Cultivates permanent personal relationships
Structured messages with detail, emphasising clarity and completeness	Tends to give simple ambiguous messages
Favours other highly verbal persons	Perceives highly verbal persons less favourably

The way different cultures address disputes provides insight into influences and innovations in the developing and shifting dynamic of dispute management. Cultural considerations are raised throughout this textbook. Where parties to a dispute process are from different cultures, or indeed the dispute practitioner's own culture is different to the parties, this will always influence the manner in which the process occurs. There are philosophical considerations that should be examined when operating in different cultural contexts. The paralanguage can add to misunderstandings as people operate from a set of assumptions that may not be reliable when applying to a different culture. McFadden refers to the three dimensions of culture as unspoken assumptions, norms and values, and explicit factors.[51]

Whether communication-dependent, law-based, relationship-focused, authority-imposing, strictly scheduled or flexible, any and each dispute management mechanism comes across a range of cultural dimensions. There is no easy solution to these differences, but awareness of them is key in adjusting the way we handle disputes for effective dispute management. As a researcher specialising in cross-cultural relations says, '[i]f you go into every interaction assuming that culture doesn't matter, your default mechanism will be to view others through your own cultural lens and to judge or misjudge them accordingly.'[52] Key areas to be aware of as influencing cross-cultural relationships include:

- communication (low v. high context)
- evaluation (direct v. indirect negative feedback)

49 Christopher A Leeds, 'Managing Conflicts Across Cultures: Challenges to Practitioners' (1997) 2(2) *International Journal of Peace Studies* 77.

50 Adapted from Edward T Hall's chart, 'Cultural Variations between Low-Context and High-Context Cultures', cited in John Barkai, 'What's a Cross-Cultural Mediator to do? A Low-context Solution for a High-context Problem' (2008) 10(1) *Cardozo Journal of Conflict Resolution* 43, 59.

51 Danny McFadden, *Mediation in Greater China: The New Frontier for Commercial Mediation* (Wolters Kluwer, 2013) 41.

52 Erin Meyer, *The Culture Map: Breaking through the Invisible Boundaries of Global Business*. (PublicAffairs, 2014) 13.

- persuasion (principles first v. applications first)
- leadership (egalitarian v. hierarchical)
- decision-making (consensual v. top-down)
- trust (task-based v. relationship-based)
- disagreement (confrontational v. confrontation-avoiding)
- scheduling (linear v. flexible time).[53]

When it comes to cultural factors some countries such as China have practised dispute management in the form of mediation for centuries, albeit in a very different form to that which is known as mediation in the West.[54] For instance, Goh makes the point that, in mediations with Chinese people, awareness of the importance of customs and rituals, along with the significance of a public apology, will have important outcomes in managing the dispute.[55] Religious facts can influence the degree of concern for the group. For instance, the dominate religious philosophy in China is Confucianism, and key moral concepts include a respect for hierarchy, masculine success, work over leisure, and a long-term pragmatic outlook.[56]

In Arab cultures, Islam provides a collectivist ideology that also applies more to high-context cultures.[57] This can be thought of in line with the discussion on low-context and high-context cultures. The collectivists, or high-context cultures, are interested in group goals, and the personal welfare of the individual is secondary.[58] Although, in considering collectivism and individualism as binary opposites, Ting-Toomey tempers this by suggesting they exist on a 'dynamic continuum',[59] which allows for a multi-layering in understanding the complexity of cultural influences.

Face theory: reputation is important to consider by saving face and giving face to oneself and the other.

An important theory to be aware of in cross cultural disputes is **face theory**. This is a reputation factor that exists in all cultures, but is taken account of in some cultures by aiming to keep disputes confidential in an effort to save face and give face to the other. Goffman first identified the concept of face as a Chinese cultural aspect and described face as 'a positive social value' one can gain during interaction with another and this can be lost, saved, or protected.[60] However, while

53 Ibid 16.

54 Guy Olivier Faure, 'Chinese Negotiators: Tradition and Modernity' (2020) 25(1) *International Negotiation* 109; see also Moore (n 2) 65–6.

55 Bee Chen Goh, *Law without Lawyers, Justice without Courts: On Traditional Chinese Mediation* (Routledge, 2016); Bee Chen Goh, 'Remedies in Chinese Dispute Resolution' (2001) 13(2) *Bond Law Review* 7.

56 McFadden (n 51) 47; Hualing Fu 'Mediation and the Rule of Law: The Chinese Landscape' in Joachim Zekoll, Moritz Bälz and Iwo Amelung (eds), *Formalisation and Flexibilisation in Dispute Resolution* (Brill, 2014) 108.

57 See, eg, Qazi Attaullah and Lutfullah Saqib, 'Mediation: Application and Functioning under Shari'ah and Law' (2017) 56(3–4) *Islamic Studies* 245; Uzma Rehman, 'Conflict Resolution and Peacemaking in Islam: Toward Reconciliation and Complementarity between Western and Muslim Approaches' (2011) 50(1) *Islamic Studies* 55.

58 Bee Chen Goh, 'On Mediation: Sino-Western Insights' in Bee Chen Goh, *Law without lawyers, justice without courts: on traditional Chinese mediation* (Routledge, 2016) 12.

59 Stella Ting-Toomey, 'Applying Dimensional Values in Understanding Intercultural Communication' (2010) 77(2) *Communication Monographs* 169, 176.

60 Erving Goffman, 'On Face-work: An Analysis of Ritual Elements in Social Interaction' (1995) 18(3) *Psychiatry* 213.

face theory has been developed, it has been shown that its usage and effect differ across cultures. Ting-Toomey and others identified differences between individualist and collectivist cultures in regard to face behaviour.[61] Face theory can mean admitting one is wrong is made difficult and will not occur in an open forum.[62] The most important consideration when dealing with generalised assertions in a cultural context is not to take one or two experiences and extrapolate to the many. We all exist in multiple cultural groups and all are subject to changes in meaning and identities over time. Therefore, every party should be considered in their individual capacity.[63] As Busch notes, cultural theory in dispute management research comes from many varied approaches:

> Goldberg clarifies that authors locate the impact of culture at different positions within a mediation process: Many mediation practitioners like for example Lederach see cultural influences rooted in theoretical mediation models. Anthropologists like Avruch instead focus on culture's influence on actual mediation practice. Besides from this, LeBaron, McCandless and Garon assume that cultures affect forms and manifestations of conflict as such.[64]

Many believe the Western-centric models of dispute management risk becoming dominated by low-context oral communication controlled by a third-party intervener in a manner that can disenfranchise high-context cultures. Mahan and Mahuna[65] are writers that propose adoption of a broader framework allowing Indigenous dispute management techniques based on high-context communicative dialogue that accommodates emotional expression through narrative and reflection.

Indigenous dispute management

With long established cultures, disputes are managed in a fashion often described as peace-keeping, to protect and sustain the community.[66] Australian Aboriginal and Torres Strait Islander peoples require awareness and cultural sensitivity in approaches to dispute management communication.[67] Cross-cultural sensitivity and competence training of dispute

---

61 See, eg, Stella Ting-Toomey et al, 'Culture, Face Maintenance, and Styles of Handling Interpersonal Conflicts: A Study in Five Culture' (1991) 2(4) *International Journal of Conflict Management* 27; John Oetzel et al, 'Face and Facework in Conflict: A Cross-Cultural Comparison of China, Germany, Japan, and the United States' (2001) 68(3) *Communication Monographs* 235.

62 See, eg, John L Graham, Mehdi Mahdavi and Navid Fatehi-Rad, 'Finding Potential Speed Bumps and Pitfalls in Buyer–Seller Negotiations in Twenty Cultures' (2020) 36(3) *Negotiation Journal* 249.

63 See, eg, Dorcas Quek Anderson, 'Court-Annexed Mediations Within Singapore: A Complex Interface Between Individual Place and the Court Environment' in Pauline Collins Victor Igreja and Patrick Danaher (eds), *Nexus between Place, Conflict and Communication in a Globalising World* (Palgrave Macmillan, 2019) 121.

64 Dominic Busch, 'Does Conflict Mediation Research Keep Track with Cultural Theory?' (2016) 4(2) *European Journal of Applied Linguistics* 181, 185 (citations omitted).

65 Laura N Mahan and Joshua M Mahuna, 'Bridging the Divide: Cross-Cultural Mediation' (2017) 7(1) *International Research and Review: Journal of Phi Beta Delta Honor* 11.

66 Goh (n 58) 2 ('Law without Lawyers'); see also Carlo Osi, 'Understanding Indigenous Dispute Resolution Processes and Western Alternative Dispute Resolution: Cultivating Culturally Appropriate Methods in Lieu of Litigation' (2008) 10(1) *Cardozo Journal Conflict Resolution* 163; Catherine Bell and David Kahane (eds), *Intercultural Dispute Resolution in Aboriginal Contexts* (UBC Press, 2004).

67 See, eg, Farzad Sharifian, 'Cultural Conceptualisations in Intercultural Communication: A Study of Aboriginal and Non-Aboriginal Australians' (2010) 42(12) *Journal of Pragmatics* 3367.

practitioners is expected. Larissa Behrendt and Loretta Kelly[68] make the distinction between inter- and intra-cultural communication and propose models for mediation relevant to the different contexts. The process they suggest for inter-cultural mediations adopts a flexible facilitation model; whereas intra-cultural mediation is about finding community connectedness and is best facilitated by Elders.

Native title matters present one of the most prominent areas where cross-cultural mediation occurs.[69] These matters are also significant in that they involve multi-parties in the dispute management. The *Native Title Act 1993* (Cth) ss 86A(1) and (2) enables the National Native Tribunal to provide for mandatory mediations in contested native title matters. It is important to note there is significant criticism of native title mediation in relation to its purported 'cultural insensitivity'.[70] Much of the literature which supports the cultural approach of native title mediation is criticised as written by white lawyers.[71] Over time, there has been refinement and learning for multi-party mediations in a cultural context.

Indigenous methods for managing disputes have been shared and influenced dispute practitioners in certain disputing areas and models. For instance, the Yolngu people of East Arnhem Land engaged in a project that shared their Mawul Rom ceremony.[72] The model entails dialogue for peace-making and harmonising of community that includes many aspects such as self-reflection and meditation.[73] Taking Indigenous knowledge to apply across broader disputing parties brings changes to how dispute management is practised. In environmental and land disputes, adopting a consensus dialogue approach to community can help dissolve dispute escalation.[74] Other influential changes have included how courts approach offending.

68 Larissa Behrendt and Loretta Kelly, 'Preferred Model for Inter-cultural Dispute Resolution' in Larissa Behrendt and Loretta Kelly (eds), *Resolving Indigenous Disputes Land Conflicts and Beyond* (Federation Press, 2008); Loretta Kelly, 'Elements of a Good Practice Aboriginal Mediation Model: Part II' (2008) 19(4) *Australasian Dispute Resolution Journal* 223, 224; R Thorne, 'Incorporating ADR into Contemporary Aboriginal Society' (Conference Paper, Second International Mediation Conference: Mediation and Cultural Diversity, Adelaide, 18-20 January 1996) 11.

69 Graeme Neate, 'Reconciliation on the Ground: Meeting the Challenges of Native Title Mediation: Part I' (2002) 5(6) *ADR Bulletin* 89.

70 See Raelene Webb, 'Whither Native Title' (2015-2016) 19(2) *Australian Indigenous Law Review* 114; Craig Jones, 'Aboriginal Boundaries: The Mediation and Settlement of Aboriginal Boundary Disputes in a Native Title Context' (Occasional Paper No 2/2002, National Native Title Tribunal, May 2002).

71 Richard D Mohr, 'Some Conditions for Culturally Diverse Deliberation' (2005) 20(1) *Canadian Journal of Law and Society* 87; Louise Anderson, 'The Law and the Desert: Alternative Methods of Delivering Justice' (2003) 30(1) *Journal of Law and Society* 120.

72 See Keren Lavelle, 'Ancient Ceremony Transformed into Cross-Cultural Mediation Training' (2005) 43(2) *Law Society Journal* 22; Samantha Newman, 'The Mawul Rom Project – An Experience of Cross-Cultural Mediation' (2004) 6(6) *Indigenous Law Bulletin* 11.

73 Djiniyini Gondarra and Sarah Blake, 'Mediation: Cultural Healing through Community Healing: The Mawul Rom Project' (National Indigenous Justice CEO Forum, 21-22 November 2008) <https://www.indigenousjustice.gov.au/resources/mediation-cultural-healing-through-community-healing-the-mawul-rom-project/>; see also Sarah Ciftci and Deirdre Howard-Wagner, 'Integrating Indigenous Justice into Alternative Dispute Resolution Practices: A Case Study of the Aboriginal Care Circle Pilot Program in Nowra' (2012) 16(2) *Australian Indigenous Law Review* 81.

74 See, eg, Rob White, 'Indigenous Communities, Environmental Protection and Restorative Justice' (2014) 18(2) *Australian Indigenous Law Review* 43; Carol Reade and Mark McKenna, 'Leveraging Indigenous Knowledge for Sustainable Workplace Harmony A Conflict Management Tool for International Managers' (2013)(September) *Journal of Corporate Citizenship* 53; AG Adebayo, Jesse Benjamin and Brandon D Lundy (eds), *Indigenous Conflict Management Strategies: Global Perspectives* (Lexington Books, 2014).

This includes considering principles of restorative justice,[75] therapeutic jurisprudence approaches, and jurisprudence of hybridity.[76] The latter is a process that evolves from the bottom up and is sensitive to not just appropriating aspects of Indigenous culture to provide an Indigenised flavour to existing justice delivery.[77]

Practitioners, when referring to Indigenous peoples, must remember there is not a single Indigenous culture, but within each continent there are diverse cultural groups. In Australia we tend to use an all-encompassing term; namely, the 'Aboriginal and Torres Strait Islander peoples'. As a practitioner managing disputes, it is essential to prepare well for a cross-cultural dispute management – whatever process is adopted. This includes not making any assumptions, observing good listening skills, avoiding stereotyping or generalising, and maintaining a self-awareness – including of one's own cultural influences. While all these factors are important, every individual must be considered as unique.

Neuroscience

In 2013, President Obama, in his speech launching the US BRAIN (Brain Research through Advancing Innovative Neurotechnologies) Initiative,[78] stated:

> As humans, we can identify galaxies light years away, we can study particles smaller than an atom. But we still haven't unlocked the mystery of the three pounds of matter that sits between our ears. But today, scientists possess the capability to study individual neurons and figure out the main functions of certain areas of the brain.[79]

Our advancing knowledge of the brain is slowly unfolding an awareness that practitioners can utilise when addressing parties in disputes. This knowledge brings a depth of awareness that permits a refinement in thinking about our approaches and processes for addressing disputes.[80]

We have already touched on the primitive brain and the role of the amygdala as the 'fight, flight or freeze' response centre. It is the place from which threats are recorded and a first response is initiated. Our body reacts to events first through the emotional or primitive brain, setting in place a complex series of physiological events when emotion is engaged. The instantaneous threat protection mechanism means the cortex – that part of our brain in which

75 See Harry Blagg, 'Restorative Visions and Restorative Justice Practices: Conferencing, Ceremony and Reconciliation in Australia' (1998) 10(1) *Current Issues in Criminal Justice* 5; Suzuki Masahiro and William R Wood, 'Co-option, Coercion and Compromise: Challenges of Restorative Justice in Victoria, Australia' (2017) 20(2) *Contemporary Justice Review* 274, for a criticism of some restorative justice approaches.

76 Paul Schiff Berman, 'Towards a Jurisprudence of Hybridity' (2010) 1 *Utah Law Review* 11, 12; Ida Nursoo, 'Indigenous Law, Colonial Injustice and the Jurisprudence of Hybridity' (2018) 50(1) *Journal of Legal Pluralism and Unofficial Law* 56.

77 Nursoo (n 76) 58.

78 National Institutes of Health, *The Brain Initiative* (Web Page) <https://braininitiative.nih.gov/>.

79 Barack Obama, 'Remarks by the President on the BRAIN Initiative and American Innovation' (Press Release, The White House, Office of the Press Secretary, 2 April 2013) <https://obamawhitehouse.archives.gov/the-press-office/2013/04/02/remarks-president-brain-initiative-and-american-innovation> [8].

80 Jeremy Lack and Francois Bogacz, 'The Neurophysiology of ADR and Process Design: A New Approach to Conflict Prevention and Resolution' (2012) 14(1) *Cardozo Journal of Conflict Resolution* 33.

thought and judgment occurs – is often not able to moderate the immediate response by thinking through the consequences of the reactive response.

Most humans, however, will learn to recognise the activation of the amygdala response, such as when anger causes the heart rate and breathing to increase, muscles to tense, and our skin to flush. When they learn to do this, they can exercise control by, for example, deliberately calming their breathing, counting to 10, or even leaving the room for a short time. Other methods can be practised to develop this ability, such as relaxation, breathing, and cognitive control techniques. This all creates a space for the cognitive brain to process the events that have given rise to the emotion and to think before reacting or speaking.

The prefrontal cortex is the part of the brain that assists in this. In particular, the left prefrontal cortex is an off switch on emotions. Acting in an executive role, it controls emotion particularly when this is not likely to result in alleviating the threat. Emotion such as anger, once aroused, can take days to dissipate. During this time, adrenaline remains in the system and it can be more easily reactivated reducing the threshold time for negative responses.

This section has only touched on the developing awareness of how the brain responds to disputes. There is a growing body of research literature that can expand practitioners' knowledge so this understanding can be used to assist parties through difficult disputes. Practitioners should maintain their knowledge in this area.[81]

Ethics

One further issue to address before leaving a discussion about disputes are ethical considerations. Ethical considerations demand the highest level of attention and often go beyond compliance with the law, and focus on what is morally correct in the given situation. Applying this high standard will ensure that, when presented with an ethical dilemma, often like a fork in the road, it will be readily apparent what direction should be taken.

Dispute management practitioners, particularly lawyers,[82] have an obligation to assist parties by advising them on the most effective steps the parties can take to manage a dispute. This requires not only the ability to diagnose the causes of a dispute but also having a well-rounded knowledge of the suitability of different processes and how they operate. Under the *Civil Dispute Resolution Act 2011* (Cth), lawyers can now face a costs order if the parties have not undertaken genuine steps to attempt to manage a dispute.[83] In creating the 'obligation to take genuine steps to resolve disputes before court proceedings are instituted', the Act also creates an obligation on the lawyers, leading to professional liability by establishing that:

> A lawyer acting for a person who is required to file a genuine steps statement must:
>
> (a) advise the person of the requirement; and
>
> (b) assist the person to comply with the requirement.[84]

81 See also Chapter 2, 23 and Chapter 4, 129.

82 *Civil Dispute Resolution Act 2011* (Cth) s 9.

83 *Civil Dispute Resolution Act 2011* (Cth) ss 12(2), (3).

84 *Civil Dispute Resolution Act 2011* (Cth) s 9.

Prior to this legislation, lawyers had no particular obligations with regard to understanding the causes of disputes or the varied processes for dispute management and parties could keep disputing until they were drained of resources.

Lawyers, as partisan advisers to clients, that are engaged in a process of dispute management must respect the role of the third-party dispute practitioner and support their role. This is also the case with the dispute practitioner. Exercising professional respect means understanding the roles each plays in the management process. Professionals should not contribute to an escalation of the parties' dispute or an extending of it beyond the earliest possible agreement.

Understanding of the process environment one is operating in is vital. For instance, if the mediation is to be a facilitative mediation then making recommendations, giving advice, or providing a decision is outside that model and is likely to be disruptive and result in complaints by the parties. Practitioners need to note their insurance terms of practice to ensure they do not stray into fields beyond their coverage.

Practitioners should not make claims, such as their success rate, in resolving disputes if this cannot be supported by evidence. In any event, such claims are best not to be made as they can raise expectations of parties.

As a partisan advisor, being an advocate for one party should involve a preference for collaboration and a focus on the problem, and not the opposing party, to ensure an approach that is conducive to dispute de-escalation and management. Being adversarial in style is not likely to help settle a matter at the earliest possible time and generally is only appropriate if litigation is the best process. Most legislative instruments now encourage attempts at genuinely settling a dispute before proceeding to litigation. Even before this legislative encouragement, judges adopted a position that supported the public policy to ensure disputes were settled as early as possible to avoid further entrenchment of the parties in their respective positions, increasing the costs to the relationships and broader society.

Justice Barr, in *Spadaccini v Grice* (2012) 32 NTLR 1, described behaviour by the parties and their lawyers that had escalated the costs in seeking an order to remove a concrete dividing boundary wall that had encroached on the plaintiffs' property by 740–790 mm. The conflict started in 2003. In 2011, the plaintiffs brought a proceeding to seek a declaration that the wall encroached on their land and that the wall be removed. Pre-trial procedure required at the time through Practice Direction 6 stated that the parties 'should follow a reasonable procedure, suitable to their particular circumstances, which is intended to avoid litigation'.[85]

Lawyers need to stay focused on acting in the best interest of their clients. This ultimately means addressing the underlying issues and managing a dispute in a manner that maintains relationships, removes obstacles to ongoing business, and addresses issues in the earliest, most cost-effective manner. Too often, the law provides only the common law-based remedy of monetary compensation. This leads lawyer dispute practitioners to seek a rights-based settlement resolution in monetary terms, often closing down the possibility for addressing the underlying issues. The acceptance that money solves all issues in an immediate settlement loses sight of the many other aspects of a dispute that raises issues such as the healing available

85 See Northern Territory Supreme Court, *Practice Direction 6 of 2009 – Trial Civil Procedure Reforms*, 11 June 2009 [29] (as amended by Northern Territory Supreme Court, *Practice Direction 10 of 2009 – Trial Civil Procedure Reform*, 5 November 2009).

from a simple apology or other solutions that parties can privately negotiate. The only limit on these solutions is the party's own creativity.

Mayer[86] has advocated staying with the dispute to manage harder issues that may never fully be resolved through a process of constructive engagement. This is a challenge to a dispute management community that is itself driven by pressures to assist parties to address disputes in short timeframes and to focus on what can be achieved as immediate solutions, leaving the harder issues for another day. Organisations that understand this and allow practitioners to engage with disputing parties in a sustained way, permitting the time needed to allow the parties to grasp the context fully and the requirements needed to avoid future disputes in a more transformative manner, support a vision needed for a paradigm shift in managing disputes.

Conclusion

The discussion in this chapter has identified when a conflict becomes a dispute and the applicability of research theory to understand key principles affecting a dispute as well as a description of models to help diagnose the causes underlying a dispute. Many think of either mediation or litigation as the primary processes for managing a dispute. However, neither prevent disputes from developing, nor do they necessarily provide transformation or address psychological issues. Other processes are available, and each brings unique characteristics to a dispute and its management. Experts and counsellors can give parties insight into the causes of their dispute and approaches to change structures and balance power. Facilitators can assist parties through improved communication and negotiation techniques. Interviewers and conflict coaches can provide parties with factual data using relevant techniques. This textbook gives you an overview of the most readily available processes.

There are many ways of thinking about disputes and what a resolution or management may be. Emotional closure is possible with appropriate acknowledgement, such as an apology or symbolic action. Some practitioners look to transform a party's dispute and understanding of their issues. This requires an engaged process to assist the parties. Some see the need only to reach a settlement based on the law, such as monetary compensation or equitable remedies. Other practitioners will seek to have underlying interests of parties met with the aim to provide a long-term solution and perhaps address power imbalance and empower parties through social justice outcomes. Knowing the aim of an intervention is important for the practitioner.

While conflict is a natural aspect of human lives, we have seen there are specific factors for practitioners to take notice of when managing disputes. There are models available to help diagnose which of the many processes available for dispute management are most effective for the dispute under consideration. One factor underpins successful dispute management, and this is effective communication. The next chapter will provide the practitioner with guidance on how to be an effective communicator in the disputing world.

86 Mayer (n 17).

EXERCISE IN APPLYING YOUR KNOWLEDGE – *SPADACCINI V GRICE*

Read *Spadaccini v Grice* (2012) 32 NTLR 1 and answer the following questions.

This case involves a neighbour dispute over a retaining wall between their properties. Rosanna Spadaccini and Michele Spadaccini, the plaintiffs, were seeking costs in the matter in relation to a prior consent judgment in their favour for $110,000. The parties combined costs in the matter had reached $900,000. Janice Grice, the defendant, and her husband (now deceased) had lived in this prestigious suburb for many years. They had built a concrete block wall some years prior to 2003, which strayed over the boundary line by around 790 millimetres at the most extensive point. The plaintiffs purchased the adjoining property in 2003 and a survey conducted prepatory to redevelopment of the site noted the encroachment of the wall. This was drawn to the plaintiffs' attention and negotiations began from there, resulting in the determinative litigation after attempts at mediation.

This case provides an excellent example of the way in which conflict can develop into a dispute and the range of processes it can go through. Entrapment is also in evidence in this dispute. Finally, Justice Barr provides an assessment of the role of the partisan legal representatives and the conduct of the matter through the various dispute management processes.

1. When did this matter change from a conflict into a dispute?
2. What signified that it was a manifest dispute?
3. Diagnose the dispute based on Moore's Circle of Conflict.
4. What would be an appropriate process for managing this dispute?
5. Apply a chosen model to hypothesise the causes underlying this dispute.
6. What was each party's position and what were their legal rights?
7. Can you describe interests that each party may have had in this dispute?
8. Document the offers made by both sides.
9. Document the lawyer's actions in this dispute, from both sides, and note whether the action deescalated or escalated the dispute.
10. Can you see a cultural impact within this dispute? How may it have been different if the parties came from the same cultural background?

2 COMMUNICATION

Learning aims

- Demonstrate understanding of interpersonal communication as an essential component of dispute management practice
- Identify and explain different models of interpersonal communication
- Demonstrate knowledge of key interpersonal skills used in dispute resolution practice
- Identify and explain challenges to effective interpersonal communication
- Explain reflective practice, emotional intelligence and issues of professional conduct

Understanding communication

Managing **communication** between parties and mastering effective communication skills are fundamental features of dispute management practice. In order to manage communication, dispute practitioners need to master effective communication skills. This chapter describes and explains some of the essential skills required for effective communication by dispute practitioners. Those skills are placed in the context of a discussion of different models of communication and the particular importance of emotion in communication. The discussion in this chapter can be applied to all the dispute management processes considered in this textbook. It is useful to begin with an examination of the nature of communication and its essential elements.

Communication: the sharing and exchange of information and meaning by verbal and non-verbal, written and other visual means, across a variety of mediums.

In dispute management processes, considerable emphasis has been given to face-to-face communication with and between parties. This form of communication is more recently aided by digital online programs, such as Zoom and Microsoft Teams. Face-to-face communication has three core aspects: the verbal message (what is said); the vocal aspect (how it is said); and the visual aspect (the way it is said). According to the distinction between verbal and non-verbal communication, the verbal aspect represents verbal communication, while the vocal and visual aspects are identified as non-verbal communication.[1]

The largest effective component of communication is visual, followed by vocalisation, which includes pitch and pace of the voice, and lastly the verbal component, or what is said. Given this relative effectiveness, the ability to convey a message to maximum effect is best achieved when face-to-face. Face-to-face communication, whether in person or via digital means, is the dominant medium of dispute management practice. As a society, however, we have become reliant on text messages, email, or short written communication. We also use the telephone, which includes vocal as well as verbal aspects, less than we did in the past. The widespread use of emoticons suggests a need to add these visual symbols to written communications in order to convey nuances of meaning otherwise absent from the basic text.

Paralanguage: the non-verbal components of communication such as pitch, tone, pace of speech, and facial expressions that convey meaning consciously or unconsciously.

Non-verbal communication, also known as **paralanguage**, consists of those oral and behavioural cues that are not spoken words; for example, intonation, pitch and pace of speaking, encouraging noises, gestures, and facial expressions. The

1 Nadja M Spegel, Bernadette Rogers and Ross P Buckley, *Negotiation: Theory and Techniques* (Butterworths, 1998) 144.

listener employs paralanguage to encourage and connect with the speaker. Head nodding is often employed to signal that the listener is following the narrative conveyed. The listener can also listen for non-verbal cues used by the speaker to convey complexity of meaning. Messages are conveyed not only by what is said but also by how it is said. Subtle differences in meaning can be conveyed, according to whether speech is high pitched or low and whether the pace is fast or slow. Examples of paralanguage include the following:

- tone, voice quality, timbre, resonance
- rate of speech
- pitch, volume intensity
- rhythm of speech
- breaks in speech: hesitation, pauses
- silence.

Interpersonal communication by verbal and non-verbal means is more than the information and subtlety of meaning conveyed. It means 'having a voice' in relationships with others. Carol Gilligan sums up what having a voice means:

> To have a voice is to be human. To have something to say is to be a person. But speaking depends on listening and being heard; it is an intensely relational act. By voice I mean something like what people mean when they speak of the core of the self. Voice is natural and also cultural. It is composed of breath and sound, words, rhythm, and language … and voice is a powerful psychological instrument and channel, connecting inner and outer worlds.[2]

Using theory and models to dissect communication

Interpersonal communication: occurs between individuals interacting at a personal level, whether face-to-face or aided through a digital interface.

Communication in dispute management emphasises **interpersonal communication** as the means by which dispute management processes are conducted. Interpersonal communication marks the field of communication that occurs between individuals at a personal level. There are various definitions of interpersonal communication in the academic literature. According to Solomon and Theiss, the

> … *inter* part of the word highlights how interpersonal communication connects people. In interpersonal communication, one person's actions both affect and reflect another person's actions … When you engage in interpersonal communication, you and another person become linked together.[3]

2 Carol Gilligan, *In a Different Voice: Psychological Theory and Women's Development* (Harvard University Press, 1982) xvi.

3 Denise Solomon and Jennifer Theiss, *Interpersonal Communication: Putting Theory into Practice* (Routledge, 2013) 5.

In the following discussion, three models of interpersonal communication are examined: the linear model, the two-way model, and a social skills model. These models provide a useful grounding for understanding how communication operates in dispute management.

Linear interpersonal communication model

A linear model of communication explains communication as the transmission of information along a linear path from sender to receiver as depicted in Figure 2.1. You can imagine the path of communicated information as similar to sound passing through a wireless transmitter. Interference, or noise, may occur along the path, interrupting or distorting the flow of information. This model relies on identification and measurement of discrete message components.[4] Imagine messages passed by Morse code during World War II. The sender would pass the message in code to a soldier who would transmit the message by machine, or channel it 'over the wire', to a recipient who would decode the message and pass it to its proper destination. As applied to dispute management practice, the linear model best describes determinative processes in which disputes are managed by third-party experts.

Figure 2.1 A linear model of communication[5]

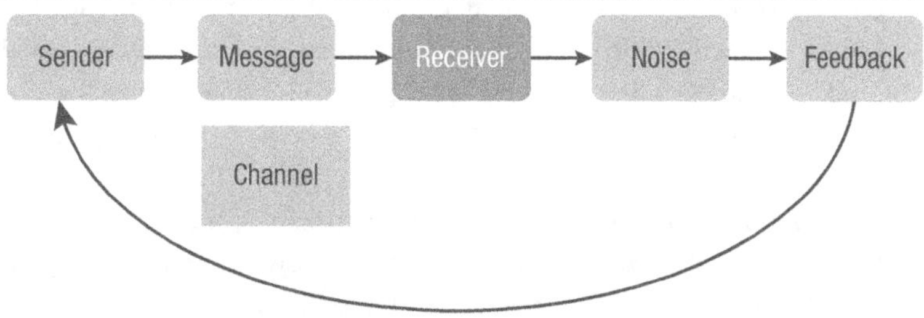

A limitation of this model of communication is the suggestion that communication moves discretely in one direction. Instead, interpersonal communication is, by definition, a two-way process. Furthermore, it will rarely involve the passage of discrete information in one event. Interpersonal communication is a process that is cumulative over time. What is said and responded to in the moment shapes the interchange of the next moments. At the same time, the communication may begin with an apparently discrete message, but is likely to be interpreted with a new or different meaning. What is communicated will depend upon the intention of the sender and the interpretation of the receiver. What is understood by both parties will ultimately involve some negotiation of meaning if shared understanding is to be achieved.

4 Owen Hargie, Christine Saunders and David Dickson, *Social Skills in Interpersonal Communication* (Routledge, 3rd ed, 1994) 19; see also Owen Hargie, *Skilled Interpersonal Communication* (Routledge 5th ed, 2011).

5 Celeste Lawson et al, *Communication Skills for Business Professionals* (Cambridge University Press, 2nd edition, 2019) 59.

Two-way communication model

This model acknowledges interpersonal communication is a two-way process of both verbal and non-verbal factors. The sender and receiver experience the whole of the communication, including feelings and attitudes.[6] This circular rather than linear process passes through encoding and decoding filters of those involved in the communication. The model includes not only the message, but the feedback and the communicative techniques involved. This entails being aware of communication at the meta-level: thinking about the communication while communicating.

Social skills model of interpersonal communication

The social skills model emphasises three key characteristics of interpersonal communication that extend our understanding beyond the linear and two-way models: acknowledgment of the social context of communication; understanding that communication is purposeful, or goal oriented; and appreciation of the role of **perceptions** in the communication of meaning.[7]

Perceptions: the understanding or interpretation given to sensory information.

The social skills model emphasises the interaction of participants in the context of their social relationships. The social identity of dispute practitioners differs according to the context of the interpersonal communication. How a dispute practitioner interacts with parties is different from how they interact with others in informal settings. For instance, a lawyer giving legal advice in a work setting is expected to give accurate legal advice. This is clearly distinguished from a lawyer providing information in an informal social setting.

In dispute management, communication with parties, dispute practitioners and other professionals is purposeful. For example, in an initial interview with parties, dispute practitioners are gathering information in order to determine a hypothesis as to the dispute's causes and the best process to assist the parties. The dispute practitioner will seek to elicit what both parties want to achieve. In communication with parties' legal representatives, the dispute practitioner will seek professional input to achieve an outcome that both parties feel they can adopt to manage their dispute.

Perceptions, or interpretations, act as a form of feedback for interpersonal communication. What is communicated is influenced initially by how the sender perceives the recipient. When a message is sent and received, how the recipient responds, both verbally and non-verbally, will influence a further response from the sender. There is ample scope in the exchange for preconceptions and misconceptions that can colour the communication and introduce the possibility of a dispute. According to Fisher and Ury, conflict is a function of differing perceptions: 'Whether you are making a deal or settling a dispute, differences are defined by the difference between your thinking and theirs.'[8] Ultimately, conflict 'lies not in objective reality

6 Spegel, Rogers and Buckley (n 1) 138.

7 Ibid.

8 Roger Fisher and William Ury, *Getting to Yes: Negotiating Agreement Without Giving In* (Penguin Books, 1981) 22.

but in people's heads'.[9] Facts may be established yet differing perceptions of responsibility can cause disagreement. Fears may be unfounded or hopes unrealistic, and both may fuel disputes.

Awareness that perceptions can be misperceptions better enables dispute practitioners to comprehend verbal and non-verbal signals used to diagnose dispute causes and to assist parties to explore their interests. Empowering and encouraging parties to consider broad options and helping them to reality test their perceptions and assumptions assists parties to reframe their dispute from a problem-solving perspective.

Dispute practitioners develop approaches to communication through training and experience. Effective communication should be evident from the first introduction, to interviewing parties and keeping them informed of the process; it is facilitated by conveying clear expectations. In all such communications, there is a need to keep an 'open mind' and to avoid making assumptions about what parties want or need. Disputes are inevitably coloured and fuelled by emotions. Recognising, acknowledging and responding to emotions are key skills employed by dispute practitioners; and examined in the discussion that follows.

Emotion in interpersonal communication

Emotion is primarily a non-verbal communication aid, although it can also certainly be verbal. It always requires acknowledgement to enable the emotional party to move into a cognitive communicative state.

Communication activates the emotional centres of the brain and so all communication is emotional. Research developments, particularly in the field of neuroscience, are leading to a new understanding of the way the brain functions. The hierarchical 'computer' image is being replaced by an understanding of the brain as a 'multiplex' non-linear organ, in which reason and emotion are holistically intertwined.[10] As outlined in Chapter 1, neuroscience indicates that the primitive emotional brain, in which the amygdala plays an important role, dictates much of our decision-making. **Neuroscience** findings are leading to acknowledgement of the importance of addressing emotion in dispute management.

Neuroscience: the study of the human nervous system.

Parties' narratives will usually contain significant emotional content that is particularly relevant to dispute management. Emotional signals can reveal the significance of situations and circumstances for a party and thereby point to their interests and needs. Emotional cues will indicate whether parties are open to moving forward and to possible compromise and whether they are satisfied with progress at any given stage. Emotional responses provide clues to how a party is feeling and thinking, and these can be displayed through the verbal, vocal and visual components of communication. Emotional cues that are visual and vocal may even contradict or modify what the party is saying verbally. In traditional legal processes, a client's emotions are treated as peripheral to the information needed for a rational-analytical approach to problem-solving. Emotions can be 'messy' and awkward for a legal practitioner and are often not considered relevant to the core facts of a

9 Ibid.

10 See also RE Cytowic, 'Synesthesia: Phenomenology and Neuropsychology: A Review of Current Knowledge' (1995)(January) *Psyche* 2; EA Phelps, 'Emotion and Cognition: Insights from Studies of the Human Amygdala' (2006) 57 *Annual Review of Psychology* 27.

matter. By contrast, being cognisant of parties' emotions enables a dispute practitioner to be alert to all sources of information and meaning creation and better able to understand the needs and interests of parties as a result.

Emotion is an inherent part of human interaction and of interpersonal communication. How one responds to emotion, whether their own or someone else's, will be a product of early conditioning and situational experience and training. As professionals, dispute practitioners need to be aware of their own emotions and how and when to display them. They must understand their own communicative response to disputes and emotions.[11] This requires a meta-awareness of one's personality, value system, and the triggers for emotions.[12] Expecting oneself and parties to be unemotional and always rational is unrealistic and limits the possibilities for dispute management. This self-awareness enables the dispute practitioner to also gain some insight to the parties' personality type. Acknowledging emotions and responding to them sensitively and constructively demonstrates active listening to parties and allows them to feel understood. Isopraxism, or following the behaviour of the other, can help a speaker feel comfortable and supported. However, this is a skilled practice that must avoid causing a party to feel belittled by mimicking. When used appropriately, this skill enhances effective dispute management.[13]

Legitimacy is an important aspect to consider in dealing with emotion. As Bolton notes, a person responds well to another whom they acknowledge is behaving in a legitimate or genuine and authentic manner.[14] Cloke[15] warns of the need to avoid 'automatic, idealized, inauthentic behaviour and sterile, bureaucratic professionalism', in order to maintain a connection to one's inner emotional self. Cloke cites Fromm:

> Today we come across an individual who behaves like an automaton, who does not know or understand himself, and the only person that he knows is the person that he is supposed to be, whose meaningless chatter has replaced communicative speech, whose synthetic smile has replaced genuine laughter, and whose sense of dull despair has taken the place of genuine pain.[16]

Practitioners need to put aside any assumptions about emotion, particularly if previously viewed as unnecessarily intrusive or irrelevant to the process of problem-solving. Reflecting back emotions is an important skill in demonstrating empathy and building trust. Parties may express a high intensity of emotion as a natural and predictable consequence of experiencing disputes; for example, frustration, sorrow or grief may be expressed by crying or an angry outburst. Alternatively, parties may exhibit deliberate restraint or an unwillingness or inability to express emotion. Where parties appear stuck or choked by emotions, moving them back to an earlier part of the discussion that was less emotional can help calm the emotional tide and

---

11 Kenneth Cloke, *Mediating Dangerously: The Frontiers of Conflict Resolution* (Jossey-Bass, 2001), specifically chapters 3, 5 and 7.

12 See also Nadja Alexander, Jill Howieson and Kenneth Fox, *Negotiation Strategy Style Skills* (LexisNexis Butterworths, 2nd ed, 2010); Roger Fisher and Daniel Shapiro, *Beyond Reason: Using Emotions as You Negotiate* (Penguin Putnam, 2006).

13 See also Pauline Collins, 'Mediators' Authentic Presence: Ways of Knowing Our Primitive Selves' (2010) 21(2) *Australasian Dispute Resolution Journal* 85; see also Chapter 1, 25, 33.

14 Robert Bolton, *People Skills* (Simon & Schuster, 1987).

15 Cloke (n 11) 53.

16 Ibid.

allow the parties to slowly move forward. Similarly, if emotions are overwhelming, non-verbal empathetic signals, such as offering a glass of water or placing the tissue box within reach, acknowledge the party's experience, demonstrating acceptance and respect. Angry outbursts can be disconcerting and give rise to defensive reactions in other parties and the practitioner. The following steps can be used to manage intense emotions:

1. Remain calm: Make a conscious decision to breathe and relax before you respond. Be conscious of your posture and facial expression – remain open and attentive. Remember isopraxism: matching appropriately the other's pitch, tone and body movements and then gradually lessening these so they join you in moving to a calmer state.
2. Take your time: Don't rush. Remain attentive and acknowledge the emotion, verbally and/or non-verbally.
3. Continue to listen: Look and act interested. Don't turn away or appear disturbed.
4. Acknowledge feelings: It is important to acknowledge the feelings expressed so that the party feels heard and the importance of their issue is understood. Identify their emotion as accurately as possible. Naming the emotion assists the party in feeling they have been heard. They can then move to a cognitive state for their continuing narrative.
5. Reframe: Use reframing to detoxify statements and lower the intensity of emotions and demonstrate that you have heard and understood. Reflect the issue back to the speaker using as closely as possible their language but neutralising inflammatory words and tone.
6. Ask questions: As the intensity of emotion dissipates, ask questions to help the party express the reasons for the emotion. This can help the other party increase their empathetic awareness.

Taking account of emotion is significant at every phase of a dispute management process. Important information can be gained from parties' expressions of emotion that is needed to identify their presenting and over-riding concerns, their interests and needs, the options for dispute management that they favour and can live with, and their ultimate satisfaction with the process and its outcome. For this reason, dispute practitioners employ skills that take into account parties' emotions. Examples of how communication skills incorporate acknowledgement of emotions are included in the discussion below.

Using communication knowledge to assist in dispute management

The following discussion identifies and explores core interpersonal communication skills used by dispute management practitioners. These skills apply across the full range of dispute resolution processes. The skills examined are:

- establishing trust and rapport
- demonstrating empathy
- active listening
- eliciting information (or asking questions and setting an agenda)

- facilitating
- checking understanding (with a focus on summaries, reflection and reframing)
- generating options
- reality testing.

These skills are not mutually exclusive. The first three in particular – establishing trust and rapport, demonstrating empathy and active listening – are core skills that should be demonstrated across the various phases of a dispute management process. Different labels are assigned to some of these skills in the literature. Active listening is also described as effective,[17] constructive[18] or reflective listening.[19] Reflection is a particular skill that embodies a non-directional approach[20] and, as such, is a component of other skills, including active listening and checking understanding. Reflection involves mirroring back to a client or party the meaning conveyed to the practitioner, including facts, opinions, beliefs, and emotional responses. Before examining these skills, barriers to effective communication and the importance of setting up a suitable space for dispute management processes are considered.

Robert Bolton identifies 12 barriers to good communication.[21] These are divided into three major categories:

1. Judging:
   - Criticising
   - Name calling
   - Diagnosing
   - Praising eventually
2. Sending solutions:
   - Ordering
   - Threatening
   - Moralising
   - Excessive questioning
   - Advising
3. Avoiding the other's concerns:
   - Diverting
   - Logical argument
   - Reassuring.[22]

These barriers may be 'well meant' by the listener. For example, judgment can suggest an attempt to put the speaker on the 'right' path, providing solutions can be an attempt to be helpful in addressing the speaker's difficulties, and avoiding engagement might be aimed towards steering the speaker into a less emotional space. Dispute management practitioners,

17 Neil Hamilton, 'Effectiveness Requires Listening: How to Assess and Improve Listening Skills' 13(2) (2012) *Florida Coastal Law Review* 145.
18 Alexander, Howieson and Fox (n 12) 117–24.
19 Carl Rogers, *A Way of Being* (Houghton Mifflin, rev ed 1995).
20 Ibid.
21 Bolton (n 14).
22 Ibid 17; see also Chapter 4.

however, need to adopt a non-judgmental attitude that communicates acceptance of a party's experience, even though they may not have had the same experience or agree with the speaker's attitude or approach.

It is interesting to note that the first two categories – judging and sending solutions – tend to be communication styles that lawyers are trained in, yet they can be barriers to interpersonal communication. For example, to say 'you are wrong' or 'that is a naïve and incorrect suggestion' is to judge and will close down communication. Moralising is a form of bias demonstrated when one says, 'you cannot possibly think that . . .' or 'really, how could that be possible?' As lawyers are trained in problem-solving, it is useful to be aware that sometimes sending advice such as, 'You need to consider doing . . .', 'I suggest . . .', Why don't you . . .', stops the party from providing any further information. It shuts the person down and can make them feel that they have not had space to voice their full story.

Cloke[23] notes that our choice of words affect the way a dispute is viewed by a party and the message it can convey. Thomas Gordon identified the power of the pronoun 'I'.[24] The single word 'I' is powerful as it directly portrays how a person feels or perceives a situation and makes defensive argument less possible as the other party is harder pressed to deny the personal expression. If, on the other hand, the word 'you' is used – such as 'you always throw your rubbish over the fence' – perhaps accompanied by some finger pointing, it is much more likely to elicit a defensive response, thus escalating the disruptive communication. Subsequent researchers have observed that careful use of the word 'we' can expand communication to achieve better outcomes by emphasising a shared problem without dividing the problem-holders.[25] Using an 'I' phrase – such as 'I am exhausted in cleaning up all the debris appearing on my side of the fence' – it is less accusative, and it also indicates not only do I have a problem but you, my neighbour, also have a problem. To mutualise the problem, a statement such as 'How can we better deal with the debris?' is more likely to lead to joint problem-solving.

Place

Place should be one of the first considerations: in other words, the place and context in which communication is occurring. This requires forethought in relation to the parties. It includes taking account of education and cultural differences. Seating arrangements are vital and, while parties may choose where they feel is comfortable, their choices may not have the best outcomes, as power imbalances and the nature of the dispute are important to consider.

Considering the environment within which the communication is taking place – the physical space, location and placement of tables and chairs is part of non-verbal communication for the parties. Be considerate of whether a formal, imposing environment or informal, comfortable space will be conducive to clear communication.[26]

The setting can encourage a cooperative approach, consistent with relational helping. Arranging the physical setting for meeting with parties' means requires preparing a room and furniture with access to amenities and tea and coffee facilities. It is useful and courteous

23 Cloke (n 11) 185.
24 Thomas Gordon, *Parent Effectiveness Training* (Wyden, 1970).
25 Wesley R Burr, 'Beyond I-Statements in Family Communication' (1990) 39(3) *Family Relations* 266.
26 See also Chapter 4, 109–110.

to ensure that water is available as well as pen and paper, so that parties can take notes. Securing uninterrupted space and time is important as it allows the parties to focus on the matter before them. Avoiding interruptions from office staff, mobile phones and distractions such as computers, unless used in the process, may seem obvious, but can often be overlooked. Providing breakout rooms and separate spaces if the dispute practitioner needs to engage in shuttle processes, or for private sessions, is best considered in advance. Washroom facilities should accommodate parties' and the dispute practitioner's needs, so they will not have to be in the same space outside the actual process; again, a simple consideration, but one that can lead to accusations of threats and bias that can be avoided with good planning.

Arranging seating around a table may be helpful, depending on the parties. A desk creates a physical barrier that suggests a powerful position, but some parties can also see it as providing safety. The main point is that seating should be factored into the setting of place to enable collaborative engagement. Where there are two dispute practitioners and two or more parties and their representatives, attention should be given to seating arrangements that place the parties in the foreground, particularly if space is limited, and adjustments for gender balancing, if appropriate.

Similar considerations are needed for technology-assisted, online dispute management to provide uninterrupted time. Familiarity with technologies required to manage the online experience smoothly and effectively requires prior training. The quality of audio and visual functions is an important consideration, particularly as online meetings do not tend to enable observations of non-verbal behaviour as readily as that achieved face-to-face. Use of break-out groups for private sessions with parties and the use of whiteboard tools can mirror the functions of face-to-face arrangements.

Establishing trust and rapport

Varied definitions of trust can be found in the literature. Moore defines trust as 'a person's capacity to depend on or place confidence in the truthfulness or accuracy of another's statements or behaviour'.[27] Boulle and Alexander define trust as 'one person's willingness to believe, to be open to, and to take risks with, another person'.[28] McAlister defines trust as 'an individual's belief in and willingness to act on the words, actions and decisions of another'.[29] These definitions identify trust as a feature that enables parties to rely upon the truthfulness and accuracy of information shared by dispute practitioners, encourages them to be guided by practitioners' expertise in managing the process, and assures them of the confidential nature of that process.[30]

27 Christopher W Moore, *The Mediation Process: Practical Strategies for Resolving Conflict* (Jossey-Bass, 4th ed, 2014) 192.

28 Laurence Boulle and Nadja Alexander, *Mediation: Skills and Techniques* (LexisNexis, 3rd ed, 2020) 59 (emphasis omitted).

29 DJ McAllister, 'Affect- and Cognition-based Trust as Foundations for Interpersonal Cooperation in Organisations' (1995) 38(1) *Academy of Management Journal* 24, 25. For identification and analysis of two types of trust (namely, calculus-based trust and identification-based trust) see Roy J Lewicki, Bruce Barry and David M Saunders, *Essentials of Negotiation* (McGraw-Hill, 6th ed, 2016) 309–15.

30 See also Robert L Swinth, 'The Establishment of the Trust Relationship' (1967) 11(3) *Journal of Conflict Resolution* 33; J Poitras, 'What Makes Parties Trust Mediators?' (2009) 21 (3) *Negotiation Journal* 307.

Research has shown that trust is a significant factor in achieving positive outcomes in dispute management processes. In a series of three studies conducted by Goldberg[31] and Goldberg and Shaw,[32] it was found that a central factor in dispute practitioner success is an ability to establish a relationship of trust and confidence with disputing parties. The first study consisted in sample of 30 mediators of which a majority of 75 per cent attributed their success, measured by achieving settlements, to an ability to establish rapport with parties, identified as a relationship of understanding, empathy, and trust.[33] In negotiations, trust has been found to encourage the sharing of information between negotiators, which in turn enhances effectiveness in achieving good outcomes.[34] Integrative negotiation processes have been found to encourage parties to see the dialogue as being about interests, relationships, and positive affect, which increases trust. By contrast, distributive negotiation processes encourage parties to view each other negatively, which reduces trust.[35] Studies have found that trust also encourages cooperative behaviour.[36]

Establishing rapport and confidence is essential to enabling a party to communicate freely and honestly. A trusting relationship can be encouraged by affirming qualifications and or credentials in the introductory phase; being transparent throughout the process by explaining the stages clearly, including the roles of participant; emphasising confidentiality overall and at relevant stages of the process; encouraging and answering questions about the process; demonstrating and maintaining impartiality;[37] and showing respect and concern throughout the process by demonstrating empathy and active listening.[38] Demonstrating empathy and active listening are central to establishing rapport and maintaining trust because these skills embody a party-centred approach to practice.

Demonstrating empathy

According to scholars in psychology, empathy is a complex concept with varied definitions according to cognitive, affective, and behavioural dimensions.[39] In essence, and for our purposes, empathy is the ability to 'stand in the shoes of another' and to understand their experience.[40] Three features of empathy are significant for dispute management practice. Empathy acknowledges the experience of another, affirms that experience as part of human experience, and recognises the emotional content of that experience. According to Carl Rogers, empathy means:

31 Stephen B Goldberg, 'The Secrets of Successful Mediators' (2005) 21(3) *Negotiation Journal* 365.
32 Stephen B Goldberg and Margaret L Shaw, 'The Secrets of Successful (and Unsuccessful) Mediators Continued: Studies Two and Three' (2007) 23 (4) *Negotiation Journal* 393.
33 Goldberg (n 31) 372.
34 Lewicki, Barry and Saunders (n 29) 313–14.
35 Ibid.
36 Ibid 309–15.
37 For a discussion of neutrality and impartiality, see Chapters 3 and 6.
38 Boulle and Alexander (n 28) 60.
39 Malissa A Clark, Melissa M Robertson and Stephen Young, '"I feel your pain": A Critical Review of Organizational Research on Empathy' (2019) 40(2) *Journal of Organizational Behavior* 166.
40 Gerard Egan, *The Skilled Helper: A Problem-Management and Opportunity Development Approach to Helping* (Cengage Learning, 10th ed, 2014) 81; see D Howe, *Empathy: What It is and Why It Matters* (Palgrave Macmillan, 2013).

> ... entertaining the private perceptual world of the other and becoming at home in it. It involves being sensitive moment to moment to the changing felt meanings that flow in this other person, to the fear or rage or tenderness or confusion or whatever that he/she is experiencing. It means temporarily living in his/her life, moving about in it delicately without making judgements, sensing meanings that he/she is scarcely aware, but not trying to uncover feelings of which the person is totally unaware, since this would be too threatening. It includes communicating your sensing of his/her world as you look with fresh and unfrightened eyes at elements of which the individual is fearful. It means frequently checking with him/her as to the accuracy of your sensings, and being guided by the responses you receive. . .To be with another in this way means that for the time being you lay aside the views and values you hold for yourself in order to enter another's world without prejudice.[41]

Empathy validates the experience of the speaker without evaluation or judgment. The role of a dispute practitioner is not to evaluate or pass judgement, but rather to acknowledge a client's or party's experience. Empathy is predicated on treating others with respect, dignity, and compassion. Empathy should be distinguished from sympathy. Sympathy is expressed when the listener enters into the experience of another.[42] If I am sympathetic to your problem, I will experience and demonstrate emotions that you are experiencing. I might join you, for example, in expressing frustration, anger, and or disappointment. There are three dangers of over-identification here for professional relationships. One is that you can lose the objectivity needed to properly assist parties in navigating the dispute process. A professional lens requires emotional detachment but not emotional unavailability. You can be emotionally connected to parties through empathy without sharing the waves of their emotions. Another is that you risk alienating a party if you later withdraw your emotional identification because you are unable to sustain it or if your perception of the situation changes. A further danger is that you will 'burn out', or in other words, cause yourself emotional, and consequent physical, exhaustion.[43]

Empathy is a learned skill.[44] It is demonstrated by communicating through speech and manner, genuine care, and concern for the speaker. As explained by Rogers: 'Another meaning of empathic understanding to the recipient is that someone values him, cares, accepts the person that he is.'[45] Rogers identified reflection as the practical demonstration of empathy.[46] Empathy can be expressed by reflecting back to a speaker the feelings s/he has communicated. This conveys an acknowledgement that the listener has understood what the speaker has communicated. Examples of responses that reflect feelings are shown in Table 2.1.

41 Carl R Rogers, 'Empathic: An Appreciated Way of Being' (1975) 5(2) *Counseling Psychologist* 2, 4.

42 See Egan (n 40) 114–15; F Strasser and P Randolf, *Mediation: A Psychological Insight into Conflict Resolution* (Continuum, 2004) 50–1; James Duffy, 'Empathy, Neutrality and Emotional Intelligence: A Balancing Act for the Emotional Einstein' (2010) 10(1) *Queensland University of Technology Law Journal* 44.D Della Noce, 'Seeing Theory in Practice: An Analysis of Empathy in Mediation' (1999) 15(3) *Negotiation Journal* 271.

43 See D S Stoyanov et al, '1117 Psychopathological Dimensions of Burnt Out Syndrome: Depression and Anxiety Correlates' (2013) 28(1) *European Psychiatry* 1.

44 Kathy Douglas and Clare Coburn, 'Students Designing Role-plays: Building Empathy in Law Students? (2009) 2(1) *Journal of the Australasian Law Teachers Association* 55.

45 Rogers (n 41) 7.

46 Carl Rogers, *A Way of Being* (Houghton Mifflin Co, rev ed 1995).

Table 2.1 Reflecting feelings

You are/were excited ...	You were angry that the proposal was not even considered ...
You seem to be sad ...	You were really upset by that behaviour...
You appear uneasy ...	You were embarrassed by those comments ...
You are/were upset ...	You found that situation confusing ...
You are/were clearly distressed ...	You were glad that happened ...

Understanding is communicated by what is said and by non-verbal acknowledgement, rather than by merely saying 'I understand'. You can never fully understand how someone feels unless perhaps you have had a very similar experience. Even those people who have very similar experiences can react differently. To say, 'I understand ...', if it is not your personal experience, is to appear dismissive. It is preferable to use reflective responses. Empathic understanding is communicated by speech and non-verbal acknowledgement. Combining speech with consistent non-verbal responses will reinforce an empathic response. Facial expressions that communicate concern and caring, and a posture that displays attentiveness and openness, will convey empathic understanding. At times, a non-verbal response is the most appropriate and effective means of communicating empathy. Silence can be effectively used to demonstrate empathy when combined with a quiet attentive posture and concerned facial expression. Furthermore, 'failure to allow periodic silence can interrupt a client's stream of association and make the client feel cut off, hurried, or pressured.'[47]

Active listening

Active listening is the single most important interpersonal communication skill for dispute management practitioners.[48] Active listening means listening attentively and being present in the moment to the person speaking. 'The goal in active listening is to develop a clear understanding of the speaker's concern and also to clearly communicate the listener's interest in the speaker's message.'[49] Active listening is intimately connected with empathy. As described by Hamilton: 'While listening can be defined as a technical ability to hear and remember what a speaker is saying, effective [active] listening requires, not only technical proficiency, but also an empathetic ability to connect with the speaker.'[50]

Active listening: being consciously attentive to the layers of meaning communicated by a speaker, including emotions, using verbal and non-verbal communication skills and demonstrating respect and empathy.

Boulle and Alexander identify three components of skill in active listening: attending skills, following skills, and reflecting skills.[51] Attending means being present and available: 'being with the client, physically and psychologically, making them feel important and trusting by use of physical attention, displays of interest, appropriate body movements, encouraging noises ("I see ...", "Uhuh ...", "Yes ...", "Oh

47 Hamilton (n 17) 158.

48 See Clare Coburn and Anne Edge, 'Listening to Each Other: The Heart of Mediation and Dialogue' (2007) 18(1) *Australasian Dispute Resolution Journal* 19.

49 Hamilton (n 17) 151.

50 Ibid.

51 Boulle and Alexander (n 28) 186–7.

really?")'.[52] Following skills are used to show the client that the listener is following what is said. The prompts above can be used, as well as refraining from interrupting, asking clarifying questions, taking notes, and summarising.[53] Reflecting skills give feedback to the speaker that what is said has been heard and understood. Reflecting means mirroring back to the speaker what has been heard in relation to the factual, feeling, relationship, and other layers of meaning communicated. Reflecting both acknowledges the content of the message and assures the client that s/he has been heard. Brandon and Robertson[54] suggest a range of verbal cues to initiate reflection (see Table 2.2).

Table 2.2 Examples of reflection

You sound/ feel . . .	It seems . . .
You believe . . .	You sensed that . . .
What you are saying is . . .	From where you stand . . .
Your point is . . .	You consider . . .
It sounded like . . .	The main concern for you is . . .
You thought that . . .	

Active listening means being attentive to the varying aspects or layers of meaning communicated by the speaker. These varying aspects include facts, interpretation, feelings, and intention. The first two components are familiar to lawyers who look for how the facts might be interpreted in the light of the law. However, differing interpretations of events are important keys to the nature and extent of disputes. Individuals may differ in their interpretation of facts and/or of the intentions of another and that difference may lead to disagreement and ultimately conflict. Focusing only on the facts of a message can cause important information to be missed. Failing to recognise the mediating effects of emotions, interpretation, and intention can result in poor or inadequate understanding. These additional components of messages are important for practitioners to actively listen out for in order to better understand a client's situation and to recommend the most appropriate dispute management process. Active listening is furthermore an essential skill for every dispute management process as the means by which parties' interests and needs are identified, options that meet those interests and needs are generated, and outcomes are negotiated.

Active listening is not a state of mind, like feeling relaxed and confident; nor does it 'just happen'. It is an activity that requires focus and effort.[55] By contrast, *inactive* listening is demonstrated by non-listening – going through the motions of apparently listening but not actually being engaged; partial listening – listening that skims the surface but may easily miss the important information the speaker wants to convey; or tape recorder listening – being able to repeat what is said but failing to be present in such a way as to connect with the speaker so

52 Ibid 186.
53 Ibid.
54 Mieke Brandon and Leigh Robertson, *Conflict and Dispute Resolution* (Oxford University Press, 2007) 151–2.
55 Egan (n 40) 81.

that they do not feel 'listened to' or 'heard'.[56] Active listening appears to be a relatively passive activity as it allows someone else to speak while we remain attentive and quiet. However, the listener actively employs non-verbal communication and paralanguage to assure the speaker that they are being heard.

Egan suggests that active listening is optimal when combined with non-verbal communication identified according to the acronym SOLER, which signals the listener to:

- ***S***quarely face the client to demonstrate involvement: this will indicate that you are present and attentive.
- Adopt an ***O***pen posture: this will indicate that you are available and open to listening to the client. Sitting with folded arms — and to a lesser extent crossed legs – suggest that you not open and available. Furniture such as a desk between you and another person can create a barrier to open communication.
- ***L***ean towards the client at times: this indicates interest and involvement to the client but should not be invasive.
- Maintain ***E***ye contact most of the time: in western cultures, eye contact conveys connection, interest and attention. Staring should be avoided as it may be intrusive and or suggest rigidity and control.
- ***R***elax as much as possible: your relaxed posture will help to put your client at ease.[57]

Two barriers to effective listening that tend to contain assumptions about what the parties identify as their concerns are internal 'fact hunting' or 'verbal battles'.[58] When fact hunting, the listener concentrates on the detail of facts and loses sight of the overall message. The main themes can be lost and with that identification of interests and needs. When engaged in internal verbal battles, instead of listening and absorbing what the other person has to say, the practitioner debates the information presented internally, its truth, reliability, relevance and or cogency, and loses track of the narrative communicated.

Eliciting information: asking questions and constructing an agenda

The purpose of questioning is to elicit information and encourage communication from a client or parties. Where that questioning resembles an interrogation or inquisition, a client or party's sense of trust in the listener and motivation to be fully responsive is negatively impacted.[59] Questions should be used cautiously and constructively. Inappropriate use of questions can act as a block to active listening and communication. Questions should not be used as a way of controlling interaction with parties, or of concealing a lack of knowledge, or to delay proceedings. Questions need to be asked in combination with active listening and within a framework of empathic understanding. There are various labels given to types of questions; for example, open and closed questions, clarifying questions, hypothetical questions, problem-solving

56 Ibid.

57 Ibid 77–8.

58 Peter Hartley, *Interpersonal Communication* (Routledge, 2nd ed, 1999) 48.

59 See Ruth Charlton and Micheline Dewdney, *The Mediator's Handbook: Skills and Strategies for Practitioners* (Lawbook Co, 3rd ed, 2014) 235.

questions, reality testing questions, and fine-tuning questions.[60] Each type has its own purpose as indicated by its name.

Distinguishing open and closed questions[61] is a basic distinction in questioning technique. Closed questions are those that can be answered by a simple 'yes' or 'no'. Open questions are those that require more thought to answer and elicit more response than simply a one-word answer. Open-ended questions allow space for the party to provide a reasoned response, giving more information than would be obtained from closed questioning. Open questions build rapport and confidence. It is always better to start with open questions to encourage the parties to share their stories. Too many closed questions early on will close down the communication. Closed questions tend to be used towards the end of a process and where more specific details or confirmation of matters is required. Open questions seek to establish the how, what, where, why, when or who of the parties' circumstances. Consider the examples below:

- 'Do you feel good about that?' v. 'How do you feel about that?'
- 'Was your idea taken up?' v. 'How did X and Y respond to your idea?'
- 'Is that important to you?' v. 'How is that important to you?'

Open-ended questions will often begin with how, what, where, why, when or who. For example:

- How did that happen?
- When do you what that to happen?
- What happened next?
- Who is the best person to contact?
- Why is that important to you?

Remembering to begin with who, what, where, why, or when is a useful practice point. However, different phrasing can be equally effective with or without the use of a question as such. For example:

- 'Describe a specific incident when that happened.'
- 'Tell me what happened.'
- 'This is clearly important to you. Tell me more.'

Open questions enable the dispute practitioner to assist parties to describe the circumstances of their dispute in their own words. This typically means encouraging them to think back to what happened. The dispute practitioner will be listening for clues to the client's or parties' interests, needs, and concerns. Narratives may contain possible legal issues and claims, but the purpose of early connection with a client or parties is to listen for what is important to them and how they frame those issues: what has offended them, troubled them, upset them; what was their role, and what was the other party's role; and what they want to happen going forward. Clues in narratives that indicate the importance of an issue include repeated words, phrases, and topics. How important an issue is to a party is indicated by the emotional intensity attached to it; and may also be indicated by positional, rigid reactions as distinct from open, if

60 Ibid 225–35.

61 Also referred to as open-ended and closed-ended questions. See Chapter 4.

tentative, gestures and responses. Dispute practitioners will be prepared with a series of questions that canvas possible issues for parties, as suggested in Table 2.3.

Table 2.3 Issues and questions

What has happened/what the incident is	What has happened to bring you here today?
Details of the incident	Can you describe to me in detail what happened?
Why the problem started	What do you think brought it on? What led to that happening, do you think?
Who was involved	Who else was there or involved at the time?
What emotions prompted their actions	What were you feeling when that happened?
How it has affected them	What impact has it had on you – your work, relationships, health?

In initial interviews with clients, lawyers will probe for sufficient facts to diagnose whether a legal action can be taken and whether there is sufficient evidence of the elements of possible legal actions. By contrast, dispute resolution practitioners are probing for the parameters of a dispute which may or may not amount to a legal action. Frequently, legal rights and obligations sit behind dispute management processes that are alternatives to litigation, but in the foreground are the clients' and parties' narratives: their interpretation of what happened, what impact it has had for them, how they see the other party, and how they would like to see the dispute managed or resolved. The role of the dispute practitioner is to navigate the narratives of parties, looking for key components of their dispute, including those shown in Table 2.4.

Table 2.4 Questions to canvas key components of a dispute

The incident/s	Who did what? Who said what?
Consequences	What happened as a result? What was the impact for the parties/any others involved?
Assumptions	What does the party think motivated the other party's conduct?
Emotions	What emotional impact has the dispute had for the parties/others affected?
Responses	What has each party done in response to the dispute?
Desired outcomes	What does each party want to see happen to manage or resolve the dispute?

Dispute management practitioners will often use a funnelling approach to questions in order to move from generalities to specifics. Directive questions may be used in combination with funnelling to direct the speaker and can be useful where a party has become 'stuck' in circular or overly emotive thinking. For example, see Table 2.5.

Notice that reflecting back or restating the essence of the client or party's initial general statement provides an introduction to follow-up questions that can provide focus, clarify information, and provide more detail. Using the reported speech of a party demonstrates active listening and enables the practitioner to acknowledge what has been said, then continue to probe for further detail and explanation. Examples of introductory phrases for reported speech are shown in Table 2.6.

Table 2.5 Funnelling directive questions

Client/party's statement	Funnelling directive questions
I was so upset!	S/he/it really upset you. Can you tell me how you felt? What bothered you about it?
He made such a mess of it.	You were unhappy with the result. What things were not done properly?
It happened all in a rush; I was flabbergasted.	It happened very quickly. What can you remember about the details?
These people are all liars!	Have you had similar experiences before? What happened then?
I am not going to apologise. It is not all my fault!	You don't see the need to apologise. How do you see each of you have contributed to the situation?

Table 2.6 Introductory phrases for reported speech

You said that . . .	You mentioned that . . .
You told me that you felt . . .	You explained that . . .
You said that you think . . .	You said that you believe . . .
You also stated . . .	You wondered if . . .

Often a dispute management process involves establishing an agenda for discussion of the parties' interests and concerns. Once a dispute practitioner has canvassed the issues raised by their client, or the parties in a joint session, they are in a position to construct a list of agenda items that can be used to structure dialogue between parties. Practitioners will look for issues that are common to the parties but about which they have different interpretations, interests and priorities. The items in an agenda should be phrased in neutral language that excludes blame or judgment. Items should avoid reference to solutions or to one party's complaints or interests. Agenda items should be broad enough to encompass 'both sides of the story' and can be confirmed by referring to each party's' view or concern about the item. Common items include 'the incident' and 'communication'. Items can be explained by referring to each party's comments and concerns about the item (see Table 2.7).

Table 2.7 Sample agenda items

Item: The incident	Rachael, you have described how the play swing 'fell apart', to use your words, when your son used it for the first time. Daniel, you have indicated that in your view the swing could not have fallen apart and the problem must have been due to faulty installation.
Item: Communication	Rachel, you mentioned that you had some difficulty getting a response from the manufacturer, represented by Daniel here today; and, Daniel, you said that your company prides itself on responding in a timely way to customers.

Once an agenda is constructed, dispute management practitioners facilitate discussion of the items by the parties with a view to exploring issues and, ultimately, generating options for possible solutions. As discussion between the parties ensues, skills in facilitating and checking understanding are needed.

Facilitating and checking understanding: summarising, restatement, and reframing

Facilitating and checking understanding are key communication skills, which if overlooked can lead not only to misunderstanding but also to an erosion of trust. They require taking the time to check in with a client or parties to ensure that what is conveyed is properly and fully understood. There are several techniques used in this context: summarising and paraphrasing; reflection and restatement; and reframing. They are all techniques that are used to feedback to a party the substance of what they have conveyed in order to confirm the practitioner's understanding and to assure parties that they have been heard.

Summarising means explaining information in a shortened form; paraphrasing means explaining something by using your own words. In the context of interpersonal communication, summarising means feeding back the main points from discussion with a client or parties. It can be used after each phase of discussion and at the end of an interview or other contact in order to keep track of issues, planned actions, and an overall view of progress. Paraphrasing is more specific and detailed. It is a technique used to feedback the substance of what is said, often in a condensed form using different words. Paraphrasing is useful during discussion to clarify and check understanding of individual issues, facts, or feelings.

Reflection and restatement (or reiterating) are subtly different from summarising and paraphrasing. As indicated in the examples of reflection above, reflection can encompass mirroring back beliefs or opinions and/or the factual, feeling, or relationship components of a message. Reflection is, however, sometimes understood as mirroring feelings, while restatement is understood as mirroring factual or other content.[62] Reflection and restatement assure the speaker that they have been heard, allow the speaker to correct or clarify what the listener has understood, validate the feelings and/or perspectives of the speaker, and enable the listener to 'round up' what has been communicated and redirect discussion if needed. Examples of introductions to restatements are provided in Table 2.8.

Table 2.8 Introducing restatements

In other words, you believe that . . .	Let me see if I understand: you propose that . . .
So, your position is . . .	So that I can be clear: Your view is . . .
You are saying XYZ – is that accurate?	You are sorry that the problem has occurred, and you are prepared to . . .

Reframing in dispute management is defined by Mayer as 'the process of changing the way a thought is presented so that it maintains its fundamental meaning but is more likely to support resolution efforts'.[63] Reframing is useful for neutralising toxic statements and for redirecting bald statements of rights and positions towards a future problem-solving focus.[64]

62 See Charlton and Dewdney (n 59) 214–16.
63 Bernard Mayer, *The Dynamics of Conflict Resolution: A Practitioners' Guide* (Jossey-Bass, 2000) 132.
64 See Charlton and Dewdney (n 59) 217–21.

Reframing is not summarising or paraphrasing, but does serve to focus attention on the key messages and provides an opportunity for a party to confirm the central messages conveyed.

Toxic words tend to evoke a defensive reaction. Reframing is often referred to as detoxifying a statement. The detoxified reframe allows the other party to consider the essential concern being conveyed. The dispute practitioner will remove offensive words, but use as much of the speaker's own words as possible in order to communicate the essence of the speaker's message. For instance, Sandra says, 'He is a pig who never completes anything properly.' A reframe might be, 'Sandra has indicated two issues: tidiness and timely completion of tasks. Can you see how you could accommodate this?' Reframing, as the example suggests, is appropriate when the party is making a complaint in strong or harsh words. Reframing provides a more constructive frame of understanding and is therefore a critical communication skill.

Generating and testing options: transitions and reality testing

Transitions are used to direct the flow of communication between parties. The aim is to encourage parties to speak to each other rather than through the dispute practitioner at key stages, such as exploration in mediation. Transitions are often best communicated non-verbally through head movements and hand gestures that can direct the flow of communication between parties. These non-verbal gestures can be accompanied by verbal transitions (see Table 2.9).

Table 2.9 Transitions

Communicating facts	Ryan, can you tell Peta what happened to cause you to withdraw your order . . .
Communicating emotion	Peta, can you explain to Ryan how you felt when you heard about the order being withdrawn . . .
Communication perspectives	Peta, tell Ryan what your understanding is in regard to purchaser's responsibilities here . . .

Having listened carefully to the parties' narratives and assisted them in exploring issues arising from those narratives, dispute resolution practitioners will typically want to explore options that move the participants forward. Processes vary as to whether emphasis is given to the parties' generation of options or to options generated by the dispute practitioner.[65] What parties want to see happen as a result of the process should be canvassed and then reality tested. Brainstorming possibilities is a useful technique to generate as many options as possible.[66] Parties can be encouraged to suggest as many as possibilities that come to mind in order to capture a creative range of solutions. These options can be later reality tested to

65 Compare, for example, the role of the mediator in facilitative and evaluative models of mediation discussed in Chapter 6.

66 See David Spencer, *Principles of Dispute Resolution* (Thomson Reuters, 2nd ed 2016) 43.

determine if they are acceptable to the other party and practically possible. Questions that assist in generating options include:

- What would you like to see happen?
- What do you think are the best options open to you?
- What is most important to you and how do you think you can secure it?
- Having heard what Ryan has to say, what options do you think are open to you?

When assisting parties to generate options, the task is to elicit what they themselves consider to be possibilities. Careful framing of questions and encouragement needs to be employed in order to avoid attempts to solve the issues for parties. Consider the different emphasis in the examples below:

- What can you suggest going forward? v. Why don't you do this?
- Is there anything else you might do? v. The best thing to do is …
- What options do you think are possible here? v. Why don't you do this?
- What might be other ways are of …? v. Have you thought about …?
- What else might work? v. I know what might work …
- What if he doesn't agree? What might be an alternative? v. He won't agree to that.

In reality testing, the dispute practitioner is 'seeking to explore with the parties the realistic result of a position they have taken or a solution they are proposing and the advantages or disadvantages of adhering to that position'.[67] Reality testing is a skill used by practitioners to test the suitability, sustainability and practicality of clients' positions and action plans. Classically, reality testing is used to draw parties' attention to their best alternative to a negotiated agreement (BATNA) or worst alternative to a negotiated agreement (WATNA).[68] BATNAs and WATNAs can encourage parties to consider the costs – whether financial, measured in time and effort, emotional and or value-driven – of failing to reach an agreement and possibly moving to a determinative process where issues are decided for them. Reality testing is a useful way to assist parties to consider the consequences of positions and plans in order to assess what they mean in practice. It is also a necessary technique in fleshing out agreements with the practical details of who will do what, when, and how? The range of techniques discussed above can be employed to reality test. Hypothetical questions are particularly useful in this regard. Hypothetical questions are generally open-ended questions. They encourage dialogue and have the added benefit of testing possibilities. As such they can be used to generate options as well as test options. They will often begin with 'What if …?' Some examples are:

- What if the other party doesn't agree to your terms?
- What if there are delays in the project?
- What if your employee refuses to meet with you?
- What if the other party takes a different view?
- What if your ex-spouse is running late to pick up the children? How should he contact you?

67 Charlton and Dewdney (n 59) 209, defined in relation to mediation.
68 See Spencer (n 66) 44–5.

Other examples using how, what or when questions are:

- How do you think Ryan will respond to that suggestion?
- What is likely to happen if you do that?
- What will happen you can't reach an agreement today?
- How can you organise that?
- When do you think you can manage that?

The focus for reality testing is to assist parties to test out the options they have generated. It is necessary for the dispute practitioner to avoid assessing or evaluating those options. The task is to assist parties to make their own assessments. Consider differences in the following examples:

- How do you think Ryan will respond to that? v. Ryan won't like that.
- How would you think about Ryan's offer? v. That offer won't work for you.
- How do you see that working? v. That's not going to work. Why don't you offer . . .?
- What needs to happen for you to be comfortable with Ryan's offer? v. You're not going to be happy with Ryan's offer unless . . .
- How practical are those arrangements going to be for you? v. Those payments are going to be difficult to meet.
- What will happen if you don't reach an agreement today? v. Things will prove difficult and expensive if you don't reach agreement today.

Positive and negative communication techniques

Positives

The good news is that well-trained communicators can become great dispute practitioners. You will gain knowledge in the dispute management processes examined in this book and understand that the manner in which you use your communication toolkit can assist each process to achieve its goals. Many of the techniques described in this chapter – such as dealing with emotions, active listening, empathy, questioning, summarising, paraphrasing, transitioning and reframing – are common features across the processes.

Negatives

The sad reality is that failure in communication is the most common factor inherent in all disputes. Many think the ability to communicate is as innate as breathing. This chapter demonstrates that there is much more to communicating well and, for dispute practitioners, this requires a great deal of practice to ensure there is no contribution to escalating a dispute because of inappropriate communication. It is perhaps unfortunate that interpersonal skills are not a greater focus in our education system. Gaining knowledge in good communication in our early life would improve society as a whole by reducing disputes.

Communication can be used for good and for bad purposes and societies suffer when it is used incorrectly. We witness a world today where truth and clarity are being turned on their heads in a post-truth society. It has probably never been more important that we each engage in developing skilful communication. As dispute practitioners, communicative ability is the artistry we provide to help others communicate what is important to them.

Special considerations

In the following discussion, we examine two important skill sets for dispute practitioners that impact the effectiveness of their interpersonal communication: emotional intelligence and reflective practice. Finally, we consider issues and strategies in dealing with difficult emotions including the use of assertiveness.

Emotional intelligence

Emotional intelligence (EI) has received growing recognition in the legal and broader dispute management literature as a set of skills required by practitioners to manage their own emotions and to respond appropriately to the emotions of parties. James, for example, argues that emotional intelligence can improve the quality of legal practice in addition to the well-being of practitioners and students.[69] Hyams advocates nurturing multiple intelligences beyond the traditional rational-analytic paradigm of law and extending to narrative and emotional intelligence.[70] Cain argues that emotional intelligence is necessary in legal practice to deal with emotions 'in the context of our relationships with clients, other attorneys, judges, witnesses, and staff'.[71] Katz and Sosa argue that EI represents one of the most important sets of competencies for negotiation practice.[72] Duffy argues that empathy and impartiality in mediation are made possible through EI.[73] Other scholars point to elements of EI as significant for mediation. Dickinson, for example, examines self-awareness in mediation practice[74] and Schreier advocates self-awareness and self-regulation in mediation.[75] Picard and Siltanen argue that competency as a mediator can be enhanced by training that builds 'in opportunities for self-reflection on individual experiences of emotion'.[76] Leary, Pillemer and Wheeler[77] argue that EI is of significant benefit for negotiators in:

69 Colin James, 'Law Student Wellbeing: Benefits of Promoting Psychological Literacy and Self Awareness using Mindfulness, Strengths Theory and Emotional Intelligence' (2011) 21(2) *Legal Education Review* 217.

70 Ross Hyams, 'Nurturing Multiple Intelligences through Clinical Legal Education' 2011(15) *University of Western Sydney Law Review* 80.

71 Paul J Cain, 'A First Step Toward Introducing Emotional Intelligence into the Law School Curriculum: The "Emotional Intelligence and the Clinic Student" Class' (2004) 14(1) *Legal Education Review* 1, 3.

72 Neil H Katz and Adriana Sosa, 'The Emotional Advantage: The Added Value of the Emotionally Intelligent Negotiator' (2015) 33(1) *Conflict Resolution Quarterly* 57, 68.

73 Duffy (n 42).

74 Mark Dickinson, 'The Importance of Transformative Mediation to the Internal Workplace Mediation Program' (2011) 22(2) *Australasian Dispute Resolution Journal* 95.

75 Lori S. Schreier, 'Emotional Intelligence and Mediation Training' (2002) 20(1) *Conflict Resolution Quarterly* 99.

76 Cheryl Picard and Janet Siltanen, 'Exploring the Significance of Emotion for Mediation Practice' (2013) 31(1) *Conflict Resolution Quarterly* 49.

77 Kimberlyn Leary, Julianna Pillemer and Micahel Wheeler, 'Negotiating with Emotion' (2013) Harvard Business Review 91(1–2) 96, 101.

- identifying emotions that they and others are experiencing
- understanding how those emotions affect their thought process
- using that knowledge to achieve better negotiation outcomes, and
- positively managing emotions; tempering or intensifying them for strategic purposes.

There are several models of EI developed in positive psychology. The most accessible model has been made popular by Goleman[78] and applied in a broad range of applied disciplines. Goleman identifies five components, or competencies, in his model of EI: self-awareness, self-regulation, motivation, empathy and social skills (see Table 2.10).[79]

Table 2.10 Goleman's model of emotional intelligence[80]

Components of EI	Definition
Self-awareness	The ability to recognise our moods, emotions and drives and their effect on others.
Self-regulation	The ability to control or redirect disruptive impulses and moods. The propensity to suspend judgement – to think before acting.
Motivation	A passion to work for reasons that go beyond money and status.
Empathy	The ability to understand the emotional make up of other people. Skill in treating people according to their emotional reactions.
Social skills	Proficiency in managing relationships and building networks. An ability to find common ground and to build rapport.

The components of empathy and social skills in Goleman's model can be mapped against the interpersonal communication skills identified earlier in the chapter.

The components of self-awareness and self-regulation in Goleman's model are intra-personal dimensions that impact interaction with others. In this context, self-awareness refers to the need to be aware of our own emotions as they are felt and displayed and the impact of those emotions on others. Self-regulation refers to an ability to control emotions. In the context of dispute management, regulation of emotions includes maintaining attention and listening actively and without judgment. A dispute practitioner might, for example, come to a meeting annoyed because they had trouble getting a parking spot, are still angry about a disagreement with their partner two days ago, or overjoyed because their football team won the night before. In these instances, and many others, a practitioner needs to regulate their emotions in order to maintain a calm, interested, and engaging presence to assist parties. Dispute practitioners also need to be aware of their reactions to parties in order to regulate those reactions and to choose appropriate responses, rather than to allow any personal bias to impact the process. Reactions include those in relation to personal characteristics (eg male, female, old, young, well presented or poorly dressed, executive or worker); behaviour (eg loud or quiet, assertive or submissive, forthcoming or reticent); values expressed (eg religious or secular, political or

78 Daniel Goleman, *Emotional Intelligence* (Bantam, 1995).
79 Ibid.
80 Ibid.

personal); positions on matters in dispute; and willingness or otherwise to compromise. Developing self-awareness assists in uncovering attitudes and responses of which a practitioner may not be fully aware. In the absence of awareness, past conditioning and emotional responses remain hidden and unchallenged. They may appear as almost instant reactions that distract the practitioner and place them off balance, or surface as unintended influences on the progress of the dispute management process.

Reflective practice

Reflective practice is a core competency across many applied disciplines[81] and integral to continuing professional education.[82] In essence, it describes learning from experience in a professional context. It is a concept deriving from the seminal work of Donald Schön.[83] Schön describes reflective practice as an 'act of professional artistry'[84] in which practice wisdom, or knowledge based on experience, has a central role in directing action. Drawing on Schön's work, Gould notes that 'practice wisdom depends upon highly developed intuition which may be difficult to articulate but can be demonstrated through practice'.[85] Schön proposes two categories of reflective practice: reflection-on-action and reflection-in-action.[86] Reflection-on-action consists of reviewing past actions with the opportunity of appraisal and evaluation in order to identify possible areas of improved performance. In reflection-in-action, use is made of direct feedback to influence and respond to a current situation. Here, the relevance of **tacit knowledge** is acknowledged as practitioners 'think on their feet'. By employing these categories, Schön depicts the actual experience of professionals in practice, probing the 'mystique of practical competence'.[87] Reflective practice is acknowledged in dispute management literature as an important element of practice. Boulle and Alexander define reflective practice as a 'tool for the improvement of practice and a way to learn by experience'.[88] It is referred to as a 'core skill' in Brandon and Robertson's generalist approach to dispute management[89] and Winslade and Monk's explanation of their model of narrative mediation.[90] A detailed consideration of reflective

Tacit knowledge: knowledge absorbed through personal contextualised experience, through doing.

81 See, eg, Siobhan Nelson, 'The Lost Path to Emancipatory Practice: Towards a History of Reflective Practice in Nursing' (2012) 13(3) *Nursing Philosophy* 202, 203; Elizabeth Smith, 'Teaching Critical Reflection' (2011) 16(2) *Teaching in Higher Education* 211, 211; Neil Thompson and Jan Pascal, 'Developing Critically Reflective Practice' (2012) 13(2) *Reflective Practice: International and Multidisciplinary Perspectives* 311, 312; Judith McNamara and Rachael Field, 'Designing for Reflective Practice in Legal Education' (2007) 2(1) *Journal of Learning Design* 66; Samantha Hardy, 'Teaching Mediation as Reflective Practice (2009) 21(3) *Negotiation Journal* 385, 393.

82 Smith (n 81) 212.

83 Donald A Schön, *The Reflective Practitioner* (Basic Books, 1983) 54–68.

84 Donald A Schön, *Educating the Reflective Practitioner* (Jossey-Bass, 1987) 12.

85 Nick Gould, 'Introduction: Social Work Education and the "crisis of the professions"' in Nick Gould and Imogen Taylor (eds) *Reflective Learning for Social Work* (Arena Gould, 1996) 1.

86 Schön (n 83) 54–68.

87 Schön (n 84) vii.

88 Boulle and Alexander (n 28) 20.

89 Brandon and Robertson (n 54).

90 John Winslade and Gerald Monk, *Narrative Mediation: A New Approach to Conflict Resolution* (Jossey-Bass, 2000).

practice appears in Lang and Taylor's classic mediation text,[91] in which the authors argue that artistry lies at the intersection of interpersonal skills used in a mediation session and thoughtful reflection during and after mediation.

Burton and McNamara[92] propose a set of reflective questions, designed for legal education, which can be used as a starting point for reflective practice in dispute management. Those questions are reproduced below.

1. What happened that most surprised you?
2. What patterns can you recognise in your experience?
3. What was the most fulfilling part of it? And the least fulfilling part of it? What does that suggest to you about your values?
4. What happened that contradicted your prior beliefs? What happened that confirmed your prior beliefs?
5. How do you feel about that experience now compared with how you felt about it at the time?
6. What does the experience suggest to you about your strengths?
7. What does the experience suggest to you about your weaknesses and opportunities for development?
8. How else could you view that experience?
9. What did you learn from that experience about how you react?
10. What other options did you have at the time?
11. What might you do differently as a result of that experience and your reflections on it?
12. What actions do your reflections lead you to?

Reflexivity is a concept related to reflective practice that extends meaning beyond awareness and review of professional practice and performance. It can be distinguished from reflection in providing a focus on uncovering the personal situatedness of the practitioner in order to limit, direct or more simply acknowledge the impact of that influence. As proposed by Fook and Askeland, in relation to research:

> Reflexivity can simply be defined as an ability to recognize our own influence – and the influence of our social and cultural contexts on research, the type of knowledge we create, and the way we create it. In this sense, then, it is about factoring ourselves as players into the situations we practice.[93]

Reflexivity is a skill that develops a practitioner's awareness of social and cultural influences that contribute to their worldview[94] and implicitly influence their approach to practice.

---

91 Michael D Lang and Alison Taylor, *The Making of a Mediator: Developing Artistry in Practice* (Jossey-Bass, 2000).

92 Kelley Burton and Judith McNamara, 'Assessing Reflection Skills in Law' (2009) 19(1) *Legal Education Review* 171, 184.

93 Jan Fook and Gurid Aga Askeland, 'The "Critical" in Critical Reflection' in Susan White, Jan Fook, and Fiona Gardner (eds), *Critical Reflection in Health and Social Care* (McGraw-Hill Education, 2006) 45.

94 Dale Bagshaw, 'Self-reflexivity and the Reflective Question: Broadening Perspectives in Mediation' (2005) 24(2) *Arbitrator and Mediator* 1.

Reflexivity is the process of looking back on oneself to acknowledge, review, and critique the social and cultural influences that define our social and cultural identities. This awareness enables practitioners to be aware of biases and preferences that could negatively impact their practice and to adjust their practice to correct for those influences. Reflexivity also opens avenues for broader critique of dominant processes, structures and discourses that influence dispute management. Broader critique enables practitioners to contribute to the ongoing development of dispute management through communities of practice.[95]

Dealing with difficult emotions

One significant difficulty in dispute management can be talking about feelings. Nevertheless, allowing parties to express emotions can assist them to uncover their needs and interests. It may be that counselling is needed for parties to explore their emotional reactions and to talk these through. Dispute practitioners are generally not counsellors, unless they are practising in specialised areas, such as part of a collaborative law specialist team or using transformative mediation or conflict coaching processes. Dispute practitioners, as has been noted, must be careful to understand their own fear of, or discomfort with emotional displays. Practitioners must avoid responses that encourage parties to suppress emotions because the practitioner is uncomfortable with emotional expression. Practitioners can become adept at active listening and staying in the moment when emotions are expressed. Conscious self-awareness assists the practitioner to acknowledge and monitor their own discomfort, if any, and to facilitate the parties' expression of difficult emotions.

Body language can betray feelings that a party may be reluctant to express. In such circumstances, a practitioner will be alert to the clues body language offers and may invite and or encourage the party to express their feelings. Giving parties an opportunity to vent feelings in a safe environment, assists them to uncover key interests and needs. Providing space for parties to express their emotions with 'I' statements and talking about how they feel enables a party to eventually move to a greater cognitive position. A common fear is that venting of emotions will produce an overwhelming emotional situation. In fact, the opposite is more often true: emotions will tend to be spent rather fed through expression in a structured, safe environment.[96]

Techniques that are useful in dealing with difficult emotions include the use of isopraxism[97] and active listening. Directive questioning can be used to take the person back to an earlier safe spot and then gradually bring them back to the place that is emotional, or to take the party forward and then return. Parties will then usually find that the next time they return to the difficult part of the communication they are more able to express themselves. Showing too much empathy or sympathy can result in a flood of emotion. In order to keep an appropriate level of professionalism, a non-verbal indication, such as silently offering the speaker a box of tissues, is sufficient to show empathy without further disrupting the communication between parties.

95 See, eg, Kathy Douglas, 'Shaping the Future: The Discourses of ADR and Legal Education' (2008) 8(1) *Law and Justice Journal* 118.

96 Eckhart Tolle, *A New Earth: Awakening to Your Life's Purpose* (Penguin, 2009).

97 See Chapter 1, 25.

Using assertiveness

The role of the amygdala in our fight, flight, and freeze responses has been discussed in Chapter 1. The following section describes how using an assertiveness technique can provide a fourth option. 'Flight' is a response in which a person runs from a dispute, and keeps moving away from the source of trouble in order to avoid accepting any responsibility for their contribution. Furthermore, when in flight, parties do not stand and assert their positions. Standing and asserting a position suggests a 'fight' response. Fighting is predicated on aggression and is a response often motivated by fear. A party with a fight response will typically jump in first with the aim of 'scaring off' the other party. A party may have experienced a fight response as effective because it places responsibility on the other party and provides little stimulus for change. Unfortunately, because it results in little change, it becomes a weakness in dealing with future conflicts.

By contrast with flight or fight responses, assertiveness can be achieved in a non-aggressive, calm manner by clearly stating the wants, needs, interests, and feelings involved. The process of assertive expression requires preparation in order to identify the concerns and preferred outcomes intended to be conveyed. An assertive message can be rehearsed and practised with a friend before delivery. The choice of place and time to deliver the message is crucial to ensure there is face-saving to both parties. It is therefore best to take place in a private space. The message should be delivered in a concise and consistent manner. It should follow this order: conveying the details and importance of the situation, then the feelings this evokes, and importantly and separately the consequences for the person affected. The aim is to be serious and objective without accusing, attacking, or providing interpretation. After delivery of an assertive response, the party making it should avoid being drawn into debate and accusation. This is done by active listening and, if necessary, reflecting back but not otherwise engaging. Reflection may mean saying, 'You think I am . . .'. If necessary, you may need to repeat the assertion several times until the other party hears what you are conveying. This will be indicated when the party agrees and concedes, such as 'Yes, that is the case, we probably need to discuss this.' Once this occurs, both parties can engage in discussion of broad strategies and option generation that may be refined into solutions. To maintain the momentum, active listening, reframing, and non-accusative language will be required.

Assertiveness process

1. Preparation
2. Assertion message: situation/feelings/consequences
3. Listen
4. Repeat steps 2 and 3 if necessary
5. Evoke strategies, options, solutions.

This assertiveness process can take complex issues and turn them into relatively straightforward issues. The following provides an example.

> Issue: You are constantly tidying up after your daughter which makes you late for work in the mornings.
> Assertive message: (combining components of situation, feelings, and consequence)
> Situation: When you leave your breakfast dishes and clothes in the bathroom
> Feelings: I feel frustrated
> Consequence: Because I have to put them away and often run late for work as a result.

Assertion requires careful preparation in advance in order to communicate in a clear, non-defensive and non-threatening manner. It also requires being prepared to repeat the message while remaining calm and in place.

Conclusion

The chapter has provided a focus on the communication skills needed by dispute practitioners. Those skills rely on theory and practice in interpersonal communication. Interpersonal communication is a branch of communication theory and practice that has particular relevance for dispute management practice. Techniques in communication must be learned and applied in a mindful way in order to obtain the best outcomes for managing disputes. How we communicate can increase the level of the dispute or it can de-escalate the intensity, if the right techniques are employed. Learning how to communicate appropriately requires application and is not often as easy as we think. A good way to start is by listening attentively to our existing patterns of communication, including our choice of words, and also to listen to others. This will tell us something about the way we and/or others respond to disputes, and whether we contribute to the escalation or de-escalation by our choice of verbal, vocal, and visual responses.

In this chapter, we examined three models of interpersonal communication. The first is a linear model that explains interpersonal communication as the transmission of information from sender to receiver in the form of coded messages. We noted that third-party intervention in determinative processes resembles this model in part. The second, two-way communication model introduces the non-verbal as well as verbal aspects in communication and suggests that it is an interactive circular process. The third model is the social skills model which sees interpersonal communication as a learned skill that occurs in a social context.

We examined the particular role of emotions in interpersonal communication and some of the barriers to effective communication. Having examined the role of interpersonal communication in dispute management, we explored specific interpersonal communication techniques. This required consideration of place, rapport, demonstrating empathy, active listening, questioning to elicit information, clarifying and facilitating understanding, and generating options and reality testing.

We examined two skill sets that provide for review and critique of practice through an emphasis on self-awareness and the impact of emotions, plus social and cultural influences: emotional intelligence and reflective practice. Finally, we considered issues in dealing with difficult emotions and the role of assertiveness. We have emphasised that the communication techniques and skills identified in this chapter form part of a toolkit that can be employed across the various dispute management processes.

EXERCISE IN APPLYING YOUR KNOWLEDGE – PETA'S FACTORY

Consider the following case study.

Peta owns a factory in which she produces bamboo material for clothing manufacture. She has developed the business over the last five years and is now supplying prominent Australian designers. She imports the bamboo fibre from Indonesia. She has exerted huge effort and expense to get the business up and running, borrowing from her parents and the bank, and is only now making a profit.

Ryan is an Australian designer who specialises in casual wear and whose designs in bamboo have become sought after, particularly with eco-friendly customers. He has recently secured a large order from a leading department store.

Ryan places an order for material with Peta to the value of $500,00.00. The order is required to be filled by 31 October.

On 30 October, Ryan contacts Peta and tells her that he needs to cancel the order. He tells her that the department store has advised him that they will cancel his order unless he accepts a 30 per cent reduction in his contract with them. He says that he is sorry, but he can't afford to go ahead.

Peta is distraught. She had just enough fibre to fulfil the order and has made it up to Ryan's specifications. She is unlikely to get any more fibre in from Indonesia, due to the COVID-19 pandemic, for months if not a year or more. She had hoped that the order would keep her going through the pandemic. She has also incurred production costs in getting the order ready. She admits that she is at least three weeks behind the due date, but she had told Ryan about the delay and he said he could manage it. She is shocked, distressed and worried for the future of her business, her employees and her family, who depend upon her.

You are asked to interview Peta as part of a dispute management intake procedure. You begin the interview by explaining your role as gathering information to later decide what dispute management option would be the most appropriate in the circumstances. You do not decide upon an option during the interview.

1. What should you be doing when interviewing Peta?
2. What models of interpersonal communication assist in understanding dispute management practice? How could you apply them to the case study?
3. What is empathy? How does active listening contribute to a demonstration of empathy? How would you use empathy in the case study?
4. How are emotional intelligence and reflective practice related to dispute management practice?

3

HISTORY AND PHILOSOPHY OF DISPUTE MANAGEMENT

Learning aims

- Describe the history of dispute management
- Explain the philosophies underpinning dispute management
- Demonstrate knowledge of how these philosophies and the history of dispute management has influenced current dispute management practice
- Explain how history and the key philosophies operate in the current dispute management world and explore the future possibilities
- Recognise special considerations applicable to dispute management and their effect on its practice

Understanding dispute management in context

This section will introduce the history and philosophy of dispute management. It provides a contextualisation to the evolving of dispute processes and the theoretical factors that arise when considering how society manages disputes.

History

Here we provide a brief introduction to the common law approach to dispute management, known as the 'adversarial approach' in the Australian legal system.[1] The adversarial process in a civil dispute entails parties presenting their competing sides usually through their legal representative – although more litigants are choosing to self-represent – to an independent decision-maker. The parties argue points of law and fact so the decision-maker can decide on the basis of a strict application of the correct law. This creates a winner and a loser, with the winner generally receiving a common law award of money. In criminal matters, the state prosecutes an alleged offender in order to uphold the criminal law. This is done according to strict rules of evidence before a judge alone, or judge and jury that must be satisfied beyond reasonable doubt of the offender's guilt. When considering the best process for managing a dispute, litigation is an essential process to have in mind. The historical development of this process reaches back to early English history. This is briefly introduced, before looking at the development of the many processes available in Australia today, which expand beyond those managed by lawyers within the adversarial system of litigation.

English beginnings

After the Duke of Normandy's conquest of England in 1066 at the Battle of Hastings, the Duke, known as William the Conqueror (r. 1066–1087 CE),[2] did not abandon the existing

1 Robert A LeVine, 'Anthropology and the Study of Conflict: An Introduction' (1961) 5(1) *Journal of Conflict Resolution* 3.

2 Ian Ward, *English Legal Histories* (Hart Publishing, 2019); William Blackstone, *Commentaries on the Laws of England* (Clarendon Press, 1765).

Anglo-Saxon system of laws that were in operation in any rupturing fashion. These laws were an amalgam of the laws developed over time in the local district and included a mix of local customs, feudal law, Danelaw, church law, remnant Roman law, and the law merchant. Instead, the one common law of England developed by gradually bringing the differences in each district into an aligned system of law for the entire country as it became centralised by the King's Courts. Citizens swore loyalty to the King, but the feudal system remained in operation. Over time, as the King's Courts became established, the people gravitated to the Courts in preference to the feudal baron's justice. Much of the history in the century following the Conqueror was unrecorded or was lost.[3] A notable exception is the *Doomsday Book* (1086), which was significant in recording the information on land ownership; somewhat like a modern day census, it documented who owned land and its usage.[4] Another, the Glanvill book, provides some of the most important surviving history recording the early pre-centralisation law.[5] However, it was not until Henry II was crowned as King (1154–89) that real changes were solidified. Three significant aspects are to be noted as deriving from this historical time and having importance to the common law systems today. These are:

1. The **Rule of Law**, a concept that evolved from significant attempts such as the barons' pressure on King John to sign the *Magna Carta* in 1215,[6] in order to control the rule of kings and place limits on Parliament and the rule by men so that laws legitimately made could be the only rule to which any person in the realm was accountable. The legitimacy of law to this day is contained by the constraints on both legislation made and promulgated through an agreed legislative process and judge-made law being regulated by the system of ***stare decisis***, controlling the ability of judges to determine and apply the law through the rules of precedent limited by the court hierarchy.
2. The growth of the legal technocrats capable of negotiating the complexities of the common law. These arose through the establishing of the Inns of Court, in which barristers and judges were trained within the ranks of professional patronage. Hierarchy of the profession was established at the inception, with Serjeants holding exclusive rights to practise in the Common Pleas and from the ranks of whom judges were appointed. The lower-level lawyers, solicitors or attorneys, were seen as the 'vipers

Rule of Law: a fundamental aspect of the legal system which effectively means citizens are subject to legitimately made law and not the whim of rulers. It has a number of aspects, including that the law is clear and promulgated in advance of its application so the citizens can know the law, that it is applied equally to all no matter their standing in society, and that all have equal opportunity to access justice.

***Stare decisis*:** the concept of precedent in which courts follow prior court decisions where the case relates to a similar matter previously decided within the same court hierarchy.

3 SFC Milsom, *Historical Foundations of the Common Law* (Butterworths, 2nd ed, 1981) 11–17.

4 See G Martin and Ann Williams, *Domesday Book: A Complete Translation* (Penguin Books, 2004); Robin Fleming, *Doomsday Book and the Law: Society and Legal Custom in Early Medieval England* (Cambridge University Press, 1998).

5 Ranulf Glanvill, *Tractatus de legibus et consuetudinibus regni Angliae* (originally published 1188) in Richardi Totteli (1st ed, 1554); Ranulf Glanvill, *Tractatus de legibus et consuetudinibus regni Angliae*, George Woodbine (ed), tr John Beams (Yale University Press, 1932). The original author is unidentified but Glanvill was Henry II's justiciar.

6 The 1215 *Magna Carta* signed by King John at Runneymede was subsequently revised in 1217 and again into its final form in 1225. See also Lawrence Goldman (ed), *Magna Carta: History, Context and Influence* (University of London Press, 2018).

and pettifoggers'.[7] The burgeoning profession used regulation to control its operation, hierarchy and behaviour right down to dress code:

> Various institutions, such as the Inns, added . . . layers of regulation to this which, for trainee barristers, meant no swords, long beards or anything Italian. And no 'curled hayr' . . . at least not at Middle Temple. Nor 'great Bryches in their Hoses, made after the Dutch, Spanish or Almon fashion'.[8]

3. The **writ** system, by which a complainant could initiate a hearing of their dispute by royal order to appear before a court. The writ provided the form necessary to initiate a legal action and, over time, these were specifically named for each cause of action being brought.[9]

Writ: a formal written document often following a standardised form that initiates court involvement in a matter.

Writs eventually became ridged forms in the 13th century. The writ helped establish both the dominance of the centralised Kings justice and an administrative practice that evolved to become a due process right and jurisdictional determinant. In turn, the formality of the writ came to limit matters that could be heard in a juridification, or ossification, of legal form in the system. The ultimate restriction on access to the King's Courts due to this procedural requirement left claimants having to resort to alternatives in order to have peaceful management of their disputes. The solution to the procedural dilemmas occurred through reference of such matters to the Chancellor, who heard and determined matters initially in an informal way based on consideration of an equitable outcome. The decisions made by the Chancellor in this manner eventually built their own system of precedents that founded the law of equity, which is still applied separately but alongside the common law in the courts in common law countries.[10] Equity breathed flexibility into a system that had become ridged and unavailable in many circumstances, and to ensure maintenance of a lawful and peaceful order for the English community. This took place over centuries. As Milsom notes:

> In the fourteenth century there was no law of England, no body of rules complete in itself with known limits and visible defects; or if there was it was not the property of the common law courts or any others. There was justice and right, absolute values; but it was not yet the lawyer's business to comprehend them in the sense of knowing what was the just and right result upon these facts and those. His business was procedural, to see that disputes were properly submitted to the appropriate deciding mechanism.[11]

The discussion so far has addressed the legal system that arrived in Australia with the British descent on the country. The Indigenous communities, of which there were over 200, had their own systems to address and manage disputes and, where possible, these have been maintained to this day. Initially there was a total failure to accept the complexity of these societies. There prevailed an inability to recognise that all communities, since they first came into

7 C Brooks, *Pettyfoggers and Vipers of the Commonwealth: The 'Lower Branch' of the Legal Profession in Early Modern England* (Cambridge University Press, 2004) cited in Ward (n 2) 54.

8 Ward (n 2) 56 (references omitted).

9 Arthur R Hogue, *Origins of the Common Law* (Liberty Press, 1986) 13: 'The number of writs increased from about 39 in the time of *Glanvill* (ca. 1189) to more than 400 in the reign of Edward 1 (1272–1307)'.

10 See, eg, *Judicature Act 1873* (UK) and *Judicature Act 1875* (UK).

11 Milsom (n 3) 83.

existence, have had to provide mechanisms by which disputes could be managed.[12] Traditionally, most disputes have been managed by less formal processes than litigation. These processes have varied based on several factors, but particularly according to the nature of the dispute and the relationship and cultural context in which the disputants have found themselves. Since the advancement of the dispute management movement there has, thankfully, been a greater willingness to listen and learn from the Indigenous peoples as to techniques that seek to peaceably manage disputes and restore harmony among groups. Some of these are referred to in Chapter 1.[13] They most often bring influences that become amalgamated with mainstream approaches to form a blended approach. Examples such as the Indigenous Courts, variously described in each State and Territory, are evidence of these influences.[14] They include less formality, inclusion of Elders for cultural awareness, an attempt to get to the underlying causes for offending and divert offenders from custodial sentencing options by linking to appropriate support services. Influences have carried to other specialist courts, such as the Drug Courts.[15] However, an amalgamation of influences can be contentious, and currently there remains ongoing calls for a National Indigenous Dispute Management Service to provide a dedicated service to strengthen communities and address the over-representation of Indigenous peoples in prisons.[16] As regards the operation of theIndigenous Courts, it is possible that more could be achieved to avoid perceptions of continued colonisation of disempowered minorities.[17] A key factor is that any dispute management process must follow the philosophy of the movement to empowerment and self-determination of Indigenous peoples.

It is clear that parties in dispute now have multiple options when seeking to address their dispute and can find guidance from many different sources, ranging from individuals to businesses operating in the disputing industry, statutory and private institutions, and specialists, such as dispute practitioners (including lawyers).

Litigation has held a status that puts it at the apex of an imaginary dispute management pyramid. In Australia, it was the established basis for all lawful management of disputes

12 For an early historical account, see Jerome T Barrett and Joseph P Barrett, *A History of Alternative Dispute Resolution* (Jossey-Bass, and Wiley 2004).

13 See, eg, Chapter 1, 31.

14 See, eg, *Sentencing Act 2017* (SA) s 22 enabling the convening of an Aboriginal Sentencing Conference known as a 'Nunga Court'; *Magistrates' Court (Koori Court) Act 2002* (Vic); Queensland Courts, *Murri Courts* (Web Page) <https://www.courts.qld.gov.au/courts/murri-court>; Circle Sentencing in New South Wales Part 7 (Circle Sentencing Intervention Program) of the *Criminal Procedure Regulation 2017* NSW; the Australian Capital Territory Galambany Court, 2004; see also Mary Westcott, 'Murri Courts' (Research Brief No 2006/14, Queensland Parliamentary Library, April 2006); see also Michael S King, 'Therapeutic Jurisprudence Initiatives in Australia and New Zealand and the Overseas Experience' (2011) 21(1) *Journal of Judicial Administration* 19.

15 See, eg, Ryan Kornhauser, 'The Effectiveness of Australia's Drug Courts' (2018) 51(1) *Australian & New Zealand Journal of Criminology* 776.

16 See, eg, *Joint ATSILS Proposal to the Commonwealth Attorney-General for the Establishment of a National Aboriginal and Torres Strait Islander Dispute Management Service*, (2010) <http://www.atsils.org.au/wp-content/uploads/2014/11/Joint-ATSILS-National-Aboriginal-and-Torres-Strait-Islander-Dispute-Management-Service-Proposal-Nov-2010.pdf>.

17 See, eg, Bridget McAsey, 'Critical Evaluation of the Koori Court Division of the Victorian Magistrates' Court' (2005) 10(2) *Deakin Law Review* 654; Aleksandra Miller, 'Neighbourhood Justice Centres and Indigenous Empowerment' (2017) 20(1) *Australian Indigenous Law Review* 123.

through the public courts. However, it is used by society to resolve only a small percentage of disputes. Studies indicate that only 5 per cent of claims are filed in court and, of those, less than 5 per cent actually go to trial.[18] Although only a small percentage of disputes end in litigation, the increased size and complexity of society has generated a litigation 'explosion' with the result that courts have experienced difficulties in handling their workloads. Delays, increasing costs, and the general adversarial nature of litigation mean that disputants look elsewhere for justice. The modern era has also brought with it a decline in reliance upon the traditional supports of the church, community elders, and the family. It is against this background that the movement to dispute management began to develop in earnest in its modern form.

It is enlightening to reflect on how legal systems slowly transform themselves over time. This cannot often be seen when working from within the system, but needs the benefit of a helicopter historical view encompassing the bigger picture. In reflecting on the development of the common law, Milsom indicates:

> Centralisation and specialisation proceeded together. But the pattern which hindsight can see was not being consciously drawn at the time. Institutions begin in expedients. An immediate problem arises: an immediate solution is found. Nobody can know that the solution will later be seen as the origin of something, or the problem as the effective end of something else.[19]

The big paradigm shift in addressing dispute management emerged as a movement in the United States in the mid-1970s.[20] The much criticised unwieldy litigation system lead to the establishment in New York of the Centre for Public Resources to promote other forms of dispute management.[21] These dispute management processes became transposed into many Western countries through the 1970s and 1980s, including in Australia. The changes arose with parties looking for more peaceable ways of addressing disputes that could be achieved quickly, cheaply, and without destroying relationships. Criticisms concerning the formal court systems win/lose outcomes meant many parties either never resorted to the courts or stopped relying on the formal legal system. This paradigm change, resulting in the enthusiastic uptake

---

18 See Kenneth Hayne, 'The Vanishing Trial' (Speech, Supreme and Federal Courts Judges Conference, 23 January 2008) <https://cdn.hcourt.gov.au/assets/publications/speeches/current-justices/haynej/haynej_23jan08.pdf>. Thomas J Stipanowich, 'ADR and the "Vanishing Trial": The Growth and Impact of "Alternative Dispute Resolution"' (2004) 1(3) *Journal of Empirical Legal Studies* 843. For current figures based on the filing of a cause of action in the Australian Federal Courts, refer to the Federal Court of Australia Annual Reports (Workload Statistics) <https://www.fedcourt.gov.au/about/corporate-information/annual-reports/2018-19>. For the position in the United States, see Howard M Erichson, 'Settlement in the Absence of Anticipated Adjudication' (2017) 85(5) *Fordham Law Review* 2017; Judith Resnik, 'Lawyers' Ethics beyond the Vanishing Trial: Unrepresented Claimants, De Facto Aggregations, Arbitration Mandates, and Privatized Processes' (2017) 85(5) *Fordham Law Review* 1899.

19 Milsom (n 3) 26.

20 Thomas O. Main, 'ADR: The New Equity' (2005) 74 *University of Cincinnati Law Review* 329, 334: 'In April 1976, acknowledging a certain amount of "deferred maintenance" in the courts, Chief Justice Burger convened the National Conference on the Causes of Popular Dissatisfaction with the Administration of Justice.'

21 CPR Institute for Dispute Resolution, 'General Counsel Forum on ADR Practice In the 21st Century' (2000) 18(4) *Alternatives* 67; Russ Blumer 'Alternatives to the High Cost of Litigation' (2005) 23(7) *Alternatives* 110.

of dispute management processes, has seen our universities increasingly offering courses to educate dispute management practitioners in law and other disciplines.

The role of the state in controlling the administration of justice has resulted in an embracing of privatising dispute management by allowing parties individually to attempt to peacefully address their disputes through mechanisms outside the courts, or indeed the specific domain of lawyers. Governments and policymakers have enthusiastically taken up the dispute management movement's promise of quicker, cheaper, more informal outcomes and ease of access by parties to dispute management processes. It has provided a way for governments to be seen to be responding to criticisms of the formal court system and access to justice.[22] Courts also saw the value of using other forms of dispute management to relieve the cost and congestion in the courts. The processes used have often been adopted from the history of different cultures. Traditional informal processes of dispute management were refined, experimented with, adapted and hybridised in order to provide suitable dispute processes.[23] These have been revived and transformed into processes that have become formalised such as mediation, conciliation and arbitration. Early successes encouraged the growth of the movement. This has burgeoned into the dispute management options available today and the many processes described in this book. The privatised management of disputes works in combination with, and is supported by, the state's public system of justice when managing disputes. It has resulted not only in the introduction of voluntary but in some cases, compulsory mediation or other settlement procedures at an interlocutory stage of a litigated dispute. It has brought with it both positive and negative aspects when addressing access to justice and the principle of the Rule of Law. Both are addressed later in this chapter.

With its continued growth, dispute management has become accepted by the commercial community to the point where most commercial entities now insert mandatory dispute management clauses into their contracts. Thus, any dispute arising under the contract is initially dealt with by processes other than litigation. Various dispute management schemes have been instituted by government,[24] as well as by professional and community bodies to cater for a wide variety of disputes ranging from the inter-personal to the international.[25] This transformation of the public formal system of justice sees dispute management becoming a corporatised or privatised system.

Changes in the legal system are evidenced through the expansion of in-house mediation and other dispute management programs that attempt to address disputes without outside assistance or the use of legal interventions. This has led to the growth of businesses offering private dispute management processes including complaint management. The cost of disputes to business operations and reputation means value exists if disputes can be addressed in-house at the earliest opportunity.

22 See, eg, David Spencer and Michael Brogan, *Mediation Law and Practice* (2006) 27–31; *Inquiry into Alternative Dispute Resolution and Restorative Justice: Final report of the Victorian Parliament Law Reform Committee* (Parliament of Victoria Law Reform Committee, 2009).

23 See, eg, Keren Lavelle, 'Ancient Ceremony Transformed into Cross-Cultural Mediation Training' (2005) 43(2) *Law Society Journal* 22–3; Akanmu Gafari, Jesse J Benjamin and Brandon D Lundy (eds), *Indigenous Conflict Management Strategies: Global Perspectives* (Lexington Books, 2014).

24 See Chapter 12.

25 See, eg, Graham Allison, 'Preventing Nuclear War: Schelling's Strategies' (2018) 34(3) *Negotiation Journal* 291, for its use in the international domain.

In the United States, there has been a rapid growth in public companies using judicial and mediation services. This specialised growth area has developed with retired judges and barristers offering high-end negotiation and expert evaluative style mediation. These companies, and others like them, solicit the best and brightest judges by financial enticement to provide confidential and quick assistance for those organisations with high-cost disputes. A consequence of these developments is the reduction in services being sought from lawyers. Although, in Australian society, negotiation often conducted through lawyers has been the most commonly used means of dispute management, and lawyers are developing skills in the range of available dispute management options, including initiating the development of such processes.[26]

Senior Executive Appraisal Mediation

An example of senior barristers or retired judges assisting with managing disputes can be found in the use of mini-trial processes or an approach used in Australia referred to as **Senior Executive Appraisal Mediation (SEAM)**. This usually involves a legally trained impartial third party in a triadic dispute process and is used in matters more likely to proceed to litigation. The understanding is that the parties may overcome a dispute quickly if representatives with authority to settle are educated about the strengths and weaknesses of each side's case. Such processes are most useful for disputes involving mixed law and fact; for example, where there is a breach of contract, challenge to proprietary rights, product liability or tortious claims.

Senior Executive Appraisal Mediation (SEAM): a legally trained, impartial third party in a triadic dispute process (in matters that are more likely to proceed to litigation) conducting a voluntary and non-binding process in which each side presents a highly abbreviated summary of their case to senior officials of each party who are authorised to negotiate a settlement of the dispute, somewhat like a mini-trial.

SEAM is a structured voluntary and non-binding process in which each side presents a highly abbreviated summary of their case to senior officials of each party who are authorised to negotiate a settlement of the dispute. A neutral advisor sometimes presides over proceedings and will give an advisory opinion if asked to do so. This process helps the parties clarify exactly what is in dispute and the expert opinion assists in assessing what is the likely outcome, particularly if the matter was to proceed to litigation. Such processes are similar to independent expert appraisal, although note they use a mechanism that adopts aspects of adversarialism.

SEAM usually involves the following steps:

1. The parties determine whether to appoint a neutral advisor, and if so, the identity and role of that neutral advisor.
2. The parties agree on the procedure and the timetable of the proceedings. Strict time limits are imposed on every step in the proceedings.
3. Each party's advocate prepares their best case, sometimes with limited discovery of the other party's documents.
4. Each advocate then presents the best case to the panel. The panel comprises the authorised decision-maker for each of the parties and the neutral advisor, if one was decided on. The presentation can include statements from witnesses, documents, and visual aids. Only the panellists may ask clarifying questions during the presentations. The strict time limits induce the parties to focus on key issues.

26 See, eg, Chapter 9 and Stu Webb's role in the development of the collaborative law process.

5. After each party has presented their best case, each party may present a rebuttal of the other party's case. The parties may agree that the advocates, witnesses and experts for the parties, as well as the panellists, ask questions of the other party during rebuttal.
6. After the rebuttals, there is often an open question-and-answer session.
7. The neutral advisor then issues their opinion, if required to do so.
8. The authorised decision-makers enter settlement negotiations based on the information and insight gained.

If settlement is not reached, additional negotiation sessions may be scheduled. Alternatively, the parties may agree that the neutral advisor adopt the role of mediator or appraiser, or otherwise actively assist the management of the dispute.[27]

Independent expert appraisal

Independent expert appraisal is a triadic process whereby the parties select an independent and impartial expert (appraiser) to formulate an opinion on the matters in dispute. Often, having an expert opinion on specific matters in dispute can clarify the issues and indicate possible early solutions to parties before the dispute escalates. The appraiser takes an active, inquisitorial role to identify and understand the issues in dispute and provide the parties with a report. The process may range from a formal inquisitional hearing involving detailed questioning in examination of witnesses by the expert, to an entirely informal assessment by the expert, using information provided by the parties.

Independent expert appraisal is particularly appropriate for disputes over issues of fact, quantification, valuation, specification, or the demarcation of responsibilities relating to a particular industry or profession. Expert opinions can be very effective where the parties in dispute agree on the chosen expert and their opinion is highly regarded.[28] This process is used mainly in a commercial context, such as in the construction industry and in disputes over international commodity agreements. It is a process frequently used as an adjunct to the mediation of commercial disputes. The fact that the appraiser is already an expert on the subject matter in dispute is an obvious advantage as it saves time educating a neutral in the complexities of the subject area.

At present, the Australian Commercial Disputes Centre is the major agency which provides this process although it may also be accessed through others such as The Bar Association schemes.

As with arbitration, the source of the parties' agreement for independent expert appraisal is normally a dispute management clause in the pre-dispute contractual documentation between the parties. The clause will usually stipulate that the expert is to act as an expert and not as an arbitrator. This is to try to ensure that the rights and obligations under the *Commercial Arbitration Acts* are not attracted.

27 Ian Hanger, 'Senior Executive Appraisal Mediation' (2000) 3(4) *ADR Bulletin* 45; Adele Carr, 'Senior Executive Appraisal: Will the Mini-trial Cement Its Place in Alternative Dispute Resolution?' (2018) 28 *Australasian Dispute Resolution Journal* 235.

28 David Spencer and Samantha Hardy, *Dispute Resolution in Australia: Cases, Commentary and Materials* (Thomson Reuters, 2014) 330–7.

An essential difference between an appraiser and an arbitrator is that the latter has a duty to act judicially. Thus, an arbitrator must manage the dispute by hearing the parties' evidence and arriving at a binding decision based on that evidence and according to objective standards. An appraiser actively investigates and questions the parties to seek out facts and arrives at a valuation or appraisal based on their own personal knowledge and expertise without obligation to hear argument from the parties. The expressed and implied intention of the parties is also relevant. The independence of the expert has been found by the Supreme Court of Victoria to be both actual independence from both parties and an appearance of independence to avoid apprehension of bias.[29] The parties may agree that the appraiser's opinion is to be final and binding, or non-binding and advisory only. In the latter case, the opinion will be used in subsequent settlement negotiations between the parties, or in arbitration or litigation should settlement not be achieved.

The Australian historical development

In Australia, the growth of dispute management is marked by significant developments starting from Federation and continuing through to current times, with the formation of organisations and bodies that have promoted dispute management processes.[30] This history does not cover pre-Federation nor the Indigenous cultures' rich history of dispute management, but it must be recalled that this history is ongoing and influences our systems post-Federation.[31]

1904 – The Commonwealth of Australia established the Commonwealth Court of Conciliation and Arbitration to specifically deal with employer and employee disputes. This body has gone through various transformations. Various Courts of Conciliation were created by State legislation.[32] The *Workplace Relations Act 1996* (Cth) was the first time mediation was referred to for employer/employee disputes.

1970s – Federal government and State governments introduced the office of the Ombudsman as an impartial independent investigator of complaints regarding generally public statutory bodies. The Ombudsman plays a mediating role in disputes and is a useful mechanism where the parties are not of equal negotiating strengths. Ombudsman positions commenced in Australia in the early 1970s, with several state ombudsman positions.[33] Over time specialised ombudsmen have been created, such as the Telecommunications Industry Ombudsman and Fair Work Ombudsman.[34]

1974 – The Consumer Claims Tribunals made provision for third-party neutrals to act as referees in disputes.

29 *500 Burwood Highway Pty Ltd v Australian Unity Ltd* [2012] VSC 596.

30 Ibid [33]–[41]. See also Peter Condliffe, *Conflict Management: A Practical Guide* (LexisNexis Butterworths, 6th ed, 2016) 123–4.

31 See Chapter 1, 31.

32 See *Courts of Conciliation Act 1892* (Qld); *Conciliation Act 1929* (SA); *Courts of Conciliation Act 1931* (Qld).

33 *Ombudsman Act 1976* (Cth); *Parliamentary Commissioner Act 1971* (WA); *Ombudsman Act 1972* (SA); *Ombudsman Act 2001* (Qld); *Ombudsman Act 1974* (NSW).

34 See, eg, *Telecommunications Act 1997* (Cth) and Telecommunications (Consumer Complaints Handling) Industry Standard 2018; *Fair Work Act 2009* (Cth).

1975 – The Institute of Arbitrators and Mediators Australia (IAMA) was established to promote arbitration and mediation dispute management processes.

1975 – The *Family Law Act 1975* (Cth) acknowledged a role for counsellors and conferences. The family law area has advanced the adoption of dispute management processes to now require mediation prior to any court hearing, and the language and tone are collaborative rather than adversarial.[35]

1980 – Community Justice Centres (CJCs) began in New South Wales.[36] The aim of the centres was to provide an informal dispute management service that offered speedy and impartial processes to the community. Victoria followed suit in 1987. A Community Justice Program was established in Queensland in July 1990 under the *Dispute Resolution Centres Act 1990* (Qld). This program reflects a similar approach to the New South Wales CJC. Using mediators trained by the organisation, the mediations provide generally fee-free services with the program funded by the state government. In Queensland, under the *Courts Reform Amendment Act 1997* (Qld), Dispute Resolution Centres may handle mediations referred to them from the Supreme, District and Magistrates Courts. The six Dispute Resolution Centres across Queensland provide services including mediation, abbreviated mediation, neighbourhood, separating couples, Aboriginal and Torres Strait Islander mediation, facilitated workplace dispute management, child protection, and adult restorative justice conferencing.[37] The Noble Park Centre, established in 1985, was one of the first mediation programs funded by the Commonwealth Attorney-General.

1986 – The Australian Commercial Dispute Centre was established to support mediation and arbitration. It has gone through several changes, including becoming the Australian International Disputes Centre (AIDC) in 2010, and the Australian Disputes Centre in 2015. The Australian Disputes Centre now has national and international reach.[38] All States and Territories passed *Commercial Arbitration Acts* which have been updated, starting in 2010 with New South Wales. Upgraded arbitration procedures exist so that arbitration may now be presented to the business and commercial community as a viable means of dispute management.[39]

---

35 *Family Law Act 1975* (Cth) s 60I; see also Rae Kaspiew et al, *Evaluation of the 2006 Family Law Reforms: Summary Report* (Australian Institute of Family Studies, 2009), regarding 2006 Family Law Reforms; Australian Law Reform Commission, *Family Law for the Future: An Inquiry into the Family Law System* (Report No 135, March 2019).

36 See *Community Justice Centres (NSW Pilot Project) Act 1980* (NSW); *Community Justice Centres Act 1983* (NSW).

37 For those wanting to explore restorative justice further see, eg, Susan L Miller and M Kristen Hefner, 'Procedural Justice for Victims and Offenders?: Exploring Restorative Justice Processes in Australia and the US' (2013) 32(1) *Justice Quarterly* 142; Annalise Buth and Lynn Cohn, 'Looking at Justice Through a Lens of Healing and Reconnection' (2017) 13(1) *Northwestern Journal of Law and Social Policy* 1; Margarita Zernova, 'Restorative Justice in the Basque Peace Process: Some Experiments and Their Lessons' (2017) 20(3) *Contemporary Justice Review* 363; Estelle Zinsstag and Inge Vanfraechem, *Conferencing and Restorative Justice : International Practices and Perspectives* (Oxford University Press, 2012).

38 See Australian Disputes Centre, *ADC History* (Web Page) <https://www.disputescentre.com.au/history/>.

39 See also Chapter 10; *Commercial Arbitration Act 2017* (ACT); *Commercial Arbitration Act 2010* (NSW); *Commercial Arbitration (National Uniform Legislation) Act 2011* (NT); *Commercial Arbitration Act 2013* (Qld); *Commercial Arbitration Act 2011* (SA); *Commercial Arbitration Act 2011* (Tas); *Commercial Arbitration Act* 2011 (Vic); *Commercial Arbitration Act 2012* (WA).

1986 – The first Australian Conference on dispute management was held in Canberra in 1986. From this, the Australian Dispute Resolution Association (ADRA) arose in 1987 as an association of academics and practitioners who promoted the benefits of dispute management processes.

1989 – Leading Edge Alternative Dispute Resolvers (LEADR) commenced in 1989, created by lawyers to facilitate the use of dispute management processes. Its aim was to promote the development and acceptance of dispute management processes in the community, and to research, educate and provide information on the topic. It had chapters in Queensland, New South Wales, Western Australia and Victoria.

1993 – New South Wales started the first Legal Aid Commission mediation programs that were closely followed in Queensland and Victoria. Many State Legal Aid offices have introduced compulsory mediation conferences, participation in which is often a pre-requisite to a grant of legal assistance.

1995 – The National Alternative Dispute Resolution Advisory Council (NADRAC), an independent non-statutory body, was founded in order to foster the growth and support of processes outside court action in civil matters. This non-statutory body, appointed by the Commonwealth Attorney-General, set national standards for mediation and mediator training, as well as ensuring accessibility to integrated mediation programs through judicial Commonwealth services. NADRAC was dismantled in 2013 as a result of the Abbott Government policies. Many of its resources can still be obtained through the Federal Attorney General's website.[40]

Late 1990s – A burgeoning tribunal growth included the establishing of state super tribunals dealing with civil disputes, administrative rights, and human rights in administering many specialised legislative domains. The first was the Victorian Civil and Administrative Tribunal established in 1998. These tribunals aid with increasing numbers of self-represented litigants. To make the provision of justice simplified and less costly, they exclude lawyers and adopt a more inquisitorial style.[41]

2000s – Specialist Aboriginal and Torres Strait Islander Courts were established in States and Territories adopting restorative approaches and therapeutic jurisprudence in the interests of diverting Indigenous Australians out of the prison system.[42]

2005 – The 2005 National Mediation Conference created a committee to develop a mediator standards and accreditation proposal.

2008 – The first National Mediator Accreditation Standards were established. These were updated in 2015 and are under review again.[43]

---

40 See Australian Government, Attorney-General's Department, *Alternative Dispute Resolution* (Web Page) <https://www.ag.gov.au/legal-system/alternative-dispute-resolution>.

41 See, eg, Bertus De Villiers, 'Accessibility to the Law: The Contribution of Super-Tribunals to Fairness and Simplicity in the Australian Legal Landscape' (2015) 39(2) *University of Western Australia Law Review* 239; Iain Ross, 'Promoting Tribunal Excellence' (2012) 21(3) *Journal of Judicial Administration* 135; Fleur Kingham, 'Reforming Queensland's Tribunals: Procedural Reform to Realise the Rhetoric' (2004) 14 (1) *Journal of Judicial Administration* 31; Guy Cumes, 'Separation of Powers, Courts, Tribunals and the State' (2008) 19(1) *Australasian Dispute Resolution Journal* 10.

42 See Indigenous Courts (n 14).

43 National Australian Dispute Resolution Advisory Council, *Who Says You're a Mediator? Towards a National System for Accrediting Mediators* (2004); Tania Sourdin, *Australian National Mediator Accreditation System: Report on Project* (2007) <http://www.ama.asn.au/The_Accredication_Report_

2011 – The *Civil Dispute Resolution Act 2011* (Cth) endorsed pre-action procedures in genuine attempts to settle disputes prior to court hearing at a Federal level.

2014 – The Australian Dispute Resolution Advisory Council (ADRAC)[44] was established, with a mix of former members of NADRAC and new members of the Council to continue and develop further the work of NADRAC by researching, advising and supporting the development of dispute management as a non-aligned think-tank.

2015 – The IAMA and LEADR amalgamated to become the Resolution Institute.

Over time, compulsory mediation schemes in respect of certain disputes have been introduced into many courts.[45] All courts now conduct a variety of pre-trial conferences using mediation principles; for example, the Queensland Supreme Court can direct case appraisal or mediation.[46] Many Magistrates Courts conduct victim-offender mediation programs and, in some instances, the magistrate has power to refer matters for mediation to the Community Justice Programs. Some judges adopt a therapeutic jurisprudence approach in their courts.[47] Law societies have promoted their own state dispute management committees that provide advisor services to government and the courts, and to train dispute management practitioners. For example, the Queensland Bar Association conducted their first 'Settlement Week' in 1992. Law school curriculums generally offer a subject on different dispute management processes.

As well as the above public indicators of the movement, the understanding and use of dispute management processes are expanding into most areas of commerce, politics, industrial relations, business, and environmental management. Notwithstanding the growing range of processes available to manage disputes, litigation still plays an important role and, although this role is being redefined, it is incorporated in this textbook as one of the obvious processes to choose from when managing a dispute. Further, the value of combining another dispute process together with litigation now occurs in Australia through the implementation of various court-connected management schemes.

An example of an off-shoot of the progressive use of dispute processes is Collaborative Practice, in which parties undertake to manage their disputes using lawyers' and other experts' skills without going to court. This is utilised in particular in family law and is aimed at supporting couples in an open and honest way to manage all aspects of their separation while

240907.pdf>. A voluntary industry self-regulated accreditation scheme accepted by stakeholders and commenced operation from 1 January 2008. See *National Mediator Accreditation Scheme (NMAS), A History of the Development of the Standards* <https://msb.org.au/themes/msb/assets/documents/a-history-of-the-development-of-the-standards.pdf>.

44 Australian Dispute Resolution Advisory Council, *The Need for a Peak Body in ADR* (2017); see also Australian Dispute Resolution Advisory Council, *ADRAC Charter* <https://www.adrac.org.au/charter>.

45 See, eg, *Federal Court of Australia Act 1976* (Cth); *Civil and Administrative Tribunal Act 2008* (ACT); *Civil Law (Wrongs) Act 2002* (ACT); *Civil Procedure Act 2005* (NSW); *Local Court Act 1989* (NT); *Civil Proceedings Act 2011* (Qld) pt 6; *Supreme Court Act 1935* (SA); *Civil Procedure Act 2010* (Vic); *Alternative Dispute Resolution Act 2001* (Tas) s 5(1); *Supreme Court Act 1935* (WA).

46 *Civil Proceedings Act 2011* (Qld) ss 40–1.

47 See, eg, Justice Ian Dearden, 'Therapeutic Jurisprudence and The District Court' (Conference Paper, Non-Adversarial Justice: Implications for the Legal System and Society Conference, 4–7 May 2017) <https://aija.org.au/wp-content/uploads/2017/08/Dearden.pdf>; cf David Kwok, 'The (im)propriety of Judicial Mediation' (2015) 26(4) *Australasian Dispute Resolution Journal* 210, for issues for the role of judges engaging in mediation.

accepting responsibility and not accentuating emotional impact on the parties and their children.[48] This particular process is outlined in Chapter 9.

Last, but not least, is the introduction of courses on dispute management at universities, in particular into the core curriculum of law schools to ensure law graduates obtain an understanding of dispute management processes in readiness for practice.[49]

Philosophy

Five philosophies

This section will address the five philosophies underpinning the dispute management movement.[50] These are key philosophies that remain essential to many dispute processes, particularly mediation.[51] Although, over time, there have been changes in the level of relative emphasis on these philosophies, they remain an essential core for collaborative dispute management processes. These philosophies are:

1. Confidentiality – This is required to encourage an environment safe for parties to make full and frank disclosure. Matters disclosed in a private dispute process should not be available to non-participants or in subsequent processes. Both parties and the third-party dispute practitioner are subject to confidentiality. This is imposed through the agreement entered into when conducting the process and may also be required by legislation. The National Mediator Accreditation Standards (NMAS) sets out mediator confidentiality obligations[52]. Legislation provides for exceptions in circumstances where parties consent, or legal issues arise such as allegations of threat or commission of offences like fraud or threat of harm. Other reasons for confidentiality to be overridden are when the administration of the process or the legal system demands, such as claims for costs in a matter and where ethical research is conducted that nevertheless maintains individual anonymity.[53] Consideration of confidentiality never prevents the review of conduct by mediators. Courts may also apply exceptions to go behind the confidentiality veil in circumstances outlined in Chapter 6.
2. Voluntariness – This was an important innovation in the early movement to empower and move to a peace-building mindset for parties. Today, it remains important for the

48 See also International Academy of Collaborative Professionals, *Collaborative Practice* (Web Page) <http://www.collaborativepractice.com> Queensland Association of Collaborative Practitioners (Web Page) <https://qacp.org.au/>.

49 Ben Waters, 'The importance of Teaching Dispute Resolution in a Twenty-first-century Law School' (2016) 51(2) *Law Teacher* 227; Pauline Collins, 'Australian Legal Education at a Cross Roads' (2016) 58(1) *Australian Universities' Review* 30; Tania Sourdin, 'Not Teaching ADR in Law Schools? Implications for Law Students, Clients and the ADR Field' (2012) 23(3) *Australasian Dispute Resolution Journal* 148; Judy Gutman, Tom Fisher and Erika Martens, 'Teaching ADR to Australian Law Students: Implications for Legal Practice in Australia' (2008) 19(1) *Australasian Dispute Resolution Journal* 42.

50 See, eg, Alessandro De Cesaris, 'Philosophy and Mediation. A Manifesto' (2019) 10(1) *Ethics in Progress* 67; Emma Dorshimer, 'What Can Anthropologists Do? Applied Anthropology in a Conflict Ridden World' (2019) *Student Publications* 708.

51 Ruth Charlton, *Dispute Resolution Guidebook* (LBC Information Services, 2000) 14–15; see also Chapter 6.

52 *National Mediator Accreditation System* (NMAS) (2015) Part III, 9 <https://msb.org.au/themes/msb/assets/documents/national-mediator-accreditation-system-2015.pdf>

53 See *Evidence Act 1995* (Cth) s 131.

parties to come into the dispute management process in good faith with a genuine desire to cooperate rather than being compelled against their preference.

3. Empowerment – Refers to the parties' ability to maintain control over the management of their dispute. This empowers the parties to find their own options to manage their situation. They are assisted to see their issues as a joint problem to be solved together. Party empowerment can assist in parties maintaining and honouring their agreement.
4. Neutrality/impartiality – The dispute management practitioner facilitates the process and does not take sides or show bias towards one party. The dispute management practitioner controls the process, but the parties control the content of the process. This requires being conscious of not treating parties differently, ensuring they have equal time and opportunity to express themselves. Avoiding using judgmental or patronising language is also a part of being impartial. For instance, the other party may feel bias if the third party expresses 'what a great idea' by commenting on a suggested option. The concept of neutrality has fallen out of favour and instead it is the practitioner adopting an impartial attitude that is important.[54] This entails the practitioner avoiding a focus on their view of what an agreement should look like, and instead helping the parties find and explore their own options. This can be difficult for legally trained practitioners as they are generally employed to provide advice on the best legal remedy for the client.
5. A unique solution – Parties can arrive at unique solutions limited only by their own creativity. This allows interests to be satisfied, not just rights. The solutions are not limited by remedies in common law (such as damages) and equitable remedies (such as specific performance and restitution). So long as the agreement is not illegal the parties can decide how they will manage their dispute. One of the more creative ways reported was in a New Zealand tech company dispute over a mobile radio network in which they resolved a £70,000 disagreement by holding the best of three arm-wrestle contests. David Ware, the beaten TeamTalk chief executive, said 'Sure, losing hurts but not nearly as much as paying lawyers' bills.'[55]

As noted in the historical development section, the dispute management movement of the 1970s–80s sprang from a radical critique of the formal justice system. Community justice centres developed, proposing dispute processes such as mediation as an alternative and peaceful manner to consensually address disputes and empower the parties at the same time. However, overtime, the philosophical underpinnings have also faced revision and critique.

Critique

Many would agree that dispute management processes have a lot to offer in the 'right' circumstances. However, being careful to fit the right process to individual disputes is always important, and one process can never be expected to be the panacea to manage all types of disputes. This textbook provides information on the range of available processes so dispute practitioners can assess what may work to help parties in their many varied disputes. Some

54 See, eg, Susan Douglas, 'Constructions of Impartiality in Mediation' (2017) 26(4) *Journal of Judicial Administration* 232.

55 Roger A McCain, *Game Theory: A Nontechnical Introduction to the Analysis of Strategy* (World Scientific, 2010) 266.

dispute management processes just may not be suitable where there are significant power differences between parties; for instance, in domestic violence cases.[56] Further, more empirical data is needed to support some of the philosophical features claimed by the dispute management movement before a full picture of the processes is enabled.

One of the major advantages of the many dispute processes is the flexibility they offer. This makes processes adaptable to the needs of the individual dispute and disputants. A concern commonly voiced, however, is that this flexibility may diminish with the growing institutionalisation of dispute processes and the standardisation of training programs for its practitioners. This has led some commentators to draw an analogy with the apparent ossification of equity which originally developed to overcome deficiencies in the common law.[57]

Party empowerment and their ability to determine their own management solutions remains a key philosophy. However, it is contested by the uptake in hybridised dispute processes, such as med-arb and arb-med, as well as using models of mediation that follow a more advisory process. Boulle and Field acknowledge the challenge, stating:

> In addition to mediators' overt and covert influences, any power disparities between parties and pressures on them to settle (such as the length of sessions, physical and emotional discomfort, attitudes of advisers, negotiation tactics and tricks and deadlines) may all reduce, rather than maximise, the parties' control within the process and over the outcome. The line between consensual and imposed outcomes is therefore sometimes blurred.[58]

The solution may be reduced to noting the ability of parties to act on the basis of their consent, being informed about the process and model being followed, and being able to choose to withdraw or continue in the process. This, however, diminishes a fundamental philosophy of party empowerment to ensuring thoroughly informed consent and genuine ability to walk away.

When this is tied with another area of contention in relation to the key philosophies, such as the questioning of the blanket applicability of principles like 'voluntariness' and 'neutrality', the importance of upholding these philosophies becomes apparent. Regarding the latter, the question arises how neutrality is implemented by dispute practitioners in reality.[59] For some, it has been taken to mean adopting a 'client-centred practice' in which the parties take ownership of the issue and the dispute practitioner assists in ensuring party self-determination.[60] The

56 Deborah Kirkwood and Mandy McKenzie, 'Family Dispute Resolution and Family Violence in the New Family Law System' (2008) 19 *Australasian Dispute Resolution Journal* 170.

57 See, eg, Main (n 20) 344.

58 Laurence Boulle and Rachael Field, 'Re-appraising Mediation's Value of Self-determination' (2020) 30(2) *Australasian Dispute Resolution Journal* 96.

59 Hilary Astor, 'Rethinking Neutrality: A Theory to Inform Practice: Part I' (2000) 11(2) *Australasian Dispute Resolution Journal* 73; Hilary Astor, 'Rethinking Neutrality: A Theory to Inform Practice: Part II' (2000) 11(3) *Australasian Dispute Resolution Journal* 145; L Mulcahy, 'The Possibilities and Desirability of Mediator Neutrality – Towards an Ethic of Partiality' (2001) 10(4) *Social and Legal Studies* 505; Rein Sikveland and Elizabeth Stokoe, 'Dealing with Resistance in Initial Intake and Inquiry Calls to Mediation: The Power of "Willing' (2016) 33(3) *Conflict Resolution Quarterly* 235.

60 See, eg, Douglas (n 54); Susan Douglas, 'Constructions of Neutrality in Mediation' (2012) 23(2) *Australasian Dispute Resolution Journal* 80; Kathy Douglas and Rachel Field 'Looking for Answers to the Mediator Neutrality Dilemma in Therapeutic Jurisprudence', (2006) 13(2) *E Law-Murdoch University Electronic Journal of Law* 177.

preference for an impartial approach,[61] seen as more realistic than the demand that a practitioner be totally neutral, has itself attracted criticism. Crowe and Field argue the notion of impartiality takes the philosophy no further than the original demand for neutrality and does not provide a sound basis for practitioners to operate ethically. They propose instead the '... better approach is to cease to treat mediator neutrality or impartiality as a guiding value of mediation practice, instead emphasising the concept of party self-determination'.[62] Establishing a code of ethical practice standards (see the NMAS in Chapters 4 and 6) has assisted in reinforcing these philosophies in practice.

Another criticism is loss of precedent as more matters are decided outside the public justice system. We rely on cases to set acceptable standards in society against which we can benchmark our actions. This is an important role of case law. For instance, the famous snail in the bottle case of *Donoghue v Stevenson*[63] most likely would never have seen inside a public court today, but from it the whole law of negligence has developed. Those countering this critique suggest if novel disputes arise or areas of law need ambiguity resolved for the public good, they are still likely to make their way to a court determination.

The issues described for the philosophies considered central to dispute management may be understood by the absorption of the movement into the existing legal system. The tendency to embrace dispute management conducted in private, behind closed doors, rather than in a public forum such as the courts, has led to many paradoxes. Governments have embraced informal processes for managing disputes to address discontent with court costs and delays and in response to the demands for access to justice.[64] This use of more informal processes by government along with the embrace by courts and uptake by the legal profession has developed what has been described as institutionalisation, or a **juridification**, of the movement with a proliferation of tribunals and alternatives to the courts when it comes to managing disputes.[65] Juridification is a term encapsulating lawyers', and the courts', invasion of the informal domain of dispute management processes and the legislating to entrench its practice and to regulate and control its methods. For instance, court-appointed mediations and some other processes are claimed to have challenged some of the philosophical justifications that had previously supported using different dispute processes. However, whenever two separate systems come into contact, both will exert influences on the other, such that the formal justice system will invariably be changed by the many dispute management processes, but these processes will also be changed through the process of institutionalisation.[66]

Juridification: the legal formalisation of the otherwise private informal domain of dispute management, such as legislation to entrench its practice and to regulate and control its method.

61 Laurence Boulle, *Mediation: Principles, Process, Practice* (Butterworths, 1996) 19–21.

62 See also Chapter 6, 184; Jonathan Crowe and Rachael Field, 'The Empty Idea of Mediator Neutrality' (2019) 29(4) *Australasian Dispute Resolution Journal* 273, 280.

63 [1932] AC 562.

64 See Cumes (n 41); Tania Sourdin and Naomi Burstyner, 'Justice Delayed is Justice Denied' (2014) 4(1) *Victoria University Law and Justice Journal* 46.

65 Ibid; P Brooker 'The "Juridification" of Alternative Dispute Resolution' (1999) 28 (1) *Anglo-American Law Review*, 1.

66 Joachim Zekoll, Moritz Bälz and Iwo Amelung (eds), *Formalisation and Flexibilisation in Dispute Resolution* (Brill, 2014) 3; David Spencer and Tom Altobelli 'The State and Dispute Resolution' in *Dispute Resolution in Australia. Cases, Commentary and Materials* (Lawbook Co, 2005) 319; Gay R Clarke and

Coy and Hedeen describe the process as one of cooption that occurs when political institutions of governance and their practices are challenged by a social movement such as the dispute management movement.[67] The outcome of such challenges entail a

> ... mix of institutionalization, social control, co-optation, and policy changes ... appropriation and resulting redefinition of movement discourse; by centrist challengers gaining inclusion at the expense of more radical challengers and without actual policy changes; by political and legal institutions appropriating the form, but not the substance of challenger practices; and by state funding strictures effectively transforming the mandates of movement initiatives ... [to] become bureaucratized and technique centered, losing ... adaptive vitality.[68]

Coy and Hedeen proceed to address scholarship. This suggests the process of cooption entails regulation and ethical code requirements being imposed on the new professionalising dispute practitioners in a manner that curbs 'deeper, more thorough critiques about the justice of the legal system, ultimately reproducing legal norms and reinforcing the hegemony of the formalized legal system'.[69] One way of addressing this is greater education of the citizenry so genuinely informed consent is possible and the parties are aware of what should happen and when the process is going off track. The enculturation of dispute processes has a long way to go. Few movies or TV series in popular culture address the options – most still portray disputes as being addressed by lawyers in an adversarial manner.[70]

How have these considerations influenced the system of dispute management used in different societies? Where are legal systems heading as a result of this significant paradigm shift in dispute management and a shift in philosophy from competitive to collaborative management of disputes?

Using history and philosophy to understand dispute management

Socio-political context

This section provides a greater understanding of the culture that has developed around dispute management and the practitioners working in the industry. Much of the culture is driven by the underpinning philosophies. This is sometimes encapsulated by a sense of cooperation over a competitive or more adversarial approach to dispute management. Factors relevant to this were identified by Morten Deutsch in his dynamic model research in 1973, referred to as the 'Crude Law of Social Relations', in which he found 'the characteristic processes and effects elicited by a given type of social relationship (eg cooperative or competitive) tend also to elicit

Iyla T Davies, 'ADR – Argument For and Against Use of the Mediation Process' (2006) *Queensland University of Technology Law Journal* 81.

67 Patrick G Coy and Timothy Hedeen, 'A Stage Model of Social Movement Co-Optation: Community Mediation in the United States' (2005) 46(3) *The Sociological Quarterly* 405.

68 Ibid 407 (references omitted).

69 Ibid.

70 'Inauguration' *The Good Fight* (Paramount Plus, King Size Productions, Kristin Bernstein and Debra Lovatelli, 2017). *The Good Fight* is a series that is one of few to introduce dispute management processes other than litigation. See for full credits: https://www.imdb.com/title/tt6193162/fullcredits.

that type of social relationship'.[71] These findings were subsequently summarised in a list of aspects that underpinned his dynamic model:

- The type of situationally determined interdependence between individuals and the psychological orientation of each individual change the probability and intensity of cooperation-competition of this individual.
- Behaviours are reciprocal: cooperative behaviours elicit cooperative behaviours from the other, and competitive behaviours elicit competitive behaviours.
- Behaviours of individuals lead to changes in psychological orientations in a manner that makes them more congruent with behaviours.
- Psychological orientations facilitate behaviours that are compatible with them.[72]

Individual orientation was something the movement in the early 1970s sought to change in order to produce greater peacebuilding. It followed the principles of democracy and non-hierarchical structures that honoured individuals' voices. A German critical theorist, Jürgen Habermas, tempered by the experience of World War II, became an influential philosopher dedicated to the ideals of democracy, the public space and in 1981 produced his influential work, *The Theory of Communicative Action*.[73] This work introduced the '**lifeworld**' notion of communicative interaction in preference to a constrained '**system world**' of strategic communication.[74] By lifeworld, Habermas refers to culture, society, and personality interacting through rational communicative action to refresh cultural knowledge, create solidarity and social identity in creating an accepted knowledge. System world is the space that enables intervention and control through mechanisms such as the media, money, and power, or, in other words, political bureaucracies and financial and market control of the means of production. The difference between the two encapsulates the different paradigms of the cooperative approach to dispute management based on negotiated consensus versus a competitive approach. Communicative action enables an equal participation in a just and fair deliberative process that preferences cooperation over coercive force used in a strategic approach driven by individual self-interests of power or financial concerns.[75] Language is an essential component of the

Lifeworld: culture, society and personality interacting through rational communicative action to refresh cultural knowledge, create solidarity and social identity in creating an accepted knowledge.

System world: the intervention and control of the lifeworld through mechanisms such as the media, money and power: in other words, political bureaucracies and financial and market control of the means of production.

71 Morton Deutsch, *The Resolution of Conflict: Constructive and Destructive Processes* (Yale University Press, 1973) 365.

72 Andrzej Nowak et al, 'From Crude Law to Civil Relations: The Dynamics and Potential Resolution of Intractable Conflict' (2010) 16(2) *Peace and Conflict* 189, 193.

73 Jürgen Habermas, *The Theory of Communicative Action: Reason and Rationalization of Society,* tr Thomas McCarthy (Polity Press, 3rd ed, 1981) vol 1.

74 See Jürgen Habermas, *The Theory of Communicative Action: System and Lifeworld: A Critique of Functionalist Reason* (Beacon Press, 1987) vol 2 183, 345.

75 Stephanie A Bryson, 'Can the Lifeworld Save Us from Neoliberal Governmentality: Social Work, Critical Theory, and Habermas' (2019) 46(3) *Journal of Sociology & Social Welfare* 63, 65:'Habermas seeks to salvage the Enlightenment project-human emancipation through reason, law, and justice – by wresting reason from the lair of the technical and bureaucratic and uniting it with language and the realm of sensual, interpretive, lived experience.'

communicative process as the significance of choosing a mediational tone in which words matter when managing disputes can never be underestimated. This support for a democratic equality has been placed under pressure by the neoliberal approach that has more recently come to dominate and is driven by individualist market forces and requirements of economic efficiency as the system world colonises the lifeworld.[76]

Neoliberal: arose as 'new liberalism' from Adam Smith's *The Wealth of Nations* in 1776, which advocated a free market for capitalism's growth. Neoliberalism advocates the market being free from government interference, increased privatisation and less state-owned service provision, replacing concepts of public good with ideas of mutual obligation.

The **neoliberal** approach since the early 1980s has been a period of privatisation and night-watchman states, in which small government as exemplified by the Thatcher and Regan era saw reduction in public civil service and state services.[77] Private providers have taken over prior roles provided by government – hence the expression 'small government'. The privatisation of justice is one example in a marketised economy. The market is seen as able to take care of itself if protected from the regulatory interference of the state. The financial events in Australia in 1991, 1999–2000, 2008 and 2011,[78] and the global pandemic beginning in 2020, have each contributed to diminishing these claims. Polanyi[79] is a vocal critic of the neoliberal evolution out of the laissez-faire liberal society, which created a world dictated to by market economic imperatives, producing an absence of authentic social relations replaced by objective accounting, now supported by artificial intelligence and big data in a techno systemised language. Notwithstanding the many commentators saying the neoliberal project or free market forces has ended as a failure, its lashing tail lives on and contributes to the disputing world, particularly for those feeling disenfranchised by the free market operation.

What this means for dispute management is that the simple objective language of politics, market, and finance (that tends to be supported by a legal system that gives undue regard to bottom lines, monetary outcomes and zero-sum bargaining) provide a dissatisfaction for parties who operate from a lifeworld perspective that engages with ethical and moral concerns. Humans can have diverse motives, needs and interests that do not fit a simple accounting language of numbers.[80] Mohr writes:

> Habermas's original 'theory of communicative action' political and legal deliberation rely upon certain ethical principles. All the parties should be heard and they should ensure that their communications are understood and are not internally contradictory. They should forego the use of force, and cooperate, with sincerity, in the search for truth.[81]

76 Jürgen Habermas, *The Post-National Constellation* (Polity, 2001); Gareth Dale, 'Double Movements and Pendular Forces: Polanyian Perspectives on the Neoliberal Age' (2012) 60(1) *Current Sociology* 3.

77 See also Susan Braedley and Meg Luxton, *Neoliberalism and Everyday Life* (McGill-Queen's University Press, 2010); Manfred B Steger and Ravi K Roy, *Neoliberalism: A Very Short Introduction* (Oxford University Press, 2010).

78 Greg O'Brien, '27 Years and Counting Since Australia's Last Recession' *Parliamentary Library Briefing Book* <https://www.aph.gov.au/About_Parliament/Parliamentary_Departments/Parliamentary_Library/pubs/BriefingBook46p/LastRecession>.

79 See Dale (n 76) 20.

80 See, eg, Dean G Pruitt, 'Tom Schelling's Contributions to Conflict Theory and Research' (2018) 34(3) *Negotiation Journal* 283; Bruce Patton, 'Managing the Value and Danger of Dualities' (2015) 31(4) *Negotiation Journal* 349.

81 Richard D Mohr, 'Some Conditions for Culturally Diverse Deliberation' (2005) 20(1) *Canadian Journal of Law and Society* 87, 89.

Criticism of Habermas extends to his reliance on humans behaving rationally and the seeking after objective truth. Certainly, a dispute practitioner must consider the suitability of parties to the process and this includes at least some form of assessment of the parties' levels of understanding and capacity for rational thinking. Dispute practitioners are more attuned to conflict and dispute theory that takes account of the developments in neuroscience and an understanding that cognitive rational behaviour in disputes requires first a consideration of the primitive brain's emotive response. This irrationality in decision-making is now well known.[82]

Notwithstanding the critics of Habermas, coming from the edges of the political boundaries the idea of a lifeworld and system world provides a vision by which to further explore the dynamic of dispute management and the nature of the politico-legal system within which they operate.

International disputes

When it comes to international conflict and disputes, the parties are states and the International Court of Justice remains a consent-based court for state parties to conduct a third-party triadic determinative dispute management.[83] After World War II, the *Charter of the United Nations* established a new regime for managing disputes and any state use of force. The system was meant to bring an era of peaceful resolution. Sadly, this has not happened, with inter-state conflicts continuing at significant levels.[84] The post-WWII power states' monopoly of the Security Council remains a permanent challenge, due to its non-democratic nature.[85] Intra-conflict and non-state party involvement in such conflicts remains taxing. The idea of **State Responsibility to Protect** (R2P)[86] has arisen as one possible way forward. However, bringing civil conflict and non-armed actors to a dispute management process is complex and a separate field of study outside the coverage of this textbook. Notwithstanding, once parties seek management of their differences, many of the processes outlined in this textbook are applicable to

State Responsibility to Protect: a global political movement to prevent conflict leading to genocide, war crimes, ethnic cleansing and crimes against humanity.

82 See, eg, Dan Ariely, *Predictably Irrational: The Hidden Forces that Shape Our Decisions* (Harper Perennial, rev ed, 2010); Carolina Feher da Silva, Marcus Vinícius and Chrysóstomo Baldo, 'A Simple Artificial Life Model Explains Irrational Behavior in Human Decision-Making' (2012) 7(5) *PloS one,* e34371; Laurence Boulle and Rachael Field, *Mediation in Australia* (LexisNexis Butterworths, 2018) 191; Emma-May Litchfield, 'It's Time We Started Talking about Neurodiversity in Dispute Resolution' *Australian Dispute Resolution Network Blog* (Blog post, 24 August 2020) <https://adrresearch.net/2020/08/24/its-time-we-started-talking-about-neurodiversity-in-dispute-resolution/>.

83 Dermot Groome, 'Adjudicating Genocide: Is the International Court of Justice Capable of Judging State Criminal Responsibility?' (2007) 31(4) *Fordham International Law Journal* 91; David Coady, Brendan Gogarty and Jeffrey McGee, 'Scientific Whaling and How Philosophy of Science Can Help Break the International Deadlock' (2018) 72(1) *Australian Journal of International Affairs* 49.

84 See also Christine Chinkin and Mary Kaldor, *International Law and New Wars* (Cambridge University Press, 2017).

85 See, eg, Madeleine O Hosli and Thomas Dörfler, 'Why is Change So Slow? Assessing Prospects for United Nations Security Council Reform' (2019) 22(1) *Journal of Economic Policy Reform* 35; Paul Kennedy, *The Parliament of Man: The Past, Present, and Future of the United Nations* (Vintage Books, 2006).

86 See also Peter Hilpold and Alex J Bellamy (eds), *Responsibility to Protect (R2P): A New Paradigm of International Law?* (Brill, 2015).

managing these larger and more complex disputes. For instance, empowering minorities, giving voice, and adopting a non-biased position as a third-party intervener are all important aspects of the underpinning philosophy of dispute management.

Other mechanisms at the international level with some 'teeth' are the World Trade Organization (WTO) and the International Criminal Court (ICC). The ICC addresses international crime and follows a litigation process, although its workings are made difficult due to reliance on state cooperation.[87] The WTO regulates world trade and deals with state disputes in trade, administering the *General Agreement on Tariffs and Trade 1994* through a judicial forum. The success of the WTO is threatened by states finding ways to bypass it, such as making bilateral agreements.[88]

The interventions of third parties seeking to settle international disputes have had varied success and many studies aim to learn from hindsight what processes may work best. Certainly, negotiation and facilitation are processes relevant to dealing with international disputes.[89]

Using history and philosophy to assist in dispute management

This section addresses areas for closer consideration when determining which process may be appropriate for a dispute by providing a contextual understanding for the current fragmentation, hybridisation, and privatisation of dispute management in a constantly reforming environment. Factors such as fairness, the changing models for processes such as mediation and the role and influence of lawyers, parties and third-party practitioners in dispute management processes are addressed.[90]

Fairness

A central theme of the movement in offering different dispute processes is fairness.[91] Underpinning this concept is the issue of access to justice. Financial resources needed to take

87 See, eg, Emma Irving, *Multi-actor Human Rights Protection at the International Criminal Court* (Cambridge University Press, 2020).

88 See also Ernst-Ulrich Petersmann, 'Between Member-Driven WTO Governance and Constitutional Justice: Judicial Dilemmas in GATT/WTO Dispute Settlement Section 2: WTO & International Trade' (2018) 21(1) *Journal of International Economic Law* 103; James Harrison and Ernst-Ulrich Petersmann, *Reforming the World Trading System: Legitimacy, Efficiency, and Democratic Governance* (Oxford University Press, 2005); Pauwelyn Joost, 'The WTO 20 Years On: 'Global Governance by Judiciary' or, Rather, Member-driven Settlement of (Some) Trade Disputes between (Some) WTO Members?' (2016) 27(4) *European Journal of International Law* 1119.

89 See, eg, Shaina D Western, 'Bargaining Power at the Negotiation Table and Beyond' (2020) 25(2) *International Negotiation* 169; Dylan Balch-Lindsay, Andrew J Enterline and Kyle A Joyce, 'Third-Party Intervention and the Civil War Process' (2008,) 45(3) *Journal of Peace Research* 345; Joakim Kreutz, 'How and When Armed Conflicts End: Introducing the UCDP Conflict Termination dataset' (2010) 47(2) *Journal of Peace Research* 243.

90 Ruth Charlton, 'A Personal ADR Retrospective – LEADR and other thing' (2013) 24 *Australasian Dispute Resolution Journal* 160; John Lande and Peter W Benner, 'How Businesses Use Planned Early Dispute Resolution' (2016) 34(4) *Alternatives to the High Cost of Litigation* 49.

91 John Zeleznikow and Emilia Bellucc, 'Legal Fairness in ADR Processes – Implications for Research and Teaching' (2012) 23 *Australasian Dispute Resolution Journal* 265.

on a dispute, particularly through the formal litigious process, are substantial. However, some disputants have the dispute come to them unbidden and have little choice. This particularly is the case with neighbourhood, tenancy, workplace, and family disputes. In many such cases, the parties feel compelled to self-represent due to the cost of a legal representative. In some situations, parties will take it as far as possible through complaint bodies that do not charge a fee, such as the Office of Fair Trading, and if they cannot get an outcome many just walk away. Some, in areas such as neighbourhood or fence disputes, will go to a lawyer and pay legal fees over some period of time for lawyer–lawyer negotiations, often to find they can have a mediated outcome in the Civil and Administrative Tribunal at little cost and in a relatively quick timeframe.[92]

However, there has been disagreement about fairness if the power imbalance of parties cannot be redressed through the process by the dispute management practitioner. In cases of physical or psychological violence, commentators have argued litigation may be preferred, or at the very least some processes may not be the most appropriate to provide a safe and fair protection of such parties.[93] However, there are those that claim this is the type of case in which a dispute process can improve communication and relationships; for instance, by turning power-over into power-with.[94] Assumptions about power imbalance must be avoided as each party interaction should be uniquely considered. Amendments to the *Family Law Act 1975* (Cth) have attempted to address the issues,[95] with funding going towards raising awareness in violence prevention and coordination between legal and health professionals.[96]

Changing processes

This leads to another area that requires consideration: namely, the changing processes for models as they develop over time. Mediation is just one process that has a number of different models (facilitative, settlement, evaluative, advisory, narrative and therapeutic). While all of these models are under the broad umbrella of mediation, the key philosophies of dispute process application operate at different levels in each model. For instance, an advisory or evaluative process, such as in the SEAM process described previously, may narrow the key philosophies of parties' empowerment and reduce the impartiality. Over time, the facilitative model, which aimed to honour the key philosophies and was supported by the NMAS in

92 See, eg, *Neighbourhood Disputes (Dividing Fences and Trees) Act 2001* (Qld).

93 Richard Delgado, 'The Unbearable Lightness of Alternative Dispute Resolution: Critical Thoughts on Fairness and Formality' (2017) 70(3) *SMU Law Review* 611; Rachael Field and Jonathan Crowe, 'The Construction of Rationality in Australian Family Dispute Resolution: A Feminist Analysis' (2007) 27(1) *Australian Feminist Law Journal* 97.

94 See, eg, Siobhan Byrne, 'Feminist Reflections on Discourses of (power) + (sharing) in Power-sharing Theory' (2019) 41(1) *International Political Science Review* 58; Rose Mirzaie, 'Divorce Mediation for Women: An Examination of Feminist Critiques' (2016) 71(3) *Dispute Resolution Journal* 161; Jordi Agusti-Panareda, 'Power Imbalances in Mediation: Questioning Some Common Assumptions' (2004) 59 (2) *Dispute Resolution Journal* 24.

95 See *Family Law Legislation Amendment (Family Violence and Other Measures) Act 2011* (Cth).

96 Vicki Waye, 'Mandatory Mediation in Australia's Civil Justice System' (2016) 45(2–3) *Common Law World Review* 214, 224. See Rachael Field and A Lynch, 'Hearing Parties' Voices in Coordinated Family Dispute Resolution (CFDR): An Australian Pilot of a Family Mediation Model Designed for Matters Involving a History of Domestic Violence' (2014) 36(4) *Journal of Social Welfare and Family Law* 392 – unfortunately funding for this successful pilot was not continued.

2008 has been diminished, with the NMAS in 2015 acknowledging the use of evaluative mediation models, or a hybridised combination of models in one mediation.[97] Dispute practitioner styles vary and practitioners should give clear advice to potential parties on the nature of the different models and how they operate in advance so parties can exercise an informed consumer choice.[98] Educating the public on these differences is essential to enable informed choices to be made. There are benefits in adopting the appropriate model or mix of models, but it is important for the practitioner and the parties to be aware of the differences and when and why the different models may be used. In a dispute involving a complex mix of facts and law, an advisory mediation may be exactly what the parties want. Lande has called for a respect between mediators when following different models.[99] He has noted the contentions over models often divides practitioners based on the background professional training of the dispute practitioner:

> At least some of the discord over facilitative and evaluative techniques is based on whether the mediators are lawyers or not, with lawyers tending toward a more evaluative approach and nonlawyers tending toward a more facilitative approach. This tension is related to conflict over control of the field between lawyers and nonlawyers.[100]

Mediation mandated by courts, referring parties to mediation, or legislative requirements for attempts to manage a dispute prior to litigation also create grounds for considering how the key philosophies are supported.[101] The voluntary nature of adopting a dispute process is less clear in mandated processes, although it has become possible to argue parties being given informed consent in the process and the right to end or agree an outcome is sufficient.[102] Others have suggested a reluctant party brought into the process can find it is useful and produces better outcomes than they had anticipated.[103] Hebdeen describes it as '... [a]ll mediations are voluntary but some are more voluntary than others'.[104]

The risk for processes conducted in a mandatory way, and that follow a settlement or evaluative model, is they may be seen as private litigation in disguise if the parties maintain an adversarial stance with a legalistic focus. This has been identified as a problem:

97 *National Mediator Accreditation System* (NMAS) (2015) Mediator Standards Board, <http://www.msb.org.au/mediator-standards>.

98 Lorig Charkoudian et al, 'Mediation by Any Other Name Would Smell as Sweet – or Would It? The Struggle to Define Mediation and Its Various Approaches' (2009) 26(3) *Conflict Resolution Quarterly* 293; Grant Morris, 'Eclecticism versus Purity: Mediation Styles Used in New Zealand Employment Disputes' (2015) 33(2) *Conflict Resolution Quarterly* 203.

99 John Lande, 'Stop Bickering! A Call for Collaboration' (1998) 16(1) *CPR Institute for Dispute Resolution* 12: 'I suggest that it would be much more helpful for adherents of differing mediation philosophies in local mediation communities to respectfully work together to concretely classify their differences as an aid to mediation consumers'.

100 John Lande, 'Toward More Sophisticated Mediation Theory' (2000) (2) *Journal of Dispute Resolution* 321, 321–2.

101 See, eg, Timothy Hedeen, 'Coercion and Self-determination in Court-Connected Mediation: All Mediations Are Voluntary, But Some Are More Voluntary than Others' (2005) 26(3) *Justice System Journal: Making Dispute Resolution Work* 273.

102 See Boulle and Field (n 82).

103 K Mahoney, 'Mandatory Mediation: A Positive Development in Most Cases' (2014) 25(2) *Australasian Dispute Resolution Journal* 120.

104 Hedeen (n 101).

> ... as we continue to burden mediation with all the things that are either good or ill in litigation, I think we're going to start to undermine its value ... we ought to use some restraints so we don't wreck this tool also.[105]

Roles for dispute process participants

Parties, participants and dispute practitioners all benefit if they have a clear understanding of their role in any dispute process.[106] Baron, Corbin and Gutman have acknowledged the possibility that the formal legal system provided by litigation in the courts and the many dispute processes are having an effect on each other:

> ... [W]e take up the Hon Michael Kirby's point that for ADR to assume all the functions of the court would be to 'throw the baby out with the bathwater'; but it would also be counterproductive for ADR to too closely assume judicial procedures. We agree that the relationship between the two processes needs to be 'correct and evolving' and the success of both hinges largely on the integrity and expertise of the personnel involved and their understanding of conduct appropriate to each process ... the borders between adversarial and ADR processes may blur; and the ways in which a lack of understanding of appropriate conduct by participants who are representing parties in mediation may detrimentally impact both processes.[107]

The importance of the participants having knowledge of what their role is and how the process works cannot be over emphasised. For lawyers, the role varies between third-party dispute management practitioners, or negotiator, mediator, collaborative practitioner, or being a partisan representative of a party. When operating as a partisan advisor, the lawyer assists both the client and mediator. This is done by advising the client in advance of the various processes available but, in particular, the details of the process model in which they will be participating. This obligation is now backed by legislative and code obligations.[108] When assisting the dispute practitioner, the **partisan lawyer** generally is helpful in seeking a good outcome based on their client's interests and in the spirit of making a genuine effort to empower the parties to manage their own dispute. Lawyers with agendas other than this includes those seeing the process as a 'fishing expedition' to identify parties' weaknesses and test evidence prior to taking a matter to litigation. This disrupts the process for the dispute practitioner and tends not to be acting in the client's long-term best interests. Other aspects that a partisan lawyer can assist with is encouraging their client to speak for themselves or if speaking on behalf of the client ensuring they tell the client's story and don't engage in long legalistic submissions. They can assist their client with reality testing any options that are generated for managing a dispute, offer legal advice on rights issues, and any costs or likely issues if management is not reached

Partisan lawyer: a lawyer who represents one party – their client.

105 CPR (2000) (n 21) 69.

106 See, eg, Chapter 6.

107 Paula Baron, Lillian Corbin and Judy Gutman, 'Throwing Babies Out with the Bathwater? Adversarialism, ADR and the Way Forward' (2014) 40(2) *Monash University Law Review* 283, 283.

108 See, eg, Law Council of Australia, *Guidelines for Lawyers in Mediations* (2019); *Australian Solicitors Conduct Rules 2015*; *Barristers' Conduct Rules 2018*; *Legal Services Directions 2017* (Cth); see also *Collins v Queensland* (2020) 61 Fam LR 160.

and another process is instigated. This assists their client in making fully informed decisions. The partisan lawyer can also advise and assist in the final agreement stage, such as drafting the terms of the parties' negotiated outcome.

For parties, the ideal is to act to support the philosophy of party empowerment. This requires parties having voice and telling their story. Nothing is more powerful than a direct communication between the parties, as it enables authentic emotional expression. More often, parties may feel nervous and, if paying for a legal representative, believe it is the lawyer's duty to speak for them. This may draw in the 'litigation in disguise' notion and diminish the philosophy of empowerment. Also, if parties are going to have to communicate in an ongoing manner, such as divorcing parents, it satisfies the philosophy of the movement's desire for a more peaceful society in assisting the parties by modelling and encouraging genuine communication.

For the dispute practitioner, particularly if they are legally trained, they must understand the changed environment and focus. To honour the philosophies of the dispute management movement, they need to alter their language to be less positional and combative. They must not attempt to take over the dispute, but remember parties' ownership and that any managed outcome belongs to the parties.[109] When conducting a triadic third-party dispute process, the dispute practitioner must ensure they are clear on the model they are adopting, fully inform the parties, and be true to the model. If offering advice in a non-facilitative model, they will need to ensure they have appropriate insurance coverage to protect against giving inaccurate advice.

Institutions also have a role in honouring the key philosophies underpinning the dispute management movement. These can be lost in a neoliberal world of accounting and cost efficiencies. This is particularly so where organisations keep statistics on the dispute practitioners' 'success rates' in achieving an agreed outcome or requiring closely managed time. Such neoliberal accountability defeats the philosophy of dispute processes and party empowerment. The dispute movement is as much about process as about outcomes. The philosophy is to help parties communicate by learning to listen, hear and address others, to take disputes from a focus on the person into a joint problem-solving narrative, and to reduce conflict in society. In time-pressured processes where the focus is shifted to outcomes, the opportunity for reinforcing more democratically peaceful societies is lost. The practitioner who is under threat of losing their position if their settlement rate is not above a certain level is being pressured and unreasonably assessed. Some parties just take longer to comprehend their best outcome or want to save face in the moment by not conceding but will subsequently approach the other side and agree an outcome before a matter is sent to another process. This factor never becomes part of the practitioner's statistics. Some legal firms now evaluate their lawyers not on lawsuits won or lost but rather when clients succeed in avoiding costly disputes or bad relationships and reputational damage because of the lawyer's approach.

Ethical considerations

The challenge for practitioners is adherence to the key philosophies when using dispute processes to sustain the movement as something other than 'litigation in disguise'. These

109 See, eg, Bryna Bogoch and Ruth Halperin Kaddari, 'Co-optation, competition and resistance: mediation and divorce professionals in Israel' (2007) 14(3) *International Journal of the Legal Profession* 115, for a discussion on the different disciplines approaches to being a dispute practitioner.

philosophies drive the ethical considerations for the dispute processes. Menkel-Meadow has explained:

> In considering what principles should inform ethical standards and rules, it is important to understand the underlying values that lay the foundation for ethical rules. With the adversary practice as the model current rules are based upon, values of zeal. . .client loyalty, partisanship, and non-accountability ... DR [dispute resolution] draws from different foundational principles – problem-solving, joint rather than individual gain, and future rather than past orientation, its underlying principles will be different. Trust, confidentiality, creativity and openness may suggest different ethical precepts and standards.[110]

Positives and negatives in the history and philosophy of dispute management

This section will deal with some of the positive and negative outcomes of the paradigm shift. We look at matters such as the critiques of the underpinning philosophies, development of precedent, neutrality, and party empowerment.

Positives

The dispute management environment presents an alternative to the rigid **positivist** formal legal system taught by law schools through appellate case law and statutory interpretation to produce adversarial lawyering. It has opened the processes to finding a way to manage disputes in flexible and tailored processes. Habermas confirms the positive, formal and legalistic operation of the law in normalising the system world within the lifeworld through its technical role that displaces moral considerations.[111] Within dispute management processes, parties are able to communicate more effectively their lifeworld, which includes morality and emotions in order to reach a mutual agreement on managing their differences that is personalised to their individual needs. This drive to democratisation and peacemaking has, however, been subjected to changing social and political developments as it negotiates its way. The privatisation and marketisation of the system world create a competitive factor that drives a developing rigidity and systemisation of the processes. Demands of the legal system and the Rule of Law also place a need for formalising of processes in order to substantiate claims of procedural justice as more providers now compete for the opportunity to work with parties in managing their dispute. In Habermas's terms, the reclaiming by dispute processes of the lifeworld is being gradually

Positivist: viewing law as deriving validity from formal legal enactment or logical rational thought applied in case law.

110 Carrie Menkel-Meadow, 'Ethics in Alternative Dispute Resolution: New Issues, No Answers from the Adversary Conception of Lawyers' Responsibilities' (1997) 38(2) *South Texas Law Review* 407, 430; Carrie Menkel-Meadow, 'The Evolving Complexity of Dispute Resolution Ethics' (2017) 30(3) *Georgetown Journal of Legal Ethics* 389.

111 See also Mathieu Deflem, 'Introduction: Law in Habermas's Theory of Communicative Action' in Mathieu Deflem (ed) *Habermas, Modernity and Law* (Sage, 2008).

absorbed into the system world. While this may sound less than positive, keeping a line of fidelity to the key philosophies described in this chapter will help anchor the dispute management world in the ethics and values that maintain the course in providing more suited processes that are quicker and cheaper, and help maintain relationships where that is the desire and need of the parties.

Negatives

The concerns raised by the changing dispute management environment often depend on where one sits. For instance, parties may see it as having many positives that these processes can maintain relationships and empower the parties by allowing for creative management options in a confidential and efficient manner. However, some in the legal profession, particularly those who were not trained in the new processes before entering the profession, can see it as a threat or invasion of the legal sector. Many have argued lawyers have taken up space without the requisite training or understanding and have brought a legalised and sometimes adversarial approach into the domain. When this happens, it runs the risk of undermining the philosophies and claims made on behalf of collaborative and cooperative processes for managing disputes. Instead, the introduction of a legalised and adversarial approach imperils the processes through an unfettered trammelling behind closed doors of the key philosophies, such that parties experiencing this will feel disillusioned and will not be advocating others adopt such processes.[112]

In the international sphere, the post-World War II institutions are changing and becoming challenged by entropy and technological advances, as world power dynamics are shifting. Zartman[113] describes a current 'system of world disorder' in which dispute practitioners will need the benefits of research underpinning their process. The processes adopted need strengthening through this research in order to understand complex and multi-party disputes.

Special considerations

This section addresses two considerations for the philosophical development of dispute management: technology and the Rule of Law. The chapter concludes with some brief considerations of where to for the future of dispute management.

Technology, online dispute management, and artificial intelligence

In the early stages of the dispute management movement, the courts sought to take an active role and the term 'multi-door courthouse' was used. As Sourdin states, this concept of the courts being a controlling centre managing the various dispute process has long passed:

112 See, eg, *National Australia Bank Ltd v Freeman* [2000] QSC 295; Laurence Boulle, 'The Dog that Did Not Bark: Mediation Style' (2001) 4(2) *ADR Bulletin* 22.

113 I William Zartman, 'Structuring in a Vacuum: Negotiating in the Current World Disorder' (2020) 25(1) *International Negotiation* 5; Annkatrin Tritschoks, 'Rethinking Justice in International Environmental Negotiations: Toward a More Comprehensive Framework' (2018) 23(3) *International Negotiation* 446.

> It is clear that the 'multi-door' approach that emerged in the 1970s was inextricably linked to the concept of the 'multi-door courthouse' and the approach was based on the assumption that the referral of disputes would take place with the court at the epicentre of the referral system. This approach, with the court as the epicentre of dispute resolution, is no longer appropriate in many jurisdictions particularly where the vast bulk of disputes are referred, resolved, and settled away from the court system and often before litigation has commenced. The more modern approach responds to the more evolved ADR system, the continuing rise in the use of ADR, a more sophisticated understanding of ADR options, and the availability of referral information on the internet and elsewhere. Rather than a 'multi-door courthouse' a 'multi option' justice system now operates.[114]

The change has not only led to multiple processes for addressing disputes, moving society inexorably closer to a collaborative problem-solving approach in addressing disputes, but it is seeing a further wave of change carried by advancing technology.[115] The growth of online dispute management (OD) is a current reality and further threatens not only the demand for high-cost legal professionals, but even judges.[116] Sourdin, who has written extensively on the subject, suggests three types of technologically driven changes:

> First, and at the most basic level, technology can assist to inform, support and advise people involved in the justice system ('supportive technology'). Second, technology can replace functions and activities that were previously carried out by humans ('replacement technologies'). Finally, at a third level, technology can change that way that judges work and provide for very different forms of justice ('disruptive technology') that can include replacing some human decision-making.[117]

The disruptive consequences of advancement in machine-based artificial intelligence (AI) is in its early stages in the 2020s. However, the COVID-19 pandemic of 2020 has hastened the uptake of technology-led solutions.[118] While basic forms such as phone conferences remain prevalent, now synchronous video platforms enable parties and dispute practitioners to be present audibly and visually while in different locations. In most situations, the process being used from negotiation through to litigation remains the same; however, it is conducted using technology. This may require some modification to accommodate the technology, but generally dispute practitioners adhere to the process being utilised.

Nevertheless, Sourdin, while acknowledging the varied functions of judges, posits that AI may have 'the potential to remove judges from an adjudicative function altogether'.[119] Fact

114 Tania Sourdin, 'The Role of the Courts in the New Justice System' (2015) 7 *Yearbook Arbitration and Mediation* 95.

115 Evan Selinger, *Confronting the Moral Dimensions of Technology Through Mediation Theory* (Springer, 2011) 287.

116 See also Tania Sourdin and C Liyanage, 'The Promise and Reality of Online Dispute Resolution in Australia' in MSA Wahab, E Katsh and D Rainey (eds), *Online Dispute Resolution: Theory and Practice: A Treatise on Technology and Dispute Resolution* (Eleven International Publishing, 2011).

117 Tania Sourdin, 'Justice in the Age of Technology: "The Rise of Machines is upon Us"' (2017) 139 *Precedent* 4, 4.

118 Tania Sourdin and J Zeleznikow, 'Courts, Mediation and COVID-19' (2020) 48(2) *Australian Business Law Review* 138.

119 Tania Sourdin, 'Judge v Robot? Artificial Intelligence and Judicial Decision-Making' (2018) 41(4) *University of New South Wales Law Journal* 1114, 1115; Tania Sourdin, B Li, and T Hinds, 'Humans and

finding is always subject to human error and courts rely heavily on investigation and uncovering the 'truth' based on facts.[120] It is a corner stone of the legal system and lawyering, which, in the common law system, adopted the adversarial dispute process as the best at refining an objective truth. Establishing this objective truth of the facts is tied to providing a fair and legitimate judgment by the decision-maker. Wendell describes this as:

> . . . legitimacy depends on truthfulness. This is the objective perspective that, I contend, is ethically obligatory for lawyers to adopt. The argument relies on the connection between lawyers as advocates and the process of reason-giving that is characteristic of legality as a distinctive mode of governance. Political ethics, including legal ethics, must begin with what Rawls calls the burdens of judgment: We must propose fair terms of cooperation with others while acknowledging reasonable pluralism, which is based on the diverse and incompatible sources of human value, as well as conflicting evidence and uncertainty about the facts bearing on the resolution of normative disagreement.[121]

Basing a justice system on the search for the truth is problematic as, in a postmodern society, much depends on whose truth and from whose perspective the 'truth' is perceived.[122] We have now moved to a post-truth society, which challenges the notion of truth and irrefutable facts.[123] The beauty of many dispute processes described in this textbook is that the philosophy of empowerment means seeking the incontrovertible one set of true facts is not the goal; rather, it is the parties coming to accept how each views their situation and reaching an accommodation of each. Perhaps this is a post-truth view of justice – placing the individual back at the centre of consideration. Certainly, in international conflict, the restorative justice approach taken in truth and reconciliation processes must reach an agreed accommodation of degrees of truth-telling. As Lingis and Komesaroff suggest,

> . . . truth must sometimes be traded off against other goods. Since truth can harm people as well as benefit them, sometimes it may be better that some facts about the past remain unknown. The most effective methods for obtaining the truth may violate the Rule of Law, personal privacy, or the right not to incriminate oneself. Such methods might be too costly in relation to other goals.[124]

Justice Machines: Emergent Legal Technologies and Justice Apps' (2020) *Precedent* 20; Tania Sourdin and R Cornes, 'Do Judges Need to be Human? The Implications of Technology for Responsive Judging' *The Responsive Judge* (2018) Spring 87.

120 W Bradley Wendel, 'Whose Truth: Objective and Subjective Perspectives on Truthfulness in Advocacy' (2016) 28(1) *Yale Journal of Law & the Humanities* 105.

121 Ibid 114.

122 Michael Kirby, 'Where Does Truth Lie – The Challenges and Imperatives of Fact-Finding in Trial, Appellate, Civil and Criminal Courts and International Commissions of Inquiry' (2018) 41(2) *University of New South Wales Law Journal* 293.

123 See, eg, Christopher Schaberg, *The Work of Literature in an Age of Post-Truth* (Bloomsbury Academic, 2018); Chris Guthrie, Jeffrey Rachlinski and Andrew J Wistrich, 'Blinking on the Bench: How Judges Decide Cases' (2007) 93(1) *Cornell Law Review* 1; see also Shai Danziger et al, 'Extraneous Factors in Judicial Decisions' (2011) 108(17) *Proceedings of the National Academy of Sciences* 6889; Andreas Glöckner, 'The Irrational Hungry Judge Effect Revisited: Simulations Reveal that the Magnitude of the Effect is Overestimated' (2016) 11(6) *Judgment and Decision Making* 601.

124 Alphonso Lingis and Paul Komesaroff, 'Truth in Reconciliation' (2011) 8(3) *Journal of Bioethical Inquiry* 239, 242; see also Philip M Bromberg, 'Truth, Human Relatedness, and the Analytic Process: An Interpersonal/Relational Perspective' (2009) 90(2) *International Journal of Psychoanalysis* 347.

Notwithstanding the complexity related to truth, AI will also affect areas of dispute management, such as negotiation, mediation, and arbitration, and those organisations acting as referral bodies. Self-help through internet sites can operate as guides, not only to dispute management options but may also provide an online AI management process for individual disputes. For instance, divorce is an area with high self-representation, and platforms guiding divorcing parties through their relationship breakdown using 'chatbots' or 'robo lawyers' present new ways of doing dispute management.[125]

Technology can be used for good and is contributing to a greater understanding of the human brain and how we create, respond to, and manage disputes through neuroscience. It is also helpful in research and testing theories and improving our understanding of how humans respond in disputes. Deutsch[126] provides a wonderful example of using computer simulation to test his early theory on Crude's Law of Social Relations. This research not only confirmed his earlier theory but provided extended insight. Technology is just a tool; however, in human hands it is also capable of being used to confound truth seeking. This has been particularly evident internationally in the disruption and interference in elections in foreign countries.[127] Therefore, the human mind and its ability to provide nuanced thinking about the human condition remains essential in how we use technology and AI, and the latter is yet to establish this level of sophistication.[128]

Dispute management processes make use of the benefits of technology in different ways and they are only briefly reviewed here due to the rapid development of the field. The concept of online dispute (OD) management includes a wide range of services from automated algorithms assessing small-value consumer complaints on online shopping sites, to online hearings and secure document management used in arbitration, to virtual courtrooms in litigation. Online and technology-assisted dispute management used to be a choice of convenience in party autonomy driven dispute management. Circumstances affecting face-to-face participation and engagement with courts or dispute management providers and professionals led to the adoption of these technologies as a mainstream solution for providing justice.[129]

In a time of fast technological development in every field, the remote handling of disputes and the use of automated or virtual dispute management have become a matter of useful practical reality, but also a source of concern. Regulation of any field is typically reactive not proactive, responding to the need for a legislative framework created by practice. This is particularly true regarding technology, which develops much faster than any legislation aiming to avoid abuse of and by that technology. The UNCITRAL has recognised the need for uniform

125 See, eg, Tania Sourdin and Bin Li, 'People are Using Artificial Intelligence to Help Sort Out Their Divorce. Would You?' *The Conversation* (22 July 2020); Bin Li, Tom Hinds and Tania Sourdin, 'Humans and Justice Machines: Emergent Legal Technologies and Justice Apps' (2020) 156 *Precedent* 20.

126 See Deutsch (n 71).

127 See, eg, Christer Jönsson, 'Revisiting the Problem of Credibility in the Age of Post-Truth' (2020) 25(1) *International Negotiation* 78.

128 See, eg, Terry Carney, 'Robo-debt Illegality: The Seven Veils of Failed Guarantees of the Rule of Law?' (2019) 44(1) *Alternative Law Journal* 4 regarding the problems in using a robo-debt collection process.

129 See also Michael Legg, 'The Future of Dispute Resolution: Online ADR and Online Courts' (2016) 27 *Australasian Dispute Resolution Journal* 227; Stefan RM Lancy, 'ADR and Technology' (2016) 27 *Australasian Dispute Resolution Journal* 168; Claire Holland and Donnalee Taylor, 'Was That Said with a Smile? Factors Influencing Effective Online Negotiations' (2016) 27 *Australasian Dispute Resolution Journal* 103.

regulation of technology-assisted dispute management, but due to the lack of political will for legal harmonisation, the resulting text takes the form of technical notes, instead of a model law or a convention.[130] The remaining gap is slowly filled by rules and soft law created by service providers and independent organisations facing market demand for safe online dispute management procedures and platforms.[131] At a time when courts across Australia are relying on online hearings held on privately owned platforms, the need for regulation is ever increasing to protect privacy and provide security and reliability.

Rule of Law

The Rule of Law is a concept essential to our legal system.[132] It has a number of aspects, including that the law is clear and promulgated in advance of its application so the public can know the law, that it is applied equally to all no matter their standing in society and that all have equal opportunity to access justice. The latter is an aspect that has received attention when considering the growing options to manage disputes. Then Chief Justice of the High Court, Robert French, when talking about the multi-door courthouse reminds of the importance of the courts as the prime dispute management forum. The courts' role goes beyond merely addressing disputes. It is the courts which exercise the judicial power provided for in our Constitution to settle controversies and in so doing make law through the case law in the common law system:

> The concept of court-annexed ADR is well established and worthy of development in a way that better integrates the various options and provides a principled basis for their connection to the judicial process. I must, however, express a reservation ... It is the courts and only the courts which carry out the adjudication function involving the exercise of judicial power. Their special position as the third branch of government is made explicit in the Commonwealth Constitution and is a matter of convention in the states. Importantly, the courts are not to be seen simply as one species of provider among a number of providers of ADR services.[133]

In this textbook, litigation is included as a process for addressing disputes. However, its special existence within our legal system as a mechanism addressing disputes is also acknowledged. The many other processes take place knowing that the ultimate ability to submit a dispute to the courts for settlement according to law remains at least to some degree. Although many matters now require parties to attempt a different process to manage the dispute or are diverted

130 See UNCITRAL, *Technical Notes on Online Dispute Resolution 2017* (Web Page) <https://www.uncitral.org/pdf/english/texts/odr/V1700382_English_Technical_Notes_on_ODR.pdf>

131 See, eg, International Bar Association, *Cyber Security Guidelines October 2018* (Web Page) <https://www.ibanet.org/LPRU/cybersecurity-guidelines.aspx>; International Chamber of Commerce Commission, *Report on Information Technology in International Arbitration 2017* (Web Page) <https://iccwbo.org/content/uploads/sites/3/2017/03/icc-information-technology-in-international-arbitration-icc-arbitration-adr-commission.pdf>.

132 See also Lisa Burton Crawford, *The Rule of Law and the Australian Constitution* (Federation Press, 2017); Brian Tamanaha, *On the Rule of Law: History, Politics, Theory* (Cambridge University Press, 2005); Joseph Raz, 'The Rule of Law and Its Virtue' (1977) 93 *Law Quarterly Review* 193.

133 Chief Justice Robert French, 'Perspectives on Court Annexed Alternative Dispute Resolution' (Speech, Law Council of Australia, Multi-Door Symposium, 27 July 2009).

to tribunals that generally prohibit representation by lawyers, they occur in the 'shadow of the law'. This phrase refers to the belief that the law as pronounced through the courts, be it interpretation and application of legislation or case law development, provides the backdrop against which all other processes for managing disputes occurs. The rights and likely outcomes, based on case law and precedent, provide a benchmark for parties if they do not address their dispute by a court determination. Mnookin and Kornhauser are often attributed with this idea of operating in the shadow of the law and, in their influential paper in 1979, they focused on the family law area.[134] The concept is now a challenged notion considered in need of a revision to acknowledge the new paradigm of broadening dispute management processes.[135] Certainly, the shadow will enlarge the closer the dispute is managed in connection to litigation, involving lawyers or under court ordered processes. Dispute management based on facts, including emotions, in neighbourhood matters or using private management, likely to be less dominated by the shadow of the law. However, where a dispute management process does not result in an agreement for management of the dispute, there is no prevention of pursuing formal legal rights and remedies.

The Rule of Law is also contested by some aspects of different dispute management processes. For instance, privatised methods such as mediation or arbitration avoid providing the opportunity for justice to be seen to be done in a public forum. Some challenge that they also contribute to the loss of guiding precedent[136] and a sense that all members of society are receiving an equality in their substantive outcomes, such as amounts of compensation or damages.[137] The trade-off is that disputes, when managed privately, can be quicker and cheaper, with any appropriate agreed outcomes unlimited by the available legal or equitable remedies, and the process can help stabilise or maintain relationships. Reputation is protected and can be an important consideration. The Rule of Law is argued by many to be supported through the additional management options, as it gives those otherwise unlikely to be able to afford and therefore access justice a viable process to manage their dispute.[138] Conversely, critics of this view argue it can reinforce a sense of disempowerment and structural differences as a form of justice for the poor.[139] When assessing substantive justice and procedural justice and the formalising of dispute processes and accreditation of dispute practitioners, the Rule of Law achieves at least a procedural uniformity that can be said to satisfy individuals' need for

134 Robert Mnookin and Lewis Kornhauser, 'Bargaining in the Shadow of the Law: The Case of Divorce' (1979) 88(5) *Yale Law Journal* 950.

135 See, eg, Jonathan Crowe et al, 'Bargaining in the Shadow of the Folk Law: Expanding the Concept of the Shadow of the Law in Family Dispute Resolution' (2018) 40(3) *Sydney Law Review* 319; Herbert Jacob, 'The Elusive Shadow of the Law' (1992) 26(3) *Law & Society Review* 565.

136 Julian Gruin, The Rule of Law, Adjudication and Hard Cases: The Effect of Alternative Dispute Resolution on the Doctrine of Precedent' (2008) 19(3) *Australasian Dispute Resolution Journal* 206; Deborah Hensler, 'The Private in Public, the Public in Private: The Blurring Boundary between Public and Private Dispute Resolution' in Zekoll, Moritz Bälz and Iwo Amelung (n 66) 45 challenges the public–private role of dispute practitioners, such as arbitrators, deciding bi-lateral investment treaty disputes when they don't have a public mandate to resolve matters of public law.

137 Mark J Rankin, 'Settlement at All Cost: The High Price of an Inexpensive Resolution?' (2009) 20(3) *Australasian Dispute Resolution Journal* 153.

138 See, eg, AKC Koo, 'The Role of the English Courts in Alternative Dispute Resolution' (2018) 38(4) *Legal Studies* 666.

139 See, eg, Delgado (n 93); Resnik (n 18); cf Carrie Menkel-Meadow, 'For and Against Settlement: Uses and Abuses of the Mandatory Settlement Conference' (1985) 33(2) *UCLA Law Review* 485.

guidance on behaviour through being subjected to the same procedures. Thus, a procedural justice is met and is sufficient. On procedural justice, Rankin suggests more research and evidence is required

> ... in acknowledging the interrelated nature of dispute resolution processes within our current legal system, it would be prudent to remember the procedural justice inclinations of most citizens. Accordingly, there is a need, within this developing system, to certify that all settlement processes are regularly evaluated by reference to certain standards of procedural justice. Given the issues already highlighted with respect to the problems encountered in adequately evaluating settlements, the extent to which this can be achieved is open to debate.[140]

Wendel has acknowledged that democratic theory and philosophy are concerns of scholars interested in dispute management and how citizens understand their rights and duties through a public acceptance established by a framework involving fair procedures.[141] Research indicates the strength of acceptance of dispute processes is dependent on the key philosophy of empowerment of parties by allowing their voice to be heard. If procedural aspects accommodate this, then justice is more likely to be accepted as having been satisfied.[142]

Conclusion

In turning to the next chapters (in which individual processes are described), it is useful to keep in mind a consideration of the future of dispute management in view of its history and core philosophies.

The terms used for the various processes seem to remain a perennial point of contention and can induce misunderstanding. As noted in this chapter, a term such as 'mediation' now encompasses many different models. The question arises: Is it time to use more specific terminology to ensure greater understanding and truly informed consent by parties? Assumptions abound that there is a common understanding in using the terminology and this remains contested.[143] Perhaps the future will come to address this problem. This textbook is an example that aims to provide clarity for all disputing parties.

Many processes seem to have become exclusive and restricted to specified fields. For instance, restorative justice principles have become almost exclusively the domain of criminal matters, although the principles can be apt for many other types of disputes. The collaborative process is almost exclusive to family disputes but could suit many areas of disputes. Will these processes evolve and grow?

The social and political environment is key to the dispute management and legal systems evolution. We introduced just some of the arguments considering the impact on democracy of a neoliberal era and how these ideological approaches affect how society responds in delivering

140 Rankin (n 137) 160.

141 Wendel (n 120) 107.

142 See also Carol Powell, 'Process Satisfaction in Mediation' (2013) *New Zealand Law Journal* 22; Tania Sourdin, *Alternative Dispute Resolution* (Thomson Reuters, 3rd ed, 2008) 18–24; Baron, Corbin and Gutman (n 107).

143 Lande (n 100) 331.

dispute management. It leads to consideration of whether the many processes in the dispute movement will become juridified and, like equity, provide a system subsumed but separate, running alongside but still part of the legal system. How will the two systems of formal and informal justice influence each other and what will be the long-term impact of technology?

Clearly, the field of dispute management is still expanding and finding its place. Room for more research exists to support and refine the claims made and provide an understanding of how society can achieve its desired outcomes in addressing inevitable disputes.[144] Assumptions need to be challenged or verified and the diversity of processes across jurisdictions has to be considered.[145]

This chapter has concluded with more questions than answers as the future requires educated predictions in an uncertain world. However, we can look to history to gain a helicopter perspective of how society can change, and systems of dispute management operate to provide justice over a longer period. It is essential to keep an eye to the bigger picture, even when buried in our day-to-day roles; as Milsom stated, '[n]obody can know that the solution will later be seen as the origin of something, or the problem as the effective end of something else'.[146]

EXERCISE IN APPLYING YOUR KNOWLEDGE – SUZI AND KAY

Suzi and Kay are keen creative artisans. Suzi makes glass jewellery and Kay is a potter. They do not have any business model, just an informal agreement to pool funds to set up a stall and regularly attend markets and sell their products. They have agreed to tend the stall on an alternate basis, but as Suzi does not drive Kay has agreed to drive them to each market and do both the set up and take down. They have also agreed verbally to put an equal amount of $1000 towards a common fund for purchase of a tent, trestle table, business cards and some art supplies for both to get started. They have agreed, as long-time friends, they will split their profits.

Suzi and Kay have attended regular fortnightly markets at three different locations on respective days of the week for some months. Unfortunately, Suzi's jewellery is proving more popular than Kay's pottery. Suzi is feeling she is being disadvantaged by the arrangement, as she is bringing in most of the money and the agreement to share the profits 50/50 is no longer to her advantage. Kay is also unhappy as she is doing all the driving using her car and petrol and feels that she is being left with a lion's share of setting up.

Kay has heard from a friend, in Suzi and Kay's circle of friends, that Suzi has been complaining about Kay and saying 'unkind' things about her.

Kay and Suzi's children go to the same school and are close friends, as are their husbands who play golf together most weekends.

Kay is very distressed about the developing tension between her and Suzi and its effect on their wider circle of friends and respective family members.

144 See, eg, Daniel Druckman, 'Looking Back and Looking Forward in Negotiation and Conflict Research' (2020) 25(1) *International Negotiation* 130.

145 Zekoll, Bälz and Amelung (n 66).

146 Milsom (n 3) 26.

Kay comes to you, a budding dispute practitioner, for advice. Apply the following three questions in giving Kay information about her options:

1. What dispute mechanisms are available to address this dispute?
2. Do these processes satisfy each of the philosophies discussed in this chapter and, if so, how? Explain your answer.
3. Give a brief outline of the history of the processes and institutions involved. Describe both competitive and cooperative processes and whether they are likely to produce a successful or unsuccessful dispute management of the dispute.

4

INTERVIEWING

Learning aims

- Describe the nature and purpose of an interview
- Develop a knowledge of the components of an interview
- Demonstrate knowledge of different types and styles of interviews
- Explain different models for interviews
- Describe, explain and demonstrate the skills and techniques required for interviewing
- Develop the ability to identify special factors that can influence an interview outcome

Understanding interviewing

This section will provide a short introduction to interviews by outlining:

1. The nature and purpose of interviewing
2. Describing types of interviews and their contribution to managing disputes
3. Identifying parties to interview in a dispute
4. Identifying components of an interview.

The nature and purpose of interviewing

Interview: a purposeful conversation to elicit certain information.

Interviewing is a process that can resolve or manage a dispute in its own right; for instance, Moore's Circle of Conflict refers to data conflicts.[1] An **interview** is a useful method to assist in managing such disputes by clarifying the data available. Interviews can be thought of as a conversation with purpose – the purpose usually being to elicit certain information. This could include assessing how accomplished the interviewee would be as a witness or it could be gaining specific facts or information. Interviewing is a key skill for all dispute practitioners and legal professionals. It requires special techniques in communication. How successful the practitioner is in achieving the purpose is dependent on their knowledge of the techniques and skills to be used and the most appropriate model to apply in the circumstances of the interview. Tillett and French describe interviewing as:

> Any form of intentional interpersonal communication in which one party (the interviewer) seeks information from the other (the interviewee).[2]

The purposes served by interviewing are generally related to disputes or uncertainties as well as in assisting clients or parties. It is a process that can be:

1 See Christopher W Moore, *The Mediation Process. Practical Strategies for Resolving Conflict* (Jossey-Bass, 3rd ed, 2003) 64–5, introduced in Chapter 1, 13, noting his later version of the Circle of Conflict also contained in Christopher W Moore, *The Mediation Process. Practical Strategies for Resolving Conflict* (John Wiley & Sons, 4th ed, 2014) 110.

2 Gregory Tillett and Brendan James French, *Resolving Conflict: A Practical Approach* (Oxford University Press, 3rd ed, 2006) 56.

- useful to clarify the issues
- part of the pre-negotiation stage and assist in determining:
  - the nature of the dispute, and
  - the best approach to take in managing the dispute
- conducted as an intake interview preparatory to conducting a dispute process
- undertaken when gaining information to assist an interviewee, such as lawyer–client interviews
- a formal investigative, or forensic interview, for laying charges, litigation or related uses
- a technique that will assist with shuttle negotiation, a form of dispute management in which the parties do not come face-to-face but communicate through a third party
- used to gain data in research.

The purpose of the interview will determine the style and approach that the interviewer will take. The purposeful conversation can occur in several different ways. For instance, for lawyers, it can range from a solicitor–client interview to cross-examination in an adversarial trial. In legal parlance, the latter is usually dealt with separately in legal texts and is not identified as a form of interview. However, it follows the nature of the interview technique in question-and-answer format although, like all interviews, it has a specialised structure based on the purpose.

The following summarises interviewing in the context of dispute management, particularly in mediation, but also in professional client/party interviews.

An interview will:

- be utilised when information beyond that available in writing is needed
- provide an interviewer with information concerning the interviewee, their issues, emotional state and other data
- assist the interviewer in understanding the nature of the dispute
- assist with clarification of the issues and the information that needs to be exchanged
- help build rapport, legitimacy and trust between the interviewer and the interviewee
- provide an opportunity for parties to ask questions and to clarify issues.

This chapter provides a grounding in the many types and purposes of interviews. There is often a best model fit for the specific requirements of the interview. Because there are a range of circumstances, from professional client interviews through to interviews within dispute management processes such as negotiation, mediation, facilitation, litigation and so on, this chapter provides a broad brush, but with sufficient detail pertinent to conducting any interview process and a number of different models to choose from. The next section addresses the types of interviewing used in relation to different purposes.

Types of interviews

While interviews can range from informal to formal, or focused verses non-focused, and structured verses unstructured, the same general components will be present in all interviews.

Unstructured interviews will be used when the information sought is more exploratory and a story-telling approach aims to invite obtaining the maximum amount of information.

Interviews conducted at a dispute analysis and diagnosing stage will generally be non-focused and non-structured and are designed to obtain the maximum information and insight into the nature of the dispute or the matter for which an interviewee is, for example, seeking legal assistance in the case of lawyer–client interviews.

At later stages in the management process, for further clarification, an interview can become focused to filter out superfluous matter and gain specific detail.

Focused and more structured interviews will be used in specialised interviews, such as police interviews of complainants and accused, or barristers asking questions in cross-examination or examination-in-chief. Interviewing a witness in a statement-proofing process before court requires assessing how well the interviewee is likely to cope with being questioned in a courtroom, but it must not result in contamination of the evidence by suggesting matters through the questioning process. Such interviews will focus closely on the purpose and outcome the interviewer is seeking. Structured interviews follow a predetermined set of questions aimed to elicit certain information.[3] They can also be used in some of the most rigidly formal structured interviews undertaken in academic research where comparable information is required.

Parties to interview

Another important factor to consider in dispute management is who should be interviewed and in what order. Key questions suggested by Moore[4] to assist in deciding the order for interviewing are:

1. Who are the most powerful or influential people in the dispute?
2. Who will be offended if he or she is not interviewed, or is not interviewed first?
3. Who should be interviewed earlier so that his or her cooperation can be used to induce others to participate in interviews?
4. Who is the person most likely to talk about the problem? Who is seeking help?

Usually, the party initiating the dispute management process will be the first to be interviewed as they are likely to be the most cooperative. When interviews are done prior to conducting a dispute process, such as mediation, the intake interviews can be done individually, or jointly, prior to the mediation. If the dispute is highly emotionally laden, or there is great power imbalance, care must be taken in the sequencing of the interviews if undertaken individually. Where it is a multi-party dispute, consider interviewing less involved parties first or invite the potential interviewees to suggest the order.

If interviewing parties together at the start of a process such as mediation, the dispute management practitioner should consider the benefits of parties informing each other of their issues, and the opportunity for the third-party practitioner to observe the party's interaction, particularly any non-verbal interaction. Such a process is also likely to increase confidence that

3 Ibid 58; see also Christopher W Moore, *The Mediation Process. Practical Strategies for Resolving Conflict* (John Wiley & Sons, 4th ed, 2014) 109.

4 Moore (n 3) 247–8.

parties are being treated equally. This is an important aspect that ensures potential power imbalance and concerns are addressed and the parties are treated fairly and equitably.

Components of an interview

Before the interview, the interviewer will have considered the process to be used in conducting the interview, the key information they are seeking, and how they will frame the questioning, as well as the best model to use to elicit this information. Interviews will be conducted where the information required cannot be obtained in a written or other form.

Consideration of the following factors before undertaking an interview should be addressed by the interviewer:

- the information required
- the interviewee's capacity
- the level of rapport sought
- the interviewee's needs.

Pre-interview

An interviewee must be contacted and provided with clear details of the purpose for the interview, how long it will take, and an agreed time and location. The manner of contact, such as a formal written letter, or command, or a more informal telephone request, can set the tone for the subsequent conversation. Will the interviewee feel discomfort and concern about the interview or is the aim to be collaborative and ensure the comfort of the interviewee? Even in police matters, having an interviewee feel as comfortable as possible will likely gain the best outcome in obtaining the information sought.[5]

The agenda or purpose for the meeting is explained at the time of the initial contact and then again when the interviewer and interviewee come together to conduct the interview. Any rights of parties – such as a right to refuse to answer questions, or seek advice, or to take a break – and confidentiality and related matters should be explained at the first opportunity and at the start of the interview.

The interview will start with informal socialising and rapport building by the third-party interviewer. Usually, the interviewer will introduce themselves, explain the reason for the interview and the process – even if this was explained during initial contact it should be repeated face-to-face. This gives the interviewee time to settle and build rapport with the interviewer before they begin the questioning process.

An interview should not be threatening when rapport building is required, nor should a cross-examination technique be used (and lawyers should guard against this in solicitor–client contact). A story-telling technique and open-ended questions are an essential part of the interview process to enable the interviewee to convey the maximum amount of information.[6]

An interviewer is likely to take notes during an interview. The reason for this must be explained to the interviewee, along with what will happen to the notes. In dispute

5 See also Georgina Heydon, 'Helping the Police with their Enquiries: Enhancing the Investigative Interview with Linguistic Research' (2012) 85(2) *Police Journal* 101.

6 See also Tillett and French (n 2) 62–7.

management processes such as negotiations or mediations, these notes are often destroyed at the end of the matter. However, if recordings or notes are to be kept for later purposes, this should be explained to the interviewee and they should be given assurance that the material will be stored in an appropriate and secure manner. Such security must be maintained over the life of the holding of such information.

Consideration must be given to non-verbal aspects of an interview. One of the significant non-verbal aspects is the location and physical setting for an interview. This includes the seating arrangements and other physical furnishings of the room. The goal is to ensure a sense of psychological and physical safety and comfort. For instance, if you are interviewing in a work injury matter relating to a fall from a height you would not place the interviewee near the windowed wall in your office on the 30th floor, even with the curtains drawn. This requires thinking about the person's circumstances and trying to eliminate the cause for discomfort. Other non-verbal aspects include your body language, voice tone, pitch and facial expressions. These convey a wealth of information and will affect the success of the interview. They are covered further later in this chapter.[7]

Roger Graef and Charles Stewart's 1982 documentary, *Police*,[8] included an episode titled 'A Complaint of Rape', which filmed a Thames Valley police interview of a complainant in a rape matter; it caused a major outcry and resulted in policy changes to police interview tactics. One of the factors drawing comment was the stark room, with cheap uncomfortable furnishings and bright glaring fluorescent lighting. The seating arrangements and posture of the detectives also drew comment. Both interviewers sat opposite the complainant – one with his ankle resting on his knee in a confrontationally aggressive manner – while the complainant, with a psychiatric history, was trying to tell her story of a rape by three strangers.

Another example was provided in the *Royal Commission into Institutional Responses to Child Sexual Abuse*,[9] in which observations were made regarding the use of barristers' chambers, with their imposing book-lined walls and grand furniture, when interviewing survivors of sexual abuse:

> Mr . . . QC and Mr . . . QC will reflect on whether their chambers are the most appropriate place to interview complainants. For many people the general environment of chambers may be threatening, if not overwhelming, and a barrister's room is unlikely to provide a sense of confidence and security for a survivor.[10]

A survivor described the experience:

> I will never forget Mr . . . chambers. It was a massive room – monstrous – it seemed to me to be the domain of an experienced legal professional. There were papers and books strewn everywhere. Mr . . . looked very comfortable but I was not.[11]

7 See also Chapter 2.

8 'Episode 3, A Complaint of Rape', Police (BBC1, 1982) <http://www.screenonline.org.uk/tv/id/464502/index.html.>

9 *Royal Commission into Institutional Responses to Child Sexual Abuse* (Web Page) <https://www.childabuseroyalcommission.gov.au/>.

10 Peter McClellan, Helen Milroy and Andrew Murray, *Royal Commission into Institutional Responses to Child Sexual Abuse* (Report of Case Study 16, August 2014) 8.

11 Ibid 39.

Being conscious of the degree of comfort conducive to achieving one's purpose in an interview means paying attention to such non-verbal attributes. Generally, the aim will be to gain useful information and an interviewee who is uncomfortable is unlikely to provide such information.

Opening phase

Again, making the setting comfortable is important. This may be the first face-to-face meeting between the parties, be it virtual or actual, and so it is important to create an appropriate degree of professional rapport. Humans will assess one another within 100 milliseconds on looks and manner, as well as communication.[12] So the window of opportunity to make a favourable impression, by either person, is miniscule. Being respectful and professional is an appropriate demeanour in most interviews.

The time should be pre-agreed, and it should be finite, but allow enough time for the interviewee to comfortably converse about the matter. Having an interviewee in a relaxed state at the start of an interview, knowing why they are there, and what they can expect takes them from a primitive brain state in which fear dominates to allow them to think in a clear cognitive brain state.[13] An interview should not be an interrogation or feel like torture.

The interview

The interview is the core reason for the purposeful conversation. The interviewer will take notes and generally commence the interview with some open or simple clarifying questions. Ideally, less interruption will enable the conveying of more information. This will depend on the model of interviewing being adopted. The next section outlines the various models further.

If the interviewee is responding well, then an interviewer will only interrupt to summarise what they have heard as a check for accuracy and any clarifying questions for points that require further information. Directive questioning[14] is useful if the narrative is running off-track or if guidance is needed to focus the interviewee on important aspects.

The latter part of the interview will generally entail more closed questions, checking details and the giving the option for the interviewee to provide any further information or ask questions. This is an important moment, as information not previously disclosed can often be disclosed at the very end of the process.

Close

The end of the interview should bring appropriate closure and not be abrupt. The interviewee has provided their time and information. Information as to any further interaction, or actions to be taken, should also be provided at this stage.

12 Janine Willis and Alexander Todorov, 'First Impressions: Making Up Your Mind after a 100-Ms Exposure to a Face' (2006) 17(7) *Psychological Science* 592.

13 See Chapter 1.

14 See Chapter 2.

Using theory and models to dissect interviewing

Theories

The following extends the discussion from Chapter 2 on communication. This enriches an understanding of communication as it addresses the purposeful conversation that occurs during interviews. Carl Rogers[15] provides ideals against which we can measure good communication, but unfortunately they are often not achieved. He refers to three aspects:

1. Genuineness or congruence – this means to be authentic. Politicians are often good studies to gauge how this can be discerned. One can note how their ability to appear genuine will often predict the public's reaction to them. Sometimes, they become too controlled by the public relations team and present as scripted and inauthentic, therefore reducing public acceptance.
2. Empathy – providing a degree of empathetic understanding shown by demonstrating an ability to feel what it may be like to be in the other's shoes. We can again think of many instances where politicians have received adverse reactions because they fail to demonstrate appropriate levels of care and come across as wooden or providing 'political' speak, rather than expressing human compassion.
3. Unconditional positive regard – simply means accepting the other person as they are and not prejudging them.

When considering interviews as a stylised component of communication, Danet's Communication Model of Dispute Processing, which has been drawn from Hymes as a sociolinguistic model, provides a useful summary of this chapter's discussion.[16] Hymes identifies eight facets in speech to which he has applied the acronym SPEAKING.[17] These summarise the considerations in interviewing. They are:

1. ***S***cene setting: the physical location of the communication. This includes the non-verbal cues derived from the furnishings and surrounds, the timing of communication, and cultural considerations
2. ***P***articipants: who is present. This includes any spectators, those who are communicating, and their roles in the communication (eg interviewer or interviewee)
3. ***E***nds: the goals of the participants and the outcome from the communication
4. ***A***ct Sequences: the speech as an event with form and content involving how something is said as much as the content of what is said

15 Carl Rogers, 'A Theory of Therapy, Personality and Interpersonal Relationships as Developed in the Client-centered Framework' in S Koch (ed), *Psychology: A Study of a Science* (McGraw Hill, 1959) vol 3; Carl R Rogers, *On Becoming a Person: A Psychotherapist's View of Psychotherapy* (Houghton Mifflin, 1961).

16 See Brenda Danet, 'Language in the Legal Process' (1980) 14(3) *Law & Society Review* 445, 493.

17 Dell Hymes 'Models of the Interaction of Language and Social Life' in John J Gumperz and Dell Hymes (eds), *Directions in Sociolinguistics: The Ethnography of Communication* (Holt, Rinehart and Winston, 1972).

5. ***K***ey: the tone of the communication
6. ***I***nstrumentalities: the medium for the communication and the style of language, including written and oral
7. ***N***orms: the rules of the communication and how speakers interpret these norms in both interaction and interpretation. Considerations of norms around when to speak, who can speak, and the order of speakers are relevant
8. ***G***enres: the form of communication, oral or written. These include interviews, negotiations, mediations, creative activity such as poems, and formal communications such as legal communication.[18]

Interviewing, whether it is taking instructions from interviewees, or proofing witnesses for a determinative litigation process, or more generally obtaining information to assist in dispute management, is a specialised form of communication. Interviewing techniques vary in accordance with the purpose for which the interview is being conducted. For instance, an interview to obtain data prior to mediation in an intake interview will be different to an interview conducted as part of an expert case appraisal.

The focus in a solicitor–client interview will be on obtaining relevant information and showing appropriate listening skills, support, and building rapport as well as clearly advising the client.[19] Evidence supports that clients, or parties, taking an active part in problem-solving and decision-making leads to a better outcome for the parties.[20] The accepted approach is known as a neutral client-centred style of interaction.[21] This means adopting a non-judgmental, neutral and empathetic approach.[22] Binder, Bergman and Price[23] adopt Carl Rogers's approach to empathy:

> Empathy . . . involves understanding the experiences, behaviours and feelings of others as they experience them. It means that [lawyers] must, to the best of their abilities, put aside their own biases, prejudices, and points of view in order to understand as clearly as possible the points of view of their clients.[24]

Sometimes, a dispute practitioner (or lawyer, counsellor and so on) will be required to deliver bad news. This should never be delivered bluntly, but should be delivered clearly and as early as practicable.[25] Forestalling and taking the long route to get to the point will not be appreciated. When information is complex or lengthy it is best to provide it in small chunks and to

18 Ibid 490.

19 See, eg, Ross Hyams, Susan Campbell and Adrian Evans, *Practical Legal Skills: Developing Your Clinical Technique* (Oxford University Press, 4th ed, 2014) 18–44 (listening and questioning), 45–62 (lawyer-client interviews).

20 Ibid 21; Gay Gellhorn, Lynne Robins and Pat Roth, 'Law and Language: An Interdisciplinary Study of Client Interviews' (1994) 1(2) *Clinical Law Review* 245.

21 Linda F Smith, 'Interviewing Clients: A Linguistic Comparison of the Traditional Interview and the Client-Centered Interview' (1995) 1(3) *Clinical Law Review* 541.

22 See also Chapter 2.

23 David Binder, Paul Bergman and Susan C Price, *Lawyers as Counsellors: A Client-centered Approach* (Westlaw Academic Publishing, 2012).

24 Ibid 40.

25 Majorie Corman Aaron, *Client Science: Advice for Lawyers on Counseling Clients through Bad News and Other Legal Realities* (Oxford City Press, 2012) 10.

pause to give time for the receiver to absorb. Professionals – for example, lawyers – should never assume the level of legal knowledge of their client. The lawyer can check in with the client about how much detail they would like but, as the client must ultimately decide based on the information given them how they want their case to proceed, the lawyer should also be satisfied they clearly understand the options. This is not achieved by just asking, 'Do you understand?' It is better to ask, 'Can you tell me what your understanding is of what I have just outlined so I can be confident all is clear?'

In mediation, an intake interview will provide information to a mediator to enable assessing suitability and hypothesising the cause of the dispute and how the parties are likely to interact in relation to power and communication styles. As an example, an intake interview prior to a mediation will have a purpose that encompasses:

- clarifying the issues
- aiding in diagnoses of the nature of the dispute – false conflicts, data conflicts, or complaints
- assessing whether psychological counselling, grieving, or conflict coaching are needed
- deciding on the best approach or process to take towards managing the dispute
- checking that all documentation required is available
- consideration of power imbalances and cultural needs.[26]

In shuttle processes used in mediation or negotiations, a form of interview is also adopted. Here, it is important the third party convey not only the content in the accurately spoken words, although in a detoxified form, but also the emotions expressed.

Models for interviewing

The following section provides a sampling of different interview models for the dispute practitioner to consider. If using interviewing as a process to manage a dispute, or even if used as part of another dispute process, the model should be adopted to suit the goal of the interview.

Motivational interviewing: a collaborative, empathetic non-judgmental model of interviewing that enables an interviewee to reach their own decision about an issue.

Motivational interviewing

Motivational interviewing has predominantly occurred in a therapeutic setting to aid in overcoming addictions and assist with change behaviour. It has been empirically evaluated and the literature confirms its success. Miller and Rollnick[27] were early exponents in developing the practice, which focused on supporting change initiative and motivation to commit to changes. They described motivational interviewing as an 'interviewee-centred, directive

26 See *National Mediator Accreditation System* (NMAS) Part III, 3.2 <https://msb.org.au/themes/msb/assets/documents/national-mediator-accreditation-system-2015.pdf>.

27 William R Miller, 'Motivational Interviewing with Problem Drinkers' (1983) 11 *Behavioural Psychotherapy* 147; William R Miller and Stephen Rollnick, *Motivational interviewing: Preparing People to Change Addictive Behavior* (Guilford Press, 1991); William R Miller and Stephen Rollnick, *Motivational Interviewing. Preparing People for Change* (Guilford Press, 2nd ed, 2002).

method for enhancing intrinsic motivation to change by exploring and resolving ambivalence'.[28]

The interview technique relies on a method of communication with five central philosophical components. These are:

1. Applying reflective listening to show empathy
2. Helping the interviewee see the gap between their conduct and their goals and values
3. Using persuasion and support rather than judgment, argument and coercion
4. Absorbing the interviewee's resistance to change in a collaborative manner instead of directing change
5. Supporting interviewee autonomy, self-efficacy, and optimism.[29]

The interviewer adopts an unconditional and collaborative approach to allow an interviewee autonomy to explore and find their own ability and desire to change in a way that closely reflects their own goals. This respects the responsibility of the individual for making their own choices and the approach helps the interviewee self-identify their desire to change and to be motivated to change. This is particularly useful in dispute management where unwanted behaviours underlie some of the causes of a dispute and when sustaining relationships is important. It may well be that a party to a dispute does not identify or accept they have any reason to change their behaviour.[30] Motivational interviewing will assist them in a supportive manner to see their need for change and to help support their motivation for change. A randomised trial study of the use of motivational interviewing techniques in family mediations showed it doubled the rate of agreements over regular mediations.[31]

The skills required must be learnt and applied in a purposeful manner, adopting a sound knowledge on the appropriate timing and words to use at key moments within the interview. Understanding what is *not* reflective, empathetic and collaborative listening may help, as these aspects should be avoided in motivational interviewing. Gordon[32] outlines 12 aspects of communication that are to be avoided in motivation interviewing:

1. Ordering or directing
2. Warning or threatening
3. Giving advice, making suggestions, or providing solutions prematurely or when unsolicited
4. Persuading with logic, arguing, or lecturing

28 Miller and Rollnick (2002) (n 27) 25.

29 Miller and Rollnick (1991) (n 27) 51–2.

30 See, eg, Ken Resnicow, Fiona McMaster and Stephen Rollnick, 'Action Reflections: A Client-Centered Technique to Bridge the WHY–HOW Transition in Motivational Interviewing' (2012) 40 *Behavioural and Cognitive Psychotherapy* 474; Antonia S Csillik, 'Understanding Motivational Interviewing Effectiveness: Contributions from Rogers' Client-Centered Approach' (2013) 41 *The Humanistic Psychologist* 350.

31 Megan Morris, W. Halford and J Petch, 'A Randomized Controlled Trial Comparing Family Mediation with and without Motivational Interviewing' (2018) 32(2), *Journal of Family Psychology* 269.

32 Thomas Gordon, *Parent Effectiveness Training: Parent Effectiveness Training: The No-Lose Program for Raising Responsible Children* (Wyden, 1970) 10.

5. Moralising, preaching, or telling interviewees their duty
6. Judging, criticising, disagreeing, or blaming
7. Agreeing, approving, or praising
8. Shaming, ridiculing, labelling, or name-calling
9. Interpreting or analysing
10. Reassuring, sympathising, or consoling
11. Questioning or probing
12. Withdrawing, distracting, humouring, or changing the subject.[33]

An example of a motivational interview sequence is provided in the following segment relating to an elderly parent resisting moving to a new place of residence to obtain a greater level of care:

Interviewer:	Mary, you are here to discuss your current situation. Can you tell me what you are thinking about this?
Mary:	I don't want to move. I have lived in my home for 35 years and I am happy and comfortable there.
Interviewer:	It sounds like a lovely home that you are comfortable and very happy in.
Mary:	Yes, I am. I am an independent person and don't believe in being a burden to others.
Interviewer:	You like to be independent and not rely on others.
Mary:	Hmm, although I know things are different now as many of my neighbours have gone it can get a bit lonely.
Interviewer:	That must be lonely with your friends having passed on or moved. How does that affect you?
Mary:	Well, it can be a few days without having talked to or seen anybody and I am not getting any younger so I don't get out as much.
Interviewer:	Is that something you like to do – get out and talk to others?
Mary:	Yes, and my son keeps saying I should go to the aged care facility where I would be among other people.
Interviewer:	On a scale of 1–10, where 1 is a desire not to move and 10 comfortable with moving, where would you say you are today?
Mary:	Around 2–3.
Interviewer:	What do you think puts you at 2–3 and not 0?
Mary:	It will be so hard to pack up my house, and it will take a lot of my money to pay for aged care housing and then my son would inherit nothing, but I know he is concerned for my happiness.
Interviewer:	So, the thought of packing and the worry of it consuming your money are important considerations. What would need to happen to move you to a 5–6 on the scale?

33 Ibid. See also Substance Abuse and Mental Health Services Administration Center for Substance Abuse Treatment. *Enhancing Motivation for Change in Substance Abuse Treatment* (US Department of Health and Human Services, 1999); see also Chapter 2.

Mary: I really cannot afford it. Although I did have a fall the other day and I was lying there for two hours before my son came.
Interviewer: That must have been very scary for you and your son.
Mary: Yes, it was and it did upset him. I don't like being a burden to him.
Interviewer: Yes, you like being independent and not having to have help or be a burden for your son. Is there any way you could see that the possibility of a burden on your son could be altered?
Mary: Well, I know if I moved to the aged care facility, he would feel more confident someone would look after me if he couldn't. But I still can't bear the thought of packing, leaving my home and the worst would be using all my money to do it.
Interviewee: The cost is a considerable concern for you?
Mary: Yes, it is. I want to leave some money for my son, not use it all up on me.
Interviewee: You love your son and have his best interests at heart. Have you discussed that concern with your son?
Mary: Oh, he says he has plenty of money and just wants me to be comfortable and cared for.
Interviewer: He seems most concerned for your happiness.
Mary: I know he is.
Interviewer: Would it help if you had more information on the actual cost and what would be involved in packing up and moving?
Mary: I guess it couldn't hurt.

The above example provides evidence of empathetic listening and reframing using motivational interviewing in rapport building, while respecting Mary's concerns. Direction or coercion is not imposed; rather, the interview follows and supports the interviewees thinking as she unveils her concerns. This is a targeted questioning that elicits change strategies, drawing out Mary's own views of the disadvantages of the status quo and advantages in change. The **importance ruler** was used. The interviewer has looked for the key indication of change thinking. This comes when Mary says she knows her son is concerned for her happiness. The series of questions following that point identify the gap or discrepancy between Mary's current position and where she might be if she did change. This is done by again referring to the importance ruler and asking for more information on the discrepancy and then summarising this back accurately. The interview script is left at the point where the interviewer is supporting Mary's change talk by empowering her ability to make change with an action reflection statement regarding obtaining further relevant information to enable a more informed decision.

Importance ruler: a useful technique to ask the question – 'on a scale of 1–10, 1 being not important and 10 being very important ...'. This can enable an interviewer to gauge where the interviewee is currently situated in their thinking about a dispute.

The aim of motivational interviewing is to assist the interviewee overcome change ambivalence through empathic listening and walking alongside, rather than directing, to empower the interviewee to find and follow their own motivations. This theory and technique is useful to many dispute management situations, but especially where a person's behaviour is contributing to a dispute. This ultimately leaves little reason for an interviewee to resist change behaviour as they have identified their issue and the way they wish to address it.

Cognitive interviewing

This approach to conducting an interview was first addressed by Fisher and Geiselman[34] in the early 1980s. It was initially designed to aid police interviews and to help the interviewee remember information. Some key philosophies apply. These include a strong focus on pre-planning, using a conversational style, and allowing more control of floor and topic to the interviewee (who speaks when, and what about) so they can follow a story-telling style with little interruption.[35] This will generally provide significantly more information than if there are many interruptive questions. To achieve this, four key aspects are required:

1. Explicitly ask the interviewee to report everything.
2. Assist the interviewee to vision the context and mentally restate all they experienced through their five senses, and not to guess what they experienced.
3. Change the temporal ordering, allowing the interviewee to go backwards to the event, or forward and backward. This helps assess the authenticity of the experience as it disrupts a constructed linear narrative.
4. Change the interviewee's perspective: have them imagine the event from the point of view of others present. Caution must be exercised here so as not to invoke imagining a victim's traumatic experience.[36]

Any questioning should be strategic to ensure the questions are framed correctly using the most appropriate style of questioning, such as open questions. Occasionally, directive questions will follow a short summary of the information presented if the story is complex and dense. These can also incorporate the temporal ordering of events by stating what has occurred in a backward and forward manner. An occasional summary helps the interviewee stay focused and feel heard and can assist the interviewer sustain the focus or proceed to a different area in the story. Using reframes that don't challenge or judge, and using appropriate silences, provides a maximum opportunity for the interviewee to recall and unfold the information they wish to impart.[37]

Allowing a story-telling approach by giving the interviewee control of the floor provides an opportunity for an interviewee to present information that previously may have not been and neither the interviewee nor interviewer had any idea was relevant to the purpose of the conversation. This is the 'unknown-unknown'. Rapport building and positive comfort levels of the interviewee assist their ability for mental recall.

Such a story-telling approach is sometimes criticised if time is a factor. However, if using an inquisitorial interrogation approach, over the same amount of time, more accurate information is likely to be provided using this technique. This is because story-telling provides a narrative,

---

34 Ronald P Fisher, 'The Cognitive Interview Method for Interviewing Co-Operative Witnesses' (Conference Paper, Second International Investigative Interviewing Conference, 2006); Ronald P Fisher and R Edward Geiselman, *Memory-enhancing Techniques for Investigative Interviewing: The Cognitive Interview* (Charles Thomas, 1992).

35 Linda F Smith, 'Interviewing Clients: A Linguistic Comparison of the Traditional Interview and the Client-Centered Interview' (1995) 1(3) *Clinical Law Review* 541.

36 Coral Dando, Rachel Wilcock and Rebecca Milne, 'The Cognitive Interview: Novice Police Officers' Witness/Victim Interviewing Practices' (2009) 15(8) *Psychology, Crime and Law* 679.

37 See Chapter 2.

rich in verbal and non-verbal information, by setting context that emphasises the interviewee's perspective. By not being interrupted, the interviewee feels rapport, respect and is comfortable in recalling information without being blocked and made to feel defensive.

Cognitive interviewing: allowing an interviewee to tell their story with minimal disruption in order to provide maximum information, with some incisive and well-informed strategic questioning only.

Cognitive interviewing should be sensitive to how memory can be distorted by the nature and type of questioning. Research has demonstrated how impressionability can lead to portrayal of what an interviewee may genuinely believe as honest answers that have been corrupted by manipulation of the brain's senses. The feelings and emotions associated with people or events can also distort the memory.[38] Naïve realism sees people thinking that others have the same world-view as they do, and find it hard to accept even objective evidence that denies their version of reality. Every person will view the world through their individual lens or schemas. Bartlett[39] instigated the idea of schemas, in which current cognitive experience is absorbed based on experience integrated in the unconscious. His work reminds us that

> ... rather than schema being cognitively neutral, 'interests and ideals' (values and beliefs), 'temperament' (dispositions) and 'character' (personality) are intrinsic to and inseparable from cognition itself.[40]

Dispute management practitioners all work within a set of professional norms and schemas can influence how facts are interpreted. Depending on the type of profession, the same 'facts' can be interpreted entirely differently. This can lead to an expected pattern of behaviour being perceived to have occurred, even if what happened was something very different. The different activity is often eradicated from the memory. Perceptions feel real to the individual and thus are hard to refute. Cognitive psychology warns of individuals' generally over-optimistic evaluation of their capabilities.[41] For interviewers, this means being conscious not to allow personal bias and perceptions to cloud the actual view of the story as it unfolds, or to pre-judge the data and evidence as presented by an interviewee. A meta-awareness and self-observation is required to work against the natural inclination to seek information that supports one's world view. This has also been labelled as an 'unconscious bias'.

The importance of the right brain intuitive, perceptive and tacit knowledge cannot be ignored and plays an essential role in decision-making by contributing and moderating purely left brain logical-ordered thinking.[42] Knowing that memory can be fallible and that it is drawn from many sources, influences, and pathways, means that an interviewer seeking truth must be sure it is constructed by using multiple viewpoints and sources.

38 Aaron (n 25) 153–4.

39 Frederick Bartlett, *Remembering: A Study in Experimental and Social Psychology* (Cambridge University Press, rev ed 1995).

40 Teresa Carla, *Rethinking Interviewing and Personnel Selection* (Palgrave Macmillan, 2015) 27.

41 Ibid 137–45.

42 Ibid; Elizabeth A Kensinger, 'Remembering the Details: Effects of Emotion' (2009) 1(2) *Emotion Review* 99; Stephanie Simpson and Signy Sheldon, 'Testing the Impact of Emotional Mood and Cue Characteristics on Detailed Autobiographical Memory Retrieval' (2020) 20(6) *Emotion* 965.

Figure 4.1 The cognitive interview process

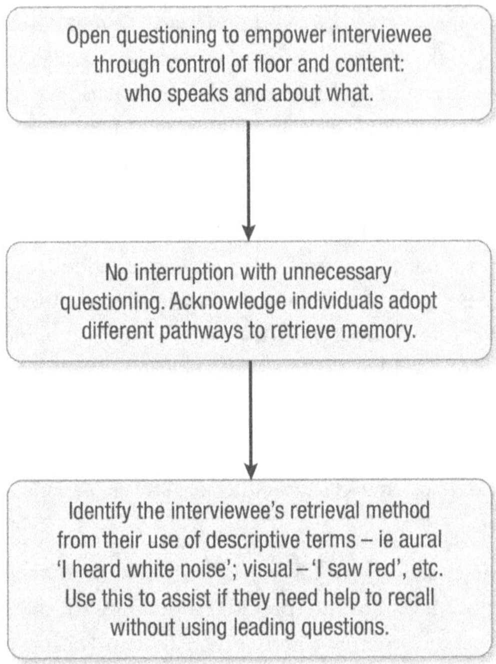

Timeline interviewing

Timeline interviewing adopts a specific process in which the interviewee may be asked to draw a timeline, although it can also be done just by their verbal description. It is often used in police settings, but is relevant to most areas of professional practice. The timeline will cover the first activity relevant to the event being discussed through to the last. Significant factors happening along that timeline are noted and described. Appropriate summarising with directive questioning can be used to assist the interviewee through this process. This is a useful technique in complex matters where many events have happened and the timing is relevant, or where the matter has unfolded over many years. The timeline is an aide to memory as it helps the interviewee prompt their memory and recall.[43] It also aides the interviewer in complex matters where events occur across an extended period. Cognitive interview techniques can also be utilised in this model.

43 Jurgita Rimkeviciene et al, 'Timelines for Difficult Times: Use of Visual Timelines in Interviewing Suicide Attempters' (2016) 13(3) *Qualitative Research in Psychology* 231; Binder, Bergman & Price (n 23) ch 6.

Figure 4.2 An example of a timeline technique used in a timeline interviewing model for a workplace dispute

T-funnels

A T-funnel model[44] is one most used in interviews in the law domain.[45] Lawyer–client interviews are generally seeking purposeful information from a client. The lawyer knows the legislative or case law in the area of concern for the client and wants to check if they have the facts that would engage the right to make a claim. For instance, it may be establishing the essential four elements for the tort of negligence to be proven: (1) was a duty of care owed? (2) was it breached? (3) did the other party's actions cause the damage? and (4) whether the other party's actions are not too remote to link to the damage suffered. The risk is the lawyer may be keen to get to these essential pieces of information and, in doing this, may disrupt the client's story and lose essential facts that mislead or require retracing questioning to establish. Following a structured process that starts with open questions and takes the information provided to form more specific questions will prevent missing important information and result in a happier client. Through actively listening to the responses to the initial open questions, the interviewer can discern several topic areas to formulate

44 See David Binder, Paul Bergman and Susan Price, 'Lawyers as Counselors: A Client-Centered Approach' (1990) 35(1) *New York Law School Law Review* 29.

45 See R Kahn and CF Cannell, *The Dynamics of Interviewing: Theory, Technique and Cases* (John Wiley & Sons, 1957) for the initial description of this model.

as an agenda on which to ask more probing questions. These areas are then covered by seeking answers to questions such as who, when, where, what, why, and how. Open questions give the interviewee a sense of control and elicit answers that provide information on personality, motivation, and aims. What is not covered in an answer can also be revealing.

This model applies questioning in a layered manner. After the initial opening questions such as 'Can you tell me about your working week?' the agenda topics are identified. These are then used to guide the questioning from the open question to open questions addressing the specific agenda topic, such as 'You mentioned you went to Sally's place on the Tuesday – what was the atmosphere like?' This topic can then be subject to a series of open and closed questions, narrowing the funnel until only specific answers are needed to paint a detailed picture on the atmosphere and mood of people present. In this manner, the details provided in answer to the probing questions are then clarified with narrow closed questions, often designed to provide a binary 'yes' or 'no' answer.[46] This process is replicated in relation to each of the agenda topics. This is likely to improve the accuracy of the information given.

Interviewers will be observant of non-verbal behaviour as well as any changes in response to the open and closed questions – the latter are often perceived as more confrontational by an interviewee.[47] If the answers shift from being forthright and explicit under open questioning to edited, evasive and deviational under closed questioning, the interviewer may feel the interviewee is being dishonest. If there is little change between the manner of answering open and closed questions, then the interviewer may draw an impression that the interviewee is being honest. Many of the cognitive interview skills are applied during this model of interviewing.

In using this approach, caution is urged to avoid becoming too formalistic. Being wooden in a neutral client-centred manner can create the opposite effect to that sought to be achieved. Empathetic responses to an interviewee must acknowledge the right level of emotion.[48] For

Figure 4.3 The funnel approach

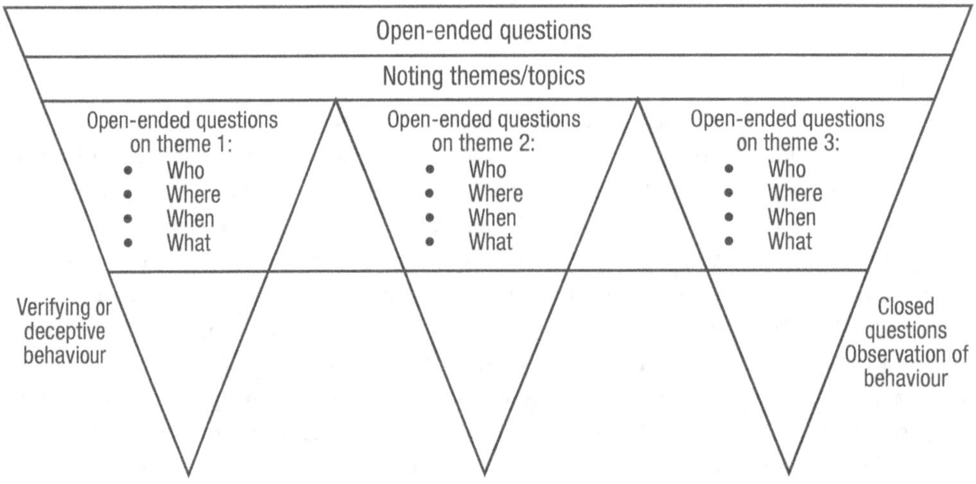

46 See Chapter 2.
47 See, eg, Hyams, Campbell, Evans (n 19) 27–8.
48 Ibid.

instance, saying to an interviewee who has just described their experience of a brutal assault as, 'That must have been unpleasant' will not be likely to impress the interviewee. If it is a disturbing or shocking description the interviewee describes, then acknowledging 'That must have been incredibly shocking and definitely disturbing' is more appropriate.

For a lawyer–client interview, once the funnel model has elicited the necessary information, the next and third stage is for the lawyer to provide the client with legal advice addressing how their factual story can result in a desirable outcome. This will involve assessing what dispute management process will best aid this and advising the client on the advantages and disadvantages of following a particular process. Hyams, Campbell and Evans make an important point when saying '[i]t is your client's agenda and needs that must take precedence'.[49] A lawyer cannot give advice to follow a process because it may be an easier option, or indeed one that brings in more income for the lawyer.

Using knowledge of interviewing to assist in dispute management

Information – why interviewing?

Interviewing as part of a dispute management process will require the interviewer to consider factors such as the positions, interests, perceptions, emotional state, suitability for the process, preparation of the interviewee, and the interviewee's specific style or needs such as cultural, religious, gender or age considerations. A clear understanding of why the interview is required and that information cannot be gained other than through an interview is essential to consider. This could be to gain an impression of the person, their personality, and communication style prior to a dispute process, such as mediation, or litigation.

Establishing key pieces of information required and the purpose for the interview prior to its undertaking are vital preparation. This can be in the form of themes or topics for conversation, rather than verbatim questions to be asked. The latter approach will interfere with authenticity and rapport and can lead to floor and topic control that blocks information flow. While one should have a clear understanding of the purpose, and perhaps some themes, it is best to not be too scripted, unless it is a formal research interview, in which case the same wording in questions must be used with each participant.

Rapport building

Despite the movie portrayal of tough courtroom cross-examination or police interrogations in interviews in which trading in tricks, threats, traps or just terror seem to be *de rigueur*, outcomes will improve if good interview techniques are applied. Using a cognitive or motivational approach sees purpose achieved more often. A professionally respectful attitude in which unconditional positive regard is shown is the ideal goal for building rapport, even in situations of interviewing someone who allegedly has done terrible wrongs.[50]

49 Ibid.

50 Gay Gellhorn et al, 'Law and Language: An Interdisciplinary Study of Client Interviews' (1994) 1(2) *Clinical Law Review* 245. A good example of this is found by viewing the video of the Interview of Colonel Russell Williams by Detective John Smith: 'Colonel Russell Williams Interrogation' (YouTube, 11 February 2018, 0:00–2:39:49) <https://www.youtube.com/watch?v=MeuidR5UNWY>.

Non-verbal: empathetic and active listening, addressing emotions

Maintaining an authentic presence and unconditional positive regard is largely achieved through non-verbal language, such as acknowledging the comfort zone of the interviewee's proxemics or physical space, taking account of cultural differences, and ensuring the interview is conducted in a manner that addresses any cultural needs. Having positive emotions, aided by using humour, can settle an interviewee and assist with their ability to take in information and respond clearly and accurately. Positive emotions can be encouraged by providing a welcoming environment with comfort and needs, such as parking, being met, and keeping to an appropriate time. There are five clear ways in which positive emotion can be attained:

1. appreciation – being heard, understood and valued
2. affiliation – having an emotional or interpersonal connectedness
3. autonomy – being free to make one's own decision
4. status – social standing, often in relation to another
5. role – often identified with one's employment.[51]

Emotion is also assuaged by reflective and empathetic listening. This is done by acknowledging emotion in a genuine way: 'That sounds like it was incredibly scary and you were very frightened by the experience' is better than 'I understand it was frightening'. The latter can come across as wooden and dismissive. Factors such as affiliation can be gained from close observation: does a person's tie or badge tell you something, and is this anything you may have in common? It can lead to small talk that a person will appreciate through feeling an empathetic connection. This can also be achieved through isopraxism or mimicking.[52] The latter is a gentle following of another person's tone pace and pitch in voice, breathing rate, and bodily positions or movements. This must be conducted with a degree of subtlety and respect or it can be perceived as insulting. However, when done appropriately, it can make the other person feel at ease, and feel a relatedness not otherwise achieved. It can also be used to move a highly emotional person into a calmer state. This is done by initially matching their breathing rate and voice level – not yelling, but using as loud a voice – and then gradually bringing the breathing and voice to a quieter and slower pace. Experienced interviewers will use these skills almost automatically.[53]

A particularly useful non-verbal technique for helping an emotional interviewee is not to stop the interview and take a break, or even verbally acknowledge the situation, but to non-verbally proffer a box of tissues and perhaps a glass of water. This does not interrupt the interviewee, but shows you are empathising with their feelings. However, if an interviewee is stuck repeating their emotions, it is important for the interviewer to accurately acknowledge

51 Roger Fisher and Daniel Shapiro, *Beyond Reason: Using Emotions as you Negotiate* (Viking, 2005) 15–21.

52 Pauline Collins, 'Mediators' Authentic Presence: Ways of Knowing Our Primitive Selves' (2010) 21 *Australasian Dispute Resolution Journal* 85; see also Aaron (n 25) 230.

53 See also Chapter 1.

the emotional experience so the interviewee can then move to a greater cognitive space to answer questions.[54]

The interviewer must also be self-aware of their own emotional reaction to the content of the matters being discussed – not only for their personal psychological benefit, but also to avoid any unwarranted influence on the interview. If the emotion appears to be overwhelming to the interviewee, then it is likely they are in a non-cognitive primitive brain state and cannot give rational or logical responses. If this appears to be the case, then taking a short break for food or rest would be appropriate.

Active listening is essential in an interview. Providing a full-facing and open body posture that shows genuine interest in hearing the other's story, taking appropriate notes, providing a quiet non-disruptive space, summarising, including acknowledging emotions, and using some questioning to clarify are all symptoms of active listening. Head nodding and regular eye contact are non-verbal indicators of active listening.[55] However, nodding frequency should be managed so it is not distracting and, if another party is present, such as in an intake interview or dispute process, then an explanation is required that your nodding does not mean agreement, but rather only that you have heard the speaker.

Questions and other techniques

Using the appropriate questions and techniques at the right time is an essential skill in interviewing. Questions generally summon a reply or response from another, unless they are rhetorical, in which case they are giving information. This section gives a brief overview of the types of questions and techniques to be used. Many have been set out in Chapter 2 on communication. However, when to use these techniques in the interview process are addressed in more detail here.

Certain forms of speech have been normalised as using questioning to control another, such as in interrogations or courtroom examinations. Danet reminds the linguistic choice of words used in questioning identifies the purpose and produces consequential responses:

> ... one can formulate a question not only in the grammatical interrogative ('What happened?') but also in the imperative ('Tell me what happened') or declarative ('I'd like to know what happened').[56]

Clearly obtaining maximum information with as little possible interjection is a technique useful in interviewing, as the models outlined above indicate. To achieve this, open questions are required to obtain the interviewee's story and build rapport and confidence in the interviewee. The possibility of providing insight and options during a reflective narrative are increased. The choice of words used in open questions will dictate success or failure. An open question can still be asked in an accusative manner, such as 'Tell us how you and Jane happened to be at the office so late.' While it allows the interviewee to use narrative in answer, it is delivered in a manner perceived as inferring some prejudgment. This will produce a more defensive answer. It is better to be fully open: 'Can you tell me about your day at work as it unfolded on the 28th?'

54 See also Chapters 1 and 2 for further information on these communication techniques.
55 See Hyams, Campbell and Evans (n 19); Chapter 2.
56 Danet (n 16) 515.

Generally, closed questions may be used towards the end of the interview when seeking more specific details or confirmation of matters. Too many closed questions early on will risk shutting down the communication, or an interviewee feeling pressured into a position that they cannot then deny without feeling like they will lose face or appear untrustworthy.

Using an interrogation interview style will include often intrusive, disruptive questioning used deliberately to unsettle a person. Such an interview may also include leading questions; namely, those that suggest the answer. However, an interviewer needs to be careful doing this, particularly if it is a forensic-type interview, such as taking a complainant or witness statement. In cross-examination, leading questions are sometimes used when the answers are not controversial and to step a witness through formalities. They can also be used to test credibility, but may incur an objection from the opposing counsel. In intake interviews preparatory to a dispute process, or solicitor–client interviews, such questions can appear accusative as they include judgment. For example: 'You have sent harassing emails previously?'; 'You decided you would only do the minimum necessary to help, didn't you?' The important consideration is that, even in a cross-examination, using challenging interrogative questions is likely to lead to a defensive shutting down by the person questioned. Approaching the questions using more tentative or less direct questioning will allow the interviewee an opportunity to provide the information ultimately being sought. For example, a series of more open questions: 'So is it possible you had previously emailed X? Can you describe what those emails were about?' or 'Can you explain your thinking around this time? Did this change what you did in the workplace? Can you describe that change?'

Directive questions are useful in interviews to prompt an interviewee if they have lost their thread of conversation, or to move them forward out of a stuck position, or perhaps they are wandering off topic. However, directive questions should be used with caution, as one does not want to prevent the interviewee from presenting unknown information that may be useful. Generally, a directive question may be preceded by a brief summary of what the interviewee has said to that point. For example: 'Thank you for explaining how you worked in 2010 and how that led to an incident in which you lost trust because your supervisor started to exclude you from meetings after that date. When you come to 2018 and the incident you mentioned earlier that was the catalyst for seeing me today, had the exclusion still been occurring?'

Clarifying questions can be framed in an open way, such as: 'Can you help me understand why . . .'. In this manner, a gentle probing can result in interests, not just positions, being unearthed. These can be further explained by clarifying: 'Why is this important to you?' There can also be closed clarifying questions used to seek a direct answer or check understanding of an ambiguous statement: 'You stated . . ., is that correct?'

Hypothetical questions can be used to assist the interviewee by evoking empathy, such as: 'If you were Joe how do you think you would have felt?' or 'If it was you that had lost that amount of money what would you have done?' This will help reality test the interviewee's assumptions, such as asking: 'Do you think there could be any other possible reason to explain Joe's behaviour?' This can assist in moving the interviewee to generating options or problem-solving thinking.

Using paraphrase or a summary to check in with the interviewee to see they have been accurately heard is appropriate if used at strategic points and used infrequently. It is important not to interrupt the flow, but necessary to ensure you have heard and understood and that the interviewee feels understood. The summary should include first acknowledging the interviewee's emotions. This not only helps their comfort, as they feel they are heard, but it allows them to focus on the cognitive aspects over the emotive once these have been acknowledged.

Circling back is a useful technique and can be used to check accuracy in what has been stated. This is done by asking a question that may have been asked previously but in a slightly different manner. It is also useful where the interviewee is talking about a difficult topic and is emotional. For instance, in interviewing a young victim of crime, if you are getting to a particularly difficult part of the story and the interviewee freezes up or is getting very emotional, you can take them back to an earlier part of their story that was safer and easier to talk about. This is 'circling back'. It helps the interviewee regain composure and then you can gently step them through, using directive questioning, back to the point at which they had difficulty. Generally, the next time around they can get through it, although you may need to do this more than once.[57]

The following are things that a good interviewer should not do:

- Do not ask accusative questions: questions that often begin with 'Why ...?' Instead, ask: 'Can you help me understand ...?'
- Do not ask questions that have many components, or many questions rolled into one: 'How did that occur? Did you ask about it or were there other factors you were considering?'
- Do not take the floor in a disruptive manner when an interviewee is telling their story.
- Do not use acronyms or jargon that confuse an interviewee, such as 'Can you state the material facts that the IRB indicated was NN and how necessary it was that it was ASAP?'
- Do not ask questions in an imprecise or ambiguous manner with too many pauses, or rephrases mid-sentence: 'Ahh ... now you said ... earlier ... ahh something about the date that happened ... I mean the date, the time that you said you thought you viewed ... I mean attended the ... umh ... property, is that ... um ... accurate?' This question followed by a 'Do you understand me?' Even though it is incomprehensible may result in the interviewee saying, 'Yes, I understand, you mean the 10th of January.' This can be inaccurate if there are a number of different relevant dates in the story and further, does it refer to viewing the property or attending the property and which property? Is there only one? Interviewees generally do not want to appear like they cannot follow the interviewer or that they are necessarily uncooperative and so will agree they understand even if they do not.
- Do not treat the interviewee as incompetent by using patronising language. Unconditional positive regard means having consideration for their age, education levels and cultural factors, but not pigeonholing them without taking account of the whole person presenting to the interviewer.
- Do not use pronouns without care. 'You' is often seen as accusative and will result in the other person becoming defensive. It is better to say 'I', as the other person cannot argue with the speaker's personal perspective: 'I need to understand ... can you assist me?' will be more conducive to an open response than 'You are saying that you did nothing to cause this?'[58]

57 See generally Chapter 2.

58 See, eg, Shane L Rogers, Jill Howieson and Casey Neame, 'I Understand You Feel That Way, But I Feel This Way: The Benefits of I-Language and Communicating Perspective During Conflict' (2018) 6 PeerJ 6: e4831.

Positives and negatives of interviewing

Positives

A successful interview achieves its purpose and can resolve a dispute without further processes being required, or can work within another process, such as litigation, negotiation, and mediation to clarify and manage the issues. The interviewee who feels they were allowed to convey their story and were heard will be more cooperative and positive towards the interviewer. If this is an interviewee, for instance, in a professional client context it can only be good for your future reputation and maintaining your client base.

For both interviewer and interviewee, a well-conducted interview allows the interviewee to express their story, needs and concerns, and an interviewer to feel they have achieved the purpose for which they undertook the interview.

Negatives

If done badly, interviews can have a negative outcome and fail to achieve the purpose of the interview. This can have consequences for interviewers in how they respond and conduct future interviews, as well as for the interviewee. For dispute practitioners and professionals such as lawyers, the party may decide to complain or certainly not return for another similar experience. Therefore, ensuring good preparation and the use of the most appropriate model is essential. Practising the relevant communication techniques should mean that the interviewer and interviewee do not have a negative experience. There will always be more challenging interviewees and contexts. Working with a co-interviewer can assist if genuine reflection is held post-interview and lessons are learnt and applied.

Special considerations

Special considerations include coverage of interviews with vulnerable persons, such as young children or persons from different cultures, as well as neuroscience, unconscious bias and ethics. How these factors affect the nature of the interview along with applying a suitable management process are discussed in the sections that follow.

Vulnerable interviewees

Vulnerable interviewees include children,[59] people with psychological disorders, or mental or physical incapacities, people with a non-English speaking background, and persons who have suffered violence, including sexual violence.

A first consideration must be identifying an interviewee as coming within the vulnerable person category. This is not necessarily an easy task, as mental and psychological disorders can take time to become apparent, and survivors of trauma or violence may not disclose this for

59 See *Murphy v Murphy* [2007] FamCA 795, for a discussion of the interviewing of young children regarding sexual abuse in a civil proceeding.

many reasons.[60] Vulnerable interviewees can be highly suggestable and keen to seem cooperative or even just passive.[61] Understanding the physical ability of an interviewee to even hear adequately is something to consider and can have significant consequences, for instance, in police interviews. In *Ebatarinja v Deland*,[62] the High Court had to consider the use of an interview with a 'a deaf mute Aborigine who ... is unable to communicate except by using his hands to ask for simple needs [and] does not know that he has been charged with murder'.[63] The Court prohibited the continuance of the committal proceeding.

The main point to note is that anyone undertaking such interviews will require specialist training, which goes beyond the reach of this textbook. Support persons must be present, particularly for children if a guardian or parent is not available, and an interpreter for people from non-English-speaking backgrounds. In dispute processes, the dispute practitioner must assure that the support person understands their role and does not disturb the outcome of the process. Sometimes, checking with the support person what risks they personally will suffer if an outcome is not achieved is a useful to ask.

Unconscious bias

Humans cannot help having preferences, prejudices, and attitudes. Awareness of this will assist in addressing the potential effects it can have on the interview. However, even when aware, it can still present as interviewer bias in that questions asked may be in a manner that tends to confirm the interviewer's view of a matter. In such cases, the interviewer needs to consciously focus on reducing judgment and increasing empathy. Being flexible and open with a degree of detachment is important to avoid corruption of the information being provided. It is the unawareness of bias that can be destructive, because if one does not know it exists then it remains unaddressed.

A good way of overcoming this is to record one's conversations or interviews for private reflection and learning, either through role plays or in genuine interviews. Such recordings must be done according to ethical requirements and should be destroyed after the interviewer has gained the necessary learning from watching their performance. The choice of words, the framing of questions, the nature of the questioning, any nonverbal or verbal expression of emotion or judgment can all be revealing of one's **unconscious bias**.

Unconscious bias: the unknown or unacknowledged bias of an individual that blocks acceptance of contrary views.

Neuroscience

Neuroscience is the study of the human nervous system and brain functions. It is changing the way we understand human interaction. Using Magnetic Resonance Imaging (MRI) enables researchers to explore the brains activity in new ways. We now know that the manner by

60 See, eg, Lorana Bartels, *Police Interviews With Vulnerable Adult Suspects* (Criminology Research Council, 2011).

61 See, eg, T Ochoa and J Rome 'Considerations for Arrests and Interrogations of Suspects with Hearing, Cognitive and Behavioral Disorders' (2009) 9(5) *Law Enforcement Executive Forum Journal* 131.

62 (1998) 194 CLR 444.

63 Ibid [3].

which we respond to facial first impressions,[64] gender and cultural bias may be hard-wired in our brain and some may have to work harder to overcome and counter initial reactions. Judgments of trust can be made within 100 milliseconds of exposure.[65] Todorov and others have found 'rapid, unreflective trait inferences from faces influence consequential decisions',[66] to the point of deciding who to elect as a candidate, and, in this research, that decisions were heavily influenced by impressions of competence. Todorov also found the competence perception has a gender bias in favour of males.[67]

When working as dispute practitioners, awareness of non-verbal impacts on others' reactivity is essential and is discussed in the non-verbal section of this chapter. Dress and presentation also have an impact. Zebrowitz and McDonald examined 500 cases in the small claims jurisdiction in the United States, and found significant favourable impacts on the outcome of a case based on the baby-facedness and attractiveness, as opposed to mature-faced individuals.[68]

The old saying, 'When in Rome, do as the Romans do', is apt to help one consider context and the impression made. The comfort level of the interviewee and judgments of competence are affected by appearance and physical attributions.[69] For example, a warm handshake of the interviewee for a job interview has been found to have positive effects on interviewer's impression and acceptance of a candidate.[70]

Two senses that have not been addressed, but that nevertheless have significant impact on our brain and our responses, are colour and smell. The impact of colour is almost universal. For instance, in the animal world, red is both an alert colour and sexual enticement – the same applies to humans. Therefore, red is not a good colour to have in a closed interview room, as the primitive brain will be dealing with a danger alert or sexual response. Other colours, such as brown, have been shown to lower cognitive activity. The best colours for interviewers are softer greys, pink, or maroon.[71]

The olfactory function – smell – evokes memory extremely well and can be used to advantage in interview rooms. Unfortunately, it is mostly neglected.[72] The unique attribute of the olfactory function is its ability to direct information straight to the limbic primitive brain

64 Clare AM Sutherland et al, 'Facial First Impressions Across Culture: Data-Driven Modeling of Chinese and British Perceivers' Unconstrained Facial Impressions' (2018) 44(4) *Personality and Social Psychology Bulletin* 521; Johan J Bolhuis, 'Neural Mechanisms of Olfactory Recognition Memory' in Johan Bolhuis, *Brain, Perception, Memory: Advances in Cognitive Neuroscience* (Oxford University Press, 2000).

65 Shanice EW Janssens et al, 'Can Processing of Face Trustworthiness Bypass Early Visual Cortex? A Transcranial Magnetic Stimulation Masking study' (2020) 137 *Neuropsychologia* 1.

66 Oh DongWon, Elinor A Buck and Alexander Todorov, 'Revealing Hidden Gender Biases in Competence Impressions of Faces' (2018) 30(1) *Psychological Science* 65.

67 Alexander Todorov et al, 'Inferences of Competence from Faces Predict Election Outcomes' (2005) 308 (5728) *Science* 1623, 1623.

68 Leslie A Zebrowitz and Susan M McDonald, 'The Impact of Litigants' Baby-Facedness and Attractiveness on Adjudications in Small Claims Courts' (1991) 15(6) *Law and Human Behavior* 603.

69 See also Carol Kinsey Goman, *The Nonverbal Advantage: Secrets and Science of Body Language at Work* (Berrett-Koehler Publishers, 2008).

70 B Farago, JS Zide and C Shahani-Denning, 'Selection Interviews: Role of Interviewer Warmth, Interview Structure, and Interview Outcome in Applicants' Perceptions of Organizations' (2013) 65(3) *Consulting Psychology Journal: Practice and Research* 224.

71 See Collins (n 52) 93–5.

72 Philipp Homan et al, 'Aversive Smell Associations Shape Social Judgment' (2017) 144(October) *Neurobiology of Learning and Memory* 86.

system. This is the region associated with memory and emotion and so enables a powerful mood stimulus, and retrieval of information important in interview contexts and social communication exchanges. The olfactory function contributes to learning and provides a fast recall cue for emotive events while also placing a person back in the location of an event.[73] The olfactory function can also be activated positively in dispute processes through the use of calming or pleasant smells from fruit or flowers. This should be used with caution and knowledge.

Ethics

It is important to remember that no matter how 'wonderful' the information one may obtain from an interview, it cannot necessarily be used if proper processes have not been followed and the person has been threatened, over borne, or manipulated dishonestly.[74] An interviewee must be respected and treated with dignity. Legal rights must be administered correctly. Professional practitioners must maintain appropriate independence in order to give the best lawful advice without fear or favour. For example, in lawyer–client interviews, the aim is to achieve the best outcome for the client – not for the lawyer. This requires approaching such relationships with the highest of ethical standards and placing the client in a fiduciary position.

Suspects participate in police interviews voluntarily and have a right to remain silent.[75] Interviews that seemingly satisfy the proper process may still be inadmissible if a court assesses the circumstances of the interview would render it unfair to the accused to use in evidence.[76] This discretion of the court is an important protection of the accused's rights, ensuring innocence of the accused until proven guilty, and helps uphold the administration of justice processes.[77] The following is a case example.

STRICKLAND V COMMONWEALTH DIRECTOR OF PUBLIC PROSECUTIONS (2018) 266 CLR 325

Facts: In December 2008, the Australian Crime Commission (ACC) was tasked to investigate allegations of criminal conduct by employees and managers of a company. However, the ACC decided to refer the matter to the Australian Federal Police (AFP) for investigation. The four defendants were interviewed by an ACC examiner in 2010. At this interview, the examiner acted contrary to the requirements of the ACC Act. He allowed up to nine AFP officers to covertly watch the interview and made recordings and transcripts available to the

73 See Donald A Wilson, Nadine Ravel and Regina M. Sullivan, *Olfactory Memory Networks: From Emotional Learning to Social Behaviors* (Frontiers Media, 2015).

74 See, eg, *Ebatarinja v Deland* (1998) 194 CLR 444.

75 See *McDermott v The Queen* (1948) 76 CLR 501; *R v Ireland* (1970) 126 CLR 321; see Brandon L Bang et al, 'Police Recording of Custodial Interrogations: A State-by-state Legal Inquiry' (2018) 20(1) *International Journal of Police Science & Management* 3, for an overview of the position in the United States.

76 See Australian Solicitor Conduct Rules 2015 r 29.9: A prosecutor must not confer with or interview any accused except in the presence of the accused's legal representative.

77 See *R v Lee* (1950) 82 CLR 133; *Burns v The Queen* (1975) CLR 258, 265 (Murphy J).

AFP and the Commonwealth Director of Public Prosecutions (DPP). At the time, the ACC investigator knew the four interviewees were suspected of crimes and, despite having refused to be interviewed by the AFP, had been threatened with criminal prosecution for failing to answer questions. The interviewees were subsequently charged with criminal offences: bribing a foreign official (Federal offence) and false accounting (State offence). The Victorian trial Judge was asked to decide whether the circumstances of the interview evidence meant the accused could not receive a fair trial. The judge determined that the interviews were authorised under the ACC Act, but notwithstanding ordered a permanent stay of the prosecutions. On appeal, the Victorian Court of Appeal unanimously reversed the decision of the trial judge holding the interviews were illegal, but nevertheless negating the stay of prosecution.

Issue: The right to silence, observation of the Rule of Law, and protection of the administration of justice. Were the interviews of the applicants conducted in a manner that permitted their use or continued prosecution of the alleged offenders?

Decision: The High Court, by 5:2 majority, upheld the initial trial judge's stay of the prosecutions (Kiefel CJ, Bell, Keane, Nettle & Edelman JJ; Gageler and Gordon JJ dissenting). The Court unanimously upheld the Court of Appeal's finding that the ACC examiner's questioning was unlawful.

Four judges noted that the interviewer's questioning breached AFP and ACC policy requirements regarding such questioning [89]–[91]. The judges held that the defendants 'suffered the forensic disadvantage of being locked into a version of events from which they could not credibly depart at trial' [75]. While the examination may be kept secret, '[t]he examinee can no longer decide the course which he or she should adopt at trial according only to the strength of the prosecution's case as revealed by the material provided by the prosecution before trial or to the strength of the evidence led by the prosecution at trial' [76].

Discussion: Ultimately, the administration of justice is a highly protected principle in which the court will observe the legislative requirements over any executive interests. If an interview is conducted outside of the legislative or common law demands, even though it may mean potentially serious offenders go unprosecuted, it will not be permitted to be used in evidence.

[Note that the anti-terror laws[78] differ as regards the rights of an interviewee and should be considered carefully if operating in that specialised field.[79]]

Interviewers should resist temptation to manipulate by exaggerating any risk or legal consequences, as such deception may well be unethical. Lawyers, and all professionals, when advising clients of options and likely outcomes must be careful to check their own positive perceptions of their capabilities compared to reality.

78 See George Williams, 'A Decade of Australian Anti-Terror Laws' (2011) 35(3) *Melbourne University Law Review* 1136; Nicola McGarrity and Jessie Blackbourn, 'Australia has Enacted 82 Anti-terror Laws Since 2001. But Tough Laws Alone Can't Eliminate Terrorism' *The Conversation* (30 September 2019).

79 See Sydney Criminal Lawyers, 'Police Cannot Persist with Questioning After Right to Silence Is Exercised' *NSW Courts* (Blog post, 23 April 2019) <https://nswcourts.com.au/articles/police-cannot-persist-with-questioning-after-right-to-silence-is-exercised/>.

For instance, the predictions by lawyers of a client's chances of success or otherwise were reported by Goodman-Delhunty, Loftus and others as often no more accurate than predictions from tossing a coin.[80] Placing oneself in the shoes of the other side and considering the matter realistically from their perspective may help overcome some of the tendency towards naïve realism and positive bias in favour of oneself or clients.[81] Honest reflection will assist in using appropriate communication techniques to ensure a client has understood advice accurately and is in a position to make genuine and informed choices. Ultimately, it is the client's choice.[82]

In any interviewing or dispute management process involving questioning, the dispute practitioner must ensure they are treating the interviewee with the required level of respect. This includes acknowledging their need for breaks or the need for a private session. Using long sessions that wear an individual down and do not enable time to take advice or reflect on a potential agreement before finally committing to the agreement is dangerous for all involved.[83]

On many occasions, interviews will bring up uncomfortable or embarrassing matters for discussion. It is appropriate to address this by identifying the possibility at the commencement of the interview. This is best addressed by explaining the reasons why the interviewer wants to discuss these matters and the purpose for which the information may be used. Explaining any confidentiality that may attach to the process is important.[84]

Recording of interviews

In forensic police interviews, video recordings are now a requirement.[85] Interviews are also often recorded when undertaking research for transcription purposes and this is done in accordance with the strict ethical obligations obtained to approve the research. Such recordings can be required to be stored in a confidential and safe manner for a number of years.[86] In other interviews, any recording should be with the consent of those recorded and advice given on how that recording will be stored, when it will be destroyed, and the purposes for which it can be used.

It should be noted that recording a person can contribute to their discomfort and make them curtail the information provided. The other option is to take notes. However, the purpose for taking notes and what is to happen to them must be clearly and honestly explained to the interviewee. Dispute practitioners will tend to avoid taking excessive notes, and will destroy

80 J Goodman-Delhunty, PA Granhag and EF Loftus, 'How Well Can Lawyers Predict Their Chances of Success' (Unpublished manuscript) cited in Aaron (n 25) 156.

81 See Aaron (n 25) 159.

82 *Legal Profession Uniform Law Australian Solicitors' Conduct Rules 2015* r 8.1: a solicitor must follow a client's lawful, proper and competent instructions.

83 See, eg, Laurence Boulle, 'The Dog that Did Not Bark: Mediation Style' (2001) 4(2) *ADR Bulletin,* 22; Chapter 6; *National Mediator Accreditation System* (NMAS) (2015), Part III, 7.6 <https://msb.org.au/themes/msb/assets/documents/national-mediator-accreditation-system-2015.pdf>.: a mediator must ensure, so far as practicable, that participants have had sufficient time and opportunity to access sources of advice or information necessary for their decision-making.

84 See *National Mediator Accreditation System* (NMAS) (2015) Part III, 4.9 <https://msb.org.au/themes/msb/assets/documents/national-mediator-accreditation-system-2015.pdf>; Hyams, Campbell, Evans (n 19) 38–42 (lawyer–client interviews).

85 See Paul Gregoire and Ugur Nedim, 'Police Cannot Persist with Questioning After Right to Silence Is Exercised' (2019) *NSW Courts* <https://nswcourts.com.au/articles/police-cannot-persist-with-questioning-after-right-to-silence-is-exercised/>.

86 See *National Statement on Ethical Conduct in Human Research 2007* (Updated 2018) (National Health and Medical Research Council, 2018).

them after the process, unless it is complex and there are sound reasons, including legislative requirements, to retain notes.

Cultural considerations

Cultural considerations are addressed in Chapters 1 and 3 and the information provided is pertinent to interviewing. Consideration must be given to the interviewee's cultural background; this should not be assumed and should be specifically appropriate to the individual. Nevertheless, the broad considerations of whether the person is from a low-context or high-context cultural is useful to have in mind.

Danet[87] outlines observations in regard to disputing that provides a basis for considering disputes in a culturally relevant manner. She makes a basic division based on whether disputes are verbal or non-verbal and provides subcategories under each. This relies on cultural preferences for disputes being managed through talking or physical action, or some combination.[88]

The non-verbal category is broken down into three domains: physical; magical such as ordeals, oaths and sorcery; and avoidance. The verbal has four categories: shaming; verbal contests (eg the Inuit song duel); settlement; and fact investigation. For verbal examples, Danet refers to the following:

> The Jale language, for instance, contains no word for settlement-directed talk apart from one Koch translates as 'shouting match.' Some societies, on the other hand, love talk for its own sake and are highly argumentative. Litigation 'looms . . . large in the lives of most sub-Saharan African peoples.' 'The Tiv are a litigious people and enjoy listening to and participating in jir [courts or moots].' The Arusha value eloquence and articulate argument.[89]

Shaming and verbal contest is nicely demonstrated in the Inuit practice of song duelling, which can take three distinct forms. These are described as (1) 'pure' play, (2) a genre in which the community uses these songs to shame and censure breaches of norms, and (3) a variety in which the parties to a specific dispute 'fight it out' in an expressive manner.[90] Hoebel, in reporting on the Inuit practice, likened it to a juridical process as the singing was constrained by convention as to style and composition patterns that aimed to entertain the audience.[91] It was not, however, designed to produce a legal entitlement; but rather as a means of determining a winner, mostly by the best 'singer' receiving the greatest support from the audience. Mansell et al[92] have described it as having parallels with the barrister's stylised 'singing' in a courtroom, convincing a jury based on who has the better speech style. However, this approach to disputes does not rely on establishing evidentially proven facts. For such disputes, Danet notes 'advocacy and argument' are essential and are found in the Western adversarial system of courtroom argument and persuasion. As to whether this approach is the best to elicit the 'truth' over the inquisitorial, questioning approach is a contested position. In any event,

87 Danet (n 16).
88 Ibid 494.
89 Ibid 494 (references omitted).
90 Ibid referring to Adamson E Hoebel, *The Law of Primitive Man* (Harvard University Press 1954) 93.
91 Hoebel (n 90).
92 Wade Mansell, Belinda Meteyard and Alan Thomson, *A Critical Introduction to Law* (Cavendish Publishing, 3rd ed, 2004) 45.

facts are constructed from interviewees' recollections and a refinement of assessing the most believable. In certain dispute processes, such as facilitative mediation, the facts are largely irrelevant to the dispute practitioner, as they guide the parties through the process and allow the parties to decide what they consider to be the facts or the matters necessary for them to reach a conclusion. In this manner, establishing 'the facts' objectively is not essential. The adversarial approach is seen as dependent on skilled controlled and closed questioning designed to test the interviewee's truth and accuracy; for example, the Funnel Model. The civil tradition of inquisitorial questioning adopts a more open and story-telling approach such as the Cognitive Model. This approach is more likely to be followed in Indigenous cultures.[93] However, as noted in this chapter, enabling the interviewees to tell their story through conversation questioning techniques is essential to dispute management across cultures.[94]

Conclusion

This chapter has provided an overview of interviewing as a dispute management process in its own right and as an important component of many dispute management processes. It has emphasised and expanded on communication covered more generally in Chapter 2 by providing detail and emphasis on aspects of communication specific to the interview process. The essential components of interviewing have been addressed and four models outlined. The chapter places attention on the interviewee in order to better enable interviewers achieve the purposes of their interviews.

EXERCISE IN APPLYING YOUR KNOWLEDGE – ROCK'N THE ROOF

Jimmy is a young boy who has become mixed up with some older youth who encourage him to get into some trouble. He was walking along a suburban street and had a habit of enjoying disturbing people and listening to the sound of throwing rocks onto roofs.

One day, Patricia was sitting in her office when a rock thrown by Jimmy missed the roof but smashed through her office window, shattering the glass all over her as she sat at her window desk. Outraged by how close she had come to being seriously injured, not to say the damage to her window, Patricia immediately called the police.

The police caught up with Jimmy but not his mates.

A solicitor–client interview is conducted with Jimmy, as well as an intake interview preparing for a third-party mediation between Jimmy, his guardian and Patricia.

1. How would the approach and questions differ for the two interviews? How would the interviewee address age and cultural considerations – assuming Jimmy was from a non-English-speaking background?
2. What would make these effective interviews?
3. What are the contemporary models for interviewing? How would they apply to the scenario?

93 Danet (n 16) 517.

94 See, eg, Allen E Ivey, Mary Bradford Ivey and Carlos P Zalaquett, *Essentials of Intentional Interviewing: Counselling in a Multicultural World* (Brooks/Cole Cengage Learning, 2nd ed, 2012).

5
NEGOTIATION

Learning aims

- Describe the key characteristics of negotiation as a dispute management process
- Demonstrate knowledge of different models of negotiation, with a focus on distributive and integrative models
- Demonstrate understanding of key practice concepts and techniques of negotiation, such as reservation price, zone of potential agreement, BATNA and anchoring
- Explain the four key principles of principled negotiation
- Explain the different phases of a negotiation process including their purposes
- Distinguish negotiation from other dispute management processes and identify its advantages and disadvantages

Understanding negotiation

This chapter addresses **negotiation** as a process of dispute management. It examines two principal models of negotiation – the Distributive and Integrative Models – and considers how these models are applied in practice. Select issues for negotiation theory and practice are canvassed. Negotiation can be a dyadic process when the negotiation occurs directly between parties, or it can be a triadic process in its own right, as third-party assisted negotiation. It can also be part of other triadic dispute processes, such as mediation, facilitation, and collaborative law.

Negotiation: a form of decision-making involving two or more parties who come together to attempt to reach agreement on contentious issues that may occur in relation to a transaction, a venture, or a dispute.

Negotiation is a process that is part of our everyday experience. We might, for example, negotiate what movie to see with a friend at the cinema, who is taking care of the children or other household duties with our partner, the best plan for our mobile phone with a provider, buying a new or used car, the purchase or sale of a property, or a pay rise with our employer. Negotiation to manage differences and allocate resources occurs in everyday life. Many instances of negotiation occur in the context of transactions, such as a purchase or sale. In that context, negotiation is often treated as synonymous with bargaining. Other instances of negotiation are brought about because of a dispute between parties. In legal matters, negotiation occurs up to 'the door of the court', and sometimes beyond – meaning that settlement options are explored as part of the process of litigation and in order to conclude a matter without a court hearing. Avoiding a final determination in court reduces the cost of legal representation, avoids the risk of having to pay the other party's costs, and allows the parties to come to an agreement that they decide. A key characteristic of negotiation and advantage of the process is that parties are empowered by the process to manage their dispute in a dyadic manner without the intervention of a third party. However, parties can seek the assistance of a third-party intervenor to facilitate their negotiation and/or the help of third-party professional representatives, such as lawyers. Dispute management practitioners can be engaged in either of these roles.

Lewicki, Barry and Saunders identity three typical reasons for negotiations: to agree on how to divide or share a limited resource, such as land, other property or time; to create something new that neither party could do on their own, such as a business venture or an innovation; or to address a problem or dispute between the parties.[1] The last of these is the primary focus of this chapter. Whatever the context for negotiation, fundamental characteristics of the process can be identified. Lewicki, Barry and Saunders indicate six fundamental characteristics of any negotiation process:

1. There are two or more parties to any negotiation.
2. There will be a conflict of needs or desires between the parties.
3. The parties negotiate by choice.
4. Negotiation carries an expectation of compromise, or 'give-and-take'.
5. Negotiation occurs when parties prefer to come up with their own solution for managing their dispute.
6. Successful negotiations require attention to tangible and intangible issues.[2]

Negotiators may be dispute practitioners engaged by one party, or each party separately, or for both parties, in order to assist with the negotiation. Negotiation may be undertaken by a third-party intervener who is an expert in dispute management or in the content of the matter under dispute. The term 'negotiator' is used here to refer to dispute management practitioners representing parties or clients.

As a dispute management option, the process of negotiation is not subject to statutory or voluntary regulation. However, where negotiation occurs as part of a process such as mediation or conciliation, it may be subject to particular standards and legislation. Negotiators' approaches and styles are informed by individual knowledge and experience. Spegel, Rogers and Buckley propose three prerequisites that all negotiators need in order to maximise opportunities for a successful negotiation. Dubbed the three A's, these are attitude, awareness, and accountability.[3] The first, a positive attitude, is consistent with a belief that a positive outcome is possible and presupposes a willingness to work towards that result. A positive attitude requires confidence, self-awareness, and thorough preparation. The second prerequisite, awareness, requires sensitivity to messages from the other party. It requires active listening and awareness of verbal and non-verbal communication, as detailed in Chapter 2. The third pre-requisite of accountability requires acceptance of responsibility. When engaged in dyadic negotiations, parties accept that any gains, or any losses, are dependent on their own actions. A dispute practitioner engaged to negotiate is accountable to the party or parties they represent for the outcome. While an outcome will not be entirely predictable, if acting for one party in the negotiation the dispute practitioner should aim to achieve the best outcome possible for that party. If negotiating between parties, the practitioner should look to achieve a negotiated outcome satisfying all parties' needs.

1 Roy J Lewicki, Bruce Barry and David M Saunders, *Essentials of Negotiation* (McGraw-Hill, 6th ed, 2016) 2.

2 Ibid 6–9.

3 Nadja M Spegel, Bernadette Rogers and Ross P Buckley, *Negotiation: Theory and Techniques* (Butterworths, 1998) 6–8; see also Nadja Alexander, Jill Howieson and Kenneth Fox, *Negotiation – Strategy Style Skills* (Lexis Nexis, 3rd ed, 2015) 6–9 on reflective practice, also examined in Chapter 2.

Using theory and models to dissect negotiation

Theory and practice in negotiation has developed from multi-disciplinary influences over the past 50 years to form a distinct academic discipline.[4] Models of negotiation have been given a range of identifiers, including adversarial, competitive, positional, distributive, interest-based, principled, problem-solving and cooperative negotiation. A repeated distinction in the literature is between distributive and integrative negotiation.[5] **Distributive negotiation** is associated with adversarial, competitive and positional concepts in negotiation. **Integrative negotiation** is associated with interest-based, principled, problem-solving and cooperative concepts.[6]

Distributive negotiation: a process in which the parties compete over the distribution of a fixed resource. Each party will establish a position as to what they think is an acceptable exchange and will compete to win that position. A gain by one party typically represents a loss to the other party.

Integrative negotiation: a process in which the parties identify their interests in the central issues in contention, as broadly as possible. The parties then cooperate to achieve maximum mutual benefit by trading across these interests to produce agreement.

An important grounding for understanding negotiation can be achieved by examining the key characteristics of distributive and integrative models.[7] Alternative models and concepts can be understood as variations of these dominant models or as applications of them in a variety of practice contexts. Distributive negotiation is characterised by bargaining in circumstances where one party's gain is the other party's loss; and where each party will take a position on what they are prepared to give or receive and at what price. Examples typically involve negotiation over a fixed resource for a price. For instance, consider real estate, business or car sales and legal claims for damages. In a car sale, the car is a fixed resource. The parties will bargain over the price, or the distribution of value, in exchange for the car. If the purchaser gains by paying less than the asking price, the seller loses that value. Integrative negotiation focuses on uncovering parties' interests beyond the issue of price and attempts to achieve mutual gains, or win-win solutions, by negotiating across a broader spectrum of interests. Consider, for example, a legal matter involving a claim in damages for breach of a building contract. Negotiation might focus exclusively on issues of fault and amounts payable in damages. Alternatively, negotiation might reveal broader interests that become useful in reaching a settlement, such as a history of business dealings between the parties, a willingness on the part of the builder to remedy the breach

4 See Andrea Kuper Schneider and Roy J Lewicki, 'The Past and Future Challenges of Negotiation Theory' (2016) 31(1) *Ohio State Journal of Dispute Resolution* 1; John Lande, 'Moving Negotiation Theory from the Tower of Babel toward a World of Mutual Understanding' (2017)(1) *Journal of Dispute Resolution* 1.

5 Richard A Luecke, *Harvard Business Essentials: Negotiation* (Harvard Business School Press, 2003) 2; see Rishi Batra, 'Using the Terms Integrative and Distributive Bargaining in the Classroom: Time for Change' (2017)(1) *Journal of Dispute Resolution* 29, which provides a review and critique of these terms in the context of developing theory and practice; Peter Condliffe, *Conflict Management: A Practical Guide* (Lexsis Nexis Butterworths, 6th ed, 2019) 204–7, which introduces variations, including structural, strategic, and behavioural approaches.

6 See Carrie Menkel-Meadow, 'Toward Another View of Legal Negotiation: The Structure of Problem-Solving' (1984) 31 *UCLA Law Review* 754; Robert H Mnookin et al, *Beyond Winning: Negotiating to Create Value in Deals and Disputes* (Belknap Press, 2000), which provides a critique of adversarial negotiation and development of problem-solving models incorporating interest-based negotiation principles.

7 See Tania Sourdin, *Alternative Dispute Resolution* (Lawbook, 5th ed, 2016) 47–53.

in a timely manner, the need to protect reputations, and/or the plaintiff's interest in avoiding the emotional as well as financial costs of a protracted dispute. These additional interests will influence, and may be integrated into, any final agreement in addition to any terms regarding the issue of monetary damages. Where appearing in this chapter, and unless otherwise indicated, positional, or competitive negotiation is treated as synonymous with distributive negotiation; and interest-based negotiation is treated as synonymous with integrative negotiation.

In theory, a central difference between these models is that distributive negotiation focuses on claiming something of fixed value, while integrative negotiation seeks to create value to add to the pool of value to be claimed.[8] Distributive negotiation is described as a zero-sum game[9] in which every gain by one party represents a loss to the other. In integrative negotiations, creative options are sought to satisfy the interests of both sides with minimal or no cost to the other.

There are good reasons to understand both models. The first is that some negotiators, including lawyers, will adopt a distributive approach combined with a highly competitive stance. Understanding that approach becomes a necessary strategy in responding to it. Secondly, an integrative approach is considered more responsive to parties' needs and hence a more refined approach to dispute management.[10] Thirdly, in practice, both models are useful options from which to choose depending on the nature of the dispute and the attitudes of the parties. A given negotiation may also display both distributive and integrative elements. An interest-based, integrative process will often close with a sharper focus on distributive aspects.[11] However, the two models differ according to their central purposes. The difference is in the orientation of the parties – whether they view the interaction as a contest and are intent upon winning or whether they adopt a more cooperative, problem-solving approach.[12] Dispute practitioners should be able to clearly identify the differences and know when it is best to use each model. The following discussion examines these models in more detail and is followed by case examples to illustrate negotiation in practice.

The distributive model

Distributive negotiations are typical where price is the paramount concern and there is no expectation of a continuing relationship between parties. As noted, the distributive model of

8 See John S Murray 'Understanding Competing Theories of Negotiation' (1986)(April) *Negotiation Journal* 179.

9 See Michael Wheeler, 'Three Cheers for Teaching Distributive Bargaining' (2012)(January) *Negotiation Journal* 73, 75, which provides a critique of this characterisation in the light of 'quasi-constant-sum games' advanced by Howard Raiffa; James K Sebenius, 'Howard Raiffa: The Art, Science, and Humanity of a Legendary Negotiation Analyst' (2017)(October) *Negotiation Journal* 283; Howard Raiffa, *The Art and Science of Negotiation* (Harvard University Press, 1982).

10 David Spencer, *Principles of Dispute Resolution* (Thomson Reuters, Lawbook Co., 2nd ed, 2016).

11 See Alexander, Howieson and Fox (n 3) 49–81, for a constructive negotiation model that incorporates problem-solving and distributive bargaining and includes exploration of interests and generation of options. The authors identify four stages to their approach: relational positioning, exploring issues and interests, generating options, and reaching solutions; see also Condliffe (n 5) 219–23, for a model that combines distributive and integrative options.

12 See Alexander, Howieson and Fox (n 3) 47–8.

negotiation is said to apply where the value at stake is fixed and each side aims to gain as much of the value as possible.[13] Dividing up a pie is used as an analogy of the zero-sum nature of the process. Each party aims to gain as much of the pie as possible, knowing any gain by one party is a loss for the other. The distributive model of negotiation is also referred to as adversarial or positional bargaining. The distributive model is signalled when parties insist upon what they want, maintaining their respective positions, without disclosing the reason/s for their position. It is not difficult to see distributive bargaining (or distributive negotiation) as representing a contest over something of value and to liken it to the adversarial nature of legal actions. As Fisher, Ury and Patton describe:

> In positional bargaining you try to improve the chance that any settlement reached is favourable to you by starting with an extreme position, by stubbornly holding to it, by deceiving the other party as to your true views, and by making small concessions only as necessary to keep the negotiations going. The same is true for the other side.[14]

The reasons behind parties' positions reveal their interests. According to an integrative, or interest-based model, when these interests are disclosed, an opportunity for more meaningful dialogue that aims to satisfy broader interests, or needs, can occur. Disclosure in the distributive model is usually seen as a weakness. A core strategy in distributive bargaining is to discover the other side's weaknesses and to exploit this to the advantage of the recipient party and to the disadvantage of the disclosing party.

The distributive model emphasises key strategic concepts that shape the interaction between parties:[15]

- The *starting point* is the initial offer or advertised amount at the start of negotiations. One party, perhaps the seller, will have an asking price and the other party, the buyer, will make an initial offer.
- The *anchor point* is the point around which negotiations oscillate. An initial offer or advertised amount will normally anchor negotiations in a way that creates a psychological advantage. However, a strong counter-offer can shift the anchor to the other side.
- The *target point or aspiration* is the price a party ideally wants to pay or receive, creating for them the maximum expected value.
- The *resistance point or reservation price* (walk-away point, or reserve) is the point or price that is the lowest a party will take or highest a party will pay. Parties will be prepared to walk away if negotiations fall outside this resistance point.
- The *zone of potential agreement* is the range between parties' resistance points, or the points at which they are prepared to walk away. These reserves are not disclosed by the parties. Although the actual zone of potential agreement may be narrow, parties negotiate in ignorance of how close or far apart they are in settling upon a price. Competition is

13 See generally Lewicki, Barry and Saunders (n 1) 28–59; Dean R Pruit, *Negotiation Behaviour* (Academic Press, 2013) 71–90; Richard A Luecke and James G Patterson, *How to Become a Better Negotiator* (American Management Association, 2nd ed, 2008).

14 Roger Fisher, William Ury and Bruce Patton, *Getting to Yes: Negotiating Agreement Without Giving In* (Penguin Books, 3rd ed, 2011) 3.

15 See Lewicki, Barry and Saunders (n 1) 34–7.

created by attempts to gauge the price the other party will settle for while aiming to gain as much value as possible.

- The *best alternative to a negotiated agreement* (BATNA) is an assessment of the cost of walking away from a negotiation in the light of other realistic options. The acronym BATNA was coined by Fisher and Ury in their book *Getting to Yes,*[16] although as a strategy, the importance of having an alternative/s to a negotiated outcome was already well known.[17] A negotiator with a strong BATNA can be a 'deal-maker' while one with no BATNA is a likely 'deal-taker'.[18] To know their BATNA, parties will ask themselves: 'What will happen if I don't reach an agreement with the other party?' Parties may also consider the worst alternative to a negotiated agreement (WATNA). To make this assessment, they consider what they would risk if they did not agree. For example, looking to buy a house by auction, a party is best to be prepared to lose the bidding at their resistance point or otherwise they would have to be prepared to pay any amount to succeed. In legal disputes, a BATNA might be litigation and bearing unknown financial and emotional costs. The ability to walk away creates a strong bargaining position. Weighing up the costs of walking away against a workable, if not optimal, agreement is a reasonable expectation and often a necessary strategy.

In situations where price is the focus, additional interests can still matter. A seller or purchaser might prefer to deal with a real estate salesperson who appears trustworthy and considerate of their needs. An ongoing relationship for a time with the seller of a business might be important to the purchaser in order to achieve an optimal handover. Overall, the quality of a product or service, the reliability of the other party and or the importance of a relationship with the other party can be as important as price.

Alexander, Howieson and Fox describe the typical strategies of distributive negotiators as:

- making sure that their opening position leaves them room to make concessions
- making the first offer in order to set the tone for the negotiation ('anchoring')
- possibly waiting for the other side to make the first offer, in order to gauge the other side's position, and whether the other side has undervalued the subject matter or because they themselves are underprepared
- being unwilling to concede on a major issue
- making concessions reluctantly and with great difficulty,
- keeping the other party's expectations low with few and minimal concessions
- making concessions slowly and at long intervals
- making ever-decreasing concessions
- using conditional-linked bargaining where appropriate

16 Roger Fisher and William Ury, *Getting to Yes: Negotiating Agreement Without Giving In* (1983, Penguin Books) 97–106; James K Sebenius, 'What Roger Fisher Got Profoundly Right: Five Enduring Lessons for Negotiators' (2013) 29(2) *Negotiation Journal* 159.

17 See James K Sebenius, 'BATNAs in Negotiation: Common Errors and Three Kinds of "No"' (2017)(April) *Negotiation Journal* 89, for a critique of common conceptions and misconceptions of a BATNA.

18 Luecke (n 5) 21.

- linking concessions to justifications which avoids changes in positions from appearing arbitrary
- avoiding sharing information with the other side until necessary; for example, externally imposed deadlines
- saying no from time to time in order to demonstrate reluctance to move on a particular issue
- not reversing or taking back concessions already made.[19]

The integrative model

The rise of integrative, or interest based, bargaining has tended to suggest that distributive bargaining can be unnecessarily competitive, its tactics sometimes unethical, and its outcomes unsatisfactory.[20] The Integrative Model of negotiation is structured to allow both sides to reach their objectives.[21] Rather than a zero-sum or win–lose game, one party's gain is not necessarily at the other party's expense. The interests uncovered in an integrative process will reveal value attached to those interests. Interests and options are explored so that each party can trade-off the things less important to them for the things they most value. Sometimes described as win–win negotiation, the Integrative Model of negotiation is more likely to produce mutual gains than the Distributive Model. However, parties will not always receive all that they want, and compromise is often a requirement.[22]

The classic example is negotiation over an orange. Using a distributive approach, one party wins the orange and the other party loses; or, at best, the orange is halved – giving each party half of what they want. Using an integrative interest-based approach, the parties explore and identify their respective interests in the orange. The example often used depicts one party wanting the orange rind for cooking and the other wanting the juice for drinking. The parties' interests in the orange differ given their respective needs for the rind and the juice. They can agree to divide the orange according to their interests: one party takes the rind and the other takes the juice. Each is 100 per cent satisfied.

The scholarship and practice of integrative negotiation has developed from Fisher and Ury's model of principled negotiation first published in *Getting to Yes* in 1981.[23] The authors developed their model from a critique of distributive, or positional, bargaining. As their method of principled negotiation is the foundation of much current theory and practice, it is useful to examine their thesis in some detail. Fisher, Ury and Patton argue that positional bargaining, though useful in anchoring a negotiation, is not efficient in producing an agreement (if one is possible) and fails to improve, and may instead damage, the relationship between the parties.[24]

19 Alexander, Howieson and Fox (n 3) 20–3.

20 See David Spencer, *Principles of Dispute Resolution* (Thomson Reuters, Lawbook Co., 2nd ed, 2016) 39–40.

21 See Lewicki, Barry and Saunders (n 1) 60–88.

22 Luecke (n 5) 2.

23 Fisher and Ury (n 16); see also L Susskind and J Cruikshank, *Consensual Approaches to Resolving Public Disputes* (Harper Collins, 1987); cf J White, 'The Pros and Cons of "Getting to Yes"' (1984) 34(1) *Journal of Legal Education* 115.

24 Fisher, Ury and Patton (n 14) 4.

As an alternative to the distributive model, Fisher, Ury and Patton propose a model of integrative or principled negotiation based upon four principles:

1. Separate the people from the problem.
2. Focus on interests, not positions.
3. Invent options for mutual gain.
4. Insist upon using objective criteria.[25]

Separating the people from the problem

Separating the people from the problem means focusing on the issues actually in dispute. In order to isolate those issues, the differing perceptions of the parties need to be heard and acknowledged. Acknowledgement of parties' emotional responses also needs to occur in order for them to focus on the issues at hand. Problems of communication between the parties can be reduced by modelling active listening and using other key communication skills considered in Chapter 2.[26]

Fisher, Ury and Patton remind us that parties are people first: 'They have emotions, deeply held values, and different backgrounds and viewpoints; and they are unpredictable.'[27] As people, parties will tend to prioritise trusting relationships based upon understanding and respect. Relationship problems, according to Fisher, Ury and Patton, are 'people problems' requiring attention to the differing perceptions and emotions and failed communication between parties. Differences can lead to misunderstandings that can fuel prejudice, negative impressions, and rigid responses. Parties may become angry, fearful and hostile as a result. Addressing these misunderstandings and the resultant emotional responses assists parties to focus on the substantive issues at hand, thus separating any negative responses to the other party from the problem confronting both parties.[28]

Focus on interests, not positions

According to Fisher, Ury and Patton's approach, the issues in dispute are not the opposing positions presented by parties. The real issues lie in the dispute between each party's 'needs, desires, concerns, and fears'.[29] These are the motivating factors behind positions, which together make up the parties' interests. Unearthing these interests enables negotiators to seek more widely for solutions. Several positions may in fact be possible as solutions to the interests identified. Shared and compatible interests as well as conflicting interests will lie behind opposing positions.[30]

Invent options for mutual gain

Generating options in integrative negotiation is significantly different from preparing for a determinative process. While legal actions are framed according to legal rights and notions of

25 Ibid 81–94.
26 See also William Ury, *Getting Past No: Negotiating with Difficult People* (Business Books, 1991).
27 Fisher, Ury and Patton (n 14) 19.
28 Ibid 22.
29 Ibid 40.
30 Ibid 42–3.

legal responsibility or fault, integrative negotiators seek options for resolving the conflict that avoid the win–lose of adversarial processes. The emphasis is not on attributing blame and determining compensation. The emphasis is on problem-solving with a view to moving forward to mutually beneficial outcomes for the parties. Fisher, Ury and Patton identify four strategies for inventing options:

1. Separate the act of judging options from inventing them.
2. Broaden the options on the table rather than look for a single answer.
3. Search for mutual gains.
4. Enable the other side to make decisions easily by putting yourself in their shoes.[31]

Insist upon using objective criteria

Insisting upon the use of objective criteria is the fourth goal advanced by Fisher, Ury and Patton in their model of integrative negotiation.[32] Objective, or external, standards can be used to persuade the other side of the fairness of the options presented for management of the dispute. Rather than simply insisting on a demand or position, communicating objective measures of what is fair serves both party's interests because it facilitates dialogue about mutually satisfactory gains. Objective criteria should be independent of each party's will and be legitimate and practical.[33] Examples of external objective criteria include legal precedents, professional standards, scientific standards, industry or company practice, market value, expert opinion, tradition or common practice and community, or moral, standards.[34]

The process of negotiation

In the following discussion, the process of negotiation is examined with particular reference to the Integrative Model. Aspects of the Distributive Model are also considered, as competitive tactics are often used in the final phases of interest-based negotiation. As noted above, the process of negotiation is not prescribed. Generally, however, there are three broad phases: preparation, negotiation, and agreement. Within these phases, there are different approaches and strategies depending on the model primarily adopted and the style of the negotiator. The discussion below is divided according to phases and strategies: preparation, establishing authority to negotiate, understanding one's BATNA, starting the process, establishing an agenda, identifying interests, creating options for mutual gain, developing objective criteria, and the agreement. Finally, reference to the need for effective communication is considered.

31 Ibid 57.
32 Ibid 81–94.
33 Ibid 85.
34 Spencer (n 20) 46.

Preparation

Preparation is critical for effective and successful negotiations. If you are a negotiator representing a party, the preparation must be thorough. Spegel, Rogers and Buckley argue that the goal of preparation is to improve the negotiator's performance by:

- creating an environment for constructive negotiation
- increasing an ability to make measured and considered responses under pressure
- increasing an ability to understand the other side and how they are operating
- enabling informed decisions during and at the completion of the negotiation process.[35]

Preparing a neutral location, or space, is ideal for negotiations. If parties are represented, the negotiators representing them are likely to arrange the meeting place. It is important to relieve tension and to foster a collaborative environment from the beginning. Having refreshments available is a simple but necessary step to signal hospitality and manage any need for refuelling as the process proceeds.

In the preparation phase, negotiators need to manage their party's expectations by reality-testing their initial demands. It is important to explain the process of negotiation to parties to assist them in understanding and following the strategies adopted on their behalf. This information, when communicated to parties, limits the potential for dissatisfaction and the possibility of complaints. Preparation includes identifying the presenting problem or need, exploring your party's interests, researching the possible interests of the other side, and exploring options for agreement through discussion with your party. The presenting problem or need may be a single issue or a more complex cluster of issues that will often include one or more legal issues. Identifying what are important issues and outcomes for your party is critical.[36]

Negotiation

It is preferable to have those with authority to reach agreement at the table. In some circumstances, parties will not want to be in the same room, particularly if animosity is high and certainly if there have been any threats of, or actual physical harm. However, in the absence of any risk, it is good practice to invite parties into the room to encourage them to participate. Luecke identifies advantages in dealing with the person/s able to authorise agreement, including:

- the reasoning of each party is heard directly by those authorised to make decisions
- the benefits of the good relationship built at the negotiating table are likely to be reflected in the agreement and its implementation
- there are fewer chances of disputes or misinterpretation of provisions in any agreement

35 See Spegel, Rogers and Buckley (n 3) 48; Alexander, Howieson and Fox (n 3) 84–103 for a systematic approach to preparation using a negotiation navigation map.

36 Ibid 10.

- if the aim is to persuade the other side to reach an agreement and avoid proceedings, your efforts could be wasted if the other party does not have authority to commit to the agreement.[37]

Understanding one's BATNA

Before actual negotiations begin, it is important to identify when a party is likely to walk away from the table without reaching agreement. A walk-away zone is dependent on a party's BATNA, or alternative to reaching an agreement with the other party. Determining a party's BATNA can be relatively straightforward and is a matter of assessing what options are open if the negotiations should fail. Working out the other side's BATNA is a more difficult task and, in the preparation phase, can only be estimated. During negotiations, it requires careful questioning about what the other side hopes to achieve and what they will do if negotiations fail.[38] Common examples of BATNA's include:

- going to court
- accepting a loss
- discontinuing business or personal relations with the other side
- keeping deposits or goods held
- facing a disciplinary tribunal
- ignoring the dispute and letting it drag on
- seeking another dispute management process.[39]

Spencer suggests the following factors as reliable discussion points for deflating the other side's BATNA during the process:

- Adverse publicity – either as a result of continuing the dispute and litigation if commenced
- Costs – including management and administration costs to run the dispute, legal costs, opportunity costs (the cost of potential business missed while running the dispute) and the net present value of a settlement (the value today may be considerably less than the cost in the future if the matter was to drags on or is litigated)
- Lost time waiting for a hearing date and attending court and or arbitration
- Uncertainty of a judicial or arbitral decision
- Loss of relationship with the other party where this is valued.[40]

Starting the process: introductions

Introductions and opening remarks are important to 'break the ice' and set the tone for constructive dialogue. Simple introductory measures are also used to encourage early

37 Ibid 36.
38 See Spencer (n 20) 44.
39 Ibid.
40 Ibid 45.

engagement. Introductions and small talk can relieve tensions and establish connection. Reflecting the degree of formality (or informality) in the presentation and language of the other side can introduce common ground; or a preferred strategy could be to set the tone of formality for the other side to mirror. Asking for updates about recent progress, or changes, can ease the parties into discussion.[41]

If a distributive, or competitive, approach is used, negotiators will state positions, make initial offers, and even look for concessions in this early phase.[42] Taking the lead at this point is useful if setting the scene for an integrative process. In opening remarks, integrative negotiators can relieve tension by expressing respect for each side's experience and expertise, framing the task positively and as a joint endeavour, and emphasising openness to the other side's interests and concerns.[43] Some competitive posturing may occur. In response, an integrative negotiator would steer the dialogue to a discussion of guidelines about how the process should proceed and by doing so introduce a focus on interests. It can be as simple as one side making the first overture, for example:

> Can we begin by clarifying the process? I suggest that each party outlines their main issues or concerns; I can write up an agenda from that; and then you can discuss each item in turn. From that you should be able to work out the best options available.

Establishing an agenda

The next step after introductions is to set an agenda. An agenda frames discussion and enables each issue to be explored in detail before moving to the next issue. In principle, the more negotiators know about each other's issues and interests through exploring an agenda, the better the quality of solutions that are produced.[44] According to Condliffe, key objectives of formulating an agenda are:

1. providing a visible structure to the session (on a whiteboard or electronic device)
2. reframing the dispute, its content and context into less divisive and provocative terms
3. giving legitimacy and validity to each party's topics and concerns
4. objectifying the dispute so as to enable the parties to 'separate' or distance themselves from the issues
5. reducing the dispute to manageable proportions.[45]

Joint development of an agenda avoids surprises and possible embarrassment for one side if issues have been missed in preparation.[46] An agenda or tentative agenda might be drawn up from communications prior to a meeting and used to structure discussion in the meeting. The

41 Luecke (n 5) 48.

42 Alexander, Howieson and Fox (n 3) 55–60 in which the authors discuss competitive openings and compare these with a problem-solving, cooperative opening.

43 Luecke (n 5) 48.

44 See Alexander, Howieson and Fox (n 3) 66–68 in which the authors discuss exploring hidden agendas.

45 Condliffe (n 5) 246.

46 Lewicki Barry and Saunders (n 1) 135.

party who articulates that agenda could have an advantage in framing the issues. Hence, it can be useful to finalise an agenda at the face-to-face meeting. Framing issues is an important consideration both in setting an agenda, identifying and exploring interests, and generating options. Identifying issues that encompass key concerns for both parties is central to setting an agenda. A neutral yet mutual statement of issues for the agenda reduces apparent bias and facilitates discussion. Framing issues from a problem-solving perspective also shifts the focus away from attributing blame to a more constructive future-focused search for solutions. Framing of the issues is one of five factors identified by Pendergast as important in developing an agenda. The factors he identifies are:

1. The *scope* of discussions: what issues should be canvassed?
2. The *sequence* of discussions: in what order should issues be addressed?
3. The *framing* of issues: how should issues be presented?
4. The *packaging* of issues: whether issues should be considered one at a time or in groupings or as packages?
5. The *formula* to adopt: should agreement on general principles be determined first or is starting with discussion of each issue preferred?[47]

There is no 'right' agenda for any given negotiation. The agenda serves its purpose when the items enable discussion of the issues of concern for the parties and thereby facilitates the parties' communication of interests. The number of issues in a negotiation agenda is one important determinant of whether a Distributive or Integrative Model is adopted.[48] Single issue negotiations lend themselves to a Distributive Model, while a more complex set of issues will suggest use of the Integrative Model.

Identifying interests

Negotiators can rely upon an agreed agenda to frame discussion. In integrative negotiation, the aims are to identify and explore as many **interests** for the parties as are relevant, to identify how these interests are prioritized, and to assess whether they might be complementary, shared, neutral, or conflicting.[49] Understanding the other side's interests in relation to your party's interests assists in shaping options for management and agreement. It is necessary to listen for interests beyond the substantive legal issues. Identifying and exploring interests is dependent upon the use of essential communication skills especially active listening.

Interests: generally are determined by asking not what a person wants but why they want something.

Using an integrative approach, a negotiator assists the party they represent to identify their interests and to prioritise them. Exploring interests and options is part of preparation with a client as well as a phase of the actual negotiation, or the actual interaction and dialogue with the other side. Negotiators need to build in flexibility in identifying interests and options as these can change in the course of the process. Attention should also be given to estimating the other party's interests and how they would prioritise them. The distinction made by Fisher, Ury

47 WR Pendergast, 'Managing the Agenda' (1990) 6(2) *Negotiation Journal* 135.
48 Lewicki, Barry and Saunders (n 1) 121.
49 Ibid 32–3, 68.

and Patton between positions and interests underlies the distinction between distributive and integrative models of negotiation. As noted, the Distributive Model is characterised by stating a position and adhering to that position or making incremental concessions towards a target. In the Integrative Model, the focus shifts to the interests underlying parties' positions in order to open up discussion of those interests and the opportunity to explore options that facilitate mutual gains.

Identifying interests and integrating them into the process of negotiation is perhaps the most influential message from Fisher, Ury and Patton's model. Lewicki, Barry and Saunders identify four types of interests:[50]

1. *Substantive interests*
   Substantive interests are the items of value to be negotiated. These will include the division of resources and price. They may have intrinsic or instrumental value or both. A party may want something because it is intrinsically satisfying and/or because it helps achieve a longer-term goal.
2. *Process, or procedural, interests*
   These are the parties' interests in how the negotiation unfolds. One party may prefer to adopt a distributive approach as someone who likes to 'drive a hard bargain'. Another party may be mostly concerned to have a voice in the negotiations and is less concerned with the detail of the outcome. Process interests can also be intrinsic or instrumental. Having a voice may be satisfying of itself but may also enable participation and input that facilitates agreed outcomes.
3. *Relationship interests*
   Although parties to a negotiation may not have an ongoing relationship, they need to relate to one another through the negotiation process. As Fisher, Ury and Patton argue, a goal of good negotiators is to focus on the problem rather than the people.[51] They recommend that negotiators treat the other side with supportive attention: 'Listen to them with respect, show them courtesy, express your appreciation for their time and effort, emphasise your concern for meeting their basic needs, and so on.'[52] Where the parties are likely to have an ongoing relationship, they may intrinsically value the relationship for the intangible benefits it offers. There may also be instrumental benefits if the relationship continues into the future, such as future business opportunities.
4. *Interests in principle*
   These interests encompass the nature of the relationship between the parties and how they should deal with each other over the issues under negotiation. They may include issues of etiquette and cultural appropriateness. They also extend to broader issues of fairness and justice. As noted by Lewicki, Barry and Saunders: 'Certain principles – concerning what is fair, what is right, what is acceptable, what is ethical, or what has

50 Lewicki, Barry and Saunders (n 1) 80–1; see also Christopher Moore, *The Mediation Process: Practical Strategies for Resolving Conflict* (John Wiley & Sons, 4th ed, 2014) 32, in which the author identifies three kinds of interests: substantive, procedural and relationship (or psychological) interests.

51 Fisher, Ury and Patton (n 14) 54.

52 Ibid 54–5.

been done in the past and should be done in the future – may be deeply held by the parties and serve as the dominant guides to their action.'[53] Interests in principle cut across substantive, procedural and relationship interests.

Parties will usually have more than one type of interest at stake. Parties may also have different types of interests at play and these may change over the course of negotiations.[54] Interests are said to stem from more basic human needs. Scholars refer to Maslow's Hierarchy of Needs (Figure 5.1) as the stimulants for parties' interests.[55] Maslow's typology ranks human needs from the most basic and biological to higher order psychological needs. According to Maslow's hierarchy, people have a primary physiological need for survival, followed by a need for safety and security. Psychological needs for association with a group to provide love and belonging and a need for an individualised identity that promotes self-esteem are higher order needs. Finally, people need opportunities for self-actualisation in order to develop their own sense of morality, creativity, and purpose.[56] A need for financial security, for example, stems from a basic need for survival and safety. A need for recognition and praise stems from the need to maintain self-esteem. Relationship interests point to our need for society. These interests overlap with individual psychological interests and encompass, for example, a need to feel part of a group and a need to gain positive affirmation from members of the group. A need to participate actively in management of a dispute derives from a need for self-actualisation and self-empowerment. Threats to these human needs can cause disputes whether real or perceived.

Figure 5.1 Maslow's Hierarchy of Needs

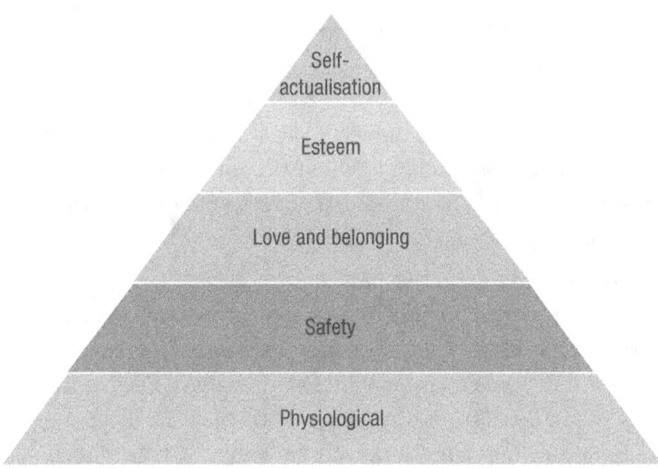

53 Lewicki, Barry and Saunders (n 1) 81.

54 Ibid 81–2.

55 Ibid 81; Laurence Boulle and Nadja Alexander, *Mediation: Skills and Techniques* (LexisNexis Butterworths, 3rd ed, 2020) 95.

56 Abraham H Maslow, 'A Theory of Human Motivation' (1943) 50(4) *Psychological Review* 370.

Exploring interests is a crucial phase for the Integrative Model and depends upon the range and depth of interests relevant to the parties and the skill of negotiators in unearthing them. There are many and varied strategies and tactics used in the face of challenging behaviours.[57] For our purposes, emphasising communication skills to elicit interests provides a core aspect. The work of generating options is assisted by a thorough exploration of issues and interests. Options may be generated during exploration of interests and noted for later discussion. Working through an agenda is useful in signalling the end of discussion about interests and a shift to option generation.

Creating options for mutual gain

Exploring the interests underlying parties' positions allows negotiators to 'expand the pie'. Rather than focusing on resources with a limited value, negotiators can uncover as many interests as possible to add to the pie. In order to satisfy those interests, negotiators search for a wide range of options that can be mutually satisfying. Fisher, Ury and Patton identify four obstacles to inventing a wide range of options:[58]

1. *Premature judgment*
   Judgment can stifle imagination. Creativity will be hampered by evaluating possibilities before they are on the table. Over-cautiousness, fear of disclosing information that might weaken a negotiating position, or feeling uncomfortable in the presence of the other side can inhibit the free flow of communication and ideas.
2. *Searching for a single answer*
   Searching for a single answer is likely to produce an impasse or an end to negotiations. Negotiators need to be firm, but flexible – firm about primary interests and needs, but flexible about how these needs and interests are met.
3. *The assumption of a fixed pie*
   Parties may enter the negotiation with a fixed idea about what they want and without having considered their own or the other side's broader interests. Their assumption can be that there is only one solution they will accept – their reserve – and that any other option misses the point. It is a negotiator's task to open dialogue about broader interests in order to generate alternative solutions.
4. *Thinking that 'solving their problem is their problem'*
   In order to craft a mutually beneficial agreement that meets both parties' needs, each party must consider the interests of the other side. The options generated by one party must not only serve their own interests but also appeal to the self-interests of the other party. It can be difficult for a party who has a significant emotional investment in a dispute and its outcome to detach enough to give attention to the other side's interests. Considering the other side's interests ultimately serves one's own because the aim is to advance one's interests, while at the same time satisfying those of the other side.

57 See, eg, Alexander, Howieson and Fox (n 3) 212–19 on how to handle hardball negotiation tactics.
58 Fisher, Ury and Patton (n 14) 57–8.

Thorough preparation enables negotiators to formulate options before the face-to-face negotiation unfolds. However, the actual discussion may rule out some options and generate others. Negotiators need to be flexible in response to dialogue from each side. Brainstorming options is a strategy emphasised by Fisher, Ury and Patton and affirmed by other scholars and practitioners.[59] Brainstorming involving both parties can be useful once the process has begun and, according to Spencer, should be considered when:

- The negotiation is failing to achieve any agreement
- There is only one option for settlement on the negotiating table, or
- The parties have run out of ideas on any one issue in dispute.[60]

Lewicki, Barry and Saunders recommend that care is taken to separate the people from the problem in option generation,[61] echoing the first of Fisher, Ury and Patton's four principles of negotiation.[62] Commenting on this principle in the context of competitive tactics, Lewicki, Barry and Saunders argue that:

> Because competitive negotiators assume an offensive posture toward the other party, they are unlikely to see the merits of a suggested alternative that comes from that party or appears to favor that party's position. It is often not possible to attack the problem without attacking the person who owns it. For effective problem solving to occur, therefore, negotiators must concentrate on depersonalizing the problem and treating all possible solutions as equally viable, regardless of who initiated them . . . Techniques for generating options that ensure anonymity may minimize the likelihood that interpersonal conflict may escalate.[63]

Spegel, Rogers and Buckley argue that to invent creative options, negotiators need to:

- separate the act of creating options from the act of evaluating them
- focus on options, not solutions
- refrain from dismissing any apparently unrealistic option as it may become a workable idea
- generate a number of options rather than look for a single answer
- search for mutual gains by looking for options that are beneficial to both parties.[64]

Using a white board, flip chart or electronic screen in a joint session to list as many options as possible, ensuring that all participants are engaged, is one technique that can reduce tensions.[65]

59 Ibid 60–3; Lewicki, Barry and Saunders (n 1) 89–90; Condliffe (n 5) 560; Alexander, Howieson and Fox (n 3) 70–1; Spencer (n 20) 43.

60 Spencer (n 20) 43.

61 Lewicki, Barry and Saunders (n 1) 89.

62 Fisher, Ury and Patton (n 14) 17–39.

63 Lewicki, Barry and Saunders (n 1) 89.

64 See Spegel, Rogers and Buckley (n 3) 27; Alexander, Howieson and Fox (n 3) 35–7; 70; Spencer (n 20) 43.

65 See Spencer (n 20) 43.

Developing objective criteria

Objective criteria: refers to facts or information that can be independently verified from another reliable source

Once generated, options can be evaluated using **objective criteria**. Objective criteria can be used to justify positions as well as to search for mutually satisfying options. The difference between the Distributive and Integrative Models becomes apparent when an integrative negotiator is open to reasoned persuasion, while a positional negotiator may not be. Objective criteria can be introduced during discussion of issues and interests as a signal for the evaluation of options later. In preparation, negotiators will identify objective criteria that validate and justify options for their party. They need to be open to reasoned arguments from the other side as to relevant criteria and to negotiate appropriate and acceptable standards. Standards of fairness, for example, vary from individual to individual. Asking the other side directly about how they would measure fairness in the circumstances opens up discussion. Pressure can be brought to bear by bribes, threats, a manipulative appeal to trust, or simply a refusal to budge.[66] 'In all these cases, the principled response is the same: invite them to state their reasoning, suggest objective criteria that you think apply, and refuse to budge except on that basis. Never yield to pressure, only to principle.'[67]

Agreement

The aim of negotiation is primarily to reach agreement, unless it is used as a delaying or obstructive tactic as part of another agenda. Agreement, however, may or might not be reached. If a final agreement is not reached, it may be possible to treat the initial meeting as the first of a series, or to treat items of agreement as tentative until further negotiations are held.[68] Where agreement is reached, it may be informally acknowledged by a nod, a handshake, verbal utterance, or a few written notes.[69] Constructing a written agreement provides proof of its terms and can be useful in future implementation or if further disputes arises.

Establishing effective communication

In all negotiations, effective communication is essential, as is emphasised throughout this textbook. Negotiations occur via phone, in writing (including email), using digital media – for example, Skype or Zoom – or in-person. Each requires attention to the advantages and challenges of these different mediums.[70] More than one meeting, whether face-to-face or by other means, can be required. The quality and appropriateness of communication will be crucial.[71] Unlike competitive processes, integrative negotiation encourages a free flow of information. Practical attention to establishing and maintaining effective communication is critical to the success of negotiation and can be facilitated by establishing:

- clearly defined contact points
- clearly defined levels of delegated authority

66 Ibid 91.
67 Ibid.
68 Alexander, Howieson and Fox (n 3) 77–8; Condliffe (n 5) 141.
69 Alexander, Howieson and Fox (n 3) 78–9; Condliffe (n 5) 143.
70 See Alexander, Howieson and Fox (n 3) 99–101 for a comparison of these methods.
71 See Chapter 2.

- systems for the flow of information such as email, fax, surface mail and others
- reporting mechanisms
- clearly defined meeting agendas and templates for minutes and other key documents
- an agreement not to speak about the negotiation to others including the media
- clearly defined action lists for tasks to be completed during the negotiation and for implementation of any resulting agreement
- any other simple but effective system that will facilitate the negotiation.[72]

Using negotiation knowledge to assist in dispute management

Case examples are considered in the following section. Examples of both party-to-party negotiations (case example 1) and those involving dispute practitioners representing parties (case examples 2 and 3) are used as case studies for the purposes of discussion. Each case example is analysed by identifying possible interests and options of the parties and applying key aspects of the Distributive and Integrative Models.

Case example 1 – A dyadic distributive negotiation: Jacob's job application

Case study

Jacob is a qualified solicitor with five years' experience. He responds to an advertisement for a senior solicitor with at least five years' experience with the firm of AA Legal Services on the Gold Coast. The advertisement states that the salary for the position is 'by negotiation'. He attends for an interview with a panel of the three partners in the firm and is later called to a meeting with the managing partner, Edward Langley.

At the meeting, Edward begins by thanking Jacob for coming, praises his application and interview with the partners, and tells him that the firm is happy to offer him the position. Jacob thanks him and says that he is delighted to be offered the position. Edward goes on to say: 'Now to the question of salary . . .'. Edward has been instructed by his partners to offer no more than $180,000 to Jacob and to preferably put him on for around $170,000.

Edward tells Jacob that the firm are prepared to pay him $150,000 per annum. Jacob is momentarily startled as he has been earning $200,000 per annum in Sydney. Jacob thanks Edward and tells him that he is very experienced and would be an asset to the firm, as he and the other partners are aware. He tells Edward that his current salary is $200,000 per annum and that he hopes the firm would be willing to pay what he is worth.

Jacob is moving to the Gold Coast to be near his parents who are now elderly. He knows that salaries in the major cities are higher and that costs are lower in regional areas. He would rather work for a smaller firm and avoid the very long hours he has worked in Sydney. He

72 Spencer (n 20) 47.

would prefer a salary of $190,000, as he is prepared to take a cut but won't accept anything below $175,000. Any less and he will look for a position in another firm.[73]

Discussion

The starting point, advertised price, or initial offer are concepts that can be applied to the beginning of negotiation between the parties (Jacob and Edward). The initial offer in this scenario is Edward's offer of $150,000. Jacob's counteroffer is his asking price at $200,000. These starting points from each side anchor subsequent offers and counteroffers. Typically, parties will continue negotiations within this range. An anchor point creates a psychological reference point for subsequent negotiation.[74] Edward creates a psychological advantage by making a first offer that is well below Jacob's asking price. Edward runs the risk that Jacob will walk away, but he also places him in a position where he needs to establish his worth if he wants the job at a higher salary.

The Firm					**Jacob**
Reserve	Target point	Initial offer	Asking price	Target point	Reserve
$180,000	$170,000	$150,000	$200,000	$190,000	$175,000

As the hirer, the firm's preferred salary of $170,000 is the target point – the point at which they would like to conclude negotiations. For Jacob, that target point is $190,000. The target point is also referred to as a party's 'aspiration point'. The salary point that Edward will not exceed, $180,000, is the firm's 'resistance point' or reservation price ('reserve', in a sale). From Jacob's perspective, the resistance point is the lowest salary he will accept at $175,000.[75]

While price will be a significant consideration in establishing a resistance point, whether a party walks away from negotiations is also determined by their BATNA. If Jacob needed to secure a position quickly because he had already given up his job in Sydney and needed the income, his bargaining position would be much weaker than if he was still employed in Sydney and did not need to be with his parents immediately. However, if Jacob simply needed whatever job he could get, having no alternative to Edward's initial offer, he might accept that offer. Basing his reservation price on other opportunities for a position on the Gold Coast will only be realistic if he has done his research and established that other suitable positions are available or could become available within a realistic timeframe. The firm's position would be strong if they did not need to fill the position quickly, but weaker if they did.

Parties should establish their own BATNA, but will generally not be aware of the others party's BATNA. Asking questions during the negotiation might help to gain insight. In addition, each party can research the position of the other as best they can. Prior to his meeting with

73 Adapted from Lewicki, Barry and Saunders (n 1) 34–6.

74 Luecke and Patterson (n 13) 72; Najung Kim and Hun-Joon Park, 'Making the Most of the First-Offer Advantage: Pre-Offer Conversation and Negotiation Outcomes' (2017) 33 (2) *Negotiation Journal* 153, provides an in-depth study of the anchoring effect of first offers.

75 See Sally Blount White and Margaret A Neale, 'Reservation Prices, Resistance Points, and BATNAs: Determining the Parameters of Acceptable Negotiated Outcomes' (1991)(October) *Negotiation Journal* 379.

Edward, Jacob could, for example, learn about AA Legal Services by contacting sources within the industry, checking relevant business/professional publications, reviewing any annual reports, asking questions of other employees informally, and imagining what the firm might need and prefer in a senior practitioner.[76]

The parties need to establish their starting, target, resistance points, and BATNA before negotiating. As they make concessions through the process of bargaining, parties typically give up the margin between starting and target points and come into the zone of potential agreement. The resistance point (reserve or walk-away point) is kept secret.[77] The challenge for a party or their negotiator is to gauge how much to ask or how little to offer before the other side walks away. The zone of potential agreement is the price range within which an agreement will satisfy both parties. The difference between the initial offer from Edward and Jacob's asking price is $50,000, which might suggest that agreement is unlikely. The zone of potential agreement between Edward and Jacob is actually very narrow: between $175,000 and $180,000. This zone, however, is not known to the parties because they do not know each other's reserve price. This non-disclosure creates and fuels competition between the parties.

The Firm's reserve	**Zone of Potential Agreement (ZOPA)**	**Jacob's reserve**
$180,000	← →	$175,000

It is worth noting that agreements have been found to frequently occur within 20 per cent of the anchor point, which here is Edward's initial offer of $150,000.[78] If the parties were aware of this pattern, they could calculate that 20 per cent above Edward's offer and 20 per cent below Jacob's offer will bring them to the zone of agreement. However, this pattern is not guaranteed and is therefore a gamble. Whether either party would break off negotiations after the initial exchange or later may well depend on their BATNA or WATNA.

Case example 2 – A dyadic integrative negotiation: Naomi's maternity leave dilemma

Case study

Naomi is a third-year solicitor at AA Legal Services law firm. Naomi started work with the firm 10 years ago as a law clerk. She studied law part-time online while she worked full-time with AA Legal Services. The partners were accommodating when it came to her exams, enabling her to take her annual leave beforehand to study and giving her time off to sit the exams. But she never missed a day at work unless she was sick. It took her 10 years to complete her degree and she was able to complete her practical legal training with the firm.

AA Legal Services is a small general law firm with three partners – Edward Langley, Joseph Langley, and Debra Keyes. Joseph is Edward's father and the founder of the practice. He is

76 Luecke (n 5) 18–19.
77 Lewicki, Barry and Saunders (n 1) 34–5.
78 Spegel, Rogers and Buckley (n 3) 35.

72 years of age and now works part-time, mainly in commercial matters. Edward is the managing partner and looks after general law matters, while Debra is a specialist family lawyer.

As a law clerk, Naomi worked on conveyancing and family law. Since qualifying as a legal practitioner, she has worked almost exclusively with Debra Keyes.

Naomi is pregnant with her first child and about to go on maternity leave. She had planned to take 20 weeks' leave – 2 weeks paid provided by the firm, and 18 weeks provided under the Paid Parental Leave Scheme at the minimum wage. She is thinking now that she will take the 12 months' unpaid parental leave entitlement under the National Employment Standards. She has worked out that she and her partner can manage with the first 20 weeks paid. She is tired and disappointed with a lack of support and positive acknowledgement from the partners in recent years. She plans to return to work part-time.

Naomi has asked to speak to Edward about her maternity leave several times. Each time he has been too busy and has delayed their meeting. Naomi has now requested a meeting formally by email, copied to the other partners.

Edward is aware that the firm needs to consider Naomi's maternity leave. Edward is not in favour of the Paid Parental Leave Scheme. He thinks it puts an unnecessary strain on the public purse. He has looked up the firm's parental leave policy and remembers that the two weeks was added when they needed to include something for a quality audit some years ago. He wonders what Debra's view will be. He's sure his father won't want Naomi away for too long. He feels that Naomi is placing a strain on the business at a particularly challenging time.

Discussion

Naomi's attempts to engage Edward in negotiation about her maternity leave provide a useful example of the impact of emotions on negotiation. Here, Naomi is feeling 'tired and disappointed' and frustrated by Edward's failure to address the issue. Despite negotiators' attempts to separate the people for the problem, emotions can run high in bargaining, particularly where a dispute has triggered negotiations. Fisher, Ury and Patton suggest that emotions should be made explicit and acknowledged as legitimate because: 'Emotions may quickly bring a negotiation to an impasse or an end.'[79] They also suggest that negotiators should not react to emotional outbursts but allow the other side to let off steam.[80] In addition, Spencer argues that many disputes arise from a lack of, or from mistaken, communication.[81] Negotiators therefore need to address potential communication problems during the process. Fisher, Ury and Patton identify three key communication problems: when parties are not speaking directly and clearly to one another, when parties may be speaking but not being heard by each other, and when parties may misunderstand or misinterpret the messages from the other side. Active listening is a core negotiation skill employed to prevent such problems.[82]

In separating the people from the problem, consider Naomi and Edward's contrasting perceptions (Table 5.1).

Parties may perceive the other side as a potential 'enemy' when competing for rights or resources. As a result, parties may quickly see the other side in a negative light, attributing opposing attitudes and values to them with possibly limited or no evidence. In our example,

79 Ibid 29.
80 Ibid 29–32.
81 Spencer (n 20) 46.
82 Fisher, Ury and Patton (n 14) 32–6. See also Chapter 2.

Table 5.1 Perceptions of the parties

Naomi	Edward
He doesn't understand what it's like for women.	I had no idea Naomi wanted children. I thought she was a career woman.
Parental leave in this industry is terrible. Two weeks' pay is ridiculous.	I don't think the firm can afford maternity leave.
I've worked here faithfully for 15 years. One year to look after my child at a cost of two weeks' pay is the least they can do.	We can't be expected to replace her for 12 months and keep her job open.
I'm entitled to return part-time.	Part-time work just won't work.

Naomi believes that Edward has little or no understanding of women and work, and that she is entitled and deserving of more adequate leave. Edward is concerned about financial and staffing issues and has apparently misconstrued Naomi as a 'career woman' with no interest in having a family. He sees her request for leave as a strain on the firm's resources despite her entitlements. These differences could escalate into angry emotional exchanges fuelled by poor communication. Separating the people from the problem is a pragmatic, dispassionate approach that seeks to isolate the problem, or issue, at hand from the personalised perceptions and responses of the people involved. Here, the issue is maternity leave and whether and how it can be accommodated by the firm. What the parties think or presume about each other is not central to the issue but can 'muddy the waters' if unchecked.

According to Maslow's Hierarchy of Needs, Naomi has a need for positive reinforcement from the firm, which she feels is lacking. We are told that she is tired and disappointed. If Edward uncovered this need, he might affirm her value to the firm, acknowledge her contribution over time, and assist her to plan her future contribution. Doing this might encourage her to return from maternity leave in less than 12 months.

Legal practitioners typically analyse situations in terms of legal issues, or questions about whether a fact situation establishes the elements of a legal cause of action. Negotiators need to expand their analysis to incorporate interests and needs, and possible options for satisfying them. In this way, issues are more broadly defined and become reflected in an agenda for the negotiation.

Naomi's substantive interest is in parental leave and a return to part-time work in order to achieve her goal of having a family and being able to care for her child. Edward, on behalf of the firm, will be interested in adequate staffing levels and the cost of replacements in the short or long term in order to ensure the stability of the firm.

Naomi's process interests may include wanting to voice her sense of the inadequacy of parental leave entitlements offered by the firm, her sense of currently being undervalued, and her wish to combine work and family moving ahead. At the same time, her interest in the details of her leave and return to work could be over-riding. Her position with the firm and her dependency on it could encourage an interest-based approach and would depend upon Edward's receptiveness to that approach. Naomi may not want to jeopardise her position with the firm by using a competitive approach. If Edward adopts a Distributive Model, he could miss the opportunity to understand Naomi's needs and to consider options that could be of mutual gain.

Naomi and the firm's ongoing relationship would figure strongly as relationship interests in the negotiation for parental leave and a return to part-time work. Naomi may see an advantage in continuing with the firm after the birth of her child, combining parenthood with accustomed work and a familiar work environment, despite any reservations she has about Edward's attitudes. Edward may value Naomi's 15 years' experience with the firm and the working knowledge she has acquired, the positive relationships she has developed with partners and other staff, and her enduring relationships with clients.

Naomi's interests in principle may include a fervent desire to be a parent and a positive attitude to parental leave entitlements. As a legal professional, she may expect AA Legal Services to conform to the community standards articulated via the Paid Parental Leave Scheme. Edward, on the other hand, may have a firm belief that parenthood ought to be self-funded and be more concerned with efficiencies for the firm.

To achieve a mutually beneficial solution, Naomi and Edward would need to be open to exploring options that include considering each other's interests. Naomi may be willing to walk away from her position with the firm if optimal parental leave is not granted. At the same time, if she leads with a demand for 12 months' leave without considering the impact on the firm, she may alienate Edward and cut off consideration of alternatives. If Edward does not acknowledge Naomi's interest in having a family, he might alienate Naomi and lead her to insist upon her statutory entitlements.

If the parties resort to distributive, or positional, tactics, the result will essentially be a clash of wills. Outcomes will be dependent upon the relative negotiating positions of the parties – in other words, their bargaining power. Parties may resort to power plays – intimidation, threats and other 'dirty' tactics – in order to insist upon what they want. The relative positions of the parties may leave one with very little alternative beyond accepting the other party's position. In Naomi's case, Edward is in a superior bargaining position given his power to hire and fire. Naomi would have access to remedies for unfair dismissal if Edward terminated her employment or forced her to resign (constructive dismissal). However, she is likely to be interested in maintaining her position and a positive working relationship with Edward and the firm. Rather than insisting upon her right to parental leave and remaining fixed about her plans, a more productive approach would be to base her request on objective community standards in relation to parental leave.

Fisher, Ury and Patton advise negotiators to commit to reaching a solution based upon principles rather than pressure.[83] They suggest: 'Concentrate on the merits of the problem, not the mettle of the parties. Be open to reason but closed to threats.'[84] Pressure can take various forms, including a bribe, a threat, a manipulative appeal to trust, or a single refusal to budge.[85] Looking to objective standards for resolving a problem moves the process away from each party trying to force the other to back down. The process can be shifted from distributive negotiation to a search for objective criteria. Reasoned and reasonable dialogue can be introduced about what standards are applicable and how they apply in the given situation. These standards, once accepted, can be applied independently of the will of the parties. Standards of fairness, efficiency, scientific understanding, industry-based best practice, market value, and precedents are examples.

In Naomi's case, her request can be framed by reference to the 12 months' unpaid leave provided under the National Employment Standards,[86] acknowledgement of the two weeks'

83 Ibid 83.

84 Ibid.

85 Ibid 91.

86 *Fair Work Act 2009* (Cth) ss 67–70, 76, 85.

paid leave offered by the firm, and the introduction of paid parental leave.[87] At the same time, her request should be couched in terms that acknowledge the firm's interest in a stable workforce. To that end, Naomi's request could include statements of her interest in remaining with the firm, of her ongoing commitment to the firm, and a willingness to work with Edward to reach mutually beneficial arrangements. Naomi might be able to predict that Edward would not want to accommodate her return to part-time work. Acknowledging the firm's interests and her past and future commitment to those interests could encourage Edward to be open to her return part-time. She might also be able to refer to her positive relationships with clients that could encourage or assure future business. Naomi may ultimately refer to legal precedents that indicate that, although a return to part-time work is not an entitlement, enabling it would avoid a claim of sex discrimination.[88] Distributive, or competitive, bargaining may still be used as an element of integrative negotiations and, in this case, particularly in the end stages where the focus becomes commitment to detailed terms of any agreement.

Case example 3 – Triadic composite integrative/distributive negotiation: Olivia's workplace

Olivia was employed with the firm of AA Legal Services for about 18 months. She worked as a senior solicitor with Joseph Langley in commercial litigation. When she started work at AA Legal Services, she found the partners welcoming and supportive but soon found that the volume of work meant that she had little contact with either Debra or Edward. As Joseph worked only part-time, three days per week, Olivia found that her case load became increasingly heavy.

Olivia was happy to work hard but was finding that Joseph wasn't pulling his weight. He would delegate work to her under his supervision but seemed disinterested in the progress of files and at times became confused about matters and where they were heading. More concerning for Olivia was his increasing attentions to her.

In the first few months of her employment with the firm, Joseph asked her inappropriate questions about her 'love life' and made other comments of a sexual nature. He later sent her sexually explicit emails that she found offensive. She approached Edward Langley with her concerns. He suggested that emails were probably sent as a joke and that the particular remarks she complained about were really very innocent.

At the last workplace function, Joseph tried to flirt with Olivia, made excuses to try to touch her, asked her how far up her body her tights went and told her she was beautiful while pressing his crotch against her thigh. Olivia was so distressed by this behaviour that she called in sick to work. She has sought help from her doctor, who referred her to a psychologist for counselling. She has been off work for six weeks and is afraid to return.

Preparation for negotiation to assist Olivia and Edward requires first checking that each party has authority to negotiate. Olivia would expect Edward Langley, as the managing partner, to negotiate on behalf of the firm. Olivia's negotiator would need to find out whether Edward

87 *Paid Parental Leave Act 2010* (Cth).

88 See *Hickie v Hunt & Hunt* [1998] HREOCA 8.

was authorised to make decisions for the firm or whether a possible agreement would need to be vetted by Debra Keyes and Joseph Langley. In Olivia's case, the presenting problem is sexual harassment. Using a Distributive Model of negotiation, a settlement figure would be a primary concern. Olivia's negotiator, most likely a lawyer, would begin by sending the firm a letter of demand which identifies the substance of her claim[89] and the amount she is seeking in settlement. This amount will anchor further '**without prejudice**' negotiations or preclude them if too far outside the firm's settlement range, if the firm is willing to negotiate at all. In a distributive approach, offer and counter-offer are exchanged as a contest between the parties. Leverage is sought by referring to the strength and credibility of the claim or lack thereof. Each party measures their willingness to agree against their BATNA – which in this case, is likely to be determinative court proceedings. In an Integrative Model, by contrast, preparation requires negotiators to look further than the legal claim alone and to consider the wider interests of both parties.

Without prejudice: refers to a legal privilege attached to communications that are used in negotiation of a settlement. 'Without prejudice' communications are inadmissible in a court.

In preparation, parties would consider identifying their interests and BATNAs; assessment of the other side's interests and BATNA; and establishing relevant objective criteria.[90]

Possible interests for Olivia and AA Legal Services are outlined as follows.

Substantive interests

Olivia:

- Acknowledgement of the alleged sexual harassment.
- Compensation for her 'injury'.
- Compensation for loss of earnings.
- Avoiding a protracted and costly process.
- Maintaining her reputation as a lawyer.
- Ongoing employment (with the firm or elsewhere).

AA Legal Services:

- Avoiding any public knowledge of Olivia's claim.
- Maintaining the reputation of the firm.
- Maintaining the reputation of Joseph Langley.
- Ensuring that Joseph Langley's cases are in order and there is no risk of professional liability.
- Addressing any problems in Joseph Langley's capacity to work.
- Avoiding any further legal action and minimising any pay-out and costs.

89 See *Sex Discrimination Act 1984* (Cth) as a backdrop to the negotiations.

90 See Sourdin (n 7) 59–60; David Spencer et al, *Dispute Resolution in Australia: Cases, Commentary and Materials* (Thomson Reuters, 4th ed, 2018) [3.60]–[3.100] for an introduction to the Harvard Project Seven Element Preparation Model.

Relationship interests

Olivia:

- Gaining acknowledgement from the firm's partners as to the difficulties she has experienced and the injury she has suffered: an apology from the partners?
- Gaining acknowledgement from the firm that Joseph is problematic and may be suffering confusion.
- Repair of her relationship with the firm: a return to work plan?

AA Legal Services:

- Repairing their relationship with Olivia in order to safeguard their reputation with other firms.
- Encouraging Olivia's return to work: Altering the work environment to enable this?

In preparation, negotiators can consider what might be the interests of the parties in the circumstances, based upon a reasoned assessment and past experience in related matters. Care needs to be taken, however, not to make assumptions about the parties' interests. Possibilities need to be confirmed with the party represented and the other party in the course of negotiations.

Process interests

In this example, the parties may tend to use distributive or integrative processes at work, which may produce an expectation that those approaches will be used by their negotiators. Negotiators for each party are well advised to communicate their strategies to their party in order to assist parties to follow the process. Research or past experience with a negotiator acting for the other side will enable a negotiator to gauge what tactics are likely to be used and to prepare accordingly. Where one negotiator prefers an integrative approach and the other a distributive approach, the former must be prepared to redirect negotiations by introducing discussion of interests as well as positions. The interests of the parties may dictate the approach used. If Olivia's primary goal is to return to work, her negotiator must be prepared to introduce dialogue about this interest with the other side and to help each party consider as many options as possible to fulfil that goal.

Interests in principle

Interests in principle may be particularly important to Olivia in this example. Her sense of being aggrieved by Joseph's behaviour, and the threat to her employment as a result, may offend her sense of justice. From Olivia's perspective, she may see justice in enabling her to return to work at the expense of Joseph's current role within the firm. Edward, however, might envisage Olivia's return to work as a reminder of his father's apparent fall from grace. He is likely to demonstrate an allegiance to his father and the firm. He may be most concerned to protect the reputation and economic viability of the firm. However, he may be open to options including Olivia's return to work if he can be assured of her loyalty to the firm and confidentiality about Joseph's behaviour.

To prioritise the interests suggested, the negotiator should ask Olivia what her priorities are in order to confirm or amend the negotiator's assessment. If Olivia's priority is a return to work, this would be her main goal. Her interests in this goal could be maintaining her reputation and position with the firm. Consider Maslow's Hierarchy of Needs for Olivia: these could include a need for a stable income; a need to maintain local connections for her children's schooling; a desire to remain on the Gold Coast where opportunities or alternative employment may be limited, but where she has developed strong work and social connections; and a desire to continue with the firm in order to further develop her existing investment in the work of the firm. Underlying her interest in maintaining her reputation as a lawyer is a need to maintain self-esteem often challenged by harassment from others, and as a precondition of her economic security.

A priority for the firm could be safeguarding its reputation and avoiding a scandal. Underlying Edward's allegiance to his father and the firm are his needs to ensure the firm's economic viability and status. Edward may give priority to protecting his father. The other partner, Debra Keyes, would have a similar interest in the firm's reputation and ongoing viability. She may have less allegiance to Joseph Langley and her approach might be helpful in encouraging a dispassionate view or, in other words, of separating the person from the problem.

The interests suggested for Olivia and AA Legal Services are possibilities that may change and certainly evolve as the process proceeds. Identifying interests assists negotiators to craft the negotiation according to their party's goals. Concluding a creative agreement is of no use if it does not meet the parties' interests and needs. Having identified interests, the next step is to generate options. Table 5.2 identifies a range of options open to Olivia, keeping in mind her interests and needs.

Table 5.2 Olivia's possible options

Olivia's options	Interests	Needs
Return to work	Employment/investment in the firm	Financial security Family and social
Ensuring safety at work	Employment/investment in the firm	Safety
Compensation for 'injury' caused	Acknowledgement of the problem and her experience	Self-esteem
Compensation for loss of earnings while 'on leave'	Fairness	Financial
Apology from Joseph/the firm	Acknowledgement of the problem and her experience/relationship with the firm	Self-esteem

If the firm decides that they do not want Olivia to return to work, her options are significantly reduced. Much may depend on the partners' assessment of her contribution to the firm thus far, a point that Olivia will want to bring to their attention in a positive light. The partners will also want to assess the value of her projected future contribution weighed against any difficulties they foresee in her return to work, such as arrangements to ensure her safety and what that means for Joseph's future role with the firm. Table 5.3 suggests possible options for AA Legal Services.

Table 5.3 AA Legal Services' possible options

The firm's options	Interests	Needs
Enabling Olivia's return to work including ensuring safety at work	Compliance with external quality standards including WH&S/ensuring stability of staff and contribution from Olivia	Professional esteem for the firm/ affirmation of integrity
Providing compensation for the 'injury' caused/and or loss of earnings	Avoiding a claim for sexual harassment	Financial and reputational security
Discouraging Olivia's return to work/ offering a settlement on termination wit confidentiality clause	Avoiding a claim and ensuring confidentiality	Financial and reputational security/closure

Establishing the limits of the negotiation consists of determining an aspiration level for a party, a walk-away zone (or reservation price), and a BATNA.[91] Olivia's aspiration level is her optimal outcome, her target. Here, her best outcome would be a return to work, with changes made to ensure her safety, compensation for loss of earnings while 'on leave', some compensation for the injury she perceives that she suffered, and an apology from Joseph and the firm. Notice that this should be distinguished as an optimal outcome and not a likely outcome. Negotiators will emphasise the need for compromise to a represented party. Notice also that, in this example, an amount of compensation for injury would need to be calculated as a reserve price.

The walk-away zone should be realistic and well considered.[92] Would Olivia, for example, choose to walk away if a return to work is not an option for AA Legal Services? Would she walk away if she could return to work, but without changes being made to ensure her safety? Would she abandon negotiations if there was no acknowledgement of her experience either in the form of compensation or an apology? Improving one's BATNA[93] and or deflating the other side's BATNA are strategies often used. For example, Olivia can be encouraged to consider alternatives if a return to work is not an option for the firm or if the terms of her return to work are unacceptable to the firm. One alternative might be an application to the Human Rights Commission if she finds the firm is unwilling to acknowledge her experience and to provide some amelioration. Attempting to deflate the other side's BATNA will be useful where negotiations are flagging or at the end stages of an integrative or more competitive process.

The firm's ability, or power, to refuse Olivia's return to work, places it in a strong bargaining position, given her interest in returning. That interest may change over the course of negotiations depending upon the firm's response to her perceived experience of injury. A negative, unyielding response may prompt Olivia to consider alternative options and to place more reliance on a BATNA that involves initiating proceedings. Avoiding proceedings would,

91 Spegel, Rogers and Buckley (n 3) 57–8; see also Luecke (n 5) 34–6.
92 Spegel, Rogers and Buckley (n 3) 57.
93 Ibid.

however, remain dependent on an acceptable settlement figure. Olivia's ability, or power, to damage the firm's reputation by making her grievance public improves her relative bargaining position.

The need to consider interests and options for both parties in the preparatory phase has been emphasised in this example of Olivia's dispute with AA Legal Services. A useful checklist of considerations includes:

- Do your best to identify and prioritise the interests of the other party.
- Consider what options might meet the other party's interests.
- Talk to the party about their impressions of the other side.
- Put yourself in the shoes of the other negotiator and prepare the negotiation from that perspective.[94]

In Olivia's case, the legal framework prohibiting sexual harassment is relevant for providing objective criteria for assessment of the parties' options. Given Olivia's interest in returning to work, the issue could be more broadly approached as one of expectations of behaviour at work and workplace health and safety regulations. Olivia's negotiator could introduce discussion around the firm's workplace policy and procedures encompassing workplace, health and safety, anti-discrimination, and sexual harassment. Acknowledgment of sexual harassment as a significant community problem could be mentioned in order to introduce the issue without insisting upon an admission of responsibility. When and if compensation is discussed, legal precedent can inform the negotiation as to what could be a fair settlement.

Positives and negatives of negotiation

Positives

As an alternative to litigation, negotiation is a dispute management option that provides the parties with the opportunity to craft their own agreement to manage their dispute either in a direct party-to-party dyadic manner or with the assistance of a negotiator in a triadic process. Parties avoid the imposition of a decision by a court, which will be limited to determination of the legal issues and will conclude with a finding in favour of one party or the other. Pre-trial negotiations can resemble the adversarial court process, but also offer the opportunity for an integrative process or one that combines integrative and distributive elements. Parties have more control of the process, either directly or through their representatives, given their ability to identify and explore issues and articulate the terms of any agreement. Using an interest-based process, parties are able to tell their stories and identify their own particular interests and concerns in addition to the legal issues in dispute. Parties are more likely to adhere to the terms of any agreement when they have canvassed all of the relevant issues and agreed to their own solution. Although parties may not be assured of everything they want, they have the opportunity for mutual gain and satisfaction. Finally, even if no agreement is reached, the parties

94 Ibid 61.

have the opportunity to identify and narrow the issues in dispute in preparation for further dispute management options.[95]

Negatives

Negotiating with the other party may not be the best option in some circumstances. We have noted that preparation is critical. If a party is not prepared, negotiation should be delayed or avoided. Sufficient time to explore issues and options is needed to avoid hasty errors of judgment. If sufficient time is not available, other options should be considered. If there is a significant difference in bargaining power between the parties so that one party has little or no real options, negotiation can be inadvisable. A weaker party could lose ground rather than gain anything by exposure to a highly competitive, distributive negotiation where the other party is well resourced and has relatively little to lose. Where unethical practices have led to a dispute and or unethical demands are being made, negotiating a mutually satisfactory outcome may be unlikely. Parties must be willing to reach agreement for the process to be effective. If either side is very resistant and or fails to act in good faith, negotiation is unlikely to be successful.[96]

Special considerations

Three select issues in negotiation are considered in the following section: dealing with issues of power, dealing with impasses, and dealing with difficult tactics.

Issues of power

A criticism of Fisher, Ury and Patton's model of principled negotiation is that it fails to account for imbalances of bargaining **power** between the parties.[97] Where one party is in an apparently stronger bargaining position, the impetus for that party to adopt an integrative problem-solving approach may be obviated. More powerful parties 'tend to aim higher: they tend to concede less and demand more, and they are more likely to do better in terms of outcome than the less powerful negotiators.'[98] Disparities of power across a spectrum of forms and sources can significantly impact outcomes.[99] The perception of power can be as important and as effective as any actuality.[100]

Power: the capacity to influence another or an outcome in a manner that suits the power-holder.

In simple terms, power is the capacity to make things happen. Power also connotes an ability to control what happens. In the context of dispute management, power is manifested as the ability to make decisions and to control outcomes. However, the ability to control

95 See Spencer (n 20) 29–30.

96 See Lewicki, Barry and Saunders (n 1) 7 citing JC Levinson et al, *Guerilla Negotiating: Unconventional Weapons and Tactics to Get What You Want* (John Wiley, 1999).

97 Condliffe (n 5) 217.

98 Alexander, Howieson and Fox (n 3) 144.

99 See Robert Adler and Elliot Silverstein, 'When David Meets Goliath: Dealing with Power Differentials in Negotiations' (2000) 5 *Harvard Negotiation Law Review* 1.

100 Ibid; see also Laurence Boulle and Nadja Alexander, *Mediation – Skills and Techniques* (Lexis Nexis, 3rd ed, 2020) 312.

outcomes without consideration of others precludes any real negotiation between those involved. Negotiation presumes some measure of interdependency of the parties, purposeful communication around issues at stake, and eventual compromise to some degree in order to reach agreement. Power in these circumstances is more aptly characterised as an ability to persuade,[101] or the power of persuasion, rather than an ability to control outcomes.[102] Alexander, Howieson and Fox advocate a constructive use of power, arguing that negotiators 'can use their power to create momentum for constructive negotiations, or they can use it to prevent co-operation'.[103] Research has found that a significant factor in achieving negotiated agreements and in facilitating integrative outcomes is the parties' experience of procedural fairness during the process.[104] In other words, where parties engage in a negotiation that encourages equal participation and mutual trust and respect, rather than the dominance of one party over the other, agreements are more likely to result and are more likely to be mutually beneficial.

A significant power differential in negotiation will be signalled by the parties' respective BATNAs. A party with superior resources may be able and willing, for example, to pursue expensive court proceedings or look to an alternative buyer or supplier if a proposed settlement is not favourable. Power plays can, however, be more subtle and interspersed through the various phases of negotiation. Wade[105] identifies a series of power tactics used in negotiation and mediation that demonstrate a range of manoeuvres used by parties in practice. According to Wade, the last four of the selection reproduced below are the most persuasive in practice when skilfully applied (though not necessarily advocated).

Being aware of the possibility of power plays in negotiation is an important part of preparation. Strategies in response include:

1. *Building in protections*
   Parties on the receiving end of power plays can remember their resistance point, or bottom line, while taking care to be open to creative options that may serve their interests in ways they had not considered.
2. *Being mindful of one's BATNA*
   Parties should be clear about their BATNA before beginning negotiations but also reassess this alternative as the negotiation progresses. Making a strong BATNA known to the other party and/or challenging the strength of their BATNA can counter power plays.[106]
3. *Correct the power imbalance*
   In the absence of a high-power party's transfer of power to the other side or a low-power party taking power (both rare in negotiations), referring the dispute to a third-party intervenor, through mediation, arbitration or litigation is an option.

---

101 Alexander, Howieson and Fox (n 3) 145.

102 See William Ury, 'The Five Ps of Persuasion: Roger Fisher's Approach to Influence' (2013) 29(4) *Negotiation Journal* 133.

103 Alexander, Howieson and Fox (n 3) 146.

104 Rebecca Hollander-Blumoff and Tom R Tyler, 'Procedural Justice in Negotiation: Procedural Fairness, Outcome Acceptance, and Integrative Potential' (2008) 33(2) *Law & Social Inquiry* 473.

105 John Wade, 'Persuasion in Negotiation and Mediation' (2008) 8(2) *Queensland University of Technology Law and Justice Journal* 253, 263–4.

106 Lewicki, Barry and Saunders (n 1) 508–10 citing Fisher, Ury and Patton (n 14).

Table 5.4 Types of power[107]

Type of power	Example
1. Experience and insider knowledge	'I negotiate every day; I know the tricks; and I know how things are done in this industry'
2. Persistence	'I will wear you out'
3. Emotional	'You are depressed and easily rattled: I am calm'
4. Risk-taking	'I am willing to take chances – with litigation, or finding an alternative supplier'
5. Status quo	'I have the status quo (possession of the business, children, job, mine); you have the burden of changing that status quo'
6. Scorched earth	'I don't care what happens; you can't hurt me; I have nothing to lose; my fall-back position is to burn everything'
7. Information	'I have vital information about . . . (bank accounts; manufacturing process; customer lists; judicial hobbyhorses etc) – you don't'
8. Expert	'My experts have more credibility; more experience in answering difficult questions . . . etc than yours'
9. Persuasion	'I am more articulate, charismatic, polite, multi-lingual, charming . . . than you'
10. Resource	'I have more expensive, faithful and aggressive lawyers/friends/valuers/ psychologists. I can spend more time and money on the dispute. I will drown you in paper'
11. Rights	'The "law", company policy, patterns of precedent, common behaviours of decision-makers, give me a stronger fall-back position'
12. Attractiveness	'My negotiators are more attractive, well-dressed and credible than yours'
13. Violence	'We know where you and your friends live; I cannot restrain my over-zealous relatives'
14. Structural	'This dispute will be decided or enforced in X jurisdiction where the bosses/ judges are accessible/cheap/honest/vigilant/independent *or* vice versa'
15. Confidence	'I am confident and nothing you say can sway me'
16. Humiliation	'I have the moral high ground and the approval of our cultural peers. You will be ridiculed'
17. Wild irrationality	'I (or my client) am angry, stupid and depressed: reason will not touch me' (variant of good cop-bad cop routine)
18. Time rich	'I have nothing else to do, but to continue this dispute for the rest of my/your life.'
19. Preparation	'I am organised, logical, equipped with graphs and summaries. You are a disorganised babbler'
20. Detail	'I am a detail person; you speak in vague generalities and with vague memory'
21. Association	'I have powerful allies/tribes (with whom you will have to trade)'
22. Publicity	'You fear publicity; I love any kind of publicity'
23. Skeletons-in-closets	'I will not tell them, but what if the police, customs, tax office, your spouse, social security etc find out about X'

107 Wade (n 105) 264.

Table 5.4 (cont.)

Type of power	Example
24. Alternative fall-back	'If you do not agree, then I have several alternative (suppliers, subcontractors)'
25. Future relationship	'If you are helpful now, I will be considerate, polite, generous in future dealings. If not . . . (or vice versa)'
26. Reciprocity	'You owe me, look at what I have already done for you.' 'I gave up my career, now it is your turn'

Power is differently constructed according to modernist and post-modernist perspectives, which are addressed further in Chapter 6 on mediation. Scholarly accounts of forms and sources of power are also considered in that chapter.[108]

Dealing with impasses

Impasse: when negotiating parties are deadlocked and unable to move forward to reach agreement.

An **impasse** occurs when negotiating parties become deadlocked and unable to move forward to reach agreement. An impasse may be genuine or tactical. A genuine impasse occurs when one or more parties believe that they are unable to move forward without sacrificing something important to them and feel unable to proceed.[109] A tactical impasse may occur where a party deliberately refuses to proceed in order to pressure the other party to make concessions.[110]

An impasse may also occur when one or both parties are inadequately prepared causing a stalemate; where the parties exhibit fundamental value differences on the issues at stake; where a party or parties are unable or unwilling to effectively engage in the process due to an experience of conflict avoidance or escalating anger and or fear;[111] or where mistakes are made by negotiators which increase the likelihood of an impasse. The best approach is to avoid an impasse by avoiding mistakes that could lead to one. Mistakes made by negotiators that have the potential to cause impasses include:[112]

1. *Neglecting the other party's problem*
   Negotiators who fail to consider the other party's interests will fail to craft an agreement that satisfies both parties' interests and can expect resistance from the other party. Agreement 'requires understanding and addressing your counterpart's problem as a means to solving your own'.[113]

108 See Chapter 6; Bernard S Mayer, 'The Dynamics of Power in Mediation' (1987) 16(Summer) *Mediation Quarterly* 75; Christopher Moore, *The Mediation Process: Practical Strategies for Resolving Conflict* (John Wiley & Sons, 4th ed, 2014).

109 Bernard S Mayer, *The Dynamics of Conflict: A Guide to Engagement and Intervention* (Wiley, 2nd ed, 2012) 171.

110 Ibid.

111 Lewicki, Barry and Saunders (n 1) 475–82.

112 James K Sebenius, 'Six Habits of Merely Effective Negotiators' (2001) 79 (4) *Harvard Business Review* 87.

113 Ibid 88.

2. *Focusing too much on price*
   While price will matter, an overemphasis will exclude important non-tangible interests that could lead to a stalemate. Significant non-tangible interests can include goodwill and shared expectations, a respectful fair process, and a positive working relationship.
3. *Prioritising positions over interests*
   Negotiators who claim value early and aggressively may cut off the potential for dialogue around interests, leading to an impasse.
4. *Looking for common ground at the expense of differences*
   Although common ground facilitates mutual understanding of interests, differences in those interests enable the parties to fashion creative exchanges. Different interests can give each party what they value most with minimum cost to the other party.
5. *Neglecting BATNAs*
   A strong BATNA is an important negotiating tool as it sets the threshold of an acceptable exchange. 'A BATNA may involve walking away, prolonging a stalemate, approaching another potential buyer, making something in-house rather than procuring it externally, going to court rather than settling, forming a different alliance, or going on strike.'[114] Being clear about when to walk away can produce leverage to achieve the most desirable result. Focusing on tactics to achieve a potential deal without keeping this threshold in mind can lead to a sudden impasse when negotiations are moving below a party's BATNA.
6. *Failing to correct errors of perception*
   According to Sebenius, negotiators can exhibit biased perceptions which, if not corrected, can lead to entrenched positions and possible stalemates.[115] These biases can be minimised by being aware of attitudes and reality testing. Sebenius identifies two forms of biased perception:
   - Role bias – which is exhibited by interpretation of information in strongly self-serving ways and can result in an exaggerated view of what can be achieved in negotiation. For example, parties with widely divergent views about what is achievable in an out-of-court settlement are unlikely to reach agreement.
   - Partisan perceptions – which are evident when negotiators vilify their opponents, while seeing themselves and their clients in a positive light.

Lewicki, Barry and Saunders identify several strategies to avoid and resolve impasses.[116] They suggest: coming to agreement on rules and procedures; reducing tension by active listening and separation of the parties if need be; improving the accuracy of information gathering and exchange; controlling the number and size of issues for discussion; establishing a measure of common ground where the parties can find a basis for agreement; and enhancing the desirability of options by, for example, advancing a proposal that the other party is likely to accept and offering 'sweeteners' rather than relying on threats.[117]

114 Ibid 90.
115 Ibid 92–3.
116 Lewicki, Barry and Saunders (n 1) 485.
117 Ibid 485–501; see also Alexander, Howieson and Fox (n 3) 222–34.

Dealing with difficult tactics

Impasses can arise when 'bad' tactics are used. Power plays represent some of the difficult tactics that parties can use in negotiation. Typically, difficult tactics are those used in distributive negotiations. Such tactics can raise ethical issues around good faith and honesty.[118] Some are identified here.

Bluff and threats

Generally, this tactic requires more than one negotiator. One negotiator 'presents a tough opening position, punctuated with threats, obnoxious behavior, and intransigence'.[119] This negotiator may leave the room on some pretence to enable the other negotiator to present as more amenable in an attempt to reach a quick agreement and thus avoid any more pressure for the other party. Alternatively, the tough negotiator might only speak when discussions are heading in an unwanted direction, leaving the amenable negotiator to participate when things are heading in the direction wanted. Although somewhat transparent, this tactic can be effective. It can be countered by naming it, possibly with humour, to refocus the dialogue.

Low ball/high ball (or good cop/bad cop)

Using this tactic, a negotiation will begin with a wildly unreasonable low (or high) initial offer that could never be achieved. The intent is that the extreme beginning offer will prompt the other side to re-evaluate their own opening offer and move closer to or beyond their resistance point. The risk in using this tactic is that the other party will withdraw immediately. A useful response is not to counter-offer, but rather to ask for a more reasonable opening offer from the other party, thus avoiding being anchored by the initial extreme proposal.[120]

Subterfuge/red herrings

This tactic is a ploy in which a negotiator pretends that an issue or item is of importance to them, when in fact it is not, in order to later trade it while appearing to make a significant concession. The tactic can backfire if the other party asks for concessions on other issues or items in order to give the first party what the subterfuge represents, making it difficult for the first party to refuse and redirect. Careful preparation and keen attention to the negotiation as it unfolds can reveal a red herring. If one party takes an unexpected position to begin with and or reverses a position well into the negotiations, it may signal that a subterfuge is in play. A useful tactical response is to ask the other party why their approach has changed and to limit concessions in view of the change.[121]

---

118 Lewicki, Barry and Saunders (n 1) 503–19; Alexander, Howieson and Fox (n 3) 212–22 in which the authors include a discussion of ethics and the impact of provisions under the *Australian Consumer Law*; Condliffe (n 5) 102–12 in which the author examines psychological and positional pressure tactics and 'verbal jujitsu' and advances an approach in response dubbed STAR (STop, Attend, Reframe).

119 Lewicki, Barry and Saunders (n 1) 63.

120 See, eg, RJ Lewicki and RJ Robinson, 'Ethical and Unethical Bargaining Tactics: An Empirical Study' (1998) 17(6) *Journal of Business Ethics* 665.

121 See also JP Gaspar and M Schweitzer, 'Confident and Cunning: Negotiator Self-Efficacy Promotes Deception in Negotiations' (2019) *Journal of Business Ethics* 1. See also Roger Fisher, 'A Code of Negotiation Practices for Lawyers' (1985)(April) *Negotiation Journal* 105; Carrie Menkel-Meadow and Michael Wheeler (eds), *What's Fair: Ethics for Negotiators* (Jossey-Bass, 2004).

Aggressive behaviour

Negotiators can use aggressive behaviour to push their position and attack the other side's position. Relentlessly insisting upon concessions, questioning the other side's proposals and pushing for agreement can produce significant pressure on the other side to concede. Aggressive behaviour may reach the intensity of intimidation when one party deliberately uses anger or attempts to instill fear in the other party (referring to breaches of policies, procedures or the law) in order to reach the outcome they want. A negotiator may gesture towards a lack of good faith or breach of trust in order to evoke fear or guilt in the other party and incline them to reach decisions based on emotional rather that objective considerations. A useful response to aggressive tactics or intimidation is to interrupt the negotiations and attempt to reach agreement on the process itself. Ground rules that preclude aggressive behaviour and focus on interests and needs can be communicated to the other side and established as a prerequisite for further dialogue.

Conclusion

Negotiation is a dispute management process involving two or more parties who come together to discuss issues is dispute and work toward an agreed outcome. Negotiation may occur directly between parties (dyadic) or may be assisted by dispute management practitioners (triadic) as agents for the parties. There are two dominant models of negotiation: the Distributive Model and the Integrative Model. These models are associated with positional bargaining on the one hand, and interest-based bargaining on the other. The Distributive Model is characterised by a competitive approach in which the parties compete over resources. The Integrative Model is described as a 'win–win' process in which emphasis is given to uncovering as many interests each party has beyond, but related to, the items or issues in dispute. For example, a dispute about compensation could be widened to include interests in reputation and avoiding lengthy and costly determinative processes. Adding to the pool of value to be negotiated enables each party to obtain what they most value with minimal cost to the other side. Parties will trade what is of least value to them with a view to obtaining what they value most.

There has been a trend away from distributive negotiation in dispute management since the work of Fisher and Ury, in *Getting to Yes*. Fisher and Ury developed a model of integrative negotiation that has become the foundation for integrative negotiation practice. The principles have been demonstrated in application through the case studies provided in this chapter. As a central step in the process, dispute practitioners will assist parties to identify as many relevant interests as possible. Types of interests include substantive, relationship and process interests, and interests in principle. Once interests are identified, as many options as possible are considered in order to produce optimal results for both parties. In practice, elements of both integrative and distributive bargaining tend to be used in all negotiations. Once interests and options are identified and canvassed, the process may become more competitive as parties trade interests in order to advance their own. Negotiation is a very flexible and versatile dispute management process, and it can be used informally and in a less structured manner than in other dispute management processes. Preparation is crucial in order to identify interests and options and to research and gauge the likely approach of the other side. Negotiation is also a well-established process in its own right but can be a part of many other dispute processes. For example, as noted in Chapter 6, mediation is sometimes referred to as a 'facilitated negotiation'. However, a key difference between mediation and negotiation is that a negotiator will suggest options with the authority of the party whom they represent and, in the classic model of facilitated mediation, the mediator does not provide options but instead encourages parties to suggest their own possibilities. Negotiation is also a preliminary step in determinative processes and has the advantage of enabling parties to reach mutually agreed outcomes that satisfy as wide a range of interests as possible.

EXERCISE IN APPLYING YOUR KNOWLEDGE – *JAKE V AA LEGAL SERVICES*

Jake is a law clerk, who has worked for AA Legal Services for the past five years. Jake has been assigned to work with Debra Keyes for the past nine months. He has been working with Debra in family law matters. He was previously working with Edward Langley on commercial law matters. He brought his experience in contract, bankruptcy and insolvency, succession planning and business matters generally to Debra's files. His work was well received prior to working with Debra.

Jake is 30 years of age and single. He is tall and heavy set with a tendency to be overweight. He is partial to Krispy Crème donuts. He presents as even tempered and easy going while conscientious, capable and with an eye for detail. He is not athletic or interested in going to a gym. His hobbies include computer games and online chess.

Debra is 45 years of age with 20 years of experience in family law. She is an accredited Family Law Specialist. Debra is always immaculately dressed, presents as capable and efficient, moves at a quick pace, and is known as an aggressive competitor in her field. Debra is an avid sportswoman. She runs to keep fit and is involved in local rowing and basketball teams. She is married with two children, both of whom are involved in sports.

Jake felt that Debra's attitude toward him was ambiguous from the beginning. She would grunt with appreciation when his research revealed something useful, but would frequently frown at him and comment on his appearance, saying, for example: 'Have you heard the phrase "Dress to Impress", Jake?'; 'Do you think you could comb your hair before you come to work?'; 'Would a proper shave [Jake was sporting a beard] and hair cut be too much to ask?'

Jake took the hint and tried to look more corporate. Debra responded by drawing attention to his eating habits with such comments as: 'Seriously, that food will rot your guts'; 'You can't eat those donuts without getting fat!'

Subsequently, Debra began to exclude Jake from contact with clients. He would usually follow up on the telephone and occasionally interview clients by phone on Debra's behalf. Debra would ask another law clerk, Sandra, to follow up in person for her. He found that files were being redirected to Sandra without notice to him. Debra was also asking him to follow up on more routine matters at an ever-increasing pace that left him feeling overwhelmed. Jake approached Edward Langley to express his concern. Edward told him: 'You need to shape up, Jake. Debra does things her way and you need to follow her lead.' Jake discovered from Sandra that Debra had been very critical of his work and had described him as: 'That fat, unhealthy computer nerd.' Jake had begun to feel undermined and anxious. His anxiety led to mistakes. Recently, Debra had scolded him almost hysterically when he allegedly missed a date for filing, saying: 'Your days here are numbered!' Jake insists that the relevant file had been moved to Sandra.

Jake has taken time off on 'stress leave'. He has lodged an application to Work Cover for work-related injury. He has been assessed by a medical practitioner as having a work-related stress condition. He has been referred for psychological assessment. He comes to you for assistance in negotiating with the firm. He wants to retain his job with AA Legal Services and to be reassigned away from Debra Keyes.

1. Describe in detail how would you proceed in negotiations on Jake's behalf with AA Legal Services.
2. What sort of opening remarks would you use in the negotiation?
3. What agenda would you construct for Jake's negotiation?

6 MEDIATION

Learning aims

- Explain how mediation operates as a method to manage disputes
- Demonstrate knowledge of the key characteristics of mediation
- Explain the principles guiding mediation practice
- Describe the differing models of mediation practice
- Demonstrate understanding of the steps in a facilitative mediation process
- Demonstrate a critical awareness of issues in mediation theory and practice
- Identify advantages and disadvantages of mediation for the management of disputes

Understanding mediation

Mediation is a triadic dispute management process involving a third party, the mediator, who assists parties in dispute to reach an agreement to, as far as possible, resolve their dispute. Mediation can be undertaken voluntarily, under a court order, or as a term of an existing contractual agreement. The Law Council of Australia, in its ethical guidelines for mediators, defines mediation as:

Mediation: a non-determinative dispute management process in which a mediator assists parties in dispute to reach an agreement to manage their dispute.

> ... a process in which an impartial person – a mediator – facilitates the resolution of a dispute by promoting uncoerced agreement by the parties to the dispute. A mediator facilitates communication, promotes understanding, assists the parties to identify their needs and interests, and uses creative problem solving techniques to enable the parties to reach their own agreement.[1]

According to the classic facilitative model, a mediator does not decide the outcome of a dispute. Nor does the mediator give advice on how the dispute could be managed if litigated. According to the National Alternative Dispute Resolution Advisory Council (NADRAC) (now ADRAC):[2]

> The mediator has no advisory or determinative role in regard to the content of the dispute or the outcome of its resolution, but may advise on or determine the process of mediation whereby resolution is attempted.[3]

However, blended models which include elements of advice and evaluation are now recognised in the National Mediator Accreditation System (NMAS) 2015.[4] As a preliminary step in the process of litigation, mediation:

> ... is a process in which parties to litigation are encouraged to resolve their differences, with the assistance of a trained mediator, and with the advice of independent lawyers.

1 Law Council of Australia, *Ethical Guidelines for Mediators* (2019) 3.

2 Australian Dispute Resolution Advisory Council (Web Page) <https://www.adrac.org.au/>.

3 National Alternative Dispute Resolution Advisory Council, *Dispute Resolution Terms: The Use of Terms in (Alternative) Dispute Resolution* (2003) <https://f77b663a-db93-4dd8-823d-909937839d69.filesusr.com/ugd/34f2d0_fc316a9a1bf0418eaa7211406ca292e2.pdf>.

4 *National Mediator Accreditation System* (NMAS) Part III, 10 <https://msb.org.au/themes/msb/assets/documents/national-mediator-accreditation-system-2015.pdf>; see also the discussion of advisory and evaluative models in this chapter.

> There is no compulsion on any party to agree to any proposed settlement. Even in a court-ordered mediation a party may decline even to negotiate. A mediation can have no binding effect other than by the agreement of the parties.[5]

A central principle of mediation is promotion of the self-determination of the participants. Self-determination is promoted by providing the parties with an opportunity to reach their own agreement in order to address their dispute. This principle is reflected in the definition of mediation provider under the NMAS.[6]

Mediation is the most common form of dispute management process used. Its modern development arose in order to provide greater access to justice by offering a timely and cost-effective option over litigation.[7] Mediation gained prominence as central to the Alternative Dispute Resolution (ADR) movement. With the growth of other options to manage disputes, mediation became one of a range of 'Additional' or 'Appropriate' Dispute Resolution (ADR) options.[8] More recently, the identifying language has shifted to 'Dispute Resolution', or as in this textbook, 'Dispute Management', which encompasses litigation and the full range of processes, of which mediation remains prominent. This is in recognition that dispute processes no longer sit as a counterpoint to litigation, but rather there is a continuum of processes available to manage disputes.

Mediation has similarities with processes of dispute management adopted by traditional cultures, including Indigenous Australian societies.[9] It developed as a community response to issues of access to justice in the 1970s.[10] Since that time, it has become institutionalised within our justice system, often legislated for and appearing as a process preliminary to determinative processes and outcomes.[11] Early development saw mediation and other processes of dispute management, such as conciliation,[12] annexed or connected to court processes. This development challenged the voluntary nature of mediation, which was an early defining feature.[13] Now mediation and other processes of dispute management are central components of civil litigation processes.[14] Parties may be directed or encouraged to attend mediation in order to attempt management of their dispute, including to more clearly identify the issues in dispute,

---

5 *Liprini v McIntyre* [2019] NSWSC 355, [116] (Simpson AJA).

6 *National Mediator Accreditation System: Practice Standards*, Part III, 2.2 <https://msb.org.au/themes/msb/assets/documents/national-mediator-accreditation-system-2015.pdf>

7 Access to justice issues have been more recently addressed by the growth of online dispute management processes: see Chapter 3.

8 David Spencer, *Principles of Dispute Resolution* (Lawbook Co, 2nd ed, 2016) 3–4.

9 See Chapter 1 and Chapter 3; L Behrendt, *Aboriginal Dispute Resolution* (Federation Press, 1995); National Australian Dispute Resolution Advisory Council, *Indigenous Dispute Resolution and Conflict Management* (2006).

10 See Access to Justice Advisory Committee, *Access to Justice: An Action Plan* (1994) (Sackville Report); for an historical account of mediation in Australia see Chapter 3; Wendy Faulkes, 'The Modern Development of Alternative Dispute Resolution in Australia' (2020) 30(3) *Australasian Dispute Resolution Journal* 234.

11 See *Civil Dispute Resolution Act 2011* (Cth) s 4; National Australian Dispute Resolution Advisory Committee, *The Resolve to Resolve: Embracing ADR to Improve Access to Justice in the Federal Jurisdiction: A Report to the Attorney-General* (2009), which recommended that legislation require that parties take genuine steps to resolve a dispute before commencement of any and all court proceedings, including with the use of mediation; Tina Popa, 'All the Way with ADR: Further Endorsement of ADR in Litigation' (2015) 26(4) *Australasian Dispute Resolution Journal* 218.

12 See Chapter 8.

13 Laurence Boulle, *Mediation: Principles, Process, Practice* (LexisNexis, Butterworths, 3rd ed, 2011) 559–612.

14 See *Civil Dispute Resolution Act 2011* (Cth) s 4.

before returning to court, if needed, for a determination.[15] Mediation has also developed as a key dispute management process in select statutory schemes. Prominent among these are mediation in family law matters, native title, farm debt disputes and workers compensation.[16] While attendance at mediation may be compulsory according to legal case management processes, parties can still choose whether to genuinely and actively participate.[17]

Mediation has developed over time from a fusion of influences from law and the socio-behavioural sciences. It is a process that has been described as occurring 'in the shadow of the law'[18] and more recently described as occurring in the shadow of 'folk law' or the law that people access and understand from online sources, friends and family and social media.[19] A focus on management of disputes that might otherwise be subjected to determinative processes, gives mediation its legal character. As mediation has become increasingly institutionalised, it has become increasingly a core component of legal processes. Mediation has also been significantly influenced by the behavioural sciences and theories of conflict and communication emanating from those disciplines. It has developed as a skills-based practice with ongoing theoretical critique. Although increasingly applied in the context of legal disputes, mediation has developed with significant influences from the caring professions of social work and psychology.

As a profession, mediation and mediators are not subject to statutory regulation. The varying applications of mediation under statutory schemes have their own requirements. Mediation and mediators are self-regulated in Australia under the National Mediator Accreditation System (NMAS), which was introduced in 2008 and revised in 2015.[20] Accreditation of mediators is a voluntary scheme administered by the Mediator Standards Board (MSB). The MSB is responsible for the development of mediator standards and implementation of the NMAS. The MSB approves recognised mediator accreditation bodies (RMABs), which include relevant professional associations; for example, the Resolution Institute and the Australian Mediation Association. Accreditation under the NMAS is encouraged for dispute practitioners who employ mediation in their practice. As accreditation certifies adherence to established standards of practice, parties are well advised to determine if their mediator is accredited.

Using theory and models to dissect mediation

This section is in two parts. The first part considers theoretical principles that are core features of mediation and is followed in the second part by an examination of differing models.

15 See Nadja Alexander, 'Mediation on Trial: Ten Verdicts on Court-Related ADR' (2004) 22(1) *Law in Context* 8.

16 See Chapter 12; Boulle (n 13) 404–54; Melissa Hanks, 'Perspectives on Mandatory Mediation' (2012) 35 (3) *University of New South Wales Law Journal* 929; Vicki Waye, 'Mandatory Mediation in Australia's Civil Justice System' (2016) 45(2–3) *Common Law World Review* 214.

17 Cf Joshua Taylor, 'It is Time to Abolish the 'genuine effort' and 'non-genuine effort': Certificates in Family Dispute Resolution' (2019) 33(1) *Australian Journal of Family Law* 29.

18 Chapter 3, 101; Robert H Mnookin and Lewis Kornhauser, 'Bargaining in the Shadow of the Law: The Case of Divorce' (1979) 88(5) *Yale Law Journal* 950.

19 Jonathan Crowe et al, 'Bargaining in the Shadow of the Folk Law: Expanding the Concept of the Shadow of the Law in Family Dispute Resolution' (2018) 40 (3) *Sydney Law Review* 319.

20 The National Mediator Accreditation Standards (NMAS) is available at <https://msb.org.au/themes/msb/assets/documents/national-mediator-accreditation-system-2015>.

Theoretical principles of mediation

Core theoretical principles of mediation are examined in this part. Those identified are taken from the NMAS and discussed under headings of confidentiality, voluntariness, self-determination, impartiality and procedural fairness.

Confidentiality in mediation

Confidentiality in mediation is regarded as a core principle that enables parties to be honest and candid in disclosing their interests, needs and concerns in an environment where it is safe to do so.[21]

Confidentiality in mediation means that both the parties and the mediator will treat the matters discussed as confidential, subject only to legal requirements external to the mediation. This is normally aided by the fact that the process occurs in private, with attendance by only the mediator and parties and any representatives or support persons acting on behalf of and agreed as between the parties.

Mediators will stress the confidentiality of the process during preliminary intake meetings with parties and during the introductory phase. They will often indicate that no record of the details discussed will be kept. Confidentiality will be stressed at other stages of the mediation, particularly before and after private sessions with each party. Private sessions will normally occur before the negotiation stage and enable parties to speak frankly to the mediator about possible offers and allow the mediator to reality test those possibilities with each party. Confidentiality is claimed to encourage settlements because it allows parties the opportunity for full and frank disclosure leading to more satisfactory agreements between them.

In limited circumstances, a mediator may be required to disclose the content of mediation as, for example, when a threat of imminent harm is made. For the parties, confidentiality in mediation is analogous to 'without prejudice' settlement negotiation privilege.[22] Parties may be asked to sign an agreement to mediate before mediation, which would normally contain confidentiality and privilege clauses.

Voluntariness

A key philosophy underpinning dispute processes, and mediation in particular, as noted in Chapter 3, is the parties' willingness to volunteer to mediate a dispute. This is an important feature of facilitative mediation. However, other models such as evaluative mediation may or may not rely on the parties' voluntary involvement. As mediation has been embraced by the courts and legal system, it has now become an almost standard requirement that parties trial a mediation process before they can utilise a third-party neutral in a determinative process. This

21 See Chapter 3, 82; Boulle (n 13) 673; Dominik Leimgruber, 'Confidentiality, Public Interest and the Mediator's Ethical Dilemma' (2013) 24(3) *Australasian Dispute Resolution Journal* 187; Joe Harman, 'Mediation Confidentiality: Origins, Application and Exceptions and Practical Implications' (2017) 28(2) *Australasian Dispute Resolution Journal* 106. *National Mediator Accredication System: Practice Standards* Part III, 9 https://msb.org.au/themes/msb/assets/documents/national-mediator-accreditation-system-2015.pdf.

22 *789TEN v Westpac Banking Corporation* [2004] NSWSC 594; *Field v Commissioner for Railways for New South Wales* (1957) 99 CLR 285, 291–29; see David Spencer, Lise Barry and Lola Akin Ojelabi, *Dispute Resolution in Australia: Cases, Commentary and Materials* (Thomson Reuters, 4th ed, 2018) [14.05]–[14.100], for a discussion of evidential privileges founded in confidentiality.

is often referred to as court-mandated mediation requiring compulsory attendance.[23] However, once the parties attend, they can choose how they engage. While cost consequences may apply if parties do not embrace the process, many parties find that having attended they experience benefit and choose to voluntarily engage. Given the increased reality of court-mandated mediation, the philosophy of voluntariness has moved from a question of choice as to whether to use the process to a choice of whether to fully engage once the process commences.

Self-determination

Self-determination is a core principle of mediation and synonymous with empowerment of the parties.[24] It is not defined in the NMAS but is reflected in the NMAS definition of mediation[25]. It is consistent with the character of mediation as a form of dispute management which has the central aim of assisting parties to reach their own solutions. Self-determination has long been acknowledged as a central principle of practice in Australia and overseas.[26] Lichtenstein defines self-determination as 'the individual's right and ability to make decisions and take actions to follow those decisions through'.[27] A focus on decision-making is evident in the Model Standards for Mediators used in the USA. According to that system:

> Self-determination is the act of coming to a voluntary, uncoerced decision in which each party makes free and informed choices as to process and outcome. Parties may exercise self-determination at any stage of a mediation, including mediator selection, process design, participation in or withdrawal from the process, and outcomes.[28]

A further and more nuanced understanding can be drawn from **self-determination theory** (SDT), a theory of psychological needs.[29] According to SDT, individuals have basic psychological needs that need to be fulfilled for optimal growth and well-being. These basic needs are identified as needs for autonomy, competence, and relatedness, which apply throughout the life cycle. They are also considered to be universal across cultures. Autonomy refers to an individual's experience of

Self-determination theory: an individual's need for autonomy, competence and relatedness.

23 See Jacqueline Durand, 'The Institutionalization of Mediation and its Effect on Unrepresented Parties: Is Justice Really the Goal of Court-mandated Mediation?' (2016) 29(4) *Georgetown Journal of Legal Ethics* 973; Rhain Buth, 'Zombie Mediations' (2015) 26(2) *Australasian Dispute Resolution Journal* 104.

24 See Chapter 3.

25 NMAS (n 6).

26 See, eg, Boulle (n 13) 65–7; Dale Bagshaw, 'Mediating Family Disputes in Statutory Settings' (1995) 48(4) *Australian Social Work* 4; J Coben, 'Gollum meet Smeagol: A Schizophrenic Rumination on Mediator Values Beyond Self-determination and Neutrality' (2004) 5(2) *Cardoza Journal of Conflict Resolution* 65; Nancy Welsh, 'The Thinning Vision of Self-determination in Court–Connected Mediation: The Inevitable Price of Institutionalization?' (2001) 6 *Harvard Negotiation Law Review* 1. In the NMAS 2008, mediation was described in clause 2(6) as 'essentially a process that maximizes the self determination of the participants'.

27 M Lichtenstein, 'Mediation and Feminism: Common Values and Challenges' (2000) 18(1) *Mediation Quarterly* 19.

28 American Arbitration Association, American Bar Association, and Association for Conflict Resolution, *Model Standards of Conduct for Mediators* (2005) Standard 1: <https://www.americanbar.org/content/dam/aba/migrated/2011_build/dispute_resolution/model_standards_conduct_april2007.authcheckdam.pdf>.

29 Edward L Deci and Richard M Ryan, 'Self-determination Theory' in Paul AM Van Lange, Arie W Kruglanski and E Tory Higgins (eds), *Handbook of Theories of Social Psychology* (Sage, 2012) vol 1, 416–36.

choice and volition and to a sense of integrity in making and demonstrating those choices. Competence is the sense of confidence and effectiveness in bringing about desired outcomes. Relatedness refers to a sense of closeness and connection in one's interactions with others.[30] SDT extends Maslow's theory of a hierarchy of essential human needs,[31] often referred to as underlying the parties' interests in negotiation.[32] Since assisting the parties to negotiate with each other is central to mediation, extending analysis of interests and needs using SDT is useful in conceptualising self-determination. However, an application of SDT to practice requires ongoing research.[33]

The importance that mediators place upon self-determination in practice has been evidenced in an empirical study by Douglas, which supports a relational understanding of neutrality and self-determination mediated by a postmodern understanding of power.[34] Field identifies self-determination as a core principle for ethical mediation practice.[35] Drawing on the work of Welsh in the United States, Cooper and Field identify mediation as furthering self-determination by providing opportunities for parties to:

* actively and directly participate in the communication and negotiation processes
* choose and control the substantive norms that will guide their decision-making
* create the options for settlement; and
* control the final decision regarding whether or not to settle and the terms of settlement.[36]

As a socio-legal concept, self-determination derives from a modernist view of people as autonomous individuals who are self-determining when they are able to exercise their autonomy.[37] Self-determination is, and has long been, a core principle for social work practice.[38] A related concept in law is consensuality, which emphasises informed consent and presumes the capacity of individuals to reach their own decisions. SDT, constructions of self-determination in social work, and consensuality in law rely upon a view of individuals as autonomous, self-interested, rational and motivated to fulfil their individual needs. Although SDT acknowledges an individual's need for relatedness, its emphasis is on the individual's satisfaction of his/her needs rather than relatedness, or relationships, as such. Relationships

30 Marina Milyavskaya and Richard Koestner, 'Psychological Needs, Motivation, and Well-being: A Test of Self-determination Theory Across Multiple Domains' (2011) 50(3) *Personality and Individual Differences* 387.

31 Abraham H Maslow, 'A Theory of Human Motivation (1943) 50(4) *Psychological Review* 370.

32 See Chapter 5.

33 See Alysoun Boyle, 'Self-Determination, Empowerment, and Empathy in Mediation: Rehumanising Mediation's Effectiveness' (2020) 15 *Newcastle Law Review* 5.

34 Susan Douglas, 'Neutrality in Mediation: A Study of Mediator Perceptions' (2008) 8(1) *Queensland University of Technology Law and Justice Journal* 139.

35 Rachael Field, 'Rethinking Mediation Ethics: A Contextual Method to Support Part Self-determination' (2011) 22(1) *Australasian Dispute Resolution Journal* 8, 9.

36 Donna Cooper and Rachael Field, 'The Family Dispute Resolution of Parenting Matters in Australia: An Analysis of the Notion of an "Independent' Practitioner"' (2008) 8(1) *Queensland University of Technology Law and Justice Journal* 158, 165 citing Welsh (n 26) 3.

37 Paul Spicker, 'Social Work and Self-determination' (1990) 20(3) *British Journal of Social Work* 221, 222; Dorothy J Della Noce, Robert A Baruch Bush and Joseph P Folger, 'Clarifying the Theoretical Underpinnings of Mediation: Implications for Practice and Policy' (2002) 3(1) *Pepperdine Dispute Resolution Journal* 39, 49.

38 Spicker (n 37).

naturally pose limits upon individual self-determination, whether they are relationships with others or physical, social, economic and political environments. No one can be entirely self-determining, or self-determining in an absolute sense.[39]

Limits to the self-determination of parties in mediation are reflected in core concepts associated with the differing models. Central to problem-solving models is the need for *compromise* leading to agreement.[40] In narrative models, core ideas include *social* justice[41] and *participation*.[42] Central to the transformative model are the dual aims of empowerment and *recognition*.[43] Each of these core concepts points to the relationship between the parties and an inherent limit to realising the interests of only one party given that relationship. Transformative and narrative models of mediation offer a more nuanced construction of self-determination given their focus on relationships and inter-subjective meaning creation, respectively.[44]

Boulle and Field identify several dimensions of mediation that promote self-determination: participatory involvement, procedural engagement, responsibility for outcomes, the parties' own voices, and consensuality of outcomes.[45] The authors affirm earlier work by Field,[46] drawing on the work of Astor,[47] that self-determination is safeguarded by the informed consent of the parties.[48] Under the NMAS, mediators are required, according to clause 7.4, to 'support participants to reach agreements freely, voluntarily, without undue influence and on the basis of informed consent'. The more precise nature and extent of support needed from mediators is untested. Boulle and Field argue that lawyers have a critical role in enabling informed consent through legal advice and advocacy.[49] However, not all mediation participants are legally represented or, if they are, attend mediation with partisan legal representation. The option of participating without legal representation could be argued as another dimension of mediation

39 See M Del Collins, 'Transcending Dualistic Thinking in Conflict Resolution' (2005) 12(2) *Negotiation Journal* 263 for an introduction to dualism and absolutist concepts.

40 Boulle (n 13) 62, 92; Bobette Wolski, 'The Role and Limitations of Fisher and Ury's Model of Interest-based Negotiation in Mediation' (1994) 12 (4) *Australasian Dispute Resolution* 210, 218.

41 J Winslade and G Monk, *Narrative Mediation: A New Approach to Conflict Resolution* (Jossey-Bass, 2000) 100; J Winslade, G Monk and A Cotter 'A Narrative Approach to the Practice of Mediation' (1998) 14 (1) *Negotiation Journal* 21, 25.

42 Sara Cobb, 'Empowerment and Mediation: A Narrative Perspective' (1993) 9(3) *Negotiation Journal* 245, 255.

43 Robert A Baruch Bush and Joseph P Folger, *The Promise of Mediation: A Transformative Approach to Conflict* (Jossey-Bass, rev ed, 2005) 14; Robert A Baruch Bush, 'Efficiency and Protection, or Empowerment and Recognition?: The Mediator's Role in Ethical Standards in Mediation' (1989) 41(2) *Florida Law Review* 253, 269; M Dewdney, 'Transformative Mediation: Implications for Practitioners' (2001) 12(1) *Australasian Dispute Resolution Journal* 20, 21; M Brenner, S Segel and N Serventy, 'What is "Transformative" Mediation?' (2000) 11(3) *Australasian Dispute Resolution Journal* 155, 156.

44 See Robert A Baruch Bush and Joesph P Folger, 'Reclaiming Mediation's Future: Re-focusing on Party Self-determination' (2014) 16 *Cardozo Journal of Conflict Resolution* 741; Susan Douglas, 'Neutrality, Self-Determination, Fairness and Differing Models of Mediation' (2012) 19(2) *James Cook University Law Review* 19.

45 Laurence Boulle and Rachael Field, 'Re-appraising Mediation's Value of Self-Determination' (2020) 30 *Australasian Dispute Resolution Journal* 96, 102.

46 Field (n 35).

47 Hilary Astor, 'Rethinking Neutrality: A Theory to Inform Practice – Part I' (2000) 11(2) *Australasian Dispute Resolution Journal* 73; Hilary Astor, 'Rethinking Neutrality: A Theory to Inform Practice – Part II' (2000) 11(3) *Australasian Dispute Resolution Journal* 145.

48 Boulle and Field (n 45) 102.

49 Ibid.

that promotes self-determination. Where expert legal or other advice is needed, mediators will typically refer parties for that advice at intake, or prior to the mediation session. However, the private and confidential nature of the process can pose difficulties in proving informed, or indeed genuine, consent where a settlement agreement is challenged.

ATKINS V IINET PTY LTD [2019] SASC 83

Facts: The appellant argued that a mediation agreement should be set aside for duress, unconscionability and/or mistake. The appellant relied on evidence that he suffered from chronic anxiety panic attack disorder, post-traumatic stress disorder, and dyslexia, which prevented him from understanding the mediation. He was self-represented and argued that the mediator's conduct was implicated in the impugning conduct of the respondent's legal representative, who attended the mediation.

Issue: Issues of genuine consent and the role of the mediator were raised. The appellant argued that the mediator should have stopped the mediation to establish that he was in a fit and proper state to participate.

Decision: The Supreme Court denied the appeal. In relation to the mediator's conduct, Brampton J referred to evidence that the mediator had been aware of the appellant's dyslexia and had made provision for it; had expressed concern for the appellant; and had offered to stop the process, which the appellant had declined. Her Honour referred to the written information made available to the parties which indicated that the process was voluntary and could be terminated by them at any time. She concluded that the mediator's conduct would not have been inconsistent with that information. Her Honour distinguished the legal requirements of duress from an experience of stress likely to occur in mediation. She concluded that any pressure as to time in which to conclude the mediation would not amount to duress.

Discussion: In this case, on its facts, the mediator's conduct was found not to be implicated in appellant's allegation of duress. The case raises a question, however, of what responsibility a mediator has to ensure that genuine consent to an agreement occurs in mediation. In *Atkins*, the mediator was found to have acted with awareness of, and sensitivity to the appellant's dyslexia, which negated any proof of duress. However, the case did not decide whether the mediator had a positive duty to ensure the genuine consent of the appellant.

Impartiality and procedural fairness

The impartiality of decision-makers and procedural fairness in the conduct of investigations are well recognised principles in Western systems of democracy. In the context of mediation, these concepts have been shown to have extended meanings given the influence of socio-legal constructs,[50] but they retain a reference to the idea of fairness and the absence of real or apparent bias.

50 See Susan Douglas, 'Constructions of Impartiality in Mediation' (2017) 26 *Journal of Judicial Administration* 232; *National Mediator Accreditation System: Practice Standards* Part III, 7 <https://msb.org.au/themes/msb/assets/documents/national-mediator-accreditation-system-2015.pdf>

Impartiality is commonly understood as a requirement to ensure bias in decision-making and conduct is avoided or minimised, if not eliminated. Questions of impartiality have been implicated in mediation with questions of neutrality. Neutrality is a modernist concept, which assumes that individuals can make decisions without the influence of conscious or unconscious bias. The neutral application of legal principles in deciding cases is a core principle of case law, but it is a presumption challenged by critical theorists, and particularly by feminist legal scholars.[51] The principle that mediators operate as neutral third parties has been critiqued by scholars and practitioners over the last two decades.[52] The neutrality of the mediator was originally a defining feature of mediation,[53] integral to widely accepted definitions of the process. In the first revisions to NMAS in 2012, neutrality was omitted from the definition of mediation but retained, with impartiality, as a required ethical competency.[54] In the 2015 revisions of the NMAS, understanding of neutrality was omitted as a competency and self-determination was included as a defining feature

Crowe and Field[55] argue that impartiality in mediation ought to be abandoned as an 'empty' concept that is indistinguishable from neutrality. The authors advance two arguments in support of their contention. They argue that the distinction is too technical and 'speaks perhaps to people who are steeped in the details of mediation terminology, but not to the ordinary party who comes to mediation for assistance with managing or resolving their dispute...'.[56] Secondly, they claim that impartiality, as understood as fair and even-handed treatment of the parties, encounters many of the problems identified with neutrality. Even-handed treatment of the parties has been criticised in circumstances where the parties present with an evident imbalance of power. In such circumstances, treating the parties equally, though procedurally fair, can result in substantially unfair outcomes.[57]

Despite the evident shift away from neutrality as it has been understood, as an absolute, dualist concept, requiring that either the mediator is neutral or not, dispute practitioners and

51 See, eg, Stephen Bottomley and Simon Bronitt, *Law in Context* (Federation Press, 3rd ed, 2006).

52 See Chapter 3; Astor (n 47); Hilary Astor, 'Mediator Neutrality: Making Sense of Theory and Practice' (2007) 16(2) *Social and Legal Studies* 221; Rachael Field, 'Mediation and the Art of Power (Im)balancing' (1996) 12 *Queensland University of Technology Law Journal* 6; Rachael Field, 'The Theory and Practice of Neutrality in Mediation' (2003) 22(1) *Arbitrator and Mediator* 79; Bernard Mayer, *Beyond Neutrality: Confronting the Crisis in Conflict Resolution* (Jossey-Bass, 2004); Carol Izumi, 'Implicit Bias and the Illusion of Mediator Neutrality' (2010) 34 *Washington University Journal of Law and Policy* 71; Ronit Zamir, 'The Disempowering Relationship between Mediator Neutrality and Judicial Impartiality: Toward a New Mediation Ethic' (2011) 11(3) *Pepperdine Dispute Resolution Law Journal* 1; Bernard Mayer et al, 'Panel Discussion: Core Values of Dispute Resolution: Is Neutrality Necessary?' (2011) 95(4) *Marquette Law Review* 805; Susan Douglas, 'Constructions of Neutrality in Mediation' (2012) 23 *Australasian Dispute Resolution Journal* 80.

53 See, eg, Christopher Moore, *The Mediation Process* (Jossey Bass, 1986) 6, who defines mediation as 'the intervention into a dispute or negotiation by an acceptable, impartial, and neutral third party who has no authoritative decision making power to assist contending parties in voluntarily reaching their own mutually acceptable settlement of issues in dispute'.

54 *National Mediator Accreditation System: Practice Standards* (2012) <https://msb.org.au/themes/msb/assets/documents/practice-standards.pdf>.

55 Jonathan Crowe and Rachael Field, 'The Empty Idea of Mediator Impartiality' (2019) 29(4) *Australasian Dispute Resolution Journal* 273.

56 Ibid.

57 See Douglas (n 50).

scholars continue to grapple with its application in theory and practice.[58] Ultimately, the issue is one of the power or authority of the mediator and whether that extends to ensuring substantive fairness. Given that mediation occurs 'in the shadow of the law' and given the private nature of the process, it would be reasonable to expect clear legislative guidelines for the exercise of such power.

Models of mediation

Mediation has developed as a dynamic, multi-faceted and adaptive process of dispute management. Consequently, varying models of practice have developed over time. Several typologies of models have been advanced by scholars in order to map the complexity of variations that continue to evolve.[59] Boulle provides a typology of four models: facilitative, settlement, evaluative, and transformative. He distinguishes these models according to differences in objectives, how disputes are defined, the characteristics of mediators, the mediator's role, the perceived strengths and weaknesses of the model, the model's areas of application, and other key characteristics.[60] Alexander adds the narrative model to transformative mediation under a heading of therapeutic models and considers wise counsel and traditional mediation as distinct approaches.[61] Each of these models is examined below.

The facilitative model

In facilitative mediation, the mediator conducts the mediation according to a strict process in order to assist parties to identify a comprehensive list of issues which focus on parties' interests and needs. The mediator then assists parties to identify their own creative solutions that parties can apply to the problems identified.[62] The definition of mediation provided under the NMAS is based on the facilitative model of mediation. The facilitative model is regarded as the classic, orthodox model adopted in community justice centres in Australia from the 1970s.[63] Central to the facilitative model is a distinction between the process of mediation and its content or outcome. According to this distinction, mediators are said to be in control of the process of mediation but not its content or outcome. In this way, the parties' opportunities for self-determination are claimed to be maximised. This distinction has been described as a hallmark of orthodox mediation

58 See, eg, Aonghus Cheevers, 'Neutrality in Irish Mediation, One Concept, Different Meanings' (2020) 37 (3) *Conflict Resolution Quarterly* 253; K Szejda and AS Ebesu Hubbard, 'Neutrality and Satisfaction in the Mediation Session: Party and Mediator Perspectives' (2019) 30(3) *International Journal of Conflict Management* 329; Bornali Borah, 'Being the Ladle in the Soup Pot: Working with the Dichotomy of Neutrality and Empowerment in Mediation Practice' (2017) 28(3) *Australasian Dispute Resolution Journal* 98; Mohamed Sweify, 'Mediator's Proposal and Mediator's Neutrality: Finessing the Tension' (2017) 28(2) *Australasian Dispute Resolution Journal* 129.

59 Nadja Alexander, 'The Mediation Meta-Model: Understanding Practice' (2008) 26(1) *Conflict Resolution Quarterly* 97; Boulle (n 13) 43–8; L Riskin, 'Mediator Orientations, Strategies and Techniques' (1994) 12 (1) *Alternatives to the High Cost of Litigation* 111; L Riskin, 'Understanding Mediators' Orientations, Strategies, and Techniques: A Grid for the Perplexed' (1996) 1 *Harvard Negotiation Law Review* 7; L Riskin, 'Decision-Making in Mediation: The New Old Grid and the New New Grid System' 2003 79(1) *Notre Dame Law Review* 1.

60 Boulle (n 13) 44–5.

61 Alexander (n 59).

62 Boulle (n 13) 43–5.

63 Ibid.

practice,[64] as it frames the role of the mediator and the scope of their work with parties. In practice, however, facilitative, settlement, and evaluative models vary according to how robust the mediator's interventions as to process are and how far they intrude into the content and outcome of a dispute. Newer models – the transformative and narrative models – reject the distinction between process and content or outcome as the central organising principle of practice.

The settlement model

In the settlement model, the mediator encourages the parties to reach a compromise on their positional claims. The mediator employs various strategies of persuasion, doubt creation, and pressure without adherence to any prescribed decision-making process.[65] This model employs aspects of distributive negotiation,[66] but is conducted as a triadic third-party process, in which the mediator assists the parties to manage the issues in dispute. It evokes the zero-sum game discussed in Chapters 2 and 5, in which one party's gain is the other party's loss. The difference is that, rather than the parties directly engaging in a dyadic negotiation, the process is orchestrated by a third-party mediator. The model is often employed by adopting a simplified version of the facilitative process. Parties may make opening statements, an agenda may be set, although often it will not contain many items to address, and some exploration may be covered before moving relatively quickly to negotiation. This process is suited to disputes where a monetary claim is central to the dispute and no future relationships or significant interests need to be addressed.

The evaluative model (expert advisory model)

According to the evaluative model, the mediator guides and advises the parties using their expertise. Emphasis is given to reaching settlement based upon the legal rights and obligations, industry norms and/or other objective criteria.[67] As such, this model is the antithesis of facilitative mediation, as the mediator not only controls the process but also influences substantive decisions. The evaluative model is also referred to as an expert advisory model[68] and is identified as a triadic advisor process. By contrast, the classic facilitative model is a triadic facilitative process in which mediators do not give advice.[69] Facilitative mediators are said to be distinguished from lawyers and counsellors because they do not give advice about the content of the dispute.[70] However, as noted above, blended processes are now recognised within the NMAS 2015, which includes advisory or evaluative mediation and conciliation.

ADVISORY MEDIATION

A second triadic advisory model enables mediators to give procedural advice about processes parties will encounter in the justice system.[71] This advice can extend to the statutory framework

64 Hilary Astor and Christine Chinkin, *Dispute Resolution in Australia* (Butterworths, 2nd ed, 2002) 146; see also Boulle (n 13) 35.

65 Boulle (n 13) 43–6.

66 See Chapter 3.

67 Boulle (n 13) 43–6.

68 See Chapter 3; Alexander (n 59).

69 See Tom Fisher, 'Advice by Any Other Name…' (2001) 19(2) *Conflict Resolution Journal* 197.

70 See S Roberts, 'Toward a Minimal Form of Alternative Intervention' (1986) (11) *Mediation Quarterly* 25.

71 See, eg, the model used at the Queensland Civil Administrative Tribunal (QCAT); Bobette Wolski, 'QCAT's Hybrid Hearing: The Best of Both Worlds or Compromised Mediation?' (2013) 22(3) *Journal of Judicial Administration* 154.

within which the dispute occurs, the relevant case management process instituted, and the determinative process if agreement is not reached.[72] Advice as to a probable outcome if the case is heard before a judicial officer is not given. However, emphasis can be given to the fact that the parties lose autonomy if the case proceeds since the matter is decided for them. This reality can encourage agreement. This type of mediation is more likely to occur in contexts in which the advice fills a gap otherwise filled by legal representation that is discouraged or unavailable.[73]

WISE COUNSEL AND TRADITION-BASED MEDIATION

Wise counsel mediators are selected because of 'their high standing in the community, communication ability, wisdom, sense of fairness, and ability to understand all aspects of the conflict'.[74] Wise counsel mediators evaluate the merits of the case like evaluative mediators but focus on the interests and concerns of the parties rather than their rights and positions. Tradition-based mediation is similar to wise counsel mediation, but its primary aim is restorative justice with a focus on community stakeholders as well as the parties involved.[75]

The transformative model

In the transformative model, the mediator assists the parties to deal with the underlying causes of their dispute by encouraging dialogue between them with the aim of transforming the way they relate to each other. The transformative model is one of two models that are identified as 'second generation mediation practice'.[76] Development of the transformative model is attributed to Bush and Folger.[77] The transformative model is premised on a relational understanding of human nature. According to the authors, people are both separate and connected as human beings and are by nature distressed by disputes, which 'leads and even forces them to behave toward themselves and others in ways that they find uncomfortable and even repellent'.[78] Transformative mediation aims to manage disputes by achieving transformation of disputes. This is based upon a view that people want reparation of their relationships, rather than merely satisfaction of their individual needs. Rather than depicting the mediator's role as limited to process, the mediator's role is to support the parties' desire and capacity to transform their dispute. This is achieved by supporting two primary aims of transformative mediation, characterised as shifts in empowerment and recognition.[79] Bush and Folger define these key concepts:

> In the simplest terms, *empowerment* means the restoration to individuals of a sense of their own value and strength and their capacity to handle life's problems. *Recognition* means the evocation in individuals of acknowledgment and empathy for the situation and problems of others.[80]

72 See Chapter 8 and Chapter 12.
73 See processes in the Queensland Civil Administrative Appeals Tribunal (QCAT) and the Fair Work Commission (FWC).
74 Alexander (n 59) 112.
75 Ibid 113–15.
76 Sara Cobb, 'Creating Sacred Space: Toward a Second-Generation Dispute Resolution Practice' (2001) 28 (4) *Fordham Urban Law Journal* 1017.
77 Bush and Folger (n 43).
78 Ibid 46.
79 Ibid 65–9.
80 Ibid 2 (emphasis in original).

The narrative model

The other second-generation model of mediation is the narrative model, principally attributed to Winslade and Monk[81] but also articulated by Sarah Cobb.[82] Narrative mediators are actively engaged in re-creating the reality of the parties' experiences. Mediation conversations aim to open a space for issues to be described in different terms, for positions offered within dominant discourses to be refused, and for parties to reposition themselves within the dominant discourses that they experience as problematic.[83] According to Winslade and Monk,[84] people rely on narratives, or stories, to make sense of their lives. Stories are culturally situated and shared according to various dimensions of identity. An assumption of the narrative model is that disputes are produced within competing cultural norms. Sometimes, 'stories compete with or conflict with each other. Conflict can be understood as the inevitable result of the articulation of difference.'[85] According to this model, differences that lead to conflict must be understood rather than necessarily resolved and understanding may of itself precipitate resolution. Understanding requires an appreciation of relations of power and privilege as these are constructed by, and in turn construct, dominant meanings and hence dominant discourses.[86] Discourses are conceived as social practices 'dispersed through a cultural world in linguistic forms and exerting a domination effect on what can be thought or spoken'.[87] The narrative model does not separate process and content because it is argued that 'relationship, process, and content issues are all interwoven in the very fabric of mediation'.[88]

Transformative and narrative models reject the distinction between process and content because they are based upon a social constructionist worldview. According to **social constructionism**, knowledge is not objective but rather created by people in interaction with one another. Meaning creation and discourse are the foundations of understanding and replace attempts to reduce human interaction into components of process and content.[89] As Cobb asserts:

Social constructionism: creation being constructed through people interacting to create a shared understanding of reality.

> ... once we adopt an interactionist or social constructionist perspective, the mandate to separate content from process dissolves, as mediators recognize the inevitability of their impact on the content of the dispute. This attention to the evolution of the content calls for a 'second generation' mediation practice in which mediators interact with disputants so as to evolve the conflict stories, reformulate relationships, reframe the past and rebuild the future.[90]

81 Winslade and Monk (n 41).
82 Cobb (n 42); Cobb (n 76).
83 Winslade and Monk (n 41).
84 Ibid.
85 Ibid 25.
86 Ibid 21–5; J Winslade, 'Mediation with a Focus on Discursive Positioning' (2006) 23(4) *Conflict Resolution Quarterly* 501, 501–5.
87 Winslade (n 86) 502.
88 Winslade and Monk (n 41) 15.
89 Michael Crotty, *The Foundations of Social Research: Meaning and Perspective in the Research Process* (Allen and Unwin, 1998) 42.
90 Cobb (n 76) 1029.

Differences in the models

Facilitative, settlement, and evaluative models are identified as problem-solving models of mediation[91] due to their development from problem-solving approaches to legal issues and counselling. Problem-solving is an approach adopted by care professionals that uses a defined set of interpersonal skills to assist parties to find their own solutions.[92] Many of these skills are applied to mediation practice. Problem-solving models rely explicitly or implicitly on the distinction between process and content. In the facilitative model, the mediator's role is limited to process interventions which enable them to structure the conversation between parties. In the settlement model, the mediator is more directive in managing the process and may intrude upon the content of the dispute by virtue of robust interventions which encourage and even urge the parties to make concessions. In the evaluative model, mediators are chosen for their expertise in the subject matter of a dispute. They orchestrate the process and influence both the content and outcome of the dispute by framing the issues and advising as to probable legal outcomes.[93]

The distinction between content and process in mediation is very similar to the distinction between substance and procedure in law. Lawyers tend to favour models that rely on this process/content distinction. Lawyers also tend to favour the settlement and evaluative models as these tend to be based on distributive negotiation,[94] which is consistent with the adversarial system in which they operate and are trained. Parties are more likely to be represented and accompanied by lawyers in settlement and evaluative mediations. Evaluative mediators will often be legally qualified and include barristers and judges not necessarily accredited mediators under the NMAS.[95] The core of the facilitative model is interest-based bargaining,[96] which mirrors the model of negotiation developed by Fisher and Ury.[97] Interest-based bargaining emphasises the central importance of process requiring 'those involved in negotiations to distinguish between the process and the content of negotiations'.[98] As a result, facilitative mediation is not framed by legal rights and responsibilities, although these considerations may be present as issues impacting upon the parties' interests. Typically, mediators using the facilitative model will refer parties for legal advice prior to the mediation, or partisan legal advisors may be present in the mediation.

Narrative and transformative models have been identified as therapeutic models,[99] partly because of their emphasis on transforming and maintaining relationships and partly because of their links to social science disciplines. The narrative model as articulated by Winslade and

91 Della Noce, Bush and Folger (n 37).

92 See G Egan, *The Skilled Helper: A Problem-Management and Opportunity-Development Approach to Helping* (Thomson Learning, 11th ed, 2019).

93 See, eg, KK Kovach and LP Love, '"Evaluative" Mediation is an Oxymoron' (1996) 14(3) *Alternatives to the High Cost of Litigation* 31.

94 See Chapter 5.

95 See David Kwok, 'The (im)propriety of Judicial Mediation' (2015) 26(4) *Australasian Dispute Resolution Journal*, 210.

96 See Chapter 5.

97 R Fisher and W Ury, *Getting to Yes: Negotiating Agreement without Giving In* (Houghton Mifflin, 1981); see Chapter 5, 143.

98 Astor and Chinkin (n 64) 111.

99 See Alexander (n 59) 116–17.

Monk is grounded in narrative therapy.[100] The narrative model advanced by Cobb is grounded in communication theory. Both narrative and transformative models are grounded in social constructionism, which posits a postmodern construction of reality and human relationships. These second-generation models of mediation contain a critique of modernist and positivist worldviews that arguably underpin problem-solving, facilitative, settlement, and evaluative models. Consistent with modernist conceptions, problem-solving models of mediation emphasise the importance of the individual and focus on finding a solution to the problem that brings the parties to the mediation table.[101] They assume that the parties are 'autonomous, self-contained, atomistic individuals, each motivated by the pursuit of satisfaction of his or her own separate self-interests'.[102]

Boulle describes mediation models as paradigms that 'are not so much discrete forms of mediation practice but rather ways of conceptualising the different tendencies in practice'.[103] Empirical studies affirm this view by indicating that mediators are flexible in applying principles associated with different models, particularly when incorporating therapeutic principles within a facilitative approach.[104] According to Alexander, elements of each model may be used concurrently in a given mediation session.[105] Alexander provides a useful comparison of the advantages (usefulness) and disadvantages (criticisms) of different models. Those in relation to facilitative, settlement and evaluative models are extracted and presented in Table 6.1.

Table 6.1 Advantages and disadvantages of the different models according to Alexander[106]

	Advantages	Disadvantages
Facilitative	**Useful where:** The parties have reached an impasse in negotiations. There are opportunities for creative and future-focused solutions to address the needs and interests of the parties. In multiple-issue disputes, especially where the issues comprise legal and non-legal elements.	**Criticised because:** In the absence of a mediated agreement, information disclosed during the process may be independently sourced and used in later adjudication or arbitration proceedings. May not be suitable in situations where a party/parties have inadequate bargaining power; for example, where one party has language or literacy difficulties or in cases involving domestic violence.

100 See G Monk et al (eds), *Narrative Therapy in Practice: The Archaeology of Hope* (Jossey-Bass, 1997).

101 D Della Noce, 'Seeing Theory in Practice: An Analysis of Empathy in Mediation' (1999) 15(3) *Negotiation Journal* 271, 277-8; Della Noce, Bush and Folger (n 37) 49.

102 Della Noce, Bush and Folger (n 37) 49.

103 Boulle (n 13) 43; see Carrie Menkel-Meadow, 'The Many Ways of Mediation: The Transformation of Traditions, Ideologies, Paradigms, and Practices' (1995) 11 (3) *Negotiation Journal* 217, 228.

104 Kathy Douglas, 'Mediator Stories of Tribunal Practice: Flexible and Fluid to Meet Parties' Needs' (2012) 21(4) *Journal of Judicial Administration* 237.

105 Alexander (n 59) 106.

106 Adapted from Alexander (n 59).

Table 6.1 (cont.)

	Advantages	Disadvantages
	In multiple-issue disputes, especially where the issues comprise legal and non-legal elements.	Can require greater investment of time than positional bargaining approaches.
Settlement	**Useful where:** Positional bargaining is preferred over interest-based bargaining. The outcome is more important than the relationship, or when the parties want no future relationship. Only the parties' legal representatives attend the mediation. Parties are negotiating over a 'fixed pie'. There is a single issue in dispute.	**Criticised because:** The stronger, more experienced, positional bargainer will always be at an advantage. Settlement mediation styles tend to overlook the needs and interests of the parties and their relationship. They may therefore miss chances to identify suitable options for all parties – short, medium, and long-term. When legal representatives are present, a focus on legal positions encourages (and arguably requires) them to take over negotiations for their clients. Parties are unlikely to learn how to negotiate constructively with each other in the future.
Evaluative (expert advisory)	**Useful where:** The parties are not expert in the technical matters in dispute. Useful where the parties are required to attend mediation and are not otherwise motivated. Useful where parties have unrealistic views of their relative positions. Useful where the parties need the objective view of an experienced specialist. Useful where the parties are seeking an expedited resolution of their dispute. Useful where the relational aspects of the dispute are not a priority.	**Criticised because:** When mediators provide opinions, it can be difficult to maintain the perception of impartiality. Parties who find the expert opinion unacceptable may subsequently consider the mediator biased. By focusing on rights and positions, the interests of the parties may be neglected. Parties are not coached by the mediator or by engaging in the process to develop their own conflict resolution skills. Knowing that mediators will provide an expert opinion may encourage parties to withhold information that they believe would not benefit their case. Expert advisory mediators seem to focus on a limited number of solutions that have worked in the past, rather than addressing the multidimensional and

Table 6.1 (cont.)

Advantages	Disadvantages
	unique facts of each case. Opportunities for a suitable outcome can be lost as a result. Settlement proposals by mediators may not support the parties' long-term interests or the improvement of their relationship. Expert advisory mediation does not encourage parties to acknowledge the perspective of the other side; rather, it encourages the parties to focus on their position only. Mediators who intervene in the legal or technical aspects of the dispute expose themselves to a higher risk of legal claims brought against them for the advice-giving aspect of their role.

Using knowledge of mediation to assist in dispute management

The facilitative model of mediation forms the basis of the NMAS Practice Standards. Essential training for mediators, as required under the NMAS, focuses on the facilitative model. There are several comprehensive explanations of mediation based upon this model.[107] Each identifies steps in the process with some variation from 7,[108] to 9,[109] to 10[110] steps. Variation is mainly a product of isolating or collapsing different phases; for example, exploration might include option generation in one account while the two may be separated in another account. An overview of 12 steps is provided below as an introduction to the broadest view of the process.

107 Mieke Brandon and Linda Fisher, *Mediating with Families* (Thomson Reuters, 4th ed, 2018): Laurence Boulle and Nadja Alexander, *Mediation: A How to Guide* (LexisNexis Butterworths, 2015); Ruth Charlton and Micheline Dewdney, *The Mediator's Handbook: Skills and Strategies for Practitioners* (Lawbook, 3rd ed, 2014); Peter Condliffe, *Conflict Management: A Practical Guide* (LexisNexis Butterworths, 6th ed, 2019) ch 7; Tania Sourdin, *Alternative Dispute Resolution* (Lawbook, 5th ed, 2016) ch 3; David Spencer, *Principles of Dispute Resolution* (Lawbook Co., 2nd ed, 2016) ch 3.

108 See, eg, Charlton and Dewdney (n 107).

109 See, eg, Condliffe (n 107).

110 The model used by the Dispute Resolution Centre, Department of Justice and Attorney-General, Brisbane.

The mediators' role is to orchestrate the process and by that means to structure the conversation between the parties. Boulle and Alexander identify four mediator functions in controlling the process. These are to create favourable conditions for the parties to manage their dispute; to assist the parties to communicate accurately, comprehensively and constructively; to facilitate the parties' negotiations; and to encourage settlement.[111] Before the process begins, parties will be contacted individually to assess whether the dispute and the circumstances surrounding it are suitable for mediation. An overview of intake is included. Figure 6.1 depicts a 12-step process.

Figure 6.1 12-step mediation process[112]

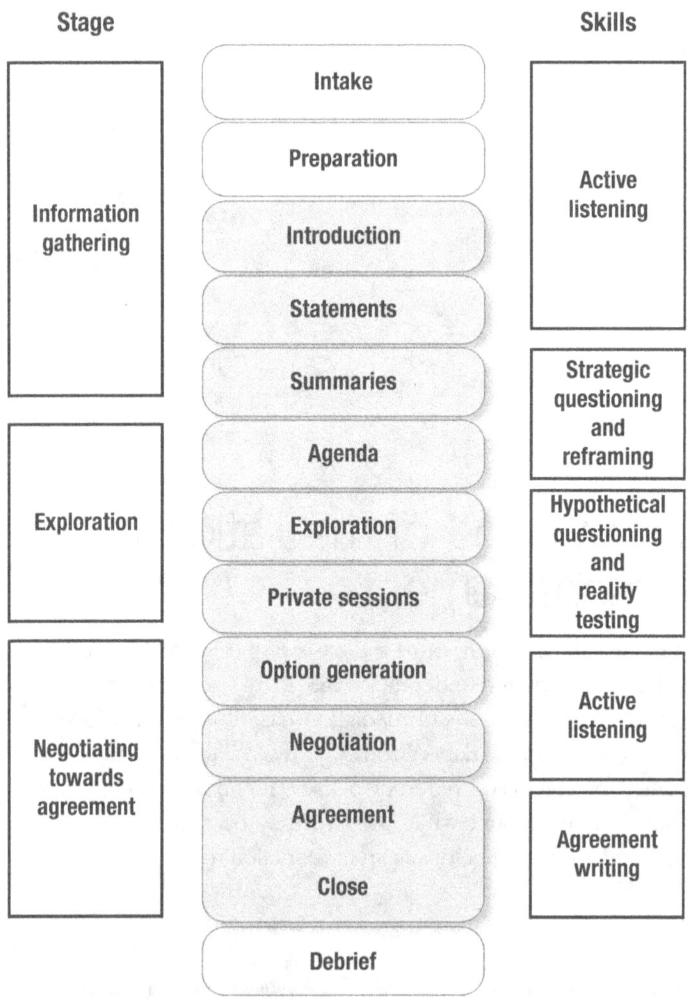

111 Boulle and Alexander (n 107) 13–15.

112 Adapted from Department of Justice and Attorney General Queensland, Dispute Management Resolution Branch, *Solo Mediation Model*, (YouTube, 25 July 2017) 0:00–12:53 <https://youtu.be/e0fZsksh1t8>.

Each step in the process is outlined below. Reference is made to skills specifically needed at each stage and depicted in the diagram above. Communication skills and techniques in Chapter 2 are relevant here. Mediation has developed as a face-to-face process for which interpersonal communication skills are a primary focus. Face-to-face sessions enable the nuances of communication, both verbal and non-verbal, to be observed by the mediator and responded to appropriately using a range of skills of which the most comprehensive is active listening. With the development of online technologies, mediation via Skype or other online platforms are emerging. The use of telephone communication via conference calls is also used particularly where parties live remotely or at some distance from one another.[113]

The classic facilitative model: 12 steps

1 Intake

As greater understanding of the dynamics of mediation has developed, intake processes have become increasingly recognised as an important first step. Intake consists of a preliminary contact with the parties, whether in person or by telephone. It includes information-gathering about the parties and their dispute, and information-sharing about the process of mediation. Parties are interviewed separately, contextual details about each party and their dispute are gathered, the process is explained to them, and their suitability for mediation is assessed. The intake can be done by the dispute practitioner who will conduct the mediation. This allows the mediator to assess what skills will be required to address any power differences, to hypothesise causes for the dispute, and to start to build rapport with the parties.[114] Irrespective of the nature of the dispute, two crucial issues need to be considered in assessing suitability for mediation. These are any questions of safety and whether each party has a willingness and capacity to engage in the process. Where one party feels unsafe in the presence of the other party, whether physically, psychologically and or emotionally, mediation is not suitable. Where one party demonstrates an evident unwillingness to participate in mediation (and perhaps has been referred to mediation by the other party, or a tribunal or court), the mediation may not be suitable. What has happened so far in terms of the nature of the dispute, the steps already attempted to manage the dispute, and what each party hopes to achieve in mediation are canvassed. Whether partisan legal representatives will attend, or other support persons, are also considered at this time. The amount of detail and emphasis varies according to the context of mediation. A set of sample intake questions is provided:

SAMPLE INTAKE QUESTIONS

1. What has brought you to mediation?
2. Who is involved with you in the dispute/problems you are experiencing?
3. Do you have any concerns about safety?

113 See also Chapter 3.

114 See also Jill Howieson and L Iriks, 'Before Mediation: Designing Processes for the Next Decade – Matching Process with the Purpose' (2017) 28(1) *Australasian Dispute Resolution Journal* 51; Dorcas Quek Anderson and Diana Knight, 'Managing the Inter-cultural Dimensions of a Mediation Effectively – A Proposed Pre-mediation Intake Instrument' (2017) 28(2) *Australasian Dispute Resolution Journal* 89.

4. Do you have concerns about your personal safety if the other party is in the same room with you?
5. Will you be comfortable to speak freely with the other party present?
6. Is there anyone else involved in your dispute that you think should also attend? What is their involvement?
7. Have you done anything to date to address the problems you have been experiencing and if so, what have you tried?
8. What do you usually do to manage disputes/problems like this?
9. What would you like to achieve from mediation?
10. What would you need from the other party to achieve the best outcome for you?
11. What if your best outcome is not agreed to by the other party?
12. How would your best outcome be achieved in practice?
13. What alternatives are there for you if the dispute cannot be managed through mediation?
14. What is the worst outcome for you, if there is no agreement reached in mediation?
15. What is the best outcome for you, if there is no agreement reached in mediation?

2 Preparation

The importance of preparation cannot be overstated even though in some settings mediators have limited time to devote to this stage. A mediator who has conducted intake interviews with the parties will understand the dispute and approaches of each party. In some circumstances, however, a mediator will have a very small window to familiarise themselves with details of the parties and their dispute. The amount of information needed will vary according to the nature of the dispute, the context of mediation, and the approach of the mediator. In the classic facilitative model, the parties have an opportunity to communicate their concerns in their opening statements. Facilitative mediators focus on the process more than the content of mediation and therefore do not need detailed information prior to the session, as this information will be elicited in the parties' own words during the process.

Preparing the space in which the session occurs is an important part of preparation. This includes configuring furniture, ensuring that tools such as pens, paper, whiteboard and or electronic devices are available and functioning. Access to separate waiting rooms and separate toilets (particularly from the mediator), tissues, water and tea and coffee facilities need to be checked. These apparently minor details are important in ensuring that the session runs smoothly without unnecessary disruption or delay.[115] Arranging furniture is particularly important. Seating around a round table is ideal. This enables parties and the mediator to seat equidistant from one another and avoids any impression of a power or status differential indicating bias that could occur if the mediator sat behind a desk.[116]

115 See, eg, David Vlock, 'Mediation Setting: The Importance of Considering Physical Environment as a Factor for Productive Mediation' (2018) 73(2) *Dispute Resolution Journal* 7.

116 See Chapter 1.

3 Introductions/mediator's opening statement

The opening statement by the mediator sets the scene for the session. It will usually include reference to key features of mediation and the mediator's role, a description of the process, and suggested ground rules. The statement should be clear and concise. Its aim is to inform and engage the parties and build rapport to reduce feelings of anxiety and uncertainty. Explanations of the steps may not be fully understood by parties at this stage and should be repeated at each phase by reference back to this overarching description so that parties can follow the process as it unfolds. The mediator may explain that the process is not a legal process, and that any agreement if reached is not enforceable unless registered in whatever form is appropriate to the context or reduced to an enforceable contract. Generally, it relies on the goodwill of the parties to adhere to it. The mediator may also refer to the fact that the process is voluntary and that parties can terminate the session at any time. Although, as noted in earlier chapters, mediation can be court mandated and therefore not always strictly voluntary. Nonetheless, engagement of the parties in the process can still be said to be voluntary in as much as they can chose whether to participate fully or not. Depending on the context of the mediation, cost consequences may be applied by tribunals or courts to encourage parties to cooperate. Mediators should refer to the confidentiality of the process, the limits to that confidentiality as required by law, and what will happen with any records of the session. Mediators may note that any agreement reached can be recorded in writing at the option of the parties.

The opening statement includes a description of the mediator's role. Here, the mediator explains that the aim of mediation is to assist the parties to reach their own agreement and not for the mediator to impose a decision on them. Mediators refer to their role as impartial third parties, who have no investment in the outcome nor in favouring one party or the other. They indicate that their role is not to give advice or to suggest solutions, but rather to assist the parties in reaching their own solutions. Mediators ask parties if they are authorised to reach agreement on the matter. This is important at this stage where a party is representing an organisation or a group; for example, a family member in an aged care dispute or a member of a body corporate in a dispute. The mediator may ask parties to sign an agreement to mediate and will explain the terms of that agreement. Mediators also refer to ground rules, such as the need to avoid interrupting each other, to enable the process to run smoothly and to demonstrate mutual respect. Mediators may ask the parties to communicate in a civil manner and to avoid inflammatory comments.

4 Parties' opening statements

In their opening statements, parties are given the opportunity to 'tell their story'. This is an important opportunity for parties to give a brief descriptive account of what brought them to mediation and to 'be heard' both by the mediator and the other party. The mediator uses this opportunity to begin to understand the issues in dispute and the parties' needs and interests. The mediator will typically take notes while demonstrating interest and engagement through (some) eye contact and a receptive active listening approach. The mediator will listen for both emotional and factual content in order to gauge both the detail of the dispute and the importance of various aspects to the parties. The party listening will have an opportunity to 'see from the other side' and may begin to understand how the dispute has been perceived by the other party and how that differs from their own interpretation. At this point, parties are generally asked to focus on the overriding reasons that have brought them to mediation. Equal time for each party is allocated for this initial statement. Parties are assured that they will have ample time later in the process to expand on the summary they provide at this stage. It may be that the mediator needs to encourage a party, who is not forthcoming, by asking some open-ended questions.

There is some evidence to suggest that the party who speaks first is at an advantage because their version of events frames the other party's statement.[117] Inevitably, however, one party will need to begin. Charlton and Dewdney suggest that it is preferable to ask parties who would like to begin and if neither party volunteers, to ask the party who brought the matter to mediation to start.[118]

Parties are asked to direct their statements to the mediator at this stage. This enables the mediator to demonstrate control of the process, while engaging and developing rapport with each party. Parties are asked not to interrupt each other, which gives each the opportunity to be heard and models the communication needed for later stages. Mediators may need to gently remind parties not to interrupt and encourage them to make a written note of any point they want to make when they have their turn to speak. The mediator can refer parties to the agreed ground rules if repeated interruptions occur. The aim of this step is not to present evidence as such and to test the veracity of that evidence, but rather to gather information from which to set out an agenda for discussion. Skills in active listening, strategic questioning, and note-taking are important for this step.

5 Mediator summaries

Either immediately after each party makes their opening statement or once both parties have completed their statements, the mediator uses their notes to summarise the statements made. The purpose of this step is threefold. It assures the parties that the mediator has heard their individual accounts and noted their issues and concerns. It enables each party to again hear the other party's story, this time through the mediator. It enables the mediator to confirm the important issues raised by each party and to demonstrate to them that their concerns have been heard and to check if any issues have been missed by the mediator. Mediators use skills in summarising, paraphrasing, and reframing in this step.[119] Mediators summarise the parties' statements by referring to both the circumstances of their dispute and their emotional responses to it. Reporting back the emotional content of parties' statements acknowledges their feelings and hence the significance to the party of their experience. As far as possible, mediators use the parties' own words to summarise their statements. This demonstrates to the parties that they have been heard and allows for identification of issues from the parties' own perspectives.

Mediators may need to reframe statements to detoxify accusations directed by one party to the other, or derogatory or inflammatory comments. Rather than repeat toxic comments,

117 Sara Cobb and Janet Rifkin, 'Practice and Paradox: Deconstructing Neutrality in Mediation' (1991) 16(1) *Law and Social Inquiry* 35.

118 Charlton and Dewdney (n 107) 27.

119 See Chapter 2.

feelings can be summarised by using such phrases as: 'You were upset by...' or 'You expressed anger toward...'. Mediators avoid communicating any assessment of the content of the statements, whether based upon rational or value judgments. The purpose here is not to gather information to enable the mediator to assess and determine the dispute, but to gather information in order to set out an agenda for further discussion between the parties. This can be difficult for those dispute practitioners trained in eliciting facts with little or no reference to emotions, such as lawyers.

6 Setting the agenda

Developing an agenda for the exploration and negotiation phases of the mediation is the next step. This is an important step as it provides the building blocks which frames the whole conversation going forward. The agenda is drawn from the parties' identification of issues, not the mediator's assessment of them. The mediator identifies the agenda from the summaries of parties' statements. In **co-mediation,** one mediator can extract themes from the summaries while the other mediator delivers them. In solo mediation, the mediator may take a few minutes to clarify for themselves what the main themes are before presenting an agenda to the parties. The items are ideally placed on a whiteboard or displayed electronically and are referred to through the course of the session. The mediator confirms with parties that the themes identified are meaningful and acceptable to them and involves the parties in deciding the order in which they will be discussed. This process takes practice, and many inexperienced mediators find it one of the most difficult steps in the facilitative model. It is important that the agenda is not limited to one or two items as this can encourage a shift to distributive negotiation. At the same time, the agenda must not be so extensive as to overwhelm and be unmanageable in the timeframe allocated.

Co-mediation: working with another mediator in pairs, rather than as a lone mediator. Co-mediators can rotate different stages of the process and provide an opportunity for reflection after the mediation.

The mediator assists parties through this step to identify issues that are of mutual concern to them, but about which they have different views that have contributed to their dispute. For example, in an aged care dispute, an agenda item of 'appropriate diet' would address one party's (a resident's) need for a different, 'improved' diet and the other party's (the aged care facility's) view that existing dietary intake is 'adequate' having regard to the needs of residents and resources available to meet those needs. The item 'appropriate diet' mutualises the issues of 'improved' diet and 'adequate' diet and enables the parties to share their views about what is an appropriate diet and how it can be achieved. Agenda items that give focus to one party's view, such as 'improved' or 'adequate' diet in the example above, should be avoided.

Legal issues may be relevant to the dispute, but unless these are identified by the parties prior to the mediation or in the information-gathering phase, the mediator should not privilege them. The mediator should instead listen for what the parties express as their underlying interests and concerns. For example, a party may have a pre-agreed arrangement with siblings to contribute to looking after an ageing parent but finds himself faced with the need to give time and attention to a new relationship. The legal status of the agreement is relevant, but a mutually acceptable solution is more likely to be found by exploring each family member's current and future needs and capacity to care for the ageing parent. Surrounding issues as well as matters in dispute are relevant here. For example, communication between the parties is often an agenda item for discussion of past problems in communication and how these may be addressed in the future. The agenda items can be framed as topics or as future-focused questions to evoke mutual problem-solving. Overall, they should be framed in neutral, mutual and forward-focused language.

7 Exploration

Once the agenda is confirmed, the parties enter the phase of exploration in which each of the issues identified are discussed in turn. In this step, the parties are asked to direct their conversation to each other. This is an important shift from channelling discussion through the mediator to encouraging direct communication between the parties. At this stage, the parties have heard each other's accounts of what has brought them to mediation and have agreed upon a list of issues to discuss. Exploration enables them to have a conversation about those issues as structured by the agenda and managed by the mediator. The mediator uses skills in paraphrasing, summarising, and transitions[120] to manage the flow of conversation and to direct parties back to the agenda items. The focus of this step is to move from the past to the present. The parties are encouraged to recount what has happened and what is happening for them in relation to each agenda item and to directly communicate that to the other party. The mediator encourages responses from the other party by using transitions which facilitate dialogue between the parties.[121] Exploration appears in the mediation diagram as the middle and central stage. Time spent in this phase is invaluable, as it enables the mediator to encourage parties to air their concerns fully and directly to the other party and to 'expand the pie' according to principles of interest-based negotiation. It encourages greater understanding between the parties and at least an appreciation of the other party's point of view, even if the same view is not held. A thorough exploration facilitates option generation and negotiation. Future options may be mentioned by parties during this phase, but they should not be tested until later. The mediator will note them with a view to returning to them in the option generation stage.

8 Private sessions

Private sessions (also referred to as 'caucuses') are opportunities for each party to speak to the mediator individually and privately. After exploration is an appropriate time to check in with the parties individually, although private sessions can be held at other times during a mediation. Care is taken to provide equal time to both parties to remove any appearance of bias, and confidentiality is reaffirmed. The mediator will inform parties that what is said in private sessions is strictly confidential and will not be brought back to the joint session by the mediator. The mediator can ask the parties who would like to go first, or perhaps choose the party who was second in making their initial statement in order to be seen to be unbiased. While one party is in private session, the other party has the opportunity for a break, but they can also be given a task, such as checking on information provided during exploration.

Private sessions provide the parties with time apart from each other and privacy with the mediator. The mediator usually begins by asking how the party considers the mediation is going. This allows parties an opportunity to communicate their sense of how likely the parties

120 See Chapter 2.
121 Ibid.

are to reach an agreement. A party might indicate that some information was unknown to them or some interpretation or attitude of the other party has surprised them. This is also an opportunity for a party to disclose to the mediator anything they have not said in the joint session that might impact the outcome, but which they have been reluctant to share with the other party. The mediator can assist the party in assessing whether the information would be helpful if revealed to the other party and whether the party concerned is able or willing to take it back to the joint session. The private session is cloaked in confidentiality to encourage open communication. For this reason, the mediator cannot bring any information from the private session back to the full mediation.

Private sessions are also used to prepare parties for option generation and negotiation. The mediator uses the agenda to ask the party their thoughts on each item with a focus on the future. The mediator supports parties to consider workable options for the future by using a problem-solving approach. The mediator will assist the party in reality testing the options by asking the party what they would like to see happen and how they think the other party would respond to any options the party suggests or that may have been raised during exploration. Clarifying and hypothetical questions can test how realistic options are in the light of the other party's expressed views, the desire for mutual agreement, and the need to consider practicalities. At this stage, a shift from hard positions to an acknowledgement of interests and needs – their own and the other party's – may be evident.

Ultimately, if a party remains positional, the mediator may ask what they will do if agreement is not reached at the end of the session. This relates to assessing one's BATNA or WATNA as discussed in Chapter 5.[122] This may encourage a party to weigh the benefits of compromise against any apparent detriments of reaching no agreement or pursuing their issues elsewhere. Some mediators will use more than one private session if the parties reach an impasse, or if later details of an agreement are decided by moving in shuttle between parties rather than in a joint session. In some models, private sessions are considered optional, and where there are time and context constraints, an opportunity for caucusing may not be possible.

9 Option generation

The stage of option generation is sometimes identified with negotiation in one step. However, there is some benefit in isolating it as a single phase. Option generation is like brainstorming, where the parties are given the opportunity to put all of the possibilities that they consider desirable and workable on the table. The mediator may not bring back any options identified in private sessions to the joint session, given the confidentiality imposed. However, the mediator will ask parties in a private session if they are willing and able to raise the options they have discussed with the mediator on return to the joint session. Openings are then created in the joint sessions for these options to be raised. Mediators use the agenda to structure this step by moving through each item and asking the parties what options for management they propose. A mediator might ask that all options are listed before they are discussed or discuss the options under each agenda item before moving onto the next. If the latter, the parties enter

122 See Chapter 5.

the negotiation stage. According to Charlton and Dewdney, option generation is an effective means of allowing parties to:

1. abandon the win/lose style of negotiation
2. promote a more creative way of thinking that is needed to reach a solution that both can live with
3. promote mutual ownership of the solution.[123]

10 Negotiation

If exploration and private sessions are thoroughly conducted, option generation and negotiation can be relatively straightforward. The mediator facilitates the negotiation employing an integrative, or interest-based, model.[124] The focus of this step is the future and enables parties to negotiate the details of options they have put forward. Options are considered according to whether they are acceptable and practicable. Details are fleshed out and become the basis of agreement. As with all steps, the context of mediation can colour the approach used. Commercial matters may become more formalised and, at this stage, references may be made to 'offers' and 'counter-offers', while Elder disputes may remain relatively informal but require attention to detail. Negotiation facilitated by the mediator at this stage has the advantages of negotiation more generally, which Spencer identifies as including:

1. Parties are in the best position to assess the impact of any proposed solution
2. Parties 'own' the process and can define its terms in any way they chose
3. Parties create their own solution and are therefore more committed to ensuring that the agreement works
4. Parties have a chance of getting part of what they want
5. Even if the dispute is not solved, parties have an opportunity to narrow the issues prior to further management processes such as negotiation or court action.[125]

11 Agreement and close

Outcomes of mediation are not necessarily legally enforceable. Generally, any agreement reached is binding in goodwill only. However, agreements will be enforceable if registered pursuant to legislation,[126] or reduced to writing in the form of a deed and hence enforceable as a formal contract. If agreement is reached, the parties are given the opportunity to evidence their agreement in writing. Whether this occurs will depend on the nature of the dispute and the context of the mediation. Where mediation occurs as part of community justice programs, agreements reached are not enforceable so that parties may chose not to conclude with a written form. However, experience suggests that most parties prefer a written record of their

123 Charlton and Dewdney (n 107) 117.
124 See Chapter 5.
125 Spencer (n 107) 25.
126 See, eg, consent orders under the *Family Law Act 1975* (Cth); *Queensland Civil and Administrative Tribunal Act 2009* (Qld) s 88.

agreement. The mediator assists parties to compose an agreement and will use the parties' own words to demonstrate and encourage their ownership. In commercial or other private disputes, a more formal agreement may be suitable. Condliffe identifies nine fundamental clauses to include in any agreement. These are: the preamble or introduction, statement of objectives, statement of tasks, amendment clause, review clause, legal review or other necessary review clause, future conflict clause, change of circumstances clause, and signature clauses.[127]

12 Debriefing

Debriefing is a step in the process where mediators have an opportunity to confidentially review the mediation and reflect on what occurred as a form of professional development. Mediators will consider what they did well, what they might have done differently, and how they can incorporate what they have learnt from the experience moving forward. Debriefing is encouraged under the NMAS Practice Standards.[128] Debriefing may occur with a co-mediator, supervisor, or colleague. Debriefing incorporates reflective practice, which is considered in Chapter 2.

Positives and negatives of mediation

Positives

Mediation provides an opportunity for parties to reach their own agreement about how to manage their dispute. As an extension of negotiation, considered in Chapter 5, mediation offers the assistance of a third party, the mediator, who has no interest in the outcome of the dispute. The mediator will ideally be trained in techniques and communication skills that support parties in managing their dispute. Reaching their own agreement enables parties to own the outcome rather than being obliged to accept an outcome imposed upon them. Parties are more likely to adhere to an agreement that they themselves have actively participated in shaping. Moreover, an agreement from which each party gains some benefit has an advantage over determinative processes, which typically find in favour of one party to the detriment of the other.

Through the process of stating the reasons for attending mediation, identifying an agenda for discussion, and exploring that agenda, parties are given the opportunity to identify and fully explore the issues confronting them. Those issues are not confined to legal issues, although these may frame or act as a backdrop to the dispute. A much wider range of interpersonal, emotional, and practical issues can be canvassed in order to facilitate a satisfactory outcome for the parties. Parties can explore what has occurred in the past, what is happening now, and what they would like to happen in the future. Parties are given the opportunity to creatively devise options going forward and to negotiate mutually beneficial outcomes.

Mediation can serve an educative function by modelling dispute management using appropriate communication skills. Mediators structure the conversation between parties by using the steps described above and by employing the communication skills described in

127 Condliffe (n 107) 349–50.

128 *National Mediator Accreditation System* (NMAS) (2015) Part III, 8.8 <https://msb.org.au/themes/msb/assets/documents/national-mediator-accreditation-system-2015.pdf>.

Chapter 2. Mediators create a safe environment by controlling the process, which assists parties to candidly disclose their interests and preferred outcomes in a confidential manner. Parties have the advantage of being heard by the other party and the mediator. A structured dialogue can assist parties to address misunderstanding and misinterpretation of events, conduct, and motives. In so doing, the emotional burden of disputes is lessened, issues are clarified, and space for negotiation is provided. Most importantly, this is a process that can manage disputes in a manner that can avoid destruction of relationships.

Negatives

Structured inequalities between the parties can lead to imbalances of bargaining power that may preclude effective mediation. Mediations between large corporations and consumers, particularly if they are repeat players, may not be suitable for mediation. In such cases, a final court determination may be required to clarify the law and ensure minority rights are protected in a public manner. Where there is a history of threatened or actual violence between the parties, mediation will be unsuitable. However, mediations can now be conducted online, by telephone, or through shuttle processes that avoid parties being in contact. Although not the same as face-to-face, these mediums for mediations can help manage the parties dispute while making them also feel safe. Mediation may not be suitable if a party has mental health concerns or there is a degree of psychological violence.[129] Court processes may be more effective in 'levelling the playing field' where imbalances of power are evident. However, court proceedings attract greater financial costs and are expensive in terms of time and emotional investment. Mediation services offered by community justice centres, or as a preliminary step in tribunal proceedings or as part of Magistrates Court matters, offer low cost and readily accessible dispute management for a wide range of matters.[130] Mediation will not be effective, however, where one or both parties are unwilling or unable to negotiate.[131] Other factors have been raised in Chapter 3.

Special considerations

In this part, select special considerations in mediation practice are examined. These are dealing with power in mediation, ethical matters, professional conduct, and lawyers in mediation.

Power in mediation

Power in mediation is a complex issue, as is the nature of power itself. Power in mediation raises issues of substantive and procedural fairness and the power of the mediator to ensure fairness in either form. This is recognised as an important issue where there is a real or perceived imbalance of power between the parties. The classic facilitative model of mediation, based upon a distinction between party's control of content and mediator's control of process,

129 See also Rebekah M Doley, 'Accommodating Common Mental Health Issues in Mediation' (2016) 27(2) *Australasian Dispute Resolution Journal* 84.

130 See also Sourdin (n 107); Chapters 8 and 9.

131 See, eg, Samantha Hardy and Olivia Rundle, *Mediation for Lawyers* (CCH, 2010) chs 1, 2.

limits the role of the mediator to orchestrating the process. The principle of party self-determination dictates that whatever the parties decide as an appropriate outcome will, by logical extension, be substantially fair. However, one party may agree to an outcome not because they think it is fair but because they feel intimidated or overborne by the other party.

The mediator can use control of the process to level the playing field as much as is possible. This would include ensuring that each party had equal time to speak, that each party was not interrupted by the other, monitoring behaviour that is outside the ground rules (for example, aggressive behaviour), and ensuring that active listening is occurring with equal attentiveness to both parties. However, the mediator has no authority, or legitimised power, to intercede on behalf of a party who enters the mediation at a disadvantage in relation to the other. Disadvantage may be evident due to existing structural imbalances of power, such as that between an employer and an employee or between a local council and a service user. Disadvantage may also be due to social and cultural factors, such as gender differences, social status and or ethnicity. Additional service referrals for counselling, financial, and legal advice prior to mediation, and interpretive services during mediation can assist in providing parties with an equal opportunity to participate. However, parties do not always seek appropriate advice and some existing inequalities may be too embedded and complex to address in the space of one or even several mediation sessions.

A stark example of imbalance occurs in family law or other matters where there has been a history of domestic violence. Where such a history exists, mediation may be considered unsuitable, unless with the consent of both parties.[132] Measures to safeguard parties include risk assessment prior to the mediation, the collaborative involvement of lawyers and other support people, and referral to support and educative services where appropriate.[133] Parties' prior interaction and/or relationship may cause one party to feel intimidated and unable to fully participate. Where this happens, mediators may be aware that outcomes are inequitable (according to their own or an objective standard), but they are not mandated to intervene.

According to existing practice standards, mediators can use their power as mediators to ensure procedural fairness but not substantive fairness. A focus on procedural fairness and ensuring safety are evident in the NMAS Practice Standards clause 6.[134] Clause 6 refers to a series of steps that the mediator can use to ensure safety, including setting ground rules, ensuring security protocols are available, and allowing parties to bring support persons. Where parties are not comfortable to meet in the same room, telephone conferencing, online mediation or shuttle mediation (where the mediator moves between the parties in different rooms) can be used. Clause 10 of the NMAS Practice Standards lists the knowledge, skills and ethical principles that a mediator must understand to be eligible for accreditation. Under that

132 See, eg, Rachael Field, 'A Feminist Model of Mediation that Centralises the Role of Lawyers as Advocates for Participants who are Victims of Domestic Violence' (2004) 20(1) *Australian Feminist Law Journal* 65.

133 See, eg, Sian Green, 'Effectively Managing the Impact of Family Violence on Mediation in the Family Law Context' (2017) 28(3) *Australasian Dispute Resolution Journal* 155; S Rice, et al, 'An Analysis of Domestic Violence Presenting to FRCs at Intake and Assessment' (2012) 23(2) *Australasian Dispute Resolution Journal* 89.

134 *National Mediator Accreditation System* (NMAS) Part III, 6 <https://msb.org.au/themes/msb/assets/documents/national-mediator-accreditation-system-2015.pdf>

clause, mediators are required to demonstrate an 'ability to manage high emotion, power imbalances, impasses and violence'.[135]

Modernism: a movement in philosophy and art during the late 19th and early 20th centuries shaped by the industrial revolution and the two World Wars. It is based on a utopian vision of human life and society and belief in progress and individual development.

Postmodern: late 1970s Western philosophical and literary reaction to modernism questioning rational scientific objectivity and moving towards subjectivity and scepticism, particularly about truth definition.

What is meant by power and power imbalances in mediation is an area of ongoing theoretical development and critique.[136] A distinction can be made between **modernist** and **postmodern** analyses of power, with a note that no one approach to power has gained acceptance throughout the mediation community. Two modernist typologies of power have been influential in the field and advanced by well-recognised scholars, Christopher Moore[137] and Bernie Mayer.[138] Mayer defines power as the ability to exert influence.[139] He identifies 13 sources of power,[140] while Moore identifies 12 forms of power exercised by mediators.

The forms and sources of power identified by Moore and Mayer respectively (Table 6.2) describe instances of personal power, as abilities and capacities demonstrated by an individual, and structural power, as power located in the social context and devolved to the individual by virtue of social position, access, and opportunity. Post-structural, or postmodern, analyses of power, reject the idea that power is identifiable, durable and measurable.[141] Following Foucault, postmodern theory sees power as a force that coheres around individuals but also circulates according to context and circumstance.[142] From a postmodern perspective, power cannot be balanced because it cannot be quantified. The benefit of a postmodern view is that power is not seen as something held by some individuals to the exclusion of others. People can be empowered to access their personal power and to disrupt power in cultural discourses which are perceived to cause them disadvantage. As described by Astor:

> All individuals have a race, a gender, a sexuality and many other aspects of identity, so that there is no essential woman, or Aboriginal person or gay man. But culture does influence the ways power is distributed, who can exercise what types of power, what can be said and by whom, which stories are recognised and which stories can and cannot be told.[143]

Whatever view of power is preferred, an ongoing issue for mediation is the proper scope of the mediator's exercise of power in addressing apparent disadvantage. Currently, the accepted and

135 *National Mediator Accreditation System* (NMAS) (2015) Part III, 10(1)(b)(vi) <https://msb.org.au/themes/msb/assets/documents/national-mediator-accreditation-system-2015.pdf>
136 See Chapter 3.
137 Christopher Moore, *The Mediation Process: Practical Strategies for Resolving Conflict* (John Wiley & Sons, 4th ed, 2014).
138 Bernard S Mayer, 'The Dynamics of Power in Mediation' (1987) 16 *Mediation Quarterly* 75.
139 Ibid 78.
140 Bernard S Mayer, *The Dynamics of Conflict Resolution: A Practitioner's Guide* (Jossey-Bass, 2000) 50–58.
141 See Hilary Astor, 'Some Contemporary Theories of Power in Mediation: A Primer for the Puzzled Practitioner' (2005) 16(1) *Australasian Dispute Resolution Journal* 30; Dale Bagshaw, 'Language, Power and Knowledge' (2003) 14(2) *Australasian Dispute Resolution Journal* 130.
142 See M Foucault, *Power/Knowledge: Selected Interviews and Other Writings, 1972–1977* Colin Gordon (ed), tr Colin Gordon et al (Harvester Press, 1980); S Best and D Kellner, *Postmodern Theory: Critical Interrogations* (MacMillan, 1991) 48–54.
143 Astor (n 141) 35.

Table 6.2 Moore and Mayer's forms and sources of power[144]

Mayer's 13 sources of power	Moore's 12 forms of power
1. Formal authority – deriving from a formal position	1. The authority and respect accorded a person experienced in dealing with conflict
2. Expert/information power – deriving from expertise	2. The ability to organise the physical environment of the mediation
3. Associational power – deriving from association with other people having power	3. The authority to organise the orderly presentation of relevant facts
4. Resource power – the control over valued resource	4. The ability to withdraw from the process if parties fail to comply with any ground rules
5. Procedural power – control over the procedures by which decisions are made	5. The persistence and optimism of the mediator
6. Sanction power – the real or apparent ability to inflict harm	6. The capacity to orchestrate the steps leading up to the mediation
7. Nuisance power – the ability to cause discomfort short of sanctioning	7. The ability of mediators to educate parties as to the process
8. Habitual power – the power of the status quo	8. The capacity to continually clarify aspects of the process
9. Moral power – power from an appeal to widely held values; and	9. Knowledge of the process and causes of conflict
10. Personal power – that which derives from a variety of personal attributes that magnify other sources of power, including self-assurance	10. Limited direct coercive power from statutory sources
11. Legal prerogative – laws, rules, regulations and customary law	11. Indirect coercive power as a result of a party's desire to gain approval from the mediator
12. Perception of power – influence exerted due to the potential to exercise power; and	12. Gendered power, resulting from perceived or actual gendered alliances between a party and the mediator.
13. Definitional power – the ability to define a situation, issue or conflict in a way which favours the person defining it.	

authorised view through the NMAS is that a mediator's power is confined to ensuring procedural fairness and does not extend to ensuring substantive fairness.[145]

144 Moore (n 137); Mayer (n 138).

145 See Mary Anne Noone and Lola Akin Ojelabi, 'Ethical Challenges for Mediators around the Globe: An Australian Perspective' (2014) 14 *Washington University Journal of Law and Policy* 145, in which the authors found that most of the mediators sampled believed they should not be concerned with the substantive fairness of a mediated outcome; see also Mohamed Sweify, 'The Art of Using Power as a

Mediation ethics

The NMAS articulates a series of ethical principles under clause 10.[146] These principles reflect and support the key philosophies of dispute management in the mediation process. They include promoting self-determination and ensuring impartiality and procedural fairness and are reinforced by references in other clauses of the NMAS.

While the Practice Standards articulated in NMAS clause 10 provide a guide to ethical conduct in mediation, in practice ethical decisions can be complex and require recourse to broader professional values and experience. Ethical dilemmas become evident where there are good reasons for conflicting courses of action that are not easily resolved by reference to existing guidelines or rules. Examples include situations where the role of the mediator precludes the giving of advice, but it is apparent that a party will be disadvantaged without advice; or ensuring that the process is procedurally fair fails to ensure an outcome that is substantially fair. In reality, ethical decision-making is not reducible to compliance with a set of rules or guidelines. As noted by Sir Gerard Brennan in relation to barristers' ethics:

> The first, perhaps the most important, thing to be said about ethics is that they cannot be reduced to rules. Ethics are not what a barrister knows he or she should do: ethics are what a barrister does. They are not so much learnt as lived. Ethics are the hallmark of a profession, imposing obligations more exacting than any imposed by law and incapable of adequate enforcement by legal process. If ethics were reduced merely to rules, a spiritless compliance would soon be replaced by skilful evasion. There is no really effective forum for their enforcement save individual acceptance and peer expectation. However, among those who see themselves as members of a profession, peer expectation is sufficient to maintain the professions ethical code.[147]

In addition to the principles provided in the NMAS, there are several approaches to identifying a set of unifying ethical principles to guide mediation practice based upon professional understanding and peer expectations. Crowe[148] articulates a model of mediation ethics drawing on moral psychology, which sees ethical judgment as a practical skill developed by repeated exposure to situational contexts. Crowe's model has three stated characteristics. It is situational rather than rule-oriented, emphasising that practice guide's principle. It is diachronic rather than synchronic, emphasising the development of organic guidelines rather than timeless rules. Thirdly, the model is community-oriented, emphasising a community of practice, rather than an individualistic endeavour. Crowe's model further acknowledges the professional nature of mediation practice, its unique contribution as a profession, and the diversity of practice approaches and models.

Tool of Influence in Mediation' (2016) 27(4) *Australasian Dispute Resolution Journal* 236; Kathy Douglas and Jennifer Hurley, 'The Potential of Procedural Justice in Mediation: A Study into Mediators' Understandings' (2017) 29(1) *Bond Law Review* 69; Jill Howieson, 'Perceptions of Procedural Justice and Legitimacy in Local Court Mediation' (2002) 9(2) *Murdoch University Electronic Journal of Law* 13.

146 *National Mediator Accreditation System* (NMAS) (2012) Part III, 10 <https://msb.org.au/themes/msb/assets/documents/practice-standards.pdf>.

147 Sir Gerard Brennan, Address to Queensland Bar Association (Speech, 3 May 1992) in Stafford Shepherd, 'One Nation, One Rule' (2012) 32(5) *Proctor* 18.

148 Jonathan Crowe, 'Ethics and the Mediation Community' (2015) 25(1) *Australasian Dispute Resolution Journal* 20.

Douglas argues that the professional relationship of trust between mediator and parties is a suitable organising principle for ethics in practice. She examines the principles associated with legal fiduciary relationships and therapeutic relationships, acknowledging the unique socio-legal development of mediation and its principles of practice. She argues that the relationship of trust between mediator and parties requires an 'other focus' on the part of the mediator who acts in the best interests of parties by facilitating their self-determination. Key socio-legal principles are incorporated into that relationship to guide mediator practice, including acting for a proper purpose, avoiding conflicts of interest, not taking sides, not directing the parties towards an outcome, being non-judgmental, and avoiding the intrusion of personal perspectives and reactions to their parties and their dispute.[149]

A contextual ethical paradigm for practice is advanced by Field. It centralises party self-determination as 'the normative and categorical aim of practice'.[150] Field proposes five guiding principles for the practice of a contextual ethical method in mediation: a thorough contextual analysis of the dispute and the parties; use of a framework of informed consent; adoption of a relational and caring ethic; adherence to the principle that mediators do not impose decisions and hence to do so would be unethical; and an overarching justification for situational action that supports party self-determination.[151] Most recently, Field and Crowe have combined their approaches to argue for a contextual approach to mediation ethics.[152]

Hardy and Rundle argue that open-ended contextual approaches can be too open ended and fluid and therefore lack appropriate guidelines for practitioners.[153] They apply a model of ethical decision-making developed by McAuliffe and Chenoweth[154] for social work practice to mediation.[155] The model is described as 'an inclusive model of ethical decision-making'. It combines recognition of four foundational principles underwriting a series of steps for ethical decision-making. The authors of the model note that ethical decision-making in social work is defined as 'the process of critical reflection, evaluation and judgment through which a practitioner resolves ethical issues, problems and dilemmas'.[156] The foundational principles, or platforms, they identify are accountability, critical reflection, cultural sensitivity, and consultation.[157]

A values-based approach to mediation provided by Ojelabi and Sourdin is based upon a platform of core values: freedom, justice, equality and peace.[158] They argue that these core values can be translated into practice through the use of a framework for decision-making and

149 Susan Douglas, 'Ethics in Mediation: Centralising Relationships of Trust' (2017) 35(1) *Law in Context* 44.

150 Field (n 35) 9.

151 Ibid 16.

152 Rachael Field and Jonathan Crowe, *Mediation Ethics: From Theory to Practice* (Edward Elgar, 2020).

153 Samantha Hardy and Olivia Rundle, 'Applying the Inclusive Model of Ethical Decision-making to Mediation' (2012) 19 *James Cook University Law Review* 70.

154 D McAuliffe and L Chenoweth, 'Leave No Stone Unturned: The Inclusive Model of Ethical Decision Making' (2008) 2(1) *Ethics and Social Welfare* 38.

155 Hardy and Rundle (n 153).

156 Ibid 49, citing Australian Association of Social Work, *Code of Ethics* (Union Offset, 2nd ed, 1999).

157 Ibid 42–3.

158 Lola Atkin Ojelabi and Tania Sourdin, 'Using a Values-based Approach in Mediation' (2011) 22(4) *Australasian Dispute Resolution Journal* 258.

action called the ERSR approach, signifying: education, recognition, support and resolution.[159] Noone and Ojelabi propose an access to justice approach to the measurement of the quality of justice in mediation.[160] The authors examine access to justice principles developed by the Commonwealth Government Access to Justice Taskforce and suggest how they could be applied to mediation. The principles they identify are accessibility, appropriateness, equity, efficiency, and effectiveness.[161]

Another approach has been to examine the ethical codes of different professions. Litaba has examined professional codes of conduct for social workers, psychologists and lawyers in an investigation of principles for the ethical practice of family dispute resolution practitioners under the *Family Law Act 1975* (Cth).[162] These varying approaches to mediation ethics draw upon differing perspectives emphasising or combining legal, socio-behavioural, and or philosophical vantage points. Each is an attempt to grapple with the interrelated questions of what ethical principles should guide dispute management professionals operating as mediators (for example, justice, equity and accountability) and what principles should guide actual instances of practice (for example, those drawn from a community of practice, critical reflection, an ethic of care and cultural sensitivity).

Professional conduct in mediation

In addition to clause 10, the NMAS addresses ethical conduct and professional relations under clause 8:[163] Mediators accredited under the NMAS are required to adhere to the NMAS Approval and Practice Standards. In addition, in order to be accredited, a mediator must be a member of a Recognised Mediator Accreditation Body (RMAB), or a member or employee of another organisation with an ethical code of conduct and a complaints and disciplinary procedure that can address complaints against mediators.[164] RMABs are approved by, and registered with, the Mediator Standards Board (MSB). The MSB is a voluntary body responsible for the development of Australian mediator standards and the implementation of the NMAS. Members of the MSB comprise RMABs, professional, government, community and consumer organisations, and education and training providers. The MSB also maintains a national register

159 Ibid.

160 Mary Anne Noone and Lola Atkin Ojelabi, 'Ensuring Access to Justice in Mediation in the Civil Justice System' (2014) 40(2) *Monash University Law Review* 561.

161 Ibid.

162 Oyiela Litaba, 'Developing Ethical Practice as a Family Dispute Resolution Practitioner' (2013) 24(1) *Australasian Dispute Resolution Journal* 36.

163 *National Mediator Accreditation System* (NMAS) (2015) Part III, 8 <https://msb.org.au/themes/msb/assets/documents/national-mediator-accreditation-system-2015.pdf>

164 *National Mediator Accreditation System* (NMAS) (2015) Part II, 2.1(h) <https://msb.org.au/themes/msb/assets/documents/national-mediator-accreditation-system-2015.pdf>; see, eg, the Resolution Institute, 'Code of Ethics', *Resources* (Web Page) <https://www.resolution.institute/resources/code-of-ethics>; and complaints-handling process: Resolution Institute, 'What Does Resolution Institute Do When It Receives a Complaint About a Member?' (2020) <https://www.resolution.institute/documents/item/4330>.

of accredited mediators under the NMAS.[165] Hence, the NMAS provides for standards of practice, standards for the accreditation of mediators, ethical codes of conduct via approval standards for RMABs, and avenues to address consumer complaints via RMABs' complaint-handling processes. Three limits to the effectiveness of this system are evident. The first is that the system is voluntary. Since accreditation under the NMAS is not mandatory, practice standards are neither universal nor uniform. Secondly, ethical codes and complaint handling systems are not uniform and can require considerable personal drive from consumers to follow through with their complaints. Thirdly, the only consequence of a failure to meet required standards is cancellation of accreditation and/or membership of a RMAB, which does not preclude continuing practice.

ADRAC has examined issues of accountability for dispute practitioners and pointed to the introduction of a national statutory disciplinary code enforceable by a recognised peak industry body as a possible measure.[166] According to ADRAC, a national statutory scheme could compel registration of practitioners, implement an enforceable range of investigative and dispositive strategies of accountability, and provide a range of remedies to aggrieved consumers.[167] In the absence of a national statutory scheme, other avenues of accountability are available through standards attaching to employment within public sector organisations and codes of conduct for professional associations of which mediators may be members.

ADRAC identifies three categories of mediators who would be subject to these additional and/or alternative requirements: mediators qualified in disciplines other than law (eg, social work, psychology, science or engineering); mediators employed as public sector employees engaged in court and tribunal annexed processes (usually mediation and conciliation); and mediators who are qualified and admitted to practice as lawyers. All three categories are encompassed by clause 8 of the NMAS. Under clause 8(1)(c)(ii) mediators are required to 'adhere to the ethical code or standards prescribed by the professional organisation or association of which they are a member or by whom they are employed'.[168]

Outside the NMAS and voluntary adherence to clause 8, it is not clear whether or when other professional codes apply unless under the terms of the respective professional codes. ADRAC recommends that professional associations enforce general standards of conduct, such as acting honestly, and enforce any specific obligations that could be said to apply to their members when acting as mediators.[169]

Mediators may act as independent contractors or as employees. Mediators working as public sector employees are subject to statutory codes of conduct. They may be qualified and

165 Mediator Standards Board (MSB) <https://msb.org.au>.

166 Australian Dispute Resolution Advisory Council, *Accountability of ADR Practitioners* (Web Page, 14 September 2016) <https://www.adrac.org.au/accountability>.

167 Ibid.

168 *National Mediator Accreditation System* (NMAS) (2015) Part III, 8.3 <https://msb.org.au/themes/msb/assets/documents/national-mediator-accreditation-system-2015.pdf>.

169 ADRAC (n 166).

admitted as legal practitioners or have other professional certification.[170] Public sector bodies owe a statutory duty to investigate complaints against their employees and can impose disciplinary action for breaches of codes of conduct. Complaints of misconduct by public sector mediators will usually be determined by internal review with the possibility of an appeal to an external review panel.[171]

In addition to the need to answer complaints, mediators can be liable in contract and/or negligence unless an immunity from suit applies. Immunity may be conferred by a clause in an agreement to mediate or where mediators act pursuant to legislation. For example, the *Federal Court of Australia Act* 1976 (Cth) s 50C provides that:

> A mediator or an arbitrator has, in mediating, or arbitrating anything referred under section 53A, the same protection and immunity as a Judge has in performing the functions of a Judge.[172]

Lawyers in mediation

Lawyers represent a particular category for consideration because they may be acting as mediators or representing clients in mediation. These are distinct roles requiring different considerations. A lawyer acting as a mediator is required to be impartial and even handed in conducing the mediation.[173] Lawyers who represent clients in mediation, or other dispute management processes, are necessarily partisan. At the same time, they need to understand the aims and principles of non-adversarial processes in order to best serve their clients.[174] Lawyers acting for clients in mediation are governed by legal professional practice rules. Whether lawyers acting as mediators are subject to the same legal professional practice rules has been the subject of debate and calls for clarification.[175] The Law Council of Australia (LCA) has published guidelines both for those acting as mediators[176] and for lawyers acting in mediations.[177]

170 See, eg, Dispute Resolution Centre (DRC) of the Department of Justice and Attorney-General, Queensland employs mediators who may be lawyers, social workers or other professionals or who may have no other professional qualification. The Queensland Civil Administrative Tribunal employs mediators in partnership with the DRC but requires those mediators to be legally qualified.

171 ADRAC (n 166).

172 *Federal Court of Australia Act 1976* (Cth) s 50C; see also *Civil Proceedings Act 2011* (Qld) s 52.

173 Law Council of Australia (LCA), 'Ethical Guidelines for Mediators' (May 2019) 3 <https://www.lawcouncil.asn.au/publicassets/a44d140e-0994-ea11-9434-005056be13b5/Ethical%20Guidelines%20for%20Mediators%20Final%2016%20May%202019.pdf>.

174 Olivia Rundle, 'A Spectrum of Contributions That Lawyers Can Make to Mediation' (2009) 20(4) *Australasian Dispute Resolution Journal* 220; Olivia Rundle, 'Lawyers' Participation in Mediation and Professional Ethical Disposition' 18(1) *Legal Ethics* 46.

175 See Bobette Wolski, 'On Mediation, Legal Representatives and Advocates' (2015) 38(1) *University of New South Wales Law Journal* 5; Bobette Wolski, 'An Evaluation of the Rules of Conduct Governing Legal Representatives in Mediation: Challenges for Rule Drafters and a Response to Jim Mason' (2013) 16 (1) *Legal Ethics* 182.

176 Law Council of Australia (n 173).

177 Ibid.

The LCA first published ethical guidelines for mediators in 1996. They have subsequently been updated and most recently in 2019. The stated aims of the guidelines are to:

1. Serve as a guide for the conduct of mediators
2. Inform the mediating parties of what they should expect
3. Promote public confidence in mediation as a process for resolving disputes.

The guidelines draw on existing codes of conduct for mediators in Europe and the United States. They address issues of impartiality, conflicts of interest, competence, confidentiality, when termination of a mediation is appropriate, assistance in recording a settlement, publicity, advertising, and fees. The LCA's guidelines for lawyers acting in mediations were also updated in 2019.[178] These guidelines begin with an outline of the role of a lawyer in mediation:

> A lawyer's role in mediation is to assist clients, provide practical and legal advice on the process and on issues raised and offers made, and to assist in drafting terms and conditions of settlement as agreed ... [it] will vary greatly depending on the nature of the dispute and the mediation process. It may range from advising a client before a mediation, to representing a client during a mediation and undertaking all communications on behalf of a client.
>
> At all times, a lawyer must pay due regard to the duties owed as an officer of the court and in the administration of justice.[179]

The guidelines address ethical issues for lawyers of confidentiality and the need to act in good faith. They also address the conduct of lawyers in deciding when to mediate, selecting a mediator, preparing for mediation, the duty to explain mediation as a process, participation during the mediation and following the mediation. Particular requirements in relation to professional conduct are provided in clause 6.3, namely:

> Legal representatives owe their opponents general duties of respect, fairness and courtesy.
>
> Lawyers must act in a professional manner and respect and obey the law including their professional rules of conduct.
>
> Lawyers must not engage in, or assist conduct that is illegal or dishonest or otherwise discreditable to a practitioner, prejudicial to the administration of justice or which might otherwise 'bring the profession into disrepute'.

The terms of clause 6.3 reflect the decision of the Legal Services Tribunal of Queensland in *Legal Services Commissioner v Mullins*,[180] which concerned the duty of honesty owed by legal practitioners to their opponents in mediation. This duty is clearly owed in traditional

178 Ibid.
179 Ibid 3.
180 *Legal Services Commissioner v Mullins* [2006] QLPT 012.

adversarial processes and, in this case, the Tribunal confirmed its application to lawyers' conduct in mediation. A summary of the case is provided below.[181]

LEGAL SERVICES COMMISSIONER V MULLINS [2006] QLPT 012

Facts: A Queensland barrister, acting for his client in a motor vehicle insurance claim, provided the defendant's insurer with an assessment of the client's future care needs and associated costs. The assessment was contained in a report obtained by his instructing solicitors from Evidex Pty Ltd. The report expressly assumed that medical reports on which it was based were correct. The claimant was rendered a quadriplegic in the motor vehicle accident. One medical report assessed the claimant's life expectancy at 20 per cent below that of a normal male of his age, then 48 years.

In a pre-mediation conference attended by the barrister, solicitor, and client, the client revealed that he had been diagnosed with cancer spots in his lungs and other parts of his body described as 'secondary cancer' for which he would be receiving chemotherapy. The barrister advised him that this new information should be disclosed to the insurer, who was likely to investigate. The client requested that the information not be disclosed unless he was under a legal obligation to do so as he wanted the matter to be settled. The barrister researched the issue and spoke to Senior Counsel. He came to the view that no ethical rules would be breached if the claimant's lawyers did not positively mislead the defendant and his lawyers about the claimant's life expectancy.

In the mediation that followed, the barrister presented a figure for future economic loss arrived at 'as per the Evidex report and reduced for contingencies by 20 per cent, including the prospect that the plaintiff may not have worked to age 65'. The claim settled at mediation. It was established that the insurer would not have settled had the claimant's cancer been disclosed.

Issue: Whether the barrister had misrepresented the claimant's life expectancy by relying on the Evidex report and thereby engaged in professional misconduct.

Decision: The Legal Practice Tribunal held that the barrister had intentionally deceived the insurer and its legal representatives about the accuracy of the assumption as to the claimant's life expectancy in the Evidex report. The Tribunal described the barrister's conduct as a 'fraudulent deception ... (which) involved such a substantial departure from the standard of conduct to be expected of a legal practitioner of good repute and competency as to constitute professional misconduct'. The Tribunal further stated that mediation should not be entered as 'an honesty-free zone'.

The barrister was reprimanded, fined $20,000 and ordered to pay the Legal Services Commissioner's costs.

181 See Bobette Wolski, 'The Truth about Honesty and Candour in Mediation: What the Tribunal left Unsaid in *Mullins*' Case' (2012) 36(2) *Melbourne University Law Review* 706; Wolski (n 175).

The instructing solicitor, who relied on the barrister's advice, was also found guilty of professional misconduct.

Discussion: This decision is indicative of the high standards of ethical and professional conduct required of lawyers and that those standards are not excluded in mediation.

Conclusion

Mediation is often referred to as a process of facilitated negotiation. It is a triadic process in which a third-party dispute practitioner assists parties to identify issues in dispute, generate options for the possible resolution of the dispute, and negotiate the terms of any agreement between them. Mediation is based upon the principle of self-determination of the parties. As such, mediation aims to promote the capacity of parties to define their own issues and options and to reach their own decisions about outcomes of the process. Mediation has become institutionalised within our justice system and is a prescribed preliminary process for many determinative processes in courts and tribunals. As a profession, mediation and mediators are not subject to statutory regulation.

In Australia, mediators are accredited under a voluntary system – the National Mediator Accreditation System (NMAS) – which is oversighted by the Mediator Standards Board (MSB). There are several models of mediation identified in the literature. The classic, orthodox model, which forms the basis of the NMAS, is the facilitative model. Variations on the facilitative model include the evaluative, settlement or advisory models. Two further models, transformative and narrative, are sometimes described as therapeutic models and are part of a second generation, or later development, of practice. Principles of mediation practice are enunciated in the NMAS Practice Standards and include: the principle of self-determination; impartiality and procedural fairness; accounting for power in mediation; and confidentiality and ethics in mediation.

Mediation is a structured process in which there are identifiable steps that structure the dialogue between parties. These can be isolated as intake, preparation, the mediator's opening statement, parties' opening statements, summaries, setting the agenda, exploration, private sessions, option generation, negotiation, agreement, and close and debriefing. Mediation is an area of dispute management practice that has received considerable scholarly critique from academics and commentary from reflective practitioners. Three areas of special consideration have been canvassed in this chapter: ethics, professional conduct, and lawyers in mediation.

Mediation has the advantage of offering an opportunity for parties to reach their own agreements without determination by an independent third party. Mediation has the further advantage of offering assistance from a trained dispute resolution practitioner whose aim is to promote the capacities of the parties to reach their own decisions and to be self-determining.

EXERCISE IN APPLYING YOUR KNOWLEDGE – KENNETH COLE'S ESTATE

Kenneth Cole aged 80 died two months ago, leaving five adult children and one minor from three marriages. His estate consists of a house, a two-bedroom worker's cottage, worth $550,000, a car worth $8,000, and cash in the amount of $250,000. Kenneth bequeathed all of his estate to his third wife, Rosemary, aged 45 years, who was living with him at the time of his death. Rosemary and Kenneth have one son, Michael, aged 4 years.

The five children from Kenneth's two previous marriages are seeking to contest the will. Kenneth had two children from his first marriage to Evelyn: Elisa aged 52 and Robert aged 48. Kenneth had three children from his second marriage to Leanne: Miriam aged 35, Eric aged 33, and Robin aged 30. Each of the five children report that Kenneth promised to provide for them on his death. Elisa is married with two teenage children and employed as a registered nurse. Robert has suffered from mental health issues since he was in his early twenties and is in receipt of a disability pension. Each of Miriam, Eric, and Robin have young families. Eric and Robin have been in and out of work for some years and mainly work in labouring jobs. Miriam has tried several businesses but is currently unemployed and supported by her partner.

Kenneth was an antique dealer until he retired at age 68. He retained a collection of antique pieces. His adult children claim that he promised some of these pieces to them. According to Rosemary, Kenneth instructed her that on his death she should allow each of the five adult children to choose one piece of furniture each but that she should keep a Chinese writing desk valued at $9,000.00.

Elisa, Robert, Miriam, Eric and Robin have each sought legal advice and have been advised that Rosemary, who lived with Kenneth for 10 years, would be entitled under legislation to the house and a proportion of the remaining assets. They have also been advised that the cost of contesting the will would be prohibitive. The five adult children nonetheless believe that they are entitled to something more than an item of furniture from their father's estate. Elisa and Miriam are referred to you for mediation. Their brothers do not want to be involved but have authorised Elisa and Miriam to negotiate on their behalf.

Antiques contested by family members are:

- An Edwardian mahogany dining setting including 8 chairs valued at $4,800.00.
- An Edwardian mahogany sideboard valued at $3,500.00.
- A rare Chinese ebony and jade inlaid writing table valued at $9,000.00.
- A set of solid silver cutlery 56 pieces valued at $4,500.00
- An antique cedar bookcase valued at $2,500.00.
- An antique cedar tallboy valued at $1,750.00.
- A large Persian rug valued at $3,800.00.
- A Wedgewood dinner set valued at $2,000.00.

Consider the private facts for Rosemary and Elisa and Miriam supplied separately to the facts above.

1. Identify six different models of mediation and according to each describe the role of the mediator.
2. What does self-determination in mediation mean?
3. What are the issues of power in mediation?
4. What is the difference between procedural and substantive fairness in mediation? Do you think mediators should ensure substantive fairness? Give reasons for your answer.
5. What ethical standards for mediation practice are contained in the NMAS?

7

FACILITATION

Learning aims

- Demonstrate knowledge of facilitation
- Explain how facilitation operates
- Describe when to use facilitation
- Identify different interventions used in facilitation and how they work and when to apply them
- Explain group communication and other theories relevant to facilitation
- Distinguish facilitation from other dispute management processes
- Discuss special considerations in relation to facilitation

Understanding facilitation

Facilitation is a word that, in its general sense, is referred to in a wide array of dispute processes. For instance, you have read in Chapter 6 (Mediation), of the facilitative mediation model, and in Chapter 5 (Negotiation), of facilitated negotiation.[1] The word is derived from the Latin word *facilis* meaning 'ease' and generally refers to any activity that facilitates the smooth flow of the matter to be addressed. However, it can also have a specific meaning and this chapter is focused on a process of dispute management described as 'facilitation'.

Facilitation: a triadic neutral third-party non-determinative process that joins communication techniques and mediator skills with sophisticated group management to assist groups in making effective decisions.

Facilitation may be used in a preventative manner in a complex situation prior to a dispute developing, or where many parties have an interest in the outcome and assisted communication can address the issue before it develops into an entrenched dispute. Facilitation can also be used to assist parties through disputes, often when those disputes bring many different stakeholder interests into play and involve public decision-making.

The actual process is flexible but nevertheless is a separately identified approach to dealing with potential or existing disputes. Given it is appropriate to numerous sizes and types of disputes, or even non-disputing situations, it must be adaptable to its context. Facilitation is sometimes described as a group mediation. Facilitation requires sophisticated group management skills and knowledge as it involves a triadic neutral third party in a non-determinative process, coupled with the skills of a mediator and common communication techniques.

Like many of the processes described in this textbook, facilitation requires parties to have a certain common interest in addressing concerns. This requires parties to have an open mind to explore emotions and perceptions as well as facts. A facilitator may also be brought to the group by one of the disputing parties being a client, or the facilitator may be in the employ of a disputing party. In these situations, the client may be a government agency or private company responsible for introducing something new by way of legislative changes, new processes, or physical changes, which require a consultative process with those impacted. In such situations, it is important for all parties to accept the facilitator as unbiased in their role, although the client

1 See, eg, D Hunter, *The art of facilitation: The essentials for leading great meetings and creating group synergy* (Jossey-Bass, 2007); Bernadine Van Gramberg, 'Facilitation in the Workplace: An Exploratory Case Study' (2001) 12 *Australasian Dispute Resolution Journal* 171.

may have expectations the facilitator will assist the client achieve their desired goal, and the facilitator may be bound to their employer's organisational values.[2] In these circumstances, it is important the facilitator follows the general facilitation process and uses their communicative skills to demonstrate that all parties are fully catered for in expressing their needs and concerns.

The following descriptions of facilitation indicate the type of process involved:

> Facilitation is a process in which the parties (usually a group), with the assistance of a dispute resolution practitioner (the facilitator), identify problems to be solved, tasks to be accomplished or disputed issues to be resolved. Facilitation may conclude there, or it may continue to assist the parties to develop options, consider alternatives and endeavour to reach an agreement. The facilitator has no advisory or determinative role on the content of the matters discussed or the outcome of the process but may advise on or determine the process of facilitation.[3]
>
> A basic facilitator fulfils her responsibility to the group by designing an effective process for the group to accomplish its work, acting consistently with the core values, identifying for the group when members have acted inconsistently (or consistently) with principles of effective group behaviour and letting the group make free and informed choices on the basis of the facilitator's interventions. In addition, a developmental facilitator helps group members learn how to identify when they have acted inconsistently with principles of effective group behaviour, how to explore the conditions that create the ineffective behaviour and how to change these conditions to generate more effective behaviour.[4]
>
> Facilitators focus on 'helping groups do better.' In doing so, they typically perform a unique service that requires that they understand group processes and that they are able to assist the group as it diagnoses and solves process problems.[5]

The definitions place a heavy emphasis on the role of the facilitator and identify two clear types of facilitation processes. One is focused on 'process alone' (often referred to as Basic Facilitation) and the other addresses both 'process and content' (often referred to as Developmental Facilitation). Process refers to the structure and how the group is to interact and make decisions to solve an issue.[6] Content is the subject matter of concern for the parties and is not generally a concern for the facilitator. In Basic Facilitation, the facilitator assists the group in addressing any immediate issues they may have. In Developmental Facilitation, the

2 Robin Saunders, 'Mediation and Facilitation – Commonalities and Differences' (2009) 20(2) *Australasian Dispute Resolution Journal* 104.

3 Australian Dispute Resolution Advisory Council, 'Facilitation' (Web Page, 5 September 2017) < https://www.adrac.org.au/facilitation>.

4 Roger M Schwarz, *The Skilled Facilitator: A Comprehensive Resource for Consultants, Facilitators, Managers, Trainers, and Coaches* (Jossey-Bass, 3rd ed, 2016); Andrew Rixon et al, 'Exploring the Language of Facilitation' (2006) 7 *Group Facilitation: A Research & Applications Journal* 21; see also John Woodward, 'Encouraging Dialogue between Large and Diverse Groups: The Emerging Field of Facilitation' (2016) 27(1) *Australasian Dispute Resolution Journal* 58.

5 Erik Shaw et al, 'In the Moment': An Analysis of Facilitator Impact During a Quality Improvement Process' (2010) 10 *Group Facilitation: A Research & Applications Journal* 4, 5.

6 Schwarz (n 4).

aim is to go to a deeper level that addresses longer term change within the group by utilising the facilitator's expert communication knowledge as appropriate to the situation.

A facilitator's role is to aid the participants by managing the process; assisting the parties to plan appropriate agendas; ensure an appropriate environment for the most productive outcome; assist parties in identifying their concerns and issues; enable the inclusive expression of parties' opinions; guide the parties in collaborative exploration of potential solutions; and understand group dynamics in order to foster consensus decisions.[7] While much of this is similar to a mediation, the difference is in the group nature of the process, which can be more open and dynamic and in which the facilitator is accepted by those involved to act neutrally and use appropriate skills and techniques that will ease the group to make effective decisions.

A facilitation can involve small numbers through to large groups. The process encourages free and open communication to enable public understanding or diminish fear by building consensus and bringing diverse views to a closer appreciation of the problem being addressed. Facilitation is much more than just a public meeting. It has a purposive structure controlled by a trained group facilitator that can bring diverse viewpoints into closer alignment to reach solutions that will provide greater benefit for all concerned. The facilitator's role will be made easier if there is goodwill, openness to listen, and the parties have appropriate empathy.[8] Facilitators have the authority to make decisions and establish a defined agreement as to whether the process is outcomes-based or a developmental facilitation that seeks to achieve a successful outcome which accommodates all interested parties.

Brief history

Forms of facilitation have been practised by humans throughout history. As a recognised process assisting in avoiding or managing disputes, it has followed the development and rise of mediation and other forms of dispute management. O'Donnell[9] has described its specific development in Queensland during the 1990s through the free services offered by the Community Justice Program of the Attorney-General's Department. Many successful facilitations were undertaken. These included facilitations around the use of the Conondale Ranges National Park for timber extraction and Indigenous community conflicts. Stakeholders in the Conondale dispute included the timber industry, conservation parties, forestry and national parks, and Indigenous communities.[10] The outcome involved compromise, but a better result for the parties in ensuring protection of the forest while maintaining sustainable development.[11]

7 John Tyrril, 'Facilitation: Corporate Decision-Making and Dispute Resolution' (1998) 9(1) *Australian Dispute Resolution Journal* 22; Sandor P Schuman, 'The Role of Facilitation in Collaborative Groups' in Chris Huxham (ed), *Creating Collaborative Advantage* (Sage, 1996).

8 Jane Elix, 'New Approaches to Adversarialism in Business and Politics – Three Facilitative Tools in Use in Australia' (2006) 17(2) *Australasian Dispute Resolution Journal* 105.

9 Marg O'Donnell, 'The Development and Delivery of Facilitation Services in Queensland, 1990 to 1996' (1997) 8(3) *Australian Dispute Resolution Journal* 162.

10 Ibid 163–5.

11 M Buchy and S Hoverman, *Understanding Public Participation in Forest Planning in Australia: How Can We Learn From Each Other?* (Australian National University Department of Forestry, 1999) 38–9; see also Lara B Fowler and Xiaoxin Shi, 'Human Conflicts and the Food, Energy, and Water Nexus: Building Collaboration Using Facilitation and Mediation to Manage Environmental Disputes' (2016) 6(1) *Journal of Environmental Studies and Sciences* 104.

Learnings from each facilitation conducted by the Community Justice Program have been taken and applied in future facilitations in an ongoing development of the process. The significance of this historical application was the provision by the state government of a freely available facilitation process for any community members wishing to access it. The experience found that certain matters were not suitable for facilitation.[12] From the experiences in the 1990s in Queensland, facilitation has grown in that state, as it has across Australia. However, it has yet to become an entrenched process as mediation, with standards, registration and a plethora of applicable legislation. Facilitation remains a developing area in which new ways of working and engaging in groups and managing multiple party issues are continually being developed.[13]

Types of disputes

Facilitation as an adaptable process is suited to many types of disputes that usually involve more than five people. Examples include:

- workplace disputes
- environmental disputes
- public matters including public policy issues
- planning processes
- organisational disputes
- contract negotiations and renegotiation
- joint venture activities
- corporate plan and policy issues
- strategic or other partnering disputes or pre disputes
- critical annual general meetings.[14]

The public sector and the corporate sector are adopting facilitation as a mechanism to avoid costly litigation if diverse interests are likely to be activated by their operations. Public disputes have some form of impact on the general public and often engage public choice around social and economic impacts and environmental or cultural concerns. A further refinement is suggested by Condliffe[15] when dealing with public issue disputes. He suggests these come in three forms: enforcement disputes, permitting disputes, and policy or law-making disputes. Enforcement disputes concern compliance with law enforcement standards, such as tree-clearing, or noise control. Permitting disputes relate to planning permissions or construction of new infrastructure such as airports and waste dumps. Policy or law-making disputes deal with the introduction of new or changing policies and new laws or regulations.[16]

12 O'Donnell (n 9) 165–6.

13 See, eg, Keith McCandless and Henri Lipmanowicz, *Leadermorphosis Podcast (Liberating Structures: Including and unleashing everyone)* <http://www.liberatingstructures.com/>.

14 Tyrril (n 7) 22.

15 Peter Condliffe, 'The Mediation of Public Issue Disputes: Seven Key Elements' (1998) 9(4) *Australian Dispute Resolution Journal* 257, 257.

16 Ibid 258.

These types of disputes can be complex due to the range of party interests. Parties often have an imbalance in terms of access to resources and any litigation is not only costly, but can delay timely management that may escalate disharmony and other unwanted consequences.

Identifying parties to a dispute in facilitation

Who should be present?

Facilitations will often require experts to provide important information that can assist in facilitation – for example, anthropologists, engineers or scientists – along with the representatives of the stakeholders from the parties attending the facilitation. In some cases, the type of expert and the spokesperson or representative of the parties will be clear from the nature of the dispute, but in other cases – for instance, cross-cultural cases – the party spokesperson will have to be identified. In a dispute dealing with parties from different cultural groups, it is important to identify the spokesperson and make sure they consent to the process and have authority to speak for the group. Likewise, where organisations are involved, key individuals who hold authority to make binding agreements on behalf of the organisation must be included. Each interested party should have appropriate representation. Ensuring all the relevant interested parties are included in a facilitation is vital.[17]

There are various methods for determining who has authority to represent the group and who may hold the power within the group; namely, the power-brokers. This can include undertaking a short survey to ensure no one is absent. Other methods include the positional approach (who is in a key position); the reputational approach (who do others identify as people 'central' to the conflict); and the decision-making approach (who previously has been involved on behalf of the group or organisation in resolving similar disputes).[18]

Multi-party and multiple parties

Most facilitations will involve multiple parties. There are differing opinions in the literature as to what constitutes a multiple party dispute.[19] 'Multi-party' refers to more than one individual or group of individuals that have a common interest or concern. 'Multiple parties', on the other hand, is where a number of individuals or groups have divergent concerns that are interrelated but oppositional, or competing, and require a negotiated compromise or collaboration. Multi-party concerns can be accommodated by facilitation of decision-making through a consensus-based dialogue that addresses issues and finds consensus by building understanding.

Multiple party disputes require understanding of the different parties' perceptions and may be addressed through a facilitation approach, ensuring each party or represented group has a separate session with the facilitator.[20] This is to allow for expression of hidden interests that may not be comfortably presented in an open dialogue forum. This private time should occur before any process is commenced and then again at appropriate intervals throughout the process, particularly

17 See Chapters 1 and 6; see also Peter Condliffe, *Conflict Management: A Practical Guide* (LexisNexis, 6th ed, 2019) 12.

18 See also Christopher W Moore, *The Mediation Process. Practical Strategies for Resolving Conflict* (Jossey-Bass, 3rd ed, 2003) 125–6.

19 See, eg, Mieke Brandon, 'Group Facilitation and Multi-party Mediation' (2010) 21(3) *Australasian Dispute Resolution Journal* 171, 178.

20 Ibid 175–6.

where parties have hostility toward others involved. This is an essential difference to *multi-party* facilitation that tends to be pre-dispute, to educate, inform and plan through the process of a Developmental Facilitation. Multiple party facilitation generally addresses an existing dispute.

Key aspects when working with multiple parties include:

- establishing the agreed purpose and guidelines for the facilitation
- enabling all parties to participate and communicate respectfully
- listening attentively and ensuring all parties are heard by others
- acknowledging what each person can and does contribute
- understanding each parties' concerns and the roles of the participants: facilitators, parties, spokespersons for parties
- creating a comfortable space and suitable interventions to ensure sharing of necessary information
- enabling the giving and receiving of constructive feedback along with an ability to have a difficult conversation respectfully
- ensuring good preparation by all, including organising of meeting times and location.

Using theory and models to dissect facilitation

This section addresses the purpose and aims of facilitation. It considers group theory and decision-making models along with facilitation styles and techniques.[21]

Decision-making styles in groups

Different models exist for facilitation and facilitators can adapt their resources to fit the individual situation. There is an absence of research on the appropriateness of any model for the different possible facilitations or even the most used approaches. No overarching training or accreditation for facilitators prevails. It is important to remember the facilitation process is not linear, but more cyclical, as tools and techniques are adapted to fit the special circumstance of each facilitation. Wayne notes: 'There is one constant for the facilitator: no matter how elegant the methods used or the skill of the practitioner, each group we work with is unique.'[22] For instance, if facilitation is to be used in a workplace, it may be useful to consider the outcomes being sought by the participants, noting there are three types of justice: procedural, distributive, and interactional. For procedural justice, the parties will be interested

21 Dorothy Wardale, 'A Proposed Model for Effective Facilitation' (2008) 9 *Group Facilitation: A Research & Applications Journal* 49; Jacob de Lichtenberg and Manuel London, 'Evaluating Group Interventions: A Framework for Diagnosing, Implementing, and Evaluating Group Interventions' (2008) 9 *Group Facilitation: A Research & Applications Journal* 37; Gwendolyn L Kolfschoten, Marielle den Hengst and Gert-Jan de Vreede, (2007) 8 *Group Facilitation: A Research & Applications Journal* 7; Jane Elix et al, 'Report on the 2006 Survey of Australian Facilitators' (2008) 8 *Group Facilitation: A Research & Applications Journal* 15.

22 David Wayne, 'Facilitation: Beyond Methods' in Sandy Schuman (ed), *The IAF Handbook of Group Facilitation* (Jossey-Bass, 2005) 21, 35.

in the processes used by the organisation when making decisions; for distributive justice, the outcome of the process is more important; and interactional justice is attentive to the respect given to the participants when making decisions in the organisation.[23] A sense of fair treatment is endemic to the human condition. If a party feels unfairly dealt with, it will not result in a good facilitation.[24]

One of the few research studies on facilitation was conducted by Rixon in 2006. This study indicated a wide range of techniques are used. It illustrated that facilitation is a process that is more creative and diverse in approach, evolving beyond the limited models available for mediation. In some cases, the techniques used were only known to the individual facilitator. However, the processes most preferred by facilitators utilised technology and the techniques they referred to were called 'World Café' and 'Appreciative Inquiry'.[25]

Important factors to consider in any facilitation

In any group (multi-party) or multiple party process, certain aspects will always be present. This section addresses some of these and the related theory that supports an understanding of the relevant aspects. For instance, **values** are inherent to all humans and are personal to the individual. Groups and organisations also espouse commonly held values. When considering conflict in line with Moore's Circle of Conflict,[26] it can be seen that values difference is a basis for disputes and is one of the harder types of disputes to manage. Therefore, understanding some of the theory behind values is important. Rokeach has defined values as:

Values: fundamental beliefs or convictions established early in life providing a hierarchical worldview of what is intrinsically important and that generally remains constant throughout a person's life.

> ... an enduring belief that a specific mode of conduct or end-state of existence is personally or socially preferable to an opposite or converse mode of conduct or end-state of existence. A value system is an enduring organization of beliefs concerning desirable modes of conduct or end-states of existence along a continuum of relative importance.[27]

Kluckholn defined values as 'a conception, explicit or implicit, distinctive of an individual or characteristic of a group, of the desirable which influences the selection from available modes, means and ends of action'.[28]

Core values are formed early in life and remain constant through most of one's life. They change only if an experience occurs that is life changing. Values exist in a hierarchical manner

23 Van Gramberg (n 1) 233–4.

24 Julie B Marcy, 'It's a Jungle Out There – The Biology of Facilitation' (2013) 12 *Group Facilitation: A Research & Applications Journal* 21, 24.

25 Rixon et al (n 4) 21–30. The most recent study was undertaken in 2006, showing a need for more research on this process. While the study sets out to conduct a reflective practice survey of the language of facilitation, it also provided useful data about the processes favoured by facilitators. The international call for participation in the survey produced 140 respondents, with 60 per cent having more than 10 years facilitation practice: Australia Dispute Resolution Advisory Council, 'Facilitation' (Web Page, 5 September 2017) <https://www.adrac.org.au/facilitation>.

26 Moore (n 18) 64–5; see also Chapter 1.

27 Milton Rokeach, *The Nature of Human Values* (Free Press, 1973) 5.

28 Clyde Kluckhorn, 'Values and Value – Orientations in the Theory of Action' in T Parsons and E Shils (eds), *Towards a General Theory of Action* (Harvard University Press, 1951) 388.

and most people have no more than five to seven core values. Conflicts between values may cause a personal crisis or cognitive dissonance. We react strongly if we feel that our core values are being threatened. Different values may lead to conflict both internally and externally between individuals, groups and whole societies.

Overcoming **groupthink**, false consensus, and unconscious bias is important to achieving an improved dialogue. Groupthink involves the group becoming influenced by the combination of the group's thinking, or a dominate member, or members, of the group which make independent contrary positions difficult to present. This can prevent the members presenting contrary views and creates a false group consensus. Unconscious bias means the unknown or unacknowledged bias of an individual that blocks acceptance of contrary views. To improve dialogue, individual values and underlying assumptions need to be considered.[29] Some facilitations may be improved by the facilitator undertaking a values-mapping or other assessment to explore the values impinging on the dispute or potential dispute. Value inventories and assessments can assist in individuals understanding their motivations and these can then be shifted to align with interests in order to find common ground.[30] Rokeach talks of terminal values, or end states, and instrumental values being those values that assist us in achieving our terminal values. Terminal values are the driving motivators of one's actions and generally do not change over one's life.[31] For instance, trust can be a significant problem for groups, and disputes will escalate as trust declines. Re-establishing trust, or at least willingness to listen, is required so that honest interpersonal dialogue can freely occur. Establishing clear norms and roles of participants can assist with restoring trust. Consideration of the overarching goals and knowledge of individuals and organisational values can re-focus the problem and remove focus from individuals or past events to interests which are easier to negotiate.

Groupthink: when a group is influenced by the combination of the group's thinking, or a dominant member, or members, of the group, making independent contrary positions difficult to present. This can prevent members presenting their true views and creates a false consensus in the group.

Facilitators must understand the clear distinction between factors, such as values, attitudes, intention, motivation, interests, morals and ethics in the following ways.

Values are fundamental beliefs or convictions influenced by behaviour and attitudes and affected by genetics, culture, significant adults (such as parents, teachers and friends) and socio-environmental factors.

Attitudes are not stable like values. Attitudes comprise our opinions and beliefs and they have three subcomponents. These are:

- cognitive – this forms the opinion or belief behind an attitude
- affective – this refers to the emotion or feeling aspect of our attitude
- behavioural – this provides the intention to act in a certain way.

Attitudes impact how we think and feel. Attitudes vary from values, in that it is possible to hold many different attitudes at once – these attitudes can often be contradictory. In our life, we

29 Brandon (n 19) 173.
30 Moore (n 18) 64–5.
31 See Rokeach (n 27) for some examples of values inventories.

make choices, and values influence how we resolve contradictions and inform why and how we set priorities and boundaries.

Intention in the law has a specific meaning that covers foresight of the consequences of one's action, or inaction, in order to achieve a particular outcome. In psychology, intention is a desire aligned with an ability. Desire is the impulse toward, and provides the ability for, potential action. Generally, this is the basis on which intention operates at the individual level.

Motivation is the internal emotional forces and urges that cause behavioural actions, whereas values are automated judgments about ends. For example, one may value receiving a law degree to earn a good income, but during a long lecture the only motivational desire present may be to leave!

Interests are things we want and are grounded in an understanding of why we want it. For example, I may have an interest in stopping a highway development,[32] and my value that underpins my interest is a healthy environment.

Morals are beliefs derived from our values that are acquired by socialisation and may be externally imposed to indicate our standards of right and wrong that constrain or influence our behaviour. For instance, while the environment is high in my value itinerary, and my interest is in stopping a highway development, my morals will determine how I go about protesting the development.

Ethics are actions generally driven by a code or standard to act in a particular way.

Other considerations when dealing with groups include paying attention to resource constraints; organisational culture; other cultural factors, such as ethnicity, gender, ideological and religious differences; and interpersonal factors, such as personality disorders, inability to listen, dominating others, and language barriers.[33]

Having a solid grounding in identifying each of these factors will enable a facilitator to apply suitable interventions and techniques during the facilitation. The facilitator can also develop awareness of the diversity in the members of a group and their learning approach in order to reinforce the importance of the different contributions brought by members to addressing the matters of concern.[34]

Models

Depending on the size of a facilitation and the degree of complexity more than one facilitator may be needed to manage the process. Where this is the case, the facilitators normally divide their roles to cover factors such as who will lead which intervention, whether they will rotate or remain in constant roles, who will record outcomes and ideas, how will individuals participate, and the role of each facilitator in ensuring this. In such an approach, the facilitators are modelling behaviour conducive to cooperation and this can create a positive atmosphere for the facilitation.

32 See also Chapter 5.

33 Brandon (n 19) 171.

34 See, eg, Keri A Frantell, Joseph R Miles and Anne M Ruwe, 'Intergroup Dialogue: A Review of Recent Empirical Research and Its Implications for Research and Practice' (2019) 50(5) *Small Group Research* 654, which provides an example of work in small group dialogue in addressing race and other differences.

A matter that has advanced to the dispute stage may well demand more than one facilitator and a more formalised approach, particularly in large groups or where there are multiple dimensions to the dispute. The model to be followed will depend on the purpose of the facilitation, which can range from being a:

- consultation to obtain suggestions and clarify information
- data exchange to advise and gather input from stakeholders and experts
- decision-making to assist groups deal with complex matters
- dispute management: to assist groups problem-solve their dispute.

A basic facilitation model

It has been noted that facilitation is a creative process the facilitator can adapt to the circumstances. The following provides a basic facilitation model as a guideline.

Step 1 Intake

Initial contact between the facilitator and known parties is often made by telephone or email to begin the information-gathering on the parties' reasons for wanting a facilitation. Face-to-face or technology-assisted meetings may follow to explore more deeply the background issues and assist the facilitator in designing the most appropriate techniques and interventions for the facilitation. At this stage, the facilitator should consider all groups that may be affected and ensure the appropriate parties are present in order to manage the issues. The facilitator will also assess the suitability of the process for application to the matter and identify potential agenda items.

The intake process not only ensures all relevant parties are consulted but builds rapport and confidence in the facilitator and the process and enables the facilitator to adopt an appropriate facilitation utilising the best tools for the participants. As Tyrril notes:

> The dynamics of meetings involving many people and differing agendas demand planning, facilitation and, at times, the skills of the mediator to resolve differences and disputes and to develop and build consensus.[35]

Step 2 Preparation

This is a vital phase in facilitation. If more than one facilitator is to be involved, the team of facilitators will meet and plan their various roles and functions. Generally, a preliminary diagnosis of the group and their needs will be undertaken. At this stage, facilitators will assess the appropriateness of possible interventions they can use.[36] Using surveys or inventories to be completed by participants in advance of the facilitation can aid in the process. If the matter concerns legal rights, interpretation of legislation, or case law, the facilitator will need to

35 Tyrril (n 7) 23.
36 Schwarz (n 4); see de Lichtenberg and London (n 21).

consider whether parties have access to legal advice, or whether having a legal expert agreed to by both sides would assist.

Setting is also an important factor to consider at this stage. Choosing a location that accommodates the size and needs of the participants is important. It should be conducive to the best outcome by providing facilities that assist with the style of facilitation to be used. For instance, O'Donnell describes

> ... the importance of ritual — of beginnings and endings, of parties eating and drinking together, and above all the importance of the process itself. People needed to find relevance and meaning in the manner in which the discussion occurred, and they needed a voice – to be heard, in their own words and tempo with kindness and respect, or at least in silence.[37]

Step 3 Commencement

At the commencement of the facilitation, there is the introduction of the facilitators and the processes to be undertaken. This stage also identifies the various parties and confirms their authority to agree any potential management options. Establishing the ground rules and outlining the process by explaining the aims of the facilitation, if identified by the intake interview, or a basic outline of the purpose of the facilitation should be made clear. This engages the parties in building rapport with the facilitator.

Step 4 Opening statement by parties

All parties, if the group is small enough, otherwise a representative chosen by each participating group, provides a statement that outlines the reason for the party's participation and the concerns they would like addressed. This should occur without interruption. The facilitator will summarise the parties' statements and seek any necessary clarification. Usually this will be done after each party's statement or where considered appropriate after all parties have made their opening statements.

Step 5 Agenda

A preliminary agenda can be formulated by the facilitator, although some will adopt processes that allow the agenda to develop from the facilitation process once it has commenced. Some facilitators may have already drafted an agenda at the intake stage or prepared the agenda after the opening statements. The agenda should be a mutualised list of the matters of concern for each of the parties or the group they represent. The facilitator may then engage the parties in deciding the order in which matters on the agenda can be addressed. Conversely, the facilitator may use the agenda items as focus points or key questions to be addressed by the interventions and techniques used during the exploration or other phases.

37 O'Donnell (n 9) 164.

Step 6 Goal statement

Facilitators can identify a goal statement that encapsulates the vision the parties are seeking in the facilitation. This step is different from other processes and helps clarify to the parties what type of facilitation is being undertaken. For instance, is it a Basic or Developmental Facilitation to build consensus? Is it pre-dispute or a dispute and, if so, what type of dispute? This assists parties to understand the real purpose of their facilitation, rather than just addressing some immediate imagined need. Assessing the success of the facilitation can then be demonstrated by reference to the goal statement in determining if all parties' needs have been met.[38]

Step 7 Exploration/intervention

This phase allows the facilitator to introduce the various intervention styles and techniques to enable the parties to discuss their issues in an exploration with each other and to generate options for problem-solving. Interventions can be planned, but can also be adopted on the spot or changed as the facilitation unfolds and the facilitator assesses that alternative approaches and techniques will assist. This is the key expertise of a facilitator; namely, one who is constantly evaluating and adapting as the session unfolds.[39] Some techniques to use at this stage are discussed in the next section of this chapter. Any intervention relies on the facilitator knowing when to intervene and what is needed to aid change.[40] This is based on the knowledge of theory and research, such as multiple parties interaction and group behaviour.

Step 8 Private sessions

Facilitators may want to check in with the parties as individual groups or stakeholders in a confidential process. This can assist in drawing out any hidden or remaining concerns that may block the negotiation phase. It also allows the facilitator pause and to gain indications from the parties whether the interventions are suitable or need to be adjusted or even revisited. Any options generated by exploration can be reality tested. The facilitator can also coach the parties in how they may introduce any matters that they wish to bring back to the main session.

Step 9 Negotiation

The facilitators will use appropriate technique and skill to bring the parties into negotiation, based on the improved understanding of the issues and to work through the options for management. If this stage is not successful, the facilitator can introduce further suitable techniques or repeat earlier interventions. A key point for facilitation is that, compared to mediation, it is not a linear process.

Step 10 Agreement, closure and debrief

A clear statement setting out any agreement reached or management of issues for future consideration should be drawn up by the facilitators or nominated party representatives. Any

38 Saunders (n 2) 107.

39 See de Lichtenberg and London (n 21).

40 See, eg, R Wageman, JR Hackman and E Lehman, 'Team Diagnostic Survey: Development of an Instrument' (2005) 41(4) *Journal of Applied Behavioral Science* 373, for a Team Diagnostic Survey to address areas where interventions may be required.

further meetings needed can be identified and agreed and any follow-up arrangements should be established. This can include agreeing to a trial period and how that would be implemented.

Addressing how to indicate to the wider world any arrangement or agreement will also be important. There may be the need for preparation of a joint media release (where wider public interest is involved) or an organisational statement (where, for instance, the organisation has been participating in a workplace facilitation).

Facilitators must manage appropriate closure of the process to aid parties in harmoniously moving forward from the facilitation. The opportunity for reflection by participants is important to ensure the parties receive feedback to guide their future interactions and aid in the implementation of outcomes. Facilitators can assist in the implementation stage and evaluate outcomes by measuring future achievements and progress.

After the closure, the facilitators, if more than one is involved, will debrief to ensure any reflective learnings for future improvement are not lost and to ensure each has an opportunity to support the other. As Brandon confirms:

> The use of reflective practice, self-empathy, mentoring and supervision is helpful for the practitioner to learn from what they did well and what they would have liked to have done differently. The integration of 'reflection in and on practice' encourages articulation of espoused theories in contrast to the theories in use. Such reflection fosters lifelong learning and creates more insightful practitioners in the future.[41]

Using knowledge of facilitation to assist in dispute management

This section will introduce techniques and interventions commonly adopted in a facilitation process, when and how to use such interventions, and general factors to consider. The techniques discussed include Open Space, Consensus, World Café, Philosophers Walk, and the Delphi Method.[42]

This chapter has outlined the types of disputes suitable for facilitation. The process is adaptable to suit many circumstances. It can be used when a dispute has developed to a stage where introducing an outsider, the facilitator, will assist by bringing greater formality and respect to the communications. Having a third-party independent facilitator assisting the dialogue between many in a multi-party dispute, or with disputes between multiple groups by utilising their specialised skills, can manage the dispute and prevent its escalation. It is particularly helpful when the facilitator brings expertise on development facilitation, working to help groups move towards a specific goal or plan by formalising option development, and aiding in any investigations that will bring the various parties to a clearer understanding of the

41 Brandon (n 19) 178 (footnotes omitted); see also Chapter 2.

42 Marcy (n 24); Jane E Haskell and Louise Franck Cyr, 'Community Facilitator Education: How Training Can Lead to Positive Impacts at the Community Level' (2011) 11 *Group Facilitation: A Research & Applications Journal* 5; David Dryden Henningsen, Miller Henningsen and Mary Lynn, 'Examining the Effect of Marginal Members in Information Sharing Groups' (2007) 8 *Group Facilitation: A Research & Applications Journal* 22.

problem or issues. Facilitators must also be able to respond to emotion. In public groups, this requires ensuring emotion is accurately acknowledged and matters raised are detoxified and summarised so that every speaker knows they have been heard and all issues raised are addressed.[43]

Factors impacting on a facilitation

Consideration of many factors will influence how a facilitator conducts a facilitation. This starts with the number of parties holding an interest in the outcome and the complexity of the matter, through to whether it is pre-dispute or in dispute, and is to be a Developmental Facilitation (content and process driven), or just a Basic Facilitation (process driven).

Internal factors

The internal factors facilitators need to consider include the group size, demographics, roles and norms, participants, and their own capability and personality.

A group may be classified as the 'whole being greater than the sum of its parts', but all groups find limitations based on the capabilities of members and the leaders that rise to influence the group's behaviour. Group cohesiveness and ultimate effectiveness is dependent on individual personality traits within the group, particularly where they drive the group's behaviour. Authoritative traits will hinder, while sociable, empathetic and self-reliance traits aid a group's effectiveness. Limitations from individuals will affect the ability of the group to engage in and achieve its task.

Heterogeneity: a heterogenic group is made up of people from diverse experiences and backgrounds.

Homogeneity: a homogeneous group is comprised of members with shared characteristics; for instance, similar backgrounds, experience, or culture.

The **heterogeneity** or **homogeneity** will also influence a group's behaviour. The more heterogeneous, the more diverse are the influences, and so creativity is required in managing potential disputes. Homogeneity will exist if a group comes from one dimension, such as the same culture, ethnic group, religion, gender, age or social class, and can lead to faster decision-making.

The norms, values, and beliefs of a group are vital for a facilitator to consider. These influence the behaviour of the group and its interpretation of other parties' behaviour. Each party will bring both explicit and implicit expectations of members and outsiders. Certain individuals are attributed roles within a group. The individual holding a specific role often has greater expectations imposed that they will conform to the norms of the group and exhibit a continuity in loyalty with any external roles the individual may carry. Non-conforming behaviour tends to attract a negative repercussion. Clarity around roles is essential to avoid disputes within the group.

Consideration of the size of the group and its impact on the ability of the group to achieve outcomes in desired timeframes is necessary. The smaller the group (around 10) the more agile and cohesive its potential. Conversely, larger groups will have a greater creative potential for problem-solving and potentially more expertise to draw on.

In any group, there will be those speaking and those who tend to remain silent, those who are active and those who are loafers (letting others do the work). A good facilitator will be

43 Saunders (n 2) 108–9.

attentive to this, and use techniques that encourage all to voice their concerns and to engage and actively contribute. This is done by recognising the different skill set an individual brings to the group. Henningsen, Henningsen and Lynn have looked at the effect of information-sharing, particularly where groups have what they describe as 'marginal members'.[44] These are members who do not contribute to a group – in other words, the loafers. They reason that there is a bias toward the group's shared information, but unshared information may be important to making viable and lasting decisions. Thus, the effectiveness of the decision-making is diminished when members do not contribute to the information pool. This problem increases the larger the group size. The following equation portrays the effect.

Functional Group size = actual group size – marginal group members.[45]

The facilitator can address group size by breaking the group into smaller working groups, and can gain information about the group prior to the facilitation through short surveys. The role of the facilitator may involve helping the group understand the internal factors that can impact on how effectively the members work together and the type of interventions required to assist in the facilitation.[46] Managing a multiple party facilitation requires use of micro and macro techniques, such as who will pay for the facilitation, how legal representatives will be involved, what is the impact of the parties' different resources, and are there existing legal orders or government legislative requirements. Shurven suggests that coordinating these factors is essential for a good outcome, but can mean significant work.[47]

One last, but vital factor, is for facilitators to be self-aware of what triggers a facilitator's emotional response, how they respond to disputing parties, their personal non-verbal communication style, and the limits of their own skills. As Shaw et al note '. . . the state of being and presence of the facilitator impacts directly on the effectiveness of any interventions . . .'.[48] Shaw et al's study addressed the effect of a facilitator's impact 'in the moment', as they make instant decisions to adjust or change interventions to address the facilitation requirements. They found that facilitators' spontaneous decisions help groups in a timely manner by responding to 'group conflict as it surfaces, and to give steady doses of encouragement and supportive feedback at each meeting so that group members can feel good about even small steps of success'.[49] The facilitator's impact is directly dependent on their skill, experience, and relationship with the parties.

External factors

A facilitator must be conscious of external factors, such as the location and physical space for the facilitation, and the nature of the client or groups (such as their organisational culture, goals and legal framework, and any reporting obligations). The latter aspects require an

44 Henningsen, Henningsen and Lynn (n 42).
45 Ibid 23.
46 de Lichtenberg and London (n 21) 39.
47 Helen Shurven, 'Multiple Party Mediation: Complexities and Strategies' (2014) 25(3) *Australasian Dispute Resolution Journal* 166.
48 Shaw et al (n 5) 4.
49 Ibid 13.

understanding of an organisation's values and vision. The goals will influence the strategies chosen. An example is where the goal of the facilitation is to reduce staff or costs. In such a case, options would not include increasing staff or spending more, and so the options available to the group become constrained. The **organisational structure** can vary and influence how decisions are reached. Structure can include bureaucratic, hierarchical, flat, democratic, authoritarian or cooperative structures and each will have an impact on how quickly decisions can be reached. A facilitation can include members from different parts of an organisation or from specific areas, which will influence options, and any reporting and decision-making. Knowing the organisation's values, policies, and procedures enables a facilitator to assist groups in identifying goals, tasks, and roles that aid the intricacies of group behaviour and team-building.

Organisational structure: the system adopted to achieve an organisation's goals. Examples can vary from bureaucratic, hierarchical, flat, democratic, authoritarian or cooperative structures.

The resources of groups are essential to consider. This can include financial, time, access to expertise, and physical resources. All have a potential to limit or extend a group's opportunities and options. Every group will have a culture comprised of unwritten, and often unspoken, standards for acceptable behaviour. These are picked up rapidly by anyone joining the group. This can lead to groupthink, or group bias and group loyalty. If a group engages in high comradery and loyalty in a desire to reduce disputes, it can risk following distorted or inaccurate beliefs.[50] Heuristics, or thinking inductively, risks being stuck in a reasoning pattern that is reliant on past experience. It increases the possibility of reaching a compromise without exploring creative and more appropriate possibilities. Being open to a dissonant, or challenging voice, and understanding the importance of critical thinking will enable healthy outcomes for the group.[51] It is necessary to be alert to subgroups that can divert and distract from the group's objectives. Marcy points out the issue of **territoriality** that often operates in multiple party disputes and personalising stakeholder groups as a means of overcoming this issue.[52] Facilitators can overcome these concerns, by using awareness activities and requiring reflection by members on how their behaviour, values, and attitudes contribute, or not, to the process.[53]

Territoriality: the monopolisation by one group to the exclusion of another.

Schwarz[54] elaborates a group effectiveness model based on a systems approach. This model proposes that there are predictable behaviours within groups and is a tool to assist facilitators in assessing what might be appropriate interventions to ensure the parties can work in a more collaborative manner. The model has three basic criteria: performance, process, and people. The elements for the parties to consider and form a hypothesis on the areas to work on to enable collaborative effectiveness require consideration of structure, process, and group context. The interconnectedness of the systems elements means that work in one area will affect others. This requires a symmetry between the relationships of each element in the

50 Marcy (n 24) 22–3.

51 Austin J Freeley and David L Steinberg, *Argumentation and Debate: Critical Thinking for Reasoned Decision Making* (Thomas Wadsworth, 11th ed, 2005) 1.

52 Marcy (n 24) 24–5.

53 See de Lichtenberg and London (n 21) 40.

54 Roger M Schwarz, *The Skilled Facilitator: A Comprehensive Resource for Consultants, Facilitators, Managers, Trainers, and Coaches* (Jossey-Bass, 2nd ed, 2002); see also Schwarz (n 4).

model. The model can provide an effective intervention by focusing the parties on the way they are working and where improvement is needed – even how to develop the model to suit their situation more exactly.

Experts

Generally, in a Basic Facilitation, the facilitators are not seen as experts in regard to the content. In some cases, they may have expertise in both the process and content, and so more is expected of them and the facilitator will adopt different processes aligned with their content expertise. This could be cultural competence, or expertise in organisational behaviour, workplace laws, or planning and engineering, for instance. In such facilitations, the facilitator can be accorded extra respect by participants, increasing trust and confidence. If this is the case, then facilitators will have to be careful to avoid any perceptions of bias towards a particular outcome. They will be required to listen and avoid making assumptions by maintaining respect for all parties.[55] A cautionary note is important to keep in mind:

> Experience suggests that experts inevitably in conceptualising the dispute, will be influenced by their own technical and philosophical frameworks. They will filter and structure information and communication based on professional constructs. They may tend to rely upon their prior knowledge or suppositions about the nature of the dispute, rather than allowing parties to teach them and each other about the dispute. The temptation for the expert is to focus on the technical aspects of the dispute and to underestimate the significance of underlying values and perceptions held by parties. I suspect that experts may also tend to lead parties to solutions.[56]

Facilitators will always be experts regarding process. The following section addresses some of the process skills and expertise required.

Facilitator qualities and skills

A survey among 140 Australian and New Zealand facilitators in 2006 indicated the majority of survey respondents were highly educated females who focus their facilitation on training, planning, and group development, working mostly for government, community and not-for-profit.[57] Key attributes indicated as essential by the respondents were 'vocal inflection, eye contact, animated facial expression … story telling … and [being] people orientated'.[58] Facilitators rate the importance of non-verbal communication as high as, if not higher than verbal communication.[59]

55 Brandon (n 19) 174.
56 C Nolan in O'Donnell (n 9) 165.
57 Elix et al (n 21) 15; Bruce W Tuckman and Mary Ann C Jensen, 'Stages of Small-Group Development Revisited' (2010) 10 *Group Facilitation: A Research & Applications Journal* 44; Shaw et al (n 5) 4.
58 Elix et al (n 21) 20.
59 Rixon et al (n 4) 25–6.

Monochronic: describes people who are punctual and orderly and to whom time is important.

Polychronic: describes people who are accepting of multiple things occurring and less rigid.

Haptics: derives from the Greek word for tactile. It refers to touch or kinaesthetic movement.

Other factors to consider in non-verbal communication include cultural differences between **monochronic** and **polychronic** time, which refers to the manner in which a group will organise their time. Monochronic people will be orderly, focused on one thing at a time, and precise in arranging meeting times and following a time schedule. Such monochromic countries or regions include Australia, Canada, Germany, New Zealand, Scandinavia, Switzerland, United Kingdom and United States.[60] Other considerations when thinking about non-verbal signals include proxemics: the personal space; and **haptics**: touch during communication. Both are factors facilitators should have awareness of and ensure they are appropriate to the parties they are facilitating. Typically, people from Western cultures like a larger proxemic distance between themselves and others and do not like personal contact. People from Pacific Island Nations, Asia and South America are familiar with close personal proxemics and touch during communication. Marcy provides metrics to evaluate non-verbal communication styles as follows:

- Eye contact: Is eye contact being made? If so, is it overly intense or just right?
- Facial expression: What is your/their face showing? Is it masklike and inexpressive, or emotionally present and filled with interest?
- Tone of voice: Does your/their voice project warmth, confidence, and interest, or is it strained and blocked?
- Posture and gesture: Are bodies relaxed or stiff and immobile? Are shoulders tense and raised, or slightly sloped?
- Touch: Is there any physical contact? Is it appropriate to the situation? Does it make you feel uncomfortable?
- Intensity: Do they seem flat, cool, and disinterested, or over-the-top and melodramatic?
- Timing and pace: Is there an easy flow of information back and forth? Do nonverbal responses come too quickly or too slowly?
- Sounds: Do you hear sounds that indicate caring or concern?[61]

Facilitators need skills that recognise these communication styles and personality traits. They will also need the skills of mediators, such as being a problem-solver to assist parties in creatively brainstorming ideas and solutions, in clarifying, reframing, summarising, as well as non-verbal communication skills. Further, facilitators will require a thorough grounding in group dynamics and behaviours along with learning and change behaviour processes.

Wardale identifies six key attributes for facilitators: 'neutrality, humility, flexibility, sincerity, professionalism and awareness'.[62] Neutrality is now a contested concept, with impartiality being favoured as it is closer to human capability.[63] In any event, an objective, non-defensive and non-judgmental position regarding the content, at least, is supported.[64] The expertise of the facilitator regarding process requires an impartial application to all parties. The use of

60 Marcy (n 24) 26.
61 Ibid.
62 Wardale (n 21) 50.
63 See Chapters 3 and 6.
64 Ibid. See also Schwarz (n 54) 41.

language that is less dictatorial and more polite demonstrates both humility and professionalism through respecting the value of all parties' contributions.

Techniques

Group development theory

An understanding of group development theory is essential for facilitators when designing an appropriate intervention. Bruce Tuckman's[65] group theory, developed in 1965, has become a common approach to understanding group dynamics. The theory proposes that there are stages in development that a group goes through – this is not always linear and can regress to earlier stages and revert when new members join a group. Moving through the stages requires each member to let go of something in return for gaining something. In 1977, Tuckman further reviewed his theory and added a final stage, acknowledging that groups may well come to an end and, in so doing, can go through another stage, referred to as 'adjourning'.[66] The identified stages are:

- forming
- storming
- norming
- performing
- adjourning.

Forming occurs when a group is in its initial meeting stages. At this time, individuals are polite and seek to avoid controversy as they observe and get to know others and their behaviour. During this phase, a tolerance for ambiguity will assist as the group seeks the natural leader. If this is contested, then cliques can begin to arise.

The *storming* phase arrives as individuals begin to assert their position and seek acknowledgement or respect for their role or contribution. Any cliques that have formed may negatively impact at this point. Generally, the group will be arriving at decision-making mechanisms and norm-creating. This can be the toughest stage for a group, with views being forcefully expressed, positions being challenged, poor communication behaviours emerging, such as poor listening, emotional reactions, defending, or withdrawing. A group can risk disintegrating at this point if they do not identify the phase as a necessary part of group development to move to the next level. Facilitators can work with groups during this stage to assist in moving forward from the destructive behaviours and agree on acceptable processes for communicating and decision-making.

Norming arrives when internal processes transition from competitive to collaborative. Cliques disband and instead identify with the whole group. Active listening and shared leadership make the group more receptive, mutually dealing with problems with greater group support and cohesiveness. This can be observed through reduced preconceptions and assumptions, greater individual self-disclosure, and sharing of tasks leading to strengthening trust.

65 Bruce W Tuckman, 'Developmental Sequence in Small Groups' (1965) 63(6) *Psychological Bulletin* 384.

66 Bruce W Tuckman and Mary Ann C Jensen, 'Stages of Small-Group Development Revisited' (2010) 10 *Group Facilitation: A Research & Applications Journal* 44.

A group will be performing at its best when it has matured to the point of strong member loyalty, with expressed warmth, openness, socialisation and collaboration between members. Such a group is less structure dependent and more accepting of individual personal expression. The group will accept individuals doing specific tasks because trust will be strong. When a group is in this phase, it may be difficult for new members to join and, if they do, the group may have to revert to some of the previous phases in a cyclical manner.

The added stage of *adjourning* acknowledges that a group that has evolved to the *performing* stage may find it difficult in accepting the life cycle of the group. This leads to an inevitable separation or termination of the group once its purpose is achieved. Separation is an important phase that requires acceptance of changes in communication as the group dissolves or individuals leave. Many other theorists have acknowledged this phase of group behaviour.[67]

A good facilitator can aid the group by identifying the phases and articulating the phase the group appears to be operating in at any time. Agreeing norms and roles early will assist a smooth transition through the various phases.

The Johari Window

Another useful tool for facilitators addressing group dynamics is the Johari Window (Figure 7.1), which explains the means by which group members achieve acceptable tolerance for why members behave the way they do. The group's levels of self-disclosure and feedback expose the degree of understanding and trust that a group holds for its members (Figure 7.2). The Window has four panes. These are the Arena, which holds the shared knowledge with open and mutual understanding; the Façade, which is non-shared knowledge of self and which can reduce group effectiveness and lead to misunderstandings; the Blind Spot, which represents an individual's attributes that they are unaware of and therefore also unaware of the consequences; and the Unknown holds the hidden.

Figure 7.1 The Johari Window[68]

	Known to self	Not known to self
Known to others	Arena	Blind spot
Not known to others	Façade	Unknown

67 See also R Lacoursiere, 'A Group Method to Facilitate Learning During the Stages of a Psychiatric Affiliation' (1974) 24(3) *International Journal of Group Psychotherapy* 342; LJ Braaten, 'Developmental Phases of Encounter Groups and Related Intensive Groups: A Critical Review of Models and a New Proposal' (1974) 7(5) *Interpersonal Development* 112; RD Mann, *Interpersonal Styles and Group Development* (John Wiley, 1967).

68 Joseph Luft, *Einführung in Die Gruppendynamik* (Klett-Cotta, 1986).

The Johari Window supports the quality of information-sharing over the quantity, and the larger the Arena the more open and effective the group is likely to be. This does not mean all individuals have to know everything about themselves and each other; rather, it should be an Arena that is appropriate to the purpose and tasks of the group.

Figure 7.2 Self-disclosure and feedback in the Johari Window[69]

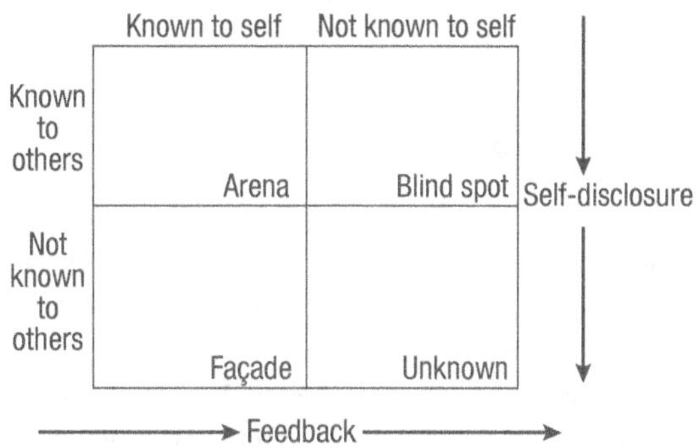

The amount of self-disclosure between individuals involves risk in sharing of feelings and facts that may make one feel vulnerable. However, sharing fears and weaknesses leads to the giving and receiving of feedback. Feedback, whether given or received, can be difficult, as it requires good communication, such as active listening and active responding. For example, if an individual is a talker, who talks over others, this can be a Blindspot and the consequence can lead to antagonism and feelings of being disrespected by those experiencing this behaviour. Making the individual aware requires giving feedback in a manner that is received and responded to respectfully. If the individual is defensive and denies they have that attribute, the problem will remain and will not become part of the Arena. It is important that self-disclosure and feedback occur equally. If there is too much feedback in comparison to self-disclosure, the Blindspot will be the largest windowpane. If, however, there is excessive disclosure and little feedback, the Façade becomes the largest windowpane. Neither situation is desirable. The preference is to enlarge the Arena by equal engagement in disclosure and feedback in order to reduce the Unknown. A technique to assist groups with this is to use a timing device, with members seated in a circle, and rotating around the circle allowing time for appropriate self-disclosure and feedback.

Working within or between groups in a facilitation means dealing with goals, roles, processes, and relationships. Problems will arise if goals are not understood, owned and agreed, and conflict will occur if the extent of their uniqueness or sharing is not clear. This also applies to overlap in role boundaries, clarity, and agreement in role obligations and the degree of autonomy and authority. The process for decision-making must make clear who holds authority, responsibility, the degree of consultation required, whether consensus or

69 Adapted from Peter Moxan, *Building a Better Team: A Handbook for Managers and Facilitators* (Gower, 1998) 4, 13.

majority vote applies, meeting processes, structure, content, and frequency required. A good leader will know to seek and be responsive to feedback. Relationships can be the most difficult to address and need respectful dealings acknowledging feelings and interests and overcoming any values and attitudinal differences in order to reach an acceptable level of understanding.

Knowledge of group dynamics is essential when deciding on the intervention to apply in a facilitation. The following section contains some of the more common interventions. The literature and websites are replete with suggestions on group interventions that facilitators may choose to use or adapt to their needs.[70]

Common interventions

Open space

Open space is a meeting technique designed to enable collaborative communication to address problems by developing creative options. Open space can lead to quicker, more efficient problem-solving than a traditional committee approach to problem-solving.

By involving the participants in synchronous, small, breakout discussion groups addressing an agenda, theme or issue, creative innovative thinking is encouraged. The small groups ideally should represent diverse participants, by mixing membership across organisational and group lines. This aspect can build relationships and trust, while quickly discovering issues to address. The process can be applied to any group size and allows all to have voice and participate, thus drawing on the knowledge and expertise of the entire group. It encourages creative non-linear thinking in problem-solving. The process can be carried out over a short time, or days if necessary.

Generally, there will be no agenda – only general themes with a set time to discuss these. The small breakout groups sit together and generate the issues important to them. Participants can move between groups, addressing issues another group may be discussing that they feel is important to offer their contribution to, or if they don't feel they are adding to the group they are with. Open space places responsibility on the individual to engage and learn and, if that is not occurring for them, they are free to leave. Usually, one member will remain with a group to record the information discussed. From this, an organic bottom-up agenda can be created.

The guiding aspects of open space are really a *laissez-faire* approach whereby whoever is present in the group is considered sufficient as they are the ones interested, concerned, and passionate enough to participate. There is no need to bring experts or others into the gathering, as the right people are the ones involved. There is no requirement for control of the discussion. The groups will bring the issues and opportunities to the surface. There is also no limitation on the group, and they can take the time needed to fully discuss and develop their options to problem-solve. This may be quick, or it may take time.

Open space discussions will conclude when:

- All issues of concern have been discussed
- The discussion has exhausted participant interest
- All critical issues are identified

70 See, eg, McCandless and Lipmanowicz (n 13); Interaction Institute for Social Change (Web Page) <http://interactioninstitute.org/developmental-facilitation/>; Schwarz (n 54).

- Issues are prioritised for action
- Relevant next steps for action are identified and volunteers agree to assist
- All the participants are provided with the matters discussed in a written form.

Open space is a technique used when groups need to uncover issues or emerging concerns and generate realistic and manageable solutions rapidly, while also building relationships and trust. It gives voice to many individuals who have an interest to provide valuable input and knowledge on matters important to all participants. Owen has developed Open Space Technology (OST) – a technology that supports use from small to very large groups, and suggests it is most useful when participants are grappling with a complex problem to which the answer is unknown and is needed in the very near future.[71]

Matters suited for Open Space facilitation include:

- providing community or organisational vision
- strategic planning
- creating new policy
- developing new infrastructure or planning changes
- building group or workplace cohesion
- providing creative problem-solving
- improving cooperation and collaboration
- managing or resolving disputes.

Consensus

A consensus approach is ideal for bringing parties to an acceptable agreement for all. However, understanding the theory underpinning consensus is not straightforward. It can relate to an organisational or whole-of-state or institution approach, a making of an agreement, or even a process.[72] Ash outlines such a process as involving:

- a group-sharing of the issues to inform each other
- discussion of the issues exploring what is needed and why it is important, including any consequences
- openness and respect allowing all ideas to be put forward
- allowing all voices time to be heard and the information to be absorbed
- exploring all options generated without judgment before due consideration
- taking time and, if necessary, a break to allow reflection on the information received
- returning to a final meeting for all groups to consensually agree to an outcome they can all live with

71 Harrison Owen, *Open Space Technology: A User's Guide* (Berrett-Koehler, 3rd ed, 2008).

72 Paul V Stock, 'Consensus Social Movements and the Catholic Worker' (2012) 5(1) *Politics and Religion* 83.

- if agreement cannot be reached at this stage, then repeating the process and taking the time needed to fill any information gaps.[73]

Quaker meeting processes provide the best example of consensus decision-making. Quaker meetings take time and result in either a consensus of thought or no agreement if one member cannot align their thinking with the others. Stock describes this process as 'based in care and recognition of the dignity of the human person'[74] in which minority interests are considered equally important as the majority. Consensus agreement such as this does not adopt a voting mechanism.

Figure 7.3 The consensus spiral process: a non-linear approach to reaching a consensus solution through identification of issues, discussion and refinement in a continually revolving process until agreement is reached

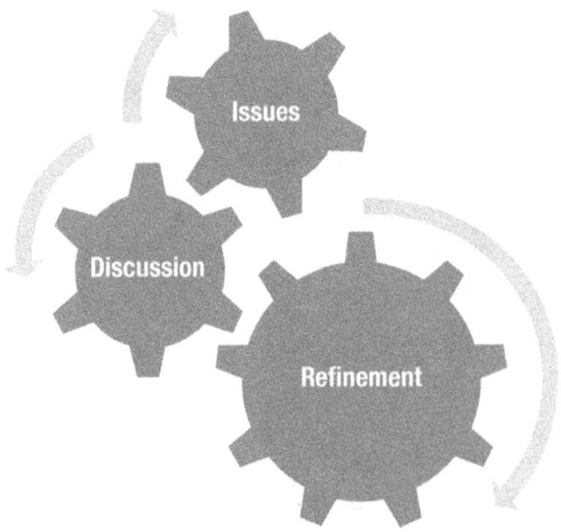

Consensus building can be difficult if the dispute is complex and advanced. Changing parties in dispute to engage in interactive negotiation is challenging. Reality testing the BATNA or WATNA[75] if an agreement cannot be reached can assist in moving the parties to engage. However, in such situations, consensus may not be an appropriate goal and other techniques should be followed.

World Café

World Café is often used by facilitators in Australia to develop collaborative conversations between groups, whether small or large, in a manner that draws on the intelligence and creativity of the minds present. The groups are asked to consider factors such as information awareness, relationships, reflection on the issues, and problem-solving options. The

73 Evan Ash, 'Adding Discussion of Issues to Mediation: Lessons from Consensus Building' *Mediate.com: Everything Mediation* (Web Page, July 2006) <https://www.mediate.com/articles/ashE5.cfm>.

74 Stock (n 72) 86.

75 See Chapter 2 for an explanation of BATNA and WATNA.

philosophy underlying this technique relies on collective insight provided by listening to the many contributions; and this in turn evolves by drawing on the intelligence gained from the deeper group reflection.

This technique needs a comfortable space to form groups around circular tables. The aim is to bring diverse people together in small group discussion in which every person is encouraged to converse and listen for deeper questions and patterns or insights in order to create a collective wisdom or knowledge.

A clear purpose, such as raising an issue to be addressed, starts the process and this can be in the form of a question from the facilitator. It requires three rounds of table sessions, lasting around 30 minutes each, in which participants in mixed groups each address the same question or further specified questions that refine and evolve from the previous round's question. One participant will stay at a table through all three rounds as the host, the other four to five participants move to different tables.

At the beginning of each round, the facilitator raises the question to be addressed, the table host then describes to the new participants what the previous rounds participants had discussed, before the new round begins their conversation. This is recorded by the table host.

A process often referred to as the 'harvest' occurs, either between each round or at the end, in which the groups have time to share the insight or 'ah ha' moments from their conversations within the group. These are recorded and then provided to the whole group for further reflection.

Important aspects include having participants who will genuinely contribute and listen for deep reflection and important ideas. Enough time should be given for each round and for participants to move between rounds. The harvest should have sufficient time and the key information sought should be gained during this process. If World Café is used early in a facilitation, it can provide rich material for the participants to explore more deeply at later stages.

Other techniques

Some other techniques facilitators can use such as the Philosopher's Walk, Reverse Brainstorming, Delphi Method and Adaptive Learning are briefly introduced here. These are only a few of the many techniques available for facilitators to draw on.[76]

Philosopher's Walk

The Philosopher's Walk helps participants literally move both bodily and in their thinking. This process can require individuals, either in pairs or alone, to walk around the room and read posted notes of the reflections already provided by the group or hold objects and speak to the thoughts they evoke in relation to the matters under discussion. This simple practice can be used when transitioning through the phases of the facilitation or moving the participants from the past to the future in thinking, to inspire creativity or lift the mood, or to allow some reflection when significant amounts of information have been presented to the group. Marcy has written on the need to consider human biorhythms, circadian rhythms, concentration span,

76 See, eg, Thomas Jordan, 'Deliberative Methods for Complex Issues: A Typology of Functions That May Need Scaffolding' (2016) 13 *Group Facilitation: A Research & Applications Journal* 57.

and other regular needs, such as food intake, when considering the ability to make good rational decisions. Such matters need to be accounted for in any planned facilitation and the Philosopher's Walk can provide a needed change of pace for participants.[77]

Reverse Brainstorming

Reverse Brainstorming turns the questions one seeks to address on their head. For instance, instead of asking 'How to solve a problem?' ask 'How can I cause the problem?' Participants then brainstorm, without challenging all the ways to create the problem. Once they have exhausted the possibilities, they then reverse the ideas into a solution for the original problem. These are then reality tested as possible outcomes.

The Delphi Method

The Delphi Method[78] is a process that was originally developed to allow a group of experts to identify the likely impact of technological weapons on warfare in the 1950s. It is useful as a predictor in forecasting likely outcomes. Overtime, it has been modified to use in consensus building. The process involves identifying a group of experts and asking them to anonymously respond to a question with their prediction. The facilitator draws these together and from this poses a second question. At this point, the group has the anonymised responses to the first question. The process is repeated, usually up to three times. This iterative process allows for free expression through the protection afforded by anonymity, but allows for identification of areas of disagreement, agreement, and eventually consensus. It can be adapted to multiple party disputes to help identify the whole group's identification of the top areas of concern by listing these concerns that are then refined over the next three rounds.[79] This works well when decision-making is required, such as generating agreement on a list of desired attributes.[80]

Adaptive Learning

Adaptive Learning requires party reflection on what has worked well in previous engagements between the parties or the group in a form of appreciative inquiry – a process that generates new approaches to old problems by focusing on strengths rather than weaknesses.[81] Examples of good outcomes can encourage positive thinking and learning. The intervention is looking to achieve transformational change.[82] The technique is useful when addressing organisational or community disputes or change. Today, the term 'adaptive learning' can also be associated with

---

77 Marcy (n 24).

78 Harold A Linstone and Murray Turoff, *The Delphi Method: Techniques and Applications* (Addison-Wesley Advanced, 1975).

79 See Lip-Wah Ho et al, 'Developing offshore Wind Farm Siting Criteria by Using an International Delphi method' (2018) 113 *Energy Policy* 53, for a different use of the process to identify areas of disagreement.

80 See, eg, Ryan T Hartwig, 'Walking the Tightrope: A Case Study of Church Leadership Team Facilitation' (2016) 13 *Group Facilitation: A Research & Applications Journal* 29.

81 See, eg, Gervase R Bushe and Neelima Paranjpey, 'Comparing the Generativity of Problem Solving and Appreciative Inquiry: A Field Experiment' (2015) 53(3) *Journal of Applied Behavioral Science* 309; Gervase R Bushe and AF Kassam, 'When Is Appreciative Inquiry Transformational?' (2005) 41(2) *Journal of Applied Behavioural Science* 161; Ronald Eugene Fry et al, *Appreciative Inquiry and Organizational Transformation: Reports from the Field* (Quorum Books, 2002).

82 See, eg, Nur Baiti Afini Normadhi et al, 'Identification of Personal Traits in Adaptive Learning Environment: Systematic Literature Review' (2019) 130 *Computers & Education* 168.

technology and its use in teaching individuals through simulations to demonstrate learning and continuous timely and responsive improvement.

Positives and negatives of facilitation

Positives

Facilitation has many advantages over other processes, not least being its adaptable nature. However, like all processes, it is suited to particular types of disputes and circumstances. A positive factor is facilitation's usefulness before a dispute occurs as a preventive approach to avoid disputes. Litigation is averted when facilitated dialogue occurs in a preventative way; for instance, such that environmental matters can be turned from protest to cooperation in a joint problem-solving dynamic.[83]

Facilitation is a popular process, with government and corporate clients using it to assist in management decision-making and negotiations, particularly where there may be multiple parties interested in the outcome. The process moves parties away from a binary oppositional position, as supported by an adversarial system such as employer versus employees, environmentalists versus corporations, and so on.[84]

Negatives

While facilitation can help diverse parties in many ways, 'it is not a panacea, a way of life, a universal cure, or a therapy. Facilitation has limits, is often not appropriate, and can, when done badly, do tremendous damage.'[85] Thus, there are numerous factors to consider when determining whether facilitation is an appropriate process. These include a failure to understand the process, cultural considerations, broken trust, lack of genuine engagement, non-party interference, and entrenched positions.

Who pays for the facilitation can be a dilemma for perceived impartiality and needs to be carefully handled. While some facilitations are free, more usually the facilitator is paid. O'Donnell noted that, in the early days of providing a facilitation service in Queensland, this became an issue:

> The question of who paid, if at all, was one of the constant moral and ethical dilemmas facing the Division. Although providing a 'free' service, the Division was expected to charge corporate clients – that is, government agencies and private businesses were expected to be able to pay their way. This frequently meant that one 'side' paid and the other(s) didn't. Despite our assurances to all of our impartiality, the paying party often felt, and showed, a greater degree of ownership and control, and the non-paying party some

83 Tyrril (n 7) 26; Elix (n 8).

84 Elix (n 8) 105, citing E Papadakis, *Environmental Politics and Institutional Change* (Cambridge University Press, 1996) 4–8, suggests that adversarial behaviour is 'widely accepted as part of a system of checks and balances and internal control' and is reinforced by a system of what he calls 'binary codes', where policy options are presented as non-negotiable opposites (eg 'environment' versus 'development' and 'conservation' versus 'economic activity').

85 P Adler, 'A Credo for Facilitators', Mediate.com: Everything Mediation (Web Page) [2] <http://www.mediate.com//articles/facilitationCredo.cfm>.

> scepticism of our neutrality. This will always be a problem for facilitators in public policy matters where the government agency does (and should, I believe) pay for dispute resolution services and the community group does not.[86]

In group dispute management processes, the third-party facilitator must be aware of party distractors. These are things that cause a person not to be fully present and to be distracted from their engagement in the process. Seemingly unrelated concerns such as face-saving, fear of appearing weak or ineffective as a leader, or concerns their leadership may be undermined are examples of such distractors.[87] Further problems with facilitation are suggested by Susskind and others,[88] and focus on three factors: where cliques form, the management of the process by the facilitator is ineffective, and the 'kaleidoscopic nature of BATNA . . . analysis'.[89] Resistance to the process can be measured by openness to new ideas, and interventions may need to focus on these issues before the parties' main concerns are addressed. Using Conflict Coaching, or leadership training can assist in these situations. Conflict Coaching is explained further in this chapter in the section 'Related dispute management processes'.

The following case study drawn from the report, *Building Strong Collaborative Relationships for a Sustainable Water Resources Future,*[90] demonstrates many facilitative techniques and provides an honest appraisal of the positives and negatives of facilitation.

> The US Army Corps of Engineers (Corps) led an initiative in 2008–09 as facilitator, coordinator, integrator and convener in order to see if water agencies, stakeholders, and levels of government could better articulate their roles and objectives. Federal and state agencies, Native American tribal representatives (invited tribal members and associations representing multiple tribes), interstate commissions, and non-government (NGOs) entities were involved in the collaborative effort. The issue at hand was how to ensure all parties could have their water needs met in an equitable and fair manner.
>
> Standardised state agency interviews and assessments were conducted, and a standard facilitation procedure was used in a series of conferences to address key questions pertaining to water planning and management. The conference methodology included: verbal and written training information for the facilitation team, careful selection of conference attendees to ensure diverse representation, nominal group and fishbowl techniques, participant worksheets, small group discussions, and interspersing discussion sessions with learning sessions.

86 O'Donnell (n 9) 165.

87 Lawrence Susskind, 'Bring Talks Back On Track with Facilitation' (2006) 9(9), *Negotiation* 4.

88 Lawrence Susskind et al, 'What We Have Learned about Teaching Multi Party Negotiation' (2005) 21(3) *Negotiation Journal* 395.

89 Ibid 402.

90 Julie B Marcy, Ada Benavides and Dale Brown, 'Collaborating for a Sustainable Water Future: A Case Study' (2011) 11 *Group Facilitation: A Research & Applications Journal* 40–48 (references omitted); *Building Strong Collaborative Relationships for a Sustainable Water Resources Future: Understanding Integrated Water Resources Management (IWRM)* (US Army Corps of Engineers, 2014) <https://aquadoc.typepad.com/files/iwrm-report-jan2014.pdf>.

The approach taken included interviews, a national assessment of water planning, and three regional conferences and one national conference to exchange ideas and information on water resources. Gatherings were also designed to see if collaborative, facilitated discussions could succeed in finding common ground for national priorities among participants with competing water needs. Approximately 350 individuals participated in the conferences.

As part of this effort, the water planning status of all 50 states was assessed during 2008 and 2009. Virtually all the states had water planning representatives who participated in telephone interviews to verify and clarify existing water resources planning and management initiatives, practices, and needs.

In addition, existing reports, management plans, and related documentation were reviewed. Forty-nine representatives of the Eastern region convened at a conference in Florida in February 2009; 80 representatives of the Western region convened in Kansas in April 2009; and 57 representatives of the Central region convened in Missouri in June 2009. Finally, 158 members of the Obama Administration, Federal and Congressional officials, and attendees representing states, interstate organisations, Tribes, and NGOs attended a national conference in Washington, D.C. in August 2009.

Attendance was by invitation in order to foster better communication and collaboration in smaller groups, and to ensure attendance by a good cross-section of key water resources entities.

Each conference was a mix of 'state of the science' briefings, best practices and current water policies coupled with formal (facilitated sessions) and informal (receptions, luncheons) discussions on key topics.

The three regional conferences were conducted in an iterative fashion, in that key speakers from the other two regions presented water resources perspectives, best practices, and lessons learned within their respective region to infuse diversity of planning and management strategies and cross-fertilise ideas.

A team of individuals from across the Corps and from CDM assisted in the interviews, conferences, and initial report preparation. A team of experienced facilitators trained and guided a cadre of support facilitators. Facilitated discussions were used to obtain desired information from the regional conference participants. Members of the facilitation support team were provided with written and verbal instructions prior to the conferences in the form of a standardised process guide outlining tasks, methods, and timelines. It included guidance on the overall process, nominal group and round robin feedback techniques, consensus building, verbal and weighted voting dots prioritisation, time management (designated times to accomplish specific tasks), and report-out preparation whereby small groups shared their key findings using a standardised reporting format.

Three small group discussion breakout sessions were used to gather feedback from the regional conference participants. Prior to each session, a lead facilitator provided the participants with an overview which included: small group member composition and logistics, objectives and expectations of the session, and discussion guidelines (cell phones off, limit 'war stories' (lengthy stories of related experiences) and acronyse (speaking in acronyms), etc). The small groups were comprised of 6–12 members as determined by the number of attendees and available facilitators, along with a facilitator and a note-taker. The composition of the small groups was intentionally diverse. Each group was requested to elect a group spokesperson (GSP) at the beginning of the session who would present their findings to the plenary group. During the session, participants were asked to use a nominal group technique to individually prepare notations on worksheets and then share their thoughts with the other attendees. This technique allowed each participant to gather their thoughts, determine items of greatest importance to communicate, and eliminate or endorse items from their list if another attendee addressed it. The use of nominal group technique and round robin feedback also helped ensure that each applicant had the opportunity to share their opinions and helped diffuse dominant personalities. Each breakout session lasted between 1.5 and 2 hours in length. Small group discussion Session A dealt with Key Water Resources Issues and asked participants to provide feedback on critical water resources needs and challenges and their associated drivers and influences. Session B dealt with Strategies to Address Current and Future Needs and built upon the top three critical water resources needs or challenges identified in Session A. Participants were requested to indicate strategies or tools currently being used to address the group's top three needs/challenges, along with additional strategies or tools they felt were needed to address them. Session C dealt with Successful Collaborations and requested feedback on:

> collaboration success stories, additional opportunities for successful collaboration/partnerships, and their perception of roles for each of Federal Government/Tribes, State Government, and Others (specified) in water resources planning and management.[91]

Upon completing the individual worksheet in each session, participants were asked to share one concise example (newspaper headline versus a full-page story) with the group using a round robin technique and recording on both paper charts and PowerPoint (PPT) slides. After the initial round, open discussion ensued during the time allotted to refine the results. The facilitator then worked with the group to consolidate similar ideas and used custom-printed, weighted voting dots (the highest value dot was placed on the item of greatest importance to them, one dot per item) to determine the top three ideas. Facilitators assured participants that all discussion notes and completed worksheets would be included in the proceeding's reports. Where needed, additional agreement was obtained via general discussion or the use of thumbs (thumb up agree, thumb down disagree and discuss, flat hand neutral). The GSP then obtained guidance from the small group on how best to present their key results in PPT form to the plenary group. The plenary group reconvened after each of the small group discussions to share results. GSPs were assembled by a lead facilitator and given approximately 5 minutes each to share key highlights from their group. They were also asked to identify the members of their group, and group members could contribute additional clarification as needed during the presentation. Plenary group members then asked additional questions on content and clarification. After each GSP had presented their results, the GSPs were asked to assemble in a fishbowl where participants sat in a small circle to share key findings while surrounded by the plenary group who observed their discussion.

The national conference began with presenting the results of the three regional conferences, along with insights from Congress and agencies involved with water planning and management. Facilitated sessions involved the plenary group and some plenary tabletop discussions. In the first session, a facilitator obtained feedback from the participants in a session titled 'Collaborative Actions as a National Team – Next Steps' to identify next steps toward improving water planning collaboration. In the second session, a facilitator obtained feedback from the participants in a session titled 'Key Regional Water Resources Needs and Strategic Actions to Move toward Our Vision' to identify remaining regional needs and steps to address them. In both sessions, the 158 participants were seated at table rounds of

91 Marcy, Benavides and Brown (n 90), 42.

eight people and a plenary facilitator asked them to initiate a table discussion on the topic. Feedback was then shared with the plenary group and responses were recorded electronically. These sessions were approximately one hour in length.

An Integrated Water Approach was developed that recognises the need for collaboration that satisfies multiple needs. Careful documentation of feedback received and learning session presentations, along with written evaluation forms, captured and assessed the work. With each progressive conference, lessons from feedback improved the process. This included adjusting worksheets, changing group spokespersons, and session times.[92]

At the national conference, two plenary facilitated sessions were used in between learning sessions. Although this was a significant effort, similar techniques could be used for smaller-scale events in which standardised facilitation methodologies are used across breakout discussion groups and to help guide less experienced facilitators.

Participant feedback provided key insights to the facilitators and reinforced their perception of disparate opinions and personalities in the groups. The facilitated small group discussion sessions of the regional conferences were highly rated, along with opportunities provided for open discussion. Providing participants with the written opportunity to recommend conference improvements or give their overall perception of the conference also revealed nuances that a standard, numeric evaluation form would not.[93]

Special considerations

This section includes topics such as confidentiality, training, use of technology, and related processes when conducting a facilitation process.

Confidentiality

One may consider that a facilitation involving large numbers of participants would make it impossible to maintain any confidentiality. However, facilitators must address this important issue and be guided by the participants. Facilitators undertake to maintain confidence about the matters they facilitate, the clients they work with, and the information obtained during the facilitation.

Often reports may be prepared or required after a facilitation. Generally, this will use data only if it is made anonymous and participants' names are not attached to the data.

A facilitation is likely to be more successful if the participants feel they can speak openly within a protected space – much like in a mediation. Participants can each sign a confidentiality undertaking and the facilitator provides a confidentiality statement when they are hired by participants. Some participants may be content to have their comments used in reports. Each facilitation is unique and the agreement on confidentiality must be discussed and confirmed by all participants at the outset. Standard exceptions to maintaining confidentiality apply, where the affected participant/s consent, or where a criminal offence is threatened, such as imminent harm of another.

92 Ibid 46.
93 Ibid; see also Fowler and Shi (n 11).

A simple sample confidentiality statement may be:

> I, Jane Doe, facilitator for a workplace facilitation between ___________ and _______________ on (dates) _______________ understand that the facilitation is a private and confidential process for each participant. I undertake to maintain the confidentiality of all participants and their commentary and actions. I will keep all such information private and confidential.

Training

Training as facilitators is provided at universities and by private providers in Australia.[94] The Australasian Facilitators Network (AFN), established in 1998, is an association of around 1,000 facilitation professionals from Australia, New Zealand, South-East Asia and the Pacific. It offers regular professional development programs.[95] However, Australia is not as advanced as the United States in superintendence of the process.

The International Association of Facilitators (IAF) was established to 'promote, support and advance the art and practice of professional facilitation'. It is a training provider offering accreditation programs.[96] The IAF Facilitator Competencies Framework provides a template for the skills, knowledge and aptitude of facilitators to work successfully in varied situations. The IAF sets out the five core elements a good facilitator requires, as being able to:

1. create collaborative client relationships
2. plan appropriate group processes
3. create and sustain a participatory environment
4. guide groups to appropriate and useful outcomes, and
5. Build and maintain professional knowledge.[97]

One of the dilemmas with training and accreditation for a process that is to be flexible and adaptable is the restrictions this may incur in preferencing certain models. Currently, there is no preferred model, unlike for mediation, and so facilitation remains a creative process open to advancement as knowledge of groups and communication develops. Accreditation is not demanded by clients and remains at the early stages only. As a process, facilitation is not regulated by a single body and is likely to remain more open than the mediation domain for some time. However, as the numbers of facilitators grow, and the need to distinguish services due to growing competition, the requirement for professional training and accreditation may develop and, like mediators, recognition as an identifiable profession for facilitators may in the future demand similar professional recognition.

---

94 See, eg, postgraduate subjects offered by universities, such as the University of New South Wales (UNSW) and the University of Technology Sydney (UTS).

95 Australasian Facilitators Network (Web Page) <http://www.afn.net.au>.

96 International Institute for Facilitation (Web Page) <https://www.inifac.org/>: this is an industry accreditation scheme which awards the Certified Professional Facilitator (CPF) credential to facilitators who demonstrate proficiency in the application of the IAF core competencies model.

97 International Association of Facilitators (Web Page) <https://www.iaf-world.org/site/>.

Technology

Technology operates in all areas of human interaction and, as such, can offer opportunities for facilitation to occur across time and space, bringing parties from geographical distance into the one 'place'.[98] By using technologically supported software platforms, instantaneous visual representation and data on any options generated can provide immediate indications of the likely consequences. Such opportunities can aid parties in focusing on a problem-solving approach.[99] In this sense, where technology can ease communication it is a welcome addition to '. . . a field that has developed in order to help us communicate better as human beings and make more sense out of our world'.[100] Using simulations to present instantaneous responses and projections in order to test options generated or proposals for management in an adaptive learning approach is only going to add to the interventions facilitators can adopt in the uptake of computer-assisted facilitation.

Related dispute management processes

A process that is often entwined with facilitation is Conflict Coaching. This is a process that helps participants, individually, to successfully work through certain processes or disputes.[101] A facilitator can act in a coaching role or educate a group on interactivity and skills. Learning respectful communication that does not attack the person but addresses cooperatively the problem is the aim of such interventions.[102]

Brinkert[103] has proposed a Comprehensive Conflict Coaching Model (CCCM), developing an integrated dialogue-facilitation and conflict coaching design. He defines Conflict Coaching as involving

> [a] coach working one-on-one with a client to develop the client's conflict understanding, interaction strategies, and/or interaction skills.[104]

Facilitation in conflict coaching is using a facilitative, open communication style in which the third person does not offer suggestions but supports the party to positively address their dispute with ideas and action that will manage the dispute and not escalate disagreement.

The CCCM process has six essential steps:

1. Preparatory Conversation
2. Discovering the Story

98 Stephen J Thorpe, 'Online Facilitator Competencies for Group Facilitators' (2016) 13 *Group Facilitation: A Research & Applications Journal* 79.

99 Goel Lakshmi et al, 'Decision-Making In-Socio and In-Situ: Facilitation in Virtual Worlds' (2012) 52(2) *Decision Support Systems* 342.

100 Christine Hogan, *Understanding Facilitation: Theory & Principles* (Kogan Page, 2002) ch 1, 1.

101 See, eg, Karina Ewer, 'Can Conflict Coaching Make a Difference to Conflict Outcomes in Hierarchical Organisational Structures?' (2018) 28(4) *Australasian Dispute Resolution Journal* 260.

102 See Brandon (n 19) 176.

103 Ross Brinkert, 'The Ways of One and Many: Exploring the Integration of Conflict Coaching and Dialogue-Facilitation' (2013) 12 *Group Facilitation: A Research & Applications Journal* 45.

104 Ibid 46.

3. Exploring Three Perspectives
4. Crafting the Best Story
5. Enacting the Best Story
6. The Parallel Process.

Brinkert suggests Conflict Coaching is useful at all stages – pre, during, and post a facilitation process. For Brinkert, this includes the facilitator adopting relevant aspects of Conflict Coaching at the intake stage and to assist in developing an agenda. During the facilitation, Conflict Coaching can assist individuals to engage in the communication process more effectively. This can be done outside the facilitation or during private sessions. After the facilitation, Conflict Coaching can assist in adopting the agreed changes or implementing aspects of an agreement. Points to keep in mind are the confidentiality and impartiality aspects in considering whether to have the same facilitator also engage in private Conflict Coaching with the parties. Mostly, this is not desirable. However, if it occurs, then the level of transparency in advising other stakeholders needs to be addressed. Understanding that Conflict Coaching is distinct from facilitation is vital.[105]

Schwarz indicates how facilitation fits within a range of related options for dispute management. In this way, facilitators can merge into conflict coaches. Which process is appropriate as a facilitator role is determined by the issues the parties or group are trying to address. It is essential to recall that the group is not always developing in a linear way and will need to circle back to earlier phases. However, in the forming stage, they are needing assistance in getting to know each other, preventing cliques from forming, and understanding roles and tasks. If there is a position identified as conflict, or perhaps at the storming stage, then structure and task clarity and positive support may help prevent this developing into a dispute or assist in moving to the performing stage. Coaching can assist a group or parties understand they are moving through stages that normalise the experience and guide them to reflect and develop mechanisms to overcome the problem.[106]

Conclusion

Facilitation is a growing area and one ripe for research as the theories of group and human behaviour, along with change and adaptation, are developing. New technologies are adding to the possibilities and understandings for facilitators to explore and adapt their skills. Facilitation offers assistance across a broad spectrum of potential conflicts and areas of disputes. These can range from helping organisations develop creative solutions to complex problems, to assist employees' mutual understanding and collaborative engagement in the organisations work, creating a detailed action plan for stakeholders, building relationships and trust, and improving decision-making.

105 Ibid 48–9.

106 See Noelene Salmon, 'Cutting Edge . . . Cutting the Cost: The Business Case for Conflict Coaching in a Government Workplace' (2017) 28(1) *Australasian Dispute Resolution Journal* 64, for a case study on using Conflict Coaching.

EXERCISE IN APPLYING YOUR KNOWLEDGE – WATER AND TOPSOIL

A community of farmers situated in a valley, in which the rich topsoil is the equivalent of only 3 per cent of quality soil in the world, has worked over 17 years together to ensure the ground water, together with above ground water, is managed and sustained. This is to ensure all of the farmers in the community have an equitable and sustainable supply of water into the future. They can farm the area, producing food continuously and indefinitely, due to the rich soil and continued water supply. AZ Mining Company has discovered the area has rich coal deposits and wants to establish a large open-cut coal mine in the valley. Work is scarce and the government is keen to utilise its raw resources to ensure continued energy supply, royalty income on the raw resources, and jobs for the members of their electorates.

1. Following the basic facilitation model outlined in this chapter, prepare a plan to facilitate a community meeting about this development.
2. What are the likely values of the stakeholders? How would you assess this?
3. Is there any possible synergy and how could you move the parties to greater collaboration?

8

CONCILIATION

Learning aims

- Describe conciliation in the context of dispute management
- Differentiate between conciliation and other processes
- Identify the types of dispute that can be conciliated
- Identify and explain conciliation models
- Determine when conciliation is an appropriate dispute management process
- Describe the role of the conciliator
- Identify and explain relevant considerations in conciliation such as good faith

Understanding conciliation

This section will provide an overview of conciliation as a dispute management process that is both alike and different from mediation. Conciliation is a triadic, potentially advisory, non-determinative process. It is possibly the hardest process to give a clear definition as it is a relatively flexible process and is often adopted in prescribed legislative schemes that can vary considerably. It therefore has to be approached in a contextualised manner. The history of conciliation in Australia will reveal the reason for it being different from its international counterpart. The chapter will not go into discussing actual disputes submitted to conciliation but will use examples to differentiate between conciliations from a procedural point of view.

The word 'conciliation' can be used in a general sense to encompass different dispute management processes, depending on the context and jurisdiction. The terminology has evolved over time in different directions, both domestically and internationally. As indicated, this makes conciliation one of 'the most problematic of all dispute resolution processes because the term is used variably to refer to a broad range of processes'.[1] On one hand, especially internationally, conciliation is sometimes understood as a mere synonym for mediation, with little or no difference between the two, as the process itself and the nature of the ultimate outcome are identical: '[t]he process is virtually identical to mediation. There is no international or national consistency over the terminology, so the terms "conciliation" and "mediation" can be used to describe the same process.'[2]

While conciliation as a process may appear similar to mediation, there are a number of differences as this chapter will indicate. One is the greater likelihood the third-party neutral takes on an advisory role. Internationally, it is recognised that in some cases 'the conciliator may express an opinion on the merits of the dispute and may ... suggest a solution'.[3] In jurisdictions where advising the parties on the substance of their dispute is also a natural part of mediation, as in an advisory mediation model, this add-on element does not make conciliation any different from mediation. In jurisdictions where mediation is a purely facilitative method,

1 Hilary Astor and Christine Chinkin, *Dispute Resolution in Australia* (Lexis Nexis Butterworths, 2nd ed, 2002) 85.

2 Susan Blake et al, *A Practical Approach to Alternative Dispute Resolution* (Oxford University Press, 4th ed, 2016) 347.

3 Ibid.

this advisory component will provide a differentiation between mediation and conciliation.[4] In Australia, mediation is facilitative and conciliation is evaluative and mainly statute-based. However, there is a frequent practice of parties approaching retired judges for 'mediation' precisely because they can assess the issues and express a legal opinion on them. It is debatable whether that method could qualify as mediation, conciliation, or indeed as mini trial, but the practice reflects the minefield that inconsistent dispute management terminology can bring.

Conciliation arrived early in Australia, as a result of the great industrial disputes in the 1890s. Conciliation and arbitration were adopted to address large-scale industrial and employment disputes when collective bargaining failed. Under the *Conciliation and Arbitration Act 1904* (Cth) that established the Commonwealth Court of Conciliation and Arbitration, if collective bargaining proved ineffective or impossible, the industrial tribunal could compel the parties to conciliation. If the conciliation failed, the tribunal could then impose an arbitrated settlement.[5] This was probably the earliest formal dispute process adopted after Federation in Australia. Conciliation and arbitration became 'the only forms of industrial regulation to be accorded express recognition in the Constitution ... expressly endors[ing] conciliation and arbitration as the preferred means of preventing and settling industrial disputes'.[6] Indeed, s 51 (xxxv) of the *Constitution* provides that:

> The Parliament shall, subject to this Constitution, have power to make laws for the peace, order, and good government of the Commonwealth with respect to:
>
> ... (xxxv) conciliation and arbitration for the prevention and settlement of industrial disputes extending beyond the limits of any one State.

After the 1970s, conciliation also spread across areas of commercial disputes, family law, and discrimination. Even though family law conciliation evolved from counselling, the industrial relations history and the constitutional recognition meant that conciliation became perceived as statute-based and often 'compulsory' in Australia. As a result, 'terms are often ambiguous and can refer to different settings, processes, or types of disputes'.[7] The word 'conciliation' became a generic term for almost any consensual, non-adversarial dispute process – failing to distinguish between conciliation, mediation, or appraisal[8] – such that 'there is, regrettably, little consensus among conciliation providers as to what, precisely, conciliation means'.[9] The variety of legislation adopting the label 'conciliation' and then prescribing a process that varies between each piece of legislation has resulted in ADRAC stating: '... where conciliation has legislative provenance it cannot, as a matter of law, simply mean what an organisation or

4 See, eg, Chapter 3, 75.

5 David Spencer et al, *Dispute Resolution in Australia. Cases, Commentary and Materials* (Thomson Reuters, 4th ed, 2018) 271.

6 Breen Creighton, 'One Hundred Years of the Conciliation and Arbitration Power: A Province Lost?' (2000) 24(3) *Melbourne University Law Review* 839; Spencer et al (n 5) 271.

7 National Alternative Dispute Resolution Advisory Council, *Dispute Resolution Terms: The Use of Terms in (Alternative) Dispute Resolution* (2003) <https://f77b663a-db93-4dd8-823d-909937839d69.filesusr.com/ugd/34f2d0_fc316a9a1bf0418eaa7211406ca292e2.pdf>.

8 Astor and Chinkin (n 1) 85.

9 Spencer et al (n 5) 268.

dispute resolution provider says it means. Its meaning must derive from the law which makes provision for it.'[10]

NADRAC and its successor, ADRAC, have attempted definitions of conciliation. According to NADRAC, conciliation is[11]

> ... a process in which the parties to a dispute, with the assistance of a dispute resolution practitioner (the conciliator), identify the issues in dispute, develop options, consider alternatives and endeavour to reach an agreement. The conciliator may have an advisory role on the content of the dispute or the outcome of its resolution, but not a determinative role. The conciliator may advise on or determine the process of conciliation whereby resolution is attempted, and may make suggestions for terms of settlement, give expert advice on likely settlement terms, and may actively encourage the participants to reach an agreement.[12]

NADRAC subsequently added a note, acknowledging that

> ... there are wide variations in meanings for 'conciliation', which may be used to refer to a range of processes used to resolve complaints and disputes including:
>
> - Informal discussions held between the parties and an external agency in an endeavour to avoid, resolve or manage a dispute;
> - Combined processes in which, for example, an impartial party facilitates discussion between the parties, provides advice on the substance of the dispute, makes proposals for settlement or actively contributes to the terms of any agreement.[13]

Conciliation in Australia can also be a service provided by private organisations as well as a compulsory mechanism mandated by legislation. Accordingly, NADRAC provided a separate definition for 'statutory conciliation' as the dispute process that 'takes place where the dispute in question has resulted in a complaint under a statute. In this case, the conciliator will actively encourage the parties to reach an agreement which accords with the advice of the statute.'[14] In a discussion paper, the Law Institute of Victoria has proposed, '[t]he term "Conciliation" should be dropped from all but statutory applications. All current forms of usage can be accommodated in the proposed re-defining of "Mediation".'[15] This, however, would render the Australian terminology impossible to reconcile with the international terminology.

There is agreement among relevant stakeholders that conciliation needs to be differentiated from mediation for several reasons. In addition to clarity, empowerment is mentioned as a relevant rationale, where the blurring between the two would 'allow a stronger advisory role for the third party, and inevitably detract from the ownership of the conflict and its outcome, by the parties in dispute'.[16]

10 Australian Dispute Resolution Advisory Council, 'Conciliation: A Discussion Paper' (2019) 12.

11 Adopted by the Australian Standards Board as *AS 4608-2004: Dispute Management Systems* in 2004 withdrawn in 2017.

12 NADRAC (n 7) 5.

13 Ibid 5.

14 Ibid 10.

15 National Alternative Dispute Resolution Advisory Council, *ADR Terminology: Responses to NADRAC Discussion Paper* (2002) 26.

16 Ibid 17.

ADRAC took a concerted effort recently to address the conundrum of defining conciliation in the Australian landscape, admitting that the NADRAC attempted definition overlapped so significantly with that of mediation that it made it difficult to actually identify conciliation. Following extensive empirical research, ADRAC proposed a new definition:

> Conciliation is a confidential, non-determinative dispute resolution process, usually established by legislation. A conciliator is expected to ensure that the terms upon which a dispute is resolved accord with a particular set of norms or principles applicable to the dispute. Conciliators normally possess expertise in the area under dispute, and provide advice to disputants when considered appropriate.[17]

This definition highlights the element of a statutory scheme for conciliation noting it 'reflects the statutory provenance and treatment of conciliation',[18] even though not all conciliations are statutory in Australia, as noted. In light of this, the authors of this book propose an alternative definition of conciliation, to encompass the different forms conciliation may take:

> Conciliation is a non-determinative, informal dispute resolution process in which a conciliator may use a range of communication techniques characteristic to negotiation and mediation in a flexible manner to assist and in some cases advise parties to a dispute or a complaint with the purpose of reaching settlement. The process of conciliation is sometimes prescribed by specific legislation applicable in specialised jurisdictions or by internal rules of private or public organisations.

The first part of this definition is broader than the one proposed by ADRAC – to some extent overlapping with that of advisory or facilitative mediation. Conciliation is a flexible process that has similarities to mediation, but also enough differences to distinguish it as a process. The differentiation proposed is in the flexibility of the techniques used, which can depart from the steps prescribed for mediation to adapt to the needs of each dispute on a case-by-case basis. Conciliation differentiates from mediation through the involvement of a third party that may or may not be completely neutral as elaborated under the role of the conciliator later in this chapter. The conciliator takes a more active role in generating options and reality testing parties to move them to an agreement. When conciliation is the dispute management process prescribed by statute for a certain type of dispute, that agreement must fit within the legislative scheme.

Abductive reasoning: the logical process of reaching the most likely conclusion based on the factual information to hand. For example, what 'looks like a duck, swims like a duck, and quacks like a duck' would likely mean it is a duck.

Characteristics of conciliation

Conciliation as a dispute management process in general remains difficult to define precisely 'because its distinguishing features remain elusive'.[19] Unlike most other dispute management processes, conciliation cannot be clearly identified based solely on its characteristics. Ideally, identifying a dispute management process should be achieved through its legal or common definition or a simple 'duck test' of **abductive reasoning**. In this case, however, no law defines

17 ADRAC (n 10) XIII.
18 Ibid XII.
19 Ibid 1.

conciliation beyond a very general level; there is no 'ordinary meaning' for conciliation that would be comprehensive enough to cover all models used and labelled as 'conciliation'.

As there is no single uniform concept of what conciliation is, the characteristics of the different conciliation processes will also vary.[20] However, ADRAC notes, '[m]ediation and conciliation share a number of common features but they are not two sides of the same coin – they are separate and different'.[21] Accordingly, the following characteristics are noted as a general, rather than strict, guide in identifying a conciliation process:

1. *Non-determinative*: Similar to mediation, conciliation is not a determinative process. Its management of a dispute depends on the parties' agreement. While the process itself may or may not be voluntary, the parties can withdraw from it at any time without reaching a solution.

   This characteristic helps differentiate conciliation from adjudicative processes like arbitration, but it does not make it different from mediation.
2. *Informal and flexible*: From a procedural point of view, conciliation is considered to be less formal than mediation, being classified more like an assisted negotiation.[22] Conciliation does not necessarily involve the meeting of the disputing parties, as the conciliator may adopt 'shuttle diplomacy'.[23] Conciliators rely on many of the common dispute practitioner communication techniques as outlined in Chapter 2. The in-house conciliator training will determine the model conciliators use.
3. *Facilitative/advisory/evaluative*: Conciliations can follow a process that varies from facilitative to evaluative.[24] Nevertheless, the majority of conciliators and conciliator entities identify their processes as facilitative. Facilitation is an important part of conciliation, mainly serving the purpose 'to achieve fulfilment of the public interests underpinning the applicable legislation'.[25] Despite this, the term 'conciliation' is used where the dispute management practitioner has an advisory role and expresses an opinion on the parties' claims and positions. This also implies expert knowledge from the conciliator on the subject of the dispute, enabling the conciliator to evaluate the strengths and weaknesses of a party's position in the dispute.

   Given that mediation can also be facilitative (albeit facilitation may manifest itself differently in mediation from conciliation), advisory or evaluative, and advisory processes also include dispute management processes like expert appraisal, case appraisal, mini trial, and early neutral evaluation, these characteristics are also unable to differentiate conciliation from other methods. Trying to distinguish between facilitation and advice-giving is recognised to be 'a somewhat unstable and elusive point of distinction' as it cannot be described as a triadic facilitative process in such cases.[26]

20 Ibid.

21 Ibid 12. See also Mieke Brandon and Tom Stodulka, 'A Comparative Analysis of the Practice of Mediation and Conciliation in Family Dispute Resolution in Australia: How Practitioners Practice Across Both Processes' (2008) 8(1) *Law and Justice Journal* 194.

22 See NADRAC (n 15) 22.

23 David Spencer, *Principles of Dispute Resolution* (Thomson Reuters, 2nd ed, 2016) 144.

24 See ADRAC (n 10) 40, for the statistics on whether conciliation conducted within an entity is facilitative, evaluative, directive, adjudicative or other.

25 ADRAC (n 10) XII.

26 ADRAC (n 10) 30.

4. *Rights-based*: Conciliation is often perceived as handling a dispute from a rights-based perspective, as opposed to the interest-based approach characteristic to mediation. However, from ADRAC's 2019 data collection it appeared that only 86 per cent of the conciliating entities indicated that the subject of conciliations they conduct is predominantly rights-based.[27] Conciliations focusing on rights are typically those that are statute-based and designed to handle complaints for breach of legal rights, but even those conciliations will include facilitative techniques. Conciliation can, however, easily be differentiated from determinative triadic rights-based processes like arbitration and litigation.
5. *Statute-based*: Since '[c]onciliation is widely used throughout Australian statutory schemes',[28] within Australia a statutory ground is often one of the main characteristics that assists in identifying a process as conciliation. This feature is based on the historic recognition of conciliation as a suitable way of managing disputes involving significant public interest.[29] Against this is the reality that 'private conciliation' exists.[30] However, ADRAC, in its study, could identify very little information about private conciliation; that is, conciliation provided by non-statutory bodies that may not be provided for in legislation, but rather under their private rules, like clubs, sports or religious organisations, political parties, private or public corporations, or the Australian Financial Complaints Authority.[31] Consequently, while a statutory label assists in classifying some processes as conciliation, it is not available for all conciliations. A further complication is that some statutory schemes refer to conciliation which allows for a determination, and some statutory non-determinative schemes use the term 'mediation'.[32]

Figure 8.1 Flexible levels of interventionism allow for a broad spectrum of processes in conciliation

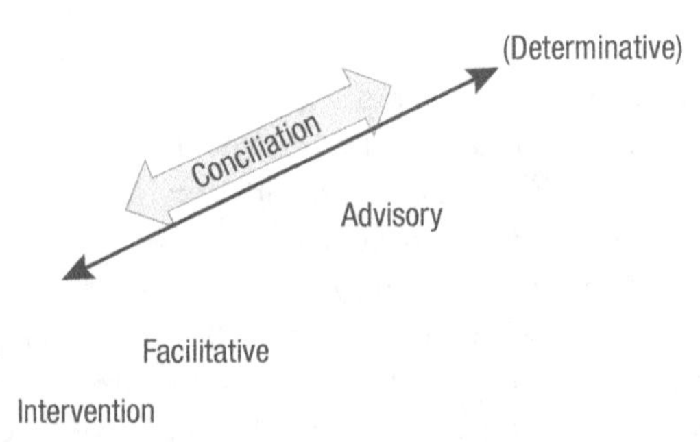

27 ADRAC (n 10) 40.

28 Spencer (n 5) 146.

29 ADRAC (n 10) 13.

30 Ibid 51.

31 See Australian Financial Complaints Authority, *Attending a Conciliation Conference* <https://www.afca.org.au/public/download.jsp?id=7523>; Australian Financial Complaints Authority, *A Guide to Conciliation Conferences* <https://www.afca.org.au/public/download.jsp?id=7570>.

32 See Chapter 12.

The model used by the Administrative Appeals Tribunal and described in the next section reinforces some of the key distinguishing features of conciliation. These differentiate conciliation from mediation and other processes:

- The parties do not choose the conciliator.
- The conciliator can oscillate from private party sessions to joint sessions in a manner that suits the conciliator.
- The conciliator can advise the parties, and suggest options.
- The conciliator can strongly challenge parties using reality-testing techniques to test strengths and weaknesses.

Using theory and models to dissect conciliation

As discussed in the previous section, conciliation is a varying process and no generalised model can be readily claimed. Conciliation may be both facilitative and advisory in an anti-discrimination dispute; it may shift between outcome- and process-focused in a family dispute depending on the context and the specific issues that need to be dealt with.[33] Conciliation may also be a simple, structured, facilitated negotiation moving between positional and interest-based negotiation in a workplace dispute or it may be a blended process resembling med-arb.[34]

There are currently 96 laws that refer to conciliation in Australia, many of which entrust a conciliation function to an identified entity.[35] However, none of these laws provide a definition or description of conciliation[36] and 60 per cent of the designated entities do not provide any significant information on their websites about their conciliation,[37] which makes identifying models and processes challenging. It can also be a source of uncertainty for parties in conciliations. Practice directions and regulations provide some guide, but there is also an apparent significant difference between the legislative frameworks and what is happening in practice.[38]

Nevertheless, common elements for a conciliation process have been identified by the ADRAC study, namely:

- a relatively high number of conciliations involve legal representation
- attending the conciliation is frequently compulsory under the applicable law
- conciliation is confidential
- the majority of conciliations appear to take 'around two hours', with only a small minority requiring more than a day
- written procedures are used in about half the cases, with the other half using procedures flexibly
- some entities 'bundle' conciliation, commonly with mediation and conferencing.

33 See Brandon and Stodulka (n 21).
34 For further information on med-arb, see Chapter 10, 324.
35 ADRAC (n 10) 15, Appendix 7.
36 Ibid 24.
37 Ibid 20.
38 Ibid 21.

There is a recognised difference between complaint conciliation and dispute conciliation. In a dispute, both parties are in the dispute knowingly. In a complaint, however, there is one party that has a grievance against the other, who may or may not know that there is even a dispute, but nevertheless becomes engaged in the conciliation either voluntarily or based on statutory obligations.[39]

All entities that manage complaints and disputes through conciliation have their own version of the process adapted to suit the type of disputes and disputants they are servicing. Their models and procedures can vary greatly; therefore, this textbook can only provide a guiding understanding of conciliation. In practice, the exact conciliation model and process will depend on the jurisdiction within which a dispute falls and the rules under which that dispute is submitted for conciliation. As indicated at the beginning of this chapter, we provide an overview of the conciliation model of the Administrative Appeals Tribunal (AAT) as that is used for a broad range of civil disputes.[40]

The AAT Conciliation Model

The AAT Model uses conciliation to 'review a wide range of decisions made by government ministers, departments and agencies under Commonwealth laws',[41] subject to such decisions being placed within the jurisdiction of the AAT by an Act, regulation, or other legislative instrument. Currently, there are over 400 such instruments placing decisions under the jurisdiction of the AAT for review, applying principles of **administrative law**.[42]

Administrative law: the law that governs decision-making by the bodies of the executive arm of government.

This vast array of legislation provides an outlet for those subject to conciliations made under the legislation who may be disgruntled with the outcome of the matter, how it affects them, or how the conciliation was conducted. These include disputes related to freedom of information, licencing, the National Disability Insurance Scheme, tax,[43] veterans' entitlements, military compensation, and workers compensation, to name a few.

Under the AAT Model, a conciliator may:

- give advice on the case management process or the practice of the AAT
- offer opinions as to the issues both factual and legal, in dispute between the parties

39 Spencer et al (n 5) 17.

40 See the Australian Human Rights Commission for another model used in Australian conciliations: 'Conciliation – How It Works', *Australian Human Rights Commission* (Web Page) <https://www.humanrights.gov.au/complaints/complaint-guides/conciliation-how-it-works>.

41 See also 'Steps in a Review', *Administrative Appeals Tribunal* (Web Page) <https://www.aat.gov.au/steps-in-a-review>.

42 This list indicates all matters subject to review by the AAT, not that every review would go to conciliation.

43 Decisions made by the Australian Taxation Office (ATO); Australian Charities and Not-for-profits Commission; Australian Financial Security Agency; Australian Prudential Regulation Authority; Australian Securities and Investments Commission; Companies Auditors Disciplinary Board; Tax Practitioners Board.

- give advice about the costs implications and other non-legal consequence
- ask parties to explain any decision-making constraints.[44]

This indicates a clear difference from facilitative mediation. While there may be some similarity to evaluative mediations, it remains a different process as noted in this chapter mostly due to its legislative guidelines and obligations.

The AAT Model includes five steps, discussed below:

1. Preparation and conciliator's opening statement
2. Parties' statements
3. Joint explanatory session and discussion
4. Private meetings
5. Concluding joint session.[45]

Preparation and conciliator's opening statement

As with all dispute management processes, preparation is paramount. Some of the questions the parties should ask themselves at this stage are:

- strengths and weaknesses of their own position
- strengths and weaknesses of the other party's position
- likelihood of the Tribunal decision-maker agreeing or not agreeing with their position
- likely costs if the dispute goes to a Tribunal hearing.[46]

The introductory remarks from the conciliator provide a brief description of the role of the conciliator and participants, the conciliation process, and any ground rules.

Parties' statements

It is common for the complaining party to attend a conciliation accompanied by their legal representative. The responding decision-making agency is also commonly represented by an instructing officer and a legal representative. Accordingly, the parties' opening remarks may start with a summary made by the applicant's representative with any additional comments made by the applicant, followed by the same from the respondent's representative and agency officer. The scope of these statements is to outline the dispute from their respective perspectives.

Joint exploratory session and negotiation

At this stage, the conciliator provides a summary and an agenda, identifying emerging interests, needs and options for use later in the conciliation. The conciliator takes an active role in summarising views and options. The conciliator may also discuss the strengths and weaknesses of the parties' cases. More importantly, however, the conciliator will try to get the parties

44 Administrative Appeals Tribunal *Conciliation Process Model* <https://www.aat.gov.au/AAT/media/AAT/Files/ADR/Conciliation-process-model.pdf>.

45 Ibid.

46 See also Administrative Appeals Tribunal , *Conciliation Preparation Toolkit* <https://www.aat.gov.au/AAT/media/AAT/Files/ADR/Conciliation-Preparation-Toolkit.pdf>.

to communicate directly with each other, encouraging cooperative interest-based negotiation rather than distributive negotiation.

The conciliator, together with the parties, will aim to clarify the parties' interests to serve as the basis for joint problem-solving. A key difference from most mediations, particularly facilitative meditation, is that the conciliator may raise options for agreement. Parties can take a break from the joint session to consult and instruct their lawyers. Further joint sessions may be conducted if necessary to explore or refine possible outcomes.

Private meetings

Overall, private meetings are an important component of conciliation. As research has revealed, conciliation is more about 'dealing with [the parties] individually rather than necessarily getting them to hear each other, because that's more mediation than conciliation'.[47] The AAT Model provides that 'the conciliator may hold private meetings with each of the parties',[48] leaving it open as an option to be utilised when necessary. This would appear to be a more flexible use of private sessions than occur in most mediations. The conciliator also reality tests suggested options during the private session. Just like in the previous step, the conciliator may advise on potential outcomes and evaluate the strengths and weaknesses of each party's case.

Concluding joint session

Depending on the success of the private meeting(s), the return to additional joint sessions may or may not occur. At this stage, the conciliator may have to assist the parties to narrow down the dispute to any remaining issues that can be managed. If agreement is reached, the conciliator will facilitate the final negotiations and assist in defining and fine-tuning the terms of the agreement.

Outcome

Conciliation appears to be a very effective dispute management process.[49] However, if settlement is not achieved, the dispute can continue to be further dealt with internally in the agency involved or referred to another body. More conciliations tend to be followed by a determinative litigious process than in other processes such as mediation, due to legislative design. This may well encourage parties to ensure an outcome from the conciliation held in the shadow of this possibility.[50]

Overall, the majority of conciliation outcomes are forward-looking, with only a minority being past-focused.[51] Under a regulatory framework, the outcome is, in principle, in line with the norms and principles of that framework. Some laws expressly state that the outcome 'must align with what could have been ordered by way of a contested adjudicated outcome'.[52] However, research has indicated that practice does not necessarily align with this expectation.

47 ADRAC (n 10) 44.
48 Administrative Appeals Tribunal (n 44) 2.
49 See ADRAC (n 10) 37, for statistics on the success rate of conciliation.
50 Ibid 31.
51 Ibid 41.
52 See, eg, *Land and Environment Court Act 1979* (NSW) s 34(3)(a).

While such an expectation is implied from the statutory nature of the conciliation, most statutes do not expressly require adherence to their own norms and standards. The lack of clarity raises the question as to what happens if the parties agree on an outcome that is contrary to the applicable statutory scheme. Depending on the dispute and the legislative framework, the conciliator may be unable to endorse a settlement agreement even if it appears to satisfy the parties or complainant. It is worth noting, however, that a recent study revealed 'the possibility that some conciliation entities may not be conducting conciliations in conformity with legislative intent' with close to 27 per cent of conciliating entities 'not discourag[ing] settlements which are inconsistent with the applicable legislative framework'.[53]

If the parties reach an agreement during the conciliation, the matter ends with the settlement. The terms of the agreement are put in writing, signed by all parties, and sent to the Tribunal. The Tribunal will then issue a consent decision based on the agreement if the terms of the agreement are consistent with a decision the Tribunal can make, and the Tribunal thinks it is appropriate to make that decision.

The matter may proceed on to a hearing by the Tribunal if the parties cannot agree on an outcome. In that case the Tribunal makes a third-party neutral determination. If the conciliation was partially successful, assisting the parties to narrow down the issues in dispute, only those remaining issues will be sent to the Tribunal for a hearing.

Using knowledge of conciliation to assist in dispute management

What disputes to conciliate

Specialist entities, such as the AAT and state administrative tribunals,[54] specialist courts,[55] and many private organisations are all conducting conciliations in a great range of disputes. In deciding whether to use conciliation, the AAT recommends the following criteria are taken into account:

- Are commercial considerations important?
- Do the parties desire to keep the dispute confidential?
- Would the parties benefit from advice on possible settlement options?
- Is there a conflict in expert opinion or evidence?[56]

It appears only around 50 per cent of statutory conciliations are concerned with parties who would be likely to want to maintain an ongoing relationship. This may be a point of difference with choosing conciliation over mediation.[57] As ADRAC observed, 'it is difficult,

53 ADRAC (n 10) 42.

54 See, eg, New South Wales Civil and Administrative Tribunal, Victorian Civil and Administrative Tribunal, and Queensland Civil and Administrative Tribunal.

55 See, eg, Land and Environment Court (NSW), Family Court of Australia, and Federal Circuit Court.

56 Administrative and Appeals Tribunal, *Alternative Dispute Resolution (ADR) Guidelines* (2006) <https://www.aat.gov.au/landing-pages/practice-directions-guides-and-guidelines/alternative-dispute-resolution-guidelines>.

57 ADRAC (n 10) 33.

if not impossible, to discern any underlying denominator(s) which explain why parliaments across Australia have chosen to subject particular disputes to conciliation'[58] and not to other processes. Accordingly, the parties to conciliation are a mix of individuals and corporate bodies.[59]

The 2019 ADRAC consultation resulted in a long list of dispute types that are subjected to conciliation, a non-exhaustive representative list of which includes:

- Indigenous Australian land rights
- access to information
- anti-discrimination
- apprenticeships and vocational training
- building disputes
- complaints against architects
- consumer affairs
- disability services
- equal opportunity
- essential services (operations and access)
- family disputes
- healthcare complaints
- human rights
- land and environment
- liquor licencing
- occupational safety
- offences by children
- privacy
- public sector employee grievances
- road freight issues
- small business disputes
- strata titles
- superannuation
- surveyor complaints
- telecommunications industry
- tenancy
- threatened species protection
- workers' compensation
- workplace relations.[60]

The role of conciliators

Another distinctive feature of conciliation is that the parties have no say in the identity of the conciliator or the conciliation process model. The conciliator is nominated by the conciliating entity and is commonly a public official that is a member of that entity's staff.[61] The role of a conciliator will depend entirely on the regulatory framework in which that conciliator operates, even though the legislation may often be vague on this aspect. It does, however, often confer the conciliation entity with the right to enforce compliance with the norms and standards established by regulation as a way of serving the public interest.[62] This, in turn, determines what process conciliation will follow in a given case and what role the conciliator has in that case.

Operating under a statutory framework leads to conciliators being 'regarded as a system representative'.[63] While conciliators are facilitative in assisting the disputing parties to manage their dispute, they are not necessarily neutral and independent to both parties of the dispute.

58 ADRAC (n 10) XI.
59 Ibid 41.
60 See, eg, ADRAC (n 10) Appendix 7 for the full list of disputes and their legislative basis for conciliation.
61 ADRAC (n 10) 39.
62 Ibid 26.
63 ADRAC (n 10) 3.

Research has found that approximately 71 per cent of conciliators were not independent from the conciliating entity.[64] However, a common element is that the conciliator has no determinative power, nor is an advocate for either of the parties. The conciliator is, however, 'both using power and seeking to empower, and the strategic choice for the conciliator is to know when to move from one mode to the other'.[65] For this reason, conciliators may often be seen as tough or 'unreasonable' and 'heavy-handed' when they exercise pressure to stay within the limits of the legislative and administrative framework under which they conciliate.[66] They nevertheless must show procedural and psychological fairness as essential skills. As with any human interaction, prejudice and unconscious bias can be an issue in conciliation. The ability to recognise and control bias is essential, as unconscious bias can negatively affect the feeling of empowerment of the parties and the outcome of the process.[67]

In principle, conciliators are expected to ensure that the outcome will be in line with the statutory or regulatory framework under which the conciliation is conducted. This provides the conciliator with a degree of authority and means they cannot be completely disinterested in the outcome. The conciliator must be guided by legislative requirements rather than the disputants' position and interests when suggesting an outcome.

Conciliators are often expected to possess expert knowledge in the area of the dispute. Legal training and knowledge may also be important, depending on the field and jurisdiction. This expertise is used to evaluate the parties' claims, advise the parties on the implications of the legislative framework, and recommend suitable outcomes. Accordingly, a conciliator 'will be an expert or someone with knowledge [and] may give expert advice or information'.[68] Conciliators may, and are often required to, 'make suggestions for terms of settlement and provide advice on those terms'.[69] Interestingly, however, empirical research has revealed 'reluctance by some conciliators to accept that advice-giving was a role in conciliation even when authorised'.[70]

Conciliators may also refrain from educating the parties on their role and the process to a degree similar to that practised in mediation. As a preliminary issue, a dispute management practitioner is often expected to explain their own role in the process to the disputing parties. In conciliation, however, this faces two challenges: (1) parties are often unfamiliar with conciliation; and (2), as shown earlier, even the law and experts struggle to define conciliation. Consequently, as a conciliator noted in the empirical study conducted by ADRAC, '[w]e don't really explain because some people don't really know what a conciliator is. We get called many other names, a consultatory, or sometimes I say I'm a mediator because they understand that better.'[71]

64 Ibid 40.

65 Spencer et al (n 5) 281.

66 Ibid citing David Bryson, 'And the Leopard Shall Lie down with the Kid: A Conciliation Model for Workplace Disputes' (1997) 8(2) *Australasian Dispute Resolution Journal* 245.

67 Louis M Marlin, 'Overcoming Bias in Mediation' [2017] (August) *Advocate: Journal of Consumer Attorneys Association for Southern California* <https://www.advocatemagazine.com/images/issues/2017/08-august/reprints/Marlin-article.pdf>.

68 National Alternative Dispute Resolution Advisory Council, *A Fair Say: Managing Differences in Mediation and Conciliation: A Guide for All Involved.* (Attorney-General's Department, 1999) 1.

69 Spencer (n 5) 144.

70 ADRAC (n 10) 40.

71 Ibid 14.

In addition to the general task of providing expert knowledge and recommendations on a possible outcome, conciliators have a wide range of other roles prescribed by the relevant laws and rules under which a conciliation may take place. These include:

- to encourage settlement of disputes as expeditiously as possible
- to provide administrative review of decisions
- to identify systematic issues giving rise to disputation
- to facilitate mutually acceptable agreements
- to issue recommendations
- to exercise power to give directions
- to assess the parties' genuine attempt to conciliate.[72]

Positives and negatives of conciliation

Positives

Conciliation does not have to operate under prescribed procedural rules, rather only an overarching statutory scheme or internal regulation. Depending on the level of intervention the conciliator may adopt in a given case (subject to the applicable laws/rules), the triadic process is flexible in the many ways by which it can shift along a continuum leading from facilitative negotiation, through to advisory, all the way towards a determinative process (without actually necessarily making a final determination).

This flexibility, as noted, is perceived as both a positive and a negative. NADRAC observed, an advantage of '... conciliation is that it can be flexible enough to allow people of diverse backgrounds to resolve a dispute in a way that is comfortable for them'.[73] At the same time, the regulatory requirement to adhere to predetermined norms and principles is (or at least should) secure 'outcomes which accord with the norms and principles enshrined in the statutory scheme'.[74] This can appease parties' sense of receiving like and equal treatment and thus procedural fairness.

Negatives

The varying levels of interventionism given to conciliators make definition of this process and identification of a general model difficult, as has been discussed in this chapter. Although the problem-solving orientation is in principle beneficial, the wide discretion conciliators have on how to conduct the proceedings is not necessarily positive for the process. The literature flags some criticism of the wide role of conciliators, namely:

- idiosyncratic styles and inconsistent outcomes, which can lead to conciliator 'shopping' by parties in the private sphere
- time pressures reduce the ability to explore the parties' underlying interests thoroughly

72 Spencer (n 5) 144.
73 NADRAC (n 15).
74 Ibid 27.

- repeat players (usually the decision-making agency) have too much power, which can feed the unconscious bias of a conciliator
- on the other hand, imbalance of power can result in conciliators becoming advocates for less powerful parties
- pressure or threats used by conciliators feeling required to achieve high settlement rates
- conciliators mismanaging the transition between their different legislative roles.[75]

While the list above was created with workplace disputes in mind and similar criticism is often raised against mediation, these criticisms are more relevant in conciliation. This is because in an advisory conciliation there is greater potential to influence and manipulate parties to satisfy the legislative obligations.[76] In conciliation, where the third-party neutral has both influence and authority to suggest a solution, focusing on the aim of achieving an outcome and ignoring the role procedure has in protecting power balance can create room for abuse of power.[77] The position of a conciliator and their required knowledge in the field of the dispute allows (and indeed, requires) the conciliator to identify strengths and weaknesses of each party's position. Any flagging of weaknesses can then potentially be taken advantage of by the other side, which may lead to further power imbalance.

Special considerations

Good faith

The AAT Model expressly requires the parties to act in **good faith**, including that there be a 'genuine effort' to uphold basic principles of dispute management such as demonstrating behaviour like:

Good faith: as a legal principle, derived from the Latin *bona fide*, the concept of acting with honesty and no intention to harm the interests or rights of others.

- adopting an honest and genuine approach to addressing a dispute by discussion
- maintaining the confidentiality of the process
- treating other parties in the process and the AAT member respectfully
- acting reasonably and fairly
- having regard to the interests of all the parties
- disclosing information relevant to the dispute in a timely fashion
- being prepared to make concessions for the purposes of the process
- endeavouring to limit the scope of proceedings by making partial concessions where appropriate
- having an open mind and a willingness to consider the interests of the other side, understand their position, and considering options generated by the other side, or the AAT Member or Conference Registrar

75 Ibid 145; see also Bryson (n 65) 246.

76 ADRAC (n 10) 26; Doris Bozin, Allison Ballard and Patricia Eastel, 'ADR: Championing The (Unjust) Resolution of Bullying Disputes?' (2019) 29(3) *Australasian Dispute Resolution Journal* 162.

77 ADRAC (n 10) 30.

- having a willingness to propose options for the management of the dispute and discuss one's position in detail
- being faithful to any agreement reached.[78]

Failing to attend a conciliation without reason and/or notice is considered to be inconsistent with good faith, but withdrawing from conciliation is not. Acting and engaging in the conciliation in good faith does not require a party to agree to a final outcome, to act against their own interest or in the interest of the opposing party, but it does exclude unethical conduct.

Confidentiality

Like most dispute management processes, conciliation is, in principle, a confidential process.[79] As a general rule, it means keeping discussions private, keeping evidence undisclosed outside the conciliation, and keeping any information provided during the conciliation secret. Accordingly, conciliation sessions can only be attended by the parties, their legal representatives, and the conciliator. Information revealed by a party during private sessions is also confidential. The conciliator cannot 'disclose information obtained in the course of a private session unless clearly instructed to do so by the party or where disclosure is otherwise required by law'.[80]

Statements made and information disclosed within the conciliation cannot be admitted as evidence at any AAT or other court hearing, unless the parties agree.[81] Confidentiality, although based on the good faith requirement, is not absolute or guaranteed. The AAT does not specifically prohibit the disclosure of information to third parties, but parties concerned may pursue remedies for breach of confidentiality.[82]

Other dispute management processes similar to conciliation

Conciliation counselling

According to NADRAC, '[c]onciliation counselling is a term used previously to describe some of the processes used by counsellors in the Family Court of Australia to assist parties to settle disputes concerning children. The Court now uses the term mediation to describe these processes.'[83] A Family Court counselling report from the Parliament of Australia recommending that primary dispute management services remain part of the Family Court refers to

---

78 Administrative Appeals Tribunal, *The Duty to Act in Good Faith in ADR Processes at the AAT: Guidelines for Applicants, Respondents and Representatives*, (2003) <https://www.aat.gov.au/AAT/media/AAT/Files/Directions%20and%20guides/DutyToActInGoodFaith.pdf>.

79 Administrative Appeals Tribunal, *Confidentiality in Alternative Dispute Resolution Processes: Guidelines for Applicants, Respondents and Representatives* (2014) <https://www.aat.gov.au/AAT/media/AAT/Files/Directions%20and%20guides/ConfidentialityInADRProcesses.pdf>.

80 Ibid 2.

81 *Administrative Appeals Tribunal Act 1975* (Cth) s 34E.

82 AAT (n 78), citing Megarry J in *Coco v AN Clark (Engineers) Ltd* [1969] RPC 41, 47.

83 NADRAC (n 7) 5.

'conciliation counselling', 'reconciliation counselling', 'separation counselling', and 'crisis counselling' in its analysis. It differentiates and defines conciliation counselling as one restricted to children's matters, helping parents to reach practical parenting agreements.[84]

Conferencing

For the sake of clarity, conferencing also needs to be mentioned when discussing conciliation. Terminology can be confusing as 'conciliation conference' can refer to the conciliation meeting, whether face-to-face, over the phone or by other communication method, in which the parties attempt to manage their dispute. 'Conference' on its own, however, is a term used to indicate an often standard preliminary process at Civil and Administrative Tribunals, as distinct from conciliation.[85] When inspecting the dispute processes listed by the different state and territory Civil and Administrative Tribunals, one can notice that there is information only about conferencing (or compulsory conferences) on the websites of the Victoria, Queensland, South Australia, Western Australia, Northern Territory and the ACT Tribunals, while the New South Wales Tribunal provides information about conciliation only as part of the procedures available.

While the AAT provides detailed information on both in its Freedom of Information Review procedures, the differences between conference and conciliation are minor.[86] They are both identified as a private, informal meeting arranged to talk about the matter, discuss evidence, see whether the dispute can be managed without a hearing and, if not, talk about what happens next.[87] This is much like a case conference or case management[88] undertaken often by a registrar of a court in an attempt to either finalise a matter listed for hearing or at least narrow the issues to be decided. The noticeable difference is that in conciliation the strengths and weaknesses of the parties' cases are also considered and the discussion on whether an agreement can be reached goes into exploring possible options for such outcome.

Conclusion

Conciliation sits between mediation and arbitration/litigation as a triadic process. In Australia, conciliation is mostly a statutory, evaluative dispute management process that resembles mediation, uses negotiation techniques, and has expert advisory input from the third-party neutral who ensures that legal rights and obligations are observed. As an institutionalised process, conciliation is developed organically to serve the needs for the type of disputes that the organisation utilising this process addresses. For this reason, conciliation can vary in detail

84 See House of Representatives Standing Committee on Legal and Constitutional Affairs, 'To have and to Hold: Strategies to Strengthen Marriage and Relationships' (1998) 241.

85 See, eg, Administrative Appeals Tribunal, 'Alternative Dispute Resolution (ADR)' (Web Page) <https://www.aat.gov.au/steps-in-a-review/other-decisions/alternative-dispute-resolution-adr>.

86 Administrative Appeals Tribunal, ' Conferences' (Web Page) <https://www.aat.gov.au/steps-in-a-review/freedom-of-information-foi/conferences>; Administrative Appeals Tribunal 'Conciliation' (Web Page) <https://www.aat.gov.au/steps-in-a-review/freedom-of-information-foi/conciliation>.

87 See Administrative Appeals Tribunal 'Conferences' (n 85); Administrative Appeals Tribunal 'Conciliation', (n 85).

88 See Chapter 10 and Chapter 11.

from organisation to organisation. Whether conciliation suits a certain dispute is not so much a personal choice as it is a decision made by the legislator. In private organisations, the suitability of disputes for conciliation is rendered by the organisation. Outside of organisational frameworks there is little to no conciliation in Australia; in that environment, the same advisory and/or evaluative process is qualified as advisory or evaluative mediation, instead.

The growing number of dispute categories that are directed to conciliation before they can access the courts is testament to the efficiency of the process. The balanced mix of observing rights and interests and adopting a flexible procedure to achieve a solution with minimum cost means conciliation brings the best of both worlds: managing disputes effectively and providing access to justice. As the response to the NADRAC discussion paper on dispute management terminology noted, 'clear and consistent distinctions are vital not just for regulatory purposes' but also to avoid confusion.[89] Whether the lack of clarity in defining the process is an issue, given the advantages in its flexible nature, is a matter for ongoing debate.

EXERCISE IN APPLYING YOUR KNOWLEDGE – *SINQUEST FINANCE PTY LTD AND ASIC*

Mr Sinquere arrived in Australia five years ago. He had been a financial advisor in his prior country of residence. He was wanting to make a new life and advance his station in life so he set up the company Sinquest Finance Pty Ltd with a view to being advisor on superannuation and help clients set up their self-managed super funds.

Mr Sinquere only sought to be a limited financial advisor, to provide the following information to clients:

(a) Provide financial product advice for the following classes of financial products:
   (i) Self-Managed Superannuation Fund
   (ii) A person's existing holding in a superannuation product
(b) Provide class of product advice for the following classes of financial products:
   (i) Basic Deposit Products
   (ii) General Insurance Products
   (iii) Life Risk Insurance Products
   (iv) Simple Managed Investment Schemes
   (v) Securities
   (vi) Superannuation.

Mr Sinquere met a roadblock in his plans when he applied for an Australian Financial Services Licence. He had not undertaken any further training since arriving in Australia. Mr Sinquere's licence application was considered by the Australian Securities and Investment Commission (ASIC) and refused.

He had been given the opportunity to provide further evidence and attend a hearing by ASIC. However, he found the process daunting and could not afford a lawyer. His English language was not of a high standard and when asked to produce evidence of his training he provided his 20-year-old Financiers Diploma from his prior country.

89 NADRAC (n 15) 15.

Mr Sinquere feels the decision was not reached fairly and his opportunity for a fair hearing was breached. He has come to you seeking assistance in obtaining his licence.

1. What is the avenue that Mr Sinquere can take to appeal ASIC's decision?
2. What advantages and disadvantages apply if this matter is conciliated?
3. Describe the conciliation process.
4. Prepare an opening statement on behalf of Mr Sinquere.
5. Prepare an opening statement on behalf of ASIC.

9 COLLABORATIVE PRACTICE

Learning aims

- Describe a Collaborative Practice process
- Explain the benefits of a Collaborative Practice process
- Describe the model and any variations
- Demonstrate knowledge of the theory and principles of Collaborative Practice
- Demonstrate understanding of when Collaborative Practice is ideal to use
- Identify special factors that can influence Collaborative Practice
- Describe aspects important to adopting a Collaborative Practice

Understanding Collaborative Practice

Collaborative Practice (CP) goes beyond the idea of lawyers just adopting a certain style of communication and instead describes another way of practising law by following a specific process. This section provides an introductory description of Collaborative Practice.

> **Collaborative Practice:** a dyadic two-party, with legal representatives, advisory negotiation following a collaborative model. Other professional disciplines may be involved in the negotiation.

Collaborative practice refers to a process in which lawyers for both parties act as legal advisors, yet they do so in a very different manner to the traditional adversarial approach. CP was developed to deal with family disputes, and despite being applicable to many other types of disputes, it has somewhat inexplicably remained concentrated in the area of family law. CP as adopted by collaborative lawyers can be seen as sitting part-way between mediation and litigation.

CP may follow varied models but all models involve lawyers and, in some cases, neutral experts from disciplines, such as financial planners, tax advisors, and psychologists, that assist the parties through a series of meetings in which agendas are set to address the parties' issues. In family matters, for instance, issues might include financial, property, parenting, and relationship concerns. The lawyers, other professionals, and parties meet to jointly problem-solve the dispute. Generally, a series of four to seven meetings address pre-agreed business agendas. The meeting agenda is settled in advance between the parties and their lawyers. All information needed is made available cooperatively prior to the meeting. CP adopts interest-based negotiation in which competitive strategies and tactics are excluded.

> **Disqualification clause:** a clause that prohibits a legal representative that has acted for a party in the CP to continue to act as their representative if the CP does not result in an agreement and the matter proceeds to litigation. This clause is often said to be the most distinctive feature of CP.

Key to CP is the willingness of the parties to engage in a collaborative and genuine problem-solving process. To this end, the parties sign a participation agreement that contains a **disqualification clause**, requiring the collaborative lawyers to not act for them, nor be a witness, should they fail to agree their issues and the matter moves from CP to litigation.

A significant difference to other dispute management processes is the active inclusion of other professionals, such as financial planners, accountants, tax advisors, child psychologists or other collaboratively trained experts. These professionals can join the process from the beginning or as needed to assist in problem-solving. Sometimes, a communication-neutral expert assists with agenda setting, meetings, and throughout the process to aid communication flow.

CP is a faster process than waiting for court hearing dates to be set, and provides the parties with greater control, while ensuring they have their own legal representative guiding them. While CP is not necessarily cheap, it saves on costs in terms of being able to see different experts for different aspects of the dispute at the one time. This factor should be considered when comparing the cost of CP with the cost of lawyers' fees for a family matter. CP aims to maintain relationships and is focused on the parties managing their issues so that a family separation can occur in a more amicable and quicker manner.[1]

Using theory and models to dissect Collaborative Practice

This section outlines some of the history of CP and the reason CP has developed to deal with the problems of the adversarial management of disputes. This section also provides an outline of the key philosophical and theoretical principles underpinning CP.

Theory of Collaborative Practice

CP arose out of the frustrations of a family lawyer in the United States, Stuart Webb, in the 1990s.[2] He found practising in family law a soul-destroying experience and believed there had to be a better method for managing family issues. From this came the movement that has become CP. Over the years, as CP has spread across the world, differences have arisen in the process and the approach has been developed and refined. Other early enthusiasts include Pauline Tesler[3] who further developed the ideas of Webb and became an advocate for the benefits of CP in managing disputes.

CP is most advanced in the United States. The passing of the *Uniform Collaborative Law Act* indicates this.[4] The process is relatively new in Australia, having first arrived here in the early 2000s. Marilyn Scott was one of the pioneer academic practitioners to introduce the process in Australia and Justice Robert Benjamin of the Family Court of Australia was another

1 See generally Pauline Tesler, *Collaborative Law: Achieving Effective Resolution in Divorce without Litigation* (American Bar Association, 3rd ed, 2017); Forrest S Mosten, *Collaborative Divorce Handbook: Helping Families Without Going to Court* (Jossey-Bass, 2009); Stuart G Webb and Ronald D Ousky, *The Collaborative Way to Divorce: The Revolutionary Method That Results in Less Stress, Lower Costs, and Happier Kids – Without Going to Court* (Plume, 2007); Daye Gang, 'Collaborative Practice and Poverty: Contextualising the Process and Accommodating the Market' (2016) 27(3) *Australasian Dispute Resolution Journal* 158.

2 Stu Webb and Ron Ousky, 'History and Development of Collaborative Practice' (2011) 49(2) *Family Court Review* 249.

3 Pauline H Tesler, 'Collaborative Family Law' (2004) 4(3) *Pepperdine Dispute Resolution Law Journal* 317.

4 The original *Uniform Collaborative Law Act 2009* (United States model legislation) was amended in 2010. The history of the drafting and enactments by States and a Legislative Information Kit and Bill Tracking Information is at *Uniform Law Commission* (Web Page) <https://www.uniformlaws.org/home>. As of 3 November 2019, 19 jurisdictions have enacted the statute; see, eg, Patrick Foran, 'Adoption of the Uniform Collaborative Law Act in Oregon: The Right Time and the Right Reasons' (2009) 13(3) *Lewis & Clark Law Review* 787.

early advocate.[5] There is now a CP website and professional membership association available in most Australian States, as well as a national professional membership group of collaborative practitioners.[6] No legislation specifically guides CP practitioners, but practice rules do exist.[7] At an international level, the International Academy of Collaborative Professionals (IACP) supports a worldwide network of practitioners, with a vision to transform dispute management.[8] It holds an annual forum, conducting research, providing resources on CP, and supporting its network of members. Membership of all CP groups extends beyond lawyers to encompass the range of professional disciplines that work together with disputing parties.

Empirical research is limited in the area of CP, with most literature providing practical descriptions of the process in order to raise awareness with practitioners. A few empirical studies have been undertaken, mostly outside Australia. One such study was completed by Julie Macfarlane in Canada and North America.[9] Taking a 'thick description' approach using 16 collaborative case studies, Macfarlane interviewed both the lawyers and the parties involved in a dispute in a time-lapsed manner. The interviews were held at the beginning, middle, and end of the process. The study was thorough, and its findings were pertinent to the different manner in which CP is conducted between the sample groups and the factors motivating the use of CP for parties and lawyers. The study examined the significance of changing style from an adversarial to an interest-based negotiation and using different communication techniques such as acknowledging emotions and providing advice when the other party is in the room. Findings from Macfarlane's study indicated that lawyers are drawn to CP in the following circumstances: it is a better fit to their values and they wish to better service their clients; the importance of being able to acknowledge and negotiate with emotions was evident; the need to develop consistent standards and appreciate different motivations between practitioners and parties (the latter being far more pragmatic as regards time; costs and reaching settlement) were relevant.[10]

5 Marilyn AK Scott, 'Collaborative Law: Dispute Resolution Competencies for the "New Advocacy"' (2008) 8(1) *QUT Law Review* 213.

6 *Australian Association of Collaborative Professionals* (Web Page) <https://www.collaborativeaustralia.com.au/about/>; *Collaborative Practice Canberra* (Web Page) <http://collaborativepracticecanberra.com.au/>; *Collaborative Professionals (NSW) Inc.* (Web Page) <http://collabprofessionalsnsw.org.au/>; *Queensland Association of Collaborative Practitioners* (Web Page) <https://qacp.org.au/>; *CollaborativeSA* (Web Page) <http://collaborativesa.com.au/>; *Victorian Association of Collaborative Practitioners* (Web Page) <https://vacp.com.au/>; *Collaborative Professionals WA* (Web Page) <http://www.collaborativeprofessionalswa.com.au/>. The NT and Tasmania are the only jurisdictions in Australia with no professional association at the time of writing.

7 Law Council of Australia, *Australian Collaborative Practice Guidelines for Lawyers: Including the Collaborative Practice Standards for Training and Collaborative Practice Standards for Trainers* <https://www.lawcouncil.asn.au/docs/3d898735-0641-e711-93fb-005056be13b5/1103-Policy-Guideline-Australian-Collaborative-Practice-Guidelines.pdf>.

8 International Academy of Collaborative Professionals (Web Page) <https://www.collaborativepractice.com/>.

9 Julie Macfarlane, *The Emerging Phenomenon of Collaborative Family Law (CFL): A Qualitative Study of CFL Cases* (Department of Justice Canada, 2005).

10 Ibid; John Lande, 'Practical Insights from an Empirical Study of Cooperative Lawyers in Wisconsin' (2008) (1) *Journal of Dispute Resolution* 203.

Other studies include Sefton's[11] empirical research in the United Kingdom, Schwab,[12] and the IACP. Lande provides a good overview of these.[13] He notes the IACP's Client Experience Survey, describing the following as important considerations when deciding to follow a CP method:

> ... quality of the outcome, focus on clients' most important concerns, tailoring of the process to clients' situation, respectfulness and non-adversarial nature of the process, level of stress in the process, access to a team of professionals, sufficient time to address clients' concerns, and control over the outcome. Cost was regarded as 'somewhat' to 'very important' in choosing CP.[14]

There is a challenge to lawyers being involved in the process if they lack training, knowledge and support as the approach in CP is entirely different than adversarial lawyering. Tesler has described the necessary 'paradigm shift':

> Collaborative lawyers have much to learn and much to unlearn in order to get good at this work. The place where that learning most often happens is in two systems that emerge spontaneously wherever CP flourishes: case-specific interdisciplinary collaborative teams, and local – interdisciplinary CP groups.[15]

Tesler indicates this shift encompasses the entire contact between lawyer and client starting from the intake interview, the type of questions asked, and the approach to instructions, including the differences and challenges of a litigation or collaborative path. The values of the disputing parties and their interests, such as resources, will assist the practitioner in this regard if they are more aligned.

Key philosophical principles underpin the theory of CP. Fundamentally, these include maintaining or supporting trust and respect. These are attributes one may think would be lacking in disputing parties. However, consideration of the ongoing relational needs of the parties and others connected to them, such as children, together with an aversion to public airing of a dispute and considerations of time and costs, mean parties can be motivated by a desire to maintain or develop trust and respect.

In negotiations that remain confidential to the parties and their dispute management team, this leads to two vital principles:

1. openness
2. transparency.

---

11 Mark Sefton, *Collaborative Law in England and Wales: Early Findings: A Research Report for Resolution* (Resolution, 2009) cited in Connie Healy, 'Dispute Resolution through Collaborative Practice: A Comparative Analysis' (2015) 27(2) *Child and Family Law Quarterly* 173.

12 William H Schwab, 'Collaborative Lawyering: A Closer Look at an Emerging Practice' (2004) 4(3) *Pepperdine Dispute Resolution Law Journal* 351.

13 Lande (n 10).

14 Ibid, 261 citing Linda K Wray, 'What You Should Know about the Cost of Collaborative Cases and Clients' View of Cost in Discussing Collaborative Practice with Potential Clients (Using the IACP Research to Correct Misperceptions and Put Cost into Context)' (2010) 6 *Collaborative Connection* 1.

15 Pauline H Tesler, 'Goodbye Homo Economicus: Cognitive Dissonance, Brain Science, and Highly Effective Collaborative Practice' (2009) 38 *Hofstra Law Review* 635, 636; see Julie Macfarlane, 'The Evolution of the New Lawyer: How Lawyers are Reshaping the Practice of Law' (2008) *Journal of Dispute Resolution* 61.

The negotiations are open as they are face-to-face in the presence of each party, their lawyer, and other relevant professionals. A protected and comfortable space is provided for the parties to engage in frank and open communication. All professionals are trained in CP to ensure they support the key philosophies of the process. Transparency means information-sharing and honest communication are essential aspects to work toward creative problem-solving that empowers the parties to reach a mutually acceptable solution accommodating shared interests and needs. Parties are empowered by the control they exercise in the information-sharing within a legal backdrop that ensures all parties, lawyers, and other professionals are working toward a legal and mutually assured outcome.

Practitioners in dispute management that have both legal and mediation training are often more suited to CP, as they already have the skills and tools in communication to assist parties to identify their underlying needs and interests. Their training in techniques such as reframing, detoxifying language, and letting the parties brainstorm options for their own unique way of managing a dispute, while withholding judgment, are consistent with a collaborative, transparent, interest-based negotiation.

Models of Collaborative Practice

There can be different models of CP, based on decisions about when to introduce other professionals into the process: some start only with each party's lawyers and call on other experts as and when required. This has been referred to as the 'LEGO Model', adopting a construction approach as and when needed to strengthen the problem-solving ability of the team.[16] Other models start with a group of relevant experts, such as lawyers, financial planners, and trained child specialists or counsellors. This model is a 'multi-disciplinary team approach'. Some practitioners prefer this model as it avoids having to adjust the team to accommodate new people when trust is a highly valued aspect of the process. All professionals in CP must have prior training in the unique skills required. The North American Collaborative Divorce Model utilises two communication-neutral coaches: a financial planner and a parenting or child consultant. Other models adopt just one communication-neutral expert. Some models will always use a communication neutral from the start – such a person calls the meetings and helps refine the agendas and the communication throughout the process.

Here we outline the basic model for CP.[17]

The basic model starts with the client seeking a collaborative lawyer trained in CP and then proceeding to agreeing to use the CP process. The parties deal with their dispute privately, and it never has to go to court, other than obtaining court orders in terms of their agreed outcomes. (This will depend on the other parties agreeing to use a collaborative practitioner and process.)

16 Nancy J Cameron, Susan Gamache and Doreen Gardner Brown, *Collaborative Practice: Deepening the Dialogue* (Continuing Legal Education Society of British Columbia, 2nd ed, 2014); Claudia Lanzetta, 'Mediation/Collaborative Law: Exploring a New Combination in Alternative Dispute Resolution in Cases of Divorce and Domestic Violence' (2019) 20(2) *Cardozo Journal of Conflict Resolution* 329, 350.

17 See Forrest S Mosten, 'Collaborative Law Practice: An Unbundled Approach to Informed Client Decision Making' (2008) (1) *Journal of Dispute Resolution* 163, 182, for a good overview of models; Sheila M Gutterman, *Collaborative Law: A New Model for Dispute Resolution* (Bradford, 2004); Scott (n 5).

Intake interview

When a collaborative practitioner identifies CP as suited to the party and their dispute, they will have to know that the opposing party is inclined to use CP. This requires a party approaching a CP trained lawyer that can work with the other party's lawyer in the collaborative process. CP will not be possible if one party wishes to adopt an adversarial management process or one party is self-represented. Other factors such as allegations of violence, psychological impediments or power differences that are hard to accommodate may also factor in a decision not to use CP. These factors must be vetted and acknowledged when assessing the suitability of CP to manage the dispute. For instance, in family matters, agreements will be reached as to property division and parenting. The parenting agreement may require revisiting as the child ages and the collaborative team can meet to address these needs as they occur.

Collaborative lawyers must fully inform the parties of the disqualification clause, which is a possible risk if the matter does not settle, as the parties would have to start afresh in briefing a new legal team.[18] The type of retention agreements can vary, but are generally signed by all parties, including the practitioners, depending on local country or region practice.[19] Wolski has noted that ethical concerns in the United States relating to **privity of contract** mean that the best solution is for each lawyer to execute a separate limited retention agreement with their client instead of a four-way participation agreement with both lawyers and parties. There should be a two-way participation agreement between the disputing parties, with their legal representatives only indicating their representation of clients and, if needs be, signing with this understanding.[20]

Privity of contract: only the parties to a contract have rights and duties under the contract, not third parties.

Initial meeting

Once both parties and their legal advisors choose CP, they establish an initial meeting time and place to agree on a preliminary agenda that covers the issues. Lawyers and possibly communication-neutral professionals prepare their client for the process and initial meeting. This also occurs between each meeting, with a debrief being held after each meeting. It is important to establish the agenda for the next meeting and clarify or identify remaining issues. The lawyers can also confer between meetings with each other and other professionals on the team on procedural issues. However, all negotiation occurs only when all are present.

Document exchange

Before the meetings, any documentation or reports required for the negotiation are provided in a timely manner for the other party. Failure to disclose can result in a termination of the CP. The good faith nature of CP means documents beyond those normally disclosed in a discovery process may require an exchange. Confidentiality covers CP negotiations in the same way it operates in everyday legal situations.[21] The CP occurs on a 'without prejudice' basis. If a matter goes to litigation, then, as in any non-adversarial process, any matter that can be proven by

18 See Lande (n 10) 218–219; Mosten (n 17).
19 Scott R Peppet, 'The Ethics of Collaborative Law' (2008) (1) *Journal of Dispute Resolution* 131.
20 Bobette Wolski, 'Collaborative Law: An (Un)ethical Process for Lawyers?' (2017) 20(2) *Legal Ethics* 224.
21 The *Evidence Act 1995* (Cth) s 131 sets out the basis for confidentiality and any exceptions.

other means is open to discovery by the lawyers in the litigation process. Some collaborative agreements may remove meeting outside the actual face-to-face meetings, thus affecting client privilege and confidentiality. If this is the practice, then the parties have to be made fully aware of these changed conditions in order to give informed consent to this particular process.[22]

Meetings

The meetings can be held in a mutually agreed and suitable meeting space or rotate between offices of the dispute practitioners. The number of meetings required depends on the number and complexity of the issues to be addressed. The CP can take anywhere from three to seven meetings of around two to three hours, but there is no constraint in the number of meetings. The parties and professionals agree on the timing and place for meetings.

Each meeting will deal with the agenda items set for discussion and negotiation. Agendas are prepared in agreement with the parties prior to each meeting. Uniquely, through an assisted negotiation process, the parties' legal advisors and the parties themselves work in the same direction to generate creative and mutually accepted outcomes for each party's needs. The lawyers follow an interest-based negotiation approach, not a rights or positional approach. The participation agreement and disqualification clause assist both the lawyers and the parties to remain focused on reaching solutions. While moving into another dispute management process, such as an adversarial one is never precluded, the collaborative professionals are motivated to assist the parties to creatively find an agreement in order to avoid the possibility of having to adopt another dispute management processes such as litigation.

Post-meeting debriefs between the lawyer and their client on progress and needs for the next meeting, and between the lawyers on general procedural matters may occur after a joint meeting. For instance, both lawyers will agree on the agenda proposed and consider whether the parties are ready to address the matter. This may include consideration of information provided by other professionals present at the meetings. Clear and accurate minutes are distributed to all parties shortly after each meeting to confirm any agreements reached. The lawyers, or the communication neutral, if one is involved, undertake confirmation of the next meeting.

Options

The lawyers and professionals assist parties in generating options through brainstorming and then reality testing the generated options. Unlike a facilitative mediation, CP allows the lawyers and other professionals present to put forward possible options. The options must aim to satisfy both parties' interests so, unusually in this sense, both lawyers are working for both parties. Such an approach can generate far more creative solutions than the regular outcomes occurring in meditation. As lawyers are trained problem-solvers they can enjoy the challenge to satisfy both parties, feeling the satisfaction that they have achieved a mutual benefit for both sides rather than gaining a result for one at the expense of the other. Once all options are transparently and thoroughly explored, relying where necessary on professional expert information provided by the professionals present or sought for this information, the parties reach a mutually agreed solution.

22 Macfarlane (n 15) 69.

Agreement

When all issues are addressed, the management approach achieved by the parties is incorporated in a legally binding agreement. The lawyers can seek a court order or Binding Financial Agreement to support the final agreement reached. Agreement can occur over just a few months. At all times, the process is conducted in a transparent and respectful manner between the parties and those present while total confidentiality encircles the process in order for the parties to feel confident in their final agreement.

Using knowledge of Collaborative Practice to assist in dispute management

This section will address what is unique about CP and look at its purpose and aims within the range of dispute management processes.

A collaborative meeting (if it is just two parties and their legal advisors is sometimes referred to as a 'four-way meeting') operates in a respectful manner in an environment that feels comfortable and less formal than a courtroom. The critical difference to all other dispute management processes is the transparency with which both legal advisors are working towards an outcome suitable to both parties, and so are communicating directly with the other party and their legal team in front of their own client. This has been likened to a six-way communication, involving communication party-to-party, legal advisor to legal advisor, legal advisor to own client, and legal advisor to opposing party. In such a negotiation, bluff and positional bargaining are not options. Any mistakes cannot be used for the other party's advantage and all errors require correction as soon as they are identified. This honesty builds trust and confidence in the parties and the process. Threats such as 'See you in court' are non-existent and any inflammatory or toxic language is minimised, if not eradicated, through the practitioners' ability to guide interest-based communication and discouraging their client from using insulting language. Parties are always present in the face-to-face meetings, which facilitates the greatest communication through all verbal and non-verbal communication channels. In CP, there is minimal written correspondence.

The process is found to benefit parties through empowering them to communicate their interests and adopt problem-solving approaches that focus on the problem rather than the opposing party. The parties see that each is obtaining the necessary legal advice in a transparent manner and as needed. The parties have a large degree of control over the regularity and timing of meetings and the content of the agenda and issues to be addressed.

The opportunity for parties to focus on their issues in a holistic and integrated manner, rather than a segmented way, is supported through having access to the professionals they may require guiding them in their problem-solving. The respectful approach ensures agreement is reached confidentially and that it satisfies both parties to the maximum extent possible and without threats of court action. Agreements reached in this manner are more likely to be sustainable.

Bryan[23] supports the idea of using CP where repairing relationships is more important than a zero-sum game, in which success by one party is at the other's loss. Areas such as workplace

23 Kathy A Bryan, 'Why Should Businesses Hire Settlement Counsel' (2008) (1) *Journal of Dispute Resolution* 195.

disputes and medical error are suggested as suitable as they involve systemic issues of harm in which long-term solutions are sought beyond mere fault-finding.[24]

Positive and negative outcomes using Collaborative Practice

Positives

Positives of CP include finding a way to manage disputes that maintains ongoing and more harmonious relationships. This is particularly useful, for instance, in family disputes where children are involved. The benefits to the parties are many. The parties gain understanding through professional assistance with their issues, and they maintain control, while a confidential, creative, problem-solving approach ensures their future needs are met within a legal framework. Parties are empowered by the process and can feel more confident in addressing subsequent issues that may arise, having gained skills in problem-solving and interest-based negotiation.

Dignity, respect, and trust are essential attributes of CP and appreciation of these see parties able to maintain such values beyond their dispute. Many parties in family disputes are pleased to know there is an option other than the Family Court process, which does not receive ideal press, and which imposes demands as regards process and timelines along with considerable costs over an indefinite period. Parties in CP know they can arrive at unique solutions tailored to their needs and ensure other third parties to the dispute, such as children, grandparents, employees or business partners, are given due consideration. A fair settlement is likely to be longer lasting and less emotionally demanding, as CP allows greater party control over all these aspects.

Positives also accrue to the dispute practitioners that operate in the CP domain. Much of the literature acknowledges the collegial relationships with others working in the field, with improved outcomes for parties, including lawyer–client relationships and work–life balance. This occurs through greater potential for management and control over meeting scheduling and better cash flow and party support as parties can actually see the beneficial work being done.[25]

Stress levels and expectations can be high, particularly in family disputes, for both the parties and the practitioners who are obligated to work within a complex and dynamic legal domain where sanctions apply when criteria are not met. Through CP, lawyers can gain pleasure from finding solutions that provide disputing parties with creative outcomes they had not anticipated. CP is not possible unless all parties can reach a desirable outcome, and this drives the focus of all involved to work together.

Negatives

There are very few negatives to CP. The effect of the disqualification clause, which is mostly seen as a positive, is considered by some as a negative, or ethical, concern. In a positive way,

24 Ibid 197.

25 Scott (n 5); Marilyn Scott and Pauline Collins, 'The Challenges for Collaborative Lawyers in Providing CP Processes' (2017) 31(1) *Australian Journal of Family Law* 27.

the disqualification clause is an encouragement that bolsters the lawyers, other professionals, and parties' commitment to remain focused on problem-solving and being resourceful in finding appropriate solutions, rather than resorting to an easy impulse to threaten to withdraw and go to court. Enabling the option to turn to litigation may seem a disincentive to continue problem-solving when it gets hard. However, this challenge inspires parties and professionals to remain at the table and to pull in the same direction to adopt creative solutions.

The negatives of the use of the disqualification clause are apparent when the cost of starting again with a new legal team, if an agreement cannot be reached, is considered. This is costly and means delays will occur, as well as requiring rapport building with different dispute practitioners. The Australian Collaborative Practice Guidelines for Lawyers provide:

> 63. Upon termination of the collaborative process, the representing collaborative practitioners and all other professionals working within the collaborative process are prohibited from participating in any aspect of the contested proceedings between the parties.[26]

Macfarlane's research investigated the impact of the disqualification agreement on the negotiation style and found that the lawyer–client relationships in relation to control and responsibility, privilege, and advocacy were areas demanding greater research. For instance, if an agreement cannot be reached due to one party's obstinacy, and the other party has limited resources, the threat to go to litigation creates power issues and pressure on a party to agree to terms that may not be suitable for them.

Not all matters are suited to CP, and the practitioner is under an obligation to screen parties carefully before suggesting that CP is appropriate.[27] If this is not done properly, then a power imbalance may occur where a party feels that the pressure to go to litigation may force them to settle on unsuitable terms. Making sure all parties are fully informed of the CP process is essential.[28]

Special considerations

The following addresses areas of special consideration when engaging in CP.

Client awareness and use of Collaborative Practice

One of the drawbacks of CP is a lack of party awareness of the process. It is anticipated that, as time passes and more people are educated on its benefits, CP will rapidly grow in demand. If one party engages an adversarial lawyer and the other party wants to use CP, it is not possible to follow CP unless the other party can be informed of its availability. Research is limited in this area, but consideration of legal practitioners' concerns over loss of clients due to the disqualification clause in CP are thought to contribute to a lack of uptake, particularly in non-family

26 Law Council of Australia: *Australian Collaborative Practice Guidelines for Lawyers* (n 7).

27 See, eg, Henry Kha, 'Evaluating Collaborative Law in the Australian Context' (2015) 26(3) *Australasian Dispute Resolution Journal* 178, 182.

28 John Lande and Forrest S Mosten, 'Collaborative Lawyers' Duties to Screen the Appropriateness of Collaborative Law and Obtain Clients' Informed Consent to Use Collaborative Law' (2010) 25(2) *Ohio State Journal on Dispute Resolution* 347; Mosten (n 17).

disputes.[29] The early studies raised a number of factors that can influence the uptake and success of CP.[30] These included legal practitioners' attitude towards CP – in particular, the changes it brings to the lawyer–client relationship, the requirement of increased trust between lawyers acting for both parties, how to relate to professionals contributing from other disciplines, and ensuring appropriate screening of parties prior to commencing the process.[31] CP practitioners have questioned the screening process, finding their own assurance levels and confidence with the process may affect whether parties are screened in or out. Scott and Collins found that parties who have experienced violence were perhaps suited to CP, and the screening that may have excluded these parties on this ground must not be due to the practitioner's levels of confidence in operating within the process.[32]

Differences to other processes

Interest-based negotiation techniques are used in CP, but CP is much more than a monadic or dyadic negotiation.[33] When lawyers undertake a *negotiation* for parties in a dispute, they only advise their client in a confidential manner using a bargaining tone and this advice is often only through written communication. In CP, lawyers and other professionals are present, and all negotiations are conducted through a pre-agreed agenda in a face-to-face meeting, in an honest and open manner, with advice provided verbally from practitioners where necessary.

CP differs from *mediation* in several ways. In a mediation, parties may or may not have legal representatives. A mediator following a facilitative mediation model does not give legal advice. The legal representatives in a mediation model are not working with both their client and the other side's client towards an outcome that satisfies both parties in the manner that CP requires.

CP differs from *arbitration*, as a third-party neutral does not make a decision. The parties control any final agreements they may reach. As such, it is not a determinative process. The parties have the assistance of numerous professionals in achieving an outcome that works for them.

In some models of CP in the United States, a mediator, external expert, or even arbitrator can be utilised by the parties to help with communication or settle specific issues.

Further, CP is not the same as 'cooperative lawyering'[34] or lawyers acting in a collaborative manner. Cooperative or collaborative behaviours are different to CP, in that the former processes do not have a disqualification clause, and also that CP follows a process in which all professionals have been specifically trained.

29 Pauline Collins and Marilyn Scott, 'The Essential Nature of a Collaborative Practice Group for Successful Collaborative Lawyers' (2017) 28(1) *Australasian Dispute Resolution Journal* 12.

30 See, eg, Sefton (n 11); MacFarlane (n 9); Lande (n 10).

31 Lande and Mosten (n 28).

32 Scott and Collins (n 25), 35–6; see also Nancy Ver Steegh, 'The Uniform Collaborative Law Act and Intimate Partner Violence: A Roadmap for Collaborative (and Non-Collaborative) Lawyers' (2009) 38(2) *Hofstra Law Review* 699.

33 See Chapter 1.

34 Lanzetta (n 16).

Collaborative Practice groups

Collaborative Practice group: provides a support and learning network for members trained as CP professionals in a local region.

Early research recognised that CP-trained professionals could not operate effectively without the support of a strong **Collaborative Practice group**. The group provides many important functions for practitioners: it enables ongoing learning and development, keeps members up-to-date with latest developments, assists in further training and credentialing, and develops the necessary trust between practitioners to sustain a strong functioning CP community. It improves understanding between multi-disciplinary teams. Without the practice group, CP cannot survive.[35] All collaborative practitioners belong to a practice group. These groups are located through the various State collaborative practitioner websites and memberships comprises of all those professionals in that region or local area who hold themselves out as collaborative practitioners.

Types of disputes

The uptake of CP in areas beyond family disputes has been limited. No clear explanation exists as to why this is. It is possible that lawyers' lack of understanding and training in the process, as well as parties' absence of knowledge of what is involved, have failed to drive its greater uptake. CP is a process suitable to any type of dispute and is particularly relevant if ongoing relationships are necessary.

The emphasis on ongoing relationships has clearly been the reason for its successful uptake in family disputes. CP allows parents to be focused on protecting their children from emotional repercussions, to accept that relationships breakdown without a need to focus on blame, and to look to the future and achieve a harmonious way forward for all parties involved. Honesty and trust remain at a certain level in these situations, and the communication and problem-solving process used during CP helps parties in their future interactions with each other.

However, the emphasis on relationships does not have to solely relate to the family. Many commercial and business disputes occur in an environment where relationships must be maintained. CP can help businesses problem-solve through arranged meetings, with the necessary professionals present to manage the dispute in a quick, confidential and transparent environment, while being assured of legal entitlements. One area that has seen some uptake in Australia is in wills and estate disputes. Other areas that could benefit from CP include workplace, planning, environment, building, business, commercial, and partnership disputes. Businesses are always sensitive to the cost associated with disputes through reputational damage, lost productivity and revenue and CP helps with each of these.

Costs

Cost is another factor that makes many types of disputes (as mentioned above) suitable to CP. For instance, if a business restructure is necessary, then the legal and accounting costs in negotiating the outcome can be addressed through the tax system as possible deductible

35 Collins and Scott (n 29).

expenses. If a tax and/or accountant practitioner is present during CP, then they can provide immediate advice to the parties as to this cost-saving benefit. The costs and fees of professionals involved in CP are negotiated as part of the process and are addressed at the outset. Hourly rates are possible, but so are other methods of payment. The important aspect is that the cost of the process is shared and transparent, with both parties being aware of the costs each are incurring from the outset. The shorter time span taken in reaching an outcome is one factor alone that reduces parties' costs.

The lawyers' income should not be affected, as when one matter ends, they have more time for other matters and are still billing for their hours worked. Parties that have experienced CP are often advocates for their collaborative lawyers and dispute professionals and recommend them to other disputing parties. This provides an assured client base and successful business.

The Australian Collaborative Practice Guidelines for Lawyers set forth the criteria on which costs are agreed in Guidelines 64–8.[36]

When is Collaborative Practice unsuitable?

CP may not be a suitable process in cases of high emotion, where trust is entirely broken, where violence or threats of violence have occurred, where revenge is high on a party's agenda, where a party is an inveterate liar, where a party has a psychiatric illness or personality disorder, or where there is drug or alcohol addiction that affects a party's capacity to be rational. Large power imbalances, whether due to financial capability or psychological issues, can present difficulties for CP. Parties who believe they can use the process to manipulate or avoid giving financial or other information to the other party soon discover this is not the case. The lawyers involved should detect all of these types of situations and make an assessment as to which dispute management process is suitable, including whether CP would work in such cases.[37]

While the situations just described may present as a barrier to using CP, they should not be automatic grounds for exclusion. Each case needs careful consideration, as some may benefit from having a multidiscipline approach applied to their problem. It may be that where complexities or power balance issues arise, the assistance of other professionals are called for and together can work to achieve a successful outcome that aids the parties more than an adversarial process could.

Self-represented parties will clearly not be suited to CP. This is one reason CP and those practising in the domain are looking at offering their services pro bono in order to increase access to CP.[38] Legal Aid and other funding mechanisms become relevant when considering the costs of providing justice to disputing parties, including enabling the opportunity to adopt CP by a broader cross-section of the community.

36 Law Council of Australia (n 7): Charges for Services ss 64–8.

37 Lande and Mosten (n 28).

38 Clarissa Rayward, 'Is There a Place for a Pro Bono CP Clinic in Australian Family Law?' (2014) 14(1) *Collaborative Review* 14.

Regulatory environment and ethical considerations

As noted previously, at this stage there is no legislated provision for CP in Australia. Certainly, no *Uniform Collaborative Law Act*[39] such as in the United States, exists. However, lawyers and other dispute practitioners who claim to be CP practitioners require training in CP. Collaborative lawyers must not hold themselves out as CP practitioners unless they follow these Guidelines.[40] The Guidelines include information on the manner in which practitioners promote their services so as not to create false expectations of the process.[41]

The regular professional practice rules and ethical requirements apply to all lawyers, including collaborative practitioners. For this reason, extra care must be taken in the collaborative setting.

In the United States, some lawyers follow the outline of CP but have abandoned the disqualification clause. This means if agreement cannot be reached, the same legal advisors can proceed to represent their clients in litigation. This variation is referred to as **cooperative lawyering.**[42] It is a style not addressed in the literature in Australia under this name. Limited retention agreements or unbundled services are concepts arising out of the United States and relate to lawyers' responses to client demands.[43] For instance, clients may have limited funds or only need legal assistance to negotiate a settlement, not to litigate, and so may contract a lawyer for that aspect alone, hence the term 'unbundled service'. Mosten has described unbundled services as 'the client is in charge of selecting one or several discrete lawyering tasks contained within the full-service package'.[44] It is now a widespread practice and, in Australia as in other jurisdictions, is understood as a way of giving access to justice through the provision of discrete lawyering for specific needs of clients in order to reduce their costs. Unbundled legal services are also called '"discrete task assistance", "á la carte legal services", "limited scope services", "decomposition" and "disaggregated legal services"'.[45]

Cooperative lawyering: involves lawyers using an interest-based approach when negotiating, but if this is not successful in managing a dispute, they can proceed to represent the parties in litigation.

Technology has enabled assistance to parties through online education, self-help checklists, and ways of obtaining legal assistance at low cost. The approach is client-centred rather than lawyer-centred. This approach may be limited to settlement negotiation assistance only – much like CP – rather than the provision of the full range of traditional legal assistance that includes litigation advocacy.

In the Australian context, Wolski has raised concerns for CP based on the notion of conflicting interests where a lawyer is driven by settlement and whether this is against the best interests of the client.[46] The ethical issues surrounding the use of the disqualification

39 *Uniform Collaborative Law Act 2009.*

40 Law Council of Australia (n 7), 71.

41 Ibid 69.

42 See, eg, Ver Steegh (n 32); Lande (n 10); Barbara Glesner Fines, 'Ethical Issues in Collaborative Lawyering' (2008) 21(1) *Journal of American Academy of Matrimonial Law* 141, 148.

43 See Forrest S Mosten, *Unbundling Legal Services: A Guide to Delivering Legal Services A La Carte* (American Bar Association Law Practice Management Section, 2000).

44 Ibid 1.

45 Pascoe Pleasence et al, *Reshaping Legal Assistance Services: Building on the Evidence Base. A Discussion Paper* (Law and Justice Foundation of New South Wales, 2014).

46 Wolski (n 20).

clause and settlement-versus-adversarial advocacy have been extensively explored in the United States, with the conclusion that CP does not offend ethical requirements of lawyers' professional conduct codes.[47] However, the question remains: is settlement always going to be in the best interests of the parties? This leads to the question: who decides what is in the parties' best interests? The answer to this depends on whether we look at purely addressing legal entitlements and rights, or the bigger picture such as party costs, time, emotions, and relationship needs.

Conclusion

CP demonstrates the creative ways disputes can be managed and that just one innovative individual can develop a new way of doing things. This burgeoning approach to dispute management presents a unique alternative to litigation and other processes. It has distinctive benefits. The drawbacks to CP relate to how to increase awareness by encouraging parties and practitioners to implement this way of managing disputes, and ensuring professional practice and ethical requirements keep apace of this process.

EXERCISE IN APPLYING YOUR KNOWLEDGE – JACK AND CATHY'S FAMILY

Jack and Cathy's relationship had ended after Cathy told Jack she wanted to start a relationship with another woman. Jack was initially distraught, believing their life together had been happy and would continue forevermore. Jack was a prominent academic and Cathy was an actress. They also operated a drama school for children.

Both Jack and Cathy agreed they did not want their separation to be hostile or draw any public commentary. They had heard about a Collaborative Practice process and so both independently sought out lawyers who knew about this process.

Jack felt uncomfortable about their three children witnessing their mother in a lesbian relationship.

Cathy, in a confidential meeting with her lawyer, indicated that she was worried Jack's 'traditional' view of the world would distort her children's acceptance of her new partner and their relationship.

Cathy's lawyer saw that Jack was a 'traditional' conservative man with views he was not afraid to express. He also was used to having people see things his way.

In the pre-meeting planning, Cathy's lawyer raised her concern with Jack's lawyer, Brenton.

Brenton agreed that both parties needed to feel comfortable and empowered so they could fully express their views for any agreed outcome to be sustainable.

Their second son, Mark, had a speech impediment and stutter and both parents were concerned that this had worsened since their separation.

Financially, they were undecided about what to do with the drama school. It had only just started to break even and Cathy's new partner, Shona, was a teacher at the school. So, Cathy wanted the business to continue.

47 See Scott R Peppet, 'The Ethics of Collaborative Law' (2008) (1) *Journal of Dispute Resolution* 131; Fines (n 42).

Cathy and Shona wanted to commit to their relationship and moved in together.

Initially, Jack and Cathy had a shared parenting arrangement in which the children changed households each Wednesday. This worked well for a while, but the two eldest boys, Christian, aged 15, and Mark, aged 13, wanted to live with their Dad and to visit their mother when they could. Pete, aged 9, was happy to change households each Wednesday.

Since Shona moved in with Cathy, there have been some upsetting incidents, such as money disappearing from Shona's purse. This has put a strain on the relationship.

As a CP lawyer:

1. Describe what other professionals could usefully be present in the business meetings and why?
2. What would you do about Cathy's concerns as:
   (a) Cathy's lawyer, and
   (b) Jack's lawyer?
3. What advantages would this process have over the normal family law process for family dispute management?
4. How can CP accommodate third parties?

10 ARBITRATION

Learning aims

- Demonstrate knowledge of arbitration as a method to manage disputes, with special focus on commercial contracts
- Recognise the sources of norms regulating commercial arbitration
- Identify the specific procedural steps of commercial arbitration
- Demonstrate the ability to apply the theory of arbitration to managing disputes
- Explain viable and appropriate arbitration agreements and discover defective clauses
- Recognise potential pitfalls when engaging in arbitration and post-award proceedings
- Demonstrate the ability to assess the suitability of arbitration for a dispute

Understanding arbitration

This section will provide an introduction to arbitration as a triadic determinative dispute management process. It includes:

- a definition of arbitration
- a brief history explaining the development of the mechanism and how it came to its current global recognition and success
- the main classifications
- who can arbitrate what and when
- and what regulates arbitration in its most known commercial form.

Definition and development of arbitration

Arbitration: a triadic determinative process in which a third-party neutral is mandated by the disputing parties to make a decision regarding the dispute between them based on evidence and law. The decision is private, final, binding, and enforceable.

Arbitration is a private process chosen and paid for by the disputing parties. It involves a third-party neutral chosen by the parties to make a decision regarding their dispute, following a procedure also chosen by the parties. The process results in a final and binding outcome that is enforceable, similar to a court judgment. Based on its characteristics and legal recognition, on the continuum of dispute management methods arbitration sits between mediation and litigation, with characteristics shared with each, yet different from both.

Arbitration appears in ancient mythology, with arguments between Greek gods and Egyptian divinities being addressed by a neutral in a final manner. Historically, arbitration has been noted between private individuals, as well as between states. In the first form, a town elder, a rabbi, a sheik, a local leader, or just a trusted, respected member of the community was often asked to decide a disagreement as a simple, informal, fast, and easy way of dealing with differences. In disputes between states, arbitration was a preferred, peaceful way of settling disputes already in the Antiquity in Greece, Rome, Persia, and Mesopotamia.[1]

Commercial and inter-state arbitration initially both developed along the same principles and procedures. Arbitration between foreign investors and a host state was also established

1 Gary Born, *International Commercial Arbitration* (Kluwer Law International, 2nd ed, 2014) 8–19.

based on commercial arbitration to provide a neutral platform and equal procedural footing in an otherwise imbalanced power set-up. Over time, proceedings involving a sovereign state (whether inter-state or investor-state) have departed from the market-driven commercial arbitration. Public interest and internal government structures demand specific processes. As a result, these different forums, while still labelled as 'arbitration' of some sort, have developed into distinct fields. Although some characteristics are still shared, this chapter will focus only on commercial arbitration, not explicitly dealing with inter-state or investor-state arbitration.

Arbitration in Australia has its origins in the English arbitration tradition developed in mediaeval times.[2] The reason behind that development was the same as for all other private dispute management: over-crowded courts battling with back-logs, much like many courts today. Australia, however, has known dispute processes resembling arbitration even before colonisation. In the absence of courts as we now know them, Aboriginal and Torres Strait Islander communities managed disputes with tribal Elders performing an arbitrator-like role. These processes were simple and efficient, based on trust and respect, as most ancient arbitrations used to be.

Today, arbitration is much more complex and a lot more regulated than its ancient form, but it is also formally recognised by legal systems. In Australia, arbitration is regulated by different Acts, depending on whether the dispute is domestic or international. Domestic cases fall under the scope of the *Commercial Arbitration Acts* of each State and Territory. International arbitration is regulated at the Federal level by the *International Arbitration Act*.[3] The legal framework is increasing the regulation of arbitration at the expense of some of its advantages, like flexibility, but it is also making arbitration appreciated as more secure and predictable. Trust in the system attracts a growing number of more complex and higher value disputes. These, in turn, demand more regulation for an even higher level of security and predictability. As a result, arbitration is changing its core characteristics due to the ever-changing market demand and ongoing legislative and industry developments.

Classification of arbitration

Arbitration can be classified into different categories based on several criteria. The relevance of this classification is to identify the legal framework in which a particular arbitration case operates, as everything depends on the applicable law.

Based on nationality

Arbitration cases can be national/domestic or international depending on the parties or the business relationship involved in the dispute. According to the *Commercial Arbitration Act* of each Australian state and territory:

> An arbitration is 'domestic' if:
>
> (a) the parties to an arbitration agreement have [...] their places of business in Australia, and
>
> (b) the parties have [...] agreed that any dispute that has arisen or may arise between them is to be settled by arbitration, and

2 Doug Jones, *Commercial Arbitration in Australia* (Thomson Reuters, 2011) 4–9.

3 *International Arbitration Act 1974* (Cth).

> (c) it is not an arbitration to which the Model Law (as given effect by the International Arbitration Act 1974 of the Commonwealth) applies.[4]

The *UNCITRAL Model Law on International Commercial Arbitration* (*Model Law*) referred to in the quoted text above defines an arbitration as international, if:

> (a) the parties to an arbitration agreement have [. . .] their places of business in different States; or
>
> (b) one of the following places is situated outside the State in which the parties have their places of business:
>
> (i) the place of arbitration if determined in [. . .] the arbitration agreement;
>
> (ii) any place where a substantial part of the obligations of the commercial relationship is to be performed or the place with which the subject matter of the dispute is most closely connected; or
>
> (c) the parties have expressly agreed that the subject matter of the arbitration agreement relates to more than one country.[5]

Accordingly, an arbitration between two parties residing within Australia is deemed to be domestic, unless the contract in dispute has a significant international element or the parties expressly agree that the dispute has a foreign element, and/or it should be arbitrated outside their home jurisdiction. An arbitration between parties residing in different States or Territories of Australia still qualifies as domestic arbitration.

Based on subject matter

Depending on the claim that is arbitrated, we can classify arbitration as commercial, labour, construction, consumer, investment, family arbitration, or other. The relevance of this classification is, again, in identifying the legal framework specific to that particular type of arbitration, but also in identifying whether a particular type of dispute can be submitted to arbitration at all. For example, property and financial claims related to a family dispute can be submitted to 'a process (other than the judicial process) in which parties to a dispute present arguments and evidence to an arbitrator who makes a determination to resolve the dispute'[6] but a divorce cannot be decided in arbitration.

According to all Australian *Arbitration Acts* (both domestic and international), an arbitration is commercial if it is about 'matters arising from all relationships of a commercial nature, whether contractual or not'[7] in a broad sense. A non-exhaustive list of examples includes

> trade transaction for the supply or exchange of goods or services; distribution agreement; commercial representation or agency; factoring; leasing; construction of works; consulting;

4 *Commercial Arbitration Acts* s 1(3).

5 *UNCITRAL Model Law on International Commercial Arbitration*, UN Doc A/40/17, annex I and A/61/17, annex I (adopted on 21 June 1985, amended 7 July 2006) (*UNCITRAL Model Law on International Commercial Arbitration*) art 1(3); see also Albert Monichino and Alex Fawke, 'International Arbitration in Australia: 2017/2018 in Review' (2019) 29(2) *Australasian Dispute Resolution Journal* 215.

6 *Family Law Act 1975* (Cth) s 10L.

7 *Commercial Arbitration Acts* s 1(6); footnote 2 in the *UNCITRAL Model Law on International Commercial Arbitration* incorporated in the *International Arbitration Act 1974* (Cth).

engineering; licensing; investment; financing; banking; insurance; exploitation agreement or concession; joint venture and other forms of industrial or business cooperation; carriage of goods or passengers by air, sea, rail, or road.[8]

Based on its organisation

One of the most important differentiations to be made in commercial arbitration is the one between **ad hoc** and institutional arbitration.

Ad hoc: Latin: 'for this'. In arbitration, a procedure created for a particular dispute, outside of the framework of an arbitral institution.

The criterion to determine whether an arbitration is ad hoc or institutional is the proceeding's organisation: whether it is administered by the parties themselves or by a specialised institution providing arbitration services. Given that arbitration only exists if the parties agree to arbitrate a dispute, in a sense every arbitration is created for the particular purpose of that dispute, but ad hoc arbitrations are free of institutional constraints.

Once the parties decide to arbitrate a dispute, they have to decide whether to opt for ad hoc or institutional arbitration. A comparison of the characteristics of these two types of arbitration (Table 10.1) can assist that decision.

Table 10.1 Comparative list of characteristics of ad hoc and institutional arbitration

Ad hoc	Institutional
• Maximum flexibility in procedure	• More rigid procedural rules
• Procedure dependent on the parties' cooperation	• Security of the proceedings provided by the institution
• Time decided by the parties	• Time imposed by the institution
• Lower costs	• Predictable costs

Considering these characteristics, ad hoc arbitration is more suitable when:

- special tasks need to be entrusted to the arbitrators or special procedures are needed for which there are no standard institutional rules
- the parties are ready to assume a greater role in shaping the procedure
- there is agreement between the parties on how to run the process in a time and cost-effective way (ie they have an overall good relationship and the disagreement is only one of substance).

Institutional arbitration is more suitable when:

- the dispute fits a type of arbitration commonly administered by an institution
- the parties cannot agree on anything, including the procedure needed for an effective arbitration
- the parties don't have enough understanding of arbitration to shape the process
- the parties don't want to assume the role of creating and running the procedure themselves.

8 *Commercial Arbitration Acts* s 1(6); footnote 2 in the *UNCITRAL Model Law on International Commercial Arbitration* incorporated in the *International Arbitration Act 1974* (Cth).

Time and cost are usually not decisive factors on their own in this selection. While ad hoc arbitration may be cheaper for not having to pay the administering institution, cost efficiency depends on the overall efficiency of case management, as everything is paid by the parties.

Arbitral institutions are service providers created to cater for disputing parties. They only administer, not decide, the disputes. The administrative framework that institutions provide is built around internal organs – usually a board and a secretariat with counsel handling the cases. The tasks performed by arbitral institutions include:

- supervising the proceedings registered to the institution, ensuring that procedural rules and timeframes are observed
- intermediating and recording the official communication and exchange of written submissions between the parties and the arbitrators
- ensuring that the tribunal is constituted – providing a fall-back procedure if the parties fail to appoint the arbitrators and providing a procedure for challenging and replacing arbitrators, if necessary
- ensuring that the fees and cost advances are secured, so that the case is not blocked for reluctance to pay for a hearing room or the arbitrators' fees
- performing administrative tasks like booking a hearing room or organising transcripts
- possibly also verifying the decisions rendered in the case, ensuring that they are in line with the applicable procedural rules.

The main arbitral institution in Australia is the Australian Centre for International Commercial Arbitration (ACICA)[9] hosted in Sydney at the Australian Disputes Centre (ADC).[10] ADC focuses on domestic, while ACICA focuses on international arbitration. Other institutions often limit their services to a specialist area or to parts of arbitration only, without providing full administration of cases. The Perth Centre for Energy and Resources Arbitration (PCERA),[11] for example, specialises in disputes in the energy and resources sector. The Melbourne Commercial Arbitration and Mediation (MCAM) Centre[12] provides venues that can cater for the specific needs of arbitration. The Resolution Institute[13] offers arbitrator accreditation and appointment services as well as a set of arbitration rules parties can freely use, but it does not administer cases.

There are many local, regional, and international arbitration service providers all around the world. There are two international organisations that have a significant presence in Australia through their local branches. The Chartered Institute of Arbitrators (CIArb)[14] is a professional organisation providing accreditation to arbitrators that is also frequently asked to recommend arbitrators for appointment, but it does not administer cases. The International Chamber of Commerce (ICC), the world's largest business organisation, has a dispute management section that offers services in a range of dispute management processes, including

9 *Australian Centre for International Commercial Arbitration* (Web Page) <https://acica.org.au/>.

10 *Australian Disputes Centre* (Web Page) <https://www.disputescentre.com.au/>.

11 *Perth Centre for Energy and Resources Arbitration* (Web Page) <https://pcera.org/about-pcera/>.

12 *Melbourne Commercial Arbitration and Mediation Centre* (Web Page) <http:/www.mcamh.com.au/>.

13 *Resolution Institute* (Web Page) <https://www.resolution.institute/>.

14 *Chartered Institute of Arbitrators* (Web Page) <https://www.ciarb.org/>; *Chartered Institute of Arbitrators Australia* (Web Page) <https://www.ciarb.net.au/>.

arbitration. The ICC International Court of Arbitration[15] is the largest arbitral institution in the world. Even though the ICC Court of Arbitration can handle cases held all around the world, regional branches are used mainly to assist with local arbitrator appointments, organising venues and logistics, not the actual administration of cases – which is done by counsel based at the ICC headquarters in Paris.

In choosing an arbitration service provider, the factors to consider will be similar to choosing between ad hoc and institutional arbitration. They will depend on the individual needs of each case and follow a cost-benefit analysis of the services offered and the associated costs. A combination of convenience and reputation often plays a significant role in choosing one institution over another.

Parties to arbitration

The fact that arbitration is based on party autonomy determines the parties to arbitration in two ways:

1. The arbitration agreement is a contract; therefore, a party must have legal capacity to enter into a contract to agree to arbitrate.[16]
2. Only a party who gave consent to the arbitration agreement can be a party to the arbitration based on that agreement; third-party non-signatories may be bound by an arbitration agreement in some circumstances only, under various theories borrowed from other fields of law.[17]

Parties in arbitration are regularly called 'claimant' and 'respondent' (or 'defendant'). The claimant is the party that initiates the arbitration, while the respondent is the one against which the request for arbitration is filed. The respondent may have its own claims against the claimant – called 'counterclaims' – but these do not change the overall status of the parties.

Since disputes are often complex, arising between several parties, and/or from several connected contracts, arbitration is often between more than just two parties. As arbitration is subject to consent, arbitrators do not automatically have the same authority as courts to join related issues in a single arbitration. To avoid parallel proceedings in multi-party and multi-contract disputes, many arbitral institutions now provide specific rules allowing for the consolidation of cases and for the possibility to join additional parties to an existing arbitration.[18]

15 *ICC International Court of Arbitration* (Web Page) <https://iccwbo.org/dispute-resolution-services/icc-international-court-arbitration/>.

16 As a rule, capacity is determined by the home law of the party. However, the law of the contract and the law of the place of enforcement may also be relevant to recognise that capacity.

17 See Stavros Brekoulakis, 'Rethinking Consent in International Commercial Arbitration: A General Theory for Non-Signatories' (2017) 8(4) *Journal of International Dispute Settlement* 610; Vicky Priskich, 'Binding Non-Signatories to Arbitration Agreements – Who Are Persons "Claiming through or under" a Party?' (2019) 35(3) *Arbitration International* 375 for more on third-party non-signatories.

18 See, eg, *ACICA Arbitration Rules Incorporating the Emergency Arbiter Provisions* (Australian Centre for International Commercial Arbitration, 2016) <https://acica.org.au/wp-content/uploads/Rules/2016/ACICA-Arbitration-Rules-2016.pdf> arts 14–15.

Arbitrability

Arbitration is a forum similar to court. As such, for an arbitral tribunal to solve the merits of a case, the tribunal needs to confirm first that it has jurisdiction over that case. Due to the contractual nature of arbitration, **arbitrability** depends on two aspects:

Arbitrability: the ability of an issue to be decided in arbitration.

1. Substantive arbitrability depends on whether the subject matter of the dispute can be arbitrated. The issue in dispute must be something the parties are free to contract around and which is not reserved for the exclusive jurisdiction of the courts. Substantive arbitrability is regulated through mandatory statutory provisions and differs from country to country.[19] In Australia, reference to arbitrability restrictions is made in both the *Commercial Arbitration Acts*[20] and the *International Arbitration Act*.[21]
2. Procedural arbitrability depends on whether the agreement to arbitrate covers the issue in dispute sufficiently to provide a valid and effective basis for arbitral jurisdiction. A deficient arbitration agreement, or one that is limited to issues not including the one in dispute, may make that dispute non-arbitrable even if the subject matter could, otherwise, be arbitrated.

Using theory and models to dissect arbitration

Philosophical and legal characteristics of arbitration

Arbitration can mostly be identified from being labelled as such. The name itself, however, does not make a process arbitration without its distinctive set of characteristics. Since most of these characteristics are shared with other dispute management processes, the key is in the unique combination of these characteristics that differentiate arbitration from other methods.

1. *Party autonomy.* As a rule, arbitration is a voluntary process, similar to most mediations and negotiation. Party autonomy is the cornerstone of arbitration, allowing disputing parties to choose to submit their dispute to arbitration. This also means that parties must agree to arbitrate, as arbitration depends on the parties' valid consent to the process.

   Party autonomy also means that the parties can choose or design the procedure to follow, as litigation and court rules do not apply. In a cross-border setting, party

19 See *Casaceli v Natuzzi SpA* (2012) 292 ALR 143, for an Australian analysis on what is 'capable of settlement by arbitration' and related mandatory law.

20 *Commercial Arbitration Acts* s 1(5) states that '[t]his Act does not affect any other Act by virtue of which certain disputes may not be submitted to arbitration', with no particular reference to what that 'other Act' may be. The relevant 'other Act' must be researched depending on what the issue in dispute is in a particular case; see also Mia Louise Livingstone, 'The Arbitrability of CCA Claims: The Australian Approach to Enforcing Arbitration (or Exclusive Jurisdiction) Agreements' (2012) 23(1) *Australasian Dispute Resolution Journal* 14.

21 *International Arbitration Act 1974* (Cth) s 2C makes express reference to the *Carriage of Goods by Sea Act 1991* (Cth), which only allows certain claims falling within the scope of that Act to be decided in court or in arbitration conducted in Australia (thereby limiting the arbitrability of those issues).

autonomy also extends to the free choice of the state in which and under the laws of which to arbitrate.

2. *Time and cost efficiency*. Although arbitration is a private process paid for entirely by the parties, the possibility to tailor-make the process to best suit a dispute can make it both time and cost efficient. Flexibility of the procedure also means that choices must be made carefully, and boundaries set up early on, so that a reluctant party cannot abuse the process by delaying tactics. The efficiency of arbitration will be different for each case. It will depend on the complexity of the case, the extent of collaboration between the parties, the procedural rules that will govern the proceedings, the efficiency of the arbitral institution (if any), and availability and efficiency of the arbitrators.
3. *Neutrality*. Like mediation, conciliation, or even litigation, arbitration involves a neutral third party. Neutrality in arbitration combined with the flexibility and party autonomy are the basis for the parties' right to choose their third-party neutral for a dispute. Called an 'arbitrator' or 'arbitral tribunal', this neutral does not need to be a lawyer. They can be appointed based on expertise, experience, availability, and trust vested in their professionalism and qualifications. Dispute practitioners who are appointed as arbitrators operate under strict conditions of independence and impartiality.

   In an international setting, 'neutrality' is also understood as the party autonomy securing the choice of a jurisdiction in which to arbitrate a dispute. The right to choose to arbitrate in a neutral jurisdiction means that the arbitration can be held in a country that is not connected to any of the parties or the relationship from which their dispute arises.
4. *Confidentiality*. There is a general understanding and expectation that, unlike litigation, arbitration brings the advantage of full and absolute confidentiality. While this can be an advantage over litigation, confidentiality is neither guaranteed nor absolute in arbitration. There is no implied duty of confidentiality, meaning that the parties must either expressly agree to keep arbitration confidential or choose arbitration rules that provide for confidentiality. There may also be limitations to a confidentiality agreement, if mandatory statutory provisions impose an obligation to disclose information; for example, based on public interest or based on financial and corporate law reporting obligations.

   Confidentiality applies differently to the different aspects within arbitration that must be identified to avoid a presumption of absolute secrecy. One must differentiate between the secrecy of the existence of the arbitration between the parties, the confidentiality of documents involved, the privacy of hearings, and secrecy of the existence and/or of the content of the resulting outcome. In arbitration there is no binding precedent as in common law litigation. Since arbitration decisions do not become law, they do not have to be made public. The general availability of confidentiality can protect disputing parties' industry secrets and reputation but can also render research and consistency across decisions challenging. To counterbalance this, there is a growing trend internationally to report arbitral decisions, if needed in an anonymised form. Anonymised reporting secures both confidentiality and transparency, contributing to consistency across arbitration decisions.
5. *Enforceability*. Unlike in many other private dispute management processes, the outcome of arbitration is a final and binding decision that can be enforced similarly

Arbitral award: a decision rendered in arbitration through which the arbitrator(s) rule on a procedural or substantive question in a final, binding, and enforceable manner.

to a court judgment. While settlement is a desired, but not a guaranteed outcome in mediation, an **arbitral award** is an inherent component of arbitration, bringing the dispute to an end for the parties through the decision rendered. An award can be based on the parties' settlement, like a settlement agreement achieved through mediation, but is not dependent on such settlement. Instead, arbitrators have a mandate to address the dispute in a final manner based on the evidence presented by the parties, and that outcome is enforceable.

The binding nature of arbitration also means that the agreement to arbitrate, once validly made, can be enforced so that the chosen procedure would lead to an enforceable outcome. A party that agreed to arbitrate a dispute cannot unilaterally change its mind and decide to litigate instead; the court would enforce the arbitration agreement by sending the parties to arbitrate. Also, unlike in mediation where either of the parties can walk away from the process at any time and declare it unsuccessful, an arbitration can only be terminated by the withdrawal of all claims or by a decision rendered.

Theory

One of the more challenging, technical legal aspects of arbitration is that it is subject to a combination of sources of norms that regulate arbitration. These sources are primarily party autonomy, arbitration rules, arbitration laws, and international conventions. Soft law, general principles of law, and the arbitrator's discretion may also be relevant sources, depending on the case.

Party autonomy

As mentioned before, party autonomy is the basic principle of arbitration, originating in its contractual nature. Party autonomy is reflected in:

- the freedom to opt for arbitration in the first place
- the freedom to determine or to choose the procedural rules to govern the arbitration procedure
- in international arbitration, the freedom to choose the applicable arbitration law and the **seat of arbitration**.

Seat of arbitration: the legal home of an arbitration, determining the legal framework in which the process is held, the 'nationality' of the resulting decision, and the courts that may have a role in that arbitration. Not necessarily the same as the physical place where arbitration hearings are held.

Party autonomy is expressed through contractual agreements, mainly in the arbitration clause. Its most obvious manifestation is in ad hoc arbitration, where the parties create and conduct the entire process themselves. The risk of such broad freedom is that the parties may fail to agree or may create procedures that are inoperable. A manifestation of party autonomy that does not bear the same risk is to choose pre-drafted arbitration rules.

Arbitration rules

Arbitration rules are a set of provisions developed usually by arbitral institutions to regulate the procedure of cases submitted to that institution. Not to be confused with arbitration laws, the arbitration rules do not have statutory authority, as they are created by private entities. An arbitration case will be governed by the rules chosen by the parties by either submitting the case to an arbitral institution or by adopting a set of rules available for use and capable of operation outside of an institution. Either way, the choice is regularly made by expressing it in the arbitration agreement.

To assist ad hoc arbitration, there are arbitration rules specifically created for proceedings that are not administered by an institution. The *UNCITRAL Arbitration Rules*[22] were created in 1976 as an 'off-the-shelf' procedural framework for parties who did not wish to make use of arbitration service providers, to avoid procedural mistakes and deadlocks. The *UNCITRAL Rules* have since been revised and amended to stay up to date with developments in the field and current requirements of international arbitration practice. Some institutions also use the *UNCITRAL Rules* either by adopting them as their own or as an alternative to their own rules, offering parties the option to choose between the two.

Arbitration laws

Party autonomy, whether designing or choosing a pre-existing set of rules, is not unlimited and is never the only source of norms regulating arbitration. No arbitration exists in a legal void; all arbitration cases fall under some statutory provision. Statutes regulating arbitration are often referred to as ***lex arbitri***.

lex arbitri: Latin for the 'law of arbitration'. This refers to the statutory provisions regulating arbitration in the jurisdiction where the arbitration is taking place.

All the domestic and international *Arbitration Acts* in Australia are based on the *UNCITRAL Arbitration Model Law*,[23] developed in 1985 and updated in 2006 to contribute to the global legislative harmonisation of arbitration. The *Model Law* origin of the *Arbitration Acts* is relevant, because the interpretation of its provisions should be done with regard to that international origin, even in a domestic setting.[24]

The *UNCITRAL Arbitration Model Law* is also an 'off-the-shelf' text. However, while the *UNCITRAL Arbitration Rules* are provided for arbitrating parties and institutions, the *Model Law* was created for states to adopt as their arbitration legislation. Consequently, the *Model Law* itself is not a direct source of norms regulating arbitration but becomes a source if and to the extent to which it is implemented as state law in a jurisdiction. Given that there are over 100 jurisdictions that base their arbitration laws on the *Model Law*,[25] the *Model Law* becomes a useful tool for comparative analysis. Interpretation of a *Model Law*-based statute is also aided by UNCITRAL guidelines and explanatory texts, further contributing to a harmonised, even if not uniform, legal framework across jurisdictions.[26]

22 *UNCITRAL Arbitration Rules* GA Res 68/109 (adopted 16 December 2013) (*UNCITRAL Arbitration Rules (2013)*).

23 *UNCITRAL Model Law on International Commercial Arbitration*, UN Doc A/40/17, annex I and A/61/17, annex I (adopted on 21 June 1985, amended 7 July 2006).

24 See *Subway Systems Australia Pty Ltd v Ireland* (2014) 46 VR 49.

25 For a current list of how many states adopted the *UNCITRAL Model Law*, see 'Status: UNCITRAL Model law on International Commercial Arbitration (1985), with Amendments as Adopted in 2006', *United Nations Commission on International Trade Law* (Web Page) <https://uncitral.un.org/en/texts/arbitration/modellaw/commercial_arbitration/status>.

26 'Explanatory Note by the UNCITRAL Secretariat on the 1985 Model Law on International Commercial Arbitration as Amended in 2006', *United Nations Commission on International Trade Law* (Web Page) <http://www.uncitral.org/pdf/english/texts/arbitration/ml-arb/MLARB-explanatoryNote20-9-07.pdf>.

Arbitration laws are applicable to a dispute to the extent that they are either chosen by the parties or made mandatory in application by the legislator. In an Australian domestic arbitration, the relevant *Commercial Arbitration Act* will automatically be applicable as a result of that Act's scope of application defined in pt 1 s 1. In international arbitration, parties can freely choose where and under what international arbitration law to arbitrate. Despite their statutory authority, not all provisions of an arbitration law are of mandatory application even when that Arbitration Act governs an arbitration. To support and leave room for party autonomy, arbitration laws operate as a framework providing limited mandatory elements and a range of backup solutions for when party autonomy fails.

International conventions

Similar to the *UNCITRAL Model Law*, international conventions become applicable only as adopted by states as part of their national legislation. Nevertheless, conventions are often considered separately due to their source of origin.

The most important convention in arbitration is the *New York Convention*,[27] having over 160 state parties. The *Convention* is the main instrument providing arbitration global recognition. Specifically created for regulating only international arbitration, its principles and procedures are, however, reflected in the domestically applicable *Model Law*-based *Arbitration Acts* as well. In essence, the *New York Convention* and the corresponding *Model Law* provisions create a framework under which states and their courts will recognise arbitral agreements and give force to arbitral awards. The *Convention* entered into force in Australia in 1975 and is incorporated in the *International Arbitration Act*.[28]

Soft law

Finally, a category of sources of norms that also frequently affect arbitration are so-called soft law provisions. These are regulations which do not qualify as arbitration rules in the strict sense but are developed by private organisations to assist arbitration practice. They can regulate an arbitration either by the parties expressly making them applicable (through party autonomy), or by the arbitral tribunal relying on them as guidelines of non-mandatory application (through the tribunal's discretion).

The most referred to soft law provisions in arbitration are those developed by the International Bar Association (IBA) providing ethical rules and codes of conduct, and guidelines for conducting certain proceedings.[29] ACICA, for example, makes express reference to the IBA rules on evidence, on conflicts of interests, and on party representation.

27 *United Nations Convention on the Recognition and Enforcement of Foreign Arbitral Awards* (1958) (*New York Convention*).

28 See *International Arbitration Act 1974* (Cth) s 2D.

29 International Bar Association, *IBA Guidelines on Conflict of Interests in International Arbitration* (2014) <https://acica.org.au/wp-content/uploads/IBA_Guidelines/IBA-Guidelines-on-Conflict-of-Interest.pdf>; International Bar Association, *IBA Guidelines on Party Representation in International Arbitration* (2013); International Bar Association, *IBA Rules on Taking of Evidence in International Arbitration* (2010); International Bar Association, *Guidelines for Drafting International Arbitration Clauses* (2010).

Hierarchy of the sources of norms

The fact that arbitration can be governed by a combination of several sources of norms may appear confusing, raising the question of which one is more relevant over another in any given case. There are two approaches to solving this: the chronological cause-and-effect order in which these norms become applicable; and the hierarchical basis on which they operate.

From a chronological point of view, party autonomy always comes first, as the necessary first step to opt for arbitration and make the basic choices of where and under what rules to arbitrate. Once these choices are made, however, the mandatory provisions of the chosen laws and rules will override any party-created or chosen provision, hence restricting party autonomy (see Table 10.2). The non-mandatory provisions of the law governing arbitration will give preference to party autonomy manifestations and will only act as gap-fillers for anything the parties or their chosen rules fail to regulate. Finally, the discretion of the arbitral tribunal serves the purpose of identifying any additional norms (most often soft law) necessary to regulate any outstanding matters.

Table 10.2 The hierarchy of sources of norms regulating arbitration procedure

Hierarchy	Sources of norms
1	Mandatory provisions of *lex arbitri*
2	Arbitration rules chosen by the parties
3	Party agreements regulating arbitral procedure
4	Non-mandatory provisions of *lex arbitri*
5	Procedural discretion of the arbitral tribunal

Using knowledge of arbitration to assist in dispute management

This section will focus on practical procedural steps taken to complete an arbitration: starting with the drafting of an arbitration agreement that forms the basis of arbitration; continuing with the arbitration process itself including the appointment and mandate of the arbitrators; and closing with the rendering of the award that puts an end to the case. The post-award phase, while inherently linked to arbitration, is not included in this section, as it is a distinct court procedure to be discussed separately.

The arbitration agreement

Arbitration is contract-based, so there must be an arbitral agreement to have arbitration at all. The *Model Law* contains the definition adopted in both the domestic and international *Arbitration Acts* in Australia, namely:

> Arbitration agreement is an agreement by the parties to submit to arbitration all or certain disputes which have arisen or which may arise between them in respect of a defined legal relationship, whether contractual or not.[30]

30 *UNCITRAL Model Law on International Commercial Arbitration* art 7.

Parties can agree to arbitrate when first entering a contractual relationship or when a dispute arises between them. The agreement for a future arbitration is usually called an 'arbitration agreement' or 'arbitration clause' in a commercial contract. The agreement to arbitrate an existing dispute is sometimes referred to as a 'submission agreement'.[31]

Scope

An arbitration agreement serves the purpose of providing authority to an arbitral tribunal to decide a dispute. It defines the scope and the limits of that mandate and is an essential requirement for arbitral jurisdiction. If there is no valid arbitral agreement, there is no arbitration. If there is a valid agreement, the arbitration will be limited to the scope given by the wording of that agreement. Accordingly, for the agreement to cover all possible issues of a future dispute, its wording needs to be broad, rather than limited. A submission agreement can be more specific, given the existence of the dispute for which it is drafted. However, a broader language may be more beneficial even for a submission agreement, as additional claims and issues may arise during the arbitration, which should not risk falling outside the scope of a narrowly defined agreement to arbitrate.

The arbitration agreement also serves the purpose of:

- defining the type of arbitration
- identifying the arbitration rules
- identifying the seat of arbitration and with that the *lex arbitri*
- defining the number of arbitrators and their qualifications, if any
- selecting the language of the arbitration, if necessary.

There are additional components an arbitral agreement can have, but these are the most essential ones for efficient use of party autonomy. Arbitration can also be initiated based on a bare minimum agreement expressing the choice of arbitration and nothing more. However, in that case, an arbitral institution approached with the claim or the arbitrators appointed or a state court would have to fill the gaps and define what the parties should have chosen upfront – all of which costs additional time and money and eventually renders arbitration less efficient.

Validity requirements

As any contract, an arbitration agreement is subject to validity conditions. Party autonomy allows the parties to choose what law will determine the validity of their arbitration agreement, but such choice is rarely expressed.[32] As a default rule, an arbitration agreement must satisfy the validity requirements of the arbitration law from the seat where the arbitration occurs. Accordingly, the validity of an agreement leading to a domestic arbitration in Australia would be tested under the *Commercial Arbitration Act* from the State or Territory where the

31 Nigel Blackaby et al, *Redfern and Hunter on International Arbitration* (Oxford University Press, 6th ed, 2015) 72.

32 For the internationally recognised test to apply in determining the law to govern the arbitral agreement, see *Sulamérica Cia Nacional De Seguros SA v Enesa Engenheria SA* [2013] 1 WLR 102, and the more recent *Enka Insaat ve Sanayi AS v OOO Insurance Company Chubb* [2020] EWCA Civ 574.

arbitration is taking place; an agreement for international arbitration in Australia would be tested under the *International Arbitration Act* (Cth).

An arbitration agreement must satisfy both substantive and formal validity conditions. The substantive conditions are:

1. The parties must have legal capacity to agree and enter into arbitration.
2. The agreement must be to arbitrate existing or future disputes. Arbitration cannot be used to obtain an enforceable award if there is no real dispute. This is designed to avoid pretend claims that may be used, for example, for money laundering.
3. The dispute must be 'in respect of a defined legal relationship, whether contractual or not'.[33] Delictual liability or tort claims may also be submitted to arbitration.
4. The dispute must be arbitrable – with reference to substantive arbitrability to be tested under the law of the seat of arbitration,[34] but also under the law of the place where enforcement of the award will be sought.[35]

An arbitration agreement must also satisfy formal validity conditions. In Australia, both the domestic and international *Arbitration Acts* reflect Option 1 of the *UNCITRAL Model Law* definition for an arbitration agreement,[36] which includes the requirement for

> ... an agreement to be 'in writing'. The written form is defined as being recorded in any form, meaning only that it cannot be an oral agreement. Electronic communication, exchange of submissions not contesting arbitral jurisdiction, or incorporation by reference to a document containing a valid arbitration agreement, all satisfy the condition of an arbitration agreement to be 'in writing'.[37]

Arbitration agreements or clauses that do not satisfy the validity requirements or are even just ambiguous enough to cause difficulties in their implementation are often called 'pathological clauses'.[38] Consequences of **pathological arbitration agreements** can range from time and costs wasted on interpreting unclear or contradictory provisions all the way to procedural non-arbitrability in case of fatal pathologies.[39] The most common causes of pathological arbitration agreements are too much specificity (ie 'over-lawyering'), ambiguity or inconsistency within the agreement, or insufficient understanding of the arbitration process.

Pathological arbitration agreements: a term introduced by Frédéric Eismann to describe a clause referring to arbitration in a sufficiently defective way to require debated interpretation and which makes observance of the arbitration agreement difficult or impossible.

33 *UNCITRAL Model Law on International Commercial Arbitration* art 7.

34 *New York Convention* art II(1).

35 Ibid art V(2).

36 *International Arbitration Act 1974* (Cth) s 16(2) states that '[. . .] arbitration agreement has the meaning given in Option 1 of Article 7 of the Model Law'. Section 7(3) of every *Commercial Arbitration Act* states that 'The arbitration agreement must be in writing'.

37 See the *Commercial Arbitration Acts* ss 7(4)-(8) for domestic arbitration; *UNCITRAL Model Law on International Commercial Arbitration* arts 7(3)-(6) Option 1 for international arbitration.

38 Frédéric Eismann, 'La Clause d'arbitrage Pathologique' in *Commercial Arbitration Essays in Memoriam Eugenio Minoli* (Unione Tipografico-editrice Torinese, 1974).

39 See also Jiangtao Qian and Liang Guo, 'The Validity and Remedy of the Pathological International Commercial Arbitration Agreement' (2019) 2(5) *Frontiers in Educational Research* 109.

To avoid the risks of pathological agreements, parties can obtain guidance from soft law on how to draft a clause[40] or use so-called 'model clauses'. Most arbitral institutions offer such model clauses on their websites or they are incorporated in their arbitration rules. Many of these model clauses follow the same pattern of including the basic necessary elements of an arbitration agreement with room for the parties to customise the details. Using one institution's model clause but choosing another institution to administer the arbitration may render the clause pathological for the purposes of that particular case if the model clause includes elements that cannot work in a different institutional setting.

A model clause example (not from any particular institution):

> Any dispute, controversy, or claim arising out of or relating to this contract, or the breach, termination, or invalidity thereof, shall be finally settled by arbitration at ... (name of institution) in accordance with the ... (name of the arbitration rules) in effect on the date of this contract, by ... (one or three) arbitrators appointed in accordance with the said Rules.
>
> The seat of arbitration shall be ... (name of the place where the arbitration will take place).
>
> The language to be used in the proceedings shall be ... (identify language, if needed).
>
> The dispute shall be solved based on ... (the law governing the contract/merits of the case).

Model arbitration process

The arbitration process itself is the phase between the filing of a request for arbitration until the rendering of a final award deciding all parts of the dispute. Party autonomy governing this phase secures the flexibility and adaptability of arbitration to a given case.[41] The model used for this chapter is that of regular commercial arbitration, but shorter, so-called 'fast track' or expedited arbitration may be an option where imposing strict time limits suits a less complex case.[42]

An arbitration process including only two parties is commonly composed of the following steps:

1. Filing a request for arbitration and identifying arbitrator by the Claimant
2. Filing an answer to the request for arbitration and counterclaims (if any) and identifying arbitrator by the Respondent

40 See, eg, International Bar Association 2010 (n 29).

41 *Commercial Arbitration Acts* s 19(1) and *UNCITRAL Model Law on International Commercial Arbitration* art 19(1) state that 'the parties are free to agree on the procedure to be followed by the arbitral tribunal in conducting the proceedings', only subject to the mandatory provisions of the Act.

42 See, eg, Australian Centre for International Commercial Arbitration, *ACICA Expedited Arbitration Rules* (2016) <https://acica.org.au/wp-content/uploads/Rules/2016/ACICA-Expedited-Arbitration-Rules-2016.pdf>.

3. Appointing the presiding arbitrator (if tribunal of three) and/or confirming the establishment of the arbitral tribunal
4. Preliminary meeting/conference
5. Issuing Procedural Order 1 or Terms of reference
6. Submission of written memorials and request for production of documents (if any)
7. Oral hearing (if any)
8. Submission of post-hearing briefs
9. Deliberation
10. Rendering of the award
11. Correction and/or interpretation of the award (if necessary).

Formation of the arbitral tribunal

The first major step after an arbitration is initiated is the formation of the tribunal. Not to be confused with the arbitral institution administering the case, the arbitral tribunal is composed of the individual arbitrators mandated to decide on the merits of the dispute. In forming a tribunal, the elements to consider are the number of arbitrators, their qualifications, and the appointment procedure.

Number of arbitrators

Disputing parties can freely decide on the number of arbitrators. Arbitration rules and laws commonly provide that the number of arbitrators should be uneven and not more than three. Preference is generally given to a single arbitrator, unless the size and complexity of the case requires a panel of three. In Australia, the *Arbitration Acts* provide for a default approach, should the parties fail to decide on the number of arbitrators. This is generally one arbitrator for domestic cases[43] and three arbitrators for international cases.[44] The criteria for the parties to decide whether to have one or three may include those in Table 10.3.

Table 10.3 When to choose a sole arbitrator or an arbitral tribunal

Sole arbitrator	Arbitral tribunal
• Simple case, limited number of small issues, not of too high value	• Complex case, multiple issues or too big value
• Easier administration, faster, cheaper process	• More difficult to coordinate, slower, more expensive process
• Appointment made together by the parties or by an appointing authority	• Separate party-appointed arbitrators
• No balancing factor – if there is an error, there is no co-arbitrator to notice	• Higher certainty that the decision is correct

43 *Commercial Arbitration Acts* s 10(2).
44 *UNCITRAL Model Law on International Commercial Arbitration* art 10(2).

Qualifications

Qualification requirements for arbitrators can be set by the *lex arbitri*, the arbitration rules, and by the parties themselves. In Australia, 'any natural person having legal capacity may be appointed as an arbitrator ... There is no requirement that the person be legally qualified, possess special experience, or be an Australian citizen or a resident'.[45] As noted, arbitrators do not have to be lawyers, but many are. Many also possess arbitration qualifications and accreditation to raise their profile and demonstrate expertise. The only universal legal requirement for arbitrators in both domestic and international cases is that they must be independent and impartial.

In addition to the legal requirements, the parties may define any qualification requirements for their arbitrators. Considerations to make when deciding on the individual characteristics of arbitrators:

- professional qualification – parties should opt for someone who knows arbitration, and understands the procedure and the legal consequences of arbitration (if technical expertise is needed in a case, that can be supplemented by an expert witness)
- knowledge and experience – preferably in arbitration, but also in the subject matter of the dispute
- availability – to schedule and address the case within a reasonable time (which can be challenging with highly sought-after arbitrators)
- language command – in international cases.

Appointing arbitrators

Party autonomy generally secures the parties' right to appoint the arbitrator(s), but institutional rules may restrict the procedure and the timeframe within which appointment happens. As a general rule (unrelated to any particular institution):

- a sole arbitrator is appointed by mutual agreement between the parties
- a tribunal of three arbitrators is appointed by each party appointing one arbitrator and the two party-appointed arbitrators (also called co-arbitrators) appointing the presiding third arbitrator (sometimes called the Chair of the tribunal)
- the arbitral institution (or the tribunal itself in ad hoc arbitration) will then confirm the formation of the tribunal and set the start date of their mandate.

Appointing authority: a person or entity authorised by the parties or the applicable rules or the *lex arbitri* to appoint an arbitrator in case, for any reason, a party does not make an appointment.

Arbitration rules and laws provide for fallback procedures to ensure that lack of agreement between the parties does not block the formation of the tribunal. In case any of the parties or the two arbitrators fail to make an appointment, a so-called '**appointing authority**' steps in. Who will have this authority depends on the arbitration rules. If no such authority is designated, the court at the seat of arbitration can make an appointment as a last resort solution.

45 Michael Pryles, 'National Report for Australia (2018)' in Lise Bowman (ed), *ICCA International Handbook on Commercial Arbitration* (Kluwer Law International, 2019) 104.

The mandate of arbitrators

The arbitrator's powers originate in the mandate conferred to them by the parties and by the arbitration law. This mandate defines what a tribunal can do (powers) and what a tribunal must do (obligations).

Powers of an arbitral tribunal include:

1. Taking procedural steps reserved to the role of arbitrator:
   - issue procedural orders – order the production of documents, submission of written briefs, presentation of evidence
   - administer oaths when hearing witnesses
   - issue interim measures of protection – to preserve evidence, protect assets, or secure the costs of arbitration
   - inspect and physically examine the object or site in dispute.
2. Making determinations the parties failed to make:
   - establish the procedural steps
   - determine the applicable procedural law
   - determine the language
   - determine the law governing the merits.[46]

Obligations of an arbitral tribunal include to:

- decide the merits of the dispute (subject to valid jurisdiction)
- act with due care – to perform as arbitrator with proper skill and care
- act promptly – a general duty often included in arbitration rules apart from the specific procedural time limits
- act judicially – to respect the rules of **due process**
- not facilitate any criminal activity – if discovering that the arbitration is for criminal purposes, dismiss the claim and/or inform the relevant authorities (depending on the nature of the crime and the legislation regulating that crime).[47]

Due process: a legal principle based on fairness, providing that the procedural and substantive rights of the parties in a dispute must be observed.

Preliminary case management conference

Once the tribunal's mandate is confirmed, the tribunal will have to determine the procedural framework of the case. This commonly occurs during a preliminary meeting often called a 'case management conference'. There is no universal rule for holding a preliminary conference, although many institutional rules require one and arbitrators often find it useful even when it is not imposed. It does not have to be a face-to-face meeting and is often held via tele- or videoconference for the sake of time and cost efficiency.

The scope of this meeting is to establish the procedural steps, the timeline to follow, any common grounds, the issues to be decided, and the type of evidence to be used. It is meant to create an overall framework that makes the arbitration predictable and easier to manage,

46 Blackaby et al. (n 31) 306.
47 Ibid 319.

avoiding dilatory tactics. The tribunal may record the outcome in a document called Terms of Reference or just include the agreed terms in the minutes of the meeting. The meeting is often also followed by a Procedural Order instructing the parties on the next step (eg make written submissions within an agreed number of days).

Written submissions

Submissions made in arbitration can bear different names; for example, memorial, memorandum, brief, statement, claim, response, counterclaim, pre- and post-hearing briefs. Their form may also vary, and they can serve different purposes and differ in content. They are, however, different from 'pleadings' that are characteristic of litigation.[48]

Written submissions also serve the purpose of determining the running of time. The timeline of submissions is set by the arbitrators depending on the needs of the case, and within time limits frequently imposed by the arbitration rules. Based on the time of the submissions, they can be:

- sequential submission by one party followed by a response from the other party
- simultaneous submissions from both sides, meaning that they are made at the same time (these are more common when the tribunal wants clarifications and not arguments, or when there is no clear allocation of roles between the parties).

Written submissions are often more important in arbitration than oral arguments. Arbitrators will use the written submissions when deliberating and when drafting the award. Consequently, counsel drafting the written submissions should take account of some practical considerations to assist the arbitrators in their decision-making. These include:

- numbering and identifying the different submissions for easier reference
- organising submissions with a logical structure and headings
- stating claim(s) clearly – identifying and defining what the tribunal is requested to decide
- identifying the relevant facts and legal grounds of the claims
- writing in plain English, in a clear and easy to follow manner, to convince the arbitrators.

Evidence in arbitration

The evidentiary procedure in arbitration is similar but not identical to court procedure. Due to the flexibility of arbitration and the very different practices preferred by different arbitrators, institutions and counsel, evidence in arbitration is the most difficult area to regulate in a uniform manner. Arbitration laws will commonly only require that '[t]he parties shall be treated with equality and each party shall be given a full opportunity of presenting his case'.[49] Beyond this rule of due process, the arbitrators have 'the power to determine the admissibility, relevance,

48 For an explanation on the difference between pleadings and memorials, see Australian Centre for International Commercial Arbitration Practice & Procedures Board, *ACICA Explanatory Note: Memorials or Pleadings?* (2020) <https://acica.org.au/wp-content/uploads/2020/08/ACICA-Explanatory-Note_-Memorials-or-Pleadings.pdf>.

49 *Commercial Arbitration Acts* s 18; *UNCITRAL Model Law on International Commercial Arbitration* art 18.

materiality and weight of any evidence'[50] with no further direction on how to administer that evidence. Procedure for taking evidence in arbitration should be fixed at an early stage of a dispute and in line with the arbitration rules' requirement for time and cost efficiency.

The category of evidence is the same as in court proceedings (ie documents, witnesses, experts, inspection of the objects), but it is important to determine early each of the following:

- the necessity, procedure of obtaining, format, scope and submission deadline of documents
- the necessity of witnesses and/or of experts, their preparation and hearing procedure, the scope and limit of their statements
- any confidentiality protection of evidence.

The use of experts will depend on the applicable rules and the legal tradition from which the parties, their counsel, and the arbitrators come. The common law tradition is for each party to have its own expert witness, while civil law traditions usually have one independent expert appointed to assist the tribunal by answering questions directed to finding the truth.

The arbitral tribunal can order the production of evidence by the parties. Ordering document production by one party to serve as evidence for the other party is possible in arbitration, but not as frequent as in common law litigation. The tribunal, however, cannot compel third parties to produce evidence or to appear as witness in a case, as the tribunal's mandate and authority is limited to the parties to the arbitration. If such authority over third parties is needed, the court from the seat may assist in obtaining the evidence.

Hearings

Hearings in arbitration are not compulsory; small cases can be addressed by 'documents only' arbitration – a flexibility commonly provided by arbitration rules and backed up by arbitration laws.[51] If there is a hearing, there may also be a pre-hearing conference, used in complex cases to prepare and organise the content of the hearing.

Arrangements to organize the hearing are made either by the arbitral institution, by the parties, or by the arbitral tribunal. The place of hearing will be determined by practical considerations. Logistics to consider when organising a hearing include the need for:

- a hearing room
- ancillary rooms for parties, witnesses, breaks, arbitrator deliberation
- minute taking or transcription facilities and staffing
- communication and office equipment
- translator/interpreter
- accommodation.[52]

50 *Commercial Arbitration Acts* s 19(3); *UNCITRAL Model Law on International Commercial Arbitration* art 19(2).

51 *Commercial Arbitration Acts* s 24(1); *UNCITRAL Model Law on International Commercial Arbitration* art 24(1).

52 For considerations characteristic to virtual hearings, see Australian Centre for International Commerical Arbitration, *ACIA Online Arbitration Guidance Note* (2020) <https://acica.org.au/wp-content/uploads/2020/05/ACICA-Online-Arbitration-Guidance-Note.pdf>.

Participating at a hearing requires no approval for the arbitrators and the parties, but the parties' legal representatives (if companies) or lawyers will need representation documents or a power of attorney to attend. Junior members of a law firm, trainees, etc not directly representing a party, as well as any other person not related to the case or the parties (eg interns of the arbitral institution, students, etc) can only attend if permission is granted by the parties. The administrative secretary, court reporters, translators, all need to be formally appointed to the case with the acceptance of the parties and can attend hearings in that role. If a party's behaviour makes the hearing impossible or if a party generates serious delays or is not cooperating to try to block the proceedings, the tribunal can conduct an **ex parte** hearing.

Ex parte: Latin for 'from the part'. This refers to proceedings or a hearing conducted in the absence of a party.

Arbitration hearings lack the formalities characteristic of courtroom proceedings. All participants are seated throughout the hearing, with no need for counsel to stand at any point. Arbitrators are addressed as Mr/Madam Arbitrator or, more commonly, by their name (and any professional title they may use). Any formalities in communication are based on respect, not rigid rules. The hearing room arrangement (see Figure 10.1) is meant to serve practical efficiency.

Figure 10.1 Typical boardroom style arbitration hearing room arrangement

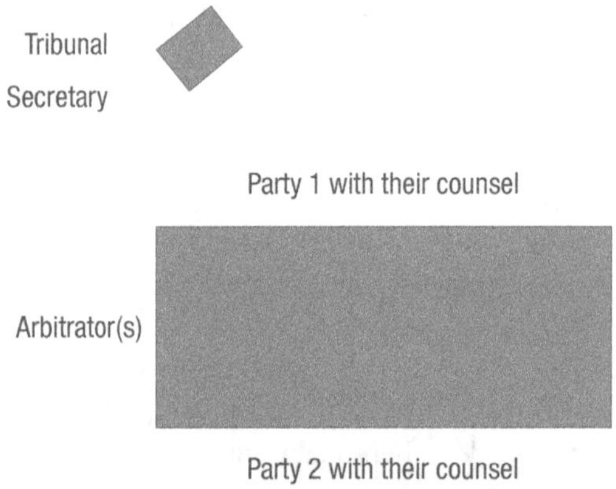

Advocacy in arbitration is similar to litigation, with the focus on clearly stating the claim and the arguments based on facts, law and persuasive authority. Opening and closing statements should be short, not repeating written submissions. To assist the tribunal in its deliberations and award drafting, closing oral submissions are often replaced by post-hearing briefs.

The nature and extent of witness examination differ between common law and civil law expectations and procedures, but internationally there is a tendency to keep oral examinations shorter if written statements are provided in advance. Unlike in some common law courts, in arbitration there is no need to use witnesses to prove the existence and reality of other evidence (eg documents) and witness testimony will usually have less weight than a document. Hearings may include witness conferencing and expert conferencing (also called confrontation or 'hot-tubbing') as a pragmatic way of identifying common grounds and contradictions to advance the tribunal's work. Witness preparation or cross-examination may not be accepted, depending on the legal culture of those involved. These are aspects that should be decided as part of the preliminary conference.

Decisions of the tribunal

One of the most important elements of the arbitral proceedings consists in the tribunal's decisions. These are documents with strict legal consequences. For efficiency of the proceedings, simple matters of procedure can be decided by the presiding arbitrator alone; all other decisions must be made by the entire tribunal. The primary term used in relation to decisions rendered in arbitration is the 'arbitral award' – a term for which there is no definition in statute. A decision will not become an award from being labelled as such; instead, what qualifies an arbitral decision as an award is:

- its finality – disposing finally of an issue decided, whether procedural or substantive
- its enforceability – being allowed under the law to oblige a party to perform the decision.[53]

Whether a decision is enforceable is determined by the arbitration law; whether it is final will be determined by the tribunal rendering it (and subject to the arbitration law and rules allowing such a decision to be final).

Categories of awards

There are several different types of awards to assist in managing the dispute:

- *Interim awards* – usually dealing with jurisdiction, applicable law, interim measures, but not the merits of the dispute
- *Partial awards* – dealing with only some of the substantive issues to be decided but not yet closing the proceedings
- *Final awards* – the last decision rendered after the administration of evidence and the parties' arguments, deciding on all (outstanding) issues, closing the arbitration and ending the tribunal's mandate
- *Default/ex parte awards* – rendered in the absence of the respondent due to its lack of engagement
- *Consent awards* – if the parties settle their dispute at any point during the arbitration, the parties may ask the tribunal to incorporate their settlement agreement in an award to make it enforceable.[54]

The rendering of an award

Rendering of an award is preceded by the arbitrators' deliberation – a confidential process ensuring both the equality of arbitrators and that a decision is reached free of outside influence and without undue delay. Once deliberation is complete, the arbitrators will draft the award to reflect their agreed position with regard to the issues decided. Decisions should, ideally, be

53 For a more detailed analysis on the characteristics of arbitral awards, see Born (n 1) 2923–37.
54 Blackaby et al. (n 31) 507.

unanimous, but majority decisions are accepted under all *Arbitration Acts* in Australia[55] and under most arbitration rules around the world. Unlike in litigation, the dissenting arbitrator is not required to draft a dissenting opinion, only to indicate disagreement by a statement in this regard explaining the refusal to sign the award.

Arbitration rules and laws define validity requirements for arbitral awards. These commonly require that the award:

- is in a written form
- is reasoned
- indicates the date and place
- includes the signature of all arbitrators (or the reason for the absence of a signature).

Awards also need to include elements that make it identifiable and enforceable:

- identification of the parties, of the tribunal, of the institution (if any), and of the claim(s)
- confirming arbitral jurisdiction and identifying the basis for it, including the arbitral agreement – whether disputed or not
- procedural history – dates and summary of submissions, events, hearings
- decision on the merits – clearly stating the resulting obligations the parties must perform
- decision on costs.[56]

The arbitral award is communicated to the parties (in ad hoc arbitration) or to the arbitral institution (which may review it and then communicate it to the parties). In some instances, the parties may request within 30 days of delivery of the award for the award to be corrected in regard to clerical, typographical, or computational errors only, its unclear provisions to be interpreted, or decisions on any omitted claims to be supplemented.[57] Finally, to be recognised in some jurisdictions, arbitral awards may be required to be deposited with the court from the seat. This is not a common requirement for subsequent international recognition of the same award.

Res judicata: Latin for 'a thing adjudicated'. An issue being decided in a final manner by an authority recognised by law to have a judicial function.

Estoppel: a legal prohibition that prevents claiming or stating a self-contradiction or something that has already been established.

The effect of a validly rendered arbitral award is one of ***res judicata***. Similar to a court judgment, the **estoppel** effect on existing disputes will depend on a triple identity test: same parties, same subject matter, and same claim for relief. On subsequent disputes the effect is one of issue estoppel: one cannot contradict a fact or legal consequence of a fact that has been decided in an earlier arbitration, even if the cause of action is now different. Unlike court judgments, however, arbitral awards have no direct effect on third parties, as the tribunal's authority is limited to the parties to the arbitration. For the same reason, arbitral awards do not constitute binding precedent. Nevertheless, arbitration 'case law' – not in the

55 *Commercial Arbitration Acts* s 29(1); *UNCITRAL Model Law on International Commercial Arbitration* art 29.

56 See Micha Buhler, 'Awarding Costs in International Commercial Arbitration: An Overview' (2004) 22(2) *ASA Bulletin* 249, for the different approaches tribunals can take when deciding on costs.

57 *Commercial Arbitration Acts* s 33; *UNCITRAL Model Law on International Commercial Arbitration* art 33, with similar or identical provisions commonly reflected in institutional rules – see *AICA Arbitration Rules Incorporating the Emergency Arbitrator Provisions* (n 42) arts 41–43.

common law meaning of binding precedent, but as jurisprudence more broadly – may have an indirect effect by being considered as persuasive authority in subsequent cases.

Recognition and enforcement

Recognition and **enforcement** are usually not separated, even though 'an award may be recognised without being enforced'.[58] Enforcement, on the other hand, includes the recognition of the award.

> **Recognition:** recognising the award for its estoppel effect for when a new identical claim is filed.
>
> **Enforcement:** imposing the performance of the dispositive orders of the award.

The procedure for recognition and enforcement and the possible grounds for refusing them are governed by the law where enforcement is sought. This place is determined by where the losing party has assets against which an award could be enforced.

In over 160 jurisdictions, recognition and enforcement of foreign arbitral awards is regulated by the *New York Convention*. In addition to this, in over 100 jurisdictions the *UNCITRAL Model Law* regulates the recognition and enforcement of arbitral awards regardless of their country of origin – in Australia, it is relevant for enforcing domestic awards.[59] Both the *Model Law* and the *New York Convention* have consistent grounds for refusing recognition and enforcement. These grounds allow for only a limited judicial review of arbitral awards. The same grounds are relevant for requests to set aside arbitral awards in *Model Law* jurisdictions.

The following grounds are considered automatically by the court:

1. non-arbitrability of the subject-matter of the dispute[60]
2. the award violates public policy.[61]

Other grounds to be considered, only if raised and proven by a party, include:

3. lack of capacity to conclude an arbitration agreement[62]
4. no valid arbitration agreement[63] – last check on jurisdiction
5. lack of notice of appointment of an arbitrator or of the arbitral proceedings[64] – due process principle, procedural irregularity

58 Ibid.

59 *UNCITRAL Model Law on International Commercial Arbitration* arts 35–6.

60 *UNCITRAL Model Law on International Commercial Arbitration* arts 34(2)(b)(i), 36(1)(b)(i); *New York Convention* art V.2(a).

61 *UNCITRAL Model Law on International Commercial Arbitration* arts 34(2)(b)(ii), 36(1)(b)(ii); *New York Convention* art V.2(b). Public policy is a concept subject to different interpretations, so the *International Arbitration Act 1974* (Cth) s 8(7A) provides additional clarification for the Australian application of the *New York Convention*:

> To avoid doubt and without limiting paragraph (7)(b), the enforcement of a foreign award would be contrary to public policy if:
> (a) the making of the award was induced or affected by fraud or corruption; or
> (b) a breach of the rules of natural justice occurred in connection with the making of the award.

62 *UNCITRAL Model Law on International Commercial Arbitration* arts 34(2)(a)(i), 36(1)(a)(i); *New York Convention* art V.1(a).

63 Ibid.

64 *UNCITRAL Model Law on International Commercial Arbitration* arts 34(2)(a)(ii), 36(1)(a)(ii); *New York Convention* art V.1(b).

6. inability of a party to present its case[65] – due process principle
7. the award deals with matters not covered by the submission to arbitration or not falling under the scope of the arbitral agreement, applying a law not chosen by the parties, or awarding more or something else than what was claimed[66] – arbitrators exceeding their jurisdiction
8. composition of the arbitral tribunal or conduct of arbitral proceedings contrary to the agreement of the parties or, failing agreement, to the *lex arbitri*[67] – party autonomy principle

An additional ground for refusing recognition and enforcement (not relevant for setting aside) is:

9. the award was annulled or suspended or is not binding[68] – set aside at the seat of arbitration or still open to appeal.

If an arbitral award is not set aside and is not refused recognition and enforcement, the party that prevailed in the arbitration can have the executing organs from the jurisdiction where the losing party has assets coerce that losing party to perform the orders of the award (ie pay the amounts or perform the actions ordered).

Positives and negatives of arbitration

Enforcement of an award may be the successful ending of a dispute, but arbitration is not a one-size-fits-all solution to any and all disputes. Whether arbitration is or is not suitable for a scenario depends on the characteristics of arbitration matching the needs of that dispute. A dispute practitioner advising a party about how to manage a dispute must consider these characteristics to identify and advise the party about the most suitable process. For legal practitioners, failing to do so attracts the professional liability of the legal practitioner.[69] When compared with non-adjudicatory dispute management processes, the common characteristic is that it involves a third-party neutral and is flexible in procedure. The main difference is that arbitration provides a final and binding, enforceable decision for the parties in their dispute management, whether they like the outcome or not.

A further distinction is that in arbitration the dispute is decided based on rights and obligations determined by law or equity principles, regardless of the parties' interests and underlying needs. Arbitration manages the dispute without addressing the underlying interests between the parties, which may last beyond the arbitration. For this reason, arbitration may not be ideal if the parties wish to maintain an ongoing relationship which could be jeopardised by an arbitral award declaring winners and losers based on strict legal grounds. It may, however,

65 *UNCITRAL Model Law on International Commercial Arbitration* arts 34(2)(a)(ii), 36(1)(a)(ii); *New York Convention* art V.1(b).

66 *UNCITRAL Model Law on International Commercial Arbitration* arts 34(2)(a)(iii), 36(1)(a)(iii); *New York Convention* art V.1(c).

67 *UNCITRAL Model Law on International Commercial Arbitration* arts 34(2)(a)(iv), 36(1)(a)(iv); *New York Convention* art V.1(d).

68 *UNCITRAL Model Law on International Commercial Arbitration* art 36(1)(a)(v); *New York Convention* art V.1(e).

69 See Chapter 12 for more on professional liability and indemnity insurance.

be ideal if the parties only wanted a decision by an independent third party that they feel manages the dispute in a manner that enables each to move on with their business.

When compared to litigation, the main difference between these two determinative processes consists in the control parties can have over the process. They both result in a binding decision; therefore, a dispute can either be arbitrated or litigated, but not both. Since arbitration cannot be combined with litigation, if seeking a triadic determinative and binding method, the only real (either/or) choice to make is between these two processes.

Positives

Advantages of arbitration over litigation:

- When the subject matter of the dispute is highly technical, the parties can appoint arbitrators with an appropriate degree of expertise and experience they can trust – an option that is not available in litigation.
- Arbitration is often faster than litigation in court, as parties can set strict timeframes and the arbitrators can be selected based on their availability and efficiency.
- Arbitration can be more flexible, adaptable to the needs of a given dispute and the parties, with cheaper costs usually closely connected to the time efficiency of the proceedings.
- Generally, arbitration is a one-step dispute process, with very limited grounds for review and quick enforcement available, making it less exposed to delaying appeals.
- Arbitral proceedings, evidence used, and arbitral awards can be kept confidential, providing protection to industry secrets and business reputation that are not readily available in litigation.
- Awards are generally easier to enforce internationally than court judgments, due to the world-wide adopting of the *New York Convention*.[70]

Negatives

Disadvantages compared to litigation:

- In non-negotiated contracts (like consumer, employment, or insurance contracts) an arbitration agreement is not created by genuine voluntary consent: one of the parties gives up its right to access the courts without having a real say on the procedure.
- The parties need to pay for the arbitrators' fees, which adds a layer of legal costs that may be prohibitive, while access to court may be cheaper – without considering legal fees.
- When there are multiple arbitrators on the panel and complex issues involving extensive evidence and submissions, juggling hearing schedules and processing of an excessive amount of materials may render arbitration longer than litigation.

70 See Blackaby et al. (n 31) 28.

- The very limited avenues for appeal mean that an erroneous decision cannot be easily overturned.
- In a few legal systems not manifesting pro-arbitration court practice, arbitral awards may be more difficult to enforce than court judgments – if a party has assets only in such a jurisdiction, then arbitration may not be a suitable method to address a dispute with that party.[71]

It seems that most characteristics of arbitration can become both an advantage and a disadvantage, depending on the circumstances. An arbitration is as good as the parties, their counsel, and the arbitrator(s) make it. The ultimate benefit consists in party autonomy: the freedom of choice in jurisdiction, applicable law, procedure, and the arbitrators. Confidentiality, being more protective in sustaining future relationships, reputation, and industry secrets is an added bonus.

Special considerations

This section is dedicated to technicalities and some legal aspects of arbitration that are not vital for a general understanding of the process, as well as some details to assist in differentiating between arbitration and other similar or connected dispute management processes.

The role of courts before arbitration

Even though arbitration is a private process, state courts may have a role in this process to secure access to justice and to secure the legal recognition of arbitration as a binding mechanism. The basic rule excluding all court intervention other than those regulated by the *lex arbitri* is contained in the *UNCITRAL Model Law on International Commercial Arbitration* art 5[72] stating that '[i]n matters governed by this Law, no court shall intervene except where so provided in this Law'. In both domestic and international arbitrations conducted in Australia, 'court' means the Supreme Court of each State and Territory where the arbitration is held.[73] For international arbitration, the Federal Court of Australia also has jurisdiction.[74] Which law determines the role of courts will ultimately depend on the phase at which a state court may have a role.

Court assistance may be needed even before an arbitration is properly started, in several matters:

1. *Enforcement of the arbitration agreement.* If a party files a suit to any court and the other party presents an arbitration agreement which on its face seems to be valid and functional, the state court will compel the parties to arbitrate. It will also leave the issue of arbitral jurisdiction to be decided by the arbitral tribunal.[75]

71 Ibid 31.

72 Replicated in the *Commercial Arbitration Acts* s 5.

73 See, eg, definitions under the *Commercial Arbitration Acts* s 2(1) and *International Arbitration Act 1974* (Cth) s 22A, subject to some exceptions referring to the Magistrates Court, as listed in the *Commercial Arbitration Acts* s 6(2).

74 *International Arbitration Act 1974* (Cth) s 22A(c).

75 *UNCITRAL Model Law on International Commercial Arbitration* art 8(1) or corresponding provision of the arbitration act from the jurisdiction in which the state court was approached in the first place.

2. *Appointment of arbitrators.* If any of the parties fails to appoint its arbitrator or the two party-appointed arbitrators fail to appoint the presiding arbitrator and there is no appointing authority, the court from the seat of arbitration can make the appointment.[76]
3. *Challenge of arbitrators.* A decision rejecting a challenge to an arbitrator can be submitted to the court from the seat for final decision.[77]
4. *Challenge of arbitral jurisdiction.* A decision by an arbitral tribunal to reject a challenge to arbitral jurisdiction can be submitted to the court from the seat of arbitration for final decision.[78]

Court assistance during the arbitral proceedings

Courts may order measures assisting and supporting arbitration but may also be disruptive of arbitration. The overall tendency today is towards pro-arbitration assistance, if necessary.

Interim measures

Interim measures are frequently requested to preserve evidence or assets, and generally to maintain or restore the status quo pending the outcome of the arbitration. Modern *Arbitration Acts* give wide powers to arbitral tribunals, while also indicating that

> [i]t is not incompatible with an arbitration agreement for a party to request, before or during arbitral proceedings, from a court an interim measure of protection and for a court to grant such measure[79]
> and that [a] court shall have the same power of issuing an interim measure in relation to arbitration proceedings [. . .] as it has in relation to proceedings in courts.[80]

While an arbitral tribunal may order an interim measure,[81] the enforceability of such order is a debated point.[82] In addition, such measure cannot be directed against any third party. A state court does not face this limitation. For these reasons, it may be best in some cases to seek the interim measure from the court, not the arbitrators. The conditions for granting an interim measure are the same regardless of whether ordered by a court or an arbitral tribunal and consist in the cumulative satisfaction that:

- not ordering the measure would cause a harm not adequately repairable through damages and more significant than the harm potentially caused to the other side by ordering the measure

76 Ibid arts 11(3)(a), 11(3)(b), 11(4), or any corresponding provision of the arbitration act from the seat.
77 Ibid art 13(3).
78 Ibid art 16(3).
79 Ibid art 9.
80 Ibid art 17J.
81 Ibid art 17.
82 Cf *UNCITRAL Model Law on International Commercial Arbitration* art 17H; see also Jonathan Hill, 'Is an Interim Measure of Protection Ordered by an Arbitral Tribunal an Arbitral Award?' (2018) 9(4) *Journal of International Dispute Settlement* 590.

- the party requesting the measure is likely to win on the merits of the claim related to the measure (only having to prove that its claim is not frivolous).[83]

Taking of evidence

Due to an arbitral tribunal's authority being limited to the parties to the arbitration, court assistance is frequently needed for ordering the appearance of witnesses and production of documents held by a third party. The *UNCITRAL Model Law* provides the general rule,[84] which is then further detailed in the Australian domestic and international *Arbitration Acts* to suit the specifics of the local legal environment.[85]

Finally, as procedural orders in arbitration are not enforceable as awards, courts also have the authority to allow for the disclosure of confidential information if:

1. the public interest in preserving the confidentiality of arbitral proceedings is outweighed by other considerations that render it desirable in the public interest for the information to be disclosed, or
2. the disclosure is no more than is reasonable for that purpose.[86]

Prohibiting disclosure is subject to the same conditions in reverse.

Court review of arbitral awards

While before and during the arbitral proceedings court assistance may or may not be necessary, the role of courts becomes stricter and unavoidable in the post-award phase. Arbitration is a private process, but arbitral awards can only be challenged, reviewed, recognised and enforced by courts. Since this phase concerns courts only, no longer being a private process shaped by the parties, party autonomy has no influence over the process or the grounds to be considered.

Called a challenge, recourse, appeal, annulment, or setting aside, the process of asking a court to set aside an arbitral award in full or in part is the only avenue to review it outside of arbitration.[87] This challenge can only occur at the seat of arbitration and is regulated by the law from the seat, which in Australia is different for domestic and international arbitration. In domestic arbitration, the parties to an arbitration may agree to an appeal or one of the parties may apply to the court for leave to appeal against the arbitral award.[88] This is not available for

83 *UNCITRAL Model Law on International Commercial Arbitration* art 17A.

84 Ibid art 27.

85 *Commercial Arbitration Acts* s 27A and *International Arbitration Act 1974* (Cth) s 23 provide for the possibility to apply to a court to issue a subpoena.

86 *International Arbitration Act 1974* (Cth) s 23G; *Commercial Arbitration Acts* s 27I.

87 *UNCITRAL Model Law on International Commercial Arbitration* art 34:

Application for setting aside as exclusive recourse against arbitral award.

(1) Recourse to a court against an arbitral award may be made only by an application for setting aside in accordance with paragraphs (2) and (3) of this article.

88 *Commercial Arbitration Acts* s 34A.

international arbitration cases. The *International Arbitration Act* includes only the limited grounds available for setting aside under the *Model Law* – the same grounds as listed for refusing recognition and enforcement above – and no right to appeal on the merits.

Depending on the ground of the challenge, the applicable law, and the conclusion reached by the court, the outcome of a challenge can be one of the following:

- Confirm the award – not accepting the grounds of challenge.
- Refer the award back to the tribunal for reconsideration – if there is a possibility to amend the award so that the ground for challenge can be eliminated.
- Vary the award – the court to perform the modification requested.
- Set the award aside in whole or in part – if the award or part of it cannot be saved.

In principle, if an arbitral award is set aside, the parties will have to start a new action either in another arbitration or in court (if the reason for setting aside was the lack of arbitral jurisdiction). If an arbitral award is not set aside, the winning party can proceed to ask for its recognition and enforcement.

Challenges in arbitration

In addition to the arbitration process described in the previous section, there are procedural steps that may be necessary, but which do not form part of every arbitration. Challenges within the arbitration process, for example, only become relevant if a procedural element does not satisfy its legal requirements.

An objection to any perceived irregularity must be raised as soon as the facts serving as ground for that challenge become known. If a party fails to submit its challenge within the legal timeframe, that party 'shall be deemed to have waived his right to object'[89] and will not be allowed to raise the same objection at a later stage. The waiver principle applies to every procedural right to object against anything in arbitration. This is, essentially, an estoppel principle meant to avoid abuse of rights and process.

Challenge to jurisdiction

Arbitral jurisdiction can be and often is challenged. A challenge to jurisdiction can be:

- *Total* – when the arbitral agreement is invalid or inoperable; when all the issues in dispute fall outside the scope of the arbitration agreement; when the subject matter of the dispute is not arbitrable; or when a party to the dispute is not a party to the arbitration agreement on which the arbitral jurisdiction is based.
- *Partial* – when the tribunal appears to exceed its jurisdiction with regard to only part of the claims or issues.[90]

Considering that the arbitrators' jurisdiction is based on the parties' agreement, questioning the mandate itself would logically mean that the tribunal cannot do anything until its mandate is

89 *Commercial Arbitration Acts* s 4; *UNCITRAL Model Law on International Commercial Arbitration* art 4.
90 Blackaby et al. (n 31) 335.

Competence-competence: an arbitral tribunal's inherent authority to decide on its own jurisdiction.

Separability: the self-standing nature of an arbitration agreement, allowing for it to be considered and assessed as a separate contractual relationship even if it is included as a clause among many in a contract.

clarified. However, the **competence-competence** and the **separability** doctrines provide a solution.[91]

Called 'severability' in the United States, the autonomous nature of an arbitration agreement means that it can survive the invalidity of the main contract and it can be governed by a different law than the law governing the rest of the contract. It also means that it can confer jurisdiction to arbitrators to arbitrate questions of validity of the main contract, as well as to decide over their own jurisdiction. Accordingly, under both the *Commercial Arbitration Acts* and the *International Arbitration Act*, '[t]he arbitral tribunal may rule on its own jurisdiction, including any objections with respect to the existence or validity of the arbitration agreement'.[92]

Generally, a challenge to jurisdiction is dealt with as a preliminary issue, before and without looking into the merits of the dispute. Should the tribunal find that it has no jurisdiction, normally that is the end of arbitration and the tribunal will not decide on the merits. An arbitral tribunal's decision to reject jurisdiction cannot be appealed. The remaining solutions available to the disputing parties are either to litigate or to construct a new arbitration – subject to arbitrability and a new, valid consent to arbitrate. Should the tribunal decide to have jurisdiction, that decision can be submitted for judicial review within 30 days to the court from the seat of arbitration.[93]

Challenging an arbitrator

The other challenge that can become relevant during an arbitration is the challenge against an arbitrator. If an arbitrator does not satisfy qualification requirements or is suspected of bias, the party concerned about the arbitrator can challenge that arbitrator. The common grounds for challenging an arbitrator are:

- lack of independence or impartiality
- issue connection – even if impartial and independent, if an arbitrator is acting as counsel in a case involving a similar issue, that role raises doubt about the capability of deciding on such an issue in an unbiased way
- lack of qualification – required by the parties or by the applicable law
- incapacity – legal, mental or physical.

Independence is tested through an objective test assessing whether there is any relationship between the arbitrator and the parties to the case. Not all relationships with a party will lead automatically to a person being unsuitable to act as an arbitrator, but laws usually do not assist in determining what relationship is or is not acceptable. Instead, soft law offers some guidance

91 See further John J Barcelo, 'Who Decides the Arbitrator's Jurisdiction – Separability and Competence – Competence in Transnational Perspective' (2003) 36(4) *Vanderbilt Journal of Transnational Law* 1115.

92 The former reproducing, the latter giving effect to the provision of *UNCITRAL Model Law on International Commercial Arbitration* art 16(1).

93 *Commercial Arbitration Acts* s 16(9); *UNCITRAL Model Law on International Commercial Arbitration* art 16(3).

in qualifying different levels and types of relationships – the most known being the *IBA Guidelines on Conflicts of Interest in International Arbitration*.[94]

Impartiality is evaluated through a subjective test assessing actual or apparent bias. It is harder to assess, but bias is always an excluding factor for an arbitrator. The threshold for the test may be different in different jurisdictions. In Australia, it is defined as 'real danger of bias'.[95] If an arbitrator is connected to any of the parties, normally that arbitrator would not accept appointment. However, if the relationship is not of a serious nature that would raise conflict of interest, the arbitrator must only disclose the connection so that the other party can decide whether to accept that circumstance or not.

Arbitration laws commonly leave it to the parties to define the challenge procedure, only providing for a default procedure in the absence of party-determined steps. Arbitration rules, however, frequently include mandatory challenge procedures to secure the timely constitution of a tribunal and to avoid the process being blocked by an uncooperative party. A challenge must be submitted in writing, indicating the detailed reasons for the challenge, and within a limited time from the appointment or from when the challenging party became aware of the facts justifying the challenge. In institutional arbitration, the challenge must be submitted to the institution and is decided by an internal organ of the institution. Rarely – more commonly in ad hoc arbitration – the challenge is decided by the arbitral tribunal.

If a challenge is successful, the challenged arbitrator will be removed. The case then can either go ahead with a truncated tribunal (if the challenge came at a very late stage in the proceedings or if the rules provide for this option), or the parties can fill in the vacancy using the same appointment mechanism as the initial one or other procedure provided by the rules. If a challenge is unsuccessful, the challenging party can ask the court from the seat of arbitration to review this decision.

Non-commercial arbitration and hybrid methods

A final 'special consideration' to have when studying arbitration is to be aware of arbitrations that fall outside of the commercial theme used for this chapter. The word 'arbitration' is often used in connection with institutionalised processes involving states or state entities that were developed together or from commercial arbitration but bear sufficiently distinctive characteristics to identify as a different process. For example, the World Trade Organization Dispute Settlement Body (WTO DSB) provides an out-of-national-court dispute settlement mechanism to manage trade quarrels between the member states. This dispute settlement is often named 'WTO arbitration'. Disputes between foreign investors and host states are often regulated by the *International Centre for Settlement of Investment Disputes (ICSID) Convention*, providing for 'treaty-based arbitration' or 'investment arbitration'. Both these fields are under ongoing development and review[96] and are recognised as systems that depart from the characteristics of commercial arbitration between private entities.

94 International Bar Association (2014) (n 29).

95 *Commercial Arbitration Acts* s 12(5); *International Arbitration Act 1974* (Cth) s 18A(1).

96 See, eg, United Nations Commission on International Trade Law, 'Working Group III: Investor-State Dispute Settlement Reform at the UNCITRAL' (Web Page) <https://uncitral.un.org/en/working_groups/3/investor-state>; see also Robert McDougall, *Crisis in the WTO: Restoring the WTO Dispute Settlement Function*

Commercial arbitration is also often incorporated in so-called 'hybrid' methods, most commonly involving mediation as the other component. The names are self-explanatory in indicating the sequence in which the two processes are combined:

- med-arb: mediation followed by arbitration, if the dispute could not be settled within the mediation in full or in part
- arb-med: mediation conducted after arbitration has been initiated, usually with the arbitral tribunal staying the proceedings for the duration of the mediation, so that if settlement is reached the dispute ends with a mediated settlement agreement and the arbitration is closed with no award
- arb-med-arb: a combination of arb-med and med-arb, where if the mediation conducted during the arbitration proves to be unsuccessful the arbitration resumes and the parties are bound by an award rendered by the tribunal; arb-med-arb can also be used to reduce the issues in dispute, eliminating those that can be settled and only leaving to arbitration those that need the arbitrators' decision.[97]

Terminology used in identifying a hybrid is not universal. The essential differences between the different sequences consist mainly in how the process starts (ie with mediation or arbitration) and what the legal qualification of the final outcome is (ie a settlement agreement or an arbitral award – whether by consent or rendered by the tribunal).

Another crucial consideration in a hybrid process involving arbitration is whether the same person acts as an arbitrator and mediator at different stages or the two roles are taken on by different individuals. The arbitrators' independence and the parties' equal opportunity mean that an arbitrator should not have any separate communication with the parties regarding the dispute at any time and all information needs to be presented to the arbitrator in a way that allows the opposing side to respond to it. A mediator, however, has separate communication with the parties and can receive confidential information from the parties in private sessions. If the same person acts as mediator and arbitrator at different stages of the same dispute, that neutral has to follow different rules in the different roles. The neutral also needs the parties' express and repeated consent for every change of role, not presuming that an initial appointment is valid after another process has been interjected.[98]

Conclusion

Overall, arbitration is as good as one makes it. As a determinative triadic process, it adopts an evidence and rights-based model resulting in an enforceable decision. As such, arbitration resembles litigation and so it can be burdensome, time and money consuming, and it does not address the human conflict underlying the dispute. As a party autonomy driven process that

(Centre for International Governance Innovation, 2018); Jorge A Huerta-Goldman, Antoine Romanetti and Franz X Stirnimann, *WTO Litigation, Investment Arbitration, and Commercial Arbitration* (Kluwer Law International, 2013).

97 See Thomas Stipanowich, 'Arbitration, Mediation and Mixed Modes: Seeking Workable Solutions and Common Ground on Med-Arb, Arb-Med and Settlement-Oriented Activities by Arbitrators' 26 *Harvard Negotiation Law Review* (forthcoming 2021).

98 See, eg, *Ku-ring-gai Council v Ichor Constructions Pty Ltd* [2018] NSWSC 610.

provides the freedom to choose the arbitrator decision-makers, to shape the procedure, to use technology for efficiency, and to design the rules of evidence to best serve a case, arbitration can provide a quick and cost-efficient private outcome. Party autonomy, on the other hand, also means that the parties bear the consequences of their choices. The global enforceability of the resulting awards makes arbitration the prime process adopted for international commercial disputes. Whether arbitration is the best process to manage a dispute depends on the dispute's characteristics and the parties' priorities. It is not a one-size-fits-all solution to everything, but if done properly it can be a most effective process providing an outcome that enables an enforceable decision.

EXERCISE IN APPLYING YOUR KNOWLEDGE – *DC MUSIKA V SOUND SPEC*

Sound Spec Pty Ltd is the Australian subsidiary (in Melbourne) of a Chinese manufacturer of sound recording and processing equipment registered in Shanghai under the same name.

Dannie Campden is an Australian sole trader based in Sydney providing services of music directing and recording under the trade name DC MusiKa.

Dannie decided to diversify her portfolio to sell equipment her clients use for live performance. She contacted Sound Spec in Shanghai to inquire about possible deals for importing microphones, PA systems and speakers, and various stage gear. Sound Spec confirmed the availability of everything she needed, and they negotiated a price to lead to repeat orders. As a final step, Sound Spec advised Dannie to arrange for delivery from the Australian subsidiary, as it would be more time and cost efficient, while the price per item would be as negotiated directly with the manufacturer. Dannie had to fill out an online order form on the website of the Melbourne-based Sound Spec to organise the delivery. To receive the delivery at her home address, she filled the form under her own name. The price was then paid by bank transfer from the accounts of DC MusiKa directly to the parent company in Shanghai.

After a while, Dannie started receiving complaints from her clients on the reliability of some of the microphones she sold. She contacted Sound Spec in Melbourne and was directed to the technical assistance department in Shanghai. Failing to achieve an acceptable response, Dannie decided to sue Sound Spec – partly to recover the loss the defective goods caused to her small business, and partly to protect her reputation. Looking through her paperwork, she found the following clause included in the Standard Terms and Conditions received from Sound Spec Shanghai together with the confirmation of items and price negotiated:

> Should users of our products be dissatisfied with our services, we will try to satisfy them by submitting our differences to alternative dispute resolution, following which the consumers can go to mediation/conciliation/arbitration. The dispute should be administered by the Shanghai Arbitration Commission, for having exclusive authority over all disputes of Sound Spec. As a sign of goodwill, Sound Spec accepts to arbitrate on neutral grounds in Singapore. The decision, to be moderated by Sound Spec, will be performed immediately. Should the parties be unsatisfied with the outcome of the process, the China International Commercial Court or the corresponding Consumer Court of the consumer will have the final power to settle the case, with no further appeal.

A different arbitration clause was included in the Standard Terms and Conditions Dannie had to click to accept when filling in the online order from Sound Spec Melbourne:

> If a dispute arises regarding an order placed with Sound Spec Pty Ltd and it cannot be solved by negotiation, the dispute will have to be solved through IAMA or CIArb arbitration, administered by ACICA. The parties may have the chance to name one arbitrator each. The chairman must be a technical expert chosen by Sound Spec. Although Australian arbitration is preferred, the famous arbitration rules of the ICC should be followed, if necessary, as the most developed in the world. No court should intervene in the arbitration, but if the arbitrators fail to solve the dispute, the respected courts of Victoria will be required to decide on the dispute submitted to arbitration. The final arbitration decision cannot be further reviewed by any court.

Dannie is confused by these two clauses, undecided as to where to take her claims, and requires your advice.

1. Identify the pathologies from both clauses above, explaining and analysing the defects and their possible consequences.
2. Identify which arbitration agreement should be applicable and why (if any).
3. Try to 'save' the clause that you find applicable.
4. Advise Dannie on an alternative arbitration agreement.
5. Advise Dannie on the arbitral procedure she can expect under the rules you suggest.
6. Advise Dannie on the possible final steps, should she be successful in arbitration.

11

LITIGATION

Learning aims

- Explaining litigation's place as an integral part of dispute management systems
- Describing the role of courts and judges within the Australian legal system
- Describing and identifying relevant court jurisdiction
- Developing the ability to navigate the procedural steps of Australian civil litigation
- Describing the legal relevance of litigation steps
- Demonstrating the ability to assess the suitability of litigation for a dispute

Understanding litigation

Litigation: a neutral third-party determinative process conducted through state courts that applies a formal process in reaching a final and binding, enforceable decision on parties' disputes, based on legal rights and obligations.

Rule of Law: a legal tradition comprising several principles that together prescribe that rights and freedom are secured through laws, which must be respected in order to maintain stability in society.

In too many dispute management textbooks, **litigation** is omitted entirely. We think, however, that litigation must be considered as an integral part of the full spectrum of dispute management processes available when handling disputes, not separately from other methods. This chapter provides an overview of litigation in the context of the many options available for dispute management. The level of this introduction to litigation is prepared with the awareness that Australian law degrees dedicate full courses to litigation, procedure and evidence in both civil and criminal jurisdictions. This chapter covers only essential aspects of litigation.

Litigation is a rule and code dense area where the law determines both the parties' substantive rights and obligations, as well as the procedure to follow to have those rights and obligations recognised in court. In a society built on the **Rule of Law**, access to justice is secured through the courts but the process is strictly regulated.

Historically, litigation and dispute management were strictly separated and differentiated from each other, with litigation being considered the main avenue in addressing disputes. Other processes were grouped together and labelled as 'alternative dispute resolution' as in opposition, providing an alternative to litigation. Litigation was seen as the dominant way to guarantee a path to justice. In the dispute pyramid depicting ways in which people deal with disputes,[1] litigation has been placed at the top as the primary method, with the body of the pyramid being composed of other processes. It is still a common perception, especially among practising lawyers. It remains a misperception that 'legal advice and litigation play a larger part in handling disputes than they do in practice'.[2] In reality, disputes have always been managed by a range of different processes, litigation taking only a small part of the overall number of cases even in a litigious culture. The importance and efficacy of litigation, however, was perceived as far exceeding that of other methods, primarily due to a separation of litigation from dispute management processes and the preponderant

1 Hilary Astor and Christine Chinkin, *Dispute Resolution in Australia* (Lexis Nexis Butterworths, 2nd ed, 2002) 44. See Chapter 3.

2 Astor and Chinkin (n 1).

focus on litigation in mainstream culture and law curricula. Such separation and primacy are culture-dependent, as a characteristic of the perceived Western, adversarial (litigious) approach to disputes.

With dispute management becoming an integrated part of the justice system, this perception is changing. In many fields, processes previously labelled as 'alternative' have become the primary methods promoted and offered through the court system. The primacy and 'top position' of litigation is, accordingly, more frequently questioned. The many processes available do not diminish the value or relevance of litigation, nor do they deny litigation as a process available in the range of dispute management mechanisms. Rather, litigation is now integrated in a system where emphasis on a particular process depends on its effectiveness rather than on overall perception of dominance.

It is in this context that this chapter offers an overview of litigation, to serve as a basis for comparison with other dispute management processes, and to enable dispute practitioners to form an educated choice when opting for one process over another to best manage a dispute. With most courts and tribunals using several different approaches in addition to litigation, identifying and differentiating their characteristics, procedures, and legal consequences becomes more important than ever. This textbook sees litigation as a relevant process in appropriate situations, rather than in competition with other ways of managing disputes.

Definition and scope of litigation

Litigation is the process through which a claim is brought to a court of law to be decided through judgment. That 'claim' may be brought by a government authority or by a private entity or individual. It may be asking for criminal sanctions, equitable remedies (such as specific performance), declaration of rights and obligations, or monetary relief. Accordingly, litigation can operate in either criminal or civil cases.

A criminal case consists of a prosecution brought to court by police or government agency representing the State or Commonwealth against an individual or legal entity for an offence against the law. Such agency can be the Public Prosecutor, but the prosecution is conducted on behalf of the Queen, which leads to the prosecutor being called 'the Crown'. In writing, this is often represented by an 'R' from the Latin *Regina* (Queen) or *Rex* (King). If either a judge (if judge alone or in lower court trial) or a jury (in the case of indictable offences) finds the accused (also called a defendant) guilty of the offence **beyond reasonable doubt**, the court can punish the offender through its judgment and sentencing. Punishment may consist of a fine, community service, good behaviour bond or imprisonment. This chapter will focus on civil litigation and will only discuss criminal cases for the purposes of differentiating them from a civil case.

Beyond reasonable doubt: the standard of proof required in a criminal case in order to convict, meaning that the decision-maker on the facts must be convinced by the evidence presented and have no reasonable doubt that the person to be convicted is guilty. Due to the presumption of innocence that is an important principle in the Rule of Law, this is a high standard.

A civil case can be between individuals, legal entities, and the government in any combination, each of them being called a 'party' to the case. The party bringing the claim can be referred to as 'plaintiff', 'claimant', or 'applicant', depending on the case and the court in which the matter is heard. The party against which a claim is brought is commonly called a 'defendant' or 'respondent'. A party asking for a judgment to be reviewed by a higher court is called an 'appellant' in both civil and criminal cases; the opposing party is the 'respondent'.

Balance of probabilities: the standard of proof required in a civil case in order for a claim to prevail, meaning that the decision-maker must be convinced by the evidence that a statement of facts is more likely to be true than not. It is a balancing exercise – as represented by the scales of justice – where the court weighs up the evidence to decide which version of the truth claimed is most probably true.

Generally, a civil case will be heard and decided by a single judge or a panel of judges on appeal.[3] Civil litigation serves the purpose of deciding a dispute as regards the rights and obligations of the parties involved and commonly involves one party seeking a remedy from the other party. The burden of proof in civil litigation is on the **balance of probabilities** and as such is less onerous than the burden in criminal cases. Family, commercial, financial, employment, and housing disputes are common examples of cases subjected to civil litigation.

The Australian legal system

To understand litigation, one must first understand the context provided by the legal system in which litigation occurs. The Australian legal system inherited the English common law system.[4] As such, it is also similar to the legal systems of the United States, New Zealand, Canada, and India. Australia has a federal structure established by the *Constitution of the Commonwealth of Australia*,[5] so all three arms of government (legislature, executive and judiciary – see Figure 11.1) exist both at state and at federal level. In a federal system, the powers are shared between the central government and the regional governments of the states and territories. Accordingly, both state and federal parliaments are able to make laws, and the Governor-General and the state

Figure 11.1 Separation of powers in Australia[6]

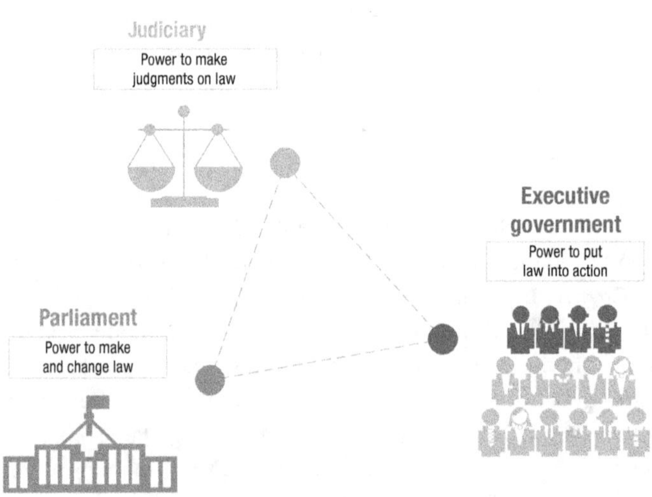

3 In civil cases dealing with tortious defamation claims, however, a small jury of four may determine whether a plaintiff has been defamed; for example, a civil jury consist of four people in NSW, six to eight people in Victoria, and seven in Tasmania.
4 See Chapter 3.
5 *Commonwealth of Australia Constitution Act 1900* (Imp) (*Commonwealth Constitution*).
6 'Separation of Powers: Parliament, Executive and Judiciary', Parliamentary Education Office (Web Page) <https://peo.gov.au/understand-our-parliament/how-parliament-works/system-of-government/separation-of-powers/>.

Governors implement that legislation and administer the affairs of government at federal and state levels, respectively. Each of the three arms of government have specific domains of activity. Put at its simplest, the legislature makes the laws in parliament, the executive administers the law, and the courts interpret and apply the law. In **common law systems** – as opposed to civil law countries – the courts can also make law through case law. In order to prevent power residing in one domain, the three arms act as a check and balance on each other through what is known as the **separation of powers**.

Common law system: a country in which the legal system adopts certain judicial decisions as a source of law – as opposed to 'civil law countries' where law originates exclusively from statutory provisions.

Separation of powers: a doctrine under which the three arms of government have separate roles and are free from influence from the others: the legislature makes the law; the executive administers the law; and the courts interpret and apply the law. The more separated the three branches are the better they operate, while a checks and balances system ensures that none of the three domains possess excessive power.

Statutes (also called legislation) are laws made by parliament (state or federal). The validity and the application of these laws are determined by the courts. At the federal level in Australia, the High Court of Australia and other federal courts are established under Chapter III of the *Constitution*. Similarly, state and territory courts are established under the state and territory Constitutions. The courts make legally enforceable judgments about legal rights and obligations. There are also statutory regulatory bodies and tribunals responsible for regulating specific areas and ensuring that individuals and businesses comply with legislation.[7] Royal commissions and other inquiry bodies can be established by the Governor-General (federally) or by Governors (within states) to investigate and report on compliance with specific areas of law.[8] These bodies can observe an adversarial type approach to hearing evidence and some take an inquisitorial approach.

The common law (also called case law or judge-made law) is a body of judgments serving as precedent, filling a gap where legislation does not regulate or does not regulate in sufficient detail an aspect raised in a dispute. A precedent is binding if it originates from a superior court that is higher in the hierarchy of courts, and it is persuasive if it originates from a superior court that is not higher in the same hierarchy of courts. The doctrine of *stare decisis*, which means that courts stand by previous decisions, refers only to the reasoning leading to the decision (***ratio decidendi***) regarding the issue in dispute, not to tangential discussion of any additional aspects (***obiter dicta***).

With the increased coverage of statutory provisions, reliance on judge-made common law is becoming less frequent, but principles and tests developed by case law are still relevant for interpreting legislation and applying it to specific facts. Legislation and common law coexist or legislation overrides common law depending on the legislator's intention. Ultimately this is a power limited only by the *Constitution*. The judiciary, however, decides on the effect of laws and by this further develops common law around legislation through judgments rendered in litigation creating a system of public precedents.

The judiciary – comprised of the judges and magistrates operating in the courts – is independent from the other two branches of power as supported by the separation of powers doctrine. Judges are appointed by the executive government at federal or state level

7 Eg, the Australian Competition and Consumer Commission (ACCC) ensures that competition, fair trading, and consumer protection laws are observed; the Australian Securities and Investments Commission (ASIC) is in charge of corporations and financial markets; the Australian Prudential Regulation Authority (APRA) regulates financial institutions, the bank, insurance and superannuation industry; and the Therapeutic Goods Administration (TGA) regulates medicines and medical devices.

8 See the *Royal Commissions Act 1902* (Cth) for the powers of a royal commission.

Ratio decidendi: Latin for 'reason'. As a legal concept, it is the reason in law that a decision in a case stands on; the component that provides precedent.

Obiter dicta: Latin for 'by the way'. As a legal concept, it refers to any statements made by a judge that do not directly justify the decision and as such do not form the *ratio decidendi* in a decision and therefore are not part of the precedent of the decision.

Jurisdiction: the scope of authority to decide a case. Originating from the Latin *juris* (law) and *dictio* (to declare) words.

respectively, depending on the court for which appointment is made. Judges of the High Court are appointed by the Governor-General, which is part of the parliament and the executive. However, neither parliament nor the government (ie the legislature and the executive) can influence the decision-making of judges. In order to secure judicial independence, the tenure and remuneration of judges is guaranteed by the *Constitution*.[9] The Judicial Conference of Australia, a representative body of the judiciary, further protects the independence and integrity of the judicial office.

Court jurisdiction and hierarchy

The **jurisdiction** of a court over a certain type of dispute is determined by constitutional provisions, which are then affirmed through legislation made in the respective state and territory or Commonwealth jurisdictions. As outlined in the other chapters, most civil cases may be subjected to dispute management either based on the parties' free choice, by statutory recommendation, or through compulsory processes. Most criminal and some civil disputes, however, are retained within the exclusive jurisdiction of the courts, as identified by relevant statutes.

In the case of courts, this scope of authority is determined by legislation identifying the purpose for which a court was created. Jurisdiction is also determined by geographical limitations, by the type of parties in a case, by the type of case, and by the amount in dispute (or in criminal cases, by the severity of the offence and its corresponding maximum penalty). Accordingly, jurisdiction is classified into subject matter and territorial jurisdiction. The latter is determined by the defendant's location in civil matters[10] and by the location of the incident or of the plaintiff in criminal matters. In addition, jurisdiction is differentiated between original and appellate level, based on whether the dispute is heard anew or as an appeal against a decision of the original court. In order to identify which court has jurisdiction over what dispute, we must classify courts based on a range of different criteria. The Australian court hierarchy is presented in Figure 11.2.

State and federal courts

The court system matches the dual state-federal system. Federal courts have jurisdiction in matters concerning Commonwealth laws made under the powers enunciated in s 51 of the *Constitution*. State and territory courts have jurisdiction in matters concerning laws beyond the areas covered by s 51. Exceptionally, if both levels of legislation provide for it, state courts may, in some circumstances, exercise jurisdiction under Commonwealth laws.[11]

9 *Commonwealth Constitution* s 72.

10 This domain of the law is addressed by conflicts of laws principles that decide the appropriate jurisdiction to cover disputes. See also Michael H Hoffheimer, *Conflicts of Law* (Aspen Publishers, 4th ed, 2019).

11 See further KH Bailey, 'The Federal Jurisdiction of State Courts' (1939–41) 2(2) *Res Judicatae* 109 for a detailed analysis of the federal jurisdiction of state courts.

Figure 11.2 A generalised representation of the hierarchy of Australian courts and tribunals with no regard to specific state and territory structures, which may vary

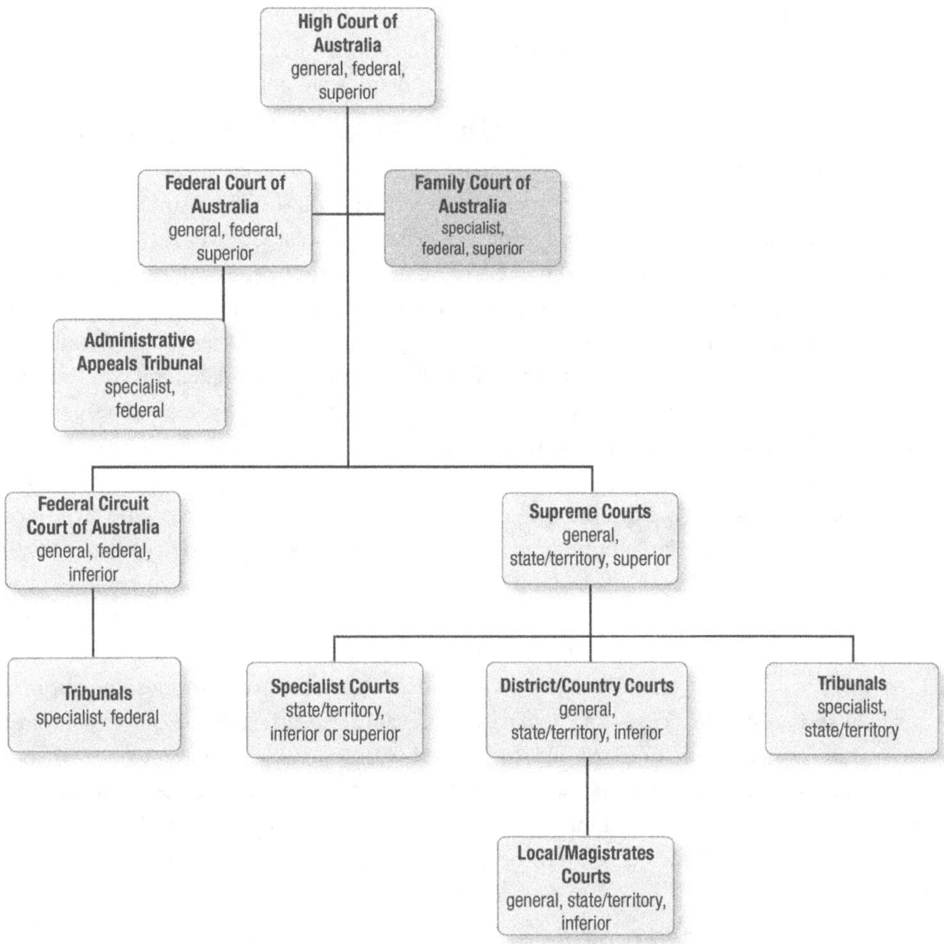

There are four federal courts:

1. Federal Circuit Court of Australia: as the lowest level federal court, it hears less-complex disputes in family, administrative, admiralty, or industrial law, bankruptcy, copyright, human rights, migration, privacy and trade practices
2. Family Court of Australia: The Family Court was abolished in February 2021 and its jurisdiction has merged with the Federal Circuit Court to create the Federal Circuit and Family Court of Australia. It was a specialist court dealing with family disputes only, and heard appeals on family law matters from the Federal Circuit Court[12]

12 Exceptionally, in Western Australia, the Family Court is a state court. In all other states and territories, the Act merging the Family Court with the Federal Circuit Court is the *Federal Circuit and Family Court of Australia Act 2021* (Cth).

3. Federal Court of Australia: it hears appeals from the Federal Circuit Court of Australia, as well as matters related to bankruptcy, corporations, industrial relations, native title, taxation and trade practices laws
4. High Court of Australia: as the highest court of Australia, its role is 'to decide cases of special federal significance including challenges to the constitutional validity of laws and to hear appeals, by special leave, from federal, state and territory courts'.[13]

State courts can vary, but there are commonly three courts of general jurisdiction and several specialist courts in each state and territory. The lower general courts are located in most major towns and cities and are called Local Court in New South Wales and in the Northern Territory, or Magistrates Court in the other states and territories. They are presided over by judicial officers called 'magistrates' and hear minor civil matters of up to a certain monetary threshold[14] and the majority of criminal and summary prosecutions under a certain penalty level, mostly up to a maximum of two years' imprisonment. There is no jury in the Local or Magistrates Courts.

All states, with the exception of Tasmania, have an intermediate level general court; there is no intermediate level court in the Northern Territory and the ACT. These courts are generally called District Courts, except in Victoria where it is called a County Court. These intermediate level courts are presided over by judges and have jurisdiction over civil cases of a value above the threshold of the lower court, up to the threshold of the Supreme Court,[15] and over more serious criminal offences. The intermediate level courts have both trial and appellate jurisdiction. Cases heard at this level may involve a jury in criminal matters or in tortious cases of defamation.

Each state and territory has a Supreme Court, presided over by a Chief Justice. As the highest superior courts of general jurisdiction in Australian States and Territories, the Supreme Courts hear serious criminal cases and civil cases of a value exceeding the threshold set for the inferior court.[16] Supreme Courts may also be vested with federal jurisdiction to hear matters under Commonwealth law. Supreme Courts represent the pinnacle of the State court hierarchy for the purpose of *stare decisis* of binding precedent. The only higher court is the High Court, and this court is part of the state and territory courts hierarchy for the purposes of precedent.

General and specialised courts

As a general rule, every matter is within the jurisdiction of the Supreme Courts of the states and territories as courts of general jurisdiction, unless specifically excluded. Within this generalised system, many state superior courts have special divisions to handle commercial disputes and class action claims.[17]

Matters excluded from the general jurisdiction fall within the jurisdiction of specialised courts as identified in the empowering legislation establishing each court. At the federal level, the Family Court of Australia was a specialist court until it was abolished in 2021 and its jurisdiction transferred to the Federal Circuit Court. It is now called the Federal Circuit and Family Court. The Industrial Relations Court was also a specialist federal court, but its

13 High Court of Australia (Web Page) <https://www.hcourt.gov.au/>.
14 See, eg, A$100,000 in NSW.
15 Between A$100,000 and A$750,000 in NSW.
16 Above A$750,000 in NSW.
17 See further discussion on class actions below.

jurisdiction has been transferred to other courts, mainly to the Federal Court of Australia,[18] and the Court ceased to exist in 2018. In most states and territories, specialist courts are the Children's Court, Coroner's Court, Drug Court, Aboriginal Courts,[19] and courts established for land, planning and environment, or other matters as needed in a given state or territory.[20]

Inferior and superior courts

The main superior courts in Australia are the High Court, the Federal Court of Australia, and the Supreme Courts of the states and territories. Some of the specialised courts are also considered to be superior, like the Land and Environment Court of New South Wales, the Industrial Relations Commission of New South Wales, and the Industrial Court of Queensland. The highest court in Australia is the High Court of Australia, while the highest court in each state and territory is the Supreme Court of that state and territory. All courts that are not identified as superior, including intermediate courts, are considered inferior courts. The place of a court in this hierarchy determines the authority of a decision for other courts – the higher in the hierarchy a court is, the greater the authority their decisions have for other courts. Accordingly, decisions of the High Court are binding on all lower courts. High Court decisions are not binding in subsequent High Court cases, only highly persuasive.

Tribunals

At this stage, tribunals must be mentioned in order to obtain a clear understanding of the judicial system. Tribunals are not courts, although they share many characteristics with courts, but also important differences. Tribunals are established by legislation to decide disputes in specific areas of law at both federal and state levels. Their emergence and integration in the system was an attempt to provide cheap and accessible justice in an increasingly expensive and time-consuming litigation environment. Tribunals may hear matters that were previously heard by courts, provide a review of administrative decisions made by government authorities,[21] or regulate professional disciplinary standards.[22]

Tribunals are, in principle, independent from the executive government, but are made up of 'members' instead of judges or magistrates, and these members are appointed for limited terms by the executive government. Unlike litigation in courts, cases at tribunals are conducted under more informal procedures often adopting a more inquisitorial approach, and members have the freedom to depart from strict rules of evidence and may restrict the participation of lawyers. The decisions, however, must be made according to law and must be reasoned. Tribunal decisions can usually be appealed on a question of law to a court, such as the District Court, the Supreme Court, or the Federal Court – depending on the placement of the tribunal in the overall hierarchy.

Federal tribunals include the Administrative Appeals Tribunal (discussed in Chapter 8), the Fair Work Commission, Australian Competition Tribunal, Copyright Tribunal of Australia,

18 As a result of the *Workplace Relations and Other Legislation Amendment Act 1996* (Cth).

19 See Chapter 1, 31; Chapter 3, 73. See also Australian Law Reform Commission, *Recognition of Aboriginal Customary Law* (Report No 31, June 1986) ch 29.

20 See further Michael Moore, 'The Role of Specialist Courts: An Australian Perspective' [2001] *Federal Judicial Scholarship* 11.

21 See Chapter 8 for details on the operation of the Administrative Appeals Tribunal.

22 See Chapter 12 for more on professional conduct.

Defence Force Discipline Appeals Tribunal, Defence Force Remuneration Tribunal, National Native Title Tribunal, and Veterans Review Board. State and territory tribunals are commonly listed together with the state and territory courts and vary depending on the particular needs of that jurisdiction.

Using theory and models to dissect litigation

This section will outline some relevant theories on how to approach litigation and will provide the basic civil procedure steps as a model to give an understanding of how litigation works in practice.

Theory

As we explained in Chapter 3, the formal legal system in common law countries was developed with courts providing the main outlet for managing society's disputes.[23] The law of evidence and civil procedure has developed over centuries to support and sustain the litigation process. A goal of the process is to determine truth by the application of objective rational criteria to verifiable and probative evidence. In this way, one party could be seen as more supported in their claims and, in time, supported by legal precedents that were argued to apply to their circumstances in a reasoned way. This search for the truth in a formalised manner constrains the type of evidence and the manner in which it can be presented to the third-party neutral, the judge.

The rights of the parties are a key factor supported by legal theory to maintain fairness and justice. This had led to variations in the way legal professionals practice in the litigation process. Barristers that represent parties in court are instructed by solicitors but decide independently how to deliver a case and evidence. The schools of thought range from the legal professional as warrior – one who will defend your rights to the limit of the law – through to an ethics of care practitioner – one who will consider their responsibility to behave in a certain manner acknowledging the interrelatedness of society, and virtue ethics, which considers the individuals ethical motivations.[24] A lawyer or barrister's ideological and theoretical view will, accordingly, affect how a case unfolds. The use of language, the level of aggressiveness, and lawyering ethics all influence the advocacy style of a barrister and play a significant role in the handling of witnesses. While judges appreciate rational and clear legal analysis, 'hard-nosed' lawyering is criticised for intimidating witnesses and presenting emotions as irrelevant, denying the human side of a case.[25]

A guiding approach is provided by the development of the Model Litigant Policy.[26] Created by the Attorney-General's Department to regulate the way government agencies should act in

23 See Chapter 3.

24 See, eg, Christine Parker, 'A Critical Morality for Lawyers: Four Approaches to Lawyers' Ethics' (2004) 30 (1) *Monash University Law Review* 49; Susan Daicoff, 'The Future of the Legal Profession' (2011) 37(1) *Monash University Law Review* 7.

25 See, eg, *Ellis v Trustees of the Roman Catholic Church for the Archdiocese of Sydney* [2007] HCATrans 697 (16 November 2007); see also Tony Foley, 'Institutional Responses to Child Sexual Abuse: How a Moral Conversation With Its Lawyers Might Contribute to Cultural Change in a Faith-based Institution' (2015) 18(2) *Legal Ethics* 164.

26 See *Legal Services Directions 2017* (Cth) app B.

litigation, the Policy became the basis for guidelines developed across all State and Federal courts to serve as 'model litigant rules'. These rules provide guidance on:

- acting honestly, consistently, and fairly in the handling of claims and litigation
- dealing with claims promptly
- making an early assessment of the government's prospects of success
- paying legitimate claims without litigation
- not taking advantage of a claimant who lacks resources
- not relying on a merely technical defence against a claim
- considering dispute management processes.[27]

Due to its complexities, litigation is approached with thorough and strategic planning. For this reason, lawyers are considered to be a necessary part of litigation. Developing a litigation strategy requires reviewing and preparing the case through specific steps:

- identifying causes of action, issues, and elements of the case
- identifying the facts and obtaining evidence
- researching relevant law and theory
- developing a case theory – narrative of facts and how they prove or disprove the case
- work out the law and evidence on each issue one by one
- draft submission – opening and closing
- prepare evidence – documents and witnesses
- prepare for hearing.[28]

Judges and juries

Judges play an increasing role in how litigation unfolds. In Australia, most civil cases are heard by one judge as the third-party neutral. Judges have legal qualifications and are commonly appointed after extended service as barristers or occasionally as law academics or solicitors. Judges are addressed as 'Your Honour' and referred to as 'Justice' or 'The Honourable Justice (Surname)'; in writing they are referred to as '(Surname) J'. The role of a judge is to decide a case by either interpreting how a law applies to a factual situation or (in the absence of legislation) by developing a new way to deal with a factual situation. If the court is composed of more than one judge, it is only the decision of the majority that constitutes the precedent; there is no requirement for unanimous decisions. Dissenting minority opinion(s), although not becoming part of the precedent, do shape the development of law through their influence. As the introductory chapter of an entire book dedicated to great dissents notes, '[t]o be a great

27 See *Analysis of the Model Litigant Rules* (Australia's Magna Carta Institute, 2020).

28 See Michael Mills, *Dispute Resolution: A Practitioner's Guide to Successful Alternative Dispute Resolution*. (Thomson Reuters, 2018) 481–559, for a detailed description of how to prepare for a case in an adjudicative process.

dissent, an opinion must hold some future importance. It may never be agreed with but it cannot be ignored'.[29]

There have been opinions that the ultimate function of a judge 'to find out the truth and do justice according to the law'[30] is not served well by the adversarial system.[31] Australia's civil justice system is considered to be adversarial, following on its Medieval English origins. Traditionally, an adversarial model meant that a dispute is between the parties who are primarily responsible for advancing the case. The judge is not actively engaged in how the dispute unfolds but passively observes how the case is run by the parties and decides on the parties' (and their barristers') presented evidence.

As opposed to this, an inquisitorial system – originating from Roman law and more characteristic to civil law countries – involves a more proactive judge engaged in fact-finding, selection of experts, and examination of witnesses. The Australian Law Reform Commission, however, in reporting about the advantages and disadvantages of the adversarial system in 2000,[32] found 'limited utility' in comparing the two systems, noting that there is 'a significant degree of convergence in the way both common law and civil law countries now approach civil procedure'.[33]

Litigation in Australia does maintain an adversarial style, but there is growing power granted to judges to proactively control the advancement of a case for the sake of case management to provide effective justice. Case management and efficiency-driven procedural rules are developed by rules committees dominated by judges. Today, the level of engagement of judges is more driven by fair and efficient access to justice principles than the historic divide and categorisation of legal systems in rigid boxes.

A judge may decide on the law only or on the matter as well if the case does not require trial by jury. In criminal trials, a jury is composed of everyday citizens called to jury duty. People that are eligible and qualify for jury service are randomly selected from the electoral roll through an automated computer program and are notified in writing. The role of a jury is to establish the facts based on the burden of proof on evidence presented being beyond reasonable doubt while being guided by the judge.[34] Jury service is compulsory and is governed by the *Jury Act* of each State and Territory.

Juries are more commonly used in criminal than in civil cases. Less serious ('summary') criminal proceedings are heard by a magistrate or judge alone, without a jury, while serious criminal cases (indictable offences) have a jury of 12 across all Australian jurisdictions. Juries

29 Andrew Lynch, 'Introduction – What Makes a Dissent "Great"?' in Andrew Lynch (ed), *Great Australian Dissents* (Cambridge University Press, 2016) 1.

30 Andrew Hemming and Tania Penovic, *Civil Procedure in Australia* (Lexis Nexis Butterworths, 2015) 15, citing *Jones v National Coal Board* [1957] 2 QB 55, 63.

31 Ray Finkelstein, 'The Adversarial System and the Search for Truth' (2011) 37(1) *Monash University Law Review* 135.

32 Australian Law Reform Commission, *Managing Justice: A Review of the Federal Civil Justice System* (Report No 89, February 2000).

33 Ibid 107. See also PD McClellan, 'Civil Justice Reform – What Has It Achieved?' [2015] *New South Wales Judicial Scholarship* 5.

34 See Graham Fricke, 'Trial by Jury' (Research Paper 11, Department of the Parliamentary Library, February 1997) for a detailed discussion of jury trials.

are only used in limited civil cases, which vary from jurisdiction to jurisdiction.[35] The size of the jury in civil cases also varies between states.[36]

Model of litigation

Litigation as a dispute management process is driven by procedure and rules of evidence. While similar across courts, there are variations applicable to the particular court in which the litigation occurs. Procedural, as opposed to substantive rules are the vehicle providing 'the critical infrastructure necessary to vindicate substantive rights and achieve access to justice'.[37] All major courts have their own set of rules establishing procedure, primarily laid down in the foundational legislation establishing that court. Supreme Courts also have an inherent jurisdiction to regulate their own processes and to issue Practice Notes or Practice Directions to ensure efficiency, but only on matters of procedure. Some procedural rules and many Practice Notes have no legislative authority, but most of them are classified as subordinate or delegated legislation to avoid challenges to their validity. The rules of the Federal Court and of the Supreme Courts still reflect their English origins, while the rules of the High Court have developed to suit its current function being primarily an appellate court.

Some courts also have standard Practice Directions or Practice Notes that provide detailed guidance on that court's case management scheme and set timetables and procedural steps the parties are expected to adhere to. This is an area given special instruction in law degrees in courses generally referred to as 'Civil Procedure'. Despite the many different sources of norms regulating civil procedure, the general course of litigation is overall identical across Australia. Rules of procedure are governed by the concept of procedural fairness, serving the overarching principles of natural justice, which all Australian courts and tribunals apply.

Pre-litigation steps

While litigation is available and accessible to parties, legislation requires certain pre-litigation steps to be completed before accessing the court. The rationale for these steps is for the court system to be used efficiently, for judicial resources not to be wasted on unnecessary litigation, and to ameliorate the traditional adversarial culture associated with dispute management. Traditional textbooks instruct practitioners to write a 'letter before action' to the other party before filing for litigation in the hope that the dispute may be solved via solicitor negotiation, without litigation. With the growing recognition of other dispute management processes, this expectation has now been included in civil procedure legislation as a more substantial requirement.[38] Now every jurisdiction in Australia gives direction to parties to make use of dispute management processes before litigation either to manage the dispute, or to properly identify the issues to be decided in court.

The *Civil Dispute Resolution Act 2011* (Cth), building on the work of NADRAC, is a prime example at the Federal level of this requirement. Its object is 'to ensure that, as far as possible,

35 With the exception of South Australia, where juries are only used in criminal cases.

36 See n 3.

37 Hemming and Penovic (n 30) xix.

38 *Civil Dispute Resolution Act 2011* (Cth) s 6 requires parties to take 'genuine steps' to resolve their dispute prior to resorting to litigation.

people take genuine steps to resolve disputes before certain civil proceedings are instituted'.[39] Similar provisions exist in all State and Territory civil procedure legislation. The most common steps across jurisdictions are:

- Pre- and post-mediation conferences in different variations involving the parties and/or their legal representatives, and mediator or conciliator
- Joint mediation involving all participants
- Private sessions involving only one party with their legal representative and mediator
- Case appraisal conferences
- Settlement conferences involving the management of some matters
- Referral of issues for judicial determination or to expert appraisal, conference, arbitration, or a special referee
- Final determination of all matters – ultimately this may be a court decision.[40]

The expectation to take reasonable steps to address a dispute before litigation has increased alongside the development of case management schemes and the growing use and recognition of dispute management in general. Changes to State and Federal legislation led to all courts having the power to order parties to engage in mediation or another similar process even if the parties do not wish to do so.[41] Pre-litigation dispute management may serve the benefit of courts but not necessarily the benefit of parties if applied as a blanket manner, instead of on a case-by-case basis. Managing disputes as a tool for creating a harmonious and just society[42] is in every government's interest. However, if a matter is suitable for litigation, then the extension of the time and costs of engaging in another process before obtaining a court judgment should be carefully assessed. It must be weighed against the reality that out-of-court dispute management has been recognised as efficient and effective regardless of the parties' initial interest in the process. Even reluctant parties often discover the value in the opportunity to manage a dispute confidentially, without further damaging relationships and escalating costs, or to select from a wider range of dispute management processes than litigation could provide. This is an appreciation reflected and confirmed by the high success rate of dispute management regardless of whether it was court ordered or voluntary.[43]

Pre-litigation processes must be demonstrated to the court but are not a pre-condition for court jurisdiction. Failure to comply with these steps does not impede parties to access the court. Instead, the court may take this failure into account when awarding costs. Legal

39 Ibid ss 3, 6, 12.

40 Hemming and Penovic (n 30) 74.

41 See Chapter 6 and Chapter 12; *Federal Court of Australia Act 1976* (Cth) s 53A; *Civil Procedure Act 2005* (NSW) ss 26, 38; *Supreme Court Act 1979* (NT) s 83A; *Civil Proceedings Act 2011* (Qld) s 43; *Supreme Court Act 1935* (SA) s 65; *Supreme Court Civil Procedure Act 1932* (Tas) ss 37A, 37B; *Supreme Court Act 1986* (Vic) ss 24A, 25(1)(e)–(ea); *Supreme Court Act 1935* (WA) s 69.

42 See, eg, Tracey Raymond, *Alternative Dispute Resolution as a Tool for Social Change: A Discussion of Issues and Evidence* (Australian Human Rights Commission, 2008).

43 See Kathy Mack, *Court Referral to ADR: Criteria and Research* (Australasian Institute of Judicial Administration and the National Alternative Dispute Resolution Advisory Council, 2003); Nicky McWilliam et al, *Court-Referred Alternative Dispute Resolution: Perceptions of Members of the Judiciary: An Overview of the Results of a Study* (Australasian Institute of Judicial Administration, 2017).

practitioners may also face professional liability for costs for failing to take a client through a preliminary dispute management process before filing for litigation.[44]

Originating process and service

Litigation must be commenced by filing documents in the court having subject matter and territorial jurisdiction over the claim and the parties. The exact form and content of the originating process, as well as the documents that need to accompany it depend on the nature of the claim and are determined by the court rules that vary between jurisdictions. The originating process must contain endorsements that inform the defendant of the nature of the dispute, of the claim, the requirement to respond, and the consequences of failing to do so. The originating process must also be accompanied by paying of fees to the court. These are also specified in court rules or regulations, together with other court fees.

Service is the process of handing over the documents of originating process to the defendant and taking any subsequent steps the court rules may require. Rules regulating the service of an originating process are included in the civil procedure rules of the relevant jurisdiction. As a general rule, an originating process must be served personally on the defendant. Service outside of Australia is commonly done through diplomatic channels, based on the *Convention on the Service Abroad of Judicial and Extrajudicial Documents in Civil or Commercial Matters* (1965).[45]

A court is vested with jurisdiction over a particular claim based on the service of originating process, which is both necessary and sufficient to create such jurisdiction, as long as the subject matter and the plaintiff fall within the authority of that court. Nevertheless, the **transient rule of jurisdiction** allows for jurisdiction based on service even if that may be inappropriate. This rule is ameliorated by the court's discretion to decline proceeding with the claim if it finds that the forum is 'clearly inappropriate'.[46] Service is the first step of informing the defendant about the existence of a claim against them and as such is a precondition to any further step against a defendant. The only exception to this is when ex parte applications are allowed due to extreme urgency.

Transient rule of jurisdiction: a rule that allows for jurisdiction to be created by service on a non-resident of the state who may be physically temporarily passing through that forum state.

Pleadings

The defendant's response to being served is generally to file and serve a notice of appearance, indicating an address for future service. However, once a defendant has been properly served with the originating process, the case can, in principle, proceed regardless of whether the defendant responds or not. If the defendant does nothing, the case will proceed to a default judgment. If the defendant enters an appearance, the parties will exchange **pleadings** (ie statements of claim and defence) to define the issues in dispute. Pleadings are the documents submitted by the parties in which they define their claims and defences and present their

Pleadings: documentation prepared by the parties defining their claims and defences and outlining their arguments and supporting facts.

44 See, eg, *Civil Dispute Resolution Act 2011* (Cth) s 12.

45 *Convention on the Service Abroad of Judicial and Extrajudicial Documents in Civil or Commercial Matters* (concluded 15 November 1965, entered into force 10-II-1969) <https://www.hcch.net/en/instruments/conventions/full-text/?cid=17>.

46 *Oceanic Sun Line Special Shipping Co Inc v Fay* (1988) 165 CLR 197.

arguments and facts on which those claims are based.[47] Unlike the arbitration memorials, pleadings in litigation do not set out the complete factual and legal case early on. Initial pleadings provide limited, mainly factual information, while evidence, legal arguments and authorities are submitted later, in a staggered format. The first pleading is the statement of claim, usually delivered with the originating process, followed by the defendant's statement of defence, submitted after or together with entering appearance. Pleadings define the matters in dispute and bind the parties to those matters at trial. They are characteristic to the adversarial system, allowing the parties to 'set the court's agenda'.[48]

Court rules regulate the content and form of pleadings. The statement of claim must include the claim and the material facts that indicate the complete **cause of action** presented in a succinct manner. No immaterial or unnecessary facts should be included in the pleadings, but alternative and inconsistent claims and defences are permitted. Similarly, no legal claims can be made without factual support in the pleadings. Parties may be required to specify the legal ground on which they rely for their claim or defence. Since the facts have to so strictly relate to the legal basis of the claim, it generally requires a legally trained person to write and file a statement of claim.

Cause of action: a set of facts that satisfy the legal requirements for making a claim, creating the right to legal action for that claim.

The statement of defence must contain an answer to every allegation made in the statement of claim. The defendant may accept or dispute the claim or may file a counterclaim or claim a set-off. If the defendant does not respond to the facts presented in the statement of claim, those facts are considered to be admitted. However, the presumption that silence means acceptance is only applicable up to (and including) the defence, not for subsequent pleadings.

Pleadings are often amended, and parties may request further particulars to understand the facts better. Pleadings are considered to be closed when the last pleading is submitted, at which stage the issues to be determined by the court should be clearly defined. This preparatory phase for litigation is designed to narrow the issues in dispute and save court time and thus public money. It tends to have become highly juridified and technical such that legal representation is desirable, similar to arbitration. This costs the parties money as the agenda setting is all done through written documentation – unlike in mediation, where the agenda-setting phase is more simply and efficiently reached and can include non-legal aspects of a dispute. As pleadings define the framework of a case, the parties' failure to state the facts on which their position is based is a frequent criticism that has caused debate around rethinking pleadings entirely.[49]

Evidence

Litigation, similar to arbitration and other adjudicative processes, has a rights-based approach to disputes. The third-party neutral decides the parties' claims by assessing the extent to which

47 See, eg, Anna Katzmann, 'Pleadings and Case Management in Civil Proceedings in the Federal Court of Australia' [2015] *Federal Judicial Scholarship* 23 for how to write good pleadings.

48 Hemming and Penovic (n 30) 295.

49 See, eg, Elizabeth Thornburg and Camille Cameron, 'Defining Civil Disputes: Lessons from Two Jurisdictions' (2011) 35(1) *Melbourne University Law Review* 208.

evidence provided by the parties supports their claim or not. Unlike in arbitration, however, there are extensive rules of evidence applicable in litigation. Generally, they are included in the respective Commonwealth, State, and Territories *Evidence Acts* which are broadly consistent.[50] This law is further developed through the common law and courts' interpretation of the statutes. As a general rule, a party making a claim must provide evidence to prove that claim.

To prove facts, a party has to present evidence consisting of documents, objects and/or witness testimonies. Nevertheless, having the burden of proof does not mean that a party can only provide evidence that they possess. A party may file an **interrogatory** consisting of written questions to the other side, the answers to which then become evidence. Similarly, a party may file a notice to admit, requiring the other side to admit certain facts in the pleadings.

Interrogatory: a formal series of questions put by one party in a dispute to the other side in order to refine the facts and matters in dispute. The answers must be provided in writing, are considered to be made under oath, and then can be used as evidence against the party providing them.

One aspect of evidence to consider is the need for expert evidence. This can take a number of forms such as a single court-appointed expert or – more commonly in adversarial systems – expert witnesses engaged by each party separately, which can sometimes turn into a contest of the experts.[51] Experts are required to establish their expertise and then give an opinion on a matter in contention that strictly falls within the limits of their expertise. Expert witness codes of conduct[52] set the rule that experts must be and remain impartial.[53] Yet, there is a common criticism that expert witnesses may act as advocates making a party's case.[54] There have been some rather notorious difficulties with expert evidence in criminal cases in Australia.[55]

Discovery and privilege

Rules also allow for pre-trial access to documents, objects and information held by the other side or a third party in order to ensure that the court can obtain all facts relevant to the dispute.

50 *Evidence Act 1995* (Cth); *Evidence Act 2011* (ACT); *Evidence Act 1995* (NSW); *Evidence (National Uniform Legislation Act) 2011* (NT); *Evidence Act 1977* (Qld); *Evidence Act 1929* (SA); *Evidence Act 2001* (Tas); *Evidence Act 2008* (Vic); *Evidence Act 1906* (WA).

51 See also Stephen Cordner et al, 'The Uniform Evidence Act and Australian Judges Ability to Assess Properly the Validity and Reliability of Expert Evidence' (2020) 52(3) *Australian Journal of Forensic Sciences* 243; Victorian Law Reform Commission, *Civil Justice Review* (Report No 14, 1999) 482.

52 See *Court Procedures Rules 2006* (ACT) sch 1; *Uniform Civil Procedure Rules 2005* (NSW) sch 7; District Court of Western Australia, *Practice Direction No 21: Expert Evidence*, July 2020; *Uniform Civil Procedure Rules 1999* (Qld) div 2; Supreme Court of Tasmania, *Practice Direction No 1 of 2016: Expert Witness Code of Conduct*, 5 January 2016; *Supreme Court (General Civil Procedure Rules) 2015* (Vic) r 44.01; *Federal Court Rules 2011* (Cth) pt 23; *Family Law Rules 2004* (Cth) div 15.5.3; Supreme Court of South Australia, *Practice Direction 5.4: Expert Witnesses,* 13 March 2014.

53 See also *Evidence Act 1995* (Cth) pt 3.3; *Federal Court Rules 2011* (Cth) pt 23; Federal Court of Australia, *Expert Evidence Practice Note (GPN-EXPT)*, 25 October 2016, Annexure A: Harmonised Expert Witness Code of Conduct.

54 See George Golvan, 'Each to Their Own: Addressing the Problem of Expert Witness Partiality' (2006) 80 (9) *Law Institute Journal* 56; Justin Gleeson, 'The Judge, the Advocate and the Expert Witness – Revisiting the Seminal Views of Sir Owen Dixon in the Modern Context' (2016) 48(4) *Australian Journal of Forensic Sciences* 366.

55 See, eg, A Howe, 'Imagining Evidence, Fictioning Truth – Revisiting (Courtesy of O. J. Simpson) Expert Evidence in the Chamberlain Case' (1997) (3) *Law Text Culture* 82; Stephen Cordner, 'Expert Opinions and Evidence: A Perspective from Forensic Pathology' (2015) 17(2) *Flinders Law Journal* 263.

Discovery: preliminary procedure characteristic to litigation in common law systems through which a party can obtain from the other side or third parties the disclosure and production of documents or objects needed to prove a fact relevant to the issue in dispute.

Subpoena: an order made by a court (or other entity authorised by law to issue subpoenas) through which a person is compelled to give evidence or produce documents.

Privilege: a rule protecting the confidentiality of sensitive documents and information, allowing the possessing party to refuse producing that document or information as evidence under certain circumstances.

Discovery allows the parties to search for relevant documents within reasonable limits by providing a list of documents requested to the other party or issue **subpoenas** to a third party holding the documents.

The person holding the documents must disclose them by either providing them to the requesting party or allowing the documents or objects to be inspected. The obligation to disclose documents or objects is only limited by **privilege**. Legal privilege provides for the confidentiality of documents presented to a lawyer for the purposes of obtaining legal advice or to an expert in preparing for litigation.[56] A party is also exempt from disclosing information that would subject them to criminal penalty. Finally, 'without prejudice' privilege protects communication to encourage parties to seek advice from legal practitioners in order to encourage a genuine attempt to settle a dispute. It is also designed to protect this communication from being used as evidence in subsequent litigation. Such communication, to fall within the without prejudice privilege, must have a direct connection with an attempt to negotiate a settlement, but it does not necessarily have to be an offer or an attempt to achieve a compromise.[57]

Confidentiality and non-disclosure agreements common in commercial relationships are not a basis for resisting disclosure ordered by the court. Nevertheless, if a case proceeds to hearing, parties may apply for suppression or non-publication orders to the court based on such agreements. Often, however, discovery may lead to an increased motivation to settle or engage in out-of-court dispute management processes. Knowing the strengths and weaknesses of the parties' position through the evidence discovered can be a strong basis for reassessing the risks and benefits of proceeding with litigation. This can lead to the phenomenon described as settlement in 'the shadow of the courts'.

Case management

In addition to the compulsory pre-litigation attempts to manage a dispute prior to the court determination, there are also processes put in place during litigation that support a non-adversarial dispute management. Case management is a process designed to ensure that litigation is conducted efficiently and expeditiously. Originating from the United States, where it is called 'case flow management', case (or caseload) management was raised in Australia first as part of law reform discussions in the 1980s.

Case management processes vary between jurisdictions, but they are all designed to speed up litigation. Case management may involve four main components:

1. setting up tracks for specialised court supervision depending on the complexity, urgency, and subject matter of a dispute and allocating cases to a suitable track for specialist expertise and case management
2. setting time limits

56 See *Glencore International AG v Commissioner of Taxation* (2019) 265 CLR 646, confirming that legal professional privilege is an immunity, not an actionable legal right.

57 *Hera Resources Pty Ltd v Gekko Systems Pty Ltd* [2019] NSWSC 37.

3. directions hearings and orders made to narrow down the issues in dispute, exchanging documents and information to reduce the scope and extent of discovery and pleadings
4. sanctions for breach, allowing judges to dismiss a case, move it to a dormant case list, or impose adverse cost orders in case of repeat and unjustified failure to adhere to timetables and directions made.

Cases are allocated to a judge, or a list of judges, for the purpose of the case being monitored and advanced, directed to other dispute processes and settlement if possible, or advanced to trial as soon as possible. Directions orders are made at direction hearings – also called conference hearings, status hearings, or case evaluation hearings depending on the court and the stage at which the hearing takes place. Throughout the case management phase, parties may have to attend several such hearings. The courts generally have a broad power to make any order that is considered appropriate for fair and speedy delivery of justice.[58] The parties are often directed to comply with a timetable for the necessary procedural steps and time limits may also be set for when the first and last directions hearing should take place.

Trial

According to the *International Covenant on Civil and Political Rights*,[59] all persons have a right to a fair and public hearing.[60] In most jurisdictions, the parties must file and serve a certificate of readiness or notice of entry for trial. If the court is satisfied that both sides have properly prepared their case and evidence, the court will set a hearing for the parties to present their evidence, cross-examine witnesses, and make submissions based on the evidence presented.

As noted, most civil cases are heard by a judge sitting alone, with jury trials being the exception in civil litigation. The judge as a third-party neutral will make a decision based on the evidence presented. Procedural fairness is a cornerstone of the trial process, but the right to a jury in a civil matter is subject to a wide range of exceptions and qualifications. As a rule, hearings are conducted in open court, although the court may order a confidential hearing or make confidentiality orders to protect, for example, commercially sensitive information or intellectual property.[61] Litigants are not required to be represented by a legal practitioner, but failure to attend a trial may attract adjournment or dismissal of the proceedings. Unrepresented litigants are increasing in number, due to the cost of legal representation. This is presenting unique issues discussed under the 'Costs' section below.

Mostly a solicitor will instruct a barrister to present the parties' cases in trial, although solicitors may do this depending on the court and different jurisdictions. The control of evidence presentation and procedural requirements means the communication in trials is highly constrained and formal. Nevertheless, lawyers will have their own style of communicating. This can range from being quite adversarial to more cooperative.[62]

58 See, eg, Tina Popa, 'All the Way with ADR: Further Endorsement of ADR in Litigation' (2015) 26(4) *Australasian Dispute Resolution Journal* 218.

59 *International Covenant on Civil and Political Rights*, opened for signature 16 December 1966 (entered into force 23 March 1976) (*ICCPR*).

60 Ibid art 14.

61 See, eg, *Interpharma Pty Ltd v Eli Lilly and Company* [2008] FCA 1422.

62 See Parker (n 24).

Outcomes

Consent judgment: a judgment based on the agreement between the parties, when the defendant agrees with the plaintiff's claims or the parties settle their dispute during litigation.

Calderbank offers: offers made in a genuine attempt to settle a matter on a without prejudice basis excepting as regards costs.

Civil litigation may end in a number of different ways before or following trial. Before trial, some cases will be settled through other dispute management processes. In this case, the claim (or the defence) may be discontinued or withdrawn, or the case may be settled and the court asked to make a **consent judgment**. Offers for settlement during litigation may take two forms:

1. Informal offers, commonly called **Calderbank offers**.[63]
2. Offers of compromise made in accordance with the court rules.

Summary judgment: a judgment rendered for one party against another without a full trial.

Default judgment: a judgment rendered when the defendant does not participate in the proceedings and does not respond to the statement of claim.

On the other hand, some cases will be closed through early disposition by the court for either substantive or procedural reasons. On reasons related to the merits of the case, where a claim or a defence has no reasonable prospects of success, the defendant or the plaintiff can apply for a dismissal by **summary judgment**. Similarly, in case of vexatious litigants, the court may either stay proceedings or prohibit the vexatious litigant from instituting proceedings without the court's leave.[64] On procedural grounds, if a party fails to comply with rules of procedure, including those on time limits, the court may render a **default judgment**. The court may also dismiss a claim for want of prosecution if a party delays the proceedings with intention or with no excuse, or when the delay may cause serious prejudice to the defendant. All these are strong reasons to consider whether litigation is, indeed, the suitable process to handle a dispute, as an early disposition means the end of a potentially time and cost consuming litigation without managing the dispute itself.

Should a case proceed to trial, the judge will provide a determination regarding the matter in dispute. Outcomes from litigation are limited to a small range of options in equity or common law or statutory financial damages. These do not encompass the open options available based on the parties' creativity in other dispute management processes.

In the case of a jury trial, available only in limited situations, the jury will reach a verdict on the facts finding in favour of one or more of the parties, assess factual issues and, in civil matters, the amount of damages claimed. In civil cases, based on that verdict, the judge will then deliver a judgment that is the final and binding determination of the court concluding the proceedings. In criminal cases, the jury decides the guilt or innocence of a defendant and the judge provides a sentence.

In case of a trial heard by a judge sitting alone, the judge will deliver the verdict as part of the judgment. The judgment must be reasoned, but the reasoning is separate from the operative part, which is the actual ruling that may be appealed. The judgment also needs to be authenticated, usually by the court registrar who signs and seals the document and it is then entered in the court records or judgment book. After that stage, the decision is final and 'beyond recall' by that court, subject only to corrections to eliminate clerical errors or

63 *Calderbank v Calderbank* [1975] 3 WLR 586.

64 See, eg, *Conomy v Maden* [2019] HCATrans 41 regarding vexatious litigants.

subsequent appeals to a higher court. For judgments to be recognised as precedent, they also need to be reported by councils of law reporting who authorise the publication of report series. Unreported cases are still recognised, but do not serve as precedent.

Setting aside and appeal

The review of court judgments in civil litigation is available only through setting aside procedures and appeal. A judgment may be set aside by the issuing court if it was obtained by fraud, rendered against good faith, or if new evidence is discovered after the trial.[65] An appeal, on the other hand, must be filed to a superior court and must be based on a significant and relevant error of fact or error of law in the first instance judgment. Depending on the court, leave to appeal may have to be sought before the court will entertain the appeal hearing.[66]

The appellate division of State Supreme Courts is either the Court of Appeal or the Full Court of the relevant Supreme Court. These are appeals by way of **rehearing** and are typically heard by three judges, or for certain cases by a panel of five. The High Court of Australia hears '**strict appeals**' subject to special leave to appeal, as the ultimate court of appeal. In some cases, an appellate court may also hear an **appeal de novo**. The type of appeal available in a given case depends on the statutory provision conferring the right to appeal.

Based on a rebuttable presumption that a judge renders a correct decision, the onus is on the appellant to demonstrate that the judge in the court of first instance exercised discretion incorrectly. A judgment will not be set aside solely because a different decision could have been reached.[67] Similarly, an appellate court will be reluctant to reverse a jury's or a trial judge's findings of facts, as they had the benefit of seeing and hearing a witness first-hand. However, if the appellant demonstrates that there was an error in the evidence admitted and in reaching the decision, the appeal court will make its own assessment of the facts.[68]

If the facts are not disputed, the appellant may argue that the trial judge made an error of law in reaching the decision either by applying the wrong principle or incorrectly applying the law to the facts. In doing so, the appellant would have to demonstrate the correct legal principles and that, based on those, the outcome would be different than the outcome reached by the trial judge. No decision on a question of fact can be challenged based on an alleged error of law.

If the parties settle their dispute during appeal, the court will make a consent order. If the appellate court is unable to make a judgment on appeal, it can order a

Rehearing: judicial procedure by which a party may ask the Court of Appeal of a State or Territory or, in some cases, the Full Court of the Federal Court, to review the evidence and the transcripts of the court of first instance, admit new evidence if any, and apply the law as it exists at the time of rehearing. In this sense, the appellate court is exercising original jurisdiction if the appellant demonstrates that there is an error in fact or in law in the judgment appealed.

Strict appeal: judicial procedure by which a party may ask the High Court of Australia or, in some cases, the Full Court of the Federal Court of Australia, to find that the judgment appealed was incorrectly decided based on the law that existed at the time of judgment and the evidence presented to the court of first instance. No change of law or new evidence can be considered in a strict appeal.

Appeal de novo: judicial procedure by which a case is heard anew as if in an original cause.

65 See *Clone Pty Ltd v Players Pty Ltd (in liq)* (2018) 264 CLR 165, for analysis on setting aside.

66 See Pamela Stewart and Anita Stuhmcke, 'Open Justice, Efficient Justice and the Rule of Law: The Increasing Invisibility of Special Leave to Appeal Applications in the High Court of Australia' (2020) 48(2) *Federal Law Review* 186, for a critical analysis of special leave to appeal in the High Court on the administration of justice.

67 See *House v The King* (1936) 55 CLR 499, 504.

68 See *Pell v The Queen* (2020) 376 ALR 478, for an analysis on error made by a jury where evidence was contradictory (in a criminal case) and the burden of proof in appeal.

new trial. The court will, however, need to balance the finality of litigation against the need for justice between the parties, which renders ordering a new trial a last resort solution available only to satisfy an imperative need for justice.[69]

As the judgment of a court is presumed to be correct and enforceable, an appeal does not automatically stay or postpone the enforcement of the judgment appealed. Nevertheless, the court may order a stay of execution in some cases if the appellant demonstrates that allowing the enforcement would cause a significant injustice.

Enforcement

Once the court formally enters the judgment, the judgment or order can be executed. A successful plaintiff has a range of avenues available to enforce a judgment depending on the identity of the party against which the judgment is made and depending on the nature of the order. Non-monetary judgments can be executed through sequestration, writ or warrant of possession or delivery, substituted performance and committal. Monetary judgments can be enforced through **writ of *fieri facias***, charging order to create a security over the debtor's property, garnishment to have money taken from the judgment debtor's bank accounts or wages, or the appointment of a receiver to have the judgment debtor declared bankrupt.

Writ of *fieri facias*: Latin for 'writ of execution' to seize and sell property belonging to a debtor.

If the judgment debtor is a company, the judgment creditor can issue a statutory demand. If the statutory demand is not responded to within 21 days, the successful plaintiff can apply to the Supreme Court to declare the debtor company insolvent for being unable to pay its debts and, accordingly, wound up. Therefore, a 'win' in court does not immediately translate into the desired outcome such as compensation. This still has to be pursued and may never be fully obtained. Before entering into litigation, it is therefore appropriate to consider whether the desired outcome can realistically be achieved.

Using knowledge of litigation to assist in dispute management

This section will assist in deciding whether litigation is the appropriate avenue for managing a dispute by identifying who can be a party to litigation, when, and how; the time and cost it takes to litigate; and what could be the right reasons for going to trial.

Parties and causes of action

In principle, anyone with legal personality has the capacity to be a party to litigation. To be party to a particular litigation, however, a person must have standing and a valid cause of action. To have standing, the requirement is for a person to have a specific legal right or a real and special interest in the subject matter of the proceedings.[70] Several causes of action can be joined at the plaintiff's choice (permissive joinder), and a court also has discretion to order

69 See *CDJ v VAJ* (1998) 197 CLR 172; *Orr v Holmes* (1948) 76 CLR 632.

70 The Hon Brian J Preston, 'Standing to Sue at Common Law in Australia' (Conference Paper, Joint Seminar on Legality of Administrative Behaviours and Types of Adjudication, 11–13 April 2006).

several trials to be joined if the joinder is convenient to the court or to the parties (joinder by leave). All these joinder possibilities represent a significant difference compared to arbitration, the other primary determinative method available for commercial disputes.

Persons that are not a party may intervene, seeking to become party to a litigation, or may ask to participate in the proceedings as **amicus curiae**. Amici curiae will not become party to a case and will not have the right to file pleadings, lead or examine evidence, but may make submissions to assist the court or to support a party's position. Although the rules of procedure do not regulate the role of amici curiae or the circumstances in which they should be allowed to participate, a court will accept submissions from such third parties if it is considered to be in the interest of justice. For example, if the parties 'are unable or unwilling adequately to protect their own interest, or to assist the court in arriving at the correct determination of the case'.[71] In the landmark case of *TCL Air Conditioner (Zhongshan) Co Ltd v Judges of the Federal Court of Australia*,[72] the Attorneys-General of the Commonwealth, New South Wales, Victoria, Western Australia, Queensland, and South Australia were interveners, while the Australian Centre for International Commercial Arbitration, the Institute of Arbitrators and Mediators Australia, and the Chartered Institute of Arbitrators Australia all submitted amicus curiae briefs, as the stakes to the recognition of arbitration as a dispute management process were very high.[73]

Amicus curiae: Latin for 'friend of the court' (pl: amici curiae), describing a person who has no direct connection to the dispute but has an interest in the issue and can provide information, expertise, or analysis to assist the court in its decision.

Timelines

There are two aspects of time being relevant in litigation. On the one hand, limitation periods are set by legislation commonly known as *Limitation Acts*, defining the timeframe within which action must be initiated. These timeframes are a matter of substantive law rather than procedure, and they vary in length depending on the underlying cause of action. For example, the general limitation period for an action in torts or contract is six years. However, the limitation period starts running from a different starting point, as in tort the cause of action can be identified from the time the damage was suffered, while in contract from the time of the breach of contract.

Failure to initiate a claim within a limitation period results in a bar to action, unless the limitation period has been suspended or extended. Correspondingly, the expiry of a limitation period is a procedural defence, unless the defendant is estopped from relying on the limitation period.[74] Therefore, litigation may or may not be an available option, depending on the time that passed since the dispute arose and the limitation period imposed for the claim. Limitation periods being established by mandatory substantive legislation, will also be applicable for raising a claim in arbitration.

71 *Kruger v Commonwealth* (1996) 3 Leg Rep 14.

72 (2013) 251 CLR 533.

73 The case challenged the constitutionality of the *International Arbitration Act 1974* (Cth), which is based on the *UNCITRAL Model Law on International Commercial Arbitration*, serving as base for all State and Territory *Commercial Arbitration Acts* and the *Arbitration Acts* of 111 jurisdictions globally.

74 See generally Peter Handford, *Limitations of Actions: The Laws of Australia* (Lawbook, 4th ed, 2017).

On the other hand, once initiated, court proceedings are governed by strict timetables imposed by the court or by court rules. These are procedural timeframes serving the purpose of efficiency and predictability and are commonly identified as part of case management. Timelines for civil claims can vary considerably, as they depend on the complexity of the case, the volume of evidence, and the extent of court hearings needed. Commercial disputes in specialist courts may be decided within one year, while class action proceedings may take more than five years. Expedited court proceedings are available in some courts if the requesting party can justify the need for that case to take precedence over others the court hears. Time is a factor every litigant must consider when deciding on a dispute management process. Litigation, out of all the processes, generally tends to take the longest before a decision may be reached by the third-party decision-maker, although arbitration has become similarly time consuming due to the complexity of cases submitted to it.[75]

Costs

Costs – monetary or otherwise – are often a decisive factor in choosing a dispute management process. The monetary costs of litigation depend on the size and the complexity of the case and consist of two main categories:

Retainer: an agreement by which a client contracts specific services from a lawyer in exchange for paying a fee.

1. Solicitor–client costs resulting from **retainer** governed by the contract between lawyer and client
2. Costs ordered by the court either on an ordinary basis (party/party costs) or on an indemnity basis (solicitor/client costs).

How those monetary costs are allocated at the end of the dispute is subject to broad discretion from the court. As a general rule, in Australia 'costs follow the event' – meaning that the party succeeding in the litigation can recover its costs from the losing party, although rarely in full. Indemnity costs are commonly awarded against a party whose unreasonable behaviour delayed the proceedings. For example, the refusal of a Calderbank offer for no reason may entitle the party making the offer to obtain indemnity costs at the end of the proceedings. Courts can also order interest on both damages and costs.

A defendant may ask the court to issue a security for a monetary costs order if there is indication that the plaintiff will not have funds to satisfy a costs order. If the court is satisfied from the totality of circumstances that ordering a security for costs is justified and the plaintiff fails to pay the security ordered, the court will stay the proceedings until the order is satisfied.

Other costs to consider are non-monetary and these can have long-term effects. They include the loss of business relationships, reputation, and emotional costs. These may be forgotten in the ferment of a dispute, perhaps because they are hard to put a monetary value on. However, they should not be ignored when assessing the best process to manage a dispute.

75 Thomas J Stipanowich, 'Arbitration: The New Litigation' (2010) (1) *University of Illinois Law Review* 1.

Res judicata and estoppel

Litigation, as a determinative process, is designed to end in a final and binding decision that stops the same claim from being raised again. Principles of *res judicata* and different types of estoppel were developed to support this finality. Triggered by the closing of a case, these principles have effect by restricting the possibility of initiating a new case. Unlike in arbitration, a court judgment binds every person, regardless of whether that person was a party to the dispute in which the judgment was rendered. These rules of public policy serve the public interest by preventing any party from re-litigating claims and re-opening matters that have been decided by a competent forum. *Res judicata* has the effect of turning a cause of action into judgment, as a result of which no court can allow for a subsequent proceeding on the same claim once this cause of action estoppel is raised as a defence.[76]

An issue estoppel, on the other hand, may be raised if a fact or issue has been decided in a previous case even if the cause of action has been different.[77] Finally, an Anshun estoppel may stop a party from litigating an issue that should have been raised in a previous case but wasn't. This latter estoppel is at the discretion of the court, which may allow for the proceedings if circumstances justify the failure to have raised those issues in the past litigation.[78]

The corresponding principle in criminal law is what is commonly called as 'double jeopardy'. While the term does not have a single meaning and can be applied at different stages of criminal proceedings,[79] the general principle is that no offender should be tried twice for the same offence. The common law principle, originating from three related principles of legal theory and reflected in state and territory legislation, is the subject of controversy.[80] Designed to secure the finality of verdicts and the reliability of the justice system, public opinion has been questioning its value when it comes to allegedly wrongful acquittals.[81] As a result, Criminal Codes and *Crimes Acts* have been amended in most States and Territories to allow, in the interest of justice, for someone to be charged anew for a serious offence, where previously they have been acquitted, if there is new and compelling evidence in the case.

The broader impact of *res judicata* and estoppel principles, as well as the binding precedent characteristic of judgments from superior courts, are all factors to consider when choosing between different processes. While an arbitral award may be easier to enforce internationally than a foreign court judgment, domestically it is only court judgments that will bind everyone and contribute to the development of common law. Similarly, although out-of-court settlement serves a public interest by reducing litigation costs to the parties, reducing the need to fund courts from taxpayers' money, and making courts more accessible by reducing their overall load, litigation also serves the public interest by performing a role that only the

76 See *Henderson v Henderson* (1843) 67 ER 313.

77 See *Carter v Walker* (2010) 32 VR 1.

78 See *BC v Minister for Immigration and Multicultural Affairs* [2002] FCAFC 221; *Ling v Commonwealth* (1996) 139 ALR 159.

79 *Pearce v The Queen* (1998) 194 CLR 610.

80 Andrew Haesler, 'The Rule Against Double Jeopardy' (Conference Paper, Lawyers Reform Association Seminar Series, 18 June 2003). These three principles are: the doctrine of *autrefois acquit* and convict acting as a defence to any new charge that is identical in fact and law; the rule that nobody should be tried twice on the same facts; and the principle that the court can prevent prosecution if it would result in an unfair trial.

81 See also Michelle Edgely, 'Truth or Justice? Double Jeopardy Reform for Queensland: Rights in Jeopardy' (2007) 7(1) *Queensland University of Technology Law and Justice Journal* 108.

judiciary and no other dispute management forum can: the constitutional function of developing and applying the common law.[82]

The public policy is to end disputes, hence in the eyes of the law a decision in litigation is designed to resolve the dispute. The question has to be asked: from whose perspective it is 'resolved'? Certainly, from society's perspective the legal system is designed to resolve or end disputes. However, if it is from the perspective of the parties, whether a winning or losing party, the real dispute that led to litigation may not have been resolved, but it has been managed. Whether other different disputes will open up between the parties based on unresolved conflicts between them remains a possibility.

Positives and negatives of litigation

Just like any dispute management process, litigation is neither the ultimate solution nor is it a forum to be avoided. According to extensive empirical studies conducted across several jurisdictions,[83] litigating in court is the exception in how people and businesses are most likely to handle their disputes. This raises the question as to why some initiate court proceedings while others do not. Large corporations may use litigation as part of a negotiating tactic, using the threat of court proceedings as leverage in moving the dispute forward out of court. However, more corporate institutions are realising the many advantages of not choosing to litigate.

Inexperienced disputants may initiate court proceedings due to lack of awareness of other options. The different objectives people hope to achieve also have an impact on whether to initiate and pursue litigation, with monetary claims making up the vast majority of litigated claims. Either way, initiating litigation does not necessarily mean that the litigation will proceed through the entire process, nor guarantee the desired outcome. Consequently, most initiated litigation is likely to be settled before trial.[84]

Whether litigation is appropriate for a certain dispute depends on many factors that will be specific to the individual dispute. The negative and positive characteristics must be compared to the negatives and positives of the range of other dispute management processes available.

Positives

A positive shift in how efficiently courts handle civil cases has occurred due to the introduction of case management. Active case management reduces costs and delays and improves access to justice by reducing case load and ensuring efficient use of judicial resources overall. On the other hand, case management reduces party control over litigation and puts the judge in a more proactive role, which has 'transform[ed] the judicial role from passive decision-maker to accountable manager of the justice system'.[85] This represents a move from the traditional perception of adversarialism towards a greater dispute management perspective.

82 See, eg, Michael Windeyer, 'Settlement in Court-Connected ADR and the Constitutional Function of the Judiciary: An Imbalance between Two Competing Public Interests' (2017) 28(2) *Australasian Dispute Resolution Journal* 135.

83 Astor and Chinkin (n 1) 44–49.

84 See, eg, David Lionel Spencer, 'The Vanishing Trial Phenomenon' (2005) 43(8) *Law Society Journal* 58.

85 Justice Ronald Sackville, 'From Access to Justice to Managing Justice: The Transformation of the Judicial Role' [2002] *Federal Judicial Scholarship* 9.

There were opinions that case management may undermine impartiality and that, by making case management more important than the parties' right to argue a claim and defence, case management will become a barrier to justice.[86] The overarching purpose for civil proceedings established in all jurisdictions[87] now renders the parties' right to justice on the merits of their dispute, subject to the overriding scope of an efficient justice administration. It puts the collective need for an efficient and trustworthy justice system, above the desire of the individual to use the court as a personal battlefield. Years after case management has been introduced in all Australian jurisdictions, it is safe to conclude that the discipline imposed through the timelines and sanctions available reduce abuse of process by disputants.

Despite the costs and time needed for litigation, and regardless of the advantages of other dispute management processes, litigation may be more suitable in some disputes. The incorporation of human rights principles in civil procedure through the right to a fair hearing[88] also aims to increase access to justice. Parties may not be capable of addressing a dispute due to the nature or history of the dispute, or due to their inability to negotiate, or the unavailability of a mutually acceptable outcome. In some cases, a party may have a strong legal case or right and therefore not be inclined to settle a matter. Minorities may feel a need to litigate to establish essential rights through a public judicial decision in their favour. In some cases, other dispute management processes may not be a solution because the outcome is relevant to others beyond the few direct parties to the dispute. For example, where a matter affects third parties, where a matter needs to be dealt with publicly or collectively (eg because there is need for public sanctioning of conduct), where the decision needs to have precedential value, or a point of law needs public clarification and certainty, private dispute management process may not be the best option.[89] In all these cases, litigation may not only be desirable, but the only avenue providing the desired outcome.

Negatives

Time and cost efficiency are the most frequently raised arguments against litigation and in favour of other dispute management processes. The increase of dispute management popularity and the adaptability to market- and user-demand of other processes do put courts in an unusual position. Their procedural rules are, in most cases, set in strict regulation that is not flexible and as easy to amend as the processes of private providers of dispute management services. Procedural reforms aimed at tackling excessive delays identified increased court control as a possible solution, coupled with **self-executing orders** to secure certainty and trust in the proceedings and avoid wasting public resources.

Self-executing order: an order dismissing a claim or a defence if the requesting party fails to comply with an instruction of the court within a set timeframe.

86 See Victorian Law Reform Commission (n 51).

87 See *Federal Court of Australia Act 1976* (Cth) s 37M(1); *Civil Procedure Act 2005* (NSW) s 56(1); *Civil Procedure Act 2010* (Vic) s 7; and reflected in the rules of civil procedure in all other States and Territories.

88 Originating from the *ICCPR*, the right to a fair hearing has been incorporated in the ACT and Victorian legislation.

89 See Chapter 3, 85.

There is a dichotomy between a need to lighten the load of courts in order to increase their efficiency and the desire to 'compete for more business',[90] which impacts on the way litigation procedure is handled. Empirical studies have revealed that despite an increase in population and the prediction that litigation will increase, the overall workload of courts has decreased.[91] The reasons behind this change may include introducing expedited procedures for commercial cases; shifting jurisdictions from higher courts to lower courts and tribunals; increase of class actions pulling together a large number of previously individual claims; an increase in litigation costs including growing legal fees; and an increase in the use of 'docket' systems. However, the predominant reason for this change is an increase in the use of dispute management, both outside of and incorporated in the court and tribunal systems, facilitating early settlement.

The technicalities of litigation procedure and the need for understanding and arguing the legal relevance of facts in order to make a strong claim or defence are also negatives of litigation (although the same can be said about all rights-based adversarial processes). While legal services are available as a principle, there are a significant number of self-represented litigants (SRL) in all courts, indicating that the cost of legal representation is unaffordable to many. Research suggests that the unaffordability of legal assistance renders litigation less effective overall.[92] Even though access to justice is not dependent on legal representation, Legal Aid arrangements can prove unsatisfactory, and litigating as SRL brings challenges both to the parties and to the judiciary. Many parties simply abandon their legal rights; some will pursue them on their own and struggle to find their place and way in the justice system.[93] Their counterparts experience increased costs and time spent due the SRL's lack of legal skills. Negotiation and litigation strategy are more difficult and settlements more rare when one of the parties is an SRL. Judges, on the other hand, experience their cases taking longer when they involve SRLs, and court staff struggle to balance their obligation of providing information against the SRL's need or expectation to receive legal advice.

Special considerations

Interim relief

Mareva injunction: a temporary order prohibiting a party from moving or disposing of assets until legal proceedings are completed.

Interim relief[94] is not common in civil litigation. A court may be asked to grant an injunctive relief to prevent the litigation from being frustrated either before or during proceedings. Injunctions may be requested for:

- prohibiting a party from acting in a certain way to preserve the *status quo* (prohibitory injunction). For example, freezing orders or **Mareva injunctions** are ordered to protect assets from being disposed of by the defendant.

90 Tania Sourdin, *Alternative Dispute Resolution* (Thomson Reuters, 5th ed, 2016) 296.

91 Ibid.

92 Liz Richardson et al, *The Impacts of Self-Represented Litigants on Civil and Administrative Justice: Environmental Scan of Research, Policy and Practice* (Australasian Institute of Judicial Administration, 2018).

93 Senate Legal and Constitutional References Committee, Parliament of Australia, *Legal Aid and Access to Justice* (Report, June 2004) 181; see also James Goh, 'The Self-Represented Litigants' Challenge: A Case Study' 43(1) *Alternative Law Journal* 48.

94 For more on interim reliefs, see Chapter 10 'Interim measures'.

- ordering a party to perform a certain act (mandatory injunction). For example, search orders, also called Anton Piller orders, are made for preliminary discovery, allowing the requesting party to enter the other party's premises and inspect, remove, or copy documents that might form evidence.

The applicant needs to demonstrate that there is a serious question of law in dispute, that granting the injunction is favoured by the balance of convenience, and that damages would not be an adequate remedy. The applicant will also have to provide an 'undertaking as to damages', promising to compensate the defendant for damages suffered as a result of the injunction if the injunction proves to have been unjustified. Applications for an injunctive relief are commonly made without notice to the other party and in an emergency regime.

Class actions

Class action: a claim brought by a plaintiff on behalf of a group of people who could all file individual claims against the same defendant in relation to the same issue.

Class actions are a peculiar construction and type of litigation involving groups as parties. While this could have been discussed under the heading 'Parties and causes of action', class actions are so unique and out-of-the-ordinary proceedings that they do not warrant a place within ordinary litigation theory and procedure.

Class actions have been introduced to Australia as a federal representative proceeding regime through the *Federal Court of Australia Act 1976* (Cth), followed much later by Victoria from 2000,[95] New South Wales since 2011[96] and Queensland starting from 2017.[97] A class action requires three cumulative conditions to be satisfied:

1. seven or more persons to have claims against the same person
2. the claims of all those persons to be in respect of, or arise out of, the same, similar or related circumstances
3. the claims of all those persons to give rise to a substantial common issue of law or fact.

The main characteristics of the Australian class action regime are:

- unlike in the United States, Canada, and England and Wales, in Australia there is no certification requirement (ie the proceedings do not have to be judicially certified as appropriate to be brought as a class action)
- individual or 'sub-group' issues are allowed within a class action, with no requirement that the common issues predominate over the individual ones
- class members may be defined by description, rendering every individual that fits that description a class member, unless they opt out of the proceedings
- class members are immune from having costs orders rendered against them in case the respondent prevails in the proceedings, which may only recover costs from the lead applicant.[98]

95 *Supreme Court Act 1986* (Vic) pt 4A.
96 *Civil Procedure Act 2005* (NSW) pt 10.
97 *Civil Proceedings Act 2011* (Qld) pt 13A.
98 See Colin Loveday and Andrew Morton, 'Australia' in Caroline Collingwood (ed), *ICLG: The International Comparative Legal Guide to Class & Group Actions* (Global Legal Group, 10th ed, 2018) 18–24. Available at <https://www.claytonutz.com/articledocuments/178/ICLG-Class-and-Group-Actions-Australia-2017.pdf.aspx?Embed=Y>.

Costs and funding are key drivers in the development of the class action regime. As the Law Reform Commission noted in the recent *Inquiry into Class Action Proceedings and Third-Party Litigation Funders*

> ... as the class action regime has matured, commercial third-party litigation funding has become a particular feature of the Australian class action landscape. Litigation funding has largely filled the lacuna created by the absence of a satisfactory mechanism to protect principal applicants from adverse costs orders.[99]

Given the costs of litigation, there are several ways in which a plaintiff or a group of plaintiffs can fund their endeavour to seek justice through court, as third-party funding of claims is permitted in Australia.

Conditional cost agreements are permitted within certain limits. Law firms often offer 'no win, no fee' agreements to both individual and group members who could otherwise not afford to pay legal fees. Under this construction, the fees are only payable in case of a win, while if the case is lost the client will not have to pay the lawyer. The retainer agreement may include a provision for payment of an 'uplift' fee in addition to professional costs in case of win, but such arrangements are only permitted under strict court supervision. Contingency fees, characteristic to the United States, where a percentage of the total amount won is taken by the lawyer, were traditionally not permitted in Australia. Victoria recently moved to allow lawyers to charge contingency fees in class actions, an initiative condemned by the Law Council, arguing that the system would 'adversely affect litigants' interests and lawyers' ethical duties'.[100]

The prohibition on contingency fees does not apply to litigation funders that have no prior interest in the proceeding. Third-party funding is a profitable industry specialised in investing in litigation, especially in class actions. Funding agreements are commercial contracts under which the funding organisation advances all costs of litigation and agrees to cover any adverse costs orders in exchange for a percentage of any amount obtained through judgment or settlement after the costs of the proceedings have been reimbursed.

Although in principle the availability of third-party funding constructions should make the justice system more accessible, litigation funding is an investment that does not assist small litigants. Conditional cost arrangements make litigation more accessible for those who do not represent an attractive investment for external funders, but those services are dependent on law firms. Litigation insurance is not common, but is available, for example, as an 'adverse costs insurance'.

Cross-border litigation

Cross-border disputes pose a particular challenge when choosing a suitable dispute management process. International arbitration, only available for commercial disputes and settlements originating from international mediation, may or may not be enforceable where

99 Australian Law Reform Commission, *Integrity, Fairness and Efficiency – An Inquiry into Class Action Proceedings and Third-Party Litigation Funders* (Report No 134, December 2018) 49.

100 Law Council of Australia, 'Contingency Fees Opposed by Law Council' (Media Release, 13 March 2020).

needed.[101] Therefore, if a binding outcome that can be enforced across borders is needed, litigation may be the only remaining avenue to consider. Cross-border litigation is an area of law not intended to be covered within this textbook. Aspects that are relevant to this chapter include service outside of the jurisdiction of any Australian court, transnational interim injunctions, obtaining evidence from Australia for foreign proceedings, and the enforcement of foreign judgments in Australia.

All Australian courts have rules permitting service outside their jurisdiction, but the criteria and the procedures vary between jurisdictions. Service overseas may be done through diplomatic channels or based on the *Hague Convention on Service Abroad of Judicial and Extrajudicial Documents in Civil and Commercial Matters 1965*,[102] reflected in the legislation of most states and territories.

Transnational freezing orders may refer to foreign assets in aid of Australian litigation (worldwide orders) or to Australian assets in aid of foreign litigation. Australian courts may also take evidence for foreign proceedings, under the *Hague Convention on the Taking of Evidence Abroad in Civil or Commercial Matters 1970* (*Hague Evidence Convention*).

Finally, the enforcement of foreign judgments in Australia is governed by both statutory provisions in the *Foreign Judgments Act 1991* (Cth) (for money judgments) and common law principles (for non-monetary judgments). Enforcement also depends on the origin of the foreign judgment. Australia has reciprocal agreements for the enforcement of judgments with 35 countries listed in the *Foreign Judgments Regulations 1992* and is a party to the bilateral treaty for the *Reciprocal Recognition and Enforcement of Judgments in Civil and Commercial Matters 1994* with the United Kingdom. Australia is not party to the *Hague Convention on the Recognition and Enforcement of Foreign Judgments in Civil and Commercial Matters 1971* – which has only five parties.[103] At the time of writing this chapter, the new *Hague Convention on the Recognition and Enforcement of Foreign Judgments in Civil or Commercial Matters 2019* has not yet entered into force.

Foreign judgments that do not fall under statutory provisions or an international treaty may be enforced under common law principles if the Australian court is satisfied that the foreign court has exercised proper jurisdiction. The defendant may object to the enforcement if it can demonstrate that the judgment was obtained by fraud, is contrary to Australian public policy, or it was rendered in breach of principles of natural justice.

Conclusion

Overall, litigation can be perceived as one of two opposite extremes, depending on one's personal and educational background: either it is the only real avenue to obtain access to justice, or it is the most damaging process humans could utilise in addressing disputes. Even in a litigious, adversarial society, litigation is rarely liked or praised by anyone else other than a

101 The *United Nations Convention on International Settlement Agreements Resulting from Mediation*, opened for signature 7 August 2019 (entered into force 12 September 2020) is too young to have its effectiveness tested in practice.

102 *Convention on the Service Abroad of Judicial and Extrajudicial Documents in Civil or Commercial Matters*, opened for signature 15 November 1965 (entered into force 11 February 1969).

103 Information correct as of 14 February 2021.

subset of legal professionals. This dislike is not the dislike of disputes in general, but rather of litigation itself, as other dispute management processes are commonly accepted as valuable and useful experiences by disputing parties and by society at large.

In reality, litigation is neither a miracle solution nor a damnation to avoid at all costs. It is a triadic determinative process constantly shaped and fine-tuned over centuries to serve individuals and society. It is evident from this chapter that this has resulted in it being a highly ordered, formal, and legalised process. The growing recognition and emphasis on other processes forced the system to 'compete' for disputes to manage. This has meant an improvement in its efficiency and processes, while maintaining the credibility of the constitutional system and maintaining the Rule of Law. Understanding the process and the ultimate scope it serves can help see litigation as one option that parties can use to manage their dispute.

EXERCISE IN APPLYING YOUR KNOWLEDGE – *MEMBERS OF LIVING LAND V THE HORNET*

The Hornet of Truth (also called *The Hornet*) is an exclusively online investigative newspaper priding itself for publishing fact-checked news, whistle blower statements and leaked documents related to crimes and controversial events from rural and regional Australia. It mainly focuses on medium and small towns under the motto 'Don't be blinded by big city lights, also notice the small-town crimes!'

In the issue of 10 February, *The Hornet* published an article claiming to be based on confidential information leaked by an employee of the Murrumbidgee Council in Northern New South Wales. Excerpt of the article reads as follows:

> **A wolf in a sheep's skin, Living Land adopts illegal methods to pursue allegedly noble goals.**
>
> The activist group Living Land has been pushing producers in regional NSW and Queensland to adopt allegedly 'land-friendly' methods in their large-scale farming despite farmers' arguments that the methods they advocate for are neither feasible nor sustainable at that scale. At the latest AGM, the members of Living Land (registered as a not-for-profit organisation) have voted to use the 1 Million Dollars they recently secured from a private sponsor to 'lobby' the Muckross Council to impose restrictions on the water use of Eden. Eden is the largest farm in the region, owned by the Carmichael family – one of the oldest and most respected families in the area and, not accidentally, one of the most influential opponents of the methods advocated by Living Land. Attempting to bribe members of Council to force the hands of the Carmichaels stands contrary to the moral and ethical values the group claims, but actions speak louder than words.

As a result of this article, several families that were known to be active members of Living Land were exposed to aggressive verbal attacks by workers employed by Eden, received anonymous death threats, and even had their small organic farms vandalised during the night. One such family that feared for the safety of their small children in this heated environment left to stay at a relative in Brisbane until the issue is sorted.

Those affected approached *The Hornet* through a collective letter sent to the only email contact available on *The Hornet's* website, asking the newspaper to publish a rectification and apology clarifying that Living Land openly advocates for water restrictions as necessary to maintain the health of the river that serves the entire region; that no bribe was ever offered or given by Living Land or its members to anyone; and that small farmers that signed up as members of Living Land are there to share knowledge and resources in sustainable farming and have no decision-making power, which is held by the NGO's Board of Directors.

The Hornet did not respond to the request. In the following edition, however, the Editor-in-Chief, Mr Long, included a short follow-up in the Editorial when stating that

> It is thanks to *The Hornet* and its revealing investigations that criminals like the infamous Living Land group end up implicitly admitting their shady businesses by running from the consequences of their own actions, like rats run from water clearing and feeding the land they claim to protect.

In the days following this editorial, a small experimental permaculture farm was severely damaged by a fire lit by unidentified individuals. The arsonists left a note splashed across the main house's front wall in red paint, saying 'DEAD RATS IN LIVING LAND'.

A group of the families affected by these events, including the owners of the burned-down permaculture, approached you to help them put together a legal action against *The Hornet*. They want to claim damages for defamation from both the newsletter and Mr Long, the Editor-in-Chief. Initial investigation revealed the following: the company owning *The Hornet* is registered in Toowoomba, Queensland, at an address where there is only an empty old house. It is likely that all employees of the newspaper work remotely, given the exclusively online nature of the business. The owners of the company appear to be Mr Long himself and a certain Ms Duffy, both having their residential address at 87 Sunset Pl in Ipswich, Brisbane. *The Hornet* does not seem to have any considerable assets, but Mr Long appears to be the owner of an exclusive spa centre run by his girlfriend. Rumour has it, they are in the process of transferring the spa centre to the girlfriend's name.

The questions and issues you face are the following:

1. Is litigation the best option to attempt to manage this dispute. Justify your answer. What other processes could usefully be adopted?
2. Could the small group initiate class action for defamation on behalf of all members of Living Land?
3. Which court would have jurisdiction over the defamation action?
4. Describe all the documents, along with their purpose, that can be used in the litigation process and that would be necessary in this case.
5. How could *The Hornet* be validly served with the claim?
6. Can the assets of Mr Long be frozen to serve as security for a later enforcement? If so, what would the process and conditions be for such an order?

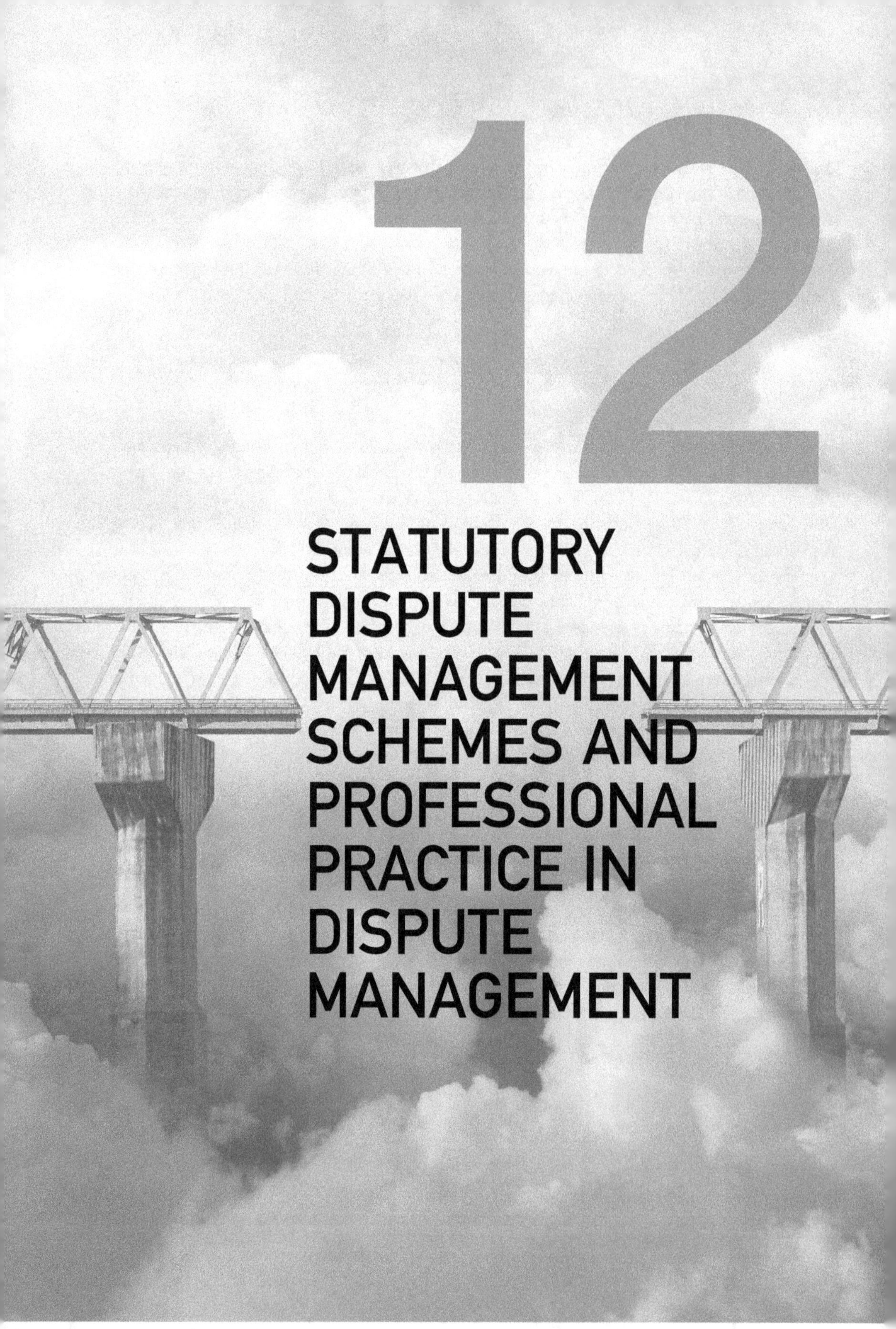

12 STATUTORY DISPUTE MANAGEMENT SCHEMES AND PROFESSIONAL PRACTICE IN DISPUTE MANAGEMENT

Learning aims

- Demonstrate awareness of statutory dispute management schemes
- Describe how statutory schemes may differentiate from other process
- Explain how statutory schemes fit in the overall management of disputes
- Apply a specified statutory scheme to practical scenarios
- Demonstrate understanding of the different roles, and obligations across dispute management practice

Understanding statutory dispute management schemes

It should now be apparent from this textbook that most dispute management processes are subject to party autonomy, with disputing parties voluntarily engaging in processes that appear to be most suitable (and are available) for that type of dispute. However, not all dispute management processes are a matter of free choice. For certain types of disputes regulated by mandatory statutory provisions, choice is restricted or non-existent. Chapter 8 provided insight into a statutory scheme used by the Administrative Appeals Tribunal (AAT) to describe conciliation. Similarly, the substantive arbitrability section of Chapter 10 showed that some disputes are retained in the exclusive jurisdiction of courts. Overall, statutory dispute management means that some disputes can only be addressed through a predetermined process as prescribed by mandatory statutory provisions regulating the field in which the dispute may arise.

Some of the statutory schemes are not determinative, leaving the outcome to be consent dependent. In others, not only the process, but the outcome as well are equally enforceable. This chapter will provide an overview of some of the statutory schemes that exist in Australia. The main statutory dispute management processes used to show how these schemes and the voluntary methods supplement each other to create an effective and efficient dispute management system will be determinative. Other statutory schemes will also be presented to the extent of their specific legislative framework, scope, and brief process.

The last part of the chapter will end this textbook by providing insight into the practical aspects of working as a dispute management practitioner: the roles and jobs available, the qualification and accreditation requirements for those roles, and the good and bad parts of practising in a rewarding, but demanding field.

Using theory and models to dissect statutory dispute management schemes

Theory

Statutory dispute management describes a particular prescribed method for a particular type of dispute. The range of disputes for which statutory schemes are prescribed is constantly evolving, as are the types of schemes and the processes that are preferred by the scheme. As such, if a scheme adopts a particular process, such as conciliation or mediation, then the key theory underpinning those processes is to be found in the chapters that deal with these processes. For this reason, this section will only cover the scope and legislative objective of some of the schemes, the particularities of the statutory process, and the expected outcome these schemes provide.

Models

This section cannot provide one fundamental model but instead provides an overview of some of the different models adopted by different statutory schemes.

Adjudication of payment claims in the building industry

A triadic determinative statutory dispute management process is available for parties claiming payment for construction work or related goods or services provided. Under a scheme called 'security of payment' (SOP), claims for payments owed under a construction contract are subject to adjudication according to the *Building and Construction Industry Security of Payment Acts* of each State and Territory.[1] The adjudicator is a third-party neutral specifically trained to decide construction payment claims within the narrow scope of the Acts. As such, they are not a judge or a general court. Which State's law governs the adjudication is determined by the place where the construction work is carried out, not by the place of the contract or that of the parties. Ultimately, the purpose of construction adjudication is to enable a fast and efficient management of disputes without the need to resort to lengthy and expensive litigation, but without depriving the parties of the opportunity to access a determinative process.[2]

Progress payment: a payment to which a person is entitled for having completed a predetermined part or the entirety of a construction work contracted.

Pay when paid: contract clauses that make payment of a subcontractor due only when the main contractor has been paid.

Adjudication exists separately and in addition to any dispute management processes included in the contract. The Acts do not allow opt-out contractual agreements from adjudication. As a statutory scheme, adjudication is the dispute management process for such claims even if it is not included in the construction contract on which the claim is based. The Acts also provides for a statutory right to **progress payments**, regardless of whether such progress payments are provided for in the contract and does not allow for '**pay when paid**' provisions. Accordingly, the obligation to pay originates from statute and the adjudicator only certifies the amount to be paid, if any. The Acts have a broad application, even when there is no actual contract between the parties on the construction work provided. The statutory scheme enables a party that is entitled to receive payment to obtain that payment through a fast, inexpensive, and simplified procedure.

1 *Building and Construction Industry (Security of Payment) Act 2009* (ACT); *Building and Construction Industry Security of Payment Act 1999* (NSW); *Construction Contracts (Security of Payments) Act 2010 (NT); Building Industry Fairness (Security of Payment) Act 2017* (Qld); *Building and Construction Security of Payment Act 2009* (SA); *Building and Construction Industry Security of Payments Act 2009* (Tas); *Building and Construction Industry Security of Payment Act 2002* (Vic); *Construction Contracts Act 2004* (WA).

2 See, eg, *Building Industry Fairness (Security of Payment) Act 2017* (Qld) s 78(2), which allows for the choice between recovering the amount owed in court or applying for the adjudication of the amount owed.

Contributing to the cost efficiency is that in adjudication the parties are not always legally represented. As such, they will not always be able to make or use legal arguments and principles that may be relevant to their case. The adjudicator, although not necessarily qualified as a lawyer, is expected to have sufficient knowledge of relevant legal concepts and basic principles of contract law to make an appropriate determination. This, however, does not make the adjudication an inquisitorial process. The adjudicator is not allowed to rely on cases, facts or analysis that were not raised by the parties; nor should the adjudicator decide the value of work based on their own experience instead of the parties' submissions.[3] 'The express obligation [of the adjudicator] is "to decide", not "to inquire".'[4] This puts a significant onus on the parties to the adjudication to justify their claims and defences, both in facts and in law. The absence of legal representation is often counterbalanced by the fact that parties in adjudication are frequently trained and experienced in the construction industry, including payment obligations and related disputes.

Adjudication follows a strict sequence of procedural steps prescribed by the applicable Act. As such it is not the same as a normal litigation process, but it is transformed into a much more simplified stylised adjudication. In particular, the adjudication application must be preceded by a **payment claim** sent by the claimant to the respondent. If the respondent does not intend to pay the full amount claimed by the date claimed, the respondent must serve a **payment schedule** to avoid the statutory debt that would arise under the Act. If the respondent fails to serve a payment schedule, the respondent becomes liable for the claim. If the respondent fails to pay the amount claimed, the claimant can submit an application for adjudication to an Authorised Nominating Authority (ANA) within the timeframes provided by the applicable Act.

Payment claim: a document requesting payment that identifies the amount claimed, the construction work to which the amount relates. An invoice can be a payment claim.

The claimant must submit all documents relevant to deciding the claim, and only those documents properly referred to in the written submission. The claimant must demonstrate that the amount of progress payment claimed is owed and the respondent's failure to engage in the process does not lead to a default decision in favour of the claimant. The claimant must also demonstrate that the construction work contracted was carried out and was not paid, the work has the value claimed, and that a payment claim and the adjudication application were served on the respondent. In this sense, adjudication is similar to arbitration, where the respondent's failure to respond does not automatically imply acceptance of the facts and claims presented by the claimant.

Payment schedule: a document responding to a payment claim that identifies the amount the respondent proposes to pay (if any) and if the proposed payment is less than the amount claimed, includes the reasons for the difference.

The respondent that has been served with an adjudication application and a notice of acceptance by an adjudicator can file an adjudication response within the timeframe provided in the applicable Act. This response, however, can only be made if the respondent has provided a payment schedule and cannot include reasons that were not raised in the payment schedule. This does not mean that the adjudication response must be a mere copy of the previous payment schedule. The respondent may argue that the claimant is not entitled to the amount claimed for reasons set out in the payment schedule, as long as the

3 *Ostwald Brothers Pty Ltd v Jaylon Pacific Pty Ltd* [2016] QSC 240.
4 *Bezzina Developers Pty Ltd v Deemah Stone (Qld) Pty Ltd* [2008] 2 Qd R 495, [34].

payment schedule includes reports, test results, or any material evidence of the defects in work completed. The claimant cannot respond to the adjudication response; its response, if any, had to be made to the payment schedule. In this regard, the procedural steps of the adjudication are far more limited than in litigation processes.

A qualified and independent adjudicator nominated by the ANA will assess the merits of the claim most commonly based on documentary evidence only. The process is subject to strict time limits that cannot be extended. The aim of the scheme is to provide for fast and effective management of claims by being more informal and restricted in time and therefore less expensive. The adjudicator will value the works and services provided, interpret the construction contract, decide issues of law, and whether the work performed complies with the requirements of the construction contract. The adjudicator is authorised to carry out an inspection, although such inspections are rarely needed in practice. Since adjudicators cannot rely on their own expertise to interpret results, they prefer to rely on an expert report provided by a party to better understand the submissions. The adjudicator may call for a conference with the parties; however, these are equally rare.[5]

The adjudicator's decision, also called a 'determination', governs the amount to be paid by the respondent to the claimant, the date at which this payment must be made, and the interest rate applicable to the amount payable. The adjudicator must also decide whether the claim is frivolous or vexatious and whether they have jurisdiction to adjudicate the application, regardless of whether either of these were raised by the respondent. The determination may also include a decision on the allocation of the adjudication costs (the fees of the nominating authority and the fees of the adjudicator) between the parties. An adjudication decision must be reasoned, setting out the steps through which the decision was reached,[6] although the extent of reasoning required is less than that of a judgment. No matter how much work the adjudicator invested in deciding the case, the parties will only see the adjudicator's competence and reasoning from the decision, which must be limited to the analysis of the claims, the relevant Act, and the evidence provided.

The parties may settle the dispute at any time during the adjudication and they may (but are not required to) ask the adjudicator to render a decision reflecting their settlement. The adjudicator will be entitled to fees and expenses even if the matter did not result in a determination due to the parties' withdrawal or settlement. However, an adjudicator who fails to make a determination within the legal framework (generally of 10 business days) will not be entitled to the adjudicator fee or any expenses that they could otherwise claim from the partiers. The adjudicator may even be ordered to repay the fees paid by claimant.[7] The parties may, however, reinstate the adjudicator and allow for additional time to complete the adjudication instead of commencing a new one with a different adjudicator. In case the adjudicator withdraws from the appointment, the matter must be referred to another adjudicator. The strict procedural steps and extremely short timeframes are uniquely characteristic to the adjudication process adopted with a view to promote cash flow in the construction industry. Comparable procedure among the dispute management processes covered in this textbook exist only in

5 See Philip Davenport, *Adjudication in the Building Industry* (Federation Press, 3rd ed, 2010).

6 *Bauen Constructions v Westwood Interiors* (2010) 28 BCL 153, [22].

7 *Galaxy Development Pty Ltd v Civil Contractors (Australia) Pty Ltd* [2020] QSC 51.

applications for interim measures of protection in arbitration or litigation processes or in expedited arbitration[8] (although the latter does not follow quite such short timeframes as those in adjudication.)

Farm debt mediation

Farm debt is another area that is subject to a statutory dispute management scheme regulated in a more-or-less consistent way across the Australian States and Territories. In New South Wales,[9] Queensland,[10] South Australia,[11] and Victoria,[12] farm debt mediation makes it compulsory for banks and other creditors to attempt to manage debt claims through mediation before attempting debt recovery on farm mortgages. The same process is available through a voluntary scheme in Western Australia. There is no farm debt mediation scheme currently in place in the Northern Territory, Tasmania, and the ACT.

The scheme applies only to mortgages covering a farm, farm machinery, or water share. What constitutes a farm for the purposes of farm debt mediation, has been defined in a broad sense, including, for example, micro-scale migratory bee-keeping.[13] The statutory mediation scheme is administered by the Rural Assistance Authority in New South Wales, the Rural and Industry Development Authority (QRIDA) in Queensland, the Small Business Commissioner in South Australia, the Department of Economic Development, Jobs, Transport and Resources (DEDJTR) in Victoria, and the Small Business Development Corporation (SBDC) in Western Australia.

Farm debt mediation may be initiated by both the farmer and the creditor, usually a bank. The process is one of voluntary, structured negotiation assisted by a neutral and independent mediator recognised by the administering authority. The mediator facilitates the conversation between the farmer and the creditor in an attempt to reach agreement on current and future debt arrangements. Farmers are recommended to obtain independent financial and legal advice before entering the mediation. Rural financial counsellors are commonly experienced in advising and supporting farmers in farm debt mediation. Guarantors to the farm mortgage must also be informed and involved in the farm debt mediation.

Farm debt mediation is based on the facilitative mediation model,[14] with the mediator not providing any advice or recommendation on the matter in dispute. In this sense, there is no difference between farm debt mediation and any other mediation. Likewise, the process's success depends on whether the parties engage in the mediation. The only difference between farm debt and any other mediation is in farm debt mediation being imposed by legislation in order to protect the special interests of farmers. Due to this statutory nature, agreements reached through farm debt mediation may be submitted for internal review by the administering authority.

8 See Chapter 10, 'Interim Measures'.
9 *Farm Debt Mediation Act 1994* (NSW).
10 *Farm Business Debt Mediation Act 2017* (Qld).
11 *Farm Debt Mediation Act 2018* (SA).
12 *Farm Debt Mediation Act 2011* (Vic).
13 *Secure Funding Pty Ltd v Bee* [2016] NSWSC 521.
14 See Chapter 6.

Native title claims

Native title disputes are dealt with in accordance with the principle that special types of disputes have their own dispute management mechanism designated by statute. Native title is fundamentally different from land rights created through legislation enacted by State and Territory governments. Land rights consist in a freehold or perpetual lease title granted by government, while native title is a common-law based recognition of pre-existing Indigenous rights and interests in ownership of land prior to the arrival of the British colonists.[15] As these Indigenous rights and interests originate from traditional laws and customs, they also vary between Indigenous communities. The organisations and government bodies created to work on the recognition of these rights reflect the complexity of this environment.

The title of Indigenous Australians over their land according to their laws and customs was first recognised as a result of a claim lodged by a group of Meriam people from the Eastern Torres Strait to the High Court in 1982 seeking recognition of exclusive occupation and possession of Murray Island. The landmark 1992 judgment in *Mabo v Queensland*[16] served the basis for Commonwealth legislature response in the form of the *Native Title Act 1993* (Cth), establishing the National Native Title Tribunal (NNTT) and a process for claiming and recognising native title lands and waters. The role of the Tribunal, through the statutory functions of its President and Members, consists of:

- arbitral decision-making
- administrative decision-making
- conducting inquiries
- conducting mediations
- conducting reviews
- assisting parties with agreements to settle applications
- assisting parties to negotiate Indigenous land use agreements (ILUAs)
- assisting representative Aboriginal and Torres Strait Islander Bodies under the Act.[17]

The process crosses the range through negotiation to a final determination and may conclude in settlement at any stage. The procedural steps, however, are strictly regulated. A native title determination application filed in the Federal Court is sent to the Native Title Registrar at the NNTT to be 'registration tested'. This means it is to be verified whether the claim satisfies the 12 conditions set out in the NTA regarding both the form of the application and the substance of the claim.[18] If the claim passes the test, it becomes a 'registered claim' in the Register of Native Title Claims. The application must provide evidence that the claiming group has a 'traditional physical connection' to the area, continues to observe traditional laws and customs that give rise to the rights and interests the group wants recognised, and those traditional rights

15 See Chapter 3.

16 *Mabo v Queensland (No 2)* (1992) 175 CLR 1.

17 See National Native Title Tribunal, *Tribunal's Role: Overview of the NNTT* (Web Page) <http://www.nntt.gov.au/aboutus/Pages/default.aspx>.

18 See National Native Title Tribunal, *Native Title Claimant Applications: A Guide to Understanding the Requirements of the Registration Test* (Web Page) <http://www.nntt.gov.au/Information%20Publications/Native%20Title%20Claimant%20Applications_Registration%20Test.pdf>.

must be recognised by Australian law. A 2015 review of the *Native Title Act* led to the recommendation to abolish the 'traditional physical connection' condition from the registration test as inconsistent with case law and 'the reality of the lives of Aboriginal and Torres Strait Islander people who have moved away from their country in order to access employment, health services and education'[19] but this recommendation is yet to be applied in practice. The registration of the claim gives important rights to the claiming group, like the right to enter into negotiations.

The NNTT will notify the local government about a native title claim over a territory falling within that council's area, informing the local government about how to become a respondent party to the claim. The council must inform the Tribunal whether it wants to become a respondent. If all respondents are satisfied with the evidence and the proposed way their specific interests will be recognised, the parties may propose a consent determination. If the parties cannot reach agreement, the court will hear evidence in trial and make a final determination. If a determination is made that native title exists with regard to a particular area, the details of this determination will be entered into the National Native Title Register.

If a claim is unsuccessful or is withdrawn from the NNTT, it may still be decided through 'alternative settlement'. Alternative settlements can include native title and non-native title outcomes and can provide for traditional owner group recognition in areas where native title rights have been extinguished, or where it is difficult for a group to prove that native title persists.[20]

Accordingly, these are alternatives outside of the native title determination framework under the NNTT. Alternative settlement agreements are regulated under state and territory legislation[21] that do not replace the NTA but provide an alternative legal basis for recognising traditional rights and interests negotiated by Indigenous communities outside of the NNTT. Alternative settlements can take the form of negotiated settlements or Indigenous Land Use Agreements (ILUAs). A special characteristic of ILUAs is that they are registered and bind all persons holding a native title, regardless of whether they are parties to the Agreement or not.[22]

Native title claims are managed and lodged by native title representative bodies (NTRBs) and native title service providers (NTSPs) collectively also called 'rep bodies'. These were also created through the *Native Title Act* and are administered by the Minister for Indigenous Affairs. Prescribed Bodies Corporate (PBC), on the other hand, are corporations established by native title holders to manage and protect the native rights and interests. PBCs are incorporated under the *Corporations (Aboriginal and Torres Strait Islander Act) 2006* (Cth).[23] Native title claim groups can either create a new PCB or nominate an existing one to manage their native title interests. While these 'prescribed bodies' have certain obligations determined under the *Native Title Act*, their form and activity will depend on the traditional laws and customs, the location, and the size of the native title group for which they were created. PBCs must be

19 Australian Law Reform Commission, *Connection to Country: Review of the Native Title Act 1993 (Cth)* (Report No 126, April 2015) 182.

20 See Bryan Keon-Cohen, 'From "land-related agreements" to "comprehensive settlements" to "domestic treaties": An Inevitable Progression?' (2018) (January) *Pandora's Box* 43.

21 See, eg, *Traditional Owner Settlement Act 2010* (Vic).

22 See Native Title Tribunal, *About Indigenous Land Use Agreements (ILUAS)* (2014).

23 *Corporations (Aboriginal and Torres Strait Islander) Act 2006* (Cth) (CATSI Act).

registered with the National Native Title Tribunal, becoming a Registered Native Title Bodies Corporate (RNTBC) holding native title rights as a trustee or as agent for traditional owners. Despite the name change designed to identify these organisations as a corporation managing native title, they are commonly still simply called PBCs.

The primary role of RNTBCs is 'to manage and protect native title on behalf of the native title holders [and] to consult with and obtain consent from traditional owners in regards to any decisions that surrender or affect native title rights and interests'. They are

> [t]he first point of contact for government and other parties wishing to undertake activities on native title land. It acts as a bridge for traditional owners to deal with the non-Indigenous legal system, and ensures certainty for government and other parties by providing a legal entity through which they can conduct business with traditional owners.[24]

Their six primary functions are identified by the *Native Title Act* as:

1. facilitation and assistance (s 203BB)
2. certification (s 203BE)
3. dispute resolution (s 203BF)
4. notification (s 203BG)
5. agreement making (s 203BH)
6. internal review (s 203BI).[25]

The facilitation and assistance functions include preparing native title applications and to assist native title holders in consultations, mediations, negotiations and proceedings. The 'dispute resolution' functions include dispute management approaches like mediating and promoting agreement between constituents. Under the agreement making function, an RNTBC is a party to ILUAs. These functions can also be performed by statutory and non-statutory bodies and alternative service providers. Corporations that have negotiated a native title outcome through alternative settlement without a native title determination are called Traditional Owner Corporations (TOCs).

Clearly, a dispute practitioner operating in this area would require detailed training in the specialised nature of native title claims and a good level of cultural communication awareness.[26] The Attorney-General's Department can provide respondent councils involved in native title claims with assistance. It also 'provide[s] the government with legal and legal-policy advice on native title [and] also assist[s] the Attorney-General to administer the Native Title Act 1993'.[27] In 2019, the Attorney-General introduced the *Native Title Legislation*

24 Prescribed Body Corporate, *About PBCs* (Web Page) <https://nativetitle.org.au/learn/role-and-function-pbc/about-pbcs>.

25 Parliamentary Joint Committee on Native Title and the Aboriginal and Torres Strait Islander Land Account, Parliament of Australia, *Report on the Operation of Native Title Representative Bodies* (Report, March 2006).

26 See Chapter 1 and Chapter 2.

27 See Australian Government Attorney-General's Department, *Native Title* (Web Page) <https://www.ag.gov.au/legal-system/native-title>.

Amendment Bill 2020[28] with the aim to 'improve native title claims resolution, agreement-making, Indigenous decision-making and dispute management processes'.[29] The National Indigenous Australians Agency (NIAA) was also created in 2019 to implement government policies related to indigenous people. As part of this scope, the NIAA funds 14 NTRBs and NTSPs. It also hosts the indigenous.gov.au website created to connect Aboriginal and Torres Strait Islander people with relevant programs and policies of the Australian Government. Finally, the National Native Title Council (NNTC) is a non-profit membership organisation made up of regional NTRBs and NTSPs, local PBCs and TOCs.

Ombudsman complaints

Ombudsmen provide a process for the public to raise concerns about the way they have been treated by government agencies or private industry bodies, as part of a statutory scheme to manage complaints that can lead to disputes. Ombudsmen are independent agencies originating from a Swedish system providing the first formal recognition of the institution through its incorporation in the *Swedish Constitution* in 1809.[30] As the New South Wales Ombudsman Office states on its website, '[l]oosely translated, the word 'ombudsman' means "the citizen's defender" or "representative of the people",' independent from government and 'accountable to the public through Parliament itself'.[31] Beyond the handling of individual complaints, the office of an ombudsman is also expected to perform a 'critical scrutiny of public administration'[32] thereby contributing to the improvement of the organisations against which individual complaints may be formulated by the public.

Today, specialist ombudsmen are set up for each area of potential concern, separately for the public and the private sphere. Government ombudsmen are established at both Federal and State levels, each under its own relevant legislation.[33] The Office of the Commonwealth Ombudsman 'is a unique administrative law institution which falls between the standard constitutional classifications of government into judicial, legislative and executive [...] is concerned with individual complainants it acts reactively to correct defective government administration but it also has a proactive role where it assists public agencies to administering their affairs'.[34]

The Commonwealth Ombudsman investigates actions taken by Commonwealth service providers as if they were actions of the relevant government department itself. It also acts as the ombudsman for the Defence Force, Immigration, the Postal Industry, Law Enforcement,

28 At the time of writing this book, the Bill has passed both Houses.

29 Australian Government Attorney-General's Department, *Native Title* (Web Page) <https://www.ag.gov.au/legal-system/native-title>.

30 See Commonwealth Ombudsman, *Commonwealth Ombudsman Annual Report 2008-09* (2009) 137. See also Sabine Carl, 'The History and Evolution of the Ombudsman Model' in Marc Hertog and Richard Kirkham (eds), *Research Handbook on the Ombudsman* (Edward Elgar Publishing, 2018).

31 See Ombudsman New South Wales, 'Who We Are' (Web Page) https://www.ombo.nsw.gov.au/what-we-do/about-us/who-we-are.

32 Michael Kirby, 'Australia's Commonwealth Ombudsman 40 Years On: Achievements and Ten Challenges' (2017) 45(3) *Federal Law Review* 494, 503.

33 *The Ombudsman Act 1976* (Cth).

34 Anita Stuhmcke, 'Changing Relations between Government and Citizen: Administrative Law and the Work of the Australian Commonwealth Ombudsman' (2008) 67(3) *Australian Journal of Public Administration* 321, 322.

VET Student Loans, Overseas Students, Private Health Insurance, and the Australian Capital Territory. There is a parliamentary ombudsman for each State and Territory, holding government agencies and non-government organisations from that state or territory accountable for their actions.

Many industries have specialist ombudsmen created to assist in complaints against providers in that industry. Such ombudsmen services exist, for example, in aged care, banking and insurance, disability, energy and water, and telecommunications to name a few. Not all industry ombudsman services and offices are called 'Ombudsman' – some being called Commissions or Commissioners, Complaint Office or Complaint Authority – but they all provide the same independent platform for handling complaints in an informal, fair way. An industry sets up an ombudsman or complaint office because providers are required by law to be members of an independent dispute management scheme. While parliamentary ombudsmen are funded by the government, industry-based ombudsmen charge its member organisations. Nevertheless, ombudsman services are independent and impartial, providing a fair and reasonable scheme that is not on either party's side.

There is no fee to lodge a complaint with any ombudsman and there is no need for legal assistance or representation either. Ombudsmen services are typically easy to access, unhindered by complex procedural rules characteristic to other processes. All ombudsmen offices will require, however, that a complaint be attempted to be addressed directly with the public or private body against which a complaint is raised before referring the complaint to the ombudsman. The ombudsman office will often provide assistance when making a complaint to the agency directly, before taking that complaint to the ombudsman for oversight.

A typical complaint procedure consists in contacting the ombudsman office over the phone, email or by filling an online form, providing sufficient details about the entity against which the complaint is made and the factual circumstances that give rise to the complaint. The ombudsman office will then contact that agency and investigate the complaint. The ombudsman does not make decisions, but it looks into the decision that led to the complaint and makes recommendations on how that decision or the process could be improved. As there are specialist ombudsmen for every field of public and private service and they cannot go outside their designated field of authority, the most challenging task in the process is identifying the relevant ombudsman for the complaint. However, if an ombudsman is approached with a complaint in which it has no power to assist, the office will commonly refer the complaint to the right authority, advising about which ombudsman is competent in that issue. Of all the statutory schemes, making a complaint to an Ombudsman (Commission, Commissioner, Complaint Office, or Complaint Authority) is the most easily accessible and easiest process in managing (and avoiding the escalation) of disputes.

Using knowledge of statutory schemes to assist in dispute management

Statutory schemes exist at both federal and state levels. Attempts to manage a dispute before a party can initiate litigation is the most pertinent representation of the integration between a wide range of approaches to dispute management and access to justice through the courts. The AAT provides an example as it prescribes conferencing, mediation, neutral evaluation, case appraisal, and conciliation as statutory schemes for managing specific disputes in a somewhat similar way. This is through an imposed, compulsory attempt to find an amicable solution before accessing a determinative process resulting in a decision rendered by a third party neutral. Accordingly, the AAT does not include arbitration or court services, but uses statutory schemes to enable a flexible, pragmatic, and efficient approach conducive to mutually satisfactory outcomes within the given legal framework.

The following section takes the models introduced in the previous section and provides some further depth on the use of these specified schemes, the rationale behind their existence, and the way they relate to and fit in with other dispute management processes.

Construction adjudication

Construction adjudication provides an example of a determinative statutory scheme the aim of which is to provide a structured, time-barred, rights-based approach outside of state courts. It replaces (or precedes) a similarly structured, time-barred, rights-based litigation in order to improve cash flow in the industry by the increased efficiency of the limited adjudication and the radically reduced opportunities to side-track or delay the proceedings.

The adjudicator's determination is enforceable, yet it is only interim – leaving it to the respondent to try to recover the payment using arbitration or litigation if it considers that payment should not have been warranted. Accordingly, the parties retain their right to litigation or arbitration, but this right is rarely exercised.[35] The parties may, however, access another determinative process for payments that are not within the scope of statutory adjudication. Payment may, for example, be due between the parties as a contract price, as damages for breach of contract, or as liquidated damages for delay in performance. None of these can be determined by the adjudicator, who only decides on a statutory entitlement under the relevant Act to a progress payment,[36] but they can be decided in arbitration or in court.

Farm debt mediation

Farm debt mediation, although not a determinative process, is also a statutory scheme established to serve the interests and provide special protection to the agricultural community outside of courts. The 2019 *Royal Commission into Misconduct in the Banking, Superannuation and Financial Services Industry*[37] addressed concerns raised by farmers and rural communities, with the Final Report including recommendations for the agricultural sector.[38] The investigations conducted and the public hearings held by the Commission emphasised the social responsibility held by the banking and financial sector towards the special needs of Australians living and farming in remote and regional areas. The Commission

35 Davenport (n 5) 4.

36 Ibid 156.

37 See *Royal Commission into Misconduct in the Banking, Superannuation and Financial Services Industry* (Final Report, February 2019) vol 1, 23.

38 Ibid.

made recommendations directly affecting agricultural lending and services, including the recommendations to:

- establish a national scheme for farm debt mediation
- offer farm debt mediation as soon as agricultural loans are declared as distressed
- recognise that appointment of receivers on a farm loan is a 'remedy of last resort'.[39]

As a result of the Royal Commission, a National Farm Debt Mediation scheme has been proposed to harmonise the different state mediation schemes.

Native title claims

The NNTT was created to have a key role in mediating disputes without recourse to the Federal Court. The initial idea under the Act was 'that native title recognition could be accomplished through consensus and mediation'[40] but the recognition of native title has become a matter for the Federal Court instead. This was the forum that was originally seen as one of last resort. As a result, the formal recognition of native title has become subject to litigation and trial, 'unless there is agreement between the state or territory and the applicant paving the way for a consent determination'.[41] However, since 'many of the legal precedents about where native title exists or has been extinguished have already been determined', the preferred method for managing native title claims is still through negotiation and mediation, rather than litigation.[42]

Royal commissions

Although not a dispute management method as such, royal commissions are, however, worth mentioning in this textbook as a statutory scheme that may be available to address matters of great importance that become a source of disputes within society. A royal commission, also called a commission of inquiry, is an investigation formally established by the Governor-General on behalf of the Crown and on the advice of government ministers. It is not a judicial body and it does not make a decision but is an ad hoc public inquiry funded from public resources that can make recommendations to government and influence policy change.[43]

A royal commission may be called by State or Federal governments, or both together. The terms of reference of the investigation are established by the government, and the commission recommends what should change as a result of that investigation. The government also appoints the commissioners and provides the funding for the commission, but once established the commission is independent of government. This makes its investigation unrestricted by political influence. Commissioners are not serving politicians but are independent experts in the field relevant for the inquiry or retired judges familiar with hearing evidence. Royal

39 Ibid 22.

40 Palmer Kingsley, *Australian Native Title Anthropology: Strategic Practice, the Law and the State* (ANU Press, 2018) 17.

41 Ibid.

42 National Native Title Tribunal and Australian Local Government Association, *Working with Native Title: Linking Native Title and Local Government Processes* (3rd ed, August 2009) 4.

43 Michael Mintrom, 'Royal Commissions and Policy Influence' (2020) 79(1) *Australian Journal of Public Administration* 1.

commissions have broad investigative powers, including witness examinations, evidence-gathering, holding public or closed hearings, and information-gathering, including the right of entry and phone-tapping; they can also refer matters to the police. These broad powers have been raised as a source of concern by the Australian Law Reform Commission (ALRC) when analysing whether Federal royal commissions should be wholly or partially exempt from the operation of the *Privacy Act 1988* (Cth), stating that:

> Royal Commissions serve the important function of inquiring into matters of public interest. Central to the performance of this function is the ability of Royal Commissions to obtain information that may be unavailable by other means of investigation or inquiry. Although they do not exercise judicial power, they are given powers that usually are exercised by courts.[44]

The first royal commission was held in 1902, when the *Royal Commissions Act 1902* (Cth) was passed. Notable royal commissions with varying degrees in successful uptake of their recommendations include the *Royal Commission into Aboriginal Deaths in Custody 1991*; *Royal Commission into Institutional Responses to Child Sexual Abuse 2013*; *Royal Commission into Misconduct in the Banking, Superannuation and Financial Services Industry 2017*; *Royal Commission into Violence, Abuse, Neglect and Exploitation of People with Disability 2019* and the *Royal Commission into National Natural Disaster Arrangements 2020*.

As of the writing of this textbook, a total of 138 royal commissions have been held at national level, not including royal commissions systems by the different state governments. In 2009, the royal commissions system was subjected to an inquiry by the ALRC, resulting in the ALRC Report 111.[45] Ten years later, the recommendations included in the report have not yet been implemented. Royal commissions under the 1902 Act remain the highest form of inquiry potentially leading to law reforms in areas that represent a source of tension in society.

Positives and negatives of statutory dispute management schemes

Although statutory schemes limit party autonomy in some ways, they also make dispute management more structured and effective by channeling certain types of disputes towards methods and fora specifically designed for those disputes. This is generally to achieve simplification, savings, and efficiencies in processes that would otherwise cost the community and prevent it achieving desired goals. Notwithstanding the aim, there are always negatives and positives.

Positives

Whether parties are allowed, required, or strongly encouraged to have legal representatives in a statutory dispute management scheme can be considered both a positive or negative,

44 Australian Law Reform Commission, *For Your Information: Australian Privacy Law and Practice* (Report No 108, May 2008) 1299.

45 Australian Law Reform Commission, *Making Inquiries: A New Statutory Framework* (Report No 111, October 2009).

depending on the situation. In the building adjudication schemes, for example, in most states the parties are not allowed to have legal representation; similarly with statutory conciliation. This may be perceived as a negative, as parties may not be aware of their legal rights and obligations and may not fully understand the legal consequences of their actions and statement. On the other hand, both in adjudication and in statutory conciliation the third-party neutral is expected to apply and safeguard legal provisions, ensuring that the rights and obligations set in the statute under which the statutory dispute management scheme operates are respected and imposed. Through this, the lack of legal representation results in decreased costs without losing from the reliability and efficiency of the process.

At the other end of the spectrum, parties are either strongly encouraged to engage legal and/or financial advisors, such as in civil litigation or farm debt mediation. The need for this specialist assistance renders those avenues for managing disputes potentially excessively expensive. However, as a rule of thumb, the more rigid and complex the procedure for a dispute management scheme and the more evidentiary process involved, the bigger is the need for costly legal representation. Imposing or strongly suggesting legal representation that may increase costs is made in the interest of the parties facing complex procedures but may attract significant costs. Many statutory schemes are meant to eliminate this pitfall by creating compulsory, but streamlined and accessible platforms and informal procedures where access to justice is not dependent on one's financial resources.

Negatives

A perceived disadvantage of statutory schemes consists in their mandatory nature, forcing parties to adopt a predetermined process regardless of whether it is in fact beneficial to a particular scenario or not. This can turn into an expensive and time-consuming 'box-ticking' exercise, with parties or their lawyers considering that any attempt to achieve an amicable solution is not in the parties' best interests. A similar disillusionment may be caused by the limited scope and authority a statutory scheme provider has. For example, individuals may decide to not lodge a complaint to an ombudsman because the Ombudsman cannot render a decision and resolve a specific complaint.

The limited scope of statutory adjudication also means that if a construction contract gives rise to claims of both progress payments and penalties for breach of contract, these two claims would have to be subjected to two different dispute management processes (adjudication for the progress payment, and possibly arbitration or litigation for the breach of contract). This can have the undesirable effect of increasing both the time and costs invested in managing a single but more complex dispute arising from the same contractual relationship. With complex relationships and disputes, there is no one size fits all solution for everything.

Special considerations

As the last section of the book, the special considerations in this chapter will deal with professional issues such as codes of conduct and working in the industry. To close the journey of learning about dispute management, the chapter will give an overview of the different roles and jobs that exist in the field, together with the good and bad sides of working in dispute management, offering a fair insight into the professions that can serve as a realistic basis for those wanting to make an educated decision about taking up a career in this area.

Codes of conduct and professional liability

Statutory provisions or procedural regulations establish rules on professional behaviour and liability of certain dispute practitioners. Personal values are rarely specified, as they vary from one individual to another. Instead, work ethics are regulated through codes of conduct setting up a liability-based system of remedies and punishments for breaching certain professional obligations. Of those engaged in dispute management, the legal profession is likely the most strictly regulated, but adjudicators, mediators and other professions working in the area, such as psychologists, financial planners and others, are all subject to professional codes of conduct.

The Law Council of Australia developed the *Australian Solicitors' Conduct Rules* in 2011 to establish professional obligations and ethical principles for Australian solicitors. The purpose of the Rules is to 'assist' solicitors in their dealings with their clients, the courts, their fellow legal practitioners, and regulators, but 'a breach of these Rules is capable of constituting unsatisfactory professional conduct or professional misconduct and may give rise to disciplinary action'.[46] The rules have been last amended in 2015 and are adopted in the ACT, New South Wales, Queensland, South Australia, and Victoria, providing a more-or-less uniform basis for solicitors' behaviour across most of the country. The *Legal Profession Uniform Law* (NSW) and (Vic) create a uniform statutory basis for the professional behaviour of legal practitioners across these two states. The other States and Territories have their own specific rules and regulations governing legal professionals. Bar associations in each State and Territory also establish their own set of rules. Which of these statutory frameworks apply when a dispute management professional provides services for an international dispute outside their home jurisdiction is outside the scope of this textbook.

The accountability of dispute management practitioners is important to maintain a credible and reliable dispute management system overall. At the same time, those who serve as decision-makers in determinative processes must be protected from personal attacks by a losing party to ensure independent decision-making. For this reason, professional liability exists for legal practitioners but not for third-party neutrals that are considered to perform a quasi-judicial role. Third-party neutrals are provided with immunity for their actions and decisions taken in that role. Any such exemption from liability is based on the provisions regulating each role separately. If, for example, an arbitrator is mandated by the disputing parties to first attempt to mediate the dispute or alternatively to make a final and binding expert determination of an issue raised, any exemption from liability for the functions of mediator or expert determiner are not covered by the Act under which the same neutral acts as an arbitrator.

A mediator may include a liability provision in the contract with the parties under which they employ the services of the mediator.[47] The immunity in an international arbitration is provided for in the *International Arbitration Act* 1974 (Cth) s 28(1), and by the *Commercial Arbitration Act* s 39 of the relevant State and Territory for a domestic arbitration. Generally,

46 Law Council of Australia, *Australian Solicitors' Conduct Rules 2015* r 2.3.

47 See Chapter 6.

they provide '[a]n arbitrator is not liable for anything done or omitted to be done in good faith in his or her capacity as arbitrator'. A similar provision exists to protect adjudicators from liability for actions or omissions taken as part of a good faith performance of that role. That immunity, however, only protects the adjudicator if the role is performed within the strict time limits imposed by statute. As the immunity is subject to good faith observance of the obligations associated with that role, dispute management practitioners may be sued for negligence in tort.[48] For this reason, where dispute management practitioners do not benefit from statutory immunity, their professional regulations require that they are covered by a professional indemnity insurance. The degree or indemnity will be guided by the level of exposure to risk. This is greater where a dispute practitioner is giving advice, hence the need to be clear on the process and model being followed.

Public sector dispute management practitioners, like conciliators in a specialist tribunal, are subject to codes of conduct established for that organisation and may be subject to investigation and disciplinary action in their public sector employee status. Dispute management practitioners operating within other frameworks not subject to strict regulation, unlike that of the legal profession, are regularly subject to their own professional codes of conduct. However, to what extent those codes of conduct may lead to a statutory complaint or enforceable remedy falls outside of the framework of dispute management. The absence of an overarching regulatory framework to provide effective, independent accountability across all dispute management processes and platforms is often the theme of debate but is yet to be solved.[49]

Confidentiality

Confidentiality is one of the areas that is strictly regulated, but generally outside of professional codes of conduct. As an overview of the confidentiality issues presented for each dispute management process separately, it is worth reiterating the different types and sources of confidentiality and privilege that are present in dispute management. Contractual confidentiality is, to a large extent, determined and defined by party autonomy but may be limited by mandatory statutory provisions imposing disclosure obligations for tax, shareholder, or public policy considerations. In addition, information may be subject to statutory privilege when statutes prevent communication from being used outside a dispute management process, particularly in court in subsequent proceedings.

Without prejudice privilege is the confidentiality of communication made in the course of genuine negotiations conducted with a view to settling a dispute. Finally, legal professional privilege is the confidentiality of lawyer–client communication made for existing or planned proceedings. These different rules may overlap in application, with a piece of information being subject to more than one privilege. What a dispute management practitioner must identify is what information is the subject of confidentiality, what is the purpose for which the information is said to be confidential, which party is able to claim and rely on confidentiality, and against which party can the confidentiality be asserted.

48 Ibid; see also Chapter 6, 212.

49 See Lola Akin Ojelabi and Mary Anne Noone, 'ADR Processes: Connections Between Purpose, Values, Ethics and Justice' (2017) 35(1) *Law in Context* 5.

Culture and ethics

Culture and ethics have been mentioned in relation to the different dispute management processes across this book. A final note to keep in mind when addressing ethical issues in a cross-cultural environment is understanding what is the 'right' approach in each situation. Considering law, ethical rules, company values, or personal values[50] may not necessarily mean that what is considered to be the 'right' approach when filtering ethical dilemmas will also be a possible or reasonable one. The cultural context in which an ethical dilemma arises must be acknowledged even if parties operating in that context are not happy with the unwritten rules. It would be hypocritical to pretend that a party in a highly authoritarian organisation is content to not raise any concerns or make complaints, or that a party facing a dispute with local authorities in a society with deeply embedded corruption prefers to pay a bribe for finding an unofficial solution to an otherwise official issue. Ethics is a combination of laws and rules, personal and organisational values, and established customs and practices.[51] Statutory dispute management schemes like the ombudsman services are created to provide flexible platforms that bridge these differences. In other areas, soft law and guidelines are developed to bridge cultural gaps characteristic, for instance, in international disputes.[52]

The professional rules and codes of conduct determining the ethics of dispute management vary between dispute management processes, types of dispute, places of dispute, and the participants. The ethical issues will be different for a mediator in a family dispute involving domestic violence, compared to a barrister representing a corporate client in international arbitration, or a High Court judge deciding a constitutional law challenge. The same ethical dilemmas will also be different depending on the cross-cultural influences at play in a given scenario:

> Culture is critical in shaping the manner in which people perceive, evaluate, and choose options for dealing with conflict. Conflict resolution, as a cultural phenomenon, is highly connected with and dependent on a society's norms, practices, and institutions.[53]

Culture can impact on the ethical considerations governing conflicts of interest in dispute management. For example, the level of personal engagement that is acceptable between a disputant and a third-party neutral will differ significantly between cultures. In many South or Latin-American countries, a lawyer may be a close friend to a judge and have lunch with them while also having a case in front of that judge; the same would possibly lead to the expulsion from the profession of an Australian barrister. These differences in what is and is not acceptable are relevant in any dispute situation that may arise in a multicultural society like Australia.

---

50 See Lola Akin Ojelabi and Mary Anne Noone (eds), *Ethics in Alternative Dispute Resolution* (The Federation Press, 2017).

51 See also Chapter 1, 34; Chapter 4, 31; and Chapter 6, 208.

52 See, eg, International Bar Association, *IBA Guidelines on Conflicts of Interest in International Arbitration* (2014).

53 Douglas P Fry and Kaj Bjorkqvist, *Cultural Variation in Conflict Resolution: Alternative to Violence* (Psychology Press, 1996) xxii.

Roles and jobs in dispute management

To end this chapter and the textbook, there is value in looking at the different roles and jobs that exist in dispute management. Disputes exist at every level of human existence: from individuals to sovereign countries and entire geographical regions. Accordingly, dispute management is needed at all levels of the social structure. As individuals, we manage disputes on a daily basis: from negotiating with family what to have for dinner through to mediating an argument between friends, or deciding which one of our kids is responsible for a broken window. We constantly rely on facilitative, advisory, or determinative processes. Within society, managing disputes is assigned to individuals holding certain roles. Traditionally, the responsibility of managing disputes rested on the shoulders of the person holding the highest rank within the community; for instance, a wise elder. Dispute management was a task that came with the recognition, respect and trust invested in leadership. Elders, religious leaders, and kings were the ones managing disputes within the community they were leading and with other communities with which they interacted. Modern-world political leaders still manage disputes within and between sovereign entities, although today this role is seldom held exclusively by one person. Managing disputes at any level has become a profession in which there is room for different roles and qualifications.

Due to a traditionally litigation-focused perception as a form of managing disputes, roles and jobs in dispute management are often perceived as the domain of those legally trained. The reality is that only a fraction of dispute management work requires legal qualifications, and includes a wide range of professions. Managing disputes within organisations, for example, belongs to human resources, known more recently as 'people and engagement departments' or similar. Family disputes may also involve counselling to support and assist the parties with the emotional and mental challenges of the dispute and the dispute management experience. Creating rules and regulations on how to deal with disputes belongs to policymakers and those involved in legislative development. Beyond directly assisting in and managing disputes, there are also a wide range of roles that may contribute to the understanding and avoidance of disputes within society. Ombudsmen, royal commissioners, police, investigative journalists, authors, social and health workers, educators, even so-called 'influencers' and practically anyone with a public profile or sufficient exposure to have an impact on the behaviour of others can have a significant role in how society perceives and handles disputes. An academic researching and writing on disputes, for instance on the psychology of domestic violence, can have just as much impact on handling domestic violence cases as the legislator regulating the procedure and potential outcome of such cases.

Most dispute management practitioners are members of some professional organisation that provides training, networking, continuous professional development (CPD) opportunities, and professional indemnity insurance for their members. In Australia, the most well-known membership organisations for dispute management practitioners are the Resolution Institute, the Australian Dispute Resolution Association, the Australian Mediation Association, the Chartered Institute of Arbitrators (CIArb), and the Australian Association of Collaborative Practitioners. Institutions and organisations specialised in providing dispute management and dispute management services, such as the Australian Disputes Centre (ADC), the Australian Centre for International Arbitration (ACICA), Conflict Resolution Service (CRS), or the Queensland Building and Construction Commission (QBCE), also provide services for dispute management practitioners registered with those organisations. Similarly, other specialised dispute management schemes may provide specific training for their dispute practitioners. Some fields require specialised accreditation to allow for a dispute management professional to practice in that field. Such accreditations are subject to specialised training that is constantly updated to meet changes in regulation. Other fields are developing to introduce new training and accreditation schemes that were previously non-existent.[54]

Both membership organisations and dispute management service providers employ a range of additional administrative, managerial, and training staff on a casual, part-time or full-time basis, depending on the organisation's needs. With the increase of online services and training, they also regularly engage technical assistance for website and learning platform development.

Lawyers in dispute management

While clearly dispute management and dispute management practitioners are not all about law, an understanding of the legal consequences of one's involvement in these processes is important. Legal background is more common among those practising in commercial disputes and those engaged in rights-based or evaluative methods for their legal expertise. Solicitors, corporate, in-house, and government lawyers provide advice on and assist in dispute management and dispute management processes. Barristers are also commonly engaged to represent parties in dispute management processes where legal representation is required or permitted. Collaborative practitioners must be lawyers practising under specific Practice Guidelines issued by the Law Council.[55] Members of the judiciary must also be lawyers.

All legal positions are subject to admission into practice by the Supreme Court of a State or Territory and require a practising certificate from the relevant legal professional body established by State and Territory legislation. Solicitors require the completion of a recognised law degree (LLB or JD) and of practical legal training (PLT) to be admitted to practice. Barristers must, in addition in some States, also pass an entrance examination to be admitted to the Bar of a State or Territory and complete a specialist course and work with a mentor before being admitted for independent practice. Solicitors commonly work within a law firm where they advance through the ranks from graduate to associate, senior associate, then partner. Barristers, although sole practitioners, commonly work within chambers of certain specialisation and advance through the ranks from reader to junior to senior counsel. Foreign lawyers are not entitled to practice Australian law; however, they can practice in certain dispute management areas. Paralegals, clerks, and legal secretaries assisting lawyers also often possess legal education or are enrolled in law degrees while working in such jobs. No other role, other than judges in dispute management, requires formal legal qualifications.

Working in mediation and conciliation

Mediators can be both lawyers and non-lawyers. Barristers and retired judges are often engaged in settlement and in evaluative mediation, usually to assess the strengths and

54 See, eg, Resolution Institute, *Expert Determiners Policy* (2020).

55 See Chapter 9; see also Law Council of Australia, *Australian Collaborative Practice Guidelines for Lawyers* (2011), 375.

weaknesses of a case, to clarify issues, and reduce the number of claims going to a determinative process (arbitration or litigation). Mediators practising in facilitative, transformative or narrative mediation are commonly non-lawyers, and can be psychologists or social workers. Courts and tribunals, as well as some dispute management institutions, keep lists of mediators from where appointments are made, but mediators are free to accept or refuse appointments. While mediators are independent practitioners, conciliators working in statutory conciliation are commonly employed by a tribunal or entity entrusted with the statutory management of a specific type of dispute.

All mediators are expected to be accredited to practice under the National Mediator Accreditation System (NMAS):[56] 'a voluntary industry system under which organisations that meet certain criteria [. . .] may accredit mediators.'[57] Accreditation requires the completion of a nationally accredited mediator training program, successful completion of the national mediation assessment, and approval by a Recognised Mediator Accreditation Body (RMAB). Once approved, a mediator's name will be added to the Register of Nationally Accredited Mediators held by the Mediator Standards Board. Mediators practising internationally often seek international certification from the International Mediation Institute (IMI). Conciliators, although not subject to specific accreditation requirements in Australia, are also commonly expected to have completed training in mediation.

Working in adjudication

Adjudicators operate under State and Territory legislation regulating construction payment disputes. They must possess qualifications and have completed training in adjudication to be recognised and receive appointments in this role. Adjudicators are appointed by Authorised Nominating Authorities (ANA) in most States. In the ACT, New South Wales, the Northern Territory, Tasmania, Victoria, and Western Australia, the Resolution Institute is such an ANA – although in Western Australia the ANAs are called Prescribed Appointers (PA). In Queensland, appointments are made only by the Queensland Building and Construction Commission (QBCC), which administers all security of payment claims. In Queensland, the training and accreditation is controlled and organised by the QBCC, while in all other States and Territories there may be a range of providers that offer courses in the field. The ANAs also provide specialist training and accept adjudicators to their panels subject to prior accreditation.

Adjudicators often engage agents to intermediate all communication between the adjudicator and the parties. Agents do not have to be accredited or trained in adjudication but must have sufficient understanding of the adjudicator's role and responsibilities. Using an agent is recommended to avoid any concern regarding conflicts of interests or procedural fairness that may arise from the adjudicator communicating directly with a party. An agent represents the adjudicator in all communications and the adjudicator can refuse direct communication from a party by directing them to the agent. The adjudicator is also responsible for the agent's acts or omissions.

56 *National Mediator Accreditation System* (NMAS) (1 July 2015).
57 See Chapter 6.

Working in arbitration

Arbitration engages individuals in a range of roles. Directly involved in cases are the arbitrators, the parties' legal representatives, the tribunal secretary, and the arbitral institution's internal counsel handling the case if the arbitration is institutional. In addition, arbitration may also engage experts; parties may engage funding entities; and law firms assisting the parties may have an entire team of legal and support staff working in the background on a case.

Arbitrators are not required to possess specific accreditation, but many aim to obtain the qualification of 'Chartered Arbitrator' from CIArb. Many arbitrators possess legal qualifications due to arbitration being predominantly used in commercial disputes. Many more, however, come from other backgrounds (eg engineering, finance, construction, shipping, etc) and specialise in disputes in those specific fields. It is up to the disputing parties or the appointing authority to decide what expertise is most suitable for an arbitrator appointment, keeping in mind that technical expertise can be supplemented by the use of expert witnesses or tribunal-appointed experts. On the other hand, a tribunal's ability to conduct, manage, and decide a case to result in an enforceable award cannot be outsourced.[58]

Arbitrators are frequently appointed from lists held by arbitral institutions. Many institutions took the pledge 'to increase, on an equal opportunity basis, the number of women appointed as arbitrators in order to achieve a fair representation as soon as practically possible, with the ultimate goal of full parity'.[59] This is an initiative launched by Arbitral Women, a professional membership organisation created to support women in arbitration.[60] Arbitrators, however, are not employed by arbitral institutions, but are independent practitioners. For this reason, few arbitrators are arbitrators only. Most arbitrators also practice as experts in their respective fields, and can be academics or consultants.

Each of these roles is subject to its own professional practice rules, codes of conduct, and guidelines setting out legal and ethical obligations. Yet, performing different roles in arbitration may be perceived as a source of concern with some questioning practitioners' ability to switch between roles for different cases. Internationally, the potentially conflicting codes of conduct from the home jurisdiction and from the place of arbitration can be a source of confusion. For arbitrators, rules of independence and impartiality from the seat of arbitration will prevail. Counsel representing parties in a foreign arbitration, however, are still subject to the rules of conduct imposed by their home jurisdiction, where the lawyer is admitted to practice. The *IBA Guidelines on Party Representation in International Arbitration* (2013) aim to set a common base for principles of integrity and honesty driving legal representation across jurisdictions, recommending remedies for misconduct that arbitral tribunals may apply.[61]

Arbitration also engages tribunal secretaries and personal or research assistants to the arbitrators. Traditionally, tribunal secretaries were not required to possess any qualifications and were either employed by the tribunal directly or provided by an administering institution to assist the arbitrators in managing the case. Tribunal secretaries are not involved in the decision-making

58 See also Chapter 10.

59 Equal Representation in Arbitration, *Commentary to the Pledge* (Web Page) <http://www.arbitrationpledge.com/about-the-pledge>.

60 See *ArbitralWomen* (Web Page) <https://www.arbitralwomen.org/>.

61 International Bar Association, *IBA Guidelines on Part Representation in International Arbitration* (2013).

process but perform administrative tasks and occasionally draft procedural orders under the instructions of the presiding arbitrator – although the latter involvement may be controversial, as it engages the secretary in substantive, not only organisational tasks. Their roles, however, were not strictly regulated until the *Yukos* proceedings[62] brought the issue into the focus. Following a growing concern that tribunal secretaries may be used by tribunals as a second (or fourth) arbitrator, exceeding their administrative role and engaging in the decision-making process that should be within the exclusive personal mandate of the appointed arbitrators, arbitral institutions developed stricter rules to regulate tribunal secretaries. Many institutions developed training aimed at secretaries and established lists from which secretaries may be appointed.[63]

Arbitral institutions also engage a wide range of staff and independent professionals for the operation of the institution. Most institutions employ several legal counsels managing the administration of cases, as well as staff in executive, administrative, management and educational roles. Independent professionals are also engaged in honorary roles on different boards and committees of many institutions, by this ensuring professional recognition and standards to the operation of the institution.

Working in litigation: courts and tribunals

Courts are considered the biggest source of employment in dispute management. In addition to the role of judges and magistrates, courts also employ registrars, judge's associates, clerks, tipstaff, legal support staff, consultants (eg family consultants for child dispute services), and dispute management practitioners. Courts often also engage volunteers providing free non-legal support, information, and referral services. Judges and magistrates are appointed following a complicated process that changes from state to state, and is regulated by the *Public Service Act 1999* (Cth) for the Federal Courts. Magistrates are appointed for local courts to preside over a large number of smaller cases; judges are appointed for District or higher courts to hear cases and preside over jury trials. Both roles require detailed legal knowledge, the ability to apply sound judgement and to reason, and a minimum number of years spent in legal practice to qualify for appointment.

Tipstaff positions are the most common and accessible entry level opportunities into the court and tribunal system. Tipstaves provide legal research, in-court duties, and administrative support for a judge and are part of that judge's personal chambers staff. Tipstaff positions are commonly for up to 12 months but are rarely advertised publicly; selection of tipstaves is conducted directly by the judge. Judge's associates are also hired by the respective judge directly, usually for one year. A judge's associate is 'a personal and confidential aide to the Judge, in and out of court, in connection with all the Judge's concerns'.[64] Opportunities to become a judge's associate are frequently circulated within law schools to attract fresh

62 *Hulley Enterprises Limited (Cyprus) v Russia,* UNCITRAL, PCA Case No. AA 226; *Yukos Universal Limited (Isle of Man) v Russia*, UNCITRAL, PCA Case No. AA 227; *Veteran Petroleum Limited (Cyprus) v Russia*, UNCITRAL, PCA Case No. AA 228.

63 See, eg, Australian Centre for International Commercial Arbitration, *ACICA Tribunal Secretary Panel* (Web Page) <https://acica.org.au/acica-tribunal-secretary-panel/>.

64 See, eg, Queensland Courts, *Judges' Associates: The Role of an Associate to a District Court or Supreme Court Judge* (Web Page) <https://www.courts.qld.gov.au/about/jobs-with-the-courts/judges-associates>.

graduates or later year students. Registrars and judicial registrars also provide administrative and judicial support to judges and the court. A registrar is the chief administrator of a court's registry, while a judicial registrar manages both the administrative and the judicial aspects of hearings and the progress of matters in court. Judicial registrars may also exercise certain delegated powers of the court, making decisions in interlocutory hearings and case management, conducting mediations, or presiding in court over bankruptcy and migration cases.

The positives and negatives of working in dispute management

A closing section before contemplating a career in this field must address both the positive and negative aspects of a career in dispute management. Identifying priorities, core values, personality traits, internal and external motivations are all imperative before deciding to work in any job. This self-assessment and clarifying your own 'why' is even more important to work in dispute management where most of the time the job involves dealing with other people's problems with maximum professionalism regardless of your own problems.

Any work that consists in assisting others when there is a dispute in their life or business operation can take a toll on a practitioner's mental health. We must learn to temporarily put aside our own issues to be able to help others with theirs. We must also learn to help by acknowledging, but not taking on, the issues that we try to help solve. And we must learn to not lose optimism, faith in humanity, or the ability to be cheerful and empathetic due to facing so many disputes as part of our daily job.

Positives

Mediation training commonly includes a 'de-roling' exercise at the end of a role-play to avoid the participants taking on their disputes beyond the training. Getting out of the role after a role-play exercise consists in physically moving away from the place where the role was played, removing accessories that were connected to the role (if any), introducing yourself by your real name and stating how you are different from the role played, and discussing the experience of the role and the role-play from an outside perspective. Self-reflection, making sure that you left the role behind, is essential, and de-roling exercises help prepare practitioners for a practice of debriefing after real disputes.[65] As a participant to a conciliation focus group study stated: the 'debriefing process is paramount for conciliation and without it you just explode.'[66] The same observation is equally valid for most dispute management settings, although confidentiality rules may make debriefing challenging. Mentoring and engaging with other practitioners through professional events and gatherings are also effective ways of processing mentally and emotionally taxing experiences, by simply sharing and analysing them, and recognising that every colleague goes through similar challenges. Collaborative Process is exceptional in always having a Collaborative Practice Group to assist with this reflective activity.

65 See Chapter 2, 61.
66 Australian Dispute Resolution Advisory Council, *Conciliation: A Discussion Paper* (October 2019) 46.

The way we naturally and predominantly think and the way we personally deal with disputes has an impact on how we perform different roles in dispute management. Whether we are predominantly competitive, collaborative, compromising, avoiding, or accommodating in dispute situations within our own life, and the extent to which we are aware of this inclination, will have an impact on how we handle others' disputes. Whether we are natural problem-solvers or not will have an impact on how well we can perform one role or another. The ability to easily decide disputes is a necessary and welcome skill for a third-party neutral in a determinative role, but the urge to solve problems can be a curse for a neutral in a facilitative process. One of the hardest parts of being a mediator for some is to hold back a solution once they see one, and let the parties reach the conclusion on what works best for them through a potentially slower, but organic process they can feel their own.

In addition, humans naturally think in either first or third person as a predominant way of perceiving life, events, and others.[67] Those who think in first person can easily be recognised as seeing everything through their own eyes and making everything about them. Those able to abstract themselves from this and adopt a consciousness outside of their own self can relate to others and/or perceive things from an abstract, neutral perspective. Those who think in second person are those that put themselves easily into someone else's shoes, demonstrating great empathy towards others. Those who think in absolute third person are those that naturally analyse things from all possible perspectives. Everyone uses all three perspectives at different times, but has only one as their predominant way of thinking. People predominantly thinking in first person are excellent for providing expert knowledge in support of dispute management, court registrars, or adjudicators; generally, roles that require dealing more with documents than people. Roles that require the ability to understand the emotions of parties in a dispute (like that of a mediator in family dispute) will come easier for someone predominantly thinking in second person; the same natural empathy, however, will make after work debriefing absolutely vital to leave party disputes behind when leaving the office. The role of a decision-maker in more complex cases (like that of a judge or arbitrator) may come easier for someone predominantly thinking in third person, since a neutral perception is necessary to understand and evaluate all parties' positions. The same neutral perspective, however, may be insufficient where a purely rational switch in perspective is insufficient to understand the impact of power imbalance over the dispute. Dispute practitioners need to develop the ability to shift between these three different ways of thinking as a professional skill; to think in first person to perform their job within the codes of conduct of the profession, to be empathetic to understand their clients' needs and wants, and to see the other parties' point of view in order to anticipate and prepare for counterarguments.

Creating and maintaining a professional profile and an online presence that attracts clients is a vital component of the job; managing an office and finances may be too expensive to outsource; and the uncertainty of a regular income may be stressful. Yet, the ability to dissect disputes, see the issues that are the cause, recognise the possible solution, and help parties 'cure' and move on from what was poisoning their life, relationship or business, is extraordinarily rewarding.[68] Eventually, the financial rewards and the recognition will follow the hard work. Depending on your personal values and priorities, the positive impact you can have on

67 See Alla Choifer, 'A New Understanding of the First-person and Third-person Perspectives' (2018) 47(3) *Philosophical Papers* 333.

68 See Ruth Charlton, 'Mediation – My First Ten Years: 1982–1992' (2019) 29(2) *Australasian Dispute Resolution Journal* 189, for one mediator's inspirational experience.

the world by working in dispute management is likely to make all the invested time, money and effort well worth it, but this is a question best asked beforehand, not in hindsight, when setting out in your career.

Negatives

The mental challenges are not the only factor to consider when preparing for a career in dispute management. The costs of such a career can be quantified not only in monetary value, but also in time and personal sacrifices. For this, a realistic assessment of your own values and priorities is essential. Those contemplating a legal career often have an idealistic, rather than a realistic image, of the status, the money, or the fascinating work that waits for them at the end of their degree. Sometimes, this image is based on movies and the occasional sensationalist representation of star lawyers in the media; neither of which are a genuine reflection of reality. The reality, for instance, of a legal career is usually a lot less glamorous, not too profitable for quite some time, and requiring a lot more time spent reading than saving the world.

Anyone planning a career in a law firm would have to ask themselves whether they are willing to put up with a billable hour system where time is split in six-minute blocks, every small task must be clocked to be paid, workload frequently demands priority over personal and family life, and fierce competition leads to high stress levels and the risk of burn-out.[69] Recent inquiries into the common presence of sexual harassment and bullying have revealed another ugly side of the legal profession that must be fought against.[70] Those aiming for the prestige and excitement of presenting impressive, persuasive arguments in court must also ask themselves whether they are willing and capable of investing the many years it may take to get there; whether they accept dealing with 99 per cent of bland cases for the 1 per cent that is, indeed, fascinating; and accept the long hours of solitary research and preparation that goes into even the shortest argument. In addition, even a brief oral pleading may trigger stage fright and performance anxiety if you are not comfortable with public speaking. Good communication skills take a long time to develop and a lifetime to practice.[71] Finally, those looking towards a judicial appointment must ask themselves whether they are willing to put up with all the above for a long period of time until they make it to the bench, if they ever do. Whether wearing a work attire in public that was developed in the 1600s is perceived as a prestige or a painful sacrifice depends on each person's personal taste.

Despite these factors, practising as a dispute practitioner can be an extremely rewarding and fun career. Such careers can be hard work, but with satisfactions that usually don't make it to the headlines. The skills and techniques needed can take a long time to perfect, during which the financial rewards can be modest. Responsibility can be significant as people in often emotional-laden disputes require support.

69 See also Natalie Skead and Shane L Rogers, 'Stress, Anxiety and Depression in Law Students: How Student Behaviours Affect Student Wellbeing' (2014) 40(2) *Monash University Law Review* 564; Paula Baron, 'The Elephant in the Room? Lawyer Wellbeing and the Impact of Unethical Behaviours' (2015) 41 (1) *Australian Feminist Law Journal* 87.

70 See Australian Human Rights Commission, *Respect@Work: National Inquiry into Sexual Harassment in Australian Workplaces* (Report, 29 January 2020); see also Law Council of Australia, *Addressing Sexual Harassment in the Australian Legal Profession: Discussion Paper July 2019* (2019).

71 See Chapter 2, Chapter 4.

Conclusion

The many processes available to manage disputes and presented in this textbook are being taken up in legislated schemes, as samples in this chapter demonstrate. The diversity in approaches are now commonly accepted and is manifest by the pedestrian adoption in legislation.

Learning about and practising in dispute management can be challenging, but for those wishing to work as dispute practitioners, there are many exciting opportunities. The time and effort invested in professional development offer real-life dividends through professional and party recognition. While practitioners may tend to practice in one process, as a specialist in that domain, others may operate across the range of processes. The knowledge and skills a dispute management practitioner acquires are, therefore, transferrable across fields. For those choosing to work using the different processes, often lawyers, the key is to be clear which process they are adopting at the time, and which is most suited to the dispute. There certainly will always be a place for litigation and good practitioners working in this area. However, dispute management is not always about the law. It's more than that. It's about making choices that make life, relationships, and interactions better. It's about taking sometimes difficult steps to make life easier for people in dispute.

Regardless of one's view or opinion about the legal environment in which disputes are managed, the rule of law and the dispute management processes created or enabled by the law are there to serve justice. And justice is always worth working towards. Finding the space where you as a practitioner can achieve your goals will bring you joy and peace in your work to assist creating a just society.

EXERCISE IN APPLYING YOUR KNOWLEDGE – THE WORLD AGAINST NICO CATANO

Nico Catano is a builder in Lismore, New South Wales, who does most of his building work on the coast near Lismore. Les Jones, a client for whom he renovated a holiday house in Byron Bay, asked Nico whether he could build him a large showroom for his furniture business in Brisbane. Nico was not sure whether to accept the significantly larger work so far from his regular work sites but the pay offered was too tempting to refuse. He asked his regular contractors from the Lismore and Byron Bay area whether they would accept this job with him in Brisbane, telling them that given the size of the work he could only pay them in full when he got paid by the client. After some negotiations, they agreed that he would pay them for half the work from his own resources and pay the other half from what the client pays him after the work is completed. With this in mind, Nico signed a contract with Seaside Furniture Ltd for the construction of a 500 sqm showroom in Eagle Farm, Brisbane. The contract provided that Seaside Furniture would pay for all materials directly as ordered throughout the project, but the builder would only be paid upon the completion of the project to full compliance.

Nico's team spent three months building the showroom, during which work was gradually slowing down as the materials needed were being delayed. Nico suspected that the furniture business was not going too well and worried that he and his team would not get paid at the end. They almost finished the work, only waiting for the wall-size opening security windows for the shopfront, but those were being delayed. Rumour had it that the manufacturer Seethrough Safety Ltd refused to release the windows until they were paid, and the client had no money to pay for them. Joe, the concreter that Nico used, was getting irritable and told Nico that he wants his money paid in full. He has poured the slab three months ago and finished the polished internal floors more than three weeks ago and he doesn't care that the principal is delaying payment for some windows that have nothing to do with his job. Nico relies on the 'pay when paid' agreement they made before taking on the job, but Joe is determined to get his money from Nico. (Questions 1 and 2)

Eventually the windows arrived, and Nico finished the job, issuing the invoice for the entire work to Seaside Furniture Ltd. At the final building inspection scheduled two days after Nico sent his invoice, it turned out that the front windows had some microcracks and were not complying with the mandatory security requirements. The building was not found to be compliant and Les could not open the shop until the entire shopfront was replaced. He was fuming and emailed the window manufacturer demanding that the windows be replaced with compliant ones and that he be paid damages for breach of contract. The manufacturer refused to replace the windows or to pay damages, saying that the microcracks were caused by lightning that struck 1 km away from the construction site on the day after the windows were delivered. Les, determined to get the manufacturer fix the nonconformity, threatened them with legal action, to which the manufacturer did not respond. Les looked up the contract he had with Seethrough Safety Ltd and noticed the following clause:

> 34. Any disputes arising out of this contract should be settled through mediation. If mediation is unsuccessful within four weeks, the dispute will be decided by an independent arbitrator selected through the parties' mutual agreement.

Les concluded that since communication has broken down between them there is no room for any further discussion and initiated proceedings against Seethrough Safety Ltd at the Queensland Civil and Administrative Tribunal. (Questions 3 and 4)

When Nico did not get his invoice paid, he called Les asking for his money. Les told Nico that he would not be paid because the project is not complete and compliant as established in the contract. (Question 5)

To make things worse, while Nico was working in Brisbane, he neglected his own house in Lismore and a big branch from an old, hollow gumtree from his yard fell over the neighbour's house. The neighbour – Leila Patton – is furious, as she has been constantly telling Nico to cut back the tree where it was leaning towards her property, but he was always too busy working somewhere else. Now that the big branch fell, it broke the fence and went through the roof of the garage, damaging Leila's brand-new BMW X7. A small branch also broke a bedroom window next to the garage. Leila is determined to sue Nico for all the damages caused to the house and the car, as well as for medical bills she alleges she encountered due to the emotional trauma that was caused by the branch falling over her house in the middle of the night. She also wants the court to order Nico to cut down the remaining branches of the tree that are within 2 m of the property boundary. (Question 6)

1. Can Joe claim for payment of his concreting work from Nico in light of their agreed payment schedule?
2. If so, what is the appropriate forum for Joe's claim?
3. What procedural defence can Seethrough Safety Ltd raise?
4. What is the most appropriate forum where Les can submit his claims against Seethrough Safety Ltd?
5. What can Nico do to claim his money from Les?
6. What steps does Leila have to take if she wants to sue Nico in court?

Write a one-page reflection on your values, what motivates your desires for your career and what your expectations are from working in your chosen area.

INDEX

For EU product safety concerns, contact us at Calle de José Abascal, 56–1°,
28003 Madrid, Spain or eugpsr@cambridge.org.

www.ingramcontent.com/pod-product-compliance
Lightning Source LLC
LaVergne TN
LVHW080011210926
848481LV00011B/2991

* 9 7 8 1 1 0 8 7 9 4 7 1 8 *